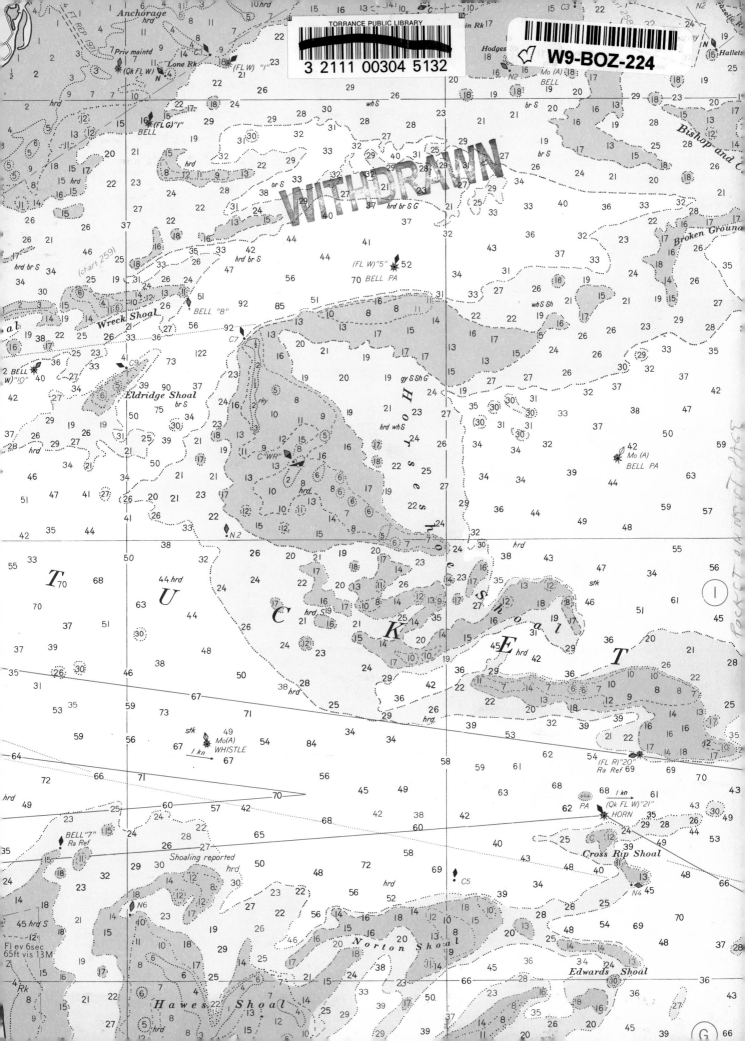

THE COMPLETE
BOOK OF
BOATING

ERNEST A. ZADIG

CONTRIBUTING EDITOR: *Motorboating & Sailing* MAGAZINE

CONTRIBUTING EDITOR: *Boating* MAGAZINE

CONTRIBUTOR: *Rudder* MAGAZINE

Popular Science MAGAZINE

AUTHOR: *Handbook of Modern Marine Materials*

Inventor's Handbook

THE COMPLETE
BOOK OF
BOATING

*An Owner's Guide to Design,
Construction, Piloting,
Operation and Maintenance*

Ernest A. ZADIG

PRENTICE-HALL, INC.

Englewood Cliffs, N. J.

Printed in the United States of America

Prentice-Hall International, Inc., London
Prentice-Hall of Australia, Pty. Ltd., North Sydney
Prentice-Hall of Canada, Ltd., Toronto
Prentice-Hall of India Private Ltd., New Delhi
Prentice-Hall of Japan, Inc., Tokyo

Library of Congress Cataloging in Publication Data
Zadig, Ernest A
The complete book of boating.
1. Motor-boats. I. Title.
VM341.Z33   623.82'31   77-98528
ISBN O-13-160143-1

Foreword

The Complete Book of Boating can be your expert alter ego, ever ready to answer questions on every phase of small boating and competent to act as a sympathetic tutor of the skills that make a good skipper.

This book is written and arranged so that you can grasp the essentials when time is pressing and then return at your leisure to delve into the subject deeply. The theories underlying all important matters are here for you to take if you want them—or to leave if your interest lies only in the mechanics.

It is an old saying among mariners that you cannot get the feel of the ocean by sitting at home with a book in your hand. True, but only one facet of the truth. Reading can forewarn and forearm you in the ways of the sea so that you can cope with them more confidently when you finally are launched.

The book is divided into seven major parts, plus glossary, and an index. The textual divisions aim at keeping closely related fields of information together for easy understanding. Thus each chapter in a section complements others in that same part. The section headings are self-explanatory; they allow you to turn directly to the general part that concerns you and from there to work down to the specific chapter that contains your facts.

Of course, you could start at page one and pleasurably read right through to the end. If you did this you would acquire all the theoretical knowledge needed to pilot a small boat safely and enjoyably and to maintain it economically.

Boating is one of the safest family sports, and power-boating is the branch of that sport which allows the easiest transition from the automobile. Yet no prudent person, regardless of his years of driving experience, would blandly get aboard a powerboat and cast off without prior study of this new element. Sailboating is a bit farther removed from the technique of auto driving and it, too, requires orientation and study. Ideally, this book should facilitate these studies and make them rewarding.

The number of boats on the waters is increasing at an ever accelerating rate. Although this does not even remotely presage traffic jams so familiar on the highways, it does mandate a knowledge of the rules and the amenities; only by observing these can everyone enjoy himself and be safe. You'll find boating rules and amenities described in full in the following pages.

If boating long since has become your permanent way of life, this book should still earn its place on your chart table. The subject matter should correlate easily with your experience and with what any boating problems you may have remaining. The text can take you to the heart of the difficulty or enable you just to laze along and clear some cobwebs from the mind.

Of one thing you can be assured: You will not find the usual technical gobbledegook between these covers. The pertinent facts are stated clearly, illustrated profusely, and presuppose no previous training for their understanding.

So, to newcomer and to old salt alike: Hail! and Happy Cruising!

E. A. Z.

South Norwalk, Connecticut

Contents

To
AUDREY
*mate, wife
and above all
sweetheart*

Introduction

I don't quite know why I am writing this introduction since my severest critic, my wife, Elise, says that she always skips the forewords, introductions and prefaces to get at the meat of the book; however, for those who do read this, *The Complete Book of Boating* is just that. Ernest Zadig, who has been writing articles for all the boating publications for years, has finally put it all together into one volume.

Not only are all the usual subjects, such as hulls, power, equipment, navigation instruments, outboards, sails and sailing, operation, anchoring, line and ropes, rules of the road, weather and safety, included but also are those subjects rarely covered in any detail, such as the legal aspects of boating; purchasing, chartering and selling a boat and maintenance and repair, which includes a delightful section on gimmicks and gadgets.

Where could you go to find such useful and interesting answers to questions such as these? Is the head on your dream boat large enough for the average-size adult? How much room is needed for the dinette? What kind of curtains should be hung in the galley? Will I be able to dry dishes when the mate is washing? Mr. Zadig answers not only these questions but many more in the section "Galley Tricks."

If you have read any of Mr. Zadig's articles, you will be familiar with his easy manner of explaining technical subjects in such a way that even the nontechnically trained person can understand them. After reading the section on diesel and gasoline engines, my wife, who cannot change a typewriter ribbon, now says that she knows the difference between them. When necessary, Mr. Zadig does get technical, but only to the extent that is required by the subject and he then explains it in nontechnical terms.

Although for more than forty years I have enjoyed boating in just about every type and size of boat, including a trick in the navy, I was amazed at how much more there is to learn. Although no one book will ever cover everything, *The Complete Book of Boating* comes close.

This book is interesting to read. You do not have to start at the beginning. Just open it up anywhere and read. Every page will add to your knowledge. If you need help on some of the subjects, then take the courses offered by the United States Power Squadrons or the Coast Guard Auxiliary. A section in the book tells you how. Enjoy "safe boating through education."

Herbert Talboys

PART I

THE BASIC BOAT

1 *Hulls—Theory and Practice*

T HE roaming of primitive man was often halted abruptly when he came to a body of water too large to cross by swimming. Nature had not adapted him particularly well for swimming; the great physical energy required to remain afloat and move ahead severely restricted the distances he could cover. So, with the ingenuity that distinguished him from the animals, man noticed that logs remained afloat without effort. Some logs even floated high enough in the water to permit weight to be carried without sinking them. It was but a short step forward to lash many such logs together into a raft.

Rafts were unwieldy and difficult to propel. True, some early civilizations made fantastic voyages with rafts, but these were merely driftings on prevailing currents. The need for a small, maneuverable marine conveyance became more and more apparent. Man found that the carrying capacity of a large log could be increased by hollowing it out; he could now sit inside the log instead of atop it. He learned that sharpening the forward end of the log reduced the muscular effort needed to paddle it to his destination.

The use of tools, or even of fire, to scoop out the log marked the beginning of the boat-building era. Refinements born of experience and of technical education advanced the hollow log to the canoe, then to the crude boat, and finally to the highly functional marine vehicles of today. The evolution placed increasing emphasis on the importance of that portion of the boat which is immersed in the water: the hull.

The shape and character of the hull determines more than merely the available space aboard. The innate safety of a vessel, its ability to struggle successfully with the elements, depends largely on its hull. Hull design may make the boat especially suitable for one body of water and yet restrict its use on another, it may cause its passengers to be transported pleasurably or uncomfortably (even though safely), it may effect an efficient use of motive power or waste a goodly portion of the fuel and benefit only meagerly from the wind's push.

Two important characteristics of hull design are buoyancy and stability. A third is the center of gravity. From these evolve the various factors that govern the motion of the vessel through its natural habitat, the water. What is buoyancy? How is stability defined and specified? Where is the center of gravity?

Buoyancy

Buoyancy was first noticed by Archimedes in ancient times. It is the power of a fluid to bear up a body that is in it. All fluids, even air, have this power to a greater or lesser degree depending upon their density. For example, seawater supports more weight per volume than fresh water because its salt makes it denser.

If you could single out a "piece" of water near the surface in a protected tank you would discover that it is stationary, it does not sink. This happens only because the water below holds it up with a force exactly equal to its own weight. This force is buoyancy.

An easier visualization of such passive opposing forces can be made by placing a book on a table. The book pushes down with its own weight; the table in effect pushes up with an exactly equal but opposite force. Result: The book does not move.

Any child knows that a steel nail, less than one ounce in weight, will sink like a plummet when dropped into water. Yet a steel ocean liner weighing thousands of tons floats majestically on the seas. The apparent mystery is

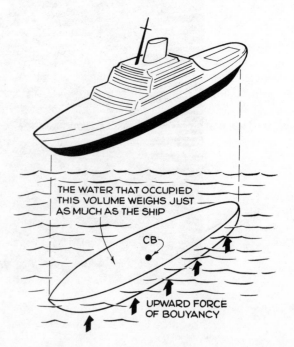

Figure 1-1: The forces of buoyancy can be considered as one upward force at the center of buoyancy CB.

no mystery at all when you apply the law of buoyancy and analyze the sketch in Figure 1-1. The water which previously had filled the space occupied by the liner's hull weighs exactly as much as the ship. The upward pressure of the surrounding water (the buoyancy) is therefore sufficient to sustain the liner and she floats.

Stated more technically, an object in a fluid (water, even air) is pushed up, or "buoyed," by a force exactly equal to the weight of the displaced fluid.

If one thousand tons of cargo were placed aboard this liner she would immerse enough deeper to displace an additional one thousand tons of water. If a giant hand squeezed the ship together so that her hull, now occupying less volume, could not displace water enough to equal her weight, she would sink, of course. It becomes a case similar to the sinking nail.

An interesting, practical, everyday exhibit of the law of buoyancy is the yacht that travels from the ocean (salt water) up a river (fresh water). Assuming that her load of fuel has not decreased sufficiently to make a difference, she will immerse deeper by approximately 3 percent in the fresh water. (Fresh water weighs approximately 3 percent less than salt water.)

CENTER OF BUOYANCY.

There is one imaginary point at the center of the "hollow" left by the liner in Figure 1-1 which is symmetrical to the entire volume. All the pressures of buoyancy that support the ship could be consolidated into one equivalent pressure at this point; this one pressure would be the sum of all the others and would produce the same effect as they do. This point is the center of buoyancy.

In any discussion of flotation, the size and shape of the displaced volume can be disregarded if the buoyant force is represented as a single pressure acting at the center of buoyancy. This force of buoyancy *always* acts vertically *upward*.

Stability

The ability to make use of the laws of buoyancy and thereby float is only one of the attributes a practical vessel must have. The vessel must also be stable, must be able to stay right side up under all reasonable conditions.

Elementary physics teaches that there are three con-

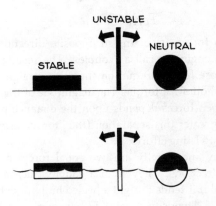

Figure 1-2: The three conditions of stability as they affect objects of common shape ashore and afloat.

ditions of stability: stable, unstable, and neutral. These are shown in Figure 1-2 and the reason for each designation is clearly evident.

Similar conditions pertain to floating bodies: The three shapes illustrated will retain their type of stability when immersed. It is a law of nature that a body in an unstable position will attempt to gain stability by moving into a stable position. Certain forces must be at work to move such an object. At least one force is always gravity.

Center of Gravity

All finite bodies on this planet have mass and are therefore attracted to the center of the earth, which is simply another way of saying that gravity acts upon them. Furthermore, a point exists in every object that can be considered the focus of gravitational pull. This point is the center of gravity.

In all discussions having to do with gravitational effects, the length and breadth of the object can be neglected if an equivalent single *downward* force is substituted at the center of gravity. The similarity of this thinking to that already used for the center of buoyancy should be noted. The marked difference is that one force (buoyancy) is *always* up and the other force (gravity) is *always* down. It can easily be imagined that a body acted upon by forces would respond by moving or even by remaining stationary if the forces neutralize each other.

Force Couple

When two forces are acting in opposite directions they form what engineers call a "couple." The resultant of a couple whose forces are not on the same straight line is a twisting motion, or torque. The magnitude of this torque for any given forces depends upon the distance between them; the greater this separation (the "torque arm"), the greater the twisting effort.

Buoyancy and gravity are two equal forces acting in opposite directions: They form a couple. Such a couple is beneficial if it tends to right a heeled hull but extremely dangerous if it tends to upset it. Either couple can happen under appropriate conditions and a skipper is forewarned and forearmed if he knows the why and the how.

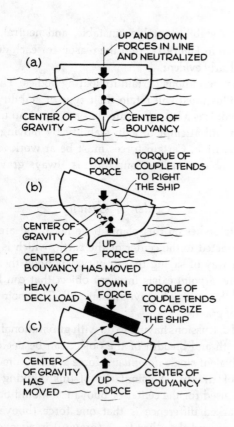

Figure 1-3: How the center of gravity (pushing down) and the center of buoyancy (pushing up) form force couples which can right or capsize a ship.

In Figure 1-3 a hull is diagrammed (a) in its normal position. The boat weight has been kept low and thus the center of gravity is low. The center of buoyancy is shown and can be verified easily on the basis of our prior explanation. The two forces, one up and one down, are equal and directly in line: They simply neutralize each other and no twisting couple exists.

At (b) the hull has been heeled over. The center of gravity of course does not move because no weight aboard has been affected. But the center of buoyancy has been moved to one side because of the different "shape" of the displaced water. (This too should be obvious from the earlier discussion.) Now we have two forces that are *not* in line acting in opposite directions. A couple must exist. This is a beneficent torque because it tends to twist the hull back into its neutral and safe position.

At (c) the torque produced by the buoyancy-gravity couple is disastrous. A heavy deck or other high-placed load has raised the center of gravity. As soon as this hull with its high center of gravity heels the least bit, the couple takes over and rapidly makes matters worse. This torque is in the wrong direction; it will increase instability and will rapidly capsize the boat. (This is a graphic warning against placing heavy weights high above the keel. It even illustrates the danger of standing up in a rowboat.)

Metacenter and Metacentric Height

Naval architects and other technicians of the world of ships coordinate the combined action of buoyancy and gravity into one term that designates the relative stability of a vessel: metacentric height. Although this term is rarely seen in pleasure boat descriptions, an understanding of it adds greatly to a basic understanding of hulls.

The metacenter is illustrated in Figure 1-4 by the point M. This point is arrived at by plotting a vertical line through the center of buoyancy when the boat is heeled *slightly* and noting the intersection of this line with the vertical taken through the center of gravity CG when the craft was in its original neutral position. The distance from the intersection M to the center of gravity is the metacentric height. In the shorthand used by naval architects, this distance is usually labeled GM.

A relatively large metacentric height makes a ship very

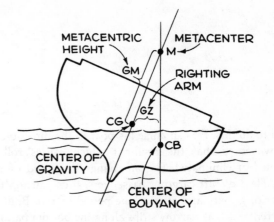

Figure 1-4: How the metacenter determines the relative stability of a ship when she is heeled.

"stiff." She snaps back sharply from any heel because the righting couple has a large lever arm and therefore develops great torque. Such action in a sea is uncomfortable for passengers and crew and ruinous to cargo, even to the structure of the ship.

On the other hand, a ship with a relatively small metacentric height is "cranky." She returns from a heel with tantalizing slowness, as though unable to decide whether to right herself or to capsize. Comparatively small changes in loading have disproportionately large effects on stability.

The foregoing conditions can be summarized in a rule: When the point M is above the point CG, the metacentric height is said to be positive; the ship has stable equilibrium and will right herself from a reasonable heel. When the point M is below the point CG, the metacentric height is negative; the ship has unstable equilibrium and will capsize from a heel. When the points CG and M coincide, the metacentric height is zero; the ship is in neutral equilibrium, with no tendency to correct a heel in either direction.

Ballast

With this understanding of buoyancy, gravity, and metacentric height, you can see that the center of gravity is a controlling factor in the safety and comfort of a boat. Furthermore, as has become obvious, the center of gravity should be low.

Often this lowering of the center of gravity can be accomplished only by the addition of weight in the bilge directly over the keel. Such weight is called ballast.

The most desirable ballast is lead, especially if it is poured in a shape that can nestle closely into the hull contour. Lead has the highest specific gravity of economically available metals; in other words, it weighs most for a given volume. But lead is expensive and everything from concrete to steel scrap is used in its place.

Ballast must be secured beyond any possibility of movement when the ship rolls and pitches. It should be stowed to avoid inaccessible cul-de-sacs in which water can accumulate and encourage the growth of rot.

Sailboats have a more acute ballasting problem because they must counteract the heeling action of the wind. Their ballast very often is in a deep extending keel.

Period of Roll

Since the forces that tend to right a ship differ with loading and design, it is logical to assume that the time it takes to complete one cycle of swinging or rolling will also vary. In this context a roll is the complete swing from one heel-over across to the opposite one and then back to the first. The time consumed for this complete movement is the "period of roll." (To be completely correct, this timing is done in still water with the heel externally applied by hauling the ship over. Taking the average of a series of rolls leads to greater accuracy.)

Every boat, from the smallest outboard to the largest liner, has a natural period of roll and this will vary with loading. An experienced skipper is aware of this and keeps himself alert for a dangerous condition known as synchronous rolling.

The period of roll of a sailboat under sail in a beam wind is obscured because the force of the wind keeps her heeled over. The effect is to steady the boat (some powerboats use a steadying sail).

SYNCHRONOUS ROLLING.

When successive waves hit broadside in exact timing with the period of roll, a condition called synchronous rolling exists. Disaster is imminent unless the situation is corrected.

Synchronous rolling can be compared to a child's swing when it is pushed at exactly the right instant during each oscillation. The arc of swing then becomes greater and greater. So with the roll of a ship; each succeeding wave pushes at exactly the right instant until the roll becomes so great that recovery from the heel is impossible.

The safe boat skipper must stop synchronous rolling as soon as he perceives it, and he has several means at hand to do this. He can angle his boat to the direction of the waves so that the resultant which causes roll is lessened or eliminated. He can change the speed of his boat. He can shift cargo or passengers, thus shifting the center of gravity and altering the period of roll. Built-in deterrents such as narrow strips along the bottom parallel to the keel and called bilge keels also help.

Experience has shown that the interplay of the boat's period of roll and the period of the broadside waves has a great deal to do with passenger comfort. Where the roll period is short and the wave period long, the boat roll is jerky, sharp, stiff, and uncomfortable. Where these two conditions are reversed the roll becomes softer, smoother, and much less tiring. The inherent roll period of a small boat often is obscured by the brute force of the waves; it is compelled to roll with the waves.

The basic physical concepts of flotation have now been covered and an understanding of actual boat hulls is in order. But, as with any voyager to a foreign land who wants to get the most from his travels, the new language must be learned.

Hull Nomenclature

The skeleton drawings of Figure 1-5 and 1-5A (for power-boat and sailboat respectively) name most of the parts of a hull and show their relation to each other. (The top-sides and interiors are treated separately in Chapter 5.) These drawings show minute details in order to explain clearly how a hull is put together. In contrast, naval designers and boat builders use a stylized form of mechanical drawings which is exact enough to provide measure-

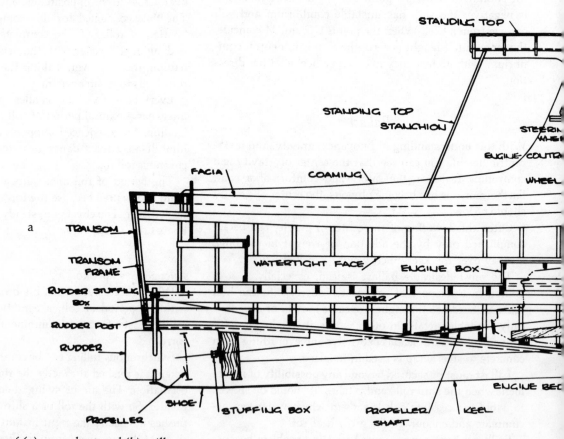

Figure 1-5: These views of (a) powerboat and (b) sailboat hulls name the various parts and show how they are joined to form a strong structure.

ments for construction. Such a layout for a hull is shown in Figure 1-6; understanding it will enable you to visualize a prospective boat completely from its mechanical views.

The view marked (b) is the "sheer," that marked (a) the "half-breadth." (Since the two halves of a hull are, or should be, identical, only one-half need be drawn.) The two views labeled (c) are the "body," one going from the bow to amidships and the other from amidships to the stern; they are generally combined on a center line as shown at (d).

The sheer view tells a great deal about the gracefulness of a hull: its height above water, its freeboard in relation to its length, the rake of its bow and its stern, the gentle upsweep or sheer of its deck line. The half-breadth view shows how wide the hull is, its beam, and how this

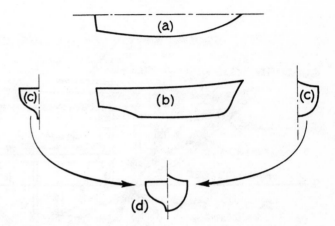

Figure 1-6: How naval architects outline a hull: (a) half breadth, (b) sheer, (c) body, (d) the combination of fore and after body.

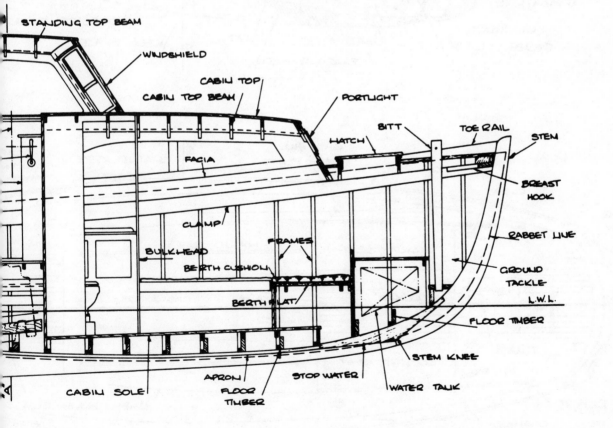

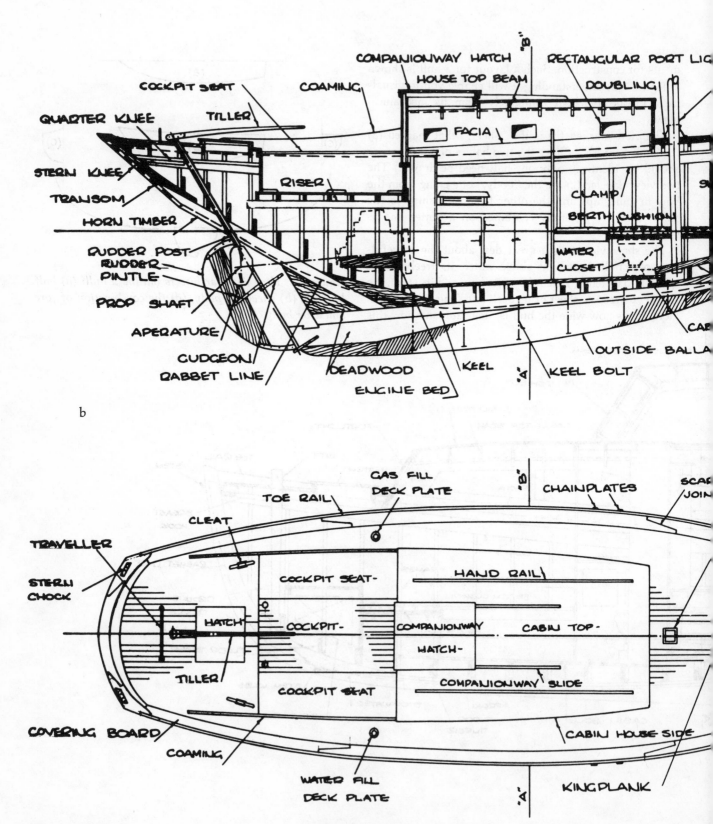

QUARTER KNEE
COCKPIT SEAT
TILLER
COAMING
COMPANIONWAY HATCH
HOUSE TOP BEAM
RECTANGULAR PORT LIG
DOUBLING
FACIA
STERN KNEE
TRANSOM
HORN TIMBER
RISER
CLAMP
BERTH CUSHION
RUDDER POST
RUDDER
PINTLE
WATER
CLOSET
PROP SHAFT
APERATURE
GUDGEON
RABBET LINE
DEADWOOD
ENGINE BED
KEEL
KEEL BOLT
OUTSIDE BALLA
CA
"B"
"A"

b

TRAVELLER
STERN
CHOCK
TOE RAIL
CLEAT
GAS FILL
DECK PLATE
CHAINPLATES
SCAR
JOIN
"B"
HAND RAIL
COCKPIT SEAT
HATCH
COCKPIT
COMPANIONWAY
HATCH
CABIN TOP
TILLER
COCKPIT SEAT
COMPANIONWAY SLIDE
COVERING BOARD
COAMING
CABIN HOUSE SIDE
WATER FILL
DECK PLATE
"A"
KINGPLANK

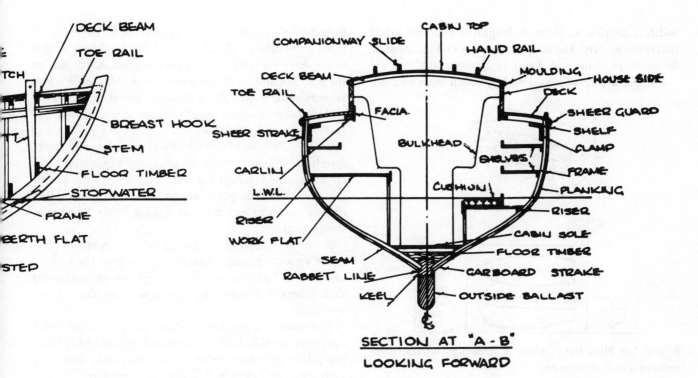

Labels on upper left diagram:
DECK BEAM
TOE RAIL
BREAST HOOK
STEM
FLOOR TIMBER
STOPWATER
FRAME
BERTH FLAT
STEP

Labels on center section diagram:
COMPANIONWAY SLIDE
CABIN TOP
HAND RAIL
DECK BEAM
MOULDING
HOUSE SIDE
TOE RAIL
DECK
FACIA
SHEER GUARD
SHEER STRAKE
SHELF
BULKHEAD
CLAMP
SHELVES
CARLIN
FRAME
L.W.L.
CUSHION
PLANKING
RISER
RISER
WORK FLAT
CABIN SOLE
FLOOR TIMBER
SEAM
GARBOARD STRAKE
RABBET LINE
KEEL
OUTSIDE BALLAST

SECTION AT "A - B"
LOOKING FORWARD

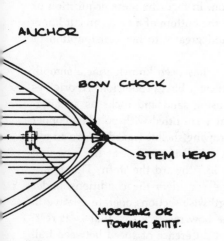

ANCHOR
BOW CHOCK
STEM HEAD
MOORING OR TOWING BITT.

SAILBOAT
NOMENCLATURE DRAWING
FOR: MR. HAL BALY, ESQ.
ATKIN & Cº

width is distributed along its length; it will spot a hull that is too squatty. The body view gives exact information on the shape of the hull at each point of its width.

Comprehension of the method by which these mechan-

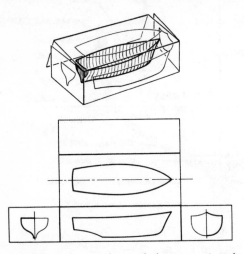

Figure 1-7: How the mechanical drawings for the blueprint of a hull are conceived.

ical drawings are conceived greatly facilitates their understanding. Figure 1-7 illustrates this method. An imaginary transparent plastic box, whose bottom is hinged along the heavy lines, is placed over the model to be drawn. The eye is then placed directly over each side and over the bottom; what it sees is drawn on the appropriate panels. These panels are then folded flat by means of the hinges, and this establishes the mutual relationships of the various views.

With a little practice, the mind can take these views and conjure up an image of the actual boat. A quick judgment is then possible about her ability to move through water with much or little resistance.

Hull Resistance

Except possibly for a float that is permanently moored, the intended purpose of a hull is to carry passengers and cargo from one place to another. Since various natural forces resist this movement, however, energy in the form of motive power (see Chapter 2) must be applied. The ideal hull design is the one that permits the easiest and

fastest motion with the least application of energy.

Nature undoubtedly anticipated the ideal hull design in the shape she gave to fast-swimming fish. A fish divides the water cleanly at its head without pushing up a wave, permits smooth flow along its sides, and then allows the parted water to come together again at its tail without forming an eddy. In other words, the fish's motion has caused a minimum of disturbance of the water and therefore has required a minimum of energy expenditure. An engineer would characterize this condition simply as efficiency. The fish has put its energy into moving ahead (the desired purpose) and not into making waves (the undesired effect).

At the present state of the art, a practical boat hull must waste a goodly portion of its motive power in the making of waves and eddies. Some hull designs are more efficient than others, but compared with a fast fish they are all very poor.

The sources of resistance to the travel of a hull through the water are skin friction, wave making, and eddy making. These retardant forces are not constant; they vary with speed and with hull shape and condition.

SKIN FRICTION.

Water has a tendency to "stick" to the sides of a moving hull and to be "dragged" along with it. This drag constitutes skin friction. Obviously, the smoother the hull, the less the skin friction. In fact, the mere acquisition of a crust of barnacles on the bottom of a boat can cut knots from her speed and add greatly to her consumption of fuel.

Since ancient times it has been known that a smooth hull is necessary for efficient boat propulsion. Aborigines smoothed their hulls using sand and rocks as an abrasive. Later, men-of-war were fitted with polished copper bottoms. The modern rowing shell is waxed before a race.

The skin friction of a hull is greatest at the bow and becomes progressively less toward the stern. This is understandable when one considers the conditions under which the various lengthwise sections operate relative to the passing water. The bow meets water that is at rest; there exists the greatest difference of speed between hull and water, and consequently the greatest drag. Gradually more and more water sticks to the sides and moves with the hull so that, as the stern is reached, some of this water is traveling almost as fast as the boat. The skin friction therefore is least at this point.

Unfortunately, in this real world work cannot be done without the expenditure of energy. This is just as true in the case of skin friction. It takes energy to drag the surrounding water along with the hull and this is supplied by the boat's motive power at the cost of fuel or by the wind at the cost of speed.

Assuming a good hydrodynamic design, little can be done to reduce skin friction and mitigate the power loss it causes. The smoothly polished hull already mentioned is one palliative. Keeping the wetted surface area of the hull to a minimum is another. Still another is to avoid hull projections, even those as small as rivet heads. Unavoidable projections such as struts and skegs should be "faired" (streamlined). The introduction of "lubricant" films of air bubbles between hull and water has also been tried. (It is believed that porpoises reduce their drag by vibrating their skins.)

Because skin friction of any hull section reduces proportionately as it is farther aft from the bow, a longer boat has the advantage over a squattier one. Nonetheless, the total skin friction of any boat is a large factor in its speed capability. Mathematically, the relationship of skin friction to hull speed is as the square for clean hulls but it can go beyond, even to the cube, for fouled bottoms. That is, the drag is four times as great when a clean hull doubles its speed (the square) but can become eight times as great for a fouled hull (the cube). An assumption here is that the wetted surface of the hull remains the same and has not been reduced by the hull's ability to climb up out of the water as speed increases, a condition known as planing. When a hull "planes," it runs with a part of its bottom out of the water.

WAVE MAKING.

A portion of every fuel dollar on a powerboat and a fraction of the wind's effort on a sailboat go into the making of undesired waves. These waves resist all increases in hull speed and are the effective barrier to the economically practical top speed of a displacement hull. (This hull designation is explained in detail on page 28.) The barrier is so definite that it can be expressed mathematically in relation to hull length.

A law of physics states that two things cannot occupy the same space at the same time. As a hull moves forward it preempts space that an instant before had been occu-pied by water. This water is pushed away in two directions, out and down, as shown in Figure 1-8. An instant

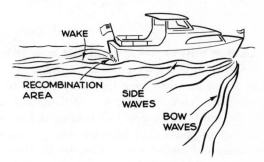

Figure 1-8: The water must part and then recombine to permit the forward motion of the boat.

later the hull vacates the space and the water rushes back to fill the void, forming waves. These waves are generated continuously during the forward passage of the hull.

Since the water is being pushed away in two directions (out and down), it is logical to expect two kinds of waves. The one moving diagonally away from the boat is the familiar bow wave. The other is the recurring "hill" of water seen alongside the hull when looking down over the rail. This side wave eventually combines with the disturbance caused at the stern; how smoothly this recombination is effected has great bearing on the total performance of the hull.

How waves are formed as the hull pushes water down can be understood from Figure 1-9. (In this illustration a stone instead of the bow has been used to push the water down initially.) At (a) is shown the deepest hollow the stone will make. Water being incompressible, it cannot absorb the "dent" as soft rubber would; instead, the pressure is transmitted into forming little "hills" on each side of the "hollow." At (b) the stone is continuing downward and no longer has any effect upon the surface. Meanwhile the force of gravity is trying to restore the original flat surface by bringing the hills down and therefore the hollows up. But the inertia of the water mass causes the hills to overshoot the surface and become hollows while the hollows likewise overshoot to become hills. The birth of waves is thus clearly shown.

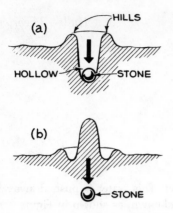

Figure 1-9: This analogy explains how waves are formed.

Water has mass or weight and to set mass in motion requires energy. Every wave can be regarded as a small packet of energy taken from the boat's power plant or from its sails. Since these waves are doing nothing to propel the hull—they are in fact holding it back—they are a waste of power. The boatman who glories in the huge waves and rooster tails thrown up by his craft is akin to the hot rodder who gauges his car by the volume of its exhaust noise.

EDDY MAKING.

Another barrier to speed and a waster of power when a hull is propelled is eddy making. The tendency to eddy making is greatly influenced by hull design, especially by the shape and size of the stern. It is an anomaly that the most popular shape of stern on present-day pleasure boats (the square transom) is the poorest from the standpoint of eddy making, while the best shape (the double-ender) has gone out of fashion. (See Figure 1-10.) The classic

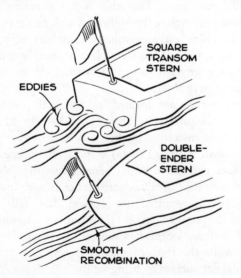

Figure 1-10: The out-of-fashion double-ender stern is hydrodynamically superior to the popular square transom. Note the bow-shaped stern of a typical double-ender.

sailboat hull, with its gracefully faired stern, assumes many of the advantages of the double-ender.

The water that was parted at the bow comes together again at the stern to resume its normal state. While the "stern" of a fish permits this coalescence smoothly, the stern of the square transom boat does not. The water coming along the sides suddenly finds a sharp break in its path, almost a void. It rushes in to fill this and swirling eddies result which become the equivalent of a backward drag. The wider and flatter the transom, the greater this suction. Power is again consumed for no useful purpose.

Disturbances from the stern plus those caused by the propellers combine with the side waves to form the total wake of the boat. Waves may combine in various ways determined by the relationships of their crests; when the crests are "in coincidence" (in phase), a phenomenon called standing waves results. These standing waves form a barrier to further increase in speed of the conventional displacement hull.

The causes of resistance to the forward motion of a hull are generally lumped together into "total resistance." This makes it possible to compare the efficiency of one hull with that of another. Obviously the better hull is the one with the lesser total resistance at a given speed; in other words, the one that requires less power to achieve a given speed.

Displacement Versus Planing

All boat hulls, whether small outboards or large cruisers, are classified into either of two general types: displacement hulls or planing hulls. (Many modern commercially built pleasure boat planing hulls incorporate features from displacement design.) A displacement hull always displaces the same amount of water; at rest or in motion its waterline does not change. By contrast, a planing hull gradually rises out of the water after it has attained a critical speed. The water it displaces becomes less and less as the speed increases. As the hull rises, the total hull resistance also drops off.

This might seem to contravene our previous section on buoyancy when it stated that the weight of water displaced must always equal the weight of the boat. The buoyancy theory still holds! The gimmick is that the planing hull acts as a displacement hull until it reaches critical speed; if it did not, it would sink. The planing hull bottom

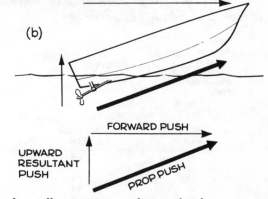

Figure 1-11: (a) This racer, with its tremendous power, is hardly touching the water. (b) A planing hull can stand on its prop because a portion of its motive power and the resultant reaction with the water raise it. (Credit—Thunderbird Boats, No. Miami, Fla.)

is so designed that a resultant from the forward motion acts to lift the boat out of the water. A portion of the effort previously supplied by buoyancy is now supplied by the engine. Nature gives nothing for nothing.

A condition similar to displacement and planing exists in all fluids, even in the air. The balloon and the airplane are familiar examples. The balloon is a displacement craft and is kept aloft by buoyancy alone; this is the reason for its large volume. The airplane is a planing craft; it is supported only by the "lift" resulting from its forward motion. It differs from the planing hull in that it cannot become a displacement type when at rest; a plane that is not moving forward fast enough "sinks."

Figure 1-11 is devoted to the why and the how of the planing hull. At (a) is a photograph of a boat of this type traveling at extreme speed, practically "standing on its tail." At (b) is a simplified diagram of the forces involved. The heavy arrow is the push supplied by the propellers and is at an angle to the surface. This is resolved into two forces, one producing forward motion and the second exerting the lifting force that is pushing the hull up a "wedge" of water.

Lateral Resistance

This term should not be confused with the hull resistance we have already discussed. Hull resistance is *detrimental*; lateral resistance is *beneficial* to the handling of a boat. Lateral resistance makes it possible for a vessel to stay on her forward course without being pushed sideways by the wind. This ability is generally obtained from a fore and aft member on the bottom called a keel. The plane of the keel is in line with the forward motion of the boat and

therefore offers minute surface to hinder movement in this direction. The surface of the keel is almost entirely presented broadside. This acts as a brake on any sideward (undesired) movement. This deterrent to sideward movement is especially important for a sailboat when the wind is from a sideward direction. Some sailboats are equipped with a centerboard, a vertical surface which is lowered to act as an additional keel. Hull resistances come into play only when there is motion—and motion implies some level of speed. How is this speed affected?

Limit on Speed

When the standing wave mentioned earlier coincides at bow and stern, it forms a barrier to a further increase in speed of a displacement hull. This phenomenon is sufficiently rigid to submit to the mathematical formulation that is given in Figure 1-12 together with some examples. At the critical speed, the hull is "locked" within the standing wave. The longer wave generated by higher speed would cause the stern to squat into the trough and the bow to point up. Any desired increase in speed thus is obtained only at the expenditure of a tremendous increase in power because the hull must climb over this hump to achieve it. Note again that planing hulls are not bound by this reasoning.

The multiplying factor (1.35) given in the equation of Fig. 1-12 is a conservative average for pleasure boats of the single hull variety. When it comes to present designs of multi-hull sailboats this factor can be doubled and sometimes increased even more. This means that the limiting hull speed for a catamaran, for instance, can be twice or more that of a mono-hull of equal length. The reason is the minimal wetted surface and ultra-fine body lines of these dual and triple hull craft.

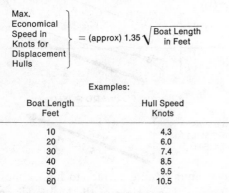

$$\left.\begin{array}{l}\text{Max.}\\\text{Economical}\\\text{Speed in}\\\text{Knots for}\\\text{Displacement}\\\text{Hulls}\end{array}\right\} = (\text{approx})\ 1.35\ \sqrt{\begin{array}{l}\text{Boat Length}\\\text{in Feet}\end{array}}$$

Examples:

Boat Length Feet	Hull Speed Knots
10	4.3
20	6.0
30	7.4
40	8.5
50	9.5
60	10.5

Figure 1-12: Displacement hulls display a direct relationship between their overall length and their economical top speed as shown by the above formula and examples.

GROUND REACTION.

The speed of a hull in shallow water also is affected by pressure patterns set up between the ground, the surface, and the moving craft. Waves generated by the motion of the boat strike the sea bottom, are reflected back, and interact with the surface waves. The various combinations of resulting standing waves sometimes help, sometimes hinder. These reactions could occur as well from the sides of a narrow channel.

Size Designations

Pleasure boats are generally identified by their length in feet. For the sake of clarity it should be noted whether this stated length is (1) between verticals erected at bow and stern, (2) at the waterline, or (3) the length along the gunwale from stem to stern.

Large ships are listed by tonnage; here again, there are different kinds of tons. Displacement tonnage is the actual weight in long tons (2240 pounds) of the water that the vessel displaces. Vessels may also be measured in gross

tons and net tons but these refer not to weight but to cubic capacity. These "tons" are equal to 100 cubic feet. The gross ton includes *all* enclosed space; the net ton takes account only of the enclosed space allotted to passengers and cargo. The displacement ton is also equivalent in weight to 35 cubic feet of seawater or 36 cubic feet of fresh water.

Hull Shapes

There are three primary hull shapes which may be used individually or in combination according to the whims of the designer: the flat bottom, the vee bottom, and the round bottom. Each has evolved over a period of time and has certain advantages: All are shown in Figure 1-13. Gull-wings, cathedrals, and similar modern forms are offshoots of these basic shapes.

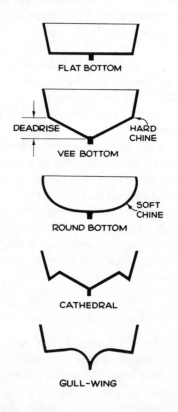

Figure 1-13: These are cross sections of the basic hull shapes.

FLAT BOTTOM.

The simplest and cheapest bottom to put on a hull is the flat; it is accordingly found on rowboats, small sailboats, and dinghies. The flat-bottom hull is easy to propel because it offers low resistance. It has minimal lateral resistance. It pounds badly in choppy water and is safe only in protected areas. A small keel is sometimes added to reduce the inherent tendency to drop off to leeward.

VEE BOTTOM.

The vee bottom is a very popular hull with pleasure boat builders and many variations are available in stock craft. The variations concern the angle of the vee, how sharply the angle diminishes toward the stern, and whether it be a simple or a compound vee. The vee has a good entrance to the water at the bow and suffers less pounding in a sea. The manner in which the center of buoyancy moves when the boat is heeled gives the vee good stability. The frames that support the outer skin can be assembled from straight sawed sections because bottom and sides meet at a sharp angle called the chine. (The significance of deadrise also is indicated in the drawings.)

ROUND BOTTOM.

The round bottom is the traditional hull that has evolved over a long period of time. The mere fact of its longevity proves that it has served its purpose safely and well. This is the most difficult construction and the frames must be sawed to shape or preferably steam-bent. All other things being equal, a curved surface is stronger than a flat plane; engineers consider the egg the sturdiest structure known for its size and weight. The round bottom is usually sharpened into a forefoot as it reaches the bow and can cut through a wave rather than pound on it and it has the least hull resistance at low and medium speeds.

MULTIPLE HULLS.

Many aboriginal tribes attached outriggers to their canoes to achieve stability in rough water. This can be thought of as attaching a small hull to the main hull by means of a leverage arm. Modern counterparts are the catamaran (two hulls) which is shown in Figure 1-14 and the trimaran (three hulls). Designers of these craft are now producing units big and sturdy enough for ocean crossing. One disadvantage of this type of construction is the limitation on usable space imposed by the necessity

Figure 1-14: Multi-hull boats claim added stability. A two-hull catamaran is shown above. (Credit—Acme Photo Service)

for dividing the internal layout between several hulls, thus losing the advantages of wide beams.

Some modern houseboats are built on a hull consisting of an assemblage of watertight hollow cylinders resembling pontoons. This is an adaptation of the multiple-hull design.

One of the inviting aspects of the multi-hulls is the increased comfort for those aboard when sailing because of the lessened angle of heel. Their wide stance (beam) enables these craft to carry the same sail as an equivalent length mono-hull but with only a fraction of the heel. Incidentally, it is a rule among the experienced multi-hullers never to let the weather hull break out of the water. (See below.)

MODERN OFFSHOOTS.

Modern designers spotted another advantage in the multi-hull concept in addition to the stability already mentioned: Resistance could be lowered by using two or more narrow hulls in place of one wide one. This was especially applicable to fast boats, those moving at considerably above traditional hull speed.

The forerunner of this thinking was the so-called sea sled. It had two narrow hulls connected by a deck which occasionally also contributed to "lift" at high speed. Shortening or eliminating this deck and then blending the hulls into a smooth cross section led quite naturally to the present cathedral and gull-wing types. Many designers incorporate the principle of trapped air lubrication, discussed earlier, in a further effort to reduce resistance and thus increase the effectiveness of horsepower or sail in providing speed.

STABILITY COMPARISONS.

Now that the factors which create stability have been explained and the various hull shapes described, you may quite logically ask: "Which hull is the safest?" There is no specific answer to that question because all are safe when properly built and intelligently handled; each may have a single facet of superiority but on total score they will all come out pretty even.

All correctly designed hulls also are stable—but stability often is a matter of degree. Some hulls can be heeled farther from their neutral point than others before the situation becomes precarious. Perhaps the best way to express this is pictorially with a diagram. The curves in Fig. 1-15 are averaged values, stylized and brought to a

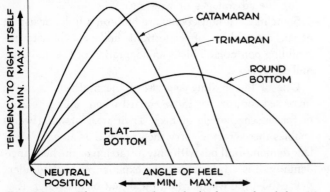

Figure 1-15: These curves show the high initial stability of the catamaran and the trimaran compared to flat- and round-bottom conventional hulls. Note however that the stability of the round-bottom hull extends for a much greater angle of heel.

single graph for ease in comparison.

The curve proves what you may already have learned from experience. A flat-bottomed boat has high initial stability over the first few degrees of heel and then tips over rapidly. The round-bottom hull can be heeled to a greater angle before it develops its maximum tendency to right itself. The surprise may lie in the two curves which portray the catamaran and the trimaran.

The maximum stability of the catamaran and the trimaran is far greater than that of the single-hull boats. This is not difficult to understand because, first of all, these vessels simulate a single-hull craft of equal length but extreme beam. Any heel rapidly increases the buoyancy of the hull being submerged and this force acts with a long lever arm. However, the multi-hulls lose their tendency to right themselves much sooner than a single-hull round bottom. A strong wind acting on the exposed underside can make this transition even sharper.

A further peculiarity relating to the stability of multi-hulls is of interest. They are in neutral stability when right side up and also when upside down. A look at the cross-sectional shape makes this statement rationally acceptable. The mono-hulls, especially those with keels, cannot remain upside down.

One of the original, often-heard claims for the multi-hulls was that they are not capsizable. This of course is not true; stupid and reckless handling can turn them over in a strong wind—and the curves explain why. Another factor is that the multi-hulls carry no ballast because the aim of the designers is to make them as light as possible to attain minimum wetted surface and consequently maximum speed. The righting ability of the tri is a bit greater than that of the cat because the tri puts its weight in the center hull and thereby achieves a lower center of gravity.

When discussing stability of boats in relation to the wind, it is important to remember how these effects relate to each other. When the wind doubles its velocity, its effect is squared; in other words four times as great. When you double the length of an identical hull, the stability goes up to the fourth power, in other words it becomes sixteen times as great. Thus, as ships get larger, all other things being equal, their ability to do battle against the elements increases at a geometric rate.

Hull Construction Methods

The skeletal constituents of all hulls are similar regardless of hull shape, but several methods are used for constructing and attaching the outer skin. This outer covering or planking can be narrow strip, carvel, lapstrake, wide sheet, homogeneous shell, riveted or welded.

NARROW-STRIP PLANKING.

This is explained by the cross-sectional view of Figure

1-16. The name is almost self-explanatory. Narrow strips of rectangular section, preferably long enough to reach from stem to stern in one piece, are fitted tightly, edge to edge, and fastened to the frames. Because of their narrow-

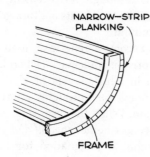

Figure 1-16: Narrow-strip planking. (Sealing compound is often applied between meeting edges.)

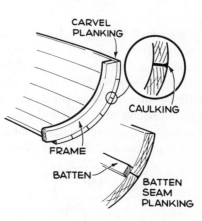

Figure 1-17: Carvel planking can be applied with or without internal batten strips. The seams are caulked.

ness, these strips can be bent to conform to the hull contour simply by clamping, without the use of heat treatment. This type of planking generally is not caulked; it gets its watertightness from the close original fit-up although the edges are often pre-coated with sealing compound for additional insurance.

Teak and mahogany are the preferred woods, although the prohibitive cost of teak restricts it to the most expensive boats. Subordinate to mahogany, and easier to come by, are white oak, douglas fir, and southern yellow pine, in that order. Heartwood is always used in preference to sapwood.

CARVEL PLANKING.

This can be thought of as similar to narrow strip in its application except that the planks are wider and the seams between planks are caulked. Carvel is the style commonly used by builders of wooden boats. Fewer planks are required to cover the surface of a given hull but this advantage is had at the cost of more difficult fitting and steam bending. The wider wood allows more secure fastening at each frame. A cross section is detailed in Figure 1-17. Wood preferences are the same as for narrow-strip planking.

An improved variation of carvel planking is called batten-seam planking. A strip of wood, a batten, is fastened on the inside over every seam to secure watertightness. The larger and better boats are also double planked; two complete layers of planking, one over the other, enclose the hull. These layers may run at an angle to each other for added strength or in any manner that does not place one seam directly over another. Canvas or plastic impregnated with sealing compound is placed between the layers by some builders.

LAPSTRAKE.

Often called clinker planking, this uses planks similar to carvel but overlaps the edges instead of butting them. Thorough fastenings, usually with rivets, are made along each overlap and this greatly increases the structural strength of the hull. There is no caulking, watertightness being achieved through the original fit-up plus a coating of compound.

A lapstrake hull rolls less than a carvel hull because the edge of each strake acts as a bilge keel. This may not be apparent immediately because the edge would seem to present an inconsequential surface. Second thought shows that the edge of a plank twenty-four feet long and only half an inch thick is the equivalent of one square *foot* of surface. This alone would offer an anti-rolling effect— and there are many planks. Lapstrake planking is shown in Figure 1-18. Wood preferences are the same as for narrow-strip planking.

WIDE SHEET.

These hull enclosures utilize plywood panels, each of which covers a fairly large area. Although this form of construction is now found only in small boats, large submarine chasers were built by this method during World War II. Because it is impractical to bend plywood into sharp or compound curves, wide-sheet construction is confined to flat-bottom or vee-bottom hulls where sides and bottoms can meet at a hard (sharp) chine.

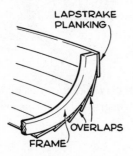

Figure 1-18: Lapstrake planking. Through fastenings, usually with rivets, are made along each overlap.

The plywood naturally is of marine grade, which means that the laminating glue is waterproof. A resorcinol glue, which results from the chemical interaction of resorcinol and formaldehyde, is the preferred adhesive. It is chemically neutral and thus has no deteriorating effect upon the wood. As a bonus it is mildly fungicidal and inhibits mold growth.

MOLDED WOOD

An offshoot of plywood construction called molded wood actually amounts to assembling the layers comprising plywood right to the shape of the hull. The individual layers of wood, being very thin and pliable, can be formed to the desired shape over the mold. The layers are assembled with their grains running at an angle (as in plywood) and adequate coatings of cement are applied between layers. The completed mass is then put under heat and pressure.

The result is a homogeneous plywood shell without the internal stresses that would result if actual plywood were bent to the required shapes. Light weight and sturdiness are achieved by this manner of construction.

HOMOGENEOUS SHELL.

This is a term intended to describe hulls that are enclosed by what is essentially one continuous skin, much like an eggshell cut in half. The material most commonly used is fiberglass although ferro-cement is making its appearance and some small boats are formed from a single thin sheet of aluminum.

Fiberglass has become a generic term although it came into being as a private trademark. Fiberglass is a sandwiched laminate in which layers of cloth and matting spun from glass fibers are thoroughly impregnated with a resinous compound. When the resin sets, or polymerizes, the structure becomes homogeneous and develops great strength. The technical designation for this material is FRP, meaning "fiber reinforced plastic."

The methods of fiberglass boat manufacture vary but almost all dispense with the frames that form the skeleton for orthodox craft. More useful internal space is thereby made available in any given-size hull. Resistance to the sidewise crushing force of the water is provided by bulkheads, the internal crosswise walls.

The layers of glass cloth and matting are laid up on a mold made to the exact dimensions of the desired hull. Heat is applied after the impregnation by the resin, whereupon a catalyst contained in the formulation cures the entire mass into a hard solid. An external coat of resin, the gel coat, provides both color and high gloss. The adaptability of fiberglass boats to mass production is apparent.

Ferrocement is a construction in which concrete forms the outer shell. When concrete is mentioned as a boat material, people think instinctively of a stone plunging to the bottom. Yet, second thought reveals that steel and other common boatbuilding metals would be open to the same false reasoning—as would any material that has a specific gravity greater than water and therefore sinks.

Ferrocement derives its name from the steel (*ferro*) reinforcing pipes, bars, wires, and netting that impart the necessary structural strength to the cement mixture. This mix consists of sand and other fine aggregates all bound together by the adhesive property of the Portland cement.

In this type of construction the entire hull is set up as a mesh skeleton of steel. The cement mixture then is forced into the mesh as a thin layer and finally troweled smooth on the outside. Frames are eliminated, as with fiberglass. (See Figure 1–19.)

Although ferrocement is only now coming to the notice of the pleasure boating public, ships were built by this method before the end of the last century. World War II saw many ferro-cement vessels in use.

RIVETED CONSTRUCTION.

This is found at present only in small aluminum boats and canoes. Adjoining sheets of the metal skin are overlapped and riveted at close intervals, sometimes with an interleaved gasket sheet to obviate leakage. Earlier large steel ships were built by the riveting technique. Modern shipyard practice has turned to hydrogen or argon electric welding for these vessels and this is true also for the large aluminum yachts. One of the advantages is the elimination of the myriads of rivet heads which increased hull resistance.

Welding is the preferred technique for metal boat construction. The skin sections are butted together and the adjoining edges are fused into a continuous piece by the heat of the electric arc. The final strength is that of a single homogeneous piece. The skin is also welded to the frames, thus giving the entire structure the rigidity of an equivalent box girder.

Many boatmen are prejudiced against metal hulls—some admittedly without any firsthand experience. They accuse the "tin cans" of transmitting exterior temperatures to the interior and say that condensation and noise are added problems. There is some truth to these accusations, especially for a single-skin hull.

Noisiness and condensation can be overcome by coating the interior with a compound made for this purpose. (The technique is akin to the undercoating of automobiles.) This coating also reduces heat transfer, making the cabins cooler in summer and warmer in winter. A double skin is the deluxe solution, especially if the between-skin space is filled with buoyant material.

Bow Shapes

The shape of the bow greatly affects the appearance of the boat but it has an even more important effect on seaworthiness and seakindliness. The vagaries of the eye make the bow that is vertical or plumb appear to be leaning aft toward the stern. A bow that slopes forward gives the feeling of speed. A blunt round nose raking slightly

Figure 1-19: In ferrocement construction a steel mesh framework is encased in cement to form the completed hull. (Credit—Motor Boating magazine)

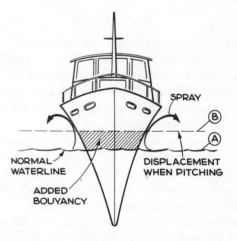

Figure 1-20: How the flared bow quickly adds forward buoyancy to mitigate pitching.

sternward gave the old oyster boats their ugly silhouette.

The flared bow has a practical purpose in addition to its beautifying effect: It deters nose diving. Figure 1-20 shows the flared bow under two conditions:(A) at its normal immersion when the craft is running on an even keel and (B) at the additional immersion caused by a violent pitch forward. It is apparent that more water has been displaced at (B) and that therefore more buoyancy has been added. This lifting power forces the bow back up to an even keel. Some of this effect would, of course, also be exercised by a straight bow but the flare magnifies the forces and lifts the bow faster. As a bonus, the flare throws spray out to the sides.

It is generally accepted that a bow's best mode of entry into the water is a sharp nose—although many liners, tankers, and warships are adopting the bulbous bow. Broadly speaking, bottom flatness at the bow tends toward pounding in a sea while high vees and rounds tend to cut through. From this it follows that the best planing designs would have a sharp vee at the bow and then gradually blend into a partial flat as the stern is reached. For a nonplaning hull the lines would fair into a modified round at the stern. An axiom to bear in mind is that any undesired disturbance at the bow is paid for in the fuel bill or in the lowered effectiveness of the sails.

Boat Woods

The first boat material was wood and it will probably retain its appeal for builders as long as there are trees to supply it. Wood floats, it is strong, and it can be worked with comparative ease. The major disadvantage of wood is that it is composed of cellulose; this means vulnerability to mold and rot and shrinkage.

The size and shape of a piece of wood are distorted by its moisture content; put more simply, wood swells and shrinks. This swelling, shrinking, and cupping always take place in a definite relation to the grain direction, however. A knowledgeable builder therefore can counter some of these ill effects by suitably aligning the grain for a proposed part.

Wood can broadly be classified as hard or soft, yet these terms do not necessarily indicate the relative strength but rather the genus of the tree. The woodsman would call these deciduous (which lose their leaves seasonally) and conifers (cone shaped evergreens) respectively. An important characteristic of both kinds is whether it be heartwood or sapwood. Heartwood is the center section of the trunk which has become close-grained and somewhat resistant to mold and rot. Sapwood is the outer section, closer to the bark, and is much more vulnerable to decay.

A conscientious builder would not consider using sapwood for a boat; he would also avoid the pith or core of the tree.

The manner in which wood is sawn from the log affects its value as boat material. A log can be fed to the saw lengthwise so that the cut is at radial angles to the growth rings; this is "quarter sawn." The saw could cut tangentially to the growth rings and this would result in "plain sawn." The cut could also be made intermediately to produce "diagonal grain." All this is shown in Figure 1-21.

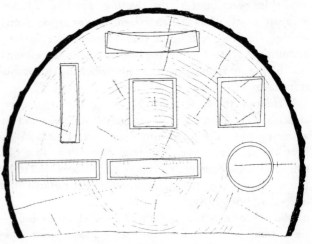

Figure 1-21: How tree trunks are sawed to become boat-building wood. The inner shapes indicate the amount and type of shrinkage to be expected.

Teak is way out in front as the wood with the finest qualities for boat building. It shrinks least, has the greatest decay and fungus resistance, responds best to finishing yet takes on a noble appearance even when merely holystoned. It is also the most expensive!

Mahogany is another fine wood for boat building. It is used today primarily for planking and transoms. There are three major sources of mahogany: American, African, and Philippine—and the quality preference is in that order. American is the "true" mahogany and has the highest natural decay resistance.

White oak finds almost universal use for the construction of hull frames. It is a tough wood that holds fastenings well yet lends itself easily to steam bending. It has medium decay resistance.

Douglas fir is a softwood that has high strength and a fairly low rate of shrinkage. It is well adapted to the making of hull stringers, engine beds, deck beams, and other structural members. Minor drawbacks are its tendency toward splitting and its retention of sap.

Southern yellow pine is the other softwood that finds much use in boat building. To some extent it is specified interchangeably with Douglas fir although it is more often found as "clamps" and the inside covering (ceiling) of a hull.

The most important factor in selecting wood for boat use, aside from correct species, is moisture content. Wood that is too green, that is, with too high a moisture content, will shrink inordinately. Wood that is too dry will expand rapidly with acquired moisture and cause bulging. Moisture content of wood is expressed as a percentage. The usually acceptable range for boat work is from 16 to 24 percent.

Hull Metals

The two metals presently in use for hull construction are aluminum and steel. Of these, aluminum is by far the more popular for pleasure boats even though steel has been a boat builder's metal since the first introduction of steam.

Aluminum owes its popularity for outdoor construction to a peculiar property: the ability chemically to protect itself. An oxide coating is formed on the surface spontaneously on exposure to atmosphere or water and this becomes a shield against further attack. Nevertheless, this alone was not sufficient to make aluminum suitable for marine use and new alloys, principally with magnesium, were developed. Only those marine alloys referred to commercially as #5050, #5154, #5083, #5005, #5454, #5086, #5052, #5456, and #6061 should be specified for boat work.

Steel does not have the self-protective property of aluminum. Although rust theoretically shields the base metal, it flakes off and exposes new surfaces to be attacked. Steel must therefore be painted and any rust should be chipped away promptly.

A rule of thumb is that steel weighs three times as much as aluminum and costs one-third as much, so that material cost in the end about balances. This of course applies only to the flat, raw metal sheet.

Hull Stresses

A vessel underway is subjected to exceedingly complex stresses and strains which its hull must be able to resist if passage is to be safe. An automobile travels a relatively flat surface; at worst it might encounter a depression on one side which places the chassis under diagonal stress. Contrarily, a boat seldom cruises on a flat sea. It traverses either a washboard or a roller coaster depending on the relative sizes of boat and wave. Only in still water is the hull uniformly supported as the designer intended. (See Figure 1-22.)

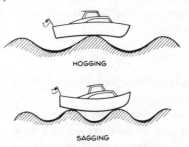

Figure 1-22: How waves can stress a hull.

When the wave is longer than the hull the weight of the boat is supported only amidships. When the wave and boat length coincide, support is had at bow and stern. The first condition encourages "hogging" and the second "sagging"; there are many intermediate positions. Many designers counter this with a resilient hull that can give a little, like a tree in a gale. A boat underway in rough weather can go through innumerable changes in its manner of support.

Trim

The fore and aft level of a hull as it rides in the water is called its longitudinal trim. Rapid alternation of this trim is called pitching. (Rapid change in athwartship trim is called rolling.)

Normal but incorrect trim can be nose-down for a particular boat. This is difficult to correct without major shifting of weight aboard. On the other hand, nose-up trim can be corrected easily with the addition of trim tabs at the stern. One such installation is shown in Figure 1-23. An innovation in trim tab application is the "joy stick"

Figure 1-23: Trim tabs can help a hull maintain proper trim under various conditions of load and speed. (Credit— Bennet Marine, Inc.)

also shown. It controls the tabs simultaneously for achieving any desired trim.

Normal athwartship trim differs greatly for sailboats and powerboats when they are underway. A well-constructed and properly loaded powerboat is expected to travel with its athwartship trim absolutely level, excepting of course any rolling caused by wave action. The height of its gunwale above the water line should be identical at directly opposite points.

However, a sailboat underway in a strong wind responds to the great sideward pressure upon its sails by heeling over, sometimes so far that its leeward gunwale is almost awash. Depending upon the relation between its course and the direction of the wind, the boat may travel in this heeled state for long periods of time. (It has been said that a true windjamming sailor is born with one leg shorter than the other to assure his standing erect on a slanting deck.)

Spray Rails

Many slow-speed hulls and virtually all high-speed hulls are built with spray rails. In appearance these rails are projecting strips running longitudinally at an angle and located at various positions on the hull. Spray rails are of greater importance and require more careful design than their simple contour would assume.

One very obvious job assigned to spray rails is to fend spray away from the hull while running. The purpose of this is comfort and visibility for those on board. But spray rails have another function, less well known yet of tremendous importance on fast boats: They keep water from climbing up the hull surface, a condition which would increase wetted area and rob power because of the added resistance.

Achieving this second function takes a combination of careful thought and experience on the part of the designer. Only certain locations for spray rails are effective on any given hull and these depend greatly on the boat's trim. (You can only deflect spray where spray exists.) Incorrect placement can aggravate rather than alleviate the spray situation and actually slow the boat down.

The cross-sectional shape of the spray rail also has great bearing on whether or not it does its job. Tests have shown that sharp corners are essential because they throw the water off. Water, aided by its capillarity, works its way around round corners and defeats the purpose of the rail.

Hull Fastenings

Many boats whose planking and frames have remained in good condition are nevertheless wrecks because their fastenings let go. These include rivets, screws, bolts, and nails. Corrosion, whether galvanic or chemical, was the enemy.

Monel and stainless steel head the list of recommended metals for fasteners. Some bronzes and some copper alloys are acceptable. Galvanized steels are borderline and are considered inferior by many builders. Brasses are not acceptable. The common shoreside hardware store fasteners are bad sailors and **never** should be used.

2   *Motive Power—*
Theory and Practice

To be of any practical value for the carrying of passengers and cargo, a hull must be fitted with a means of self-propulsion that is responsive to the operator's will. Work must be done to move the hull and this requires an expenditure of energy. The source of this energy and the method of its application determine the nature of the propulsion machinery.

Energy could be supplied by human muscle, by the wind, by fossil fuels, by electricity, and even by atomic fission or fusion. Muscle power is obvious and requires no great elaboration but the other devices can be examined more or less closely, depending upon the popularity of their use in modern pleasure boats.

At this writing atomic power is the most visionary on the list; it is doubtful that any present skipper will see use made of it within his lifetime. True, atomic submarines are roving the seas in increasing numbers and an atom-powered merchantman has circumnavigated the globe. But these are large vessels whose hulls have the buoyancy and the space to house the tremendously large and heavy protective shields that are necessary for the safety of personnel. At this stage of the art there is no foreseeable atomic power plant whose output could compete in the horsepower range usual for small boats and be adapted to pleasure craft. So, at least for now, the powerboat skipper and the atom will not be shipmates.

Electricity as a propellant for powerboats is held back by the same component that blocks its use for automobiles: the battery. No storage battery has yet been developed whose capacity as a power source comes even close to that of the smallest fuel tank. The use of electricity to propel pleasure boats is certainly not new in itself; electric launches were in operation more than a half-century ago. But these were sight-seeing boats on the lakes of amusement parks; their total mileages were insignificant and they were always handy to the charging plug.

The electric motor has kept a toehold in the pleasure-boat world to a very minor degree in the outboard field. It is still available as a low-powered propulsion unit for light rowboats on small inland lakes. These units usually consist of an electric motor and its propeller at the bottom of a transom-mounting support. (Some drive through a flexible shaft in order to avoid immersion of the motor.) The power source is an automobile storage battery charged ashore and brought aboard. These devices are for slow meandering and quiet fishing; in no sense are they competitive with standard gasoline outboards.

The electric motor does have an important place in marine propulsion but this is in the realm of large commercial and naval ships. Here the motors actually do the prop turning but they themselves are powered by large generators run by diesels or turbines. The electricity in this scheme is merely a flexible means of power transmission; the original muscle is supplied by fossil fuels.

For boats, as for automobiles, the future of electric propulsion most probably is *not* oriented to the storage battery and its hoped-for improvement. It is difficult to foresee a storage battery as easily recharged on a trip as filling a tank with gas. Even a nationwide exchange system of charged batteries for discharged ones would be cumbersome in the extreme.

Any future the electric motor has as sole power for a powerboat undoubtedly is dependent upon the fuel cell. This device takes a fossil fuel and converts it directly into electricity without the intervention of generators or other moving elements. Some fuel cells do this by burning the fuel and applying the heat to thermoelectric materials that transform the thermal energy to electric energy. Others actually dissociate the fuel into its basic elements and then set up the electron flow that characterizes an electric current.

Whatever the final method of supplying the electric current, the actual work will always be done by an electric motor. All such motors, be they pigmy or giant, operate by certain basic principles and these are explained fully in Chapter 7.

The list of possible energy sources for powerboats has thus been narrowed down to the fossil fuels, the mainstay of modern boating. Fossil fuels, such as coal and petroleum, come from the internals of the earth. Coal can be ruled out at once although Dr. Diesel ran his first engines on coal dust. (Can you imagine a powerboat mate watching aghast as a load of coal dust comes aboard?)

Petroleum means diesel oil to the diesel skipper and gasoline to the vast majority of all other skippers. The energy in these fuels is always released for practical use by "burning" but this combustion could take place outside or inside the engine. As a consequence we have two broad classes of prime movers: external combustion and internal combustion. The early naphtha launches that burned the petroleum product under a boiler to form steam which ran the steam engine are examples of *ex-*

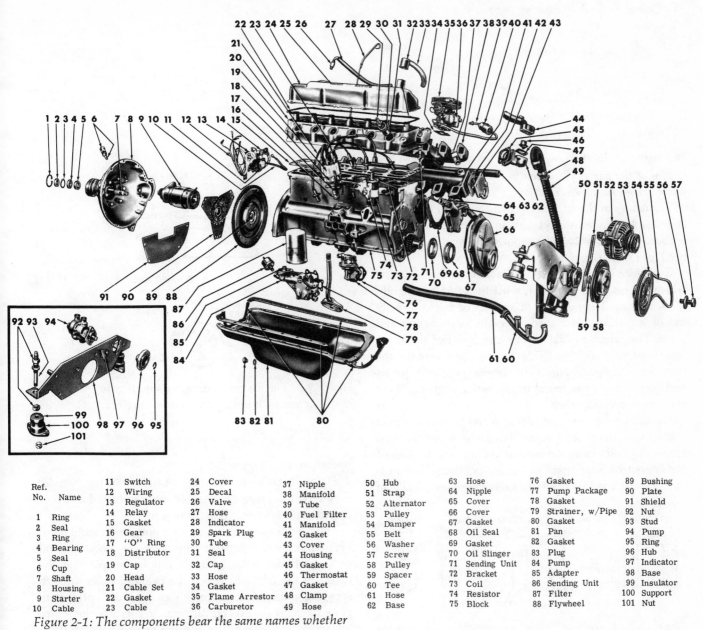

22 23 24 25 26 27 28 29 30 31 32 33 34 35 36 37 38 39 40 41 42 43

1 2 3 4 5 6   7 8 9 10 11 12 13 14 15

Ref.		11	Switch	24	Cover	37	Nipple	50	Hub	63	Hose	76	Gasket	89	Bushing
No.	Name	12	Wiring	25	Decal	38	Manifold	51	Strap	64	Nipple	77	Pump Package	90	Plate
		13	Regulator	26	Valve	39	Tube	52	Alternator	65	Cover	78	Gasket	91	Shield
1	Ring	14	Relay	27	Hose	40	Fuel Filter	53	Pulley	66	Cover	79	Strainer, w/Pipe	92	Nut
2	Seal	15	Gasket	28	Indicator	41	Manifold	54	Damper	67	Gasket	80	Gasket	93	Stud
3	Ring	16	Gear	29	Spark Plug	42	Gasket	55	Belt	68	Oil Seal	81	Pan	94	Pump
4	Bearing	17	"O" Ring	30	Tube	43	Cover	56	Washer	69	Gasket	82	Gasket	95	Ring
5	Seal	18	Distributor	31	Seal	44	Housing	57	Screw	70	Oil Slinger	83	Plug	96	Hub
6	Cup	19	Cap	32	Cap	45	Gasket	58	Pulley	71	Sending Unit	84	Pump	97	Indicator
7	Shaft	20	Head	33	Hose	46	Thermostat	59	Spacer	72	Bracket	85	Adapter	98	Base
8	Housing	21	Cable Set	34	Gasket	47	Gasket	60	Tee	73	Coil	86	Sending Unit	99	Insulator
9	Starter	22	Gasket	35	Flame Arrestor	48	Clamp	61	Hose	74	Resistor	87	Filter	100	Support
10	Cable	23	Cable	36	Carburetor	49	Hose	62	Base	75	Block	88	Flywheel	101	Nut

Figure 2-1: The components bear the same names whether the engines are large or small.

ternal combustion. Modern powerboats of course depend upon *internal* combustion engines. The principles are the same whether these engines consume diesel fuel or gasoline but there are some operating differences to be explained.

Internal Combustion Engines

All gasoline and all diesel engines generate their power in cycles of either two strokes or four strokes. (One complete movement of the piston, either up or down, is a stroke.) The dictionary states that a cycle is one complete series of continually recurring events which makes the word self-explanatory in relation to engines. In other words, one engine completes each cycle of power production in two strokes (one up, one down) while the other takes four strokes to do the same thing (one down, one

up, one down, one up). Each has its good points, its bad points, and its staunch adherents.

In layman's parlance, the two-stroke cycle is commonly referred to as the "two-cycle" and the four-stroke cycle as the "four-cycle." In the world of gasoline engines it is fairly axiomatic that the two-cycle will be met with only in the smaller sizes and in outboards. This does not hold true with diesels; some of the very large ones are two-cycle. The four-cycle engine is more complicated than the two-cycle engine and yet the workings of an internal combustion engine can be explained more easily and clearly if the four-cycle unit is taken as an example. Paradoxical but true nevertheless.

ENGINE COMPONENTS.

As the hawkers say at the football games, you can't tell the players without a program—and you can't discuss an engine without knowing the names, purposes, and shapes of the parts. The labels in the sketch of Figure 2-1 identify everything clearly.

The names of the parts are generic and hold true for all engines. A cylinder is a cylinder, in a puny 2-horsepower outboard and in a 2000-horsepower tugboat diesel. The need for familiarity is thus basic.

Cylinders. The inside of the cylinder is the surface upon which the piston slides and it must therefore be smooth, glass-smooth. The cylinder cavity can be bored directly out of a casting which also serves to locate valves and ports. The cylinder could also be a thin-walled sleeve inserted into the casting. This construction permits the metallurgy of the cylinder to be chosen specifically for its special purpose; it is found in the better engines. These cylinder sleeves are called liners.

Liners may be "wet" or "dry." A wet liner is in direct contact with the cooling water, a dry liner is not. Various forms of gasket seals are used at the top and bottom of the liners to mintain gas- and water-tightness. The various cylinder constructions are sketched schematically in

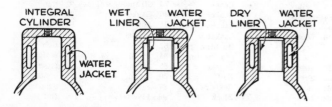

Figure 2-2: Three methods of constructing and cooling engine cylinders. The one at the left is the most common.

Figure 2-2.

Pistons. The pistons are sized for an easy sliding fit inside the cylinder. The gas-tightness necessary to avoid loss of power is achieved by piston rings that bear tightly against the cylinder wall.

The piston head is often given special shape to promote the turbulence needed for efficient fuel combustion. The pistons in small two-cycle engines carry deflectors that aid in scavenging the burned gases from the cylinder. The pistons in a good engine are carefully matched by weight as a vibration preventive.

The piston is connected to the crankshaft by a connecting rod. A piston pin (or wrist pin) gives the connecting rod freedom for its necessary swiveling motion during

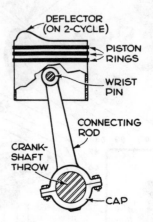

Figure 2-3: The piston transmits its motion to the crankshaft via the wrist pin and the connecting rod.

operation. (See Figure 2-3.)

Piston rings. Since the rings fit tightly in the cylinder they bear the brunt of wear. (Every motorist has heard the oft-repeated need for a "ring job.")

The rings actually serve another purpose in addition to maintaining gas-tightness: regulating the amount of oil on the cylinder walls. They do this by scraping off the excess of the oil that gets on the cylinder walls through spraying and splashing. Sometimes expander springs are placed behind the oil control rings to increase the scraping action and prevent the oil from reaching the combustion chamber, thus eliminating what is commonly called oil burning.

The piston ring obviously cannot be a solid hoop (how would it be installed?) and must have a split or gap. This gap also serves as room for expansion when the ring is hot. A gap naturally forms a tiny leak and various commercial designs attempt to minimize this; they are illustrated in Figure 2-4.

The upper piston rings maintain the compression by eliminating or greatly reducing the blow-by of the high-pressure products of combustion; these are known as the compression rings. The lower rings control the oil film on the cylinder walls and are called the oil rings. (Excess oil drains back through holes in the piston.) The drawings show what the sections of these two types of rings look like. All rings are fitted into grooves in the piston with just enough clearance for easy sliding. The best rings are

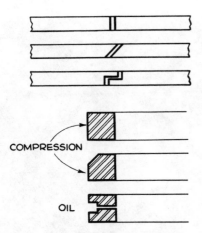

COMPRESSION

OIL

Figure 2-4: The gap in the piston ring permits installation and expansion. Holes in the oil control ring permit excess oil on the cylinder wall to drain back into the sump.

made of cast iron; steel and even molybdenum are also used.

Firm contact with the cylinder wall by the ring is maintained not only by the spring action; the high pressure combustion gases also help. Many designs permit this high pressure to get behind the ring and add its force.

Cylinder blocks. In multi-cylinder engines the cylinders are not set up separately but are cast in blocks, generally of two, three, four, or sometimes even six. (The heavy marine engines of an earlier day had individual cylinders.)

The blocks also contain the valve ports and carry the valves and their guides. The location of these valves determines the cylinder classification into "L-head," "T-head," or "overhead." The L-head has valves on only one side of the block, the T-head on both sides, while the overhead design carries the valving in the cylinder head and not in the cylinder block. The sketches in Figure 2-5 explain this.

Connecting rod. The connecting rod links the piston to the crank shaft. It transmits the lineal force exerted against the piston head by the burning fuel to the crankshaft. Since both piston and connecting rod are in reciprocating motion, designers attempt to keep their weight down as low as possible consistent with the required strength. The lower this weight, the less the vibration of the engine and the "snappier" the acceleration.

Connecting rods generally have an I-beam cross section since this affords the greatest strength with the least material. The upper end, at the wrist pin, may or may not have a bearing, but the lower end that encircles the crankshaft throw is always carefully bearinged to reduce friction.

Bearings. Bearings look simple enough, merely smooth

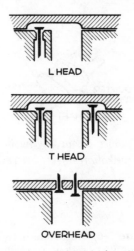

L HEAD

T HEAD

OVERHEAD

Figure 2-5: The engine is classified as "L," "T" or "overhead" by the location of its valves.

surfaces of light-colored metal, but their importance in the engine cannot be overemphasized. They must fit closely enough to prevent rattle and loss of alignment, yet loosely enough to accommodate a film of oil between the moving surfaces. The word loose is perhaps relative here because this looseness is measured in only a few thousandths of an inch.

To the casual observer of any machine it may appear that metal is sliding upon metal. If this were actually the case, disaster would result; the heat of friction would quickly destroy the surfaces. Microscopic examination would show that the metal surfaces are separated by a film of oil and never come in contact with each other if the machine is functioning properly.

The shiny metal bearings (babbit bearings) are not the only ones found in the engine. Ball bearings and roller bearings are also used in appropriate places and offer considerably less friction than the babbit.

Crankshaft. The main shaft of the engine, from which

the useful power is taken, is called the crankshaft. It transforms the push delivered by the connecting rod into a rotational force which can be used to turn the propeller.

The connecting rod is attached at an offset of the crankshaft called a throw and the length of this offset determines the "stroke" or lineal distance each piston travels.

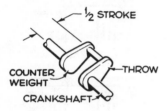

Figure 2-6: The power of an engine is taken from its crankshaft. The crankshaft offsets are called "throws."

As shown in Figure 2-6, the stroke is twice the distance from the center of the crankshaft to the center of the throw. Modern crankshafts of high-speed engines have counterweights opposite each throw to maintain balance and reduce vibration.

Valves. The cylinder space must be connected alternately to the source of fuel and to the exhaust line; this requires valves. The valves found in large modern marine engines are (universally) of the poppet or mushroom type illustrated in Figure 2-7 together with the usual assembly. (Some small two-cycle engines do not use poppet valves but substitute stationary openings or ports in the cylinder wall which the piston uncovers during its travel.)

A strong spring forces the valve head into intimate contact with its seat in the closed position and forms a relatively gas-tight closure. The valves are opened at the proper time for intake or exhaust by lobes or lifters on the camshaft.

Since the valves are subject to the searing temperatures of the burning fuel, it is evident that they must be manufactured from heat-resistant alloys; even so they would soon be destroyed without provision for cooling. The intake valve is cooled by the rush of fuel and air mixture when it opens. The exhaust valve is in a worse position because the gas rushing by it is in a flaming condition

Figure 2-7: The intake and exhaust valves open and close the passages to the intake and exhaust manifolds. The valve stems and springs are under the rockers; the push rods also can be seen. (Credit—Miami News, Photo by Jay Spencer)

and aggravates rather than cools. Whatever cooling it gets comes from its contact with its seat and its guide. (This difference in severity of service makes it possible to identify exhaust valves on sight by their condition.)

Valves, like pistons, are in constant reciprocating motion. This means that they must stop and start in the opposite direction thousands of times per minute. Inertia consequently becomes an important factor in valve operation in high-speed engines; valve weight must therefore be kept to a minimum and spring strength to a maximum.

Camshaft. The opening of each valve at the correct point in the cycle to assure optimum engine performance is done by the camshaft. The camshaft accomplishes this by having a "hill" of controlled shape at each valve position. These hills wedge the valves up as the shaft rotates either directly (as in overhead camshaft engines) or through pushrods and rockers (as in the standard engines). The camshaft is geared to the crankshaft or chain-driven by it in order to maintain the correct timing relationship.

On a four-cycle engine, the camshaft rotates at half the speed of the crankshaft. On those two-cycle engines that have poppet valves (and therefore require a camshaft), the camshaft turns at the same rate as the crankshaft. The explanation of two- and four-cycle operation on page 48 makes the need for this difference clear. A typical camshaft is pictured in Figure 2-8.

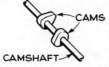

Figure 2-8: The intake and exhaust valves are opened and closed by the cams on the camshaft—directly on overhead and camshaft engines and through push rods and rockers on others.

Flywheels. Since power is produced during only a portion of each cycle, energy must be returned during the balance of the cycle to force the pistons back to their power-producing positions. This energy is drawn from the flywheel which received it originally on the power stroke.

The flywheel is thus an energy reservoir which apportions the power throughout the cycle to make a smoothly running engine. The flywheel has this ability because of its mass or weight, and the more this weight is concentrated at the rim, the more effective its operation. The limiting factor on size and weight is inertia, which will prevent quick responses to desired changes in speed.

Automobile engines have their flywheels at the rear; on marine engines this does not hold true. Some marine engines have the flywheel forward and the power takeoff aft, others reverse this procedure. The flywheel housing is of necessity a large bell-shaped enclosure, and thus the flywheel location can be ascertained at a glance.

Manifolds. The several exhaust openings in multi-cylinder engines are joined together in a common casting so that the exhaust pipe can be attached conveniently. This casting is the exhaust manifold. The intake openings are similarly joined by an intake manifold. Sometimes the intake and exhaust manifolds are in contact with each other so that the hot exhaust gases preheat the cool incoming fuel mixture.

Carburetor. Gasoline fuel cannot burn at the proper time under compression in the engine and release its energy unless oxygen is mixed with it in exactly the correct proportion. For gasoline this varies between twelve and seventeen parts by weight of air to one of fuel, the specific ratio at any time depending upon the load and the speed. Starting a cold engine requires a "richer" mixture (more gasoline), while moderate speed under low load takes a "leaner" mixture (less gasoline).

This mixing of air and gasoline was accomplished in early engines by a mixing valve; it was done quite inefficiently but well enough to get by. Many small engines such as those on power lawn mowers still use such a device.

Modern gasoline engines have their fuel mixture served to them by carburetors. These carbs are quite complicated in construction because they automatically vary the fuel-air ratio to suit the constantly changing needs of the engine. The theory and function of carburetors are discussed in detail on page 51 in this chapter.

Ignition. The fuel-air mixture in the cylinder must be ignited at a precise moment during the cycle if the maximum power is to be taken from it. This is the job of the ignition system. (Our discussion of the diesel engine on page 57 shows that these power plants are unique in not requiring an ignition system.)

The components of a standard ignition system are the spark plug, the ignition coil, the distributor, the breaker points, and the condenser. The current for operating this system can be taken from a battery or it can be self-generated in a magneto. Many of the very small engines incorporate this magneto method. (In years gone by, many of the larger marine gas engines also used magnetos, although of a different type.)

The action of the spark coil, essentially a transformer, and of the condenser (a capacitor) are explained carefully in Chapters 7 and 8. The appearance and function of a spark plug are known to every motorist.

Briefly, the breaker points initiate the spark with precise timing because the cam that actuates them is driven by the crankshaft through proper gearing. The resulting spark is routed to the correct cylinder by the distributor, which rotates integrally. What these two items look like is shown in Figure 2-9; references later in this chapter illuminate them even more clearly.

Cooling. It is an unfortunate fact of thermodynamic life that a great portion of the energy in every drop of fuel is wasted as heat—indeed *must* be wasted to comply with nature's laws. This waste heat is drawn off by the engine cooling system and eventually is transferred to the surroundings.

The cooling medium could be air, and this is used in some small automobiles and in most small appliances such as lawn mowers and chain saws. The more usual cooling medium is water. All marine engines are cooled by water and, either directly or indirectly, the waste heat finds itself

dispersed in the surrounding sea. Automobile engines are also cooled by circulating water but here the heat is eventually transferred to the air flowing through the radiator.

The cooling water circulates through a series of passages called the jacket. These are kept as close to the various hotspots of the engine as possible for efficient heat transfer. The circulation can be either raw seawater or enclosed fresh water, which then transfers its heat to the sea via a heat exchanger.

Raw seawater cooling is the simplest system but by no means the most desirable. It hastens corrosion in the engine jackets and often results in an insulating layer that interferes with the passage of heat. The closed cooling system containing fresh water is preferable.

An added advantage of the closed system is that various coolants can be circulated in place of plain water. One such could be ethylene glycol, the well-known antifreeze used in automobiles. Such coolants usually are composites of many additives which have as their purpose rust and corrosion inhibition and sometimes even the automatic sealing of leaks. The closed cooling system with its heat exchanger permits engines to function at higher, more efficient temperatures.

Gaskets. It is theoretically possible but not economically feasible to machine two metal surfaces so flat and so smooth that they will make a watertight seal when pressed together. As a substitute for this ultra-machining, a layer of comparatively soft and compressible material is placed between the surfaces to insure tightness. This material is called a gasket.

An engine has gaskets of many forms. Metal is never bolted against metal without an intervening gasket. Some gaskets are simple layers of cork cut to the required shape; others are made of asbestos; still others, such as the gasket between the cylinder block and the cylinder head, are asbestos lined on both sides with copper sheet.

FOUR-CYCLE OPERATION.

How do the conglomerate parts that have been described function together to produce useful power from a liquid fuel? What actually happens during each of the four strokes of each cycle? An understanding of these happenings means an understanding of *all* internal combustion engines, small, large, gasoline, or diesel.

The four strokes of a complete cycle are called intake,

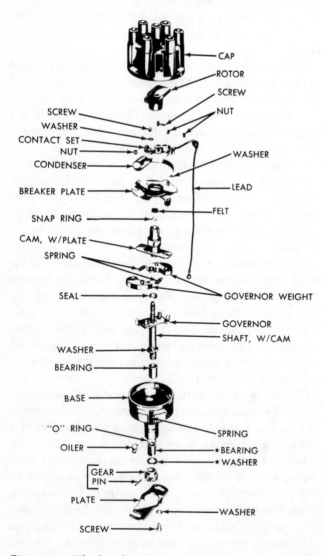

Figure 2-9: The breaker points (contacts) make and break the primary ignition circuit. The distributor routes the spark to the right cylinder.

compression, power, and exhaust—and they occur in that order. They are pictured successively in Figure 2-10. Remember that a stroke is one complete travel of the piston in *one* direction and is caused by a half-turn of the crankshaft. To complete the four strokes of each cycle of a four-cycle engine therefore takes two revolutions. From this evolves the first axiom: A four-cycle engine gets only *one* power stroke in each cylinder for every *two* revolu-

one-tenth of its original volume and is consequently under great pressure. This compressed state increases the efficiency with which power can be drawn from the fuel.

Power stroke. With the piston at the top of the cylinder, the fuel mixture under compression, and the two valves closed, everything is in readiness for the big bang that produces the power. This is initiated by a spark across the electrodes of the spark plug.

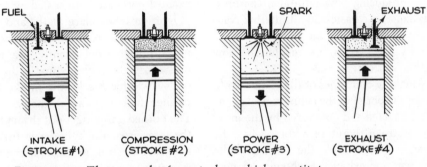

Figure 2-10: These are the four strokes which constitute the "four-stroke cycle." (A stroke is one complete movement of the piston either up or down.)

tions of the crankshaft.

Intake stroke. On the intake stroke, the piston travels from its highest to its lowest positions in the cylinder. This increases the volume, reduces the pressure below the outside atmosphere, and creates what the layman calls a suction. Since the intake valve is open during this period (the engine is built that way), thus opening the connection to the carburetor, the suction draws in a combustible mixture of fuel and air.

At or near the bottom of the intake stroke the intake valve is closed by the camshaft. The exhaust valve remained closed throughout this stroke.

Compression stroke. The momentum of the flywheel, transmitted through the crankshaft, now causes the piston to move back from the bottom to the top. Since both valves are tightly closed and the fuel mixture has nowhere else to go, compression results. The degree of this compression, called the compression ratio, is determined by the design of the engine and is not under the control of the operator.

When the piston reaches the top of its compression stroke the fuel mixture has been reduced to one-eighth or

The mixture bursts instantaneously into flames and its pressure now soars. This forces the piston down to the bottom of the stroke. Through the connecting rod and the crankshaft, this force is converted into rotation of the flywheel and into useful power.

Contrary to popular belief, the mixture does not explode in a properly running engine; it burns in an extremely fast but orderly fashion. When improper conditions actually cause the mixture to explode, it causes the annoying, destructive, and power-robbing "knock."

Exhaust stroke. The fuel mixture has now performed its mission and the useless burned gas residue must be expelled into the atmosphere. This is the purpose of the exhaust stroke.

The exhaust valve has been opened by the camshaft at the beginning of the exhaust stroke while the intake valve has been closed. The upward travel of the piston (again caused by the momentum of the flywheel) therefore pushes the exhaust gases out through the exhaust valve and into the exhaust pipe. This is the fourth of the four strokes and has completed the cycle.

The various valve conditions and the ignition were described at their theoretical positions at the end of each stroke. In actual practice the valve openings and closings and the ignition may precede or come after the exact terminal points of each stroke; these matters are determined by design. The controlling factor is that gas movement and combustion are not instantaneous but take a finite amount of time which must be compensated for.

TWO-CYCLE OPERATION.

The four steps in producing power (intake, compression, power, and exhaust) are basic and all internal combustion engines must take them. But the two-cycle engine crowds them into only two strokes, one revolution. How does it accomplish this shortcut?

The answer is by making both sides of the piston work, and by making openings (ports) in the cylinder wall act as valves when they are covered and uncovered by the moving piston. The first stroke therefore accomplishes the intake and compression steps while the second stroke takes care of the power and exhaust. Each cylinder now has one power stroke for every revolution or twice as

many as the four-cycle engine. The diagrams in Figure 2-11 should clarify this.

At (a) the piston is reaching the top, completing its first stroke, which started at the bottom. (As with all nonpower strokes, this was made possible by the momentum of the flywheel.) On its travel, the top of the piston has compressed the fuel mixture in the cylinder while the bottom of the piston has created a suction and filled the crankcase with new fuel through the one-way valve. Intake and exhaust ports are both sealed off by the piston skirt.

Ignition takes place at (b) and the resulting great increase in pressure forces the piston down and provides useful power. Concurrently, the underside of the piston pressurizes the fuel mixture in the crankcase because the one-way valve blocks the intake line. When the piston reaches the bottom at (c), the ports have been uncovered. The burned gases rush out through the exhaust port and the interior of the cylinder is further scavenged by the new fuel blasting in through the intake port. The cycle is complete; the four necessary steps have been taken in only two strokes or one revolution.

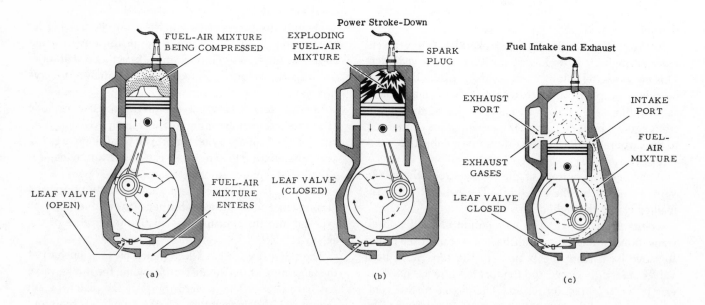

Figure 2-11: The two-stroke-cycle engine derives a power stroke from each revolution. At (a) the piston is nearing the top, is compressing the fuel mixture in the cylinder and is drawing new fuel into the crankcase. At (b) the fuel has been ignited and the piston is on its power stroke. (The one-way valve retains the fuel in the crankcase.) At (c) the piston is at the bottom of its stroke and the burned gas is being scavenged.

Two concepts make the two-cycle design possible. One is a baffle shape on the piston head. This deflects the incoming fuel mixture up and around the cylinder so that it can more effectively clean out the exhaust gas. Loop scavenging and cross-flow scavenging are popular methods of ridding the cylinder of the products of combustion; they are shown in the illustration. The second is one form of the simple one-way valve that seals the fuel mixture in the crankcase while the piston is putting it under pressure, yet allows fuel to enter on the piston's up stroke. The second axiom therefore is that a two-cycle engine gets one power stroke in each cylinder on every revolution.

FOUR-CYCLE VERSUS TWO-CYCLE.

A detailed comparison of the four-cycle and two-cycle engine features should act as a mental clarifier and facilitate decisions between the two when a power plant is being purchased.

It is evident that the two-cycle engine is simpler; poppet valves, camshaft, and gear train have been eliminated. This assumes the basic two-cycle operation, previously described, in which the crankcase is used to put the fuel under pressure. (Some large two-cycle engines sacrifice a portion of this simplicity in order to restore the crankcase to its original function as an oil reservoir.)

The two-cycle engine packs more power into a given size and weight. It has twice as many power impulses per cylinder as the four-cycle and thus its flywheel can be lighter.

The four-cycle engine has an oil sump from which a small pump can force lubricating oil under pressure to all friction surfaces. In the absence of such a sump, the two-cycle must get its lube oil as a mixture with its gasoline. This is not only wasteful but also the burning oil increases the tendency to firing-chamber and spark-plug fouling. The mixing of lubricating oil and gasoline in a fixed proportion is more bother than simply filling a tank with plain fuel. (Some fuel docks have pumps which automatically dispense a gas-oil mixture.)

The two-cycle engine is capable of faster response to an opened throttle because every downstroke of its pistons is a power stroke. On the other hand, the four-cycle is more economical with its fuel because its combustion is more efficient. Some of the incoming fuel in the two-cycle does go out the exhaust port and some of the burned gases do remain to tone down the flame.

Based on relative simplicity and complexity, it is reasonable to expect the two-cycle engine to cost less than the four-cycle engine of equivalent horsepower and service rating. A look at manufacturers' price sheets usually bears this out. The price differential is not great enough, however, to be the major reason for a choice of one or the other powerplant; indeed, in the larger size, such a choice is not even offered.

CARBURETOR FUNCTIONING.

The purpose of the carburetor on the gasoline engine is to mix fuel and air in the correct ratio. Basically this is a simple function and the earliest carburetors were correspondingly uncomplicated. Later, more sophisticated engines required continuously varying fuel mixes to keep pace with changing loads and speeds; starting had to be easy whether hot or cold; fast acceleration was required; the ever-increasing cost of gasoline demanded economical running. Satisfying these critical needs brought forth the complicated device which is today's carburetor. A representative carburetor is shown, cut open, in Figure 2-12. The component parts are labeled.

The carburetor owes its operation to a device called a venturi, and the venturi in turn depends upon a natural law first declared more than a century ago by a scientist named Bernoulli. The law states that when a fluid is in motion, the point of greatest velocity has the lowest pressure. This can be demonstrated easily; a favorite way of doing it in physics classes is with the contraption shown in Figure 2-13.

Fluid is flowing through a pipe that has a reduced center section. The fluid could be a liquid, air, or even a gasoline-air fuel mixture; it makes no difference in the operation. Pressure gauges or manometers are attached to the pipe at the points shown. The pressure is *always* lower at the center constricted portion—and the higher the velocity of flow, the lower the pressure.

The similarity between the constricted tube and the venturi in the schematic carburetor of Figure 2-14 can be seen easily. The air drawn into the engine by the motion of the pistons must pass through the venturi section at increased velocity and thus at reduced pressure. Atmospheric pressure therefore pushes fuel out of the nozzle which is in the slipstream. The action breaks the fuel into ultra-tiny droplets and mixes it with the passing air. The mixture going on to the engine has thus become a highly

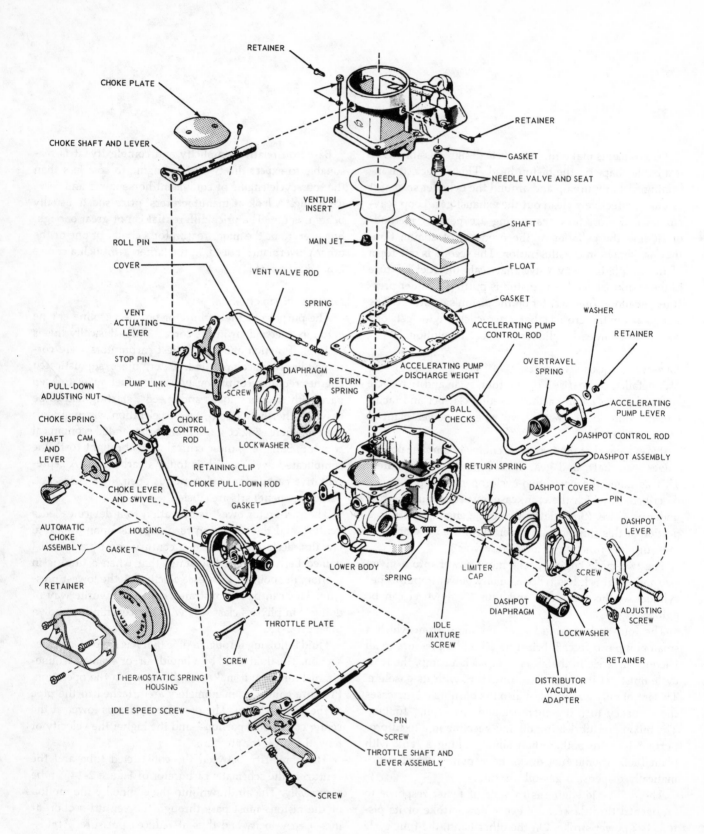

Figure 2-12: The various components of a representative carburetor are identified. (Credit—Autolite)

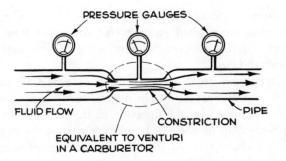

Figure 2-13: *The principle of the venturi: "The higher the velocity, the lower the pressure."*

flammable gasoline-air vapor.

The arrangement shown in Figure 2-14 assumes that the fuel is at the level of the nozzle because the difference of pressure caused by the venturi is not enough to lift

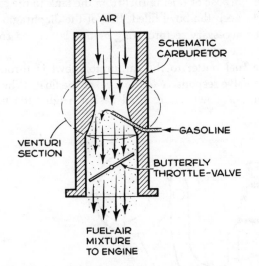

Figure 2-14: *The venturi action (lowered pressure) of the constricted throat draws in the gasoline and mixes it with the air.*

gasoline any appreciable height. This is not the case in a practical installation because the fuel tank is always lower. An auxiliary fuel reservoir called a bowl is therefore made a part of the carburetor as shown in Figure 2-15. The fuel is brought to the bowl by a pump and kept at a constant level by a float and needle valve as shown.

An engine equipped with this rudimentary carburetor would probably run passably well at only one combination of load and speed. It would certainly not start easily, it would not respond to demands for fast acceleration, and most likely it would not idle. Parts must be added to the carburetor before the engine can achieve these operational features.

At idling speed of the engine, the throttle valve (called

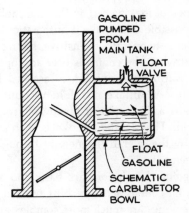

Figure 2-15: *The bowl holds a reservoir of gasoline at a level suitable to the venturi's ability to withdraw it.*

a butterfly) is almost entirely closed. The movement of air through the carburetor is minimal and the venturi is inactive and unable to feed fuel. An idle jet is therefore provided with its outlet directly under the lip of the closed butterfly. A metering pin performs the idle adjustment. Opening the butterfly renders the idling fuel hole ineffective.

If the throttle were opened suddenly in a desire for quick acceleration, our present schematic carburetor would not be equal to the task and the engine would gasp and stall. The sudden rush of air through the venturi would outdistance the fuel and the mixture would get leaner, whereas it should at that moment have been richer. This problem is solved by an addition to the carburetor called an acceleration pump. This is actually a small pump hooked to the throttle in such a manner that it squirts gasoline only with rapid throttle movements. (Do not confuse this with the regular fuel pump.)

An engine needs a very rich fuel mixture for easy starting from a cold standing condition. It would certainly not be practical to change the carburetor adjustments for every start and so a temporary expedient is used in the form of a second butterfly, called a choke, that closes off the air intake. With the choke closed, the high vacuum in the intake manifold draws gasoline from all the jets. The resultant mixture is so rich that there is danger of flooding unless the choke is used sparingly.

One method of making certain that the choke is opened as soon as possible is to make it automatic. In the automatic choke a temperature-sensitive spring keeps the choke closed when the engine is cold and opens it when the engine warms; the opening is assisted by a small piston actuated by intake manifold vacuum. The automatic choke is a development borrowed from the automotive world. The standard choke is manually opened and closed by the operator, generally through a flexible cable arrangement.

The foregoing descriptions are basic and apply to all carburetors. Of course, actual carburetors found on modern marine engines are much more complex and compact in construction, as the illustration in Figure 2-12 clearly indicates. Smooth engine performance under all operating conditions is obtained by adding high-speed jets and main jets plus complicated passages for controlled flow. In effect the fuel follows "circuits" or paths for various speeds and loads.

Carburetors are divided broadly into down-draft, side-draft, and updraft types. The names are self-explanatory and determined by the direction of the air flow. In all types the throttle valve or butterfly is nearest the engine and the choke farthest from it. The main air passage is called a throat and a single carb may have as many as four. The complete, minute details of construction of any specific carburetor can be had from the manual issued by its manufacturer.

FUEL PUMP.

The fuel pump is rudimentary as pumps go but it fulfills its purpose of raising fuel from the tank to the carburetor to keep the bowl filled. It is of the diaphragm type and the necessary reciprocating motion is derived from a cam on the camshaft.

The fuel outlet to the carburetor bowl is through a needle valve responsive to the level of the float. When the fuel in the bowl has reached design height, the needle

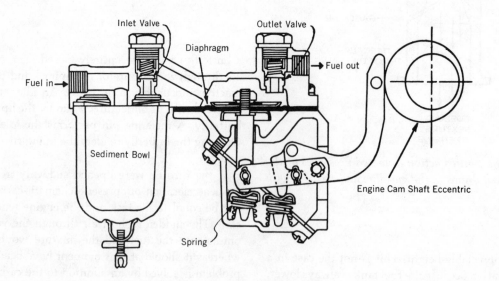

Figure 2-16: The mechanical fuel pump (shown diagrammatically and as one type actually looks) is part of the engine. An electric fuel pump operates independently on the engine.

closes the passage. (See Figure 2-15.) This blocks the fuel pump and renders it inoperative until the level recedes. The mechanical marine fuel pump is identical in construction with the one found on automobiles and is illustrated in the exploded view of Figure 2-16.

Electric fuel pumps are also found on marine installations and many skippers prefer them. These are still diaphragm pumps, but the reciprocating motion is imparted by a solenoid (an electromagnet) under the control of the ignition switch. The electric fuel pump has no *mechanical* connection with the engine.

FLAME ARRESTER.

Every motorist who has ever lifted a hood remembers the disproportionately large contraption that sits on top of the carburetor. This is the air cleaner; its function is to filter out dust and silence the air intake.

A marine engine does not run into much dust but it does operate in a location likely to be filled with highly flammable vapors from the bilge. The air cleaner has therefore given way to the flame arrester; it is shown

Figure 2-17: The flame arrester is at the air intake of the carburetor. (Ordinary automotive air cleaners are not legal for marine service.)

above the carburetor in Figure 2-17.

The use of a flame arrester is mandatory on marine gasoline engines. The requirements for the construction of marine flame arresters are much more rigid than for automotive air cleaners and they must be completely fireproof, something which the auto variety is not. Flame arresters for marine engines also must be of a type approved by the Coast Guard.

IGNITION TIMING.

The spark that initiates the power stroke must come at a precise point in the piston travel if smooth engine performance and maximum power are to be obtained. Theoretically this would be at the very beginning of the downstroke, at top dead center. But, as already pointed out, the flame takes time to travel and this must be compensated for by having the spark occur earlier. In engine parlance, the spark is "advanced."

The amount of advance is stated in degrees of rotation before the piston reaches top dead center (BTDC). An average value for marine engines would be about ten degrees. This means that the crankshaft must still rotate ten more degrees after the spark has occurred to bring the piston to its extreme top position.

Modern high speed engines are timed while running and therefore the timing requirement is specified at a certain speed: 10° BTDC @ 1000 RPM, for example. This is necessary because the automatic mechanism that governs timing while running cannot be checked at standstill. (In earlier days timing was accomplished by notching the flywheel over by hand and watching the breaker points open.) Mechanics use a stroboscopic light which is triggered by the spark; through an optical illusion this makes the mark on the flywheel apparently stand still.

Earlier we saw that a four-cycle engine has one power stroke (and one spark) in each cylinder for every two revolutions of the crankshaft. The cam that actuates the breaker points in these engines must therefore run at one-half engine speed. Since the camshaft also must be driven at one-half engine speed, these units generally are coupled together.

It follows on the basis of previous discussion that two-cycle engines must have breaker point cams driven at crankshaft speed.

How the ignition cam opens and closes the breaker points that control the current to the spark coil is shown in Figure 2-18. The cam in a single breaker installation will have as many faces or lobes as there are cylinders. The breaker points are separated (open) when the hill of the cam is under the rubbing block and in contact (closed) when the valley is in this position. The number of degrees of rotation during which the breaker points remain closed is called the dwell angle and many manufacturers specify this as a means of tune-up; it is measured electrically with specially calibrated voltmeters.

Since the ignition is advanced to compensate for the time it takes the flame to spread, it is correct to assume that this advance must vary with the engine speed. This is why automatic advances are incorporated into the timing system.

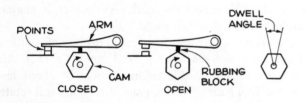

Figure 2-18: The rotation of the cam opens the ignition breaker points and a spring closes them. The relationship of point opening to piston position determines engine timing and is critical.

The basic automatic advance is centrifugal and consists of weights which actuate a lever or cam as they swing outward during rotation. They are restrained by a spring which determines the amount of advance at any given speed. Additional control is provided by a piston or diaphragm responsive to intake manifold vacuum. Since the vacuum in turn is affected by the load on the engine, this combination makes for very effective control.

Correct ignition timing is important mechanically (for smooth engine operation) and electrically (to get the full output of the spark coil), hence the attention paid to the dwell angle. The dwell angle determines the duration of time during which current flows to the coil and consequently is a major factor in determining the robustness of the spark. Although the degrees remain the same, the actual time of current flow is shorter as the speed increases. This is an unfortunate, natural, and insurmountable shortcoming which causes the spark to get weaker just when it should be getting stronger.

Attempts have been made to overcome this problem by increasing the current to the coil. This is generally self-

defeating because the breaker points will not stand the gaff. In the latest systems, transistors are used; they make and break the ignition circuit electronically upon being triggered by a very light current through the points. The most modern system eliminates points altogether and uses magnetic or electrostatic pulses without physical contact.

The very important role that the condenser (capacitor) plays at its critical connection across the breaker points should be mentioned. The condenser acts as a reservoir for current that would otherwise arc across the points when they open. It then sends this current back to force a faster collapse of the magnetic field around the coil and thereby increase the strength of the spark. A faulty condenser or the absence of a condenser will cripple the ignition.

SPARK PLUG HEAT RANGE.

Spark plugs are deceptively simple and very much alike but they have one characteristic that suits a certain plug to a certain engine—heat range.

Spark plugs are classified as cold or hot with many gradations between. The designation refers to the normal operating temperature of the center insulator and electrode. As shown in Figure 2-19, the only way that these parts can maintain a constant temperature is by shedding their excess heat to the engine block via the path out-

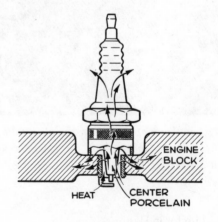

Figure 2-19: The spark plug maintains its proper temperature by shedding its excess heat along the paths shown by the arrows.

lined by the arrows. This path is a tenuous one because the porcelain electrode insulator is a poor conductor of heat; the longer this insulator, the hotter the plug will run.

A hot spark plug, meaning one with a long central electrode, installed in an engine that should have a cold one can attain a temperature high enough to pre-ignite the fuel and gradually destroy itself. A plug running too cold accumulates a sooty carbon deposit. For this reason all enginemakers specify the plugs which are best for their various models.

A clean new spark plug connected outside the engine to a spark coil fires at about 8000 volts. This same plug, installed in the engine, requires a considerably higher voltage because the compression has the effect of interposing a better insulation between the electrodes. A heavily sooted plug leaks the rising voltage and prevents it from reaching a value high enough to cause a spark; this is why fouled plugs cause engine misfiring. The correctly chosen plug, running under proper conditions, will keep burning itself clean.

Diesel Engines

Diesel power seems to mystify and overawe many skippers who, contrarily, are perfectly at home with their gasoline engines. Yet both are internal combustion engines and their points of similarity are far greater than their differences.

The diesel engine, exactly as the gasoline engine, must go through four steps in order to produce power from its liquid fuel. These, as already enumerated earlier, are intake, compression, power, and exhaust. If each step is a complete stroke, it is a four-cycle diesel; if two steps are combined in one stroke, it is a two-cycle diesel. This follows exactly the discussion of gasoline engines and the diagrams then given (Figures 2-10 and 2-11) still apply. The photo in Figure 2-20 shows a representative four-cycle marine diesel.

The similarities are so great that it is often difficult at first glance to tell a diesel from a gasoline marine power plant of the same size. Identification is established only after noting the presence or absence of ignition equipment and carburetor.

This highlights the main difference between diesel and gasoline engines: The diesel has no coils, wires, distrib-

utors, or spark plugs and it has no carburetor. Fuel injectors are located in the diesel where spark plugs would be in a gasoline engine.

The ignition of the compressed fuel-air mixture, which initiates the power stroke, is accomplished in the diesel without the help of any electrical spark. The charge is ignited by the high temperature of the compressed air in the cylinder. At first this may seem impossible, but if you take an ordinary bicycle pump, block the output nozzle with your finger and give it a few strokes, you will soon find the cylinder too hot to hold.

The air in the diesel cylinder gets so hot because of the very high pressure resulting from the high compression ratio. A gasoline engine may have a compression ratio of approximately eight, a comparable diesel will have a ratio of perhaps eighteen. This means that the content of the diesel cylinder when the piston reaches the top of its stroke has been squeezed down to one-eighteenth of its original volume and has increased its pressure eighteen times. The work done in pushing the piston up has been transformed into heat and the temperature is high enough instantly to ignite the sprayed-in fuel.

This points up another dissimilarity between the gasoline unit and the diesel: The gasoline engine draws into its cylinder a correctly proportioned mixture of fuel and air prepared by the carburetor; the diesel engine draws in air only. The undiluted fuel is sprayed into the superheated air at or near the top of the stroke and instantly burns. The resulting expansion causes the power stroke.

The much greater pressures encountered in the diesel engine put a higher stress on mechanical parts such as bearings, connecting rods, cylinder heads, and crankshafts, and these must consequently be stronger and heavier. It follows naturally that a diesel weighs more than a gasoline engine of the same output. But there are mitigating factors and the weight gap is rapidly being closed by new developments in design and metallurgy.

As a bonus from its beefed-up construction, the diesel can give workhorse service long after its gasoline competitor has thrown in the sponge. There are many records of commercial fishermen and lobstermen whose rusty diesels have been on the bottom several times but still resume their daily grind after each resurrection. And the vast majority of such engines are in the hands of mechanically unskilled operators!

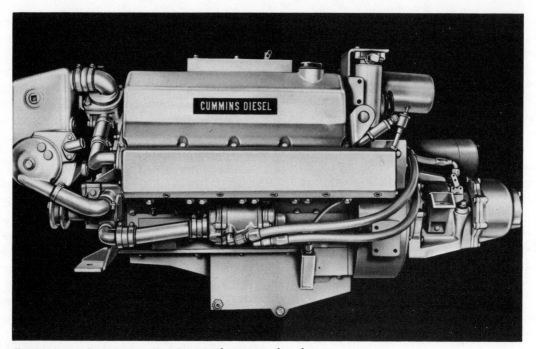

Figure 2-20: A representative four-cycle marine diesel engine. (Credit—Cummins Engine Co.)

DIESEL FUEL SYSTEMS.

It was stated earlier that the diesel engine has no carburetor and no mixing valve because its fuel needs no mixing. The only operations performed on the diesel fuel prior to its combustion are measuring, pressurizing and atomizing.

Pressurizing is necessary because the fuel can enter the cyclinder only after overcoming the high pressure which exists there at the instant of combustion. Since the cylinder pressure is made very high in order to generate ignition temperatures, the fuel pressure must be even higher; in many systems it reaches 10,000 or 15,000 pounds per square inch. One way of picturing the magnitude of such pressure is to realize that it could easily pierce the skin of a finger held before it.

Fuel atomization is resorted to in the diesel for the same reason as in gasoline engines: so each molecule of fuel has more intimate contact with each molecule of oxygen in the air. The high fuel pressure and the small orifices through which the liquid is forced favor atomizing. On the other hand, the diesel fuel has greater viscosity than gasoline and so requires greater effort to atomize it.

In addition to pressurizing and atomizing, a precisely metered quantity of fuel must be delivered to a cylinder at a precise point in the piston travel. This entails measuring and timing. Diesel engines perform this part of the job in one of four ways: the common rail, the individual pump, the distributor, or the self-contained injector. The ultimate purpose is the same for all but each arrives there differently.

Common rail. The common rail from which this system gets its name is a pipe or header that connects all the cylinder injectors. This header or rail is constantly supplied with fuel which is maintained under high pressure by a central pump. As each injector is actuated by its push rod, it acts as an opening and closing valve to pass a metered portion of this fuel in the common rail to its nozzle for spraying into the cylinder.

A schematic diagram of the common rail system is shown in Figure 2-21. To avoid fluctuations in the fuel supply when an injector opens, the main pump must have an output greater than the immediate demand. This ex-

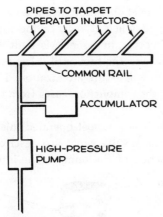

PIPES TO TAPPET
OPERATED INJECTORS

COMMON RAIL

ACCUMULATOR

HIGH-PRESSURE
PUMP

FROM FUEL TANK

Figure 2-21: A schematic diagram of the common rail diesel engine fuel system. The common rail is maintained full of fuel under high pressure.

cess is absorbed by an accumulator which has the further effect of dampening out the pump oscillations.

Individual pumps. In this system each cylinder has its individual pump which generates the necessary pressure and also does the metering. These small pumps could be separately installed at each cylinder but modern design puts them all into one compact body housing with a single drive shaft. A typical unit is shown mounted on the engine in Figure 2-22.

This system was pioneered by Bosch of Germany and the pump complex in outward appearance looks very much like the ignition magnetos this firm was building at the time. The housing contains very precisely manufactured piston pumps, one for each cylinder. The volume of fuel the pumps deliver at each stroke is controlled by the throttle or by a governor when constant speed is desired. The unit is driven at one-half crankshaft speed for four-cycle engines and at crankshaft speed for two-cycle types, in both cases with precise timing to the camshaft.

A separate tube takes the output of each individual pump to the injector of the cylinder it serves. These tubes

Figure 2-22: Piping connects the fuel injector pump to the injectors in the cylinders. The pump mechanism meters and times each "shot" of fuel. (Credit—Mercedes-Benz)

can be seen clearly in the photograph.

Distributor. The distributor system in a diesel engine does with fuel what the ignition distributor of a gasoline engine does with a spark: routes it to the right cylinder at the right time.

A central pump provides the high pressure and sends a metered amount of fuel to a rotating distributor. This distributor is precisely timed with the piston position and connects with a tube to the proper cylinder at the proper time to pass the fuel on. The tubes from the distributor to the injectors are very much like the wires from ignition distributor to spark plugs.

The self-contained injector. This system has been made standard by a leading diesel-engine maker; it is probably the simplest, the easiest to install, and the handiest for service and repair. The functions of pump, meter, and injector are all combined in a compact unit that screws into each cylinder head like a spark plug. A clear cutaway view of this device is given in Figure 2-23.

When the rocker arm strikes the tappet head of this injector, a metered amount of fuel is pressurized. When the pressure reaches a value higher than the cylinder pressure the fuel is sprayed into the cylinder in a complete circle. The timing is effected by the cam on the camshaft that actuates the push rod and rocker. The amount of fuel is regulated by the throttle rod which controls the position of the internal fuel intake port.

One criticism of the systems previously described is that the multiplicity of high-pressure tubing is costly and difficult to install and service. The self-contained injector overcomes this objection; its external tubing carries fuel only at a very low pressure. An injector unit can be removed and replaced without the necessity for subsequent bleeding and adjusting the rest of the system.

With the self-contained injectors each cylinder can be tuned to its own peak performance. Individual adjustments in the throttle linkages are provided for this purpose.

Standard injectors. The injector used with the common rail systems is cam-operated usually through a push rod and rocker arm that maintain the proper timing with the camshaft and thus with piston position. It meters the required amount of fuel from the high-pressure supply in the common rail.

The individual pump systems and the distributor systems do not require the complicated injectors that meter fuel through tappet operation. In these systems the fuel is already metered when it reaches the injectors. Consequently the injector, in essence, is built around a check valve that restrains the fuel until it has reached a critical pressure which will assure atomization. This check valve also prevents the combustion gases from backing up into the fuel lines.

In some designs a tappet-operated injector is used in place of the check valve types just described, despite the metering function of the pumps. The internal construc-

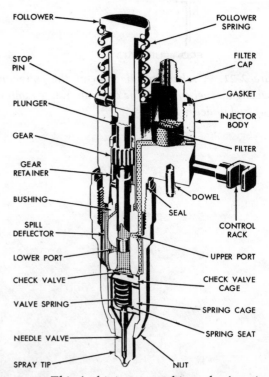

Figure 2-23: This fuel injector combines the functions of a high pressure fuel pump and metering device for engine speed control. The injector is timed and actuated by the camshaft through a push rod and rocker. (Credit—Detroit Diesel; Photo by G. M. Photographic)

tion of these injectors is such that the exact moment of fuel injection can be advanced or retarded, thus achieving timing control in response to speed or load. The mechanism of these adjustments is almost universally a series of grooves in the injector plunger which cover and uncover feed and delivery ports as the throttle is moved.

Another technical objection that has been raised to

diesel fuel systems employing long lengths of high pressure tubing is that pressure waves interfere with proper action at high speeds. Worrying about waves of pressure in tubing only a few feet long may seem like nit-picking until the time element is analyzed. Then it develops that only a few thousandths of a second are available for the gulp of fuel to travel through the pipe at top engine RPM and the matter of wave reaction comes into focus. This is one of the talking points used in favor of the self-contained injectors.

The type of spray coming from the injector nozzle plays a large part in engine performance. Each combustion chamber design has its own best spray pattern. The pattern and the atomization are governed by the size, number and arrangement of holes in the nozzle—and each manufacturer has his own panacea.

One major injector sickness is dribbling. This is a small leakage of fuel after the regular injection period has passed. Since it occurs after the initial combustion, dribbling can cause smoking exhaust and other problems. The final check valve at the nozzle is the usual culprit.

The same engine can be fitted with different injectors for different maximum horsepower outputs. The difference would be in the volume of fuel the injector squirts at maximum position. (This volume is so small that it is best measured in cubic millimeters. An average would be about one cubic millimeter for each cubic inch of piston displacement, or a ratio of about 15,000 to 1.)

COMBUSTION CHAMBERS.

Considerable variations exist in the shape of the combustion chambers of diesel engines, again the result of each manufacturer's technical decisions. Nonetheless, the trend is to the open combustion chamber because, despite its simplicity of construction, it stands up well in the matter of performance and economy.

The open combustion chamber is illustrated in (a) of Figure 2-24. It is simply a space provided either in the top of the piston or in the cylinder head or partially in both. Injection is usually at the center and forms an all-around spray.

Another form is the swirl chamber shown in (b). In this design the upward travel of the piston forces the air into violent rotation in the swirl chamber. Subsequent fuel injection and combustion and resultant expansion blast the charge out again and push the piston down. This

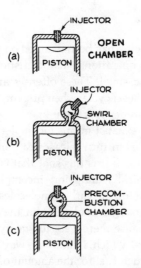

Figure 2-24: These are some of the variations in combustion chamber design found in diesel engines. The open chamber (a) is the simplest but advantages are claimed for the swirl chamber (b) and the precombustion chamber (c).

seems like a lot that must happen in the small spaces of time allotted, but it does.

Still another design is the combustion chamber pictured in (c). It differs from the swirl chamber in that only a small part of the air in the cylinder is forced into it. The combustion is started here and continued in the cylinder when the remaining fuel is squirted through the connecting hole.

DIESEL TWO-CYCLE.

The popular large two-cycle diesel engines differ from small two-cycle gasoline units in one important mechanical respect: They do not use the piston to pull in the air required for combustion. The air is forced in by a separate, external blower driven from the crankshaft.

The blower runs continuously and forces air into an "air box" surrounding the cylinder ports. When the piston uncovers these ports the air rushes in from all sides and scavenges the gases from the previous combustion out through the open exhaust valve. The maker claims this to be much more efficient than using the entire engine as an air pump for half of each cycle (as every four-cycle does). The blower shown is the Rootes positive displacement type in which the lobes of the two rotors are always in contact with each other.

DIESEL SMOKE.

The diesel engine has been damned on the road and on the water for an operational characteristic that it need not have: smoke and smell. These offenses are definitely *not* inherent in the diesel cycle; when present, they are always the result of improper operation.

Smoke in the exhaust means incomplete combustion in the cylinder: This in turn releases carbon into the air in the form of soot and it is this soot that is seen as smoke.

From a chemical standpoint, incomplete combustion means that some of the carbon molecules in the fuel did not unite with oxygen molecules in the air. This could result either because there were too many carbons or not enough oxygens, which is another way of saying that there was too much fuel for the amount of air available to burn it. This could happen when a heavy truck overloads its engine going up a hill and the extreme throttle opening injects too much fuel into the cylinders. It could happen on a boat when some restriction in the intake (or even in the exhaust system) cuts down the normal air flow. The objectionable odor is a by-product of the smoke.

A diesel engine in good condition and correctly operated does *not* have "exhaustitosis." It has the good manners to offend neither eye nor nose. A great deal of diesel prejudice by boatmen would vanish if this were more generally known. In fact, the exhaust from an ideal diesel is comparatively harmless because it contains no carbon monoxide whereas the exhaust from a gasoline engine is lethal.

HOT PLUGS.

Some diesel engines do not start as readily from a cold stand as others; it is a matter of design. These units generally use hot plugs for starting.

Hot plugs should not be confused with spark plugs, although some older diesels did use standard spark plugs for a sort of semi-diesel starting and cold running. Hot plugs, or glow plugs as they are also known, have a small platinum wire tip which heats red hot when energized by battery current. They are under the control of a starting button and are used only momentarily until the engine fires. They extend into the combustion chamber or the precombustion chamber.

DIESEL COST.

Horsepower for horsepower, the diesel engine costs more than the gasoline engine. This is an unfortunate fact of marine economics and there are some sound reasons for it.

First of all, diesels are not manufactured in quantities at all comparable with the huge production of gas engines. Thus they cannot share in all the benefits of mass production. Whether production is carried on largely by hand or by automation makes an understandable difference in cost.

The diesel must be built sturdier. Because the compression pressures are so much higher than in gasoline engines, everything must be beefed up: Bearings must be stronger, castings heavier, pistons and connecting rods must take the added thrust.

The precision of manufacture and fit is greater in the diesel. Tolerances as minute as a few *ten-thousandths* of an inch are common. This, too, is traceable to the higher pressures at which the diesel functions. Diesel manufacturers stress the economy of their engines despite the original higher acquisition cost. Diesel fuel is cheaper per gallon than gasoline. Diesel engines are sturdier and last longer under continuous use than gasoline. Under identical conditions, the diesel engine will squeeze more miles out of a gallon of fuel. Some also claim that the absence of the vulnerable electric ignition system makes the diesel more reliable.

Turbines

The turbine is the dark horse in the internal combustion race toward the ideal power plant of the future. It is as much in the race on land, for automobiles, as it is in the marine field, and it has many advantages.

The turbine has no reciprocating parts; no pistons, connecting rods, or valves go rapidly back and forth to cause vibration. Every component is in rotary motion and therefore is easily balanced statically and dynamically.

Although its method of operation is entirely different from the gasoline and diesel engines, the turbine qualifies as an internal combustion power plant for the obvious reason that it burns its fuel internally. The fuel is burned continuously, not in strokes as in its competitors.

The diagram in Figure 2-25 shows how the turbine works and depicts the principal parts. Basically the system consists of a centrifugal compressor and a turbine on a common shaft with a combustion chamber between. Once started (by high-speed cranking) the compressor forces air under pressure into the combustion chamber. Fuel enters continuously in a very fine spray and keeps burning after initial ignition by a glow plug. The extreme expansion and heat force the hot gases against the turbine blades and cause rotation. Since the turbine and compressor are interconnected, the action is cumulative and results in very high speed.

Early turbines could just about keep themselves going because the gains just barely overcame the losses. Modern design has made it possible for the turbine to put out more power than the compressor draws. This excess is the

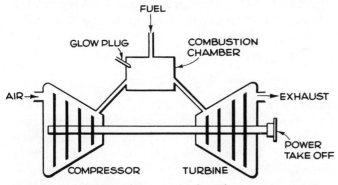

Figure 2-25: The turbine principle: The power remaining in excess of that absorbed by the compressor is available at the power takeoff.

power output of the unit and is available at the output shaft.

The turbine is essentially a high-speed device and is efficient only at very high speeds. Propellers are essentially low-speed devices. Thus a gap must be bridged for marine use of this new power plant. Nevertheless the present advanced state of the art in transmissions would seem to indicate that the gear people can do the bridging when needed without too much effort.

Turbine-driven boats finally have become available to the boatman. Several boat builders are offering stock craft so powered.

Volumetric Efficiency

The volumetric efficiency is the technical manner of stating how well a piston engine "breathes." Its ability to breathe efficiently, that is, to fill its cylinder completely on every intake stroke, to a large extent determines its power output capability.

Valves play a large part in good breathing because the intake air must rush past them. At slow speed this is no great problem but at high speed it can become insurmountable. Many high-speed engines put two intake valves in each cylinder, instead of the usual one, as a means of improving breathing. (Two regular-size valves are more feasible than one very large one.)

The volumetric efficiency is the ratio of the amount of charge actually drawn into the cylinder to the amount of charge that could be drawn in. Temperature has a bearing on this because warm air is less dense than cold air. To be completely meaningful, volumetric efficiency should be stated at a definite temperature and atmospheric pressure.

Every piston engine develops its best volumetric efficiency at some critical speed. This can be found easily from a curve of the engine's performance; volumetric efficiency peaks at the point of maximum torque.

Crankcase Ventilation

The automobile people pioneered the idea of positive crankcase ventilation and it has wisely been carried over to marine engines.

The ventilation system rids the crankcase enclosure of blow-by fumes which could condense and contaminate the lubricating oil in the sump. These vapors are drawn through a regulating valve and into the intake manifold where they mix with the fuel and are eventually burned. This is not a method intended for recouping losses because the increase in efficiency is negligible; the purpose of the scheme is the elimination of noxious vapors and the reduction of oil dilution.

At closed throttle the intake manifold vacuum is at a maximum and would draw in a disproportionate amount of the crankcase fumes unless a valve were placed in the pickup line. This valve closes at high vacuum, opens at low. The air path through the crankcase is so arranged that the entire volume is continuously being swept while the engine runs.

Compression Ratio

As was explained earlier, the fuel-air mixture is compressed before combustion; this means a higher yield of power, in other words, greater efficiency. The degree to which this compression takes place in any piston engine depends upon its compression ratio.

If cylinder volume is measured with the piston at bottom dead center and then again with the piston at top dead center, the former divided by the latter is the compression ratio. Example: Volume with piston at bottom dead center equals 80 cubic inches. Volume with piston at top dead center equals 10 cubic inches. Compression ratio equals 8.

The theoretical goal in internal combustion engine design is the highest possible compression ratio. The limiting practical factor on increasing compression ratio in a gasoline engine is the "knocking" of the gasoline. In a diesel engine it is the mechanical strength of the parts and the highest temperatures they can stand in continuous operation.

The compression ratio of an engine is fixed by its design. Some slight changes can be made by altering piston heads or gaskets.

Supercharging

Standard engines draw their fuel charge into the cylinder by the reduced pressure (suction) created when the piston moves down on its intake stroke. This is not the most efficient way. The restriction of intake valves, the inertia of the air, and other factors reduce the volumetric efficiency. The fuel mixture alternately can be forced into the cylinder under pressure. When this is done, the engine is said to be supercharged.

The supercharger is essentially a compressor driven by the engine. The drive could be a direct mechanical connection to the engine such as a chain, belt, or shaft. The compressor could also be driven by the exhaust gases, with no mechanical linkage, by a turbine; this form is known as a turbocharger.

Many believe that the turbocharger, because it is not *mechanically* driven from the engine, operates "for free." This of course would be getting something for nothing, which is strictly against nature's law. True, some degree of power wasted in the exhaust is retrieved. But the presence of the turbine in the exhaust passage raises the back pressure on the engine and this is tantamount to taking power from it.

When air is compressed, the work done on it heats it.

This is an undesirable result when supercharging because a portion of the desired benefit is negated. To overcome this, many supercharger and turbocharger installations place an intercooler in the line to the intake manifold. The intercooler is water-jacketed and removes from the air most of the heat generated by the compression.

Figure 2-26 shows a supercharger and a turbocharger. The turbocharger is an extreme high-speed device and therefore can be smaller. It has the inherent problem of disproportionately lowered output at low engine speed because the reduced volume of exhaust gas has much less driving power. Engines without superchargers are called naturally aspirated.

Engine Ratings

Many a skipper has wondered why his marine engine is so much heftier than his automobile engine of the same horsepower. The answer lies partly in the advertising flights of rhetoric that intrude into what should be a strictly engineering domain, and mostly in the realm of "duty cycle." The duty cycle is the percentage of time the engine is actually operating under load during any period of use.

The automobile engine is almost never under full-rated load. A great deal of its life is spent at moderate speed, and even in coasting, with a horsepower output far below what the catalogue says. Any attempt to take advertised horsepower from it for any length of time would surely reduce it to steaming junk. It is built for a low duty cycle.

The marine engine is on a high duty cycle. It is forever going "uphill" in the sense that it must continually work at or near its rated horsepower to push its boat through the water. On a long cruise, for instance, it may be working at high output for many hours at a stretch, without even a minute's respite. This difference in work habits dictates a difference in construction which in turn makes for increased heft—and cost.

Horsepower

The word horsepower, by itself, has a very finite meaning. To an engineer it signifies the ability to lift 33,000 pounds to a height of one foot in one minute—or any similar combination that amounts to 33,000 foot pounds per

a

Figure 2-26: The two gasoline-powered tandem racing engines (a) are supercharged. The turbocharger on the diesel engine (b) is driven by the exhaust. (Credit—Caterpillar Tractor Co.)

b

minute.

When applied to an engine the word horsepower must be qualified. Is it "indicated horsepower" or "brake horsepower" or "shaft horsepower" or "gross horsepower"? At what speed in revolutions per minute is it developed? Under what conditions of temperature and barometric pressure?

Marine engine manufacturers are generally more conservative than their automotive counterparts and are fairly honest in rating their products. Nonetheless, the layman and the skipper are not always aware of the little nuances in catalogue descriptions that can make a difference in an engine's job performance.

The figures given by manufacturers are usually gross horsepower. Such power measurements are taken on an engine stripped of all accessories not actually necessary for the trial operation. This means minus generator, water pump, fuel pump, and others.

The net horsepower is the amount actually available at the output shaft when the engine is rigged exactly as it would be in marine service. The net is the gross minus the horsepower consumed by the accessories; this is sometimes called shaft horsepower.

Most makers rate their engines at a maximum horsepower at a definite speed and let it be assumed that the test was conducted under standard conditions. Sometimes a table of horsepowers at various speeds is listed although it is more common to put this information in the form of a curve like the one in Figure 2-27. Such a curve enables a rating to be obtained for any speed. A torque curve is usually included, also as shown.

MEASUREMENT METHOD.

Horsepower is measured with an electric dynamometer, a machine that absorbs the power put out by the engine under test and gives its readings in terms of voltage and current dissipated. This is then calculated into horsepower. The photo in Figure 2-28 shows an engine under test hooked to a dynamometer.

An alternate method makes use of a device called a prony brake. This is an extremely simple setup consisting of a weighing scale and a friction power takeoff on the engine pulley. It provides an answer in foot-pounds. Adding time to the calculation converts this to horsepower.

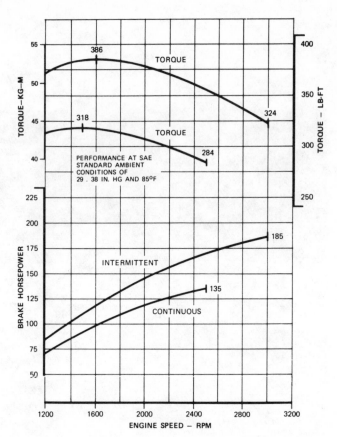

Figure 2-27: Curves like these give the full horsepower and torque capabilities of engines at every speed.

Torque

The "muscle" of an engine, its twisting ability, is called its torque. Torque is expressed in foot pounds, which means the number of pounds pressure multiplied by the number of feet radius. Example: In the preceding diagram, if the arm length were 2 feet and the scale pressure were 100 pounds, the torque would be 200 foot pounds. Note that neither speed nor time enters into the measurement of torque, although both do in measuring horsepower.

Firing Order

Multi-cylinder engines do not fire from one cylinder to the next adjacent one. To do this would result in extreme torsional vibration and very rough running. Instead, the power impulses are varied evenly back and forth along the crankshaft. A typical six-cylinder engine would fire in this order: 1-5-3-6-2-4. Most engines carry a plate showing their firing order.

Figure 2-28: The output of the engine is being determined by an electric dynamometer. (Credit—Outboard Marine Corp.; Photo by Oristano-Pearsall Associates)

Square and Over-square

An engine is called square when the number of inches of its bore (cylinder diameter) is equal to the number of inches of its stroke. An over-square engine is one in which the bore is larger than the stroke. Such extreme short-stroke engines are popular for high-speed service.

Lubrication System

An oil film must separate one moving metal surface from another. It is the duty of the engine lubrication system to maintain these oil films wherever they are required.

The oil level is maintained in a sump in the crankcase. A positive displacement pump picks it up from there through a screen and places it under pressure. The pressurized oil is then forced through a circuit of passages drilled in crankshaft, camshaft, bearings, and connecting rods. At some points a spray is directed against cylinder walls and the underside of piston heads. All oil then drains back to the sump for recirculation. (Small two-cycle engines, you will remember, get their lubrication from oil mixed with the fuel; they have no sump.)

This pressure oil distribution is the desirable one and is found on all quality engines. An alternative is the splash method; in this, the connecting rods splash through the oil sump and throw oil on the internal surfaces of the engine.

Lubricating oil, like everything else in modern life, has become highly specialized. Oil is sold in many grades, with and without additives and detergents, for various types of service. There is a special formulation intended for mixing with gasoline to lubricate two-cycle outboards. There are special oils for engine break-in and others for heavy-duty diesel service.

The American Petroleum Institute (API) has set up class designations based on the service for which the oil is intended. These are: *SA* (light duty, no additives), *SB* (medium duty, some additives), *SC* (heavy duty plus additives), *SD* (heavy duty plus anti-rust and additives) and *SE* (extreme duty meeting latest specifications plus anti-oxidants). The older designations were: *ML* (light duty), *MM* (medium duty), *MS* (severe duty), *DG*, and *DM* (for diesels).

The Society of Automotive Engineers (SAE) has established a series of viscosity standards that are designated by the numbers 10, 20, 30, 40, 50, and 60. Number 10 is the lowest viscosity, meaning that it pours most easily, and Number 60 is practically glue. The SAE also authorizes the addition of the letter *W* to the viscosity number if the oil retains its pouring ability at low temperature. (In gas stations these are commonly known as winter oils.)

The designations overlap. Thus an oil might be certified as meeting the entire series of service requirements and also two or three of the viscosity numbers. The best guide for the skipper through these labyrinthine shoals is to check the manual issued by the engine manufacturer and use the oil specified.

In a modern engine oil does more than lubricate. It helps to cool hot engine parts. It washes away any microscopic metal "chips" that wear off the surfaces. It keeps the inside of the engine clean. It prevents sludge and varnish formation. All this is a tall order. Nevertheless, it is performed reasonably well by the complex chemicals and detergents mixed with the oils at the refinery and called additives. Oil has come a long way since the early days of motoring and boating when it was simply dipped out of an open barrel—dirt, flies, and all.

Fuels

It is ironic that the modern boatman (and the motorist) is dependent upon fossil fuels laid down into the earth millions or billions of years ago. Except for a tiny percentage of power plants burning fuels derived from other sources, petroleum products run the engines of the world. From the standpoint of powerboats, these are either gasoline or diesel fuel.

The crude oil coming from the well is divided chemically (fractionated) into products ranging from natural gas to asphalt. Near the top of the list is gasoline, one of the highest fractions.

The cruising skipper who gets to gas docks run by competing companies is bombarded by a barrage of claims of superiority. The simple fact is that there is mighty little, if any, difference in the quality of gasolines. Every *large* company makes good gasoline—and how could a *small* company possibly get into the refining business, accessible only to giants, and make *any* kind of gasoline?

As every one out of his diapers knows, gasoline is available in two general grades: regular and special. The difference is largely a matter of octane number, although the special does have a few more magic additives than the regular.

The octane number is a measure of the gasoline's ability to burn in any particular engine without "knocking." The higher this number, the greater the anti-knock quality. Most regular gasolines hover around 94 while the specials can hit 100 or better. The minimum octane for any engine is usually specified by the manufacturer. Nothing is gained by using a higher octane than the engine normally requires—all advertising to the contrary notwithstanding.

Old-time skippers will remember that the only gasoline a boatman would use years ago was the "white" or colorless variety. Leaded gas of that day was unstable, especially when in contact with the copper of fuel tanks and lines, and would break down into gum; skippers avoided

ASTM Classification of Diesel Fuel Oils

	No. 1-D	No. 2-D
Flash Pt.; °F Min.	100	125
Carbon Residue; %	0.15	0.35
Water and Sediment; (% by Volume) Max.	Trace	0.10
Ash; % by Wt.; Max.	0.01	0.02
Distillation, °F 90% Pt.; Max.	550	675
Min.	-	540
Viscosity at 100 °F; centistokes Min.	1.4	2.0
Max.	2.5	5.8
Sulfur; % Max.	0.5	1.0
Cetane No; Min.	40	40

Figure 2-29: The allowable compositions of diesel fuels are shown in this table. The most important factors for good engine operation are distillation range, octane number and sulphur content. Recommended for most pleasure-boat diesels is D-1. Lowered sulphur D-2 could be second choice.

it. (An irony is that the lead actually had nothing to do with the gum although it did plate out on spark-plug insulators and caused plugs to foul.)

Present-day leaded gasolines are suitable for all power plants and, because of their uniform octane ratings, are specified by almost all engine manufacturers as a hedge against ruinous detonation. The rainbow hues available at gas docks and service stations are produced by dyes and have no function other than identification.

Diesel fuels are classified according to the American Society for Testing Materials (ASTM) Designation D975-60T. Of this listing, only the D-1 and the D-2 are considered satisfactory for the modern high-speed marine diesel engine. Listing is made on the basis of the following qualities: flash point, carbon residue, sediment content, ash, sulphur, viscosity, distillation temperature, and cetane number. Assuming a good clean fuel, the most important characteristic to check on for satisfactory diesel use is the cetane number.

The cetane number of a diesel fuel determines its ignition quality somewhat in the manner that an octane number indicates the anti-knock rating of a gasoline. The two numbers have no direct connection, however. You look for the *highest* octane number and the highest cetane number. Actually, the cetane number is the percentage of cetane contained in an equivalent test fuel with the same ignition qualities. Under the standard test this means a 13-degree ignition delay at a specified compression ratio. A cetane number of 40 is about minimum for marine diesels.

The most deleterious contaminant in fuel as far as the diesel engine is concerned is sulphur. The D-2 fuel permits a sulphur content of 1 percent and this is the maximum that a high-speed diesel engine should be asked to digest. Sulphur corrodes the exhaust system among other things. It is even more destructive when, as sulphur dioxide, it combines with water in the exhaust to form sulphurous acid. A table of values for D-1 and D-2 fuels is given in Figure 2-29.

Engine Installation

Just as a sturdy foundation is essential to a good house, a good marine engine installation depends first of all on engine stringers properly fastened to the hull and strong enough for the load. Most standard engine mounts require

that the centers of the stringers be 22.5 inches apart to accommodate the lag bolts. Clearance is needed for the oil pan.

An engine under load by a propeller attempts to turn itself in a direction opposite to the prop shaft rotation. This results in a tensional stress on the lag bolts on one side and tends to pull them out. Bolts must be sufficiently well anchored to resist this and the stringers must of course be sound.

The exhaust piping should never be smaller in inside diameter than the outlet on the exhaust manifold; larger does no harm. The piping should have a slope to the transom of one-half inch to the foot so that water cannot be trapped. It may be necessary to install an elbow at the manifold to attain this. The weight of the pipe should be supported independently of the exhaust manifold.

Engines in sailboats, including motor sailers and auxiliaries require extra precautions in their installation because they are often located below the water line. The exhaust lines frequently include a reverse bend (a tight 180° change in direction) with the U of the bend high enough to be above the waterline. This prevents water from backing up into the exhaust manifold and from there into the cylinders, which would have disastrous results. Provision is made to prevent siphoning, although the large diameter of the pipe itself is a deterrent.

Marine engines are generally installed at an angle as shown in Figure 2-30. This is done as a matter of necessity because the engine bed is higher than the propeller. This angle may not exceed the figure given by the manufacturer, however. The reason for this restriction is mainly the nature and size of the oil sump and the consequent ability of the pump to pick up oil. One manufacturer places a limit of 18 degrees from the water level for all engines.

The engine stringers are strongly fastened to the frames and the hull and for this reason are excellent transmitters of vibrational noise throughout the boat. Transmission can be reduced somewhat with rubber engine mounts that act as noise and vibration insulators. Many engines contain this rubber as an integral part of the mounting system.

Alignment of the engine with the propeller shaft is all-important. Perfect alignment means that the center line of the propshaft and the center line of the engine output

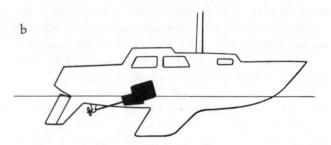

Figure 2-30: The angle (a) at which an engine must be mounted in order to line up with the propeller shaft may not exceed the manufacturer's limit. The drawing (b) shows the engine angle in relation to the boat. (Credit—Starrett Diesel)

shaft are identical; this is the target to shoot for. Manufacturers usually specify the permissible deviation from perfect for their engines.

An easy method of checking alignment without fancy instruments is shown in Figure 2-31. The check is performed at the two faces of the engine-shaft coupling with a feeler gauge or any other thin metal strip of about .003-inch thickness (or other thickness if specified). The engine is shimmed or otherwise moved until the feeler shows uniform separation all around the circle. Of course, the outside edges of the coupling must also be flush all around.

Any alignment in drydock should be considered only a temporary placement because the hull is bound to "work" a bit after launching. When the waterlogging of the hull has stabilized, the alignment procedure should be repeated. At this time all shims, wedges, and mounts are in their final positions and the lag bolts should be snugged down tight.

The cooling system requires a seawater pickup scoop outside the hull and a through hull fitting to connect it. A sea cock at this point is urgently recommended. Some engines require nothing more than a hose connection to the intake water pump but others need recirculation piping; the engine manual will give the necessary information. The connecting hose must be noncollapsible because of the suction exerted by the water pump. Figure 2-32 shows the typical plumbing for a cooling system; it also outlines the additional piping for thermostat recirculation.

Figure 2-31: Engine and shaft alignment can be checked at the coupling with feeler strips. (The final check should be made after the boat has been in the water for a time.) (Credit—Ray Krantz Photographic Illustrations)

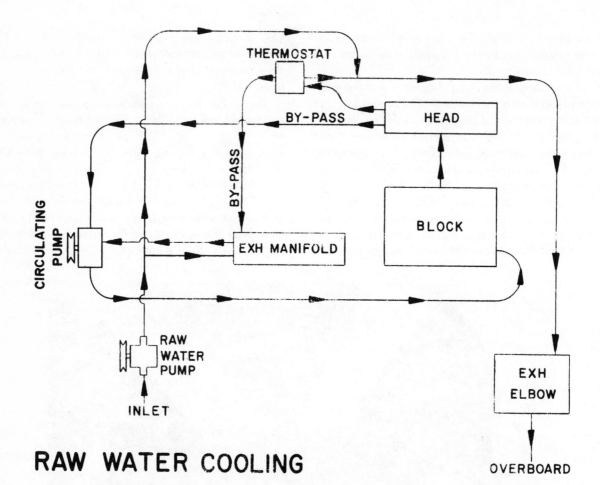

RAW WATER COOLING

Figure 2-32: Typical cooling system circuits of marine engines.

The fuel line should have a flexible section at the point of its connection to the engine fuel pump. This prevents transmission of engine vibration to the line and is good insurance against line breakage from fatigue. Incidentally, fuel filters at this point are good insurance against down time caused by clogging with sediment and scale.

Many makers recommend that batteries be placed close by the engine in order to reduce the voltage drop when the heavy starting motor load is applied. This seems slightly at variance with Coast Guard wishes but is nevertheless generally followed. Some engines also have a preferred position for the grounding lug.

The need for proper ventilation of the engine compartment has become a legal one but the fundamental requirement of a running engine for huge amounts of air must still be satisfied by proper openings, louvers, or stacks. A partially airtight enclosure will have the same effect on a gasoline engine as a partially closed carburetor choke; on a diesel it will cause smoking exhaust.

Bowden wires used for engine throttle control must have sufficient slack to take care of engine movement. (A Bowden wire is an actuating wire inside a flexible metal sheath like the old-time choke control.) The need for slack also applies to tachometer cables, electric wires,

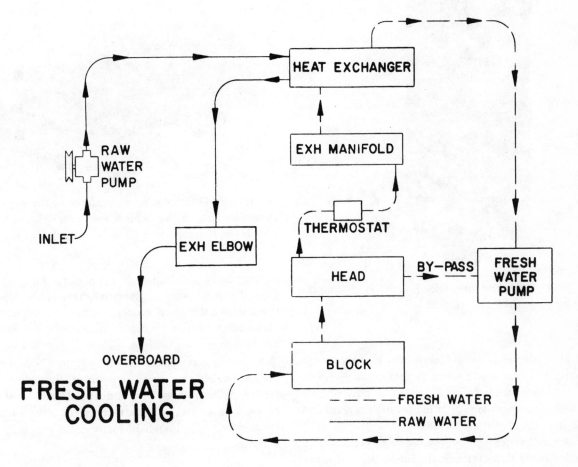

FRESH WATER COOLING

gauge lines, fuel lines and all other connections to the engine.

Engine Accessories

Many accessory devices and gadgets are available to the skipper to insure trouble-free operation of his engines or to relieve him of constant vigil over them.

ALARMS.

A ringing bell warns immediately of the absence of pressure in the lubricating system or too high temperature in the cooling system. This alarm device is simple in construction and also simple to install. It consists of a pressure-sensing switch in the oil line and a heat-sensing switch in the waterline.

FILTERS.

Water and solid contaminants in the fuel are trapped by filters placed in series with the supply line to the engine. This foreign matter is then retained in the housing until emptied. A typical unit is shown in Figure 2-33.

HEAT EXCHANGERS.

Instead of running raw water through the engine

Figure 2-33: Water and dirt in the fuel are kept from the engine by filters like this. (Credit—Fram)

Figure 2-34: Fresh water recirculates in the engine and passes its heat to the isolated raw water through a heat exchanger. (Credit—Sen-Dure Prod. Inc.)

jackets, the cooling job can be taken over by fresh water circulating in an enclosed system. A heat exchanger then passes the engine heat to an independent flow of raw water. The advantages are better temperature control and cleaner, less corroded water jackets.

The heat exchanger is simply a set of tubes in a housing. The engine water flows through the tubes, the raw water flows along the outside of the tubes. The two flows thus are entirely isolated from each other. A heat exchanger is shown in Figure 2-34.

TRANSISTOR IGNITION.

The ignition breaker points are a source of woe on all gasoline engines and a palliative in the form of transistor ignition is gaining favor on powerboats just as on automobiles. Some of the transistor systems drastically reduce the current the breaker points must handle, thus prolonging their life; one new system eliminates the points entirely.

A basic explanation of the functioning of each component of the ignition system will be found in Chapters 7 and 8.

IGNITION SHIELDING.

The interference from the ignition system of a gasoline

engine can be a nuisance for every electronic instrument from depth sounder to radio receiver. (This is another point where the diesel scores.) Sometimes the only final elimination of the erratic readings and the buzz-saw noises is complete shielding.

A shielding system is shown in Figure 2-35. This one provides shields for every component, the only fully effective method. Plugs, cables, distributor, and coil are all covered. Less effective is the insertion of resistors into the ignition wires, although in many cases this may prove sufficient.

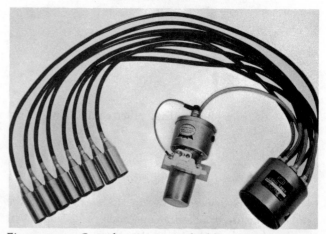

Figure 2-35: Complete ignition shielding is often necessary to eliminate noise in the radio receiver and interference with other electronic devices on board. Shown are shields for the ignition coil, distributor, cables and each spark plug. (Credit——Hallett Division of Livingston Industries)

OIL COOLERS.

One of the functions of the lubricating oil is to help cool some of the internal parts of the engine. In doing this the oil acquires heat that it must then discard or it would soon break down.

An oil cooler acts as a heat exchanger wherein the hot oil can pass its heat to cooling water. The construction is the usual piping within a housing with the hot and cold fluids separated by thin metal walls.

Marine Conversions

The automobile engine is a popular basic building block on which to assemble a marine power plant. Such units are called marine conversions. One is shown in Figure 2-36.

Figure 2-36: By replacing manifolds, pump, transmission and other parts with comparable units designed for sea duty, an automobile engine becomes a marine conversion. (Credit—Lehman Mfg. Co.)

Using a standard automobile engine has many advantages. The mass production techniques by which they are manufactured permit more economical pricing and their wide service facilities make spare parts always available. The basic engines can be purchased new from car dealers and can often be had at great savings from new cars that have been wrecked. More mechanics are familiar with them because they are in such general use.

Some manufacturers supply the marine conversions complete, ready to put into the boat. Others supply conversion kits. These kits contain all the parts that must be replaced on the auto engine to make it suitable for sea duty. The user of these kits buys his engine locally, new or used.

Certain parts of the automobile engine, the fan for instance, are obviously not used in a boat installation. Other parts are replaced with units of similar function because the original is not able to withstand marine conditions. The air filter is exchanged for a flame arrester because the former does not meet Coast Guard requirements. The water pump is replaced with one of greater capacity. The manifolds give way to ones that are water cooled. The horizontal mounting in an automobile must be reformed for the angle mounting in a hull; this would apply to carburetor as well as engine base. Sometimes the electrics must be moved to more accessible positions. The flywheel housing must be adapted to the housings of standard marine transmissions and reduction gears.

The original transmission from the automobile is never used in the marine conversions. Its reverse gear is inadequate because of its great reduction ratio. In fact, the entire transmission is not built to withstand the strain of constant transmission of full power and would soon break down.

The use of these conversions is not as farfetched as might seem. Some of the standard marine engines on the market are built on and around automobile engine blocks obtained from the auto factories. These manufacturers correctly claim that they are getting the benefit of all the research and development carried out in Detroit.

Conversions are available not only for gasoline engines but also for diesels. Here again the basis is a standard truck or tractor diesel engine made by one of the big automotive firms.

One attraction the conversion people hold out to skippers is the low cost of engine replacement. When the converted engine wears out, they advise, remove all the newly added marine parts and trade the basic engine in for a new one at the exchange price. This type of exchange "with your old one" is familiar to many motorists who do their own tinkering.

Governors

A powerboat in a heavy sea often digs its nose in and raises its propellers into thin air. At that time the engines could "run away" and destroy themselves because the throttle is wide open. A governor prevents this ruinous condition. It is geared to the engine and closes the throttle when the set speed is reached, thus preventing any further increase and damage. (The governor can do this infinitely faster than any human.)

Mufflers

Unlike automotive mufflers which are made of sheet steel, marine mufflers are often heavy iron castings, although corrosion resistant metals and special rubber are coming into use. The cooling water flows through them, helps keep them cool, and aids in the muffling of the exhaust noise.

Muffler design calls for a maximum of sound suppression and a minimum of back pressure. These two criteria are generally antagonistic, necessitating a compromise.

The Wind

The foregoing close examination of the many aspects of mechanical propulsion should not obscure the fact that thousands upon thousands of pleasure boatmen in this country prefer the wind for motive power. These sailors watch with cynical satisfaction as their motorboat counterparts dig down to pay for power which the wind gives free. Yet many of the sailor-boys carry an engine, just in case—although some do so as furtively as a fly fisherman carries his worms.

Whereas the push exerted by propulsion machinery is always directly ahead when underway, the direction of the wind's push is a matter of chance and could come from any direction without regard to intended course. The trick in sailing is to convert these randomly oriented wind forces into useful power toward a desired objective.

The instrument for making this conversion is the sail. It can accomplish the feat under the aegis of a principle in physics which states that a force can be resolved into equivalent resultant and complementary forces. Bernoulli's principle, discussed in Chapter 1, also comes into the act.

One example of the conversion is pictured in Figure 2-37, where a sailboat is apparently doing the impossible, namely, sailing against the wind. The detailed sketch shows that the wind is fathering a pulling force almost opposite in direction to itself. The secret lies in the airfoil shape which the sail is made to assume.

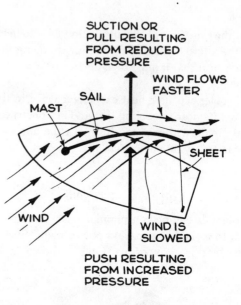

Figure 2-37: Sailing against the wind is possible. The sail must assume an airfoil shape to accomplish this feat.

The air must travel considerably faster over the convex forward face of the sail because of the curvature. Bernoulli's principle assures us that this reduces the pressure on the surface of the sail (you could call it a suction) and that therefore a forward pull is produced which the vessel can use as motive power.

Sailors have assigned names to the various segments of a circle from which the wind can blow in relation to the ship's course. These are illustrated in Figure 2-38.

It is interesting to note that the boat can exceed the speed of the wind in all angles (subject of course to its own hull speed limitations) except when she is running directly before the wind. In this juxtaposition, the wind is merely pushing. For a push to be exerted, the boat must be moving slower than the wind, in other words, must offer some resistance. Once the craft attains the speed of the wind, the pushing force vanishes.

Although a sailboat can move toward the wind, it cannot run directly into it. Under such a confrontation, no useful resultant pull can be generated; about 45 degrees off the wind is as close as most sailing ships can come. This means that the boat must be tacked (zig-zagged

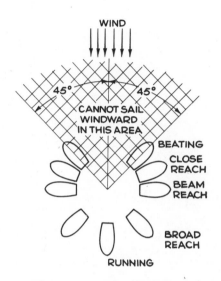

Figure 2-38: The various segments of a circle from which the wind can blow in relation to a ship's course are named here.

across the wind) when the destination is upwind. Tacking is described more fully in Chapter 14.

The powerboatman has his throttle; the sailor has his halyards and sheets. By manipulating these, he determines the area and aspect of the surface upon which the wind is to act and the nature of the resultant motive power.

Of course ships do not have brakes as motorcars do, but two propellers reversing at full throttle become a pretty good equivalent on a powerboat. The sailboat generally lacks this ability to stop short. A windjammer usually estimates the distance he can shoot forward after his sails are doused or else swings up into the wind to stop. He must substitute his skill for the stinkpotter's easy throttle manipulation. When a sailboat slides to a perfect landing at a pier, *sans* engine help, it is a thing of beauty for all to admire. Rare is the skipper whose chest does not swell after accomplishing this feat.

3 Propellers, Drives, Shafts and Gears

Engines deliver their power in the form of rotary motion, or torque. To be useful, a hull requires power in the form of a lineal push that can move it from one place to another. The most common marine device for transforming power from the first form to the second is the propeller.

The propeller is an old invention, greatly antedating the pleasure boats which today are its greatest market. A patent on a "propulsion screw" was granted in 1785 and a propeller actually pushed a ship years before the *Clermont* made her trip up the Hudson River. In fact, practical propellers were in use even before there was a through understanding of the physical principles that govern their operation and make them possible.

The propeller is basically a portion of a helix or screw. This has led to the general belief that it threads its way through the water much as a bolt turns its way through a nut. This concept is true only to a very limited extent. It takes Newton's laws of action and reaction to explain correctly the pushing force developed by a rotating propeller. Thus it becomes apparent that this seemingly simple propulsion screw is more complicated in its functioning than first thought assumed.

Although each manufacturer has his own pet formulas governing details of design, all propellers, large or small, are basically alike. Aside from the matter of size, the categories into which propellers fall are determined by their number of blades and by the direction of their intended rotation. Commercial screws are available in two-blade, three-blade, four-blade, and even five- and six-blade styles. These can be had for either right-hand or left-hand turning. Single-blade propellers have been tried

a

Figure 3-1: From wooden pattern (a) to finished propeller (c) requires many operations (b) & (c). (Credit—Michigan Wheel Company; Photos by William Andrews)

but are now only a curiosity. The photographs in Figure 3-1 show some standard props as well as some of the steps in their manufacture.

Boatmen call a propeller a wheel. Wheels are described specifically by listing these seven characteristics: diameter, pitch, bore, number of blades, rotation, style, and material. The sketch in Figure 3-2 helps to visualize each of these.

Diameter

The diameter of a propeller is the smallest circle into which the rotating wheel would fit. In a two-blade or four-blade model in which the blades are directly opposite, it is of course the distance from tip to opposite tip through the center. A more accurate measuring method, which would apply to all blade configurations, is illustrated in the aforementioned figure. In this, a measurement is taken from the center to the outermost edge of one blade; *twice* this length is the wheel diameter.

Pitch

The angle through which each blade is twisted from the flat dish position determines the pitch of the propeller.

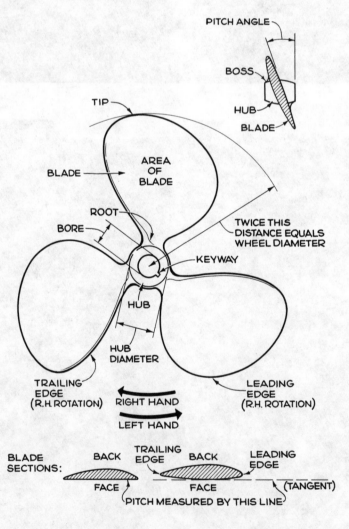

Figure 3-2: Propeller nomenclature.

Commercially, however, this twist is not specified in degrees of angle but rather in inches. The inches of pitch is the distance the propeller would move forward in one revolution if it functioned purely as a screw threading its way through solid material acting as a nut. (A propeller in actual service *never* pushes a boat ahead in one revolution a distance equal to its pitch because water is not a solid material.)

Early propeller blades were almost flat and thus maintained the same angle of twist, or pitch, from the hub to the tip. Modern blade design utilizes transverse pitch distribution. In this method the blade is not only twisted from its flat dish position but also is twisted upon itself. The pitch therefore varies smoothly from hub to tip and its designated pitch is an average effective value. (Props for airplanes are all of distributed pitch design.)

A more technical consideration of the pitch of a propeller blade divides it into three classifications: constant pitch, axially increasing pitch and radially increasing pitch. A constant pitch blade maintains the same degree of twist over its entire surface. The twist of an axially increased blade becomes greater from the leading edge to the trailing edge. The twist of a radially increasing blade increases from the hub to the tip. All these variations have the same aim: greater efficiency under certain conditions.

Bore

The hole diameter at the center of the hub that accommodates the shaft, expressed in inches and fractions, is the bore. This is not a parallel hole but is tapered and the size designation applies to the large end which faces the shaft. The amount of taper is fixed by engineering convention and is standard in the marine industry; the diameter decreases by one-sixteenth of an inch for every inch away from the large end. (The shaft naturally has a corresponding taper.)

The tapered mating surfaces offer several mechanical advantages. When the propeller is forced onto the shaft, the two units have a tendency to jam tight; this becomes effective in transmitting the power from the engine. The jamming also has a centering effect which keeps the prop true. The wheel can be "unjammed" with relatively slight pressure which makes for easy removal. The looseness that would be inevitable with a parallel hole and a parallel

shaft is eliminated.

Slippage of propeller on shaft is prevented and power transmission is aided by a "key," a metal rod of rectangular or square cross section which fits simultaneously into "keyways" in hub and shaft. The sizes of keys and keyways are also fixed by engineering convention. Sharp corners at the bottoms of keyway slots always should be avoided because these induce a concentration of stresses that could cause shaft and prop failure. Good practice dictates a smooth, radial blending of the bottom and side of the slot; the corners of the key are naturally re-

MARINE PROPELLERS HUB BORE DIMENSIONS
Taper: Per Foot = ¾"
Per Inch = 1⁄16"   Angle with centerline = 1°47'24"

Std. Taper	Dia. Small End "A"		Keyway Width "C"			Keyway Side Depth "D"		
	Min.	Max.	Nom.	Min.	Max.	Nom.	Min.	Max.
¾	.608	.610	3⁄16	.1865	.1875	3⁄32	.098	.100
⅞	.710	.712	¼	.249	.250	⅛	.129	.131
1	.812	.814	¼	.249	.250	⅛	.129	.131
1⅛	.913	.915	¼	.249	.250	⅛	.129	.131
1¼	1.015	1.017	5⁄16	.3115	.3125	5⁄32	.162	.165
1⅜	1.116	1.118	5⁄16	.3115	.3125	5⁄32	.161	.164
1½	1.218	1.220	⅜	.374	.375	3⁄16	.195	.198
1¾	1.421	1.423	7⁄16	.4365	.4375	7⁄32	.226	.229
2	1.624	1.626	½	.499	.500	¼	.259	.262
2¼	1.827	1.829	9⁄16	.561	.5625	9⁄32	.291	.294
2½	2.030	2.032	⅝	.6235	.625	5⁄16	.322	.325
2¾	2.233	2.235	⅝	.6235	.625	5⁄16	.322	.325
3	2.437	2.439	¾	.7485	.750	5⁄16	.323	.326
3¼	2.640	2.642	¾	.7485	.750	5⁄16	.323	.326
3½	2.843	2.845	⅞	.8735	.875	5⁄16	.324	.327
3¾	3.046	3.048	⅞	.8735	.875	5⁄16	.324	.327
4	3.249	3.251	1	.9985	1.000	5⁄16	.326	.329
4½	3.796	3.798	1⅛	1.123	1.125	⅜	.388	.391
5	4.218	4.220	1¼	1.248	1.250	7⁄16	.450	.453
5½	4.640	4.642	1¼	1.248	1.250	7⁄16	.950	.953
*6	4.749	4.751	1⅜	1.373	1.375	½	.517	.520
*6½	5.145	5.147	1⅜	1.373	1.375	½	.516	.519
*7	5.541	5.543	1½	1.498	1.500	9⁄16	.579	.582
*7½	5.937	5.939	1½	1.498	1.500	9⁄16	.579	.582
*8	6.332	6.334	1¾	1.748	1.750	9⁄16	.582	.585

*—1" per foot taper

Figure 3-3: Propeller hubs are bored to standard dimensions.

lieved sufficiently to fit. The table in Figure 3-3 lists standard hub bore dimensions.

Rotation

The direction of rotation of a propeller is always specified by looking at it from aft of the stern. A wheel that turns clockwise from this view is a right-hand propeller. A wheel that turns counterclockwise from this view is a left-hand propeller.

Single-screw boats are generally equipped with a right-hand propeller while twin-screw craft carry a right-hand and a left-hand wheel. The right-hand prop is on the starboard side so that the blades move away from each other at the top, the preferred practice.

Style

Every propeller manufacturer offers a wide choice of blade styles, each of which he recommends for a specific service. The configuration of a blade is derived from a combination of mathematics, empirical knowledge, and trial-and-error testing. Spectacular claims of improvement are often based on comparatively small changes in curvature, outline, or cross-sectional shape. To some degree, propeller design is still a black art in which experience is an important ingredient.

Much design and engineering effort goes into the shape of the blade tips and the cross section of the blade itself. These two points weigh heavily in the propeller's ability to resist cavitation, a condition explained on page 89.

Material

Bronze is the preferred material in the preponderant majority of powerboat installations. Various alloys of this material have been developed whose strength approaches that of steel without sacrifice of corrosion-resisting ability. Aluminum and stainless steel also serve as propeller materials, and a hard, tough plastic has come into use recently.

Casting, or its plastic equivalent, molding, is the usual method of manufacture and all of these materials are castable. Material strength is especially important in blade designs that taper down to thin, sharp sections at the trailing edge.

Commercial Sizes

Once the matter of rotation, style, and material has been decided, a propeller is characterized commercially by two numbers. The first designates the diameter in inches and the second states the pitch, also in inches. Thus a "10–13" wheel would be 10 inches in diameter with a 13-inch pitch. When diameter and pitch are equal, the propeller is gen-

erally known as square; a 12–12, for instance, would be a square wheel, while a 12–14 becomes an over-square.

Propeller Theory

It was stated earlier that a propeller performs its function under the laws of action and reaction first established by Isaac Newton. Anyone who has ever held a garden hose has demonstrated these laws to himself. When the flow is turned on, the water shoots forward (the action) and the hose pushes back against the hand (the reaction). The classical law states that every action has an equal and opposite reaction and the truth of this has been proved innumerable times in every physics class.

The propeller forces a quantity of water astern, the action, and the boat is pushed ahead by the reaction. The effectiveness of the push is dependent upon the mass or weight of the water that is moved and upon the speed of the motion. In moving this water the propeller acts like the impeller in a pump and, in fact, the entire action is akin to that in a pump that has its outer housing removed. (Propellers have been designed to work in a cylindrical shield for greater efficiency, which is simply a restoration of the pump housing.)

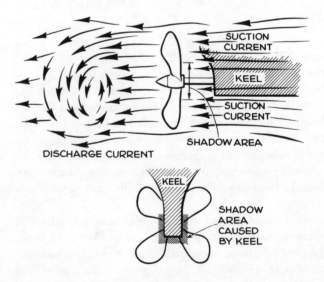

Figure 3-4: *Conditions in the vicinity of a rotating propeller. Obstructions in the suction current can cause a "shadow area" of impeded water supply to the prop.*

The sketch in Figure 3-4 shows what happens in the vicinity of a rotating propeller. The water flowing to the screw is the suction current; the water leaving the screw is the discharge current. Note that the suction current was not described as being "pulled" to the propeller; obviously water is not a solid material upon which a force of tension can be exerted. The suction current is water that is forced by surrounding pressures to replace the water pushed astern by the prop.

The free and unobstructed flow of the suction current is important to the efficiency of a propeller. In actual installations this free approach is not achieved because of unavoidable obstructions such as struts or keels or even portions of the hull. A clear-cut example of obstructed flow occurs in a single-screw boat where the keel effectively divides the suction current in two. This is illustrated in the drawing. When the propeller is close abaft, the keel projects a definite shadow area onto it in which the suction current is starved and insufficient to maintain full thrust.

The discharge current abaft the spinning propeller represents the power absorbed from the engine. The larger the mass or volume of this current and the higher its velocity, the more power expended by the engine and the greater the reactive forward thrust on the hull. The speed of the discharge current is greatest at its center; it tapers off to zero at the periphery by the friction of the surrounding water.

Theoretically, the discharge current is a cylinder of water the diameter of which is the same as that of the propeller. This condition could come about only if the surrounding water offered no friction and if the blades forced all water axially and none radially. Under actual operating conditions the discharge current is an expanding cone whose movement is soon dissipated and lost with only a wake remaining to testify to its existence.

This shape of the discharge current is the logic behind the corrective action taken by some prop manufacturers. The correction consists of cupping or curving the trailing edges of the blades as shown in Figure 3-5. The effect is to throw more water directly rearward and lose less in radial offshoots. Advantages in noise reduction and lessened vibration are also claimed.

Technical Considerations

Catalogues describe propellers by their MWR and their

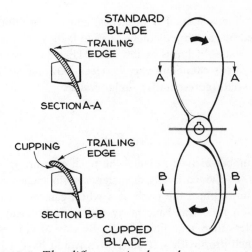

Figure 3-5: The difference in shape between a standard and a cupped blade is shown in the sectional views. The cupping contracts the discharge current and makes for more efficient propeller operation.

BTF. These abbreviations signify the mean width ratio and the blade thickness factor.

MWR.

When the average width of the blade, in inches, is divided by the diameter of the wheel, also in inches, the quotient is a decimal number called the mean width ratio. By its size this decimal quickly indicates whether the propeller to which it applies is narrow-bladed or wide-bladed. Considering all props likely to be used on pleasure boats, the MWR might be between about .1 for a knife-like narrow wheel to about .5 for the extremely wide blades of a screw for a slow commercial lugger.

The need for variations in MWR can be understood easily if you visualize what the face of the propeller blade is intended to do. The blade face "pushes" water. The wider the face, the more water it can push. The more water pushed, the greater the amount of work done and the stronger the thrust on the boat. The reasoning runs along neatly and the purpose behind MWR variations is made clear.

BTF.

The blade thickness factor is also a decimal number; it is always much smaller in value than the MWR. The BTF number represents the sturdiness or heft of a propeller blade. If a projection of the blade thickness on the center line is measured in inches, and if this number is divided by the prop diameter, also in inches, the quotient is the blade thickness factor. The BTFs of the wheels in one maker's catalogue vary between .037 and .047 and these seem representative design values.

Pitch Ratio

The number arrived at when the pitch of a propeller, in inches, is divided by its diameter, also in inches, is the pitch ratio. Since the pitch of a wheel can vary widely, the pitch ratio can have many values; it can run from much less than 1 to more than 1. By way of illustration, a 20-inch prop with a 10-inch pitch would have a PR of .5; a wheel of the same diameter but over-squared to a 24-inch pitch would figure to a PR of 1.2.

The average powerboat with a displacement hull, not too fast and not too slow, would keep its pitch ratio around 1.0. At the low end of the scale would be the wide-beamed, heavy workboat with a PR of perhaps .5; the fast, light planing hull would be at the top end with a PR approaching 1.5.

Tip Speed

This term is almost self-explanatory. It is the lineal distance the tip of the blade travels in its circle in a given unit of time, usually one minute. Since the circumference of a circle is pi (3.14) multiplied by the diameter, it is only necessary to multiply this product by the shaft revolutions per minute to get the tip speed. For instance, the blade tip of a 10-inch propeller travels 31.4 inches in one revolution (10 x 3.14) and has a tip speed of 31,400 *inches* per minute when the shaft RPM is 1000. This is a perfectly respectable answer although it is customary to divide this result by 12 to get 2616 *feet* per minute.

Excessive tip speed becomes the factor which limits the revolutions per minute at which large wheels can be driven. Each manufacturer specifies the maximum permissible figure for each of his designs. The prop loses its "grip" on the water when this speed is exceeded and what is technically known as cavitation results. A general idea of maximum tip speeds would place them between 8000 and 16,000 feet per minute, judging by manufacturers' catalogues.

Slip

It should be emphasized again that a propeller does *not* function like a screw threading its way through a solid nut and that the pitch does *not* correspond to the exact distance it will advance in one revolution. The difference between the actual advance and the pitch advance is called the slip. Obviously, since water is very thin, this slip could be any value between near zero and 100 percent, depending upon the resistance offered to the forward travel of the propeller by the hull to which it is attached.

The immutable laws of physics being what they are, some slip must occur before a thrust can be generated. For instance, a ship tied securely to a pier with its wheels turning at full power would exhibit 100 percent slip; a feather-light boat skimming along at high speed would show a very low percentage of slip.

The concept of slip is complicated by the fact that the propeller seldom works in still water. As explained in Chapter 1, the moving hull "drags" some water with it because of skin friction. This places the propeller in the equivalent of a forward-moving current and further robs it of some of its pitch advance. Thus we have apparent slip and true slip. (Many nontechnical skippers will consider both slips as one and will not go far wrong.)

Apparent slip is the easy one to calculate. The pitch in inches is multiplied by the revolutions per minute; this gives the theoretical advance in inches per minute. Dividing by 1056 reduces this to statute miles per hour.

If boat speed through the water is now measured by some independent means, the percentage of slip evolves without difficulty. It is necessary only to subtract actual boat speed from the theoretical advance and then to divide this remainder by the theoretical advance. The answer multiplied by 100 is percent of apparent slip. (True slip calculations require a knowledge of the speed of the forward flow of water into which the propeller is "biting.")

A sample calculation for percentage of slip follows: The propeller has a pitch of 10 inches and is turning at 2000 revolutions per minute. The theoretical advance is thus 10 × 2000 or 20,000 inches per minute. Dividing by 1056 brings this to roughly 19 statute miles per hour. Subtracting the actual boat speed of 15 miles per hour, determined independently, leaves 4 and dividing this by 19 equals 4/19ths or approximately 21 percent slip when multiplied by 100.

SLIP VS. EFFICIENCY.

The usual connotation of the word slip may imply a false idea when applied to propellers. To slip generally means to make a mistake or to lose something. Accordingly, many skippers believe that the larger the slip, the greater the loss in efficiency. This is not so; slip and efficiency are related very distantly if at all.

When the props start to churn on a large and heavy ship that has been at rest, the initial slip is 100 percent because the great inertia must be overcome before movement can commence. As speed is gained by the ship the percentage of slip drops and finally reaches a value at which all the forces balance.

Contradictory as it may seem, a reduction in slip under some conditions may also reduce efficiency. For instance, slip could be cut by increasing blade area or pitch but the consequently greater resistance of the prop through the water could eat up more than a commensurate amount of power. (A fair average value for slip on powerboats is 25 percent.)

Cavitation

Cavitation is often discussed, frequently encountered, and rarely understood. Yet this propeller ailment was first noticed at the turn of the century and has been the subject of study and experimentation ever since.

Cavitation occurs when the suction side of a propeller blade loses contact with the water and operates instead in a region of vapor and air. The supply of "solid" water may have been interrupted for some reason—excessive blade speed, interfering protuberances, too great pitch, or whatever.

The water in the discharge current has been accelerated by the engine and can reach any reasonable speed of which the available power is capable. But the water in the suction current can come to the propeller only as fast as the surrounding water pressure and air pressure can make it. This is sometimes insufficient to replace the water that has been pushed away. A void results on the suction (forward) side of the blade and cavitation ensues. These voids are not continuous but break down and re-form. These actions happen at lightning speeds and the droplets of water hit the blade surface like chipping hammers and pockmark it. The water vapor formed in the regions of low pressure supplies the energy for this destruction.

Once it is clearly understood that cavitation is the result of a faulty supply of water to the propeller, then the immediate causes of this phenomenon in any particular instance can be reasoned out. Too steep a pitch, for instance, moves water away faster than it can be replenished by the natural forces prevailing. Excessive speed of revolution does the same thing. Deadwood or a wide keel or even an oversized strut could partially block the suction current. Figure 3-6 portrays the cavitation forces.

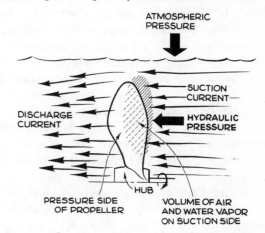

Figure 3-6: Cavitation occurs when the forward faces of the blades of a fast-revolving propeller lose contact with "solid" water. This occurs when water is pushed astern in the discharge current faster than the suction current can replenish it.

Aside from the damage to the propeller itself, cavitation can injure the engine and drive train. The sudden releases of the load permit the engine to overspeed; often even governors cannot completely subdue these rapid fluctuations.

Practical Considerations

The foregoing discussion should have made clear that the propeller is deceptively simple in its appearance yet complicated in its action when going about its business. Some of its idiosyncrasies are triggered by the manner in which it is installed and used.

It is not too great an oversimplification to say that the diameter and blade area of a propeller should relate to the power of the engine while the pitch should relate to the speed of the boat. Neither can it be denied that the selection of the proper wheel for a particular boat, despite all the available tables and formulas, is largely a matter of experience and cut-and-try. Basically, the propeller should absorb the full horsepower of the engine at its rated speed, should neither prevent that speed from being attained nor permit overspeeding.

Prop Location

The need for an unobstructed path for the suction current has already been stressed. This is easier to attain on twin-screw boats than on single-screw boats. Where the single-screw boats have a heavy keel, as on auxiliaries, the problem becomes acute and partially unsolvable.

Most modern powerboat hulls permit reasonably clear water influx to the propeller when there is a twin installation. The major obstructions are the shaft itself and the struts supporting it. The struts can be faired to reduce their interference; the shaft cannot be reduced in diameter below the size required for the fulfillment of its mechanical functions.

How much the keel on a single-screw boat impedes the suction current depends on the space between the propeller and the keel extremity. When this space is great enough for the water flow to re-form into a single stream, the interference is slightest.

Propellers must also be placed so that their tips are never closer than a minimum distance from the hull; most makers prescribe this as one-tenth of the diameter. Closer spacing can cause interference with the suction current (and cavitation) and also objectionable noise in the boat. The noise comes from the water hammer against the hull as each blade passes. The frequency or tone of this noise is equal to the number of blades multiplied by the shaft revolutions per second; it can go from a rumble to a whine.

Unequal Thrust

Ideally, the thrust of a propeller would be equal at all positions of every blade. This could happen only if the prop were placed with its disk parallel to the surface of the water and it were pushing straight down. Under actual conditions of propeller placement, where the wheel is vertical or slightly inclined, the thrust is unequal and introduces problems in maneuverability.

When the propeller disk is vertical (horizontal shaft) the inequalities in thrust arise because the pressure of the

water increases naturally with depth. Each foot deeper brings an area with greater pressure than the one above; the constant increase is dramatized by the heavy armor of the deep sea diver. A prop blade in its uppermost position is working in water of less pressure than a blade in its lowest position. There is thus a difference in thrust and a sideward component, or push, is generated which affects steering. (The undesired steering effect is neutralized with twin screws rotating oppositely.)

When the propeller disk is tilted (shaft at an angle to the surface) the above-mentioned conditions are compounded further; that is, the apparent pitch of the blade relative to its forward motion is different on the upstroke and the downstroke. Figure 3-7 should help in under-

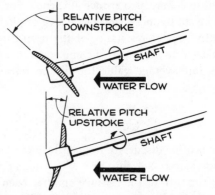

Figure 3-7: The tilt of the propeller shaft affects the apparent pitch of the propeller blade as it revolves; undesired side thrusts are generated.

standing this.

The figure also emphasizes the desirability of keeping drive shafts horizontal. Aside from the accentuation of unequal thrust, the inclined shaft wastes a portion of the propeller push. Since this push or thrust is along the line of the shaft, some of it is trying to force the stern up—and the bow down—without providing its share of forward motion.

Sailboat Auxiliary Propellers

Many sailboats and auxiliaries have an inbuilt advantage when it comes to propeller installation. Because of their deep hulls and consequently deep-set engines, these boats can install their prop shafts horizontally and thus keep their propellers vertical. Some undesired effects of unequal thrust thereby are largely avoided. Furthermore, the thrust is in a horizontal plane and completely useful in pushing the boat.

Blade Edges

The leading and trailing edges (the head and tail) of the blades have received more and more attention as the sciences of aero- and hydrodynamics have stressed their importance. The goal is a smooth entrance into each mass of water and an exit devoid of eddies. The cross section of a prop blade looks increasingly like a cut across an airplane wing; except for the density of the medium, the conditions under which both work are similar. Some representative blade and tip forms are shown in Figure 3-8.

Figure 3-8: Propeller sections and blade tips have various shapes to suit different types of service.

Miscellany

Special propeller blade shapes have been designed for use where the heavy vegetation in shallow waters would soon clog a standard screw. One so-called weedless type is pictured in Figure 3-9. It protects itself from weeds both by sloughing them off and cutting them.

Feathering propellers have their blades set in rotatable

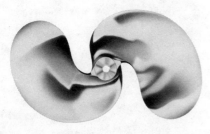

Figure 3-9: This blade shape is designed to throw off weeds that would entangle a standard propeller. (Credit— Federal Weedless Propeller)

sockets geared together to move in unison. Actuation is either through a rod inside the drive shaft or through an outside yoke. These props are often used on sailboats because in their full feathered position (infinite pitch) the blades are parallel to the direction of travel and present little drag. One is shown in Figure 3-10.

An unusual use of feathering propellers is illustrated on the Coast Guard cutter *Dallas* in Figure 3-11. This

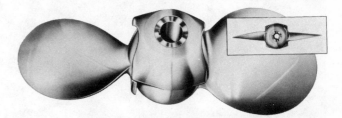

Figure 3-10: The two blades are geared together and can move from zero pitch (flat dish) to infinite pitch (shown in the inset) at which they offer minimum resistance to forward motion on a ship under sail. (Credit—Michigan Wheel Company)

ship has no reversing gear and the engines always run at constant speed. Forward and reverse as well as all boat speed changes are made entirely by changing the pitch of its driving screws.

The abrupt termination at the hub of a propeller causes undesirable eddies and reduces efficiency. This is corrected by the installation of a "fairwater," illustrated in Figure 3-12. The fairwater takes the place of the final shaft nut or locknut and is secured by a drilled pin or set screw.

Balance is important with a propeller just as it is with any heavy device that must be rotated. There are two methods of achieving balance: static and dynamic. For static balance the wheel is put on a shaft and placed on horizontal knife edges. Metal is removed from heavy sections until the wheel remains stationary in all positions.

Dynamic balance is far superior to static methods—and requires much more sophisticated and expensive equipment. The prop is mounted on a machine which spins it and electronically records the location and amount of any imbalance. (See Figure 3-1.)

An important last note about propellers: The rotation

Figure 3-11: The CG cutter Dallas *is propelled by feathering props of giant size. The ship has no reverse gear and the engines run at constant speed. All maneuvering, ahead and astern, is done by changing pitch. (Credit— U.S. Coast Guard)*

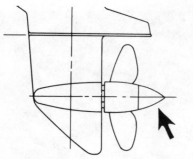

Figure 3-12: The fairwater (arrow) at the end of the pro-peller shaft helps reduce unwanted turbulence.

of a prop is determined by looking forward toward it from astern. The rotation of engines is determined by looking aft at them from forward. Thus there arises the anomaly that a left-hand prop requires a right-hand engine and a right-hand prop must be driven by a left-hand engine.

Shafts

Few skippers realize that the shaft which turns the propeller must also be stiff enough to push the boat. The thrust of the propeller is exerted against the shaft, the shaft in turn transmits it to the thrust bearing in the engine or gear box, and the engine mount transfers it to the hull. The need for shaft stiffness becomes obvious; and the longer the shaft, the greater this need. The shaft must also be hefty enough to transmit the necessary torque or twisting effort from the engine to the wheel without appreciable deformation.

SHAFT MATERIALS.

Shafts for powerboats are formed from bronze, Monel, and stainless steel—generally in that order of popularity and cost. The specific alloys are manganese bronze, stainless #304, #316, or #410, and Monel #400 and #K500. The alloying element in the stainless steel is primarily chromium. The Monel #400 is a nickel-copper combination while the #K500 adds aluminum to this duo.

The foregoing alloys are chosen for their combination of strength and corrosion resistance. All can resist the ravages of seawater as well as chemically polluted bay and lake water. This does *not* mean that they are immune to galvanic action; when placed in juxtaposition to in-compatible metals they must be protected. This is explained in Chapter 22.

A rough choice of shaft diameter is made easy with the nomograph given in Figure 3-13. If maximum engine horsepower and *propeller* revolutions per minute are known, a straight edge laid across the columns will determine optimum shaft diameter with a good margin of safety. Actual *propeller* speed is stressed as against engine speed because in most cases these two are not identical since a reduction gear usually is interposed. The critical dimensions which this shaft must have are given in the tables which accompany the nomograph. Once shaft size is fixed it is then necessary to find the correct spacing of the bearings to prevent shaft whip. The nomograph in Figure 3-14 will provide this, again with a simple straight edge.

Shaft ends are standardized and match the propeller hub standards mentioned earlier. As with the keyway in the prop hub, the keyway in the shaft looks innocuous but is all-important from a stress standpoint. Rounded corners and fillets, such as shown in Figure 3-15, should have a radius of at least 1/32 inch and as much as 3/32 inch on the larger sizes.

STUFFING BOXES.

A watertight closure that also acts as a bearing support is needed where the shaft enters the hull. This device is called a stuffing box and is illustrated in Figure 3-16. A gland nut permits tightening sufficient to exclude water but loose enough to allow rotation without excessive friction.

Older stuffing boxes carried the adjusting nut on the outside, the end toward the propeller. Adjustment required either hauling or the services of a scuba diver. The more modern design places the adjusting nut on the inside, in the bilge, where access is handy.

STRUTS.

When the shaft protrudes any distance beyond the stuffing box, supports in the shape of struts must be provided to eliminate whip. One such strut must be located directly at the propeller to act as a bearing and steady it from side thrusts. Good struts are faired to reduce water turbulence, as shown in Figure 3-17. Strut material is generally the same as shaft material. Rubber

MARINE PROPELLER SHAFT ENDS DIMENSIONS

APPROVED S.A.E. STANDARD DIMENSIONS FOR SHAFTS 3/4 TO 3 IN. IN DIAMETER

Nom Shaft Dia. A	Diameter Small End B		Taper Length C	Keyway Width D			Keyway Side Depth[a] E			Keyway Fillet Radius[b] R	Thread[c] F		End of Taper to End of Thd G	Extension Beyond Taper H	Undercut		Dia. of Pin End L	Lgth. of Pin End M	Cotter-Pin Hole		Cotter-Pin, Q		Nuts[a]			Keyway Length X
	Min	Max		Nom	Min	Max	Nom	Min	Max		Dia.	Tpi			J	K			N	P (drill)	Nom dia.	Length	Size	Plain thick, T	Jamb thick, W	
3/4	0.624	0.626	2	3/16	0.1865	0.1875	3/32	0.095	0.097	1/32	1/2	13	1 1/16	1 5/16	25/64	1/8	3/8	1/4	1 9/64	9/64	1/8	3/4	1/2-13	1/2	5/16	1 1/2
7/8	0.726	0.728	2 3/8	1/4	0.249	0.250	1/8	0.125	0.127	1/32	5/8	11	1 1/4	1 1/2	31/64	1/8	7/16	1/4	1 21/64	9/64	1/8	3/4	5/8-11	5/8	3/8	1 25/32
1	0.827	0.829	2 3/4	1/4	0.249	0.250	1/8	0.125	0.127	1/32	3/4	10	1 7/16	1 3/4	19/32	1/8	1/2	5/16	1 33/64	9/64	1/8	1	3/4-10	3/4	7/16	2 1/8
1 1/8	0.929	0.931	3 1/8	1/4	0.249	0.250	1/8	0.125	0.127	1/32	3/4	10	1 7/16	1 3/4	19/32	1/8	1/2	5/16	1 33/64	9/64	1/8	1	3/4-10	3/4	7/16	2 1/8
1 1/4	1.030	1.032	3 1/2	5/16	0.3115	0.3125	5/32	0.157	0.160	1/16	7/8	9	1 5/8	2	23/32	1/8	5/8	3/8	1 23/32	11/64	5/32	1 1/4	7/8-9	7/8	1/2	2 13/16
1 3/8	1.132	1.134	3 7/8	5/16	0.3115	0.3125	5/32	0.157	0.160	1/16	1	8	1 13/16	2 1/4	13/16	1/8	3/4	7/16	1 29/32	11/64	5/32	1 1/2	1 -8	1	9/16	3 3/16
1 1/2	1.233	1.235	4 1/4	3/8	0.374	0.375	3/16	0.189	0.192	1/16	1 1/8	7	2	2 7/16	29/32	3/16	7/8	7/16	2 3/32	11/64	5/32	1 1/2	1 1/8-7	1 1/8	5/8	3 1/2
1 3/4	1.437	1.439	5	7/16	0.4365	0.4375	7/32	0.219	0.222	1/16	1 1/4	7	2 1/4	2 3/4	1 1/32	3/16	1	1/2	2 23/64	13/64	3/16	1 3/4	1 1/4-7	1 1/4	3/4	4 7/32
2	1.640	1.642	5 3/4	1/2	0.499	0.500	1/4	0.251	0.254	1/16	1 1/2	6	2 5/8	3 1/8	1 1/4	3/16	1 1/4	1/2	2 47/64	13/64	3/16	2	1 1/2-6	1 1/2	7/8	4 15/16
2 1/4	1.843	1.845	6 1/2	9/16	0.561	0.5625	9/32	0.281	0.284	3/32	1 3/4	5	3	3 1/2	1 3/8	3/16	1 3/8	1/2	3 9/64	17/64	1/4	2 1/4	1 3/4-5	1 3/4	1	5 5/8
2 1/2	2.046	2.048	7 1/4	5/8	0.6235	0.625	5/16	0.312	0.315	3/32	1 3/4	5	3	3 1/2	1 7/16	3/16	1 7/16	1/2	3 9/64	17/64	1/4	2 1/4	1 3/4-5	1 3/4	1	6 3/32
2 3/4	2.257	2,259	7 7/8	5/8	0.6235	0.625	5/16	0.313	0.316	3/32	2	4 1/2	3 1/2	4	1 11/16	1/4	1 11/16	1/2	3 41/64	17/64	1/4	2 1/2	2 -4 1/2	2	1 1/8	6 21/32
3	2.460	2.462	8 5/8	3/4	0.7485	0.750	5/16	0.311	0.314	3/32	2 1/4	4 1/2	3 7/8	4 3/8	1 15/16	1/4	1 15/16	1/2	4 1/64	17/64	1/4	3	2 1/4-4 1/2	2 1/4	1 1/4	7 11/32

Figure 3-13: The nomograph makes selection of shaft diameter easy without calculations.

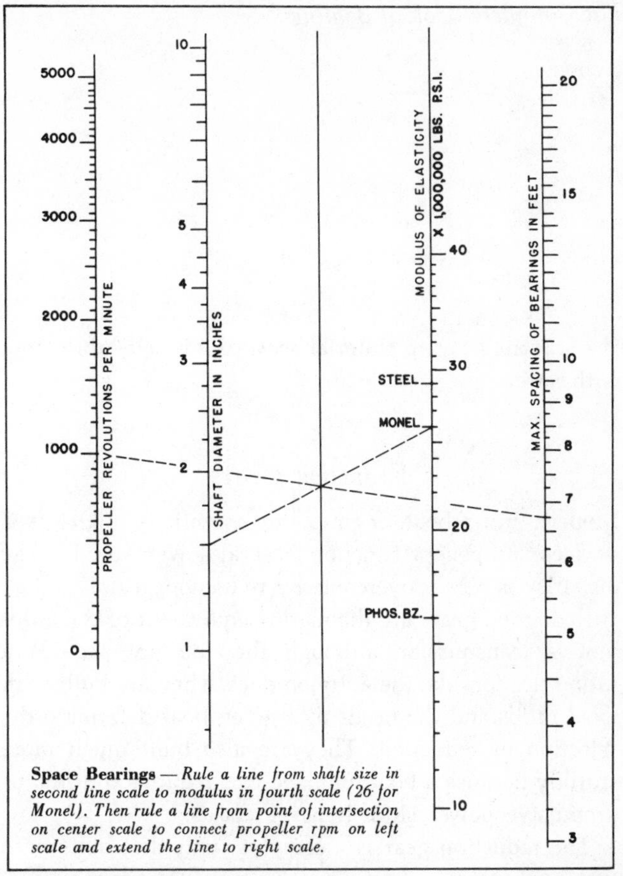
PROPELLER REVOLUTIONS PER MINUTE
SHAFT DIAMETER IN INCHES
MODULUS OF ELASTICITY
X 1,000,000 LBS. P.S.I.
STEEL
MONEL
PHOS. BZ.
MAX. SPACING OF BEARINGS IN FEET
Space Bearings — *Rule a line from shaft size in second line scale to modulus in fourth scale (26 for Monel). Then rule a line from point of intersection on center scale to connect propeller rpm on left scale and extend the line to right scale.*

Figure 3-14: Shaft bearings should be spaced according to this nomograph.

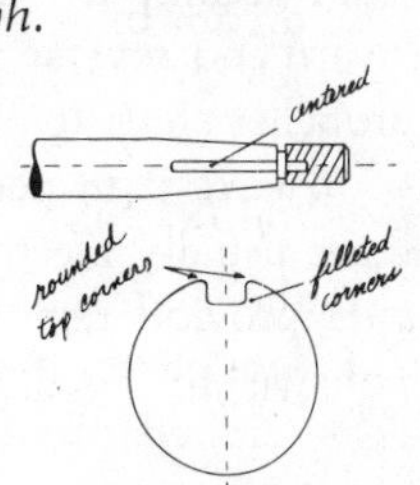
centered
rounded top corners
filleted corners

Figure 3-15: Fillets at the corners of shaft and propeller keyways remove points of otherwise high stress that cause material failure.

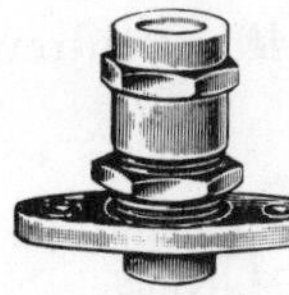

Figure 3-16: The stuffing box makes a watertight closure where the shaft enters the hull. (Credit—Manhattan Marine & Electric Co., Inc.)

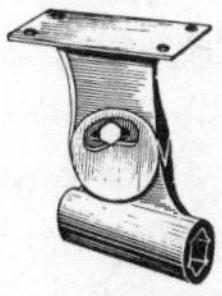

Figure 3-17: An adjustable strut aligns easily with the propeller shaft. The strut should be faired to reduce resistance to water flow. (Credit—Manhattan Marine & Electric Co., Inc.)

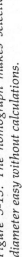

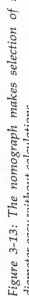

is a favorite bearing material because it is self-lubricating with water.

Reduction Gears

Modern powerboat engines are essentially high-speed devices; propellers function best at lower speeds. The disparity is nicely overcome by reduction gears.

Reduction gears are the marine equivalent of the automotive transmission although they do not provide a ratio selection like the auto job does. They are built with fixed ratios and the needs of a given boat determine the selection of reduction. They are also built much more sturdily because a boat, unlike a car, requires continuous propulsive power since it never coasts.

The reduction gear is a complete unit that bolts onto the flywheel or output shaft housing of the engine. It contains gear trains that accomplish the desired speed reduction for both forward and reverse rotation. Internal clutches connect the propeller shaft to either the forward or reverse gear train—or leave it in neutral, nondriving position. The clutches are usually mechanically operated although the finer units provide remote-controlled hydraulic systems responsive to small handles at the steering position.

Reduction gears are rated by their power-handling ability at a given speed and primarily by their reduction ratio. For instance, a 2:1 (two to one) box would turn the prop shaft at 1200 RPM when the engine is doing 2400 RPM. A typical reduction-reverse gear is shown in Figure 3-18.

Drives

VEE-DRIVES.

The engines in most powerboats are amidships and, when you think of it, it doesn't make too much sense to dump these noisy monsters into the middle of the living space. The reason for the location, of course, is to minimize the angle of the propeller drive shaft. A device called a vee-drive permits moving the engines to the stern yet maintaining the same low angle of shaft.

The vee-drive housing contains bevel gears set to angles that may vary between 10 degrees and 17 degrees, thereby offering a choice for various installations. (One maker obtains the angle with universal joints.) Lubrica-

Figure 3-18: The reduction gear reduces the comparatively high speed of the engine to the lower speed required for efficient propeller operations. (Credit—Twin Disc, Inc.)

tion and cooling are self-contained. The input flange takes power from the engine reduction-reverse gear and the output flange transmits this to the prop shaft, sometimes with additional reduction. Figure 3-19 explains the installation.

The engines in a small powerboat constitute an appreciable part of the total weight and form an important factor in the design for longitudinal and transverse stability. Therefore it may not always be possible simply to move the engines astern without strong effects on the boat's characteristics; good overall technical design must be observed.

Sailboats, auxiliaries and motor sailers, with their much deeper draft, allow the engine to be placed nearer the level of the propeller. This makes it possible to have the propeller shaft at only a very slight angle and in many cases even horizontal. As already stated, propulsive efficiency is improved by such placement.

Stern Drives (I/Os)

Stern drives achieve the same results as vee-drives, that is, moving the engines to the stern, but they accomplish this in a simpler manner. They borrow strongly from outboard engineering in doing this and are popularly

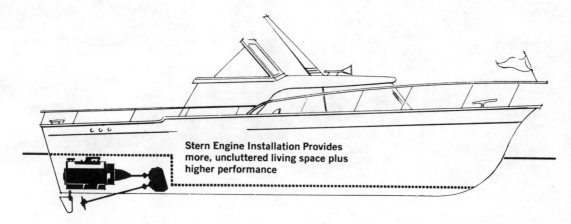

Figure 3-19: The vee drive permits boat engines to be placed in the stern, under the cockpit or in the lazarette, away from the midship living space.

known as I/Os or Inboard-Outboards.

The stern drive is a through-the-transom drive and its propeller section resembles an outboard motor without the power head. As with outboards, steering is done by swinging the prop housing and thus changing the direction of the slipstream. Also like the outboard, the angle of the prop can be changed and the wheel can even be raised out of the water for service or inspection. A complete installation is shown skeletally in Figure 3-20.

Figure 3-20: The stern drive, popularly known as an In-board-Outboard, or I/O, also permits engines to be placed aft out of the way. (Credit—Kiekhaeffer Mercury)

JET DRIVES.

Early in this chapter it was explained that the propeller functions as a pump although without a housing to confine its action. It is but a short step in technology to supply the housing, improve the prop into an impeller, and evolve with a really efficient high-velocity pump whose reactive effect, as with the original propeller, drives the boat. This is the jet drive.

Instead of operating in the water astern, as a standard propeller does, the jet drive pump is in the boat directly attached to the engine. A water scoop forward supplies the intake and a nozzle aft emits the high-velocity discharge that creates the reactive thrust. Steering and reversing are done by a combination of rudder and change in jet direction. Remembering Newton's laws of action and reaction, it should not be surprising to learn that the jet is about as effective in pushing the boat whether the stream is discharged into the water or into the air.

The need for constant water pickup by the bottom scoop restricts this drive to hull shapes that do not drag an air cushion along; the scoop must remain in solid water. The various makers have favorite positions for the pump and engine, but the principles are not altered. One type, with the pump located at the transom, is shown in Figure 3-21.

Figure 3-21: The jet drive makes use of Newton's basic law of action and reaction by shooting a high velocity stream of water sternward. The boat is steered by swinging the jet through an arc like a rudder. (Credit—Century Boat Co.)

4 *Steering Equipment and Engine Controls*

A hull, even though fully equipped with propulsion capability, does not attain practical value until after the addition of adequate systems of control. These control systems must serve two purposes: (1), to determine the speed of travel forward and reverse and (2), to choose the direction of this travel. The first purpose is met by the engine control system on powerboats and less directly on sailing vessels by sail manipulation and the second by the steering system.

A steering system can be as primitive as an oar trailing over the stern or as sophisticated as a computer that constantly ponders the effects of wind and current on the course. The usual powerboat steering equipment lies somewhere in between. Sailboats generally use the simpler means with most small craft depending upon a tiller.

So also with engine control devices. They can be as simple as a hand-operated lever sticking out of the gear box plus a wire pull for the throttle. A fancier installation combines both of these into a single little gleaming handle at the steering position which, with only finger pressure, governs everything by remote control.

Some power is required to accomplish all of these control and steering operations because of friction and other losses. This power can be supplied by the skipper's muscles—a manual control system. Alternatively, engine or battery power can be triggered to do the actual work at the skipper's bidding—a mechanical or hydraulic or electrical servo-control system.

In all cases, the size of the boat and the owner's propensity for spending money influence the final choice. The servo-controls for steering usually are simpler than the servo-controls over the engine because the latter must accommodate forward, reverse and neutral.

Rudders

The rudder is a small, vertical flat surface submerged at the after end of the hull and so supported that it can be swung from side to side. The reaction of this surface with the moving stream of water pushes the stern to one side or the other and thus steers the boat.

There are two important concepts in the foregoing description of a rudder. The first is that there must be movement of water against the rudder before it can perform its function. This movement can be the result of the boat's forward or reverse travel or it can be the slip-stream from a propeller—but there must be relative motion between rudder and water.

The second is that a boat is steered *not* by pointing its bow in the desired direction but rather by moving its stern in the *opposite* direction. This may be a bit confusing until you visualize what happens by comparing it with an automobile: A boat moving forward steers the way a car does when it is backing up. Imagine the rear end of the backing auto to be the bow of the boat and the front end to be the stern, and you have it.

Rudders are classified into two types even though they may have many small changes in outline shape to match them to the needs of various hulls. They are either "balanced" or "unbalanced." Both types are shown in Figure 4-1.

With the unbalanced rudder, the steering system must resist the full force of the water flowing against the rudder face when it is turned to either side from straight amidships. This can be a severe strain with a large rudder or even with a smaller rudder at high speed. The balanced rudder has a portion of its surface ahead of the rudder post; this forward section neutralizes a proportionate part of the water pressure and consequently lessens the strain on the steering system. The relative percentage of balance is a designer's choice and is determined by many factors.

Rudders on small sailboats are hung in a fashion to make them quickly and easily removable and replaceable. This is accomplished by downward projecting pins on the rudder called "pintles" which slide into receiving sockets on the stern called "gudgeons." (See Figure 4–1.)

Pivot Point

Close observation of a boat under hard right or left rudder will disclose that she has a pivot point. At the completion of a full 360-degree turn, the hull will have described three concentric imaginary circles. The innermost one will be the path of the bow, the outer one the path of the stern, while the central circle will show the relative travel of the pivot point. This disclosure of the vessel's crabbing action should not be surprising after the explanation that the stern is moved in order to turn the bow.

Figure 4-2 shows what happens during the maneuver just discussed. The location of the pivot point slightly forward of amidships is approximately correct for most boats. The pivot point of any hull is not permanently

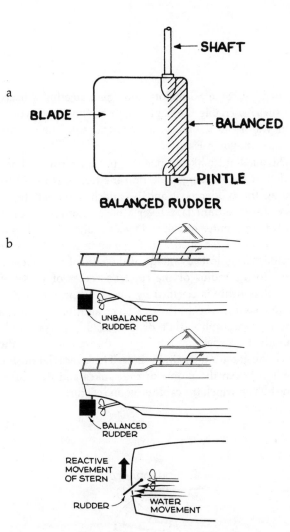

a

SHAFT

BLADE

BALANCED

PINTLE

BALANCED RUDDER

b

UNBALANCED
RUDDER

BALANCED
RUDDER

REACTIVE
MOVEMENT
OF STERN

RUDDER

WATER
MOVEMENT

Figure 4-1: The sketch at (a) explains the theory of a balanced rudder. The water movement applies a counter torque to the shaded portion and reduces the effort needed to steer. Whether balanced or unbalanced, the relative movement between rudder and water produces a reaction (b) which shifts the stern in the desired direction.

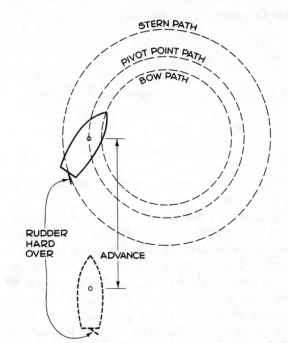

STERN PATH

PIVOT POINT PATH

BOW PATH

RUDDER
HARD
OVER

ADVANCE

Figure 4-2: Every boat has a pivot point and usually it is located slightly forward of amidships. The advance is the distance the boat will travel along its original path before beginning to turn in response to the rudder.

information for many maneuvers.

Forces Resisting Steering

One of the goals of hull design is to provide a contour that will follow a true, straight path in the water. Intentionally turning the hull away from this straight path, in other words, steering it, therefore unleashes opposing forces which resist the turn. Overcoming these forces consumes the power required for steering.

If you take a flat surface 1 foot square and move it through the water broadside at a speed of 1 knot, you encounter a resisting force of about 3 pounds. This low figure does not seem to portend much trouble. But here's the rub: As you push it faster and faster, the resisting force rises as the *square* of the speed! This means that at 5 knots the resisting force is *25 times* as great (5 × 5 = 25) and at 10 knots, *100 times* as strong (10 × 10 = 100).

Of course the rudder is never fully broadside to the oncoming water because its total travel from hard-over to hard-over is never more than approximately 90 degrees. This makes its maximum impact on either side 45 degrees. Simple trigonometry shows that the pressure on the rudder surface varies as the sine of the angle. At 45 degrees this pressure is about 84 percent of the maximum and at 0 degrees (straight ahead) it falls to zero theoretically.

The foregoing figures serve to illustrate several facts about steering: That as speed increases and especially as boats get larger with consequent greater rudder area, sizable amounts of power must be available for steering.

fixed; it will move back and forth slightly in response to changes in loading and trim.

The motion of the boat has been idealized in the solid-line portion of the sketch to show only its action during the actual circling. Under practical conditions, the rudder will have been put hard-over at the position indicated by the dotted outline of the boat. The craft will then crab along for a certain distance under the influence of inertia and other forces before the helm really takes hold. In naval parlance, this distance is called the advance; knowing its length at various boat speeds could be valuable

Human muscles cannot supply this power without mechanical help.

The simplest mechanical helper is the lever. The sailboat man attaches the lever directly to the rudder post, calls it a tiller, and multiplies his muscular effort by an amount directly proportional to the tiller's length. The powerboat man also uses the lever, but in a more disguised form. His levers take the form of rudder quadrants and steering wheels. His advantage is that steering can be done from a forward position; he need not hang onto a tiller at the stern.

Mechanical Steering Systems

A remote steering system (in addition to the rudder) consists of the rudder quadrant, the steering cables, the steering wheel, and any subsidiary hardware such as sheaves and turnbuckles. The steering cable is generally steel, preferably nonmagnetic stainless, and is sometimes interspersed with roller chain for the sprocket activation

required by some autopilots and some steering wheels. The sheaves enable the cable to go around obstructions on its way from the wheel to the quadrant. The components are shown in Figure 4-3.

The quadrant makes it possible to transform the lineal motion of the steering cable into the torque required for turning the rudder post and its attached rudder. In essence, the quadrant is a lever whose fulcrum, or pivot point, is the center of the rudder post and whose length is the radius of the quadrant. The gain in force, that is to say, the mechanical advantage, is the ratio of the quadrant radius to the radius of the rudder's center of pressure. This relationship is clarified by the sketch in Figure 4-4.

The steering wheel also is a lever and its mechanical advantage multiplies that of the quadrant. As would naturally be expected, the larger the diameter of the wheel, the greater the gain in force. The lever relationship here is between the radius of the spokes and the radius of the hub on which the cable is wound; Figure 4-5

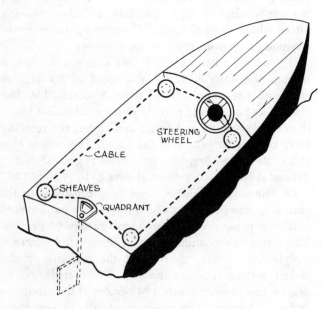

Figure 4-3: The movement of the steering wheel is transmitted to the rudder(s) via cable and sheaves.

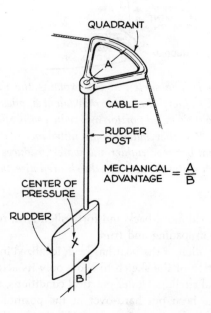

Figure 4-4: The quadrant, rudder post and rudder act together as a lever whose mechanical advantage amplifies the steering force exerted by the helmsman.

explains this. Now, if the mechanical advantage of the wheel is 10 and that of the quadrant is 3, the total force turning the rudder is 30 times the effort exerted by the skipper on the spokes.

It may seem at this point that nature has been outwitted, that something has been gotten for nothing. Nature does not give in that easily! The work done on the

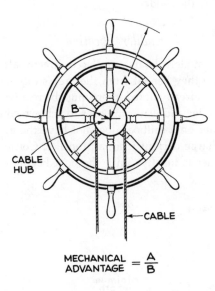

MECHANICAL ADVANTAGE = $\dfrac{A}{B}$

Figure 4-5: The steering wheel also acts as a lever; it magnifies the force exerted by the helmsman and applies it to the cable.

rudder can be no greater than the work the skipper did on the steering wheel; in fact it is less because of losses in transmission. What has happened is that the force has been multiplied but the distance over which it works has been cut proportionately; the skipper moves his wheel much farther than the rudder moves. If losses are neglected, force times distance at the rudder will always equal force times distance at the steering wheel—just as nature's law says it should.

HYDRAULIC STEERING SYSTEMS.

The cables of the mechanical system can be replaced by copper tubing containing hydraulic fluid. The steering

wheel hub on which the cable was wound is then replaced by some form of pump. A final cylinder makes the connection to the quadrant. This is a hydraulic steering system. The helmsman's muscle is still the total operating power.

The advantage of the hydraulic system is easier installation. The sheaves and the clear paths needed for the cable are eliminated; the tubing can follow any reasonable number of bends and twists and can be run in out-of-the-way places. Another advantage is irreversibility; this means that forces kicking against the rudder cannot turn the steering wheel to tire the helmsman. Further, the counter-helm needed to keep a single-screw boat on a straight course can be held without continuous physical effort at the wheel.

The pump at the steering wheel forces fluid from one tube into the other and is usually of the compact vane type. It fastens to a bulkhead and acts as support and shaft for the wheel. One type commercially available is shown in Figure 4-6.

The hydraulic pressure in the tubing is converted back to lineal motion at the quadrant by a piston in a cylinder. This is a double-acting unit, meaning that pressure can be exerted against the piston from both ends to move it in either direction. Figure 4-6 shows such a system.

As with most commercial products, some hydraulic steering systems are more elaborate than others. The simplest comprise only the wheel pump, the tubing, and the rudder cylinder. Others add to these basics such additional components as check valves, relief valves, reservoirs, and hookups for automatic pilots. The added complexity is usually installed when more than one steering station is desired.

OTHER MECHANICAL SYSTEMS.

The two lines of flexible cable used in the standard system already described can be replaced by a single cable in a housing. (Such a device technically is called a Bowden wire.) The housing enclosure makes it possible for this cable to transmit a push as well as a pull, hence the need for only one line. The enclosed cable can be run around obstructions if the bends are kept slight, thus acquiring some of the advantages of a hydraulic system.

A steering system of this type is illustrated in Figure 4-7. The steering wheel controls the cable through a 15–1 pinion-to-ring gear reduction ratio and provides this equivalent mechanical advantage in force applied to the rudder.

A kit of parts which extends main position steering to the flying bridge is shown in Figure 4-8. The upper wheel, through a series of shafts, universal joints, and gears, transmits its motion to the main wheel via a gearbox. The regular steering system of the boat takes over from the main wheel to the rudder.

Rudder Location

Rudders on modern boats are placed directly aft of propellers. Here they benefit from the prop's discharge current since, as already noted, there must be relative motion between rudder and water in order to achieve control.

The rudder on a sailboat does not have the advantage of the discharge current from a propeller. Consequently, such a rudder is inactive until the boat begins to move.

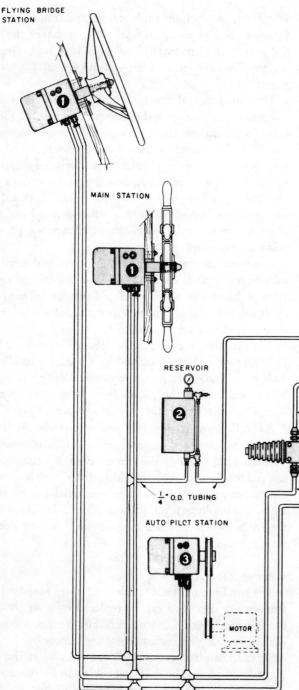
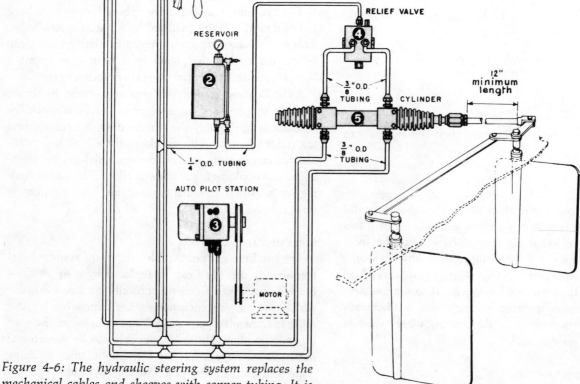

Figure 4-6: The hydraulic steering system replaces the mechanical cables and sheaves with copper tubing. It is irreversible, thus rudder reaction does not tire the helmsman. (Credit—Hynautics Co.)

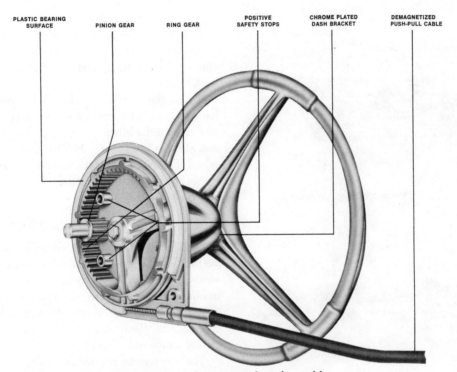

PLASTIC BEARING SURFACE   PINION GEAR   RING GEAR   POSITIVE SAFETY STOPS   CHROME PLATED DASH BRACKET   DEMAGNETIZED PUSH-PULL CABLE

Figure 4-7: Wheel movement is transmitted to the rudder by a steel wire inside a flexible housing. The housing can be routed around obstructions somewhat like the tubing of a hydraulic system. (Credit—American Chain Co.)

Sailboatmen often ameliorate this condition by moving the tiller back and forth in a sculling motion so that the rudder develops propulsive force like a fish's tail.

Rudder position in a vertical direction is also important, namely, its depth with relation to hull and keel. A few inches either way can make a substantial difference in the response of a boat. This exact placing eludes mathematical computation and is determined finally by trial and error.

Twin-screw craft carry two rudders. Occasionally a large, old twin-screw clunker will add a third rudder abaft the keel in an attempt to improve steering response. All rudders, of course, are ganged and operate in unison.

Outboard Steering

Boats propelled by outboard motors or the outboard units of I/O drives do not steer by means of rudders. In these installations the sideward push of the stern (necessary for steering) is achieved by swinging the propeller. This moves the discharge current either to right or left of amidships and supplies the steering reaction. This subject is treated fully in Chapters 12 and 13.

Tillers

The tiller, described earlier as a simple lever, is the standard steering equipment on most small sailboats. Because it is a simple lever it has some inherent peculiarities: When the tiller is swung to the left, the boat steers to the right; when swung right, the boat steers left. Although this may sound like a hazard to boat operation, the subconscious mind quickly takes over and accommodates.

The rudder in most tiller installations is hung by pins and eyes called pintles and gudgeons. These make the rudder easy to unship and replace. The construction is similar to the open-end hinges found on some cabinets which permit the door to be removed for convenience.

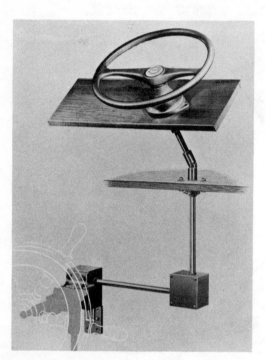

Figure 4-8: This additional installation (from a kit of parts) extends steering control to the flying bridge.

The simple lever arrangement can become cumbersome when great mechanical advantage is desired or required. In such cases, the tiller arm becomes overly long and can obstruct a good portion of the cockpit space. (The mechanical advantage is the ratio of the length from rudder post to end of the tiller to the length from rudder post to center of rudder pressure.)

Earlier days heard romantic orders to the helmsman such as "Port your helm!" and these could easily cause confusion. Today, by preference and in fact by Coast Guard dictum, the command is either "Right rudder" or "Left rudder"—clear and almost impossible to misconstrue.

The steering wheel supersedes the tiller on larger sailboats. As explained elsewhere in this chapter, the wheel affords a greater mechanical advantage.

Hard-over

The restriction of rudder swing to the specified arc already mentioned is accomplished by placing stops at some point in the steering system. Such stops could be at the wheel or at the quadrant or in between; some old, big ships have stop chains running from the rudder tip to the hull on both sides.

When the rudder reaches the stopped position, it is hard-over either to left or to right. The total travel from one stop to the other is known as hard-over to hard-over and abbreviated H/O to H/O. Three turns of the steering wheel for H/O to H/O would be about average for powerboats and motor sailers.

Automatic Pilots

A continuous watch at the wheel on a long passage can be tiresome business. Mechanical devices that relieve the strain on human mind and muscle are welcomed. These inanimate helmsmen are called automatic pilots and, truth to tell, they can steer a straighter course than the saltiest of old salts. (Bear in mind that automatic pilots do *not* "pilot"; they only steer.)

The apparently mysterious goings-on inside the components of automatic pilots are explained fully in Chapters 8 and 9. At this point only the total action insofar as it affects steering will be considered.

All automatic pilots function by constantly comparing the actual heading of the boat with a preset desired heading. The preset heading can be maintained by a magnetic compass or by a gyro compass and the difference between it and the actual track can be picked off by various means, either electric, magnetic, or photoelectric. This difference is processed into the ultimately required rudder movement. It is the faster comprehension and action of the autopilot that makes it superior to a man at the wheel.

Automatic pilots also come in various degrees of refinement and complexity and, as is usual, these bear a relationship to cost. Some autopilots are classed as hunting. These continually make slight corrections in course in order to maintain the straight track. Others are non-hunting and make intermittent corrections only after a certain allowed lapse. With skippers who have had experience, favorites are about equally divided.

The magnetic compass of automatic pilots is prone to all the ills that affect any other magnetic compass. (See Chapter 9.) It must be installed away from magnetic materials and stray magnetic fields. Some boats install it up on the mast at the yardarm, an excellent location. Gyro compass autopilots are free of these magnetic complications, but are relatively new to pleasure powerboats. One such gyro autopilot is shown in Figure 4-9.

Everyone who has steered any vessel knows that she must be given counter-rudder before the desired heading is reached in order to prevent an overswing. The amount of this counter-rudder depends upon speed, sharpness of turn, and sea conditions; with a human helmsman it is a

Figure 4-9: The gyro "brain" of this automatic pilot is free of the ills that affect magnetic compasses. (Credit—I.T.T. Decca Marine)

subconscious calculation based on his experience. Since the autopilot cannot think and acquire experience, the necessary information is dialed in and the mechanism then acts upon it.

One method of attaching automatic pilots to the steering system is through an intermediate gear on the steering wheel shaft. The autopilot drives this with a sprocket chain. Such an attachment is shown in Figure 4-10.

Since the autopilot is "blind" insofar as obstacles in the course ahead are concerned, it must be capable of being overridden by the man on watch. Some units automati-

cally go back to the originally assigned course as soon as the overriding is released. There are also fail-safe arrangements should the steering power fail. Needless to say, someone *always* should be on watch for obstacles and traffic during the time the autopilot is in control.

Power Steering

Power steering has become standard on automobiles. There is some demand for it on powerboats although it may be difficult to justify the need. One type available today is actually an offshoot of an automatic pilot installation; it utilizes the remote control box furnished with the more elaborate units. Left and right steering is done by pushing the left and right buttons and passing the work of turning the wheel on to the machinery.

A power steering system similar in principle to automobile power steering also can be had for boats. The steering wheel actuates a follow-up valve in the power unit which controls the flow of high-pressure hydraulic fluid to the actuating cylinder connected to the rudder arm. Thus, every movement of the steering wheel is faithfully amplified into a powerful torque at the rudder. The power for this system is supplied by an engine-driven pump, exactly as in the automotive units, and a heat exchanger keeps the fluid cool.

The big ships have always had power steering; human strength would be inadequate for the job. Steam engines or electrically driven hydraulic actuators turn the rudders in response to a small master steering wheel in the pilot house.

Self-Steerer

The self-steerer for sailboats is one of those simple ideas that smell of genius. In essence this device is nothing more than a husky weather vane hooked up to the tiller or rudder. It has been a boon especially to the single-handed ocean sailor because it gives him respite from his vigil at the tiller.

Like any weather vane, the vane of the self-steerer parallels itself with the wind and holds this direction with a force commensurate with its area. Cables and pulleys then keep the rudder at the desired angle for that point of sailing. Thus, in a steady wind, a course can be held without the skipper's intervention.

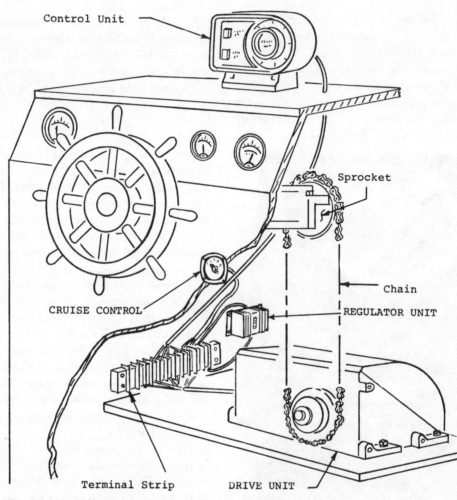

Control Unit

Sprocket

Chain

REGULATOR UNIT

CRUISE CONTROL

Terminal Strip

DRIVE UNIT

Figure 4-10: The automatic pilot turns the steering wheel through a gear and sprocket chain. (Credit—Ametek/ Calmer)

Engine Control Systems

The engine control system on a powerboat must be able to perform four operations: to change the revolutions per minute and to shift the power transmission into either forward, neutral, or reverse. The ideal way of doing this is with one small lever at the helmsman's position; less complicated methods are of course also in use.

A commercial single-lever-control unit is shown in Figure 4-11. (A dual-lever-control head is used for a twin-engine installation.) When the lever is in its central posi-

tion, the clutch is in neutral and the throttle is at idle. Moving the lever forward first engages the clutch in the ahead direction and then increases the speed of the engine. Moving the lever back from its mid-position first engages the clutch in the reverse direction and then increases the speed of the engine. Speed can be varied throughout the forward and reverse ranges without disengaging the clutch. The heart of the system is the engine control unit which accepts a single motion from the helmsman's lever and transforms it into two separate and properly timed motions, one for clutch and one for throttle.

Engine Revving

All single-lever engine control systems recognize that the engine may need to be revved up and warmed after starting and before the clutch is engaged. This is accomplished in various ways by different makers. In one, the lever slides out axially; in this position it breaks contact with the clutch and affects only the throttle. Another unit has a button which when pushed disengages the clutch from the control and retains only the throttle connection. Still another system makes use of an entirely separate cable connection to the throttle; this is manipulated solely for engine revving while the control lever is left in its central neutral position.

All systems have safety interlock arrangements that prevent clutch action at other than idle engine speed. This eliminates the possibility of machinery breakage and passenger injury should the clutch suddenly lock on to a speeding engine.

A two-lever engine control unit is for entirely independent operation of throttle and clutch. One lever controls the throttle, another one the clutch. The operating medium is hydraulic fluid transmitted through small-bore copper tubing. Several control stations can be hooked into the line to accommodate the several steering positions. This again is the now familiar pump (control head) and actuating cylinder (throttle and clutch units) design.

These engine controls can be connected in tandem so that both the main steering station and the flying bridge have command. The hookup for such a dual system, using two-lever controls, is diagrammed in Figure 4-12.

One of the more primitive steering and engine control systems is still in use on many club launches and yacht tenders. A hand lever amidships at the gunwale, opposite the engine, is connected to the rudder arm through a cable-and-sheave arrangement. This does the steering, generally with the operator's right hand. At the engine, and within reach of his left hand, is the lever for the clutch; the throttle is also within easy reach. This rig sounds as though it required a three-handed man, yet observing one of the yacht club "skippers" in action makes you wonder at the ease with which he maneuvers. Remote control problems he never has. The sketch of his equipment in Figure 4-13, and the previous illustrations of more sophisticated equipment, are the alpha and the omega of control systems.

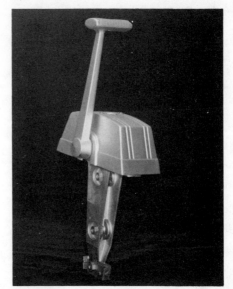

Figure 4-11: The single lever controls both clutch and throttle. It allows forward, neutral and reverse settings plus speed changes.

Sail Control

Controlling the sails on a sailboat can be thought of as the equivalent of engine control on a powerboat. The sails are raised and lowered by lines called *halyards* which control the area of sail exposed to the wind and therefore the power to be derived. The angle of the sails relative to the wind is controlled by lines called *sheets* which determine the useful resultant forward push applied to the boat. All this is discussed more fully in Chapter 11.

A bit of mechanization has also found its way into the world of sailboating in the form of rotary sail furlers discussed in Chapter 11. When sails must be reefed (reduced in area) in strong winds without this new gadget, it is done by tying the reef points, a more laborious and sometimes a more hazardous operation. Manually furled sails are rolled and tied with *stops*.

Stabilizers

The human stomach was designed to remain on an even keel and it rebels with unfortunate results when it is pitched and rolled. Operators of ocean liners and cruise ships realized this long since and equipped their craft with stabilizers. Now stabilizers have become available for powerboats even down to medium size.

Stabilizers are of two types: those which stabilize by sheer might and main and those which take advantage of sea reaction. The first type accomplishes its purpose with huge gyroscopes whose rotors weigh many tons and generate tremendous stabilizing forces. These gyros are rigidly attached to the hull with structural members that transmit the stabilizing forces and keep the vessel on an even keel. Some big ship installations are on this order.

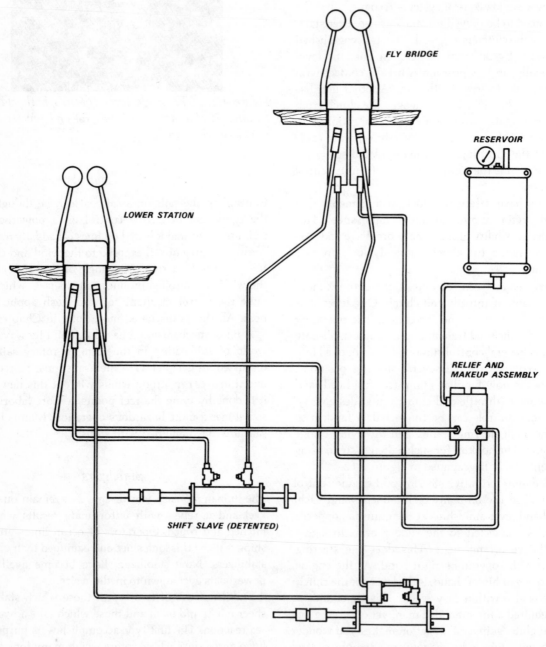

FLY BRIDGE

RESERVOIR

LOWER STATION

RELIEF AND
MAKEUP ASSEMBLY

SHIFT SLAVE (DETENTED)

THROTTLE SLAVE

*Figure 4-12: The main steering station and the flying
bridge have independent control over the engine with this
hookup.*

The second type uses a gyroscope also, but only a very small one. Here the gyro acts merely as a sensing unit; it detects an incipient roll and instantaneously sends out corrective signals which control hydraulic or electric power that alters the position of fins mounted outside the bilge. The sea reaction against these fins keeps the boat on a relatively even keel. Manufacturers claim up to 90 percent reduction in roll with such fins installed. The photograph in Figure 4-14 show the details of a bilge fin installation on a powerboat of medium size.

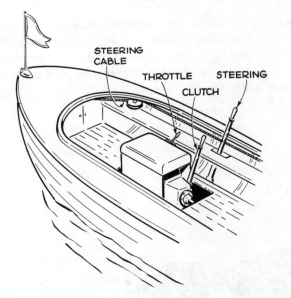

Figure 4-13: This simplest of all engine and steering control "systems" still is in use on many club launches—and works surprisingly well.

The bilge keel (see Chapter 1) is a static form of stabilizer and roll reducer that is in fairly common use. Another form of static stabilizer is lengths of angle iron attached to the bottom of the keel on both sides. Still another is the "flopper stopper" pictured and described below. These static devices are more or less effective.

Flopper Stoppers

Many skippers swear by the flopper stopper as the one and only simple device that will act as a stabilizer to pre-

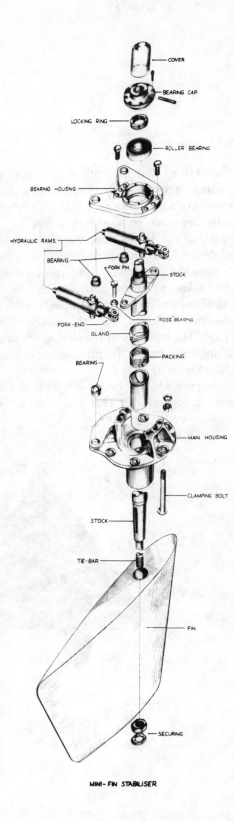

Figure 4-14: Details of the fin and of the actuating unit are shown as well as a completed fin installation on a powerboat hull. The sea reaction to changes in fin attitude keeps the hull on an even keel. (Credit—Vosper Thornycroft Group)

vent or reduce rolling. But the truth is that many other skippers swear *at* them as ineffective and clumsy nuisances. It seems to simmer down to an individual situation: on some boats they work, on some they do not.

The principle of the flopper stopper is the same as the principle of the keel—to provide resistance to undesired movement—only the flopper works in a vertical direction while the keel takes care of the horizontal. In one form, like the one illustrated in Figure 4-15, relatively large flat surfaces are submerged and held horizontal by a boom and guys. The tendency of the ship to roll imparts a sudden lifting force on the flat plate which is resisted. Ergo (you hope) no roll.

A flopper stopper which is intended for moored boats only is shown in Figure 4-16. This device can be made easily by the do-it-yourselfer.

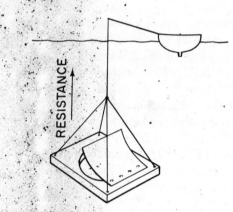

Figure 4-16: The flopper stopper shown above is a rudimentary device easily constructed by the do-it-yourselfer. It is intended for use at a mooring only and so employed will reduce roll considerably. It cannot be used while the boat is underway.

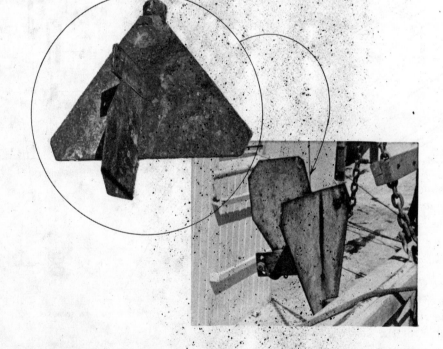

Figure 4-15: Many commercial shrimp boats use flopper stoppers like the one shown above. These vessels are super-sturdy craft and can withstand the tremendous stresses imposed on boom and rigging by these stabilizers underway. Pleasure-boat construction cannot take this punishment.

5 *Topsides and Interior Arrangements*

PERHAPS only with the exception of dinghies and life-boats, a hull cannot achieve its maximum usefulness without enclosed, protected space for the accommodation of people, cargo, and machinery. The amount of such space and its relative location form the basis for the generally accepted classification of pleasure craft: They become runabouts or cruisers or sport fishermen or houseboats or possibly even true yachts. With sailboats the position of the mast or masts determines the classification as a sloop or ketch or yawl or schooner and Chapter 11 elaborates

Chapter 1 illustrated and explained mechanical drawings that delineated the exact shape of a hull from stem to stern. These made no provision for the internal subdivision of hull space. Now we need an extended form of mechanical drawing that concerns itself only with internal and topside layouts and tells us definitely which space is used for what purpose. Such a drawing is called a deck plan.

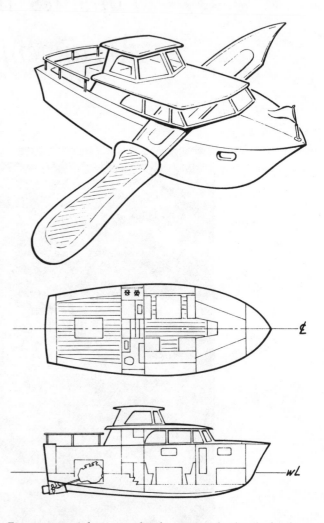

Deck Plans

Imagine a giant knife slicing lengthwise through a boat on a plane parallel to the waterline, as in Figure 5-1. If the upper portion is then discarded and the lower portion observed from above, the view will be as pictured. This view tells us clearly how the interior of the hull has been divided and where the various appurtenances have been placed. This is the deck plan. (When head room is to be shown, a *vertical* slice is made through the desired area of the boat.)

For a small boat one "slice" would probably tell the whole story; a yacht with several decks would require a slice at each level in order completely to show all facilities and especially the locations of the various connecting stairways or companionways. These several deck plans are then placed side by side, in order, beginning with the topmost. The deck plans of such an elaborate yacht are shown in Figure 5-2, together with an overall illustration of the boat.

Figure 5-1: A horizontal "slice" reveals the deck plan; a vertical cut shows the head room in each section and shows the various deck levels.

Symbols

Every profession develops an illustrative shorthand to depict items constantly used and naval architecture is no

exception. These symbols make it easy to read details on blueprints and eliminate much explanatory lettering which might otherwise be needed. (In radio, for instance, we have the two small parallel lines which denote a capacitor.) The "shorthand" symbols indigenous to the boat designer are shown in Figure 5-3.

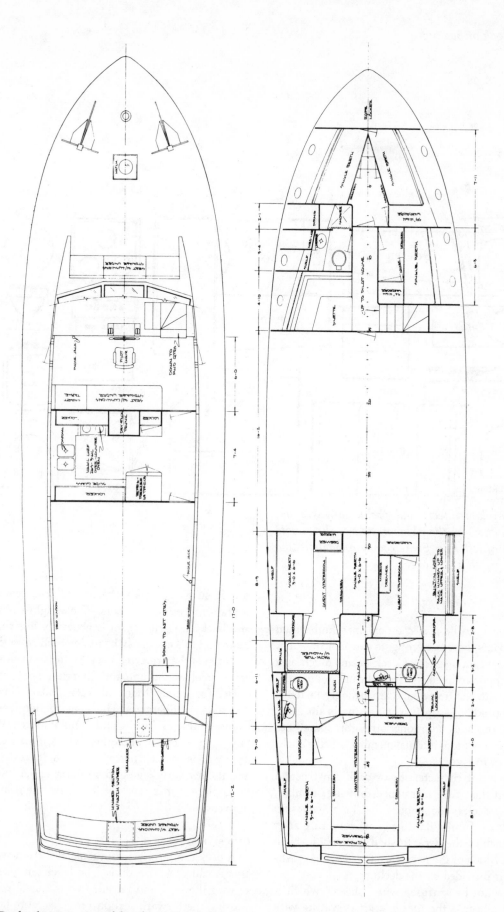

*Figure 5-2: Deck plans at several levels are needed for a
more elaborate yacht such as this beauty.*

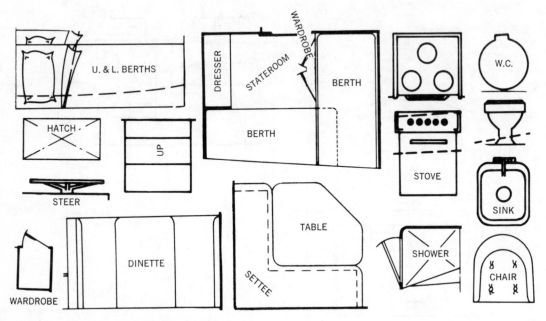

Figure 5-3: Naval architects and yacht designers use "shorthand" symbols on their blueprints and thus avoid much explanatory lettering. Some common symbols and their meanings are shown above.

Decks

The initial covering to be placed on an open hull would be the deck, and it is therefore proper to consider this first. The decking is laid on a series of deck beams much as a house floor is supported by joists. These beams are usually spaced equally with the frames and are strongly fastened to them. A longitudinal strip just under the beam ends, called a clamp, provides additional strength, sometimes with the aid of another longitudinal member called a shelf. This is illustrated in Figure 5-4.

Another important characteristic of deck construction is also shown in the above-mentioned drawing: camber. The camber of a deck is the amount that its *athwartship* shape curves down from a flat line. This curvature adds strength and enables the deck to shed water quickly in rough weather. Much of the resistance to sideward crushing of the hull is provided by the deck.

Camber must not be confused with "sheer," which is also illustrated. Sheer is the *fore and aft* curvature with the low point coming approximately amidships.

When the full sweep of a deck beam is broken by a cutout, such as a deckhouse, short "grub beams" are used as the supporting members. The weight-carrying ability of a deck at a grub beam is generally less than at a full beam and this can easily be understood from the drawing.

Wood is the preferred deck material; even some builders of steel, aluminum, and fiberglass boats show a preference for wood. (Many fiberglass boats, however, have decks also of fiberglass. This construction dispenses with frames and deck beams and gains its strength from ribbing, reinforcement and other means.) Teak is the king of deck woods. Its lustrous appearance, its resistance to rot, and its low shrinkage and swelling under marine conditions place it in a class by itself. Its one drawback is its high cost.

DECK STYLES.

A deck can be one continuous level from stem to stern; this is called a flush deck. The level can also be broken toward the bow and raised; this is called a raised deck. Raising the forward section provides more head room in the bow and makes the forepeak space more usable. The land-going equivalent might be the dormer in the roof of

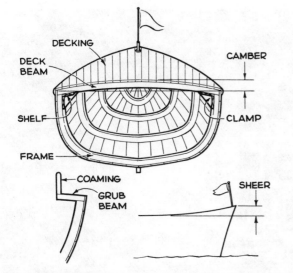

Figure 5-4: The shelf, clamp and deck beams which support the boat deck are important structural units in hull construction.

a house.

Another form of superstructure is the trunk cabin. This, too, is a device for increasing the head room below decks. The name is perfectly descriptive because it does look like a large trunk resting on the deck. The trunk usually contains windows or portholes for light and air. Trunk cabins may look natty from the outside but they are not too comfortable when judged from below. The reduced head room at the cabin sides often is a nuisance and generally relegates these areas for use as bunks. Guests newly aboard a trunk cabin boat invariably bump their noggins; it takes a bit of getting used to. Trunk cabins also waste good deck space. Figure 5-5 shows these styles.

Ceiling and Sole

A landlubber always finds his ceiling overhead but a sailor would never look upward for his. On boats the "ceiling" is the side planking on the inside of the hull that encloses the frames; it forms the cabin walls. The ceiling serves a decorative purpose by providing smooth cabin sides instead of the recurrent obstruction of frames. It also serves a minor structural purpose by stiffening the hull longitudinally.

A drawback of a ceilinged hull is the restriction to ventilation that this enclosure makes. Openings purposely made in the ceiling counteract this to some extent, but despite these measures the beneficial ventilating air flow is always reduced and the opportunity for rot increased.

A landlubber walks upon a floor but his seagoing cousin

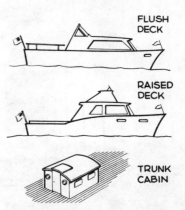

Figure 5-5: The trunk cabin has lost most of its popularity because of the inconvenience it creates in the cabin and the space it wastes on deck. The flush deck and the raised deck are current popular types.

treads on a "sole." Not the sole of his shoes—his floor is called a sole. The location determines the full name and thus we have the cabin sole and the cockpit sole. The sole is laid upon stringers and floor timbers. Again, the dryland equivalent would be the house floor and its supporting joists and beams.

Rope Locker and Lazarette

The extreme forward section of the bow, directly aft of the stem, is triangular in shape because the planking meets there and can be put to little use other than storage. Accordingly this space is almost universally used as a rope or chain locker for stowing the "rode," the lines and chains used in anchoring. The anchor winch and davit, if carried, are on the deck directly above for convenience. Ventilation of this compartment is important because wet lines find their way in even with the most careful skipper.

At the stern is another space, much more usable especially with square transoms, called the lazarette. It is gen-

erally a storage space and may contain fuel and water tanks. It may even contain engines hooked up as inboard/ outboard drives or as vee-drives. (See Chapter 3.) Here, too, ventilation is extremely important and during fair weather the solid lazarette access cover is replaced by a grating that permits air circulation. (Some modern cruisers have extended the owner's stateroom right back to the transom, sacrificing the lazarette.)

Many sailboats extend their cockpits to the extreme aft end of the hull, thereby usurping what in a large powerboat would become the lazarette. This becomes especially true when steering is by tiller.

Bulkheads

The transverse walls which divide the hull into separate spaces are called bulkheads. These bulkheads supply cross-sectional strength and may serve as partitions between cabin areas and contain doors for thoroughfare. The most important bulkheads from the standpoint of a boat's safety at sea are the watertight bulkheads.

The insurance and regulatory authorities will not accept as watertight any bulkhead that has a door, even though there may exist facilities for securing this door in an airtight manner. Their reasoning is obvious and understandable; the door might be open at the very moment when its tight closure is imperative to avert disaster. Even small holes cut in a watertight bulkhead for the passage of pipes and wires must be securely gasketed to become acceptable. (Modern small craft rely upon flotation material to keep them afloat in case of accident; larger craft depend upon their watertight bulkheads which divide the hull into buoyant compartments.)

Owners of small pleasure cruisers who use their boats solely for their own private purposes might nevertheless like to bring their craft up to the safety standards demanded by the Coast Guard for similar vessels that carry passengers for hire. The requirements are detailed in pamphlet CG-323, which is obtainable free upon request. First on the list is a watertight collision bulkhead located not less than 5 percent or more than 15 percent of the waterline length aft of the stem.

Human Dimensions

Before going into detail on the subdivision of the hull and superstructure into habitable spaces, it makes sense to study the dimensions of the potential occupants: people. Boat builders have paid more attention to the needs of the human form than automobile makers; everyone has gone through the contortions needed to enter a modern low-slung car. Even an ingenious naval architect is hard put to it when asked to provide living space for a family in a twenty-one-foot cruiser, however. It is of value, therefore, to know how much room a human needs in his various positions.

The drawings in Figure 5-6 show an average man in a standing position (or supine position), and seated. From these dimensions you can determine how wide and how long a bunk should be, for instance, or how much head room is minimal for a dinette. Naturally the designer should be generous with a few extra inches all around so that passengers will not become sardines in a can. A male was chosen to illustrate the point because men are generally larger than women. To take a small liberty with a well-known adage: If it's adequate for the gander, it's ample for the goose.

A cursory study of the dimensions immediately raises some caution signals which should be observed when inspecting a prospective boat. Since the width of people at the hip is at least thirteen inches, a walkaround deck narrower than this is going to be an impractical nuisance. Less than six feet two inches of head room in the cabin will evoke repeated cussing when heads and deck beams come into violent contact. The skipper will be uncomfortable without at least 3 feet from the back of the helmsman's chair forward to the bulkhead carrying the wheel. A bunk only twenty inches wide will feel like a straitjacket to the sleeper. Every feature intended for human occupancy should be tested against the male dimensions.

Heads

Only the location and space of the head (toilet) are discussed here; mechanical details of this human necessity are in Chapter 6. In small cruisers the head is often located in the bow just aft of the rope locker because this narrow space is not too suitable for any other purpose. When this space is part of a forward cabin the head is concealed under one of the vee bunks. Whether or not the head is above or below the waterline makes a difference in the simplicity or complexity of the plumbing. Figure 5-7 shows an installation.

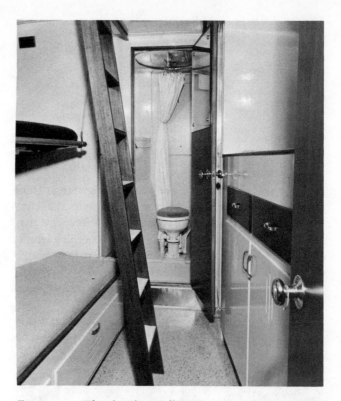

Figure 5-7: This head installation is typical for boats of medium size. Note the escape ladder for the occupants of the cabin in event of danger. (Credit—Photo by Niel C. Nielsen, Jr.)

Heads on much larger boats are located almost anywhere the designer's fancy dictates. The number of heads has become a status symbol denoting the caliber of the yacht just as the number of bathrooms characterizes the value of a house. In these more elaborate settings, the head is usually only one item in a complete bathroom containing basins and shower.

Shower Baths

Shower baths were once confined to millionaires' yachts but are now to be found even in twenty-one-footers. They are available in modular units which can be installed as part of a complete bathroom with basin and head or separately with their own walls and doors, as shown in Figure 5-8. The deck space required is approximately three feet square. The base pans are of ceramic or vinyl tile treated to present a nonslip surface. Full head room is of course necessary. Where the base is below the waterline, and this encompasses most cases, a sump pump is needed for emptying.

Berths and Bunks

The trend to family vacations and overnight stays has made sleeping accommodations important. Careful planning can make it possible for sleepers to be as comfortable

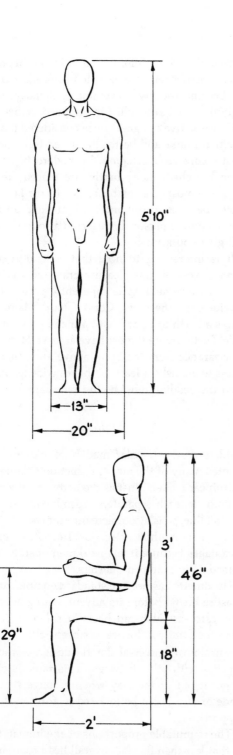

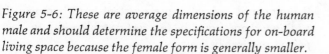

Figure 5-6: These are average dimensions of the human male and should determine the specifications for on-board living space because the female form is generally smaller.

afloat as ashore. The provisions for slumber range from conventional beds in large staterooms to dinettes that convert to double beds and vee-bunks in the forepeak that follow the contour of the hull. The average sleeping length allotted is six feet four inches, which appears to be ample on the basis of Figure 5-6. The average width is thirty-two inches but three feet would assure more comfort for a restless sleeper.

A type of berth originally developed for Pullman cars is popular at sea. In this model the backrest of a daytime

Figure 5-8: A typical shower bath (and bathroom) installation is shown in the stateroom of a cruiser.

couch swings up on hinges at its upper corners and fastens in a horizontal position. The seat and the backrest then become the lower and upper berth respectively. The sliding curtain that assured privacy in the railroad car is also borrowed.

Dinettes usually convert to double berths by sliding the seats forward to close the open space and laying the back cushions down flat. In many models the table, normally between the seats, is lowered to form a firm support for the center of the double bed.

The musty odor and mildew once typical of beds afloat have vanished with the advent of foam and rubber mattresses. Any of the air-blown plastic or rubber formulations that are immune to rot and biologic deterioration may be used. A representative plastic is polyurethane foam. Thickness averages six inches. These synthetics do not offer the luxurious comfort of eiderdown but they are much more practical and sanitary.

Long before women invaded pleasure boating, men made their beds by folding a sheet in half in order to make it serve as two. At long last that somewhat crude custom has become socially acceptable with novel sheets especially designed and split for the purpose. See Figure 5-9.

Conservative designers once considered it an unwritten rule that bunks and berths be placed fore and aft for the most comfortable sleeping. In modern boats this rule is often breeched; many berths are placed athwartship to make the most of available space. In the last analysis the choice between a fore and aft berth and an athwartship one is a purely personal matter; in a rough sea, either one will give you a tossing.

It is interesting to note that federal regulations for *licensed* vessels (not pleasure craft) also concern themselves with something as apparently personal as the beds provided for the crew. Coast Guard Manual #323 requires a berth to be at least 74 inches long and 24 inches wide. Furthermore it must have at least 24 inches of vertical clearance from the bunk above and must have direct access to an aisle at least 24 inches wide leading topsides. Even the bedding must be fire retardant.

Dinettes

Builders of the popular models of pleasure boats have adapted many of the mass production techniques used by Detroit car makers. Just as the body and the chassis of an automobile, each separately assembled, meet on the production line, so is a complete interior section lowered into a hull. This method of sectional construction has many advantages because it lets workmen operate in free space instead of in cramped quarters.

The dinette has become standard equipment on cruising pleasure boats. Before its advent, eating afloat was done on a catch-as-catch-can basis in salon or cockpit. Here again the family influence has been felt.

An almost universal dinette design is the two facing benches with table between. This table is either hinged to get it out of the way when a conversion to a bed is made or else it can be lowered to form part of the bed's support.

The immutable proportions of the human form remind us that less than five feet overall head room in the dinette is impractical and will cause constant head bumping. In addition, there should be two feet of table width for each person who is to be seated.

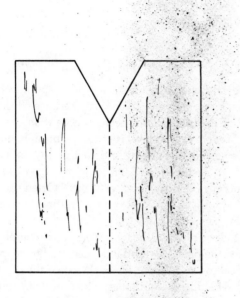

Figure 5-9: The time-honored bachelor custom of making one bed sheet serve as two now is made "legal" by this commercially available sheet that simplifies the process.

Galley

The female explosion to boating has made its greatest impact on the galley. In the bygone days when cruising was indulged in only by men, any little corner that could accommodate an alcohol stove qualified as a galley. Now the galley is a sacrosanct, separate space containing a stove and a refrigerator even more resplendent than the ones at home.

Chapter 6 is devoted to the minutiae of the galley; only the location of the galley in relation to the rest of the interior is discussed here.

In the last few years the galley has moved from its old location under the foredeck to a point adjacent to and on a level with the salon. In many designs it has gone all the way into the salon. This has been a direct result of feminine demand. As one builder put it: "The mate doesn't want to be left out of things like a paid hand while she is cooking. She wants to be able to keep up with the conversation of the guests while still keeping an eye on the stove." The views of Figure 5-10 are deck plans that show the progressive movement aft of the galley.

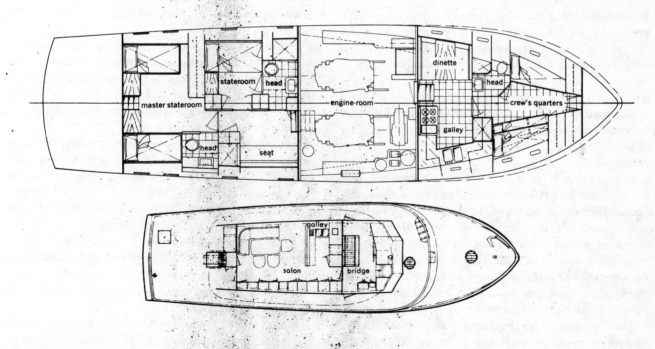

Figure 5-10: These plans show how the galley has moved from the forepeak aft into the salon in response to the feminine influence.

Kitchens ashore in modern homes are often separated from the living room by nothing more than a row of upright poles; thus, cooking odors waft about without restraint. Naval architects also apparently do not realize that preparing a meal can be a smoky, smelly business that is intensified by the cramped quarters of a boat and the consequently poorer ventilation. Grease-laden air is certain to damage drapes and furnishings. "Galley in the salon" looks and reads much better in catalogues than it works in actuality.

With the exception of the fuel tanks, the galley is the final destination of most deliveries to the boat. Packages of food, bottles of drink, and in many instances cakes of ice must be brought to it. The galley should therefore be in a location accessible to the deck so that this traffic can be handled with convenience and without messing up the boat. (Pleasure craft of earlier days had hatches leading from the deck to the interior of the icebox; ice could be stored without dripping its way through the salon.)

Cockpits

Between the open runabout which is really all cockpit, and the large cruiser, which generally has no cockpit, lie the various forms of topsides design. When cockpits form only part of the hull space, they are now invariably at the stern; the forward cockpit has disappeared—and a good thing, too, because it was a hazard in bad weather. Water coming aboard in a rough sea and filling the forward cockpit could seriously change the trim and stability of a boat.

Many cockpits on modern boats are self-bailing which is a great safety feature. The automatic bailing action is accomplished by having the cockpit sole above the waterline and providing scuppers (holes) through which the water drains out over the side. The scuppers are fitted with flaps that act as one-way valves and keep waves from pounding through. An after cockpit whose sole is below the waterline can become a hazard if a heavy following sea overtakes the boat. The water taken aboard quickly finds its way to the bilge and its sloshing then affects stability.

The best material for the cockpit sole is teak. All other boating materials are also used, from plywood to fiberglass, depending upon the construction of the boat itself and its quality level. The most important safety factor for the cockpit sole is that its surface be nonslip.

Ladders and Companionways

Ladders (seagoing stairs) or, more specifically, several steps, are common in cabin boats because efficient utilization of the hull interior decrees more than one level. The need for changes in level is generally brought about by the placement of the engine and fuel tanks, the largest permanent installations. On a larger boat there would be more and more elaborate "stairs." Often such steps are hinged to swing up and expose a "rathole" entrance to the engine compartment.

Modern pleasure boats have almost completely eliminated the plain, bare ladders once used to connect salons and cabins at different levels. We owe the disappearance of these ladders to the ladies, who found difficulty in navigating them. It's good riddance; although the ladders looked very nautical, they were also very unsafe.

Fuel Tanks

The outboard boatman has the simplest form of fuel tank: He carries aboard a two- or six-gallon container. In many cases the tank has a fitting that snaps into the fuel line and he is ready to go.

The fuel-gulping habits of powerful inboard engines make large tankage necessary in order to secure a reasonable cruising range. Large tanks introduce not only a space problem but one of trim and stability as well because of the constantly changing weight as fuel is consumed.

Designers place tanks in balanced positions athwartships or along the keel line so as to maintain proper trim. This presupposes that the tanks will be emptied and filled in a manner to retain the balance, a matter which most boatmen ignore. (Many dual tanks have self-leveling connecting piping.) One skipper of a converted eighty-five-foot Navy craft found that he could cut many hours of running time between New England and Florida if he filled his tanks to a predetermined level and then drained fuel in a definite ratio between forward and stern tanks; his secret is careful trim.

A fuel tank's location seems to have a direct bearing on its service life and safety; a tank hidden away in an inaccessible place is not going to be inspected often if at all. The tank material must be immune (or at least resistant to) rust, corrosion, and the chemical action of fuel ingredients. Figure 5-11 reproduces a table from Coast Guard Manual #323 that gives some good instructions and advice on material. It should go without saying that an object as heavy as a filled tank must be secured against breaking away in a heavy sea; it could easily punch a hole through the hull, if it got loose.

Water Tanks

The American ethic of super-cleanliness and sanitation entails the use of a great deal of fresh water for bathing and washing. This is in addition to an ingrained high requirement for drinking and cooking. The net result is a comparatively large tank for potable water.

It is not uncommon for small cruising power- and sailboats to carry two hundred gallons of water while yachts and schooners in the sixty foot plus class almost routinely have tanks up to one thousand gallons. Bear in mind that a full two hundred and fifty gallon water tank weighs more than a ton and you have an indication of how strongly this water load can affect trim.

There is another facet to the question of carrying heavy loads of water. It takes fuel to push this extra weight and fuel translates into money—unless the "fuel" is the wind. In the end, the free water aboard is not so free. There is a trend to less tankage with the addition of a water maker. (Water tank materials and water makers are discussed in Chapter 6.)

Windshields, Windows, and Ports

The wide expanse of window glass found in the modern cruiser would make an old-time salt-water sailor shudder. In his mind's eye he would see the splintered wreckage left after a wave crashed aboard in heavy weather. The saving grace seems to be that few small cruisers are ever exposed to storms. Those that venture out when the going is rough are in command of competent skippers who often safeguard their windows by covering them with plywood panels.

Some builders glaze their boats with safety glass all around and this high-strength material reduces the damage hazard. A little arithmetic that takes into account the square inches (or square feet) of glass area and the weight of water involved will show the staggering amounts of force that nature exerts.

Portlights are the traditional windows for a ship and these are often retained in pleasure craft wherever the aperture is in the hull itself. The original round shape of a portlight has changed to rectangular, both to admit more light and to add to the illusion of boat length. In judging the safety of portlights, the Coast Guard requirements for small, passenger-carrying vessels can be a good guide. These prescribe that the portlight must be fixed (not of the opening type, in other words a "deadlight") although opening may be permitted if the location is at least thirty inches above the waterline. Furthermore, portlights must be fitted with "dead" covers for use when the sea is run-

Material	A.S.T.M. specification (latest edition)	Thickness in inches and gage number vs. tank capacities for—		
		1 to 80 gallon tanks	More than 80 and not more than 150 gallon tanks	Over 150 gallon tanks
Nickel-copper	B127, Hot Rolled Sheet or Plate.	0.037 (USSG 20) [1]	0.050 (USSG 18)	0.107 (USSG 12)
Copper-nickel	B122, Alloy No. 5	.045 (AWG 17)	.057 (AWG 15)	.128 (AWG 8)
Copper	B152, Type ETP	.057 (AWG 15)	.080 (AWG 12)	.182 (AWG 5)
Copper-silicon	B97, Alloys A, B, and C	.050 (AWG 16)	.064 (AWG 14)	.144 (AWG 7)
Steel or iron [2]		.0747 (USSG 14)	.1046 (USSG 12)	.1875 (USSG 7)

[1] Nickel-copper not less than 0.031 inch (USSG 22) may be used for tanks up to 30-gallon capacity.
[2] Fuel tanks constructed of iron or steel, which is less than 3/16 inch thick, shall be galvanized inside and outside by the hot dip process.

Figure 5-11: The Coast Guard recommends the above materials and specifications for powerboat fuel tanks.

ning high. This is not an unreasonable precaution; even the *Queen Mary* can take water on her weather deck, some seventy *feet* above her waterline.

Staterooms

The word stateroom is as widely interpreted in pleasure boating as the word yacht, which once meant a magnificent creation never less than one hundred feet long. The forepeak with its cramped vee-bunks and hidden head is a stateroom; so is the owner's quarters in the stern, the size and furnishings of which more nearly merit the name.

The number of staterooms, and their size, on any given boat is the direct result of the designer's ingenuity. In a family cruiser requiring privacy for age and sex groups, this segregation can be achieved by doors when space permits and by curtains when it doesn't. Most private space on a small boat is double-purpose; for instance, the dinette becomes a double sleeper.

Sailboat design tends to minimize enclosed cabin and stateroom space. Part of this stems from the need for adequate walk space on deck all around the ship, the need for room to tend sail, and part from the lower deckhouse height mandated by swinging booms.

The most important consideration for a stateroom (assuming it has the greatest comfort possible) is a means of escape in the event of disaster. It should always be possible to leave a stateroom by more than one route and this usually means providing an escape hatch. Thus, if the aisle to a stateroom is blocked, the occupants can reach the safety of the outdoors through the hatch. Such an arrangement is shown in Figure 5-7. The hatch cover adds ventilation and its opening should be at least two feet square. In that arrangement an actual ladder is fixed permanently but more often the access steps are on the back of a door or on a bulkhead to conserve space.

Flybridges

The flybridge has become a status symbol. As a result, some small boats seem higher than they are long. This is not to deny the utility of flybridges on pleasure craft because truly each additional foot of elevation above the surface of the water allows the skipper miles of extra vision. (Each additional foot also adds to the sea-sickening arc of gyration in bad weather.)

A good flybridge installation duplicates the controls and instruments located at the lower helmsman's position. Some flybridges provide for guests in addition to the skipper; this added weight on the deck of the cabin below requires considerable structural stiffening. The weight of four or five persons this high above the waterline could also raise the center of gravity, reduce the metacentric height, and impair stability on a small boat. (See Chapter 1.)

Storage Space

Wherever humans gather, provision must be made for storing their possessions. This is as true afloat as it is ashore. It means drawers, lockers, wardrobes, closets, and even the use of empty structural spaces. Certain refinements of closure and ventilation not needed on land must be incorporated in seagoing storage spaces; a wall closet in a house never tilts to spill its contents.

Drawers can be made spillproof with locks. A more convenient method is shown in Figure 5-12. A small notch

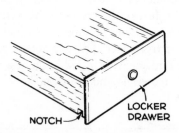

NOTCH   LOCKER DRAWER

Figure 5-12: A notch on each side, cut as shown, will prevent a drawer from unshipping in a sea. The slight lift required in opening the drawer soon becomes a habit.

is cut in each draw-rail close to the front face and as wide as the front of the cabinet is thick. In the closed position the drawer rests on this notch and is secure; to open, the drawer is lifted slightly and then pulled open normally.

A "hanging locker" is a wardrobe high enough for clothes to be hung full length; it is a great convenience and is in fact considered a necessity by the mate. The dimensions that such an enclosure must have to be serviceable can be derived from the dimensional sketches in Figure 5-13. The width of the locker, which determines

20"

MAN'S JACKET

34" (RAINCOAT 46")

18"

DRESS

39"

42"

TROUSERS

Figure 5-13: A true hanging locker must be high enough to accommodate clothes like these with a few inches to spare at the bottom.

how many garments can be hung, allows three inches for each one. A thorough spraying of each locker before use with an antimildew chemical is an excellent precaution against future loss. It is claimed that mothballs left in all drawers and lockers are a mildew deterrent, keep out mice, and "sweeten" the contents.

Locks on lockers can become a headache unless they are lubricated properly. The extremely thin, nongumming oil used in watches is the best for this purpose; finely powdered graphite available in plastic applicator tubes is also good.

Engine Space

Motive power is covered completely in Chapter 2; only the location of the engines is examined here. In the early days it was mandatory to locate the engines pretty far forward in the boat. The reason for this, aside from the requirements of fore and aft trim, was the angle of the propeller shaft. If the engines were placed too far astern, the prop would be pushing more upward than forward.

Then came two developments either of which made it possible to relegate the engines to the stern, out of everyone's way. These were the vee-drive and the inboard/outboard drive. These two have had a great influence on boat design, the former on large craft and the latter on small. Not only have they released space to better use but on cruisers especially they have taken the noise away from the passenger compartments. (Chapter 3 looks at these drives more closely.)

Despite this new freedom in engine placement, designers for the most part remain conservative and engines generally remain central. Engines under the cockpit or under the salon are made accessible for inspection and service by large, hinged hatches. When these hatches are in the salon they can become a nuisance because opening them means removing the carpeting, taking out the furniture, and losing the use of the cabin; this involved and messy procedure may be the cause of much engine neglect. The mate abhors dirty wrenches and greasy hands in the midst of her decor.

Engine spaces should preferably be bulkheaded and should certainly be sound-deadened. They must be ventilated properly to conform to Coast Guard regulations. These require that each engine (and fuel tank) compartment be fitted with at least one duct to bring in fresh air and at least one duct to exhaust fumes. The intake duct must be fitted with a cowl or pickup scoop; the exhaust duct must also have a cowl or preferably an exhaust blower. When the blower motors are actually in the compartment, they must be of the sparkproof variety. These legal requirements are given in greater detail in Chapter 25. A further requirement for good ventilation is the large quantities of air the engines need in order to keep going.

Rails

Handrails and their connecting lifelines are important safety equipment because they reduce the possibility of people falling overboard. The Coast Guard takes official cognizance of rails and issues specifications covering them but only for boats carrying passengers for hire. The pleasure boat owner is not bound by these rules but would do well to heed them nevertheless. Regulations call for rails 42 inches high on all exposed decks. Safety rails or cables must parallel the main rail at distances not greater than 12 inches below the main rail. (At fishing positions the main rail may be lowered to 30 inches.)

The bow rail is the greatest deterrent to amateur crew members going overboard with the anchor. Some designers leave a small open space in the rail at the peak of the bow as a convenience in handling ground tackle. Figure 5-14 shows rails and modular rail hardware.

Time was when a boat owner who wanted a rail would go into conference with the local plumber. Soon an agonizing array of tees and ells and floor flanges would appear together with threaded lengths of galvanized pipe. When finally erected, this plumber's nightmare was horrible to behold but it did serve its purpose of separating the passengers from the sea. Today, of course, the entire rail assembly can be purchased ready-made and beautiful and in most cases is original standard equipment.

The toe rail is not a rail in the sense just described but rather a narrow strip of wood that outlines the outer edge of the deck and is about one inch high. The rub rail serves as a fender to protect the hull from scraping against spiles and piers. It may run the full length of the hull or it may be in sections at bow and stern or at the widest beam; preferably it is faced with a stainless strip.

Seating

The human is the only animal that cannot sit down com-fortably with its own natural equipment but must have a mechanical assist in the form of an elevated bench or ledge. Because of this, boats, like homes, must provide comfortable seating.

Reference to Figure 5–6 shows that the best height for a seat is 18 inches. On a boat, as in an automobile, this is seldom achieved and compromises down to 12 inches are used. The lower the seat below the optimum 18 inches, the greater the forward leg room that must be allowed to avoid cramps.

HELMSMAN'S SEAT.

For best visibility, the ideal place for the helmsman is up on the flybridge. This vantage point gives him extended vision clear around the compass; further, the wheel here is amidships so that his position favors neither side when docking.

The best helmsman position below is on the starboard side. This location is chosen on the basis of the rules of the road which give vessels approaching on this side the right of way and thus require them to be seen promptly. This position is also helpful in docking on the starboard side; docking on the port side puts the skipper in the same situation as the motorist who cannot see his opposite fender but must "feel" its presence from experience. A neglected facility on most pleasure boats is chart space close enough to the wheel to be within the ken of the helmsman.

Masts

The mast is a primary component of a sailboat's motive power, as important to it as the crankshaft to a powerboat. Sailboat masts are completely functional and are designed for great strength despite their sometimes slender appearance. Most are of wood, some of aluminum, and in all types the diameter narrows toward the top. Masts can be an actual straight tree (trimmed down and polished, of course) or a hollow wooden laminate. Aluminum masts are always hollow tapered tubes.

Engineering-wise, the sailboat mast is an end-loaded column held in alignment by side guys called *shrouds* and fore and aft guys called *stays*. The shrouds are anchored to chain plates which in turn are fastened to the hull directly to port and starboard of the mast; turnbuckles adjust and maintain tension.

The mast on a cruiser can be considered mostly decora-

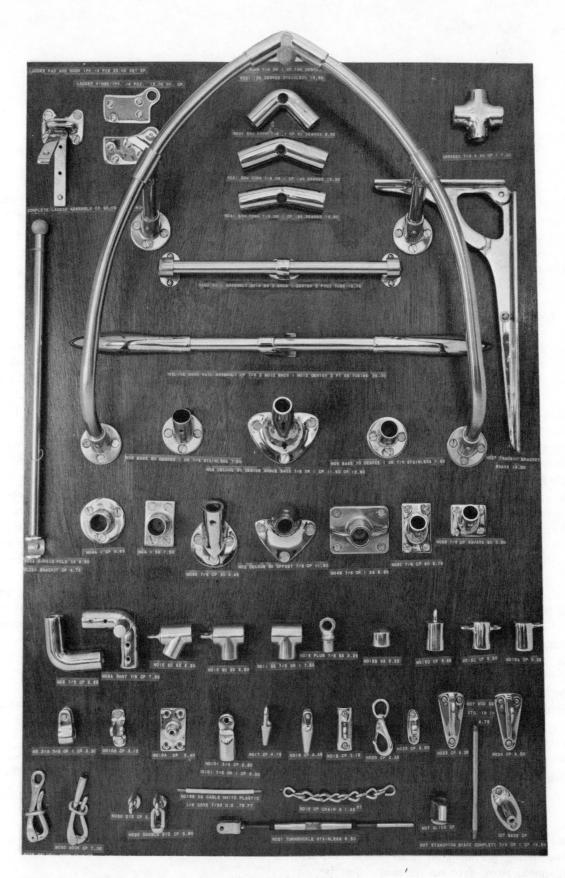

Figure 5-14: Safety rails can be assembled to fit any deck contour with these modular components fashioned from corrosion resistant materials. (Credit—Cea & Cea Marine Supply, Inc.; Photo by Harry Merrick)

tive; it lends that nautical flair which gladdens the owner. It does have nighttime utility for the carrying of anchor lights and in the daytime its yardarm can carry signal flags. Masts on boats that habitually travel canals are made to be swung down or to be unstepped for clearance under bridges.

Unfortunately, the masts on many stock cruisers are set just ahead of and flush in height with the flybridge; a pennant set at the truck (top) keeps flapping in the helmsman's face.

Insulation

Materials are available that insulate against sound and others that insulate against heat and cold while still others can do both jobs at once. Acoustical insulation has already been mentioned for use in the engine compartment; it can be equally important in the cabins. Small enclosures such as cabins can easily concentrate noise much as an organ pipe resonates sound. Research has proved that the absence of noise is a prime factor in comfort and ease.

Furnishings

It makes good nautical sense to provide lashings for all movable furniture in cabin and salon. These fastenings could be to screw-eyes sunk in the deck or in appropriate bulkheads. Any large piece free to move when the ship rolls is a potential blockbuster.

A recent news story told of the havoc wrought on an ocean liner by a piano that broke loose in a storm. If you can imagine about seven hundred pounds of concentrated hardware sliding toward you on an inclined deck, you can get the feeling of the awesome situation that arose. Of course this is an extreme case, but even an ordinary lounge chair could demolish a cabin if it got free in a sea.

Lighting

Adequate lighting brings cheer and removes that in-a-dark-cave feeling prevalent on many boats. Adequate lighting should be no problem for most boats because they spend their nights at marina piers where sufficient electric current is available. To tie into this, most pleasure craft are wired for city current in addition to battery voltage. (See Chapter 7.)

Lights required underway (running lights) are strictly specified by law and are covered in Chapter 25. Cabin and deck lights under way must be shielded in a manner that will avoid confusing oncoming mariners.

Windage

A sailboat heeling over in a breeze is a common sight but few powerboatmen realize that their craft, too, have "sail area" which affects their operation when the wind kicks up. This sail area is the projection of the boat above the waterline (the silhouette) viewed from the direction of the wind; it is greatest when the wind is abeam.

Such crosswinds can cause the boat to fall off to leeward in accordance with the wind's strength and in proportion to the craft's projected areas above and below the waterline. The area above the waterline is the sail; the area below meets the resistance of the water and resists the fall-off. The flat surface of a keel is most effective in doing this. Designers of old-time boats intended for open-water service in all weathers kept the silhouettes low. Modern builders of pleasure craft seem to have acquired some of the love for skyscrapers which imbues shoreside architects.

One aspect of windage affects the boat's speed and fuel consumption even in a dead calm. This is the resistance to forward motion offered by the head-on area or silhouette. The airplane people call this drag. If the forward area of a boat were flat, like the front of a boxy house, the drag would be the same as that of a flat plate of the same area being pushed through the air. The rounding and fairing of superstructures common to all good boat designs can reduce this drag by 20 percent or more.

The sad part of drag is that the mathematical formula expressing its effects contains a *squared* term for velocity. This means that the wind resistance of the vessel is increased *four* times when the speed is only *doubled*. The amount of horsepower he is devoting merely to pushing air may surprise the skipper blithely purring along at 20 knots.

Silhouette

Whether we judge a boat to be graceful and sleek or tubby and sluggish in appearance, we are probably making a spontaneous judgment based upon her silhouette. The corollary is that, in order to achieve a pleasing topside outline, we must take into account some of the idiosyncrasies of the eye. We must fool the eye a little, cater to its likes and dislikes.

The eye is easy to fool; compared to the ear, it is a technically imperfect device. Looked at another way, movies and TV would be impossible if the eye were as sensitive as the ear. The eye is subject to certain aberrations that must be borne in mind in arriving at a pleasing and effective silhouette.

The eye takes parallel vertical lines in a topside silhouette and makes them appear to point in different directions. Rake these same parallel lines slightly aft (for instance, masts and the forward ends of cabins), and the eye conjures up the feeling of forward speed. Rake the bowline in the opposite direction, that is, slightly forward, and the feeling of speed is increased. Make the mistake of raking the bowline slightly aft and the eye will tell you that the boat is pug-nosed and ugly. Combine aft raking masts with a fore raking bow and add a sheer line with a generous rise at the stem and the eye revels in a beautiful yacht. At any rate, the eye is democratic and accepts these nuances of design in the smallest boat as well as in the largest. Figure 5-15 corroborates these views.

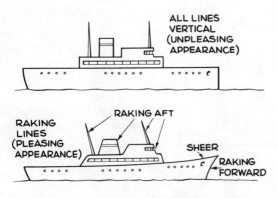

Figure 5-15: The eye does not like straight vertical lines. Note the more pleasing silhouette of the ship designed with rake and sheer.

In this matter of beautiful silhouette, sailboats really come into their own. The requirements for efficient functional wind-driven design and the prerequisites for eye appeal are almost synonymous. Thus a good sailboat almost automatically is also a thing of beauty. Sailing craft exude a grace of movement which few powerboats can equal.

Decor

Women and decor arrived on pleasure boats together. And boat builders were quick to learn that the wife's fascination with cabin decoration unlocked the husband's checkbook. As a consequence, styling that charms the feminine eye is now the dominant trend and some engineering values have been sacrificed to superficial frills—even as with automobiles ashore. Nonetheless, anyone who has seen the before and the after, the dingy cabins of yore and the miniature floating living rooms of today, must admit that, on the whole, the advent of the ladies has been beneficial.

The most striking thing about seagoing decor is that everyone realizes the value of color and is not afraid to use it. Brilliant drapes, colorful furniture, carpets that contrast or complement, all can be found in cruisers large and small. The caution on boat decoration has to do with materials; many fabrics are not good sailors. Whenever possible, the choice should be restricted to the fiberglass, vinyl, and other synthetics that are mildew- and rot-proof. It is also important to use fire-resistant or fire-retardant materials or, even better, nonflammable ones.

Amenities

Afloat or ashore, thoughtful little additions to furnishings and decor can add greatly to creature comfort. In most cases the cost of these amenities is minimal and the major problem is thinking of the right ones to have. Since one man's comfort can become another man's annoyance, the choice is a highly personal one for each boat owner.

The avid seeker after game fish will surely want a fighting chair and will feel that catching the titans of the sea is impossible without it. A bar is always welcome and by association lends an air of gaiety to every social gathering. Medicine cabinets and vanities are almost an artifact of American houses so their desirability afloat is obvious. Hi-fi and TV have also gone to sea and the sensitive mod-

Figure 5-16: The tuna tower reaches skyward far above the flybridge and affords a magnificent view around the compass that facilitates spotting fish. (Credit—Motor Boating magazine)

ern receivers have eliminated the need for an antenna installation in many cases. And nothing will swell the breast of the skipper on the bridge as much as an intercom which lets him give orders to salon, galley, or wherever without stirring from his omnipotent position of command.

Sportfisherman

A unique style of topside design called sportfishermen has evolved from the wishes of skippers who "go after the big ones." One requisite is a large cockpit with places for one or more fighting chairs and room for the wielders of gaffs and other gear. Another appurtenance of these boats is a "tuna tower"; this reaches skyward to dizzying heights and thereby affords wide visibility.

The tuna tower has a complete set of controls. This often is the third set on board, with one below and one on the flybridge. Any weight on the tuna tower has an extremely long lever arm and exerts a strong effect on stability and roll period. The photo in Figure 5-16 is typical.

Houseboats

An entirely new genus of seagoing craft has evolved in the modern houseboat and its topsides design owes more to the highway trailer than to marine lore. (Modern houseboats are also self-propelled in contrast to their earliest forebears, which were simply barges that had to be towed.)

Houseboat interiors are not restricted by the curved and arched surfaces that form the shell of a traditional boat. Walls and ceilings of rooms meet at square corners, as they do ashore, and windows of generous size admit light and air. Space and utility approximate that of a small apartment. Appliances usually are the standard type found in homes.

The subject of windage assumes increased importance with houseboats. The large, square silhouette above the waterline, and the relatively small area below it, make the houseboat more difficult to handle in a blow. Maneuvering visibility often is not as good as it might be; some houseboats take this into account by placing an additional steering position on the roof.

Many skippers, perhaps influenced by traditional boat shapes, denigrate houseboats on the matter of seaworthiness. Manufacturers, on the other hand, make strong claims for the seagoing ability of their craft and the photograph in Figure 5-17 would seem to corroborate them.

Figure 5-17: This photograph of a houseboat in a race would seem to prove that these boats can take heavy going with ease. (Credit—Bahamas Ministry of Tourism)

6 *Galley Equipment and Plumbing*

WHETHER man eats to live or lives to eat is a question that gourmets and Spartans have bandied back and forth for a long time. In either case, food must be prepared and cooked whether on land or at sea. The place for doing this on most boats is, of course, the galley.

A modern galley presupposes hot and cold running water and adequate drains for waste. These require plumbing. Since piping, tanks, and pressure units must be installed to serve the galley, it is only logical to claim the bonus and extend the plumbing to include washbasins, shower baths, and that certain appurtenance which makes for true internal organic comfort afloat and is known, euphemistically, as the head. This juxtaposition of galley and toilet, it is hoped, will not offend the squeamish skipper. (The actual physical location of the galley itself is discussed in Chapter 5.)

The lady of the house took over the galley when family cruising supplanted the stag fishing party. She wanted the floating cookery to be as much a kitchen as the one at home—and the boat designers got the message. The coffee pot, tin plates, and can opener that sufficed for the men expanded into complete sets of dishes, glasses, and tableware plus the ever-necessary skillets and saucepans. The problem of space and utility which all this presented was the impetus that brought the galley to its present highly developed state.

Seen through a woman's eyes, the galley consists of three main units around which everything else is built: the stove, the sink, and the refrigerator. That order of listing also approximates their order of importance.

Safety Precautions

The open flames and the hot materials indigenous to a galley make safety of such prime importance that a few cautions must be given right at the outset. The cooking area should have good ventilation but the burners must be protected against gusts of wind which could extinguish them. All wooden and other combustible surfaces above and immediately surrounding stoves should first be covered with asbestos or similar material and then sheathed with metal. Smokestacks should clear all woodwork by at least five inches, should have no dampers, and should be protected against rain and backdraft by hoods and smokeheads at the top. (The sailors call these top pieces Charley Nobles.) A water-iron like the one pictured in Figure 6-1

is required where the stack passes through the deck.

In many cases, the "open flames" and the "smokestacks" have been pushed into limbo by the electric stove. However, this change does not in any way lessen the need for strict adherence to the common-sense rules of safety. The red-hot heating element of an electric stove can set

Figure 6-1: A circular pool of water in this water-iron insulates the hot smoke pipe from the surrounding deck. (Credit—Manhattan Marine & Electric Co., Inc.)

fire to a curtain almost as fast as an open flame.

Curtains should be avoided in the galley at points where their ignition is even remotely possible. Complete operating instructions should be posted near each appliance to help in avoiding misuse that could lead to accident. Everything that could be turned into a hazard by the motion of the boat should be fastened securely. Lighted stoves should *never* be left unattended. A fire extinguisher should be handy on the bulkhead just *outside* the galley and ready for immediate use. (The extinguisher is placed outside so that Cookie can vamoose pronto and do the fire-fighting from a safer position.)

Stoves and Fuels

Seen through an engineer's eyes, a stove is a device for creating conditions favorable to combustion and then controlling and directing the resultant heat to a desired area. A safe marine stove must be able to perform these operations under varying conditions of gravity, namely, during the roll and pitch of a boat.

Most fuels that are used ashore can also be employed on a boat but one in particular—gasoline—is definitely prohibited. The small gasoline pressure stoves, so familiar around camp sites, are perfect for outdoor use but absolute murder in the galley. Under NO circumstance should gasoline be used aboard for cooking, heating, or any other open-flame purpose.

The permissible galley fuels are wood, coal, fuel oil, kerosene oil, alcohol, solidified alcohol, liquefied petroleum gas, and electricity. All except electricity are primary fuels.

The listed fuels are all good and the choice is a matter of cost and convenience. Wood and coal have long served the sail fraternity. Kerosene oil, fuel oil, and liquefied petroleum are more easily controlled. Alcohol can be extinguished with water in the event of accident. Electricity is the safest and cleanest. Solidified alcohol is widely available and the stoves that use it are simple in the extreme; it is too expensive for any but emergency or intermittent use, however.

Electricity is the most desirable fuel but its use is limited because of the heavy current required for any reasonable cooking speed. For small pleasure boats this means dockside use only with the further proviso that the marina wiring is adequate and not overcrowded with other users. Larger vessels that carry their own generators are of course free from the dockside limitation but they incur the inconvenience and the noise of running generating plants simultaneously with the stoves.

The housewife afloat will probably feel most at home with the liquefied petroleum gas (LPG) installation because it is the closest thing to her normal gas usage ashore. These stoves are ignited and regulated in the standard gas-stove manner and the heat they produce is not different enough from that of their city counterparts to cause any change in cooking methods.

LP Gas

Certain derivatives of petroleum can be liquefied by being placed under moderate pressure. In this manner a considerable quantity of equivalent gas can be stored in a comparatively small tank. When the pressure is released the liquid becomes a gas without further ado and burns in a regular gas burner. Technically, these gases are hydrocarbons (chemical combinations of hydrogen and carbon) and may consist of propane, propylene, isobutane, or butylene. All are known in the trade as LP gases.

A peculiarity of LP gases is that they are heavier than air. This means that any escaped gas can eventually sink down into the bilge and diffuse there much like gasoline vapor and with the same explosive potential. Since the gases themselves are practically odorless, a noxious odorant is added to act as a telltale warning of any leaks.

The LP gas situation unfortunately has been beclouded by a Coast Guard edict prohibiting the use of this fuel on vessels carrying passengers for hire. The reasoning for this is somewhat obscure because that very boat could be carrying hundreds of gallons of gasoline. Naturally, the existence of such a prohibition has raised undeserved doubts in many minds about LP gas safety and the use of LPG aboard has declined almost to the vanishing point. (The Coast Guard does *not* forbid the use of LP gas on pleasure boats.)

When the installation is made in accordance with standard technical specifications (NFPA*302), and to do this is only common sense, the use of LP gas aboard a yacht is eminently safe. Insurance companies recognize this in their premium structure and impose no penalties. From a purely practical standpoint, cooking with LP gas is simple and fast. A further advantage is the wide availability of full replacement cylinders for empty ones. Highway trailers have recognized the many advantages of LPG and are avid users.

LP GAS STOVE SYSTEMS.

The complete system for cooking with liquefied petroleum gas consists of the cylinders containing the gas, the pressure reducing regulator, the valves, the pressure gauge, the necessary tubing, and of course the stove. The interconnection of these various components is shown diagrammatically in Figure 6-2.

Gas Cylinders. The containers in which liquefied petroleum gas is supplied have been standardized down to four sizes. The two smaller ones look somewhat like metal bottles, hence the popular name, bottled gas. The cylinders are shown in Figure 6-3. The respective weight of each cylinder when filled with gas is 20 pounds, 44 pounds, 53 pounds, and 90 pounds; these provide 20, 80, 160, and 336 minimum cooking hours respectively. The usual installation is with two cylinders in tandem; this permits one cylinder to be removed for replacement without interfering with the continued use of the stove.

LP gas cylinders must always be installed so that only the vapor and not the liquid gets into the distribution tubing. Since the vapor collects over the liquid in the cylinder, this means that the gas takeoff must be above the liquid level.

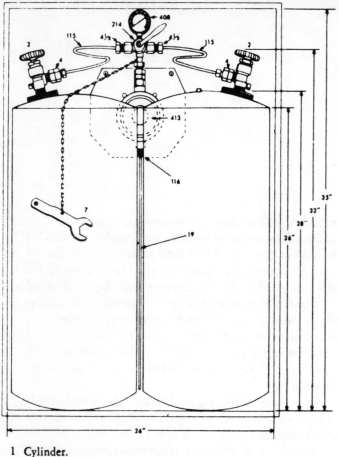

1 Cylinder.
2 Cylinder valve.
4 Connecting fitting (cylinder end).
4½ Connecting fitting (manifold end).
7 Wrench.
19 5/16" O.D. copper tubing fuel line from regulator to appliance.
115 ¼" O.D. copper tubing "pigtail".
116 Tube coupling.
214 Pressure reducing regulator manifold with throw-over valve having lever handle showing which cylinder is being used.
408 Pressure gauge.
413 Pressure reducing regulator.

Figure 6-2: The tanks, valves and regulators for an LP gas supply are interconnected as shown.

Each cylinder must have a permanently attached hand wheel on its valve so that a shutoff may be accomplished quickly without the use of a wrench. The cylinders must meet the regulations of the Interstate Commerce Commission regarding strength. They must be discarded when any corrosion or denting has weakened them or after they have been involved in a fire. Each cylinder must be secured individually with brackets or yokes.

The LP cylinders on all boats must be so located that any escaping gas cannot reach the bilge, engine compartment, or other enclosed space. The easiest way to meet this requirement is to place the cylinders topside in a suitably constructed locker. The usual manner of doing this, where the size and arrangement of the boat permits, is to build the locker on the forward deck ahead of the deckhouse. A large covering cushion then allows such a locker to do double duty as a bow seat. (See Figure 6-4.)

Other locations for LP gas cylinders are also permissible but a housing must always be provided for protection from the sun. This housing must be vented top and bottom to prevent the buildup of escaped gas. Spare cylinders, even those considered empty, are not permitted to be stored below.

The gas pressure at the LP stove is very low, about comparable to that used by shoreside appliances, and

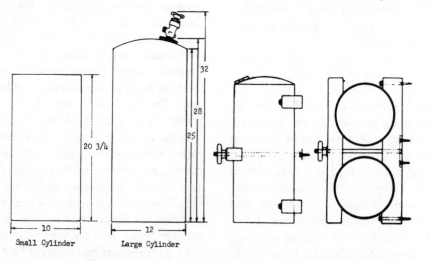

Small Cylinder   Large Cylinder

Figure 6-3: The dimensions shown above for small and large LP gas cylinders can be used as a guide in the construction of the required deck lockers. Methods of securing the tanks are also shown.

144

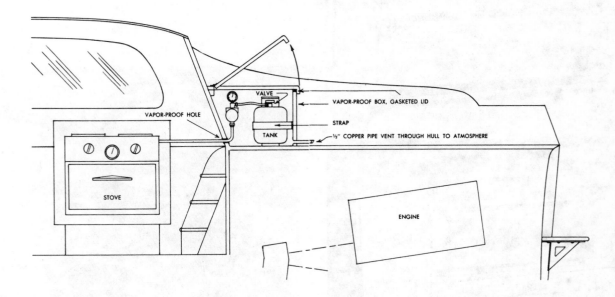

Figure 6-4: LP gas tanks must be carried above deck and protected from the sun in a suitable locker fitted with bottom vents, as LP gas fumes are heavier than air. A caution label, like the one shown, must be displayed at each appliance and also at the tank locker.

CAUTION

1. Keep cylinder valves closed when boat is unattended. Close them immediately in any emergency.
2. Be sure all appliance valves are closed before opening cylinder valve.
3. Always apply match or flame to burner and then open burner valve.
4. Close master valve whenever consuming appliance is not in use.
5. Test system for leakage at least bi-weekly and after any emergency in accordance with the following procedure:
   With appliance valves closed, the master shut-off valve on the appliance open, and with one cylinder valve open, note pressure on the gauge. Close cylinder valve. The pressure should remain constant for at least 10 minutes. If pressure drops, locate leakage by application of liquid detergent or soapy water solution at all connections. Never use flame to check for leaks. Repeat test for each cylinder in multi-cylinder system.

never exceeds a few ounces. This reduction from the very much higher tank pressure, perhaps a hundred pounds, is accomplished by the regulator valve. A diaphragm and needle valve arrangement in this unit permits only enough gas to pass to maintain the preset condition.

The pressure gauge indicates the pressure of the LP gas in the cylinder. This is not necessarily an indication of the *amount* of gas remaining in the cylinder because the pressure changes with the ambient temperature. Since the liquefied petroleum vaporizes at any temperature above 40 degrees below zero F., gas is available in any weather if there is a positive gauge reading. The exception might be an errant skipper, lost and unknowingly cruising the North or South Pole.

The Underwriters' regulations specify that two metal signs be included with every LP gas installation on any boat. These list the instructions and cautions for safe operation of the equipment. One sign must be fastened at the locker containing the cylinders and the other at the appliance which uses the gas.

LP Stoves. Except for slight changes in the combustion passages, the LP range is a counterpart of the city-gas home kitchen unit although the design is more economical of space in order to fit the usually constricted small boat galley. The burners are of the Bunsen type that suck air by a venturi action and mix it with the gas for a hot, blue flame.

Any LP range installed in a powerboat must have been approved specifically for marine service. Such approval can not be earned unless the unit contains a master packless shutoff valve that cuts the gas off simultaneously from all burners and also eliminates pilot lights. Representative ranges in various degrees of grandeur and installation are shown in Figure 6-5. Note that all models have the master shutoff valve within immediate reach at the front, in accordance with requirements.

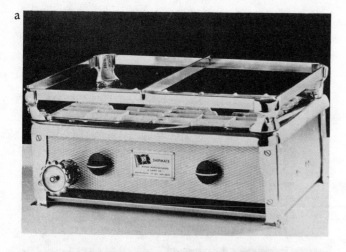

Figure 6-5: A small two-burner stove (a) and a more elaborate unit with oven and broiler (b), both approved for use with LP gas, are shown. (Note the required master shutoff valve.) The portable single burner cooker (c) is said to deliver 7,000 BTUs and can double as a cabin heater. (Credit—Shipmate Stove and Paulin Infra-red)

Alcohol and Kerosene Stoves

Alcohol and kerosene are related chemically and the stoves that burn these fuels are likewise similar in construction. Two types are offered: those with gravity feed of fuel from a tank raised above the burners and those in which air pressure forces the fuel to the burners and

atomizes it. In these latter a small hand pump supplies the air pressure and a relief valve protects against excess.

Proper combustion requires that the fuel be vaporized at the burner because it is actually the gas that does the burning. This is usually accomplished by burning a small amount of alcohol in the preheating cup under the burner (priming), thus getting the burner hot enough to cause vaporization. The cooking flame keeps the burner hot enough from then on. The action is identical with the manner in which the old-style plumber's gasoline torch was started. A pan under the stove is a safeguard against spilled priming or other fuel.

Alcohol is much the cleaner fuel, both in handling and in combustion. It has fewer carbon molecules to deposit themselves as soot and is easier to start than kerosene. Nevertheless, kerosene is thoroughly adequate if care is taken to get the burner hot enough at the start. The effect of a slight taint of either fuel in food is quite another story and always objectionable.

Electric Stoves

The newest cruisers have followed the trend in modern homes ashore and have switched to electric cooking. But the cruisers lack the ingredient which made possible the switch on land—a power line supplying unlimited power.

Many tasks can be performed economically with electricity but cooking is *not* one of them and (as pointed out in Chapter 10) neither is supplying any other kind of heat. On the other hand, the cleanliness and convenience of electric cooking makes many skippers and mates happy to overlook the economics involved. One thing which should not be overlooked is that electric stoves *cannot* be operated off any normal set of storage batteries.

There are certain eccentricities of electric stoves that must be learned and accommodated. First of all, the range of heats (except on highly sophisticated models) is not infinitely variable as it is with gas. Second, the burners stay hot for quite some time after the current is turned off; this can be an advantage to the experienced cook who turns the juice off in advance of the required cooking time. An electric range that also includes a rotisserie is shown in Figure 6-6.

Toasters

Breakfast toast has become an American way of life and few people like to abandon it just because they are cruising away from home. Toasting bread is certainly one of the simplest cooking operations, and yet it presents problems afloat because of the quick concentrated heat required.

Electric toasting is still the time-honored method. At dockside, with 120-volt city current available, toasting is a cinch with a standard home toaster. At lower voltages such as the battery, electric toasting becomes impractical because of the heavy current needed. The open-flame stoves may also be used for toasting and baking with several adapting gadgets. The bread slices must be turned manually and this may prove a chore for pampered users accustomed to automatics. You could also hold a slice of bread over an open flame with a long-handled fork.

Utensil Holders

The seagoing cook stove needs an appliance that its landlocked counterpart will never require except in an earthquake: gadgets to hold the cooking utensils in place during a rough trip. A hot liquid sliding off a galley stove can be dangerous and, at the very least, messy.

Simple devices for keeping cooking utensils in place over their burners are shown in Figure 6-6. These holders are adjustable to the size of any pot or pan and are attached easily to the stove itself or to the surrounding counter top.

Figure 6-6: Electricity is by all odds the cleanest and safest cooking "fuel." This model sports a rotisserie in addition to its oven. (Credit—Princess)

Sinks

Stainless steel and Monel are the preferred materials for galley sinks and have supplanted enamel and vitreous types on pleasure vessels. These metals do not rust, are immune to the corroding effects of most kitchen chemicals, are reasonably easy on dishes, and quickly polish up to a shipshape shine. They are widely available as modernizing replacements for galleys on older boats.

A neat installation is shown in Figure 6-7. The sink edges are flush with the counter top for easy dishwashing and to eliminate ridges that catch dirt. The lip of the sink is set in bedding compound all around to prevent seepage of water into the storage space below.

Stainless steel sinks and steel wool scouring pads are enemies; *never* the twain should meet. Manufacturers of these sinks constantly get complaints about their products "rusting"—and of course rusting on stainless steel just does not take place. In each case, investigation showed that the mate had scoured the sink with steel wool. What happened was that microscopic particles of the steel from the wool imbedded themselves into the pores of the stainless and immediately rusted, giving the appearance of a rusted sink.

The only "cure" is the use of an acid strong enough to dissolve the steel particles, yet not harmful to the sink, which will thereby restore the stainless surface.

Water Systems

The hand water pump, long a staple fixture in the galley, has gone out with the kerosene lamp; no modern mate would consider going back to the slavery of yanking that old handle up and down. Pressure water systems are now standard on all but the smallest, cabinless boats.

Thanks to the improvements and miniaturization of

electric water pumps, installing a pressure water system for the galley and associated plumbing is not difficult and not expensive. The electric current these units draw is small enough to cause no worry about battery capacity.

A pressure system supplying hot and cold water for a small boat consists of the following units: a storage tank, a water heating tank, a source of heat, the necessary piping, safety and check valves, the connecting fittings, and the electric pump. A schematic diagram showing the interconnection of all these parts is shown in Figure 6-8.

WATER TANKS.

The material of which the water storage tank and the water heating tank are made is of great importance if the water is to be used for cooking and drinking. Human taste buds are extremely sensitive to off-flavors in drinking water caused by metallic contamination or by bacterial growth. The former cannot be changed once the tanks

are installed but the latter can be controlled by cleanliness and periodic sterilization with the proper chemicals. (When purity cannot be achieved, tank water should be used for washing and bottled water for human consumption.)

The two top-ranking materials for water tanks aboard ship are stainless steel and Monel. Both are completely inert to water and impart no off-flavors. Both can be fabricated without undue difficulty, can be welded or brazed for watertight seams. Sterilizing chemicals, used in proper concentration, do not affect either. In the non-metal category, fiberglass boats often have built-in fiberglass tanks. (Some skippers claim that fiberglass imparts a disagreeable flavor to water.)

The water heating tank aboard is smaller than the one usually found supplying shoreside kitchens; it will hardly ever exceed fifteen gallons and more often is less than ten. Provision in the form of relief valves is made against

Figure 6-7: The sink is flush with the counter and set in bedding compound to prevent seepage into the locker below. (Credit—Pearson Co.)

overpressure caused by excessive heating.

A full water storage tank easily can have a weight that becomes an appreciable percentage of the boat's total displacement. Its location therefore becomes important because of its possible effect on the craft's stability. The safest location, and the one which will affect stability least, is over the keel and as low as possible. Large tanks should have baffles to reduce sloshing. The evil effects on transverse stability of uninhibited sloshing known as free surface, are counteracted best by tanks that are long and narrow in the fore and aft direction.

SOURCES OF HEAT.

Until a few years ago, the preferred source of heat for hot water on small boats was LP gas. Today gas-fired water heaters are in disfavor and most manufacturers have stopped making them. These units required a pilot light and such a flame is a hazard under small boat conditions. The final shot in the head was the Coast Guard edict banning LP gas on boats carrying passengers for hire and the consequently implied question about its safety on any craft.

One source of heat that is available free of charge when a powerboat is underway is the engine. This is waste heat that normally would go overboard; putting it to work when this can be done with simple piping is just good engineering. Marina current can take over the standby heating of the water while at dockside; most heating tanks make provision for this adaptation. Again, this standby heating is no job for the storage batteries.

PIPING.

The various components of a boat fresh water system generally come with half-inch NPT (national pipe thread) inlets and outlets and the piping of course must follow suit. (Note that a half-inch pipe has an actual outside diameter of .840 inches and bears 14 tapered threads to the inch.)

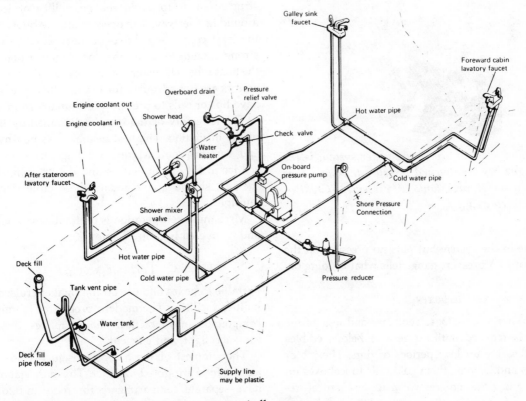

Figure 6-8: This diagram shows the interconnection of all components needed for a good hot and cold pressure water system. (Credit—Boating Industry Assn.)

The piping can be rigid or tubing or even plastic. The rigid requires a great deal of fitting of ells and tees; the tubing is therefore simpler because it is merely bent around obstacles. Plastic tubing retains this advantage and adds freedom from rot and corrosion and the ability to stretch. It thereby avoids bursting when frozen.

PRESSURE PUMPS.

The heart of the pressure water system obviously is the electric pump that produces the pressure. In order to produce pressure, these pumps must be of the positive displacement type rather than centrifugal, meaning that they employ diaphragms, pistons, progressively collapsing tubes or volumes, gears, or similar methods. (The diaphragm pumps can be run dry without damage since there is no sliding friction as with a piston in a cylinder.)

A representative pressure pump is shown in Figure 6-9. This one includes a small pressure vessel that main-

Figure 6-9: The heart of a pressure water system is the pump. This one has an attached pressure tank and thus relieves the main storage tank of pressure. (Credit—Raritan Engineering Co.)

tains pressure in the system but puts no pressure on the main water tank. A pressure gauge tells what is going on.

Iceboxes

Molds and bacteria decompose food less and less as the temperature is reduced until, at zero or below, edibles can be stored safely for long periods of time. The job of cooling foods and keeping them cold falls to iceboxes on small boats and goes progressively to mechanical refrigerators and freezers as the craft get larger and more elaborate.

The icebox is the simplest contrivance for keeping food

cold on a boat; it is also the least convenient. Ice must be purchased and lugged. Since the ice soon becomes water, provision must be made for drainage. Because the temperature in even the better iceboxes is far above freezing, ordinary foods cannot be kept very long and frozen foods cannot be kept at all. One bonus with ice: Many mates feel that vegetables and other items prone to drying keep fresher in the moist air of the old-fashioned box.

Draining the runoff from the boat's icebox would seem to be a very simple matter—and yet it is not. The simplest expedient of allowing the drain to empty into the bilge is very poor practice; this water accelerates rot and causes bad odors. The ideal answer is to drain the box overboard but this can be done without a pump only if the icebox is well above the waterline. Drip pans are no better than the human factor that remembers to empty them.

From a safety standpoint, iceboxes should be constructed so as to avoid the possibility of ice banging around in a seaway. Top openers are the safest but, again, the least convenient. Front openers should have latches strong enough to secure the doors against popping when the boat rolls. The magnetic latches found on home refrigerators are not adequate for marine duty. Shelves should have lips or rails to prevent the contents from spilling.

The longevity of the ice is determined by the quality of the insulation. The best insulation is non-hygroscopic and vermin-proof. Marina vending machines generally sell ice in fifty-pound cubes and the ice compartment of the box should accommodate these either singly or in multiples.

Mechanical refrigeration is preferable without question and is covered fully in Chapter 10.

Portable Coolers

Portable iceboxes find use on the smaller cruisers without built-in facilities. The modern process of foaming plastic compounds into practical shapes makes these coolers compact, light, and efficient.

The simplest of these coolers is just a box in which ice and food are stored together. The more elaborate units have separate compartments for food and for ice and some even add a spigoted tank for drinking water. It should be noted, however, that the ice remains heavy despite the lightening of the box.

Dry Ice

Solidified carbon dioxide, dry ice, is yet another means of storing energy to be released later for keeping foods cool for short periods. This material is extremely cold, far below zero, and cold enough to "burn" the skin when touched. Because of its low temperature, a small amount of dry ice can do a comparatively large cooling job. Dry ice is easily available because many food trucks and ice cream vendors use it; it is not expensive.

Dry ice does not melt but rather sublimes directly into a gas; there is thus no drainage problem. This gas is carbon dioxide (CO_2); it is odorless, nonpoisonous, and tasteless. Carbon dioxide quite possibly exerts a slight preservative action on food. CO_2 is *ex*haled by humans and *not* breathable by them because the oxygen is so tightly held by the carbon that the human lungs cannot break it away.

Ice Makers

The latest word in aid of afterdeck martini gulping is an electric ice maker. Such a unit is shown in Figure 6-10.

Figure 6-10: This ice maker is a boon when the sun is over the yardarm. This unit can make as many as 400 ice cubes per day—hopefully enough to satisfy the hardiest skipper. (Credit—Raritan Engineering Co.)

In essence this is a scaled-down mechanical refrigerator whose freezing cabinet accommodates only the paraphernalia needed for making, handling, and storing ice cubes.

The pictured unit can make up to four hundred ice cubes per day—and that's a lot of guests to have aboard. Installation consists only in placing the unit above, below, or into a counter and connecting two wires, plus a fresh water supply. No drain is needed because an electrically heated drip pan evaporates all the moisture that collects. (Of course this transfers the moisture into the surrounding cabin air.)

Water Purification

A cruising skipper will most likely fill his fresh water tanks at various docksides and unfortunately with water of varying degrees of acceptability. Nevertheless, the water from the galley spigot can still be sweet, pure, and tasteless. The trick can be turned by simple gadgets.

Maintaining the purity of the drinking water is a two-part job. First, the water must be filtered to remove suspended solid particles. Then it must be subjected to a chemical action in order to eliminate salts and other taste and odor contaminants which are in solution and to kill bacterial growth.

Filtration is a simple mechanical process. The water is forced through a barrier whose mesh openings are small enough to trap the undesired particles. This barrier can be cotton, paper, wire screen, or a series of closely spaced disks. The chemical part of the purification can be done in several ways. One is with a special resin that has the property to attract all contaminants in the water by ionic action. Another is with activated carbon that adsorbs or draws the contaminants into itself. Bactericides are added. The runoff in either case is equivalent to distilled water.

Water Makers

At first thought, a device for making drinking water from the sea conjures up a picture of an explorer who expects to be away from civilization for years on end and therefore must be entirely self-sufficient. But calmer thinking shows a place for this device on even a fair-sized cruiser. Every skipper has had the experience of picking up an uninviting water hose at a strange small pier, doubtful of the quality of water it would supply.

A maker of fresh water (a seawater evaporator) that could easily fit into the complex of a large engineroom is shown in Figure 6-11. Smaller units for smaller boats also are available. The unit makes use of a standard distillation

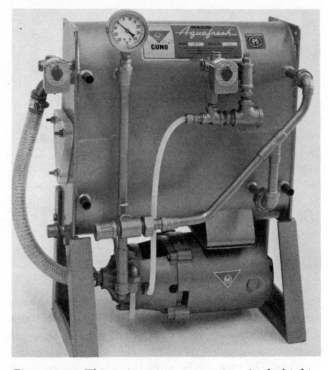

Figure 6-11: This unit turns seawater into fresh drinking water with the aid of waste engine heat. The boiling is done in a vacuum, therefore at lower temperature. (Credit —Cuno Manufacturing Corp.; Photo by Barnes Studio)

Figure 6-12: This combination stove, sink and refrigerator is a galley space saver.

process in which the water is boiled and the steam is then condensed. The heat for boiling is supplied by the propulsion engine jacket water. (You may wonder how a jacket temperature which hardly ever exceeds 160 degrees can boil water. The answer lies in creating a partial vacuum in which to do the boiling, thereby lowering the boiling point.)

One practical advantage of a water-making plant on a cruising vessel is the reduction in size and weight of the fresh-water tank which is made possible. There isn't much sense in spending the power and space needed to lug along a ton or more of drinking water when it can easily be made fresh as needed. (One shortcoming of water makers is their inability to function satisfactorily in badly polluted areas.)

Combination Units

The restricted space in the galleys of all but the most elaborate yachts has spurred designers to heed the Latin motto "Multum in Parvo," much in little. An ingenious example is illustrated in Figure 6-12. This is a combination stove, sink, and refrigerator which fits into a space only thirty inches wide.

Despite the miniaturization, the refrigerator has a frozen food compartment and is said to accommodate five

cubic feet of storage. The motor-compressor unit is accessible from the front for service. The stove has three full-size burners with front controls. The sink is equipped for pressure hot and cold water.

Galley Storage

An efficiency engineer studying the galley would start with the basic problem of storage and he would divide this into two parts. First, there must be storage space for the durable items, then for the consumable ones. The durables are pots, pans, dishes, and glassware which remain permanently; the consumables are obviously foods, both staple and perishable.

Storage space must be conveniently accessible. Galley headroom is never high enough to allow those favorite mistakes of the shoreside architects: shelves up near the ceiling where no housewife can get at them. But the marine designer often makes the opposite error: placing lockers down on the sole, within a swish of the bilge water, where they can't be looked into without lying on your stomach.

Storage space must be dry and well ventilated. If cold-water piping or drains run through a locker they should be wrapped amply with antisweat tape to avoid condensate. Doors should have positive lock catches to keep them closed; detents and magnetic catches are not sufficient in a rolling sea. Wherever possible, form fitting coamings or hollows should be provided for the articles stored. Open-front bins can be placed where lack of room rules out doored lockers.

Storage space for the durables can be considered from a modular standpoint because the sizes of dishes, cups, and glasses are pretty standard. Dinner plates are 10 inches in diameter with an occasional manufacturer running to 10 3/8 inches, just to be different. Salad plates are 8 1/2 inches in diameter. Soup plates are 9 1/4 inches in diameter. Saucers measure 5 1/2 inches across and cups 3 3/4 to 4 inches. The height of a cup is 2 1/4 inches.

Placed in stacks of eight dishes, the height of each stack is as follows: dinner plates, 3 inches; salad plates, 3 inches; saucers, 2 1/2 inches; and soup plates, 4 1/4 inches. These are actual measurements and clearance should be added all around in figuring storage requirements.

Highball and collins glasses with a 10-ounce capacity are 3 inches in diameter and 5 1/2 inches high. Glasses for old-fashioneds are the same diameter but only 3 1/2 inches high. Both of these are the standard bar type with heavy double bottoms which some mates consider to have better stability under way. These two types of glasses can take care of everything that comes out of the bar, although some drinkers may feel that such restricted service is not strictly according to Hoyle (or Barleycorn).

Although the exigencies of cramped space seldom permit it, the ideal location for dish lockers is over the counter, à la home kitchens. If a depth of eleven inches can be achieved dishes can be stacked flat inside the coaming or rail. If this depth is impossible, then it is wise to avoid some intermediate, nonmodular dimension and cut down all the way to five or six inches. In this narrower locker or bin, dishes would be stacked on edge behind suitable protective fittings.

An ingenious method of preventing rattle and breakage

is shown in Figure 6-13. Here plastic sponges are cemented to the insides of the locker doors so that they keep pressure on the dishes when the doors are closed. These inexpensive sponges also come in handy as rattle stoppers elsewhere.

Cups are best stowed upside down in fitted racks. The

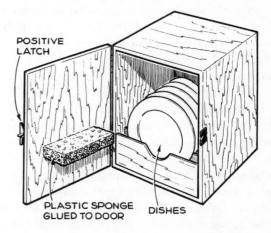

Figure 6-13: Plastic sponges make good "anti-rattlers." One application is shown for a dish locker.

next best method is to hang them individually from locking hooks but their constant swinging is annoying and requires "mooring space" like a boat swinging from its buoy. Glasses are also best held by racks, placed about three inches up from the bottom, with either square or circular holes of the right size.

Stowage

The remaining durables to be stored are the pots and pans. These can take rough handling; to a large extent they can be stacked one within the other for a great saving of space. The best material for cooking utensils is stainless steel, with aluminum a second choice; enamel ware should be avoided as chippy and impractical. Often the space below the sink automatically becomes marked for pot and pan storage because it is not very good for anything else. Many mates prefer copper bottoms on stainless steel cookware because they feel this distributes the heat more evenly.

The selection of locations in the galley for storage

of the consumables, the foods, is governed primarily by the necessity for preventing contamination and spoilage. The two enemies are moisture and vermin. The proper storage space for edibles that need refrigeration is obvious, and this location also insures against mold and bugs.

Screw-top jars with tight-fitting covers are excellent for bulk items like flour, sugar, coffee, tea, and others. The nonshatterable plastics are much to be preferred over glass. The less glass aboard, the better; even drinking "glasses" of plastic should be chosen in place of the breakable kind, if the mate will have them.

Modern food packaging which sells loaves of bread in moisture-proof plastic bags is a boon to the galley. Bread kept tightly closed in its bag, and in the fridge, keeps fresher than it would in any of the usual bread boxes. These bags can also double as tight containers for other foods and are fine for sealing the fishy aroma in with the fish and keeping it from permeating the refrigerator.

Housewives know the value of common table salt for putting out frying-pan fires; a container of it should always be handy in the galley. This will take care of little flare-ups that don't require the extinguisher. Paper towels are very handy in the galley and the holder is attached easily to a bulkhead. Some form of securing carving knives should also be installed to prevent these potential daggers from slithering around lethally. (Magnetic knife racks do not hold strongly enough to be safe at sea.)

One of the more exasperating practical jokes played on newlyweds is to send them a load of canned foods from which all labels have been removed. The mate in the galley can have the same exasperation if the canned goods have been aboard for a long time. The salt sea air seems to make labels wilt and lose their grip on things. Marking contents on can tops with an indelible marker is recommended.

A good rule in the galley is to inspect all foods carefully for vermin before stowing, in order to prevent infestation. Especial attention should be paid to groceries delivered in an old carton, a favorite traveling vehicle for the ubiquitous roach. Once aboard, he is a hard tenant to dispossess; he has survived through millions of years because he is slier than his adversaries, although modern bug killers have counteracted some of his reproductive zeal.

Mice and rats can also be expected as freeloaders aboard any boats that habitually tie up at large marinas. These rodents have learned that it is always Thanksgiving around the dockside garbage can and the brighter ones have found that the galley is even handier and cozier. It is hard to prevent their coming aboard because the hull is generally in direct contact with the slip. Traps are the ready solution; and the best trap of all has four feet and a tail and says meow. (The only difficulty with this "trap" is the disposal of the exhaust.)

Bars

As with its counterpart in the home, the seagoing bar can be anything from the corner of a shelf reserved for a bottle to an elaborate installation rivaling the corner saloon. It all depends on the space available, the affluence of the skipper, and his desire to share his potables.

Bars are classed as wet or dry, meaning with running water or without. A well-equipped cabinet bar attached to the bulkhead in the salon is shown in Figure 6-14. It has appropriate holes to keep the necessaries in place. There is, apparently, no locking device to keep the bottles out of circulation and this presupposes honest guests and tolerant hosts.

Figure 6-14: Bars on board can be anything from a bottle on a corner of a shelf to an elaborate installation. This bar is a cabinet against a bulkhead.

Iron Pots

Many skippers ban iron pots and iron skillets from the galley. Their reason for the prohibition is the possible effect on the compass. Theoretically, such effect is possible but, practically, unless the galley is directly below or adjacent to the binnacle, the effect will be negligible or nonexistent. The offenders, if any, will be the heavy, cast-iron cooking utensils; most stainless steels are nonmagnetic, as of course is aluminum.

If the galley equipment is suspected as a source of compass deviation, this can be checked by watching the card carefully on different headings while the pots and pans are carried to the forepeak or moved to the opposite side of the boat. Should they prove to be offenders, there are two avenues of cure: either get rid of them or else have them in their places when the deviation table is being prepared and see that they remain in place during a voyage.

Chemical Purifiers

Maintaining the integrity of drinking water is one of the most important means of preventing illness aboard. The water evaporators already described are the best guarantee because their output is distilled water, the purest if not the most palatable form. Chemical methods can also be used to purify drinking water.

Calcium hypochlorite ($CaOCl_2$), commonly known as chloride of lime, is a chemical often used for water purification. It is added to the water supply in the ratio of 1/4 ounce to 100 gallons and in this concentration will purify without being noticeable. (The actual disinfection is done by the chlorine released by this chemical compound.)

Tablets and pills can also be purchased to purify drinking water. These are handy to carry and available in small, controlled dosage. A typical formulation contains p-sulphomedichloroamine benzoic acid in minute concentration plus sodium borate and sodium chloride for stabilization. One of these pills dropped into a jug of doubtful water brings it to drinking condition within a half hour.

Another chemical purifier useful around the galley (and head) is sodium hypochlorite ($NaOCl$). This is usually sold in grocery stores in bottles as a 5 percent solution for laundry bleaching. This solution should *never* be used in conjunction with any ammonia-containing substance be-

cause dangerous chlorine gas could be released. The 5 percent solution is further diluted with water before being used as a general disinfectant. It is corrosive to silver, aluminum, and steel.

The five percent laundry bleach is a cheap but excellent water purifier. In concentrations as minute as one part per million this chemical can safeguard drinking water. It purifies without imposing off-flavors except in the case of water containing a high degree of suspended vegetable matter. In this latter instance the result may be water that does not taste good.

Galley Comfort

Small boat galleys are notorious for bad lighting and poor ventilation except on the newest, plushiest boats. The odorous gloom that prevails is the chief cause of incipient mutiny among mates, yet this annoying condition need not exist. The introduction of low-voltage fluorescent lamps and small, efficient blowers makes it unnecessary for the mate to bear this cross.

The fluorescents are available even for low-voltage battery lines and they are far more economical of watts for the light produced than are incandescents. The illumination is soft, kind to makeup, and soothing to the feminine psyche.

The blowers should have rotors of the squirrel-cage type; the units with fan blades do not push enough air to rid the galley of odors or enough to have any effect on comfort. (The squirrel cage must be cleaned periodically because grease clinging to the vanes changes their airfoil and reduces efficiency.)

Heads

The foregoing detailed examination of the means and equipment for the preparation and serving of food would seem to lead logically (though not esthetically) to the subject of heads. These disposal units were once simple devices for allowing human effluvia to slip overboard quietly and unobtrusively. The only controversy then surrounding heads was how they acquired their appellation.

Suddenly, heads have shed their obscurity and have become the target for widespread political activity and regulation. Many states already have promulgated strict rules to which heads must conform; all other states undoubtedly soon will join them and the federal government is working on it. As was the case with the Boating Act, an overall federal law will supersede the state dicta and therefore govern. Politicians have discovered that to do battle against heads (and their users) gains many more votes than it loses.

In the first place, it can be stated almost categorically that the plain and simple head which led directly overboard is *out*. The discharge of untreated wastes is *out*. In many localities, and their number is increasing, the discharge of *any* waste is out; it must be held aboard and discharged on land.

The present state of the art and science of waste disposal encompasses three methods of dealing with the output of a head: chemical treatment, incineration, and holding. There seems to be no common preference, since many states accept one and outlaw the others, although there is some provision for reciprocity between states. An educated guess would place the holding method as the leading contender for the ultimate universal approval.

The laws are being written not to favor any method but to specify a required result of effluent purity. If the specifications are met, then how the job was done is of no moment. This leaves the door wide open for new and improved technology and equipment.

A representative digest of the specifications for any overboard discharge is as follows: All floating and settling solids must be removed; suspended solids, no more than 50 parts per million (PPM); biological and chemical oxygen demand, not to exceed 50 PPM; not more than 50 coliforms per 100 milliliters of fluid.

Admittedly, these are tough specs. In fact they are so tough that none of the treatment devices has yet been able to meet them—hence the legal swing to on-board holding methods.

CHLORINATORS.

Heretofore the most common method of treating head discharge has been the mechanical-chemical. A solution rich in available chlorine, such as a laundry bleach, is mixed with the discharge from the head after it has been thoroughly mascerated by a revolving blade. The mix is retained for a period long enough to give the chlorine a chance to kill bacterial growth and is then sent overboard. Hopefully, the effluent has been churned into particles small enough to be inoffensive to nearby eyes and has

Figure 6-15: This is one form of chlorinator-macerator head. An electric motor drawing current from the batteries operates the unit. (Credit—Raritan Engineering Co.)

been sterilized sufficiently to prevent contamination of the water. An electric head which performs the foregoing operations is shown in Figure 6-15.

The adequacy of the sterilization often is gauged initially by the number of live coliform organisms remaining in the discharge. The coliform itself is innocuous and not the cause of any illness but it indicates the presence of excreta from warm-blooded animals and therefore the presumption of toxic germs. The coliform is used as an indicator because the test for its presence is simpler than other tests. By its very nature this test is therefore not positive; bathing beaches around New York City have not been closed despite coliform counts in the thousands—and no ill effects have ensued.

INCINERATORS.

The discharge from the head can also be subjected to extreme heat (and flame) and thus reduced to a sterile ash. The ashes are held and subsequently disposed of ashore. Since the volume of ash is small, this presents no great problem. However, the amount of heat (and flame) required rule this method out for small boats and the Coast Guard prohibits it for vessels licensed to carry passengers for hire.

The dangers of fire and flame have been eliminated in a recently developed "incineration" system which claims to accomplish a satisfactory result at low, flameless temperatures. A schematic explanation of the method and

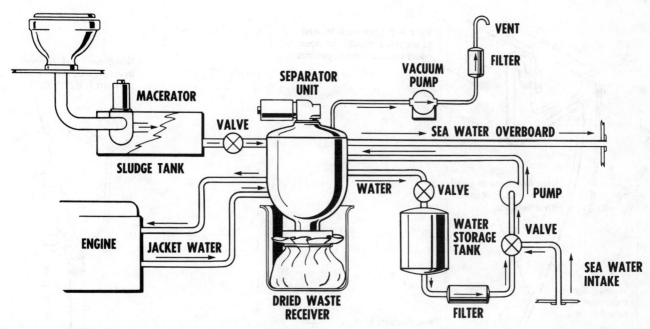

Figure 6-16: This "incinerator" system uses no fire but gets its heat from engine cooling water. The toilet effluent is macerated and then boiled off under vacuum to end up as dried waste in a disposable plastic bag.

equipment is drawn in Figure 6-16.

The heat for this system is supplied by engine jacket water. Because the temperature of the cooling water from a normally running engine is below the boiling point, the "incineration" process is carried out under a vacuum. (This is a familiar technical ploy, used also in the freshwater maker described earlier.) The final output of this newly proposed solution to the marine toilet problem is a very small volume of dried waste in a plastic, disposable bag. The maker claims that the seawater employed in the process is returned overboard completely sterile. The system could even be divorced from the sea by storing water in a tank and reusing it.

HOLDING TANKS.

The idea of holding sewage aboard in a tank is theoretically simple but putting it into practice has become complicated. The complications arise not only from the esthetic and sanitary facets of the problem but also from the specifications that various governmental agencies have laid down.

Practically speaking, holding tanks must be strong enough and safe enough for the job; there are cases on record where these installations have exploded with easily imagined results. Warning devices must indicate when the tanks are full or almost full. Discharge connections must restrict attachment only to approved shoreside emptying facilities and must make surreptitious dumping en route impossible. A schematic of an approved holding-tank installation is shown in Figure 6-17.

RECIRCULATORS.

The recirculating toilet is a variation on the holding-tank system and achieves the same purpose with greater economy of space. The unit combines a head and a holding tank into a single device and flushes itself with a small amount of contained liquid which is continuously recirculated. The principle long has been used on aircraft, where overboard dumping would prove catastrophic. A recirculating head is pictured in Figure 6-18.

A sterilizing and clearing chemical is added to the water

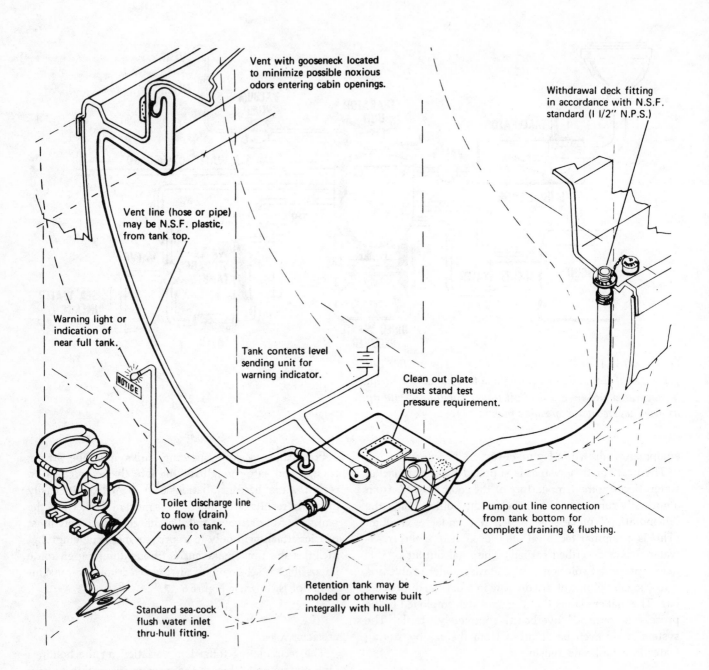

Vent with gooseneck located to minimize possible noxious odors entering cabin openings.

Withdrawal deck fitting in accordance with N.S.F. standard (1 1/2" N.P.S.)

Vent line (hose or pipe) may be N.S.F. plastic, from tank top.

Warning light or indication of near full tank.

Tank contents level sending unit for warning indicator.

Clean out plate must stand test pressure requirement.

NOTICE

Toilet discharge line to flow (drain) down to tank.

Pump out line connection from tank bottom for complete draining & flushing.

Standard sea-cock flush water inlet thru-hull fitting.

Retention tank may be molded or otherwise built integrally with hull.

Figure 6-17: The holding tank must be sturdy, securely fastened and have a vent to the atmosphere in addition to the pump-out fitting. A remote indicator must warn of a filled or nearly filled tank. (Credit—Boating Industry Assn.)

Figure 6-18: One solution to the holding tank space is this head which is its own "holding tank." (A treated chemical solution is recirculated.) (Credit—Monogram Industries, Inc.)

which is circulated. Further clearing of the liquid is accomplished by screens and other mechanical means. The power for this action is drawn from the boat electrical system. Pump-out is done via a deck fitting connected to the toilet.

Nevertheless, the holding-tank system is the only one that can guarantee zero contamination of the waters, hence its likelihood to survive other methods. (Some marinas already provide discharge service at a reasonable cost per visit and New York State is installing some coin-in-the-slot, do-it-yourself dischargers.)

In fairness to the skipper, it should be pointed out that politicians have grossly exaggerated the culpability of the small boat in water pollution. Actually, most pleasure craft are in use only a small part of the time and their heads even less. One factory at the water's edge discharges more pollutants than all the cruisers in the state—and the chemical nature of this waste is more destructive to marine life than human excreta. But the power of government is great and the skipper must bend the knee.

As often happens in similar confrontations, the loudest voices in the ecological melee are generally those with the least knowledge. Human waste deposited in large bodies of water in reasonable quantities does no harm; it is actually beneficial. This waste becomes part of the food chain for scavengers and is soon removed by them. As the waste increases, again within reason, the scavenger population increases. Only in a closely packed marina with

every boat busily pumping its head, could the situation get out of hand—and such a condition is highly unlikely. It is the chemical and industrial wastes, for which nature makes no provision, that are the danger to our future.

Galley Tricks

The mate can adapt many shortcuts from the cooks in shoreside lunchrooms and learn even more from the chefs in dining cars who serve a half-hundred meals from a space hardly twice the size of the galley in most pleasure boats. One of the secrets is preparation and another is concentration.

Coffee. A mix for instant *complete* coffee, which eliminates the need for carrying and refrigerating milk, is made easily. Into a jar with a tight screw cover place instant coffee and milk powder and sugar in the proportion of 1, 2, and 3; shake to mix thoroughly. Adding hot water to a couple of spoonfuls of this mix in a cup makes delicious hot coffee complete with "cream" and sugar. The proportions can be varied according to taste, especially by the reduction or elimination of sugar for the dietetically inclined, and the powdered milk can be replaced by the synthetic powdered cream.

Wine. A bottle of sherry wine, the domestic kind sold at moderate price in gallon jugs, provides a marvelous pepper-upper for almost every kind of cooking, from soups to sauces. French chefs never use water when wine will do. (So-called cooking wine is simply an average quality wine with enough spices added to make it immune from the liquor tax.)

If you would like to prove to yourself what wine can do for routine cooking, take standard frozen mixed vegetables and cook them in your favorite wine instead of in water. The odds are good that thereafter your galley will never be without wine.

Wine is a wonderful pan cleaner and does automatically what detergents do with scrubbing. As a bonus, wine makes the sauce while it shines the pan. The trick is accomplished by pouring a little wine into the pan, for instance, after frying liver or sautéing meat, and then letting the result cook down to sauce consistency. The sauce will be deliciously European and the black spots will have left the pan.

Bacon and eggs. Instead of cooking the bacon and the

eggs separately, the two can be done together in one frying pan and over one flame. The bacon is rendered first, with the grease progressively poured off. The egg is then dropped over the bacon and cooked to the desired turn. Sunny side up, no cover; to simulate the turned egg, cook covered.

Breading. Fish fillets are especially toothsome when breaded and so are thin cuts of veal. Chicken parts intended for deep frying also benefit from a generous breading; this makes them "Southern fried."

The coating can be prepared in toto, ready for use; in this state it will keep a day or two under refrigeration. Alternatively, the dry ingredients of the coating can be premixed and stored indefinitely to be wetted into the final form at the time of use.

The dry ingredient is general-purpose flour salted and flavored with your favorite spices: Paprika, curry powder and powdered ginger are good choices. Egg, milk and wine transform this prepared flour into the liquid coating.

To a tablespoon of the dry mix add two tablespoons of evaporated milk so that the flour is worked into a paste. Add two tablespoons of wine (sherry is good) and one egg. Beat well with a fork or a wire whip. (If the finished coating is to be refrigerated, a pinch of cream of tartar will help its keeping qualities.)

Fillets, veal, chicken parts and other meats dipped into this mixture and then coated with cracker meal (or flour) are ready right then for a hot frying pan with *hot* (just short of smoking) oil. The foods can also be coated and breaded a day in advance and kept in the refrigerator for subsequent frying. (The dipping and coating and breading can be repeated several times for those who like their vittles armor-clad.)

"Instant" heating. Cans of beans and similar edibles can be heated quickly and without using pots by placing them *unopened* directly over a low flame (after the label has been removed). But stay there with them! This is a *fast* process! Turn the can occasionally, end over end. The important thing is to listen carefully for that little click as the ends expand due to the steam inside. When you hear that click—*take the can off the fire!*

You will find that the contents taste better than usual because no flavor has been steamed away.

Mixed drinks. The complete ingredients for sours, martinis, manhattans, collins and similar drinks can be mixed in advance, including the liquor but excluding the ice, and

kept in the refrigerator in bottles. A call for a drink on board then simply means that some of the mix is poured into a shaker, ice added, and shaken. The prepared lemon juice available in the grocery store is superior to the fresh fruit for this purpose.

Crepes. Many guests find the usual omelets a little too heavy on the water but enjoy the thin French crepes. These are easily prepared, even by people who can't say *oui.* Into a bowl go one-half tablespoon of flour plus salt and spices (like cinnamon) to taste. These are thoroughly mixed with a fork. Two tablespoons of evaporated milk are added, a little at first to wet the dry ingredients completely and make a paste. Now come two tablespoons of wine and the egg. Beat well, preferably with a wire whip. For each crepe just use enough of this mixture to cover the bottom of a hot greased frying pan thinly. When the underside is done (the edges become brown) the crepe is turned with a spatula or flipped, boy scout fashion. Rolled with marmalade these are delicious; flambé them and you are in Paris. (To flambé, heat some brandy in a large spoon or metal cup, ignite, and pour over crepes.) The amounts listed above are enough for three thin crepes; the French trick is to keep them *thin.*

Soup. The bones that are usually thrown away after a chicken dinner can make a delicious soup. Once you try it, you will thenceforth turn with revulsion from the salt water and fat that masquerade as chicken soup in cans.

The chicken bones and carcass (plus cooked or uncooked gizzard, neck, legs, what have you) are placed in a large saucepan, a cup of wine is added, and then water to cover. Added are dried parsley, celery seed, paprika, onion salt, pepper, and other favorite spices in proportions to suit the taste. Simmer for several hours until reduced to soup consistency. Strain off the liquid and place it in refrigerator overnight.

In the morning this soup will have jellied (has a *canned* chicken soup ever jellied?) and the fat will have concentrated at the top. Scrape off the fat and discard it. Enjoy this soup cold, as jellied consommé, or warm, with or without rice.

Tableware. The most practical knives, forks, and spoons for boat use are those made of stainless steel in a simple design. Wooden-handled table knives, the fancy, so-called steak knives, deteriorate quickly under marine conditions unless they are of the highest quality using the hardest, seasoned woods. One advantage of the stainless knives is that they can be sharpened without destroying their rust-resisting quality; a plated knife exposes its base metal when its edge is ground.

Tableware is stowed most conveniently in segregated compartments of galley drawers. Another suggestion might be a silverware rack fastened to a bulkhead.

"Linen." The synthetic fibers, principally nylon, have taken over from natural materials such as linen in the field of sheets, pillow cases, tablecloths, and napkins. This has freed the mate from the constant battle against mildew in the linen chest, because the synthetics are not subject to this fungus attack.

The nylon table coverings are now available pretreated for "wash and wear." They can be thrown into marina washing machines, hung out to dry on a convenient line from mast to stern staff, and used without ironing.

PART II

EQUIPMENT

7 Electrical Equipment

Shoreside electricians tend to look with disdain at the electrical systems of pleasure boats; the voltages used afloat are considered too low even to be mentioned in residential wiring codes. True, marine voltages are generally in the 6-, 12-, or 32-volt category while land systems are built around 120 and 240 volts (although there may be a bit of this high-voltage circuitry aboard for dockside use). Nevertheless, the patronizing attitude is unwarranted. It takes skill and know-how to make an efficient electrical installation that will withstand successfully the rigors of its environment.

Dampness, corrosion, and vibration are the enemies of marine electrics. Direct contact with salt water, or with the damp air that carries salt, is an ever-present hazard. Any skipper whose radio has been silenced by an invisible film of conductive salt on his antenna insulator knows firsthand what sea conditions can do to electric equipment. Copper terminals and wire that have turned a beautiful green are familiar to every seafarer.

The one big difference between shore and marine electrics which demands respect and caution is the much higher current (amperage) available on the boat. It is current which does the heating and melting of wires. Fifteen amperes is about the maximum current that can do good or evil in the average home before the fuses blow. By contrast, a short circuit in the starting motor wiring, for instance, could unleash several *hundred* amperes, enough to destroy a heavy cable with a flash that easily could start a fire.

Since watts are merely the product of volts multiplied by amperes, it takes more amperes to satisfy the wattage requirements of any appliance at the lower boat voltage. Thus the wiring must be heavier because it is the amperage, not the voltage, that determines wire diameter. This should explain a question that puzzles many skippers: Why are the wires on my 12-volt boat thicker than those in my 120-volt home?

Protection against the environmental hazards already mentioned is not enough; safe boat wiring should conform to specifications laid down by Coast Guard and other safety agencies. The facts and figures of these specs will be enumerated in conjunction with the various components to which they apply. Compliance with these safety laws is not only good legality but also good sense.

DC or AC?

The first fork in the road to electrical knowledge is to decide whether a system is direct current (DC) or alternating current (AC). This decision could be important; some equipment, for instance, a transformer, will function only on alternating current and will be damaged if connected to direct current. On the other hand, incandescent lamp bulbs are not choosy and will perform equally well on AC or DC.

In the two-wire electric circuit of a direct-current system, one wire is always positive and the other always negative. Many direct-current devices (again excepting the lamp bulb) require that the polarity of their terminals be respected; the penalty for a wrong connection can range from inactivity to complete ruin. (A battery *always* delivers direct current.)

In the two-wire alternating-current system, each wire is alternately positive and negative. This switching of polarity takes place rapidly at a rate determined by the line "frequency." In the United States the common line frequency is 60 cycles per second and, since one cycle is a complete change through positive and negative, each wire goes from plus to minus 120 times in one second. This frequency corresponds to a low-pitched hum—the sound heard around much alternating-current equipment.

Alternating-current systems are subdivided into one-phase, two-phase, and three-phase; this is determined by the manner of their generation. The single-phase circuit is the most common around marinas and is carried on two wires. Two-phase and three-phase circuits require at least three wires.

The puzzled skipper, faced with two wires of uncertain parentage, can use a simple high school physics trick to ferret out their AC or DC nature. If the bared ends of the two wires are placed near each other (*not* touching) in a glass of water the resultant bubbles will identify the type of current. Bubbles at only one wire mean DC, and this wire is negative. Bubbles at both wires mean AC. If the line voltage is very low, a pinch of salt added to the water will improve the bubble visibility.

Volts, Amperes and Watts

The characteristics of electricity are measured in terms

of volts, amperes and watts; these are units just as pounds, yards, or gallons are units in other fields. The volt is the unit of potential or pressure. The ampere is the unit of the amount of current. The watt is the unit of electric power.

The voltage rating of an appliance is the factor that determines whether it can be connected safely to a certain circuit. You would not take a tire rated for only 28 pounds of air pressure and connect it without restriction to a 100-pound pressure line. Likewise, a lamp bulb rated at 12 volts can be connected only to a 12-volt circuit; any considerably higher voltage would burn it out. (Reversing the procedure, namely, connecting a 100-volt lamp to a 12-volt circuit, results merely in inactivity; the bulb would hardly glow.)

The amperage rating of a device states how much current it requires for its operation. Properly connected, it will draw that many amperes and no more, regardless of the amperage available. If the aforementioned 12-volt lamp bulb were connected to a 12-volt storage battery able to discharge hundreds of amperes, it would still draw only its rated small current and no more.

The power consumed by any device connected to an electric circuit is expressed in watts. Wattage is the product of volts multiplied by amperes. Electric utilities sell their power by the kilowatt hour, a unit which is equivalent to 1000 watts for one hour (or any other combination such as 100 watts for 10 hours).

"Volts $\times$ amperes $=$ watts" is always true for direct-current circuits. On alternating-current circuits it is true only for *resistive* appliances such as toasters or lamp bulbs; on *reactive* circuits containing motors and transformers, a reducing multiplier called a power factor is added.

The resistance to the flow of electric current is measured in ohms. Technically, a resistance of one ohm exists in a circuit when a pressure of one volt can force through a current of one ampere. This relationship, expressed in several forms, is known as Ohm's Law, after its original formulator.

Storage Battery

The storage battery is the alpha and the omega of the marine electrical system; it is the "sun" whence all light flows. It is the logical point to begin explaining electrical phenomena aboard and a thorough knowledge of its merits and idiosyncrasies is valuable.

To begin with, the common conception that the storage battery "stores" electricity is technically incorrect, although perhaps adequate for layman's use. (Only a capacitor actually *stores* electricity. See Chapter 8.) The storage battery stores chemical energy which is increased on charge and decreased and converted to an electric current on discharge.

This chemical reversibility gives the storage battery its correct technical name: secondary battery. By contrast, a primary battery, such as those used in flashlights, does not have this reversible trait. It runs down until its active material is exhausted, whereupon it is dead and must be discarded.

Two types of storage battery are available on the American market: the lead-acid and the nickel-iron-alkaline (commonly called the Edison). Chances are that the vast majority of boatmen have never seen the latter but come into daily contact with the former because this is the type used in both boats and automobiles. An Edison battery is superior in longevity, power, and ability to withstand abuse but it is much more expensive and unfortunately not compatible with extreme cold weather.

This "coming in contact" with the lead-acid battery requires a word of caution. While the shock danger from a low-voltage storage battery is negligible, two other dangers are very real. The acid (sulphuric) is highly corrosive and can damage skin and almost everything else with which it comes in contact. The gas (hydrogen) coming from the vents during charge is highly flammable and only a spark is needed to set off a junior atomic explosion. Accidentally spilled acid can be neutralized with water and ammonia or baking soda. Sparks can be prevented by providing a cover that makes it impossible to drop tools on battery terminals.

The storage battery was born about one hundred years ago when a Frenchman named Planté put two strips of lead into a glass jar containing dilute sulphuric acid. He connected the two strips to a source of direct current, thereby charging the cell, and found that it subsequently could be discharged to return current. His alternate charges and discharges formed the plates into the required chemical composition; it is interesting to note that early commercial storage batteries were actually manufactured by this same forming process.

Modern storage batteries are no longer simple sheets

Figure 7-1: The internal construction of a lead-acid storage battery. The plates are lead grids containing lead peroxide for the positive and spongy lead for the negative. The plates are insulated from each other by separators. The electrolyte is diluted sulphuric acid. (Credit—Prestolite)

of lead formed by the Planté process. The negative and positive plates are intricately cast grids of a lead-antimony alloy. The grids hold tightly packed active material, lead peroxide for the positive and spongy lead for the negative. These grid plates are then interleaved alternately but always with one extra negative plate so that negative plates will be at the two outsides of the sandwich. The internal appearance of a modern battery is shown in the cutaway view of Figure 7-1. The insulating separators which keep the plates from touching are wood, plastic, or rubber, the last being preferred.

Remember that this battery stores energy chemically and not electrically. During discharge the lead peroxide and the spongy lead both change to lead sulphate; the charging current changes this lead sulphate back to the original lead peroxide and spongy lead. During discharge the released oxygen and hydrogen combine to form water, thereby diluting the acid and lowering the specific gravity of the electrolyte. This action, too, is reversed during charging. A hydrometer is the simplest tool for checking battery condition and it depends upon this water-forming reaction. A hydrometer is shown in Figure 7-2 together with a scale of equivalent battery conditions.

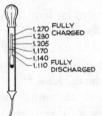

1.270 FULLY CHARGED
1.230
1.205
1.170
1.140
1.110 FULLY DISCHARGED

Figure 7-2: A hydrometer is the simplest device for checking the charge condition of a storage battery. (Beware of spilled acid!) The table lists the corrections for temperature.

BATTERY RATINGS.

Storage batteries are rated by their "ampere hour capacity" (AH). By specification this is the total number of amperes that could be taken from the battery at a uniform rate of discharge for 20 continuous hours. Thus, a 200 AH storage battery will deliver 10 amperes continuously for 20 hours and, hopefully, 5 amperes for 40 hours.

The ampere hour rating unfortunately does not tell much about the battery's ability to crank a heavy gas or diesel engine. The cranking effort requires an abnormally heavy amperage, several hundred or more, and whether or not the battery can deliver this depends upon the huskiness of the plates and the quantity of the water-acid electrolyte.

The nominal voltage of each cell in a lead-acid storage battery is two volts and this varies but slightly from complete discharge to complete charge. This small variation explains why ordinary voltmeters have no value for indicating battery condition. A specially constructed voltmeter, known technically as a suppressed zero, must be used if this manner of checking batteries is desired. Incidentally, the size of the cell affects only the ampere hour capacity; the voltage is always two, whether the cells are big or little.

BATTERY CHARGING.

A storage battery is charged by applying to its terminals a voltage slightly higher than its own. This forces current into the battery to do the chemical work that results in the energy storage. The ideal charging procedure is to supply a fairly heavy current when the battery is discharged and then to taper this down to zero as the battery reaches its full level. The charging current can come from a generator on the propulsion engine as is done on automobiles, from a separate engine-generator set, or from a marina shore supply through suitable equipment. These components are discussed later.

Overcharging—in other words, continuing the charge current after the battery is fully charged—is harmful. It knocks active material out of the grids and reduces the life span of the battery. It causes excessive evolution of hydrogen gas. It evaporates the water and requires frequent addition. Incidentally, it is never necessary to add *acid* unless some of the original electrolyte was lost through leak or accident.

An important reason for keeping a battery fully

charged is that in this condition it will not freeze under any normal winter temperatures.

A few sample figures will bring out this relationship vividly. A fully discharged storage battery will freeze at 25 degrees F., a fairly common winter temperature. If this same battery were even half-charged, the thermometer would have to sink to 15 degrees *below* zero before freezing could occur. And a fully-charged battery will resist freezing all the way down to a fantastic 95 degrees below zero! (Cold weather does, however, reduce the battery's ability to discharge.)

BATTERY LOCATION.

Ideally, storage batteries should not be located in the same compartment with a gasoline engine or a gasoline tank. Admittedly this is a goal impossible to attain with most powerboats and so alternative cautions must be applied. Mechanical strength of the hold-downs is important to prevent the batteries unshipping in a sea. The tray or container in which the batteries stand should be capable of retaining any spilled acid; for this purpose lead is best and wood heavily coated with asphaltum is passable.

The batteries should be accessible or hydrometer testing might become so great a chore that it will be omitted. Ventilation should draw off the emitted hydrogen gas before it can accumulate in dangerous quantities. Battery location should always be high enough in the hull to be beyond the reach of bilge water.

Generators

When underway, far from the electric outlets on the marina slips, the electricity for charging the batteries and keeping all the electronic gadgets aglow must be produced right on the boat. This is the function of the generator. Everyone knows that the engine turns the generator and that the generator turns out the "juice." But why does spinning something inside something else generate electricity?

Two early scientists, Hans Christian Oersted and Michael Faraday, might be called the granddaddies of the generators found today on every engine or, for that matter, anywhere else. Oersted showed the interrelation between magnetism and electricity and Faraday discovered that magnetism in motion can induce an electric cur-

rent in a wire. The sketches in Figure 7-3 show how easily anyone can repeat their important experiments. Current through the wire creates a magnetic field which affects the compass needle. Moving a wire through a magnetic field induces an electric current which is detected by the meter.

It is not a difficult path of reasoning to proceed from these two phenomena to the basic theory of a generator. If one wire carrying current can produce a weak magnetic field that is detectable only with a compass needle, then

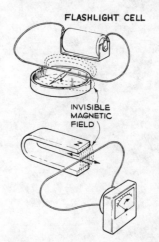

FLASHLIGHT CELL

INVISIBLE MAGNETIC FIELD

Figure 7-3: A compass needle will indicate the magnetic field around a current-carrying wire. A current is generated in a wire which is moved through a magnetic field.

obviously a coil of many turns of wire can have a cumulative effect and result in a very strong magnetic field. Similarly, a coil of many turns moved in a magnetic field generates a current that can do useful work instead of merely flicking a meter pointer.

There you have the two units that make up an electric generator: one coil of wire (the "field") that produces the necessary magnetic field and another coil (the "armature") to rotate in this field and generate the desired output current. Each of these coils can consist of many subcoils, all contributing to the total effect. A schematic of such a hookup is shown in Figure 7-4 and a cutaway view of an actual generator is also given. (The latest designs of some small generators substitute a permanent magnet which consumes no current for the usual wire-wound field.)

One thing in the sketch may still cause puzzlement: the

a

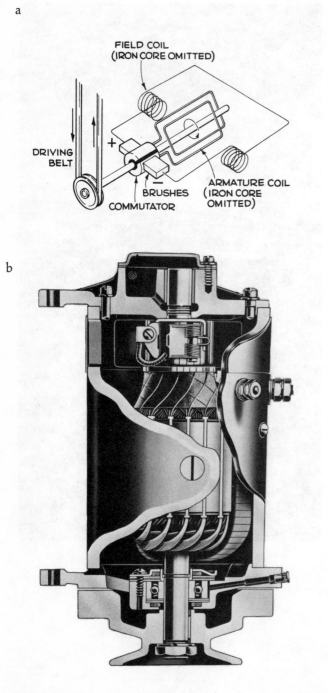

FIELD COIL
(IRON CORE OMITTED)

DRIVING
BELT

+

BRUSHES
COMMUTATOR

ARMATURE COIL
(IRON CORE
OMITTED)

b

Figure 7-4: The schematic (a) explains the action of the basic components of every electric generator and the cutaway view (b) shows an actual machine. (Credit—Prestolite)

commutator. If you analyze the movement of each side of the rotating coil you will see that they interchange positions at every half revolution. This means that the current in the wires changes its polarity every half revolution; in other words, the result is an *alternating* current. But it was emphasized that a storage battery can be charged only with a *direct* current. That's where the commutator comes in.

The commutator keeps reversing the connections of the rotating coil to the outside circuit so that one brush always picks off the positive pulses and the other takes only the negative pulses. The output is thus a direct current. For the sake of simplicity the drawing shows only two segments in the commutator. Actual generators have many—two for every coil in the rotating armature.

GENERATOR OUTPUT.

The output of a generator is determined by the speed at which it is driven and by the number of turns of wire in its various coils. The amount of wire relates directly to the physical size of the machine—and it seems altogether logical that a larger unit should be capable of greater output than a smaller. The output of a generator is controlled by varying the current in its field coils.

The relationship between speed and output introduces complications when the driver of the generator is a variable speed device such as a propulsion engine. Some form of control must be added to boost the output at slow speed and hold it within safe limits at high speed. The voltage regulator described below is just such a control. Too high a voltage in the system would quickly burn out lamps and electronic equipment. (The characteristics of the storage battery also aid the voltage regulating process.)

GENERATOR TYPES.

The current for the field coils is taken from the generator's own output in all but the very largest central station machines. This can be done in either of three ways: series, shunt and compound. The designations refer to the manner of connecting the field to the armature.

In the series connection, all the current generated by the machine passes through the field coils. In the shunt connection (the one shown in Figure 7-4), only a portion of the current is tapped off, the amount being determined by the resistance of the field winding. The compound system is a combination of these two methods. Each scheme makes the generator more adaptable to a special purpose. Most of the generators found on marine engines are shunt-connected because this is best for their function of battery charging.

VOLTAGE REGULATION.

The importance of maintaining proper voltage has been stressed in relation to both battery longevity and appliance protection. A regulating method known as the third-brush was in wide use for automotive generators until the early 1950s. This was superseded by the voltage regulator now found in all modern marine installations.

The third-brush method was actually an additional brush bearing on the commutator between the two main brushes. It supplied the field current but regulated it in such a manner that generator output could not exceed a set limit, regardless of speed increase. The main drawback of the third-brush generator was that it kept charging the batteries even after they were full, which was detrimental to battery life.

The voltage regulator is not an integral part of the generator but a separate, compact device. It continually senses the voltage in the system and reacts by sending more or less current to the field coils of the generator to maintain that voltage at its set level. This tapers the charging current because, as already stated, it is dependent upon the difference between the battery terminal voltage and the generator terminal voltage.

The older voltage regulators are electromechanical; the newer ones are transistorized. In the former, a vibrating contact controls the amount of resistance in the field circuit. The transistor regulators have no moving parts and the equivalent control is obtained electronically. The wiring diagram for a typical voltage regulator is shown in Figure 7-5.

CUTOUTS.

From the wiring diagram in Figure 7-6 it can be seen that the battery would discharge itself through the generator when the engine stopped, if this branch of the circuit were not opened. This open circuit must be maintained until the engine speed is high enough to bring the generator voltage slightly above that of the battery and then it must be closed. The opening and closing of

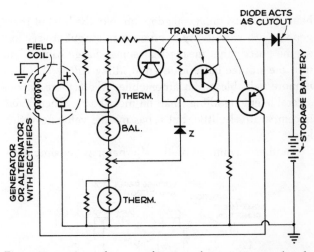

Figure 7-5: A modern, sophisticated, transistorized voltage regulator is shown together with its circuit. It has no moving parts. A simple nonmoving cutout (a diode) is also included.

the circuit to the battery is the function of the cutout.

The cutout is a switch or relay which senses not only the generator voltage but also the direction of current flow between generator and battery. Reversed flow, meaning from battery to generator, immediately opens the circuit. The cutout is generally located together with the voltage regulator. In the transistorized voltage regulator, electronic circuitry with a diode has replaced the movable contact of the obsolete cutout. (See Chapter 8.)

Wind Driven Generators

A small wind driven generator may be the answer to the problem of how to keep a sailboat's storage battery charged. Devices of this nature, although larger than practical for a small boat, have long been used by farmers without access to a power line. Small units expressly designed for marine use are now available which, with a moderate wind, will put three or four amperes into a battery.

Alternators

The generator has been replaced by the alternator on modern boats as well as on automobiles. The alternator is a generator that delivers alternating current.

The alternator has many advantages over the generator,

hence its almost universal adoption. Not the least of these good points is its ability to produce an output at very low engine speed; this means that some charge can be put into the storage batteries even at idling RPM. This trait is more valuable on an automobile, where there is considerable engine idling, than on most boats, where there is comparatively little, but it has marine value nevertheless.

Another advantage of the alternator is its simplicity.

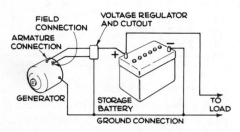

Figure 7-6: The basic connections between generator, cutout, voltage regulator and battery are diagramed. The cutout prevents the battery from discharging itself through the generator when that machine is not rotating fast enough.

The alternator has no commutator and no attendant power pickup brushes; much generator trouble centers at this point. The simplified internal construction makes possible a smaller housing for the equivalent power output and this is always welcome in the crowded engine compartment.

A little reflection on the sketch in Figure 7-4 will lead to the correct conclusion that *all* generators are alternators *internally*. The alternate movements of the coils between the north and south magnetic fields perforce generate an alternating current and only after this passes through the commutator does it become direct current. But custom labels these machines on the basis of their final *outputs*, hence "generators" or "alternators."

You will remember that storage batteries can be charged only with direct current, therefore some form of rectification must be provided at the alternator terminals. This is the purpose of the diodes incorporated in the endplate of the housing. There are usually four in a bridge circuit (see Chapter 8); this form of mounting acts as a heat sink to keep them cool.

The power winding in the generator (the armature)

revolves; in the alternator it is stationary. This enables the power to be abstracted by direct connection without any sliding contacts that introduce loss and trouble. The only moving contacts are the slip rings which carry the light field current.

The output of the alternator is controlled by varying the current in its field coils, just as in the generator. And, again, a voltage regulator does the job. Since the diodes by their very nature do not permit reverse flow of current, they eliminate the usual cutout that disconnects the battery during standstill. A bonus of this arrangement is the absence of the disturbing radio "hash" that emanates from the commutator of a generator.

Large alternators connected directly to gas or diesel engines are also found on many boats for supplying the equivalent of house current while underway. These auxiliary units permit the use of standard AC appliances like TV sets and refrigerators. The frequency is kept close to the normal 60 cycles by governing the engine; the result is not good enough for electric clocks and may even cause some flopover trouble with the television. (Equipment is described later for automatically disconnecting the auxiliary generator when the boat is plugged into the marina lines.)

Battery Chargers

The direct current required for battery charging can be obtained from an alternating current source by several methods. The simplest one, which a skipper could rig for

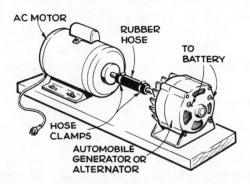

Figure 7-7: This jury-rigged battery charger takes a junkyard automobile generator or alternator and runs it with an AC motor. (It does the job but can be noisy.) If desired, a rheostat can be added in the generator's field circuit for output regulation.

himself, is shown in Figure 7-7. It consists of a small AC motor direct-connected to an automobile generator or alternator on a common base. The rig is inexpensive because the parts can come from the local junkyard—but that is its main virtue, because it is noisy in operation.

In the nonrotating, static commercial equipment, conversion is affected by rectifiers and the voltage reduction by transformers. The more sophisticated units contain sensing and regulating circuits which control the current to the battery and even shut it off on full charge.

Chargers can be mounted permanently on a bulkhead near the batteries to reduce the loss in the wiring. They should *never* be placed directly over batteries because of the explosion hazard and the possibility of corrosion. Drip shields should be provided if there is any possibility of moisture entering the unit. Very light and inexpensive battery chargers intended for home garage use are available on the market; these often have a "hot" case and are *not* suitable for marine use.

Inverters

An *in*verter changes direct current to alternating current; it is therefore the opposite of a *con*verter. Inverters are useful aboard because they enable small AC appliances like record players, fans, and shavers to be run off the storage batteries. The older inverters made use of a vibrating reed tuned to 60 cycles; the newer units are completely static and achieve their purpose entirely with solid state electronics.

The question arises: Why is a vibrator or its transistor equivalent necessary in an inverter and not in a converter? The answer lies in the nature of a transformer, and a transformer is needed to step the low-battery voltage up to the 120 required for AC appliance operation. A transformer can operate only on AC; the vibrator or the transistor breaks the direct battery current up into a simulated AC which is acceptable to the transformer. The output of a transformer is always alternating current, which is the desired end result.

Transformers

Transformers are a common sight. They range from the heavy unit on the utility pole to the engine ignition coil (yes, this too is a transformer). But transformers are always encased and, as a result, an unwarranted mystery exists about their innards.

The internal construction of a transformer is simplicity itself. It consists of two separate windings of wire on an iron core, one being the primary and the other the secondary. (In some specialized cases one winding functions as two and in still others the iron core is omitted.)

A current sent into the primary induces a voltage in the secondary. Whether this voltage is higher or lower than the primary voltage depends on the ratio of the number of turns in each. An ignition coil, for instance, has vastly more turns on its secondary than on its primary; the low battery voltage consequently is stepped up to many thousands for the spark plugs.

The generator and the transformer are akin in that both require movement between the wire and the magnetic field. In the transformer, however, the wire is stationary and the magnetic field gets a relative motion from the constantly changing alternating current producing it. The result is the same: the "cutting" of the field by the wire and the inducement of electric current.

Transformers are classified as open core and closed core. In the former, the magnetic path is partially through the air; in the latter, a closed iron loop contains the magnetism. Iron has much greater permeability than air, imposes much less restraint on the magnetic field.

Motors

The function of an electric motor is to change electrical energy into useful mechanical work. Electric motors are common on most boats and it behooves the skipper to know what happens inside that round iron gadget that runs the bilge pump, keeps the refrigerator cold, and turns the engine over for starting.

Perhaps the easiest way to understand the direct-current motor is to realize that its construction mirrors that of the direct-current generator. The two are practically identical. Supply it with current and it is a motor; drive it from the engine and it is a generator.

A motor turns because opposite magnetic poles attract each other and like poles repel. (The poles are part of the armature and the field.) A further reason is more technical: A wire carrying current in a magnetic field is always forced from the stronger to the weaker portion. The secret of *continuous* rotation is the commutator, which keeps changing the polarity of the coils on the rotating armature so that each attraction and repulsion takes place at just the right instant to maintain the motion.

MOTOR TYPES.

Motors, like generators, can be of the series, shunt, or compound type. Here again, the designation refers to the manner of connecting the field winding; each has its special characteristics. The series motor has a very high starting torque; hence, this is the type used for engine starting. Its drawback is that the load on the motor controls its speed; if the load is removed, the motor will "run away" and destroy itself.

The shunt-wound motor runs at a constant speed but lacks the very high starting torque of the series motor. This is the general service type, the all-around workhorse found on bilge pumps and many other marine components. The compound-wound motor, as might be expected, combines the features of the series and the shunt types.

A closer study of theory reveals that every motor concurrently acts as a generator while it is running. The voltage it generates is called the counter electromotive force and is opposite in polarity to the impressed voltage which drives it. The current consumed by the motor is determined by the *difference* between these two voltages and is thereby held down to a workable value. Were it not for this counter-voltage phenomenon, every electric motor would draw currents heavy enough to destroy itself.

ALTERNATING-CURRENT MOTORS.

Unless he is treading the deck of a liner, the average skipper rarely comes in contact with alternating-current motors. The few that might come within his ken are most likely the fractional horsepower motors in refrigerators and fans intended for shore use.

While alternating-current motors are just as dependent upon electromagnetism as their direct-current counterparts, their action is a little more difficult to comprehend. The small AC motors are single-phase and are fed by two wire circuits. The larger three-phase motors, which are fed by three wire circuits, are found only on heavy equipment.

The AC motors have no commutators. This makes their internal construction simpler and cheaper to build and also results in a hardier, more trouble-free machine. Since the commutator is the rotation-producing element, its

absence forces the AC motor to resort to another scheme, known as the revolving magnetic field.

The revolving magnetic field "revolves" in an electrical sense only; it does *not* turn mechanically. The electrical movement of the field magnetism pulls the rotor around with it. It is still a matter of magnetic attraction and repulsion.

The smallest AC motors, and this includes the driving mechanism in electric clocks, are of a construction known technically as shaded pole. Other constructions are "split phase," "capacitor start," "squirrel cage," and "repulsion-induction." The order in which these are listed is also the order of ascending size and power.

Relays

A relay is a remote-control switch. Although an ordinary switch is opened and closed manually, a relay performs this function through an electromagnet or solenoid which receives its impulse from a distant location. A relay makes it unnecessary to transmit the heavy currents to be controlled all the way to the control point; instead, only the light control current need be transmitted, usually at low voltage.

The most familiar relay aboard is the solenoid type that actuates the engine-starting motor. By its means a small button at the steering position can control the very heavy current required by the starting motor. Were it necessary to run this heavy current all the way to a switch by the steersman, heavy cables would be required and even then a bad voltage drop would result. A solenoid relay is shown on a starter motor in Figure 7-8; this one does the double duty of closing the starter circuit and also moving the pinion into mesh with the engine flywheel. Relays are also found in radio telephones to connect the antenna alternately to transmitter and receiver in response to the button on the microphone.

Fuses

The fuse is purposely made the weakest link in the circuit chain so that it can melt and break the circuit if its current rating is exceeded. The fuse material is a low-melting lead alloy. The cross section and length of this lead wire are carefully controlled to maintain a specific resistance. Every current passing through generates some heat; an

Figure 7-8: This solenoid relay atop a starting motor does double duty: it closes the circuit and meshes the pinion with the engine flywheel. (Credit—Prestolite)

excess current produces enough quick heat to melt the fuse element and protect the connected load.

The familiar screw-in, plug-type fuse so prevalent ashore is not considered suitable for marine use. Shipboard fuses are the so-called cartridge type in which the fuse element is enclosed in a short fiber tube with a contact ferrule at each end. The usual installation aboard is a panel which holds a number of fuses, as shown in Figure 7-9. It is wise occasionally to take each fuse out

Figure 7-9: The holder is for cartridge fuses; the screw type found in homes is not suitable for marine use. (Credit —Manhattan Marine & Electric Co., Inc.)

and replace it; the friction between ferrule and clip cuts through corrosion and reestablishes good contact.

The maximum current-carrying capacity of each fuse is derated for continuous service. For instance, the 30-ampere fuse is expected to carry only 24 amperes for a constantly connected load. This is admittedly conservative but it is always wiser to err on the side of caution when dealing with boat electrical systems. Needless to add, fuse panels should not be in hazardous locations. Fuses should *never* be placed in the ground-return circuits, only in the "hot" lines.

Circuit Breakers

A circuit breaker does the watchdog service of a fuse but in a nonself-destructive manner. Once a fuse "blows," its service life is finished. However, when a circuit breaker "blows," it can be reset instantly without any deterioration in its ability to stand guard and protect.

All circuit breakers are actuated by the current flowing through them, and each is calibrated for a certain number of amperes. They differ in the manner the overload current affects them. Some reset themselves when the overload is removed; others must be reset manually. Some emit a continuous buzzing sound to call attention to the overload. Most circuit breakers incorporate a small time delay; this prevents the heavy initial starting current of a motor from tripping the breaker. It is customary to omit fuses and breakers in the lines to heavy current consumers that are used only intermittently, for example, horns and starters.

Generating Plants

More and more cruising skippers are equipping their boats with separate generating plants instead of relying for electric power entirely on the generators attached to propulsion engines. The available choice of these generating plants is great, comprises gasoline and diesel drive, and runs from tiny units that can be picked up and carried with one hand to huskies that can put out 30 and more *kilowatts*. The output is generally alternating current because this enables standard shoreside appliances to be used aboard. What might be the two extremes of generating plants are shown in Figure 7-10. The little one delivers 300 watts of AC plus a DC winding for charging storage

Figure 7-10: The alpha and the omega of marine generating plants (300 watts and 30,000 watts) are compared. The large unit is a diesel, the small one runs on gasoline and can be carried about. (Credit—Onan Marine)

batteries; the giant is rated at 30,000 watts.

A skipper about to purchase and install a generating plant must first be able to answer a basic question: What are the total wattage requirements aboard? The loads presented by the more common household appliances that are likely to go to sea are listed in Figure 7-11. Simply add

APPLIANCE AND EQUIPMENT LOADS

Air Conditioner	1000 watts
Battery Chargers (Rectifier)	up to 800 watts
Blankets (Electric)	50 to 200 watts
Coffee Makers	550 to 700 watts
Electric Drill	250 watts
Electric Range (Per element)	550 to 1500 watts
Fans (minimum)	25 watts
Fry Pan	1000 to 1350 watts
Heater (Space)	1000 to 1500 watts
Hot Plate (Per element)	350 to 1000 watts
Iron (Electric)	500 to 1200 watts
Lights (bulbs)	as marked
Refrigerator	300 watts
Television	200 to 300 watts
Toaster	800 to 1150 watts
Vacuum Cleaner	150 watts
Waffle Iron	650 to 1200 watts
Water Heater	1000 to 1500 watts

Figure 7-11: The total electrical load aboard can be computed from the values in the above tabulation.

together the wattages of those devices that will be used at one time and be guided by the maximum. The chances are that a generating plant selected for only this sum will get by, but it is far better to add a generous allowance or even to multiply by two.

Once the size of the generating plant has been determined, the remaining question concerns the type of fuel. Should it be gasoline or diesel? The best practice is to select a driving engine that would use the same fuel as the propulsion engines do because this simplifies storage. If a cross in fueling must be made, it is far better to select a diesel plant on a gasoline boat than vice versa.

A common and often justified complaint against generating plants concerns their noisy operation. The small units with their staccato put-putting are generally considered worse offenders than the larger multi-cylinder engines whose exhaust more closely approaches a purr—albeit a loud one. This "outside" noise of the exhaust sometimes is not too annoying on board but more irritating to neighboring ships. Skipper and crew are more affected by the "inside" noise and vibration transmitted throughout the boat by structural members. One solution offered is the sound-absorbing housing shown in Figure 7-12.

The engines of the smallest generating plants are started with the pull cord long familiar on outboards and lawn mowers. The larger plants incorporate electric self-starting by providing a winding on the generator which enables it to act as a starting motor. To avoid this electrical manufacturing complication, some generating plants merely rely on standard starting motors. The best of these

Figure 7-12: A sound-absorbing cover like this one can muffle generating plant noise. (Credit—Onan Marine)

latter units offer automatic starting; turning on any electric appliance, even a small lamp, starts the generating plant and keeps it going as long as there is a demand. The most sophisticated installations have automatic transfer switches which prevent interference between the shipboard generator and the dockside power should an attempt be made to activate the two simultaneously.

Manufacturers recommend that the generating plant be installed in the same compartment with the propulsion engines. This space has been fireproofed to some extent and is reasonably well supplied with the necessary air. Furthermore, this is the heart of the boat's electrical system and all wiring radiates from there. This does *not* apply to the very small air-cooled units that have an integral gasoline tank; the location of these is restricted to weather decks.

Where the generating plant is supplied by fuel from the main tank, this should be by separate line. Placing a tee in an existing fuel line to the propulsion engines is not recommended; it could lead to a tug-of-war for fuel.

Primary Batteries

A skipper's life afloat is bound up with his storage (secondary) battery; nevertheless, he is often dependent upon *primary* batteries, for instance, in his flashlight or his transistor radio. These so-called dry batteries are not really dry because a completely dry battery is a dead battery. Moisture must exist in an electrolyte to make it operative. Of course this can be sealed hermetically in the container, hence the description as dry. The inside of a dry battery is exposed in Figure 7-13.

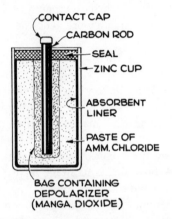

Figure 7-13: The "dry" cell (a primary battery) is not really dry but moist inside its seal. (If it were totally dry it would be dead.) A primary cell functions until its active material is exhausted; it cannot be recharged.

The electrical energy available from a dry cell is the transformation of the chemical energy set free when the electrolyte attacks the zinc. The voltage at the terminals is approximately 1½ volts and remains fairly steady until the cell's demise. As with secondary cells, size does not affect voltage but only current delivering ability.

Series and Parallel Circuits

Every device connected into an electric circuit is hooked up either in series or in parallel—and it is easy to determine which. A series connection resembles the links of a chain. A parallel connection is similar to the rungs of a ladder. Figure 7-14 shows both.

The choice of series or parallel is always governed by the technical dictum of fitting the load to the supply; it is never the result of a mere whim. The four 12-volt bulbs in the sketch require a 48-volt supply for the series connection but only a 12-volt supply for parallel. Power is neither saved nor lost in either arrangement; it remains

at 48 watts.

The rule is this: For a series connection, the voltages add but the amperes do not; for a parallel connection, the amperes add but the voltages do not. The drawback of the series connection is that when one lamp goes out they all go out—and anyone who has ever used the old-style Christmas tree lights remembers the attendant frustration.

The most ubiquitous series connection aboard is that of the storage battery. Its cells are tied together in this

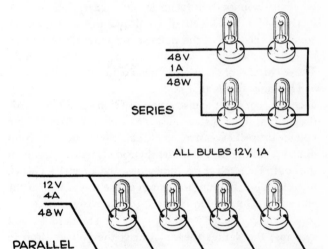

Figure 7-14: Whether in series or in parallel, the power required for each bulb and the total power needed remain unchanged.

manner in order to build up the desired boat voltage. Batteries could also be connected in parallel in order to boost their ampere capacity but this is not recommended because of inherent cell peculiarities.

Wiring Practices Aboard

Good, safe wiring aboard any boat must meet three cardinal specifications: (1) the cross section of the wire must be large enough to carry the required current without objectionable voltage drop; (2) the insulation of the wire must be able to withstand the line voltage under the particular environmental conditions; (3) the fastening of the wire in its place must be mechanically strong enough to resist vibration and other forces and its location must avoid dangerous areas. These requirements seem stringent and yet they are no more than what a skilled mechanic would employ instinctively.

WIRE SIZES.

Copper wire sizes are expressed by numbers in the American B&S wire gauge; the larger the number, the thinner the wire. Thus, #0000 is very thick (almost a rod) and #60 is very thin (like a human hair). The diameter of the wire is measured in mils, each mil being equal to 1/1000 of an inch. The approximate area of the wire, which is the important factor in current carrying, is given in circular mils. The circular mil quantity is derived by squaring the mils in the diameter; a wire 10 mils in diameter, for instance, has an area of 100 circular mils. These correlations are all tabulated in Figure 7-15.

The table shows that copper wire has a certain resistance per foot and the discussion of Ohm's Law (page 167) proves that this resistance leads to a voltage drop. Such a voltage drop, if excessive, would cause lamp bulbs to burn dim and motors to stall under their loads with consequent burnout. To avoid these difficulties, the wire size chosen must take into account the length of the run as well as the amperage. The table in Figure 7-16 removes the necessity for calculation when working with the standard 12-volt systems; the figures therein restrict the voltage drop to 3 percent, a figure most equipment can live with. Cutting the allowable length of run in half would adapt the table to 6 volts; doubling the length would take care of 24 volts, and so forth.

Solid copper wire is frowned upon for powerboat wiring because of the presumed danger of its rupture by vibration. This admittedly is slicing the meat very thin because any vibration bad enough to break the husky copper wire would probably destroy the hull first. But this is the Coast Guard view and therefore had best be heeded. Only stranded copper wire should be employed for wiring the boat.

Stranded copper wire is flexible because it substitutes many thin wires for the original single thick wire. The current-carrying ability is maintained by having the combined areas of the thin wires equal or exceed the area of the solid wire they replace. The individual strands are kept as thin as possible for the sake of flexibility and their number increases with the gauge of the conductor. For instance, a #14 B&S flexible conductor contains 19 strands while a #0000 is made up of 418 strands.

Wires smaller than #14 gauge should not be found on a properly wired sailboat or powerboat. The only exception is on boats large enough to require the use of intercoms; these instruments may be connected together with rubber or thermoplastic-covered #16 wire. Since the currents and voltages in an intercom system are minimal, this lightening of the rules does not infringe safety. The commercial "bell wire," with its wrapping of waxed cotton, used on shore for intercom work is not permissible afloat, however.

WIRE INSULATION.

The purpose of insulation is to keep the current in the wire and prevent it from leaking to adjoining surfaces. To accomplish this with a margin of safety the insulation must be able to withstand many times the voltage actually being carried by the circuit. More than that, wire insulation aboard a boat must maintain its isolating ability despite moisture and salt atmosphere.

The basic commercial insulating materials are rubber and thermoplastic compounds. The various chemical formulations of these materials determine their moisture- and heat-resisting qualities. Figure 7-17 lists all acceptable combinations, gives their commercial identifying code letters, and states the service for which they are permitted.

The use of multiple conductor cables instead of single wires is permitted with some restrictions. The restrictions apply to the armoring and sheathing of the cable; in this connection, "armor" refers to the outer protective coating and "sheath" to the underlying electrical shield.

Cables that are sheathed with lead but carry no protective armor over this should not be used. Neither should cables whose armor consists of spiral-wound, flat metal stripping. A lead sheath cable whose outer armor is a metallic basket weave is acceptable, however.

The Coast Guard establishes 50 volts as its dividing point for insulation requirements; these are less stringent below that voltage and more stringent above. Generally the only circuits aboard most small boats that carry more than 50 volts are those which distribute the shoreside power at 120 volts or self-generated power at the same voltage. Cables carrying these higher voltages should be sheathed and armored and, where the location is prone to moisture, the armor should be bronze or aluminum. The overall specification governing all these wires is "suitable for marine use."

Wire Size A.W.G. (B&S)	Diam. in Mils	Circular Mil Area	Turns per Linear Inch			Cont.-duty current single wire in open air	Cont.-duty current wires or cables in conduits or bundles	Feet per Pound, Bare	Ohms per 1000 ft. 25° C.	Current Carrying Capacity at 700 C.M. per Amp.	Diam. in mm.
			Enamel	S.C.E.	D.C.C.						
8	128.5	16510	7.6	—	7.1	73	46	20.01	.6405	23.6	3.264
10	101.9	10380	9.6	9.1	8.9	55	33	31.82	1.018	14.8	2.588
12	80.8	6530	12.0	11.3	10.9	41	23	50.59	1.619	9.33	2.053
14	64.1	4107	15.0	14.0	13.8	32	17	80.44	2.575	5.87	1.628
16	50.8	2583	18.9	17.3	16.4	22	13	127.9	4.094	3.69	1.291
18	40.3	1624	23.6	21.2	19.8	16	10	203.4	6.510	2.32	1.024
20	32.0	1022	29.4	25.8	23.8	11	7.5	323.4	10.35	1.46	.8118
22	25.3	643	37.0	31.3	30.0	—	5	514.2	16.46	.918	.6438
24	20.1	404	46.3	37.6	35.6	—	—	817.7	26.17	.577	.5106
26	15.9	254	58.0	46.1	41.8	—	—	1300	41.62	.363	.4049
28	12.6	160	72.7	54.6	48.5	—	—	2067	66.17	.228	.3211
30	10.0	101	90.5	64.1	55.5	—	—	3287	105.2	.144	.2546
32	8.0	63	113	74.1	62.6	—	—	5227	167.3	.090	.2019
34	6.3	40	143	86.2	70.0	—	—	8310	266.0	.057	.1601
36	5.0	25	175	103.1	77.0	—	—	13210	423.0	.036	.1270
38	4.0	16	224	116.3	83.6	—	—	21010	672.6	.022	.1007
40	3.1	10	282	131.6	89.7	—	—	33410	1069	.014	.0799

Figure 7-15: All the pertinent electrical characteristics of copper wire are shown in this table. (A "mil" is 1/1000th of one inch.)

Temperature is an important factor in the insulating ability of an insulating material. An insulation that performs satisfactorily at a normal temperature may break down at the same voltage when the temperature is raised. It is thus wise to consider carefully the heat-resisting characteristics of the insulation on any wire that is to be run close to the engine or other hot body.

Perfectly dry wood is a good insulator but the wood in the hull of a boat in service is far from dry. If the service is in salt water, it is a fair assumption that the wood also contains minute quantities of salt. The combination of water and salt (an electrolyte) changes the wood from an insulator to a conductor and robs it of its original ability to protect electric circuits.

WIRING FASTENINGS.

The basic rule for running electric wires around a small boat is to keep them above the bilge and to fasten them every 14 inches. Elevating the wires keeps them out of the water that is likely to accumulate in the bilge and also removes them from dangerous vapors which often seep there.

The wires must be protected at every point where they are liable to mechanical damage, such as doors, hatches, or other movable structures. This protection may take the form of removable metal coverings, preferably grounded. A covering that takes the form of a pipe or other shape which could entrap moisture must have drain holes. Wherever wires run through a watertight bulkhead, special through-fittings must be used which maintain the watertightness.

The common, double-pointed U staples, so familiar ashore, should not be employed on any vessels. It is much too easy to injure the wire's insulation with these staples and thus provide a weakened point which eventually becomes a short circuit. Metal clamps of the proper width and without sharp edges are the preferred wire holders. Plastic clamps may also be used, but it should be borne in mind that these may fail in a fire, drop the wires, and present an additional hazard.

Any wire carrying current has about itself a magnetic field. Such magnetism is detrimental to the accuracy of any nearby compass. Obviously, therefore, all wiring should be kept away from the compass; if proximity cannot be avoided, the wires should be twisted to cancel their magnetic fields and thus their magnetic effects.

Two wires may be spliced together with an insulated, UL (Underwriters Laboratory)-approved wire connector but soldering is preferable. The completed joint must be

Stranded Conductors For 12 Volt Circuits

3% Voltage Drop

Wire Size S.A.E.	20	18	16	14	12	10	8	6	4
Stranding	7x28	16x30	19x29	19x27	19x25	19x23	19x21	49x23	49x21
Circular Mil Area	1094	1568	2340	3777	5947	9443	15105	24354	38430
Circuit Current in AMPS	MAXIMUM LENGTH OF CONDUCTOR IN FEET FROM POWER SOURCE TO LOAD AND RETURN.								
1.	36.4	52.3	78.0						
2.	18.2	26.1	39.0	63.0	99.0				
3.	12.2	17.4	26.0	42.0	66.0				
4.	9.1	13.1	19.5	31.5	49.5	78.8			
5.	7.3	10.4	15.6	25.2	39.6	63.0			
6.	6.1	8.7	13.0	21.0	33.0	52.5	83.8		
7.	5.2	7.4	11.1	18.0	28.2	45.0	72.0		
8.		6.5	9.8	15.8	24.8	39.4	63.0		
9.		5.8	8.6	14.0	22.0	35.0	56.0	90.0	
10.		5.2	7.8	12.6	19.8	31.5	50.4	81.3	
15.			5.2	8.4	13.2	21.0	33.6	54.1	85.5
20.				6.3	9.9	15.8	25.1	40.6	63.4
30.					6.6	10.5	16.8	27.1	42.7
40.						7.9	12.6	20.2	32.0
50.						6.3	10.1	16.2	25.6
55.							9.2	14.7	23.3
60.								13.5	21.4
75.								10.8	17.1
90.									14.2

Figure 7-16: No calculations are needed to find the correct size wire on the basis of current drain and distance from source to load.

insulated with tape or other means to provide insulation at least as good as that of the wires being joined. The ends of stranded conductors that are to be fastened to terminals should first be formed and soldered, unless a UL-approved pressure connector lug is used. (There is an apparent difference of opinion here between the insurance group and the Coast Guard, the former banning the soldered form and the latter approving it.) Figure 7-18 pictures the UL-approved connectors and also shows how insulating tape should be applied.

A method of twisting two wires together prior to soldering is shown in Figure 7-19. This joint makes excellent electrical contact and also maintains good mechanical strength. It is a real "oldie," known to old-time electricians as the Western Union splice, but no newer wrinkle has yet surpassed it for simplicity and effectiveness. As shown, the bared wires are twisted about each other three or four times and then the ends are coiled tightly about the opposite wire. This splice is soldered easily but is also highly serviceable for temporary connections that will not be soldered.

Since the danger of corrosion and galvanic action is always present on a boat (see Chapter 22) all connectors, lugs, and other parts that are in contact with the copper wire must be of compatible metal. Copper is best, iron or steel worst.

COLOR CODING.

Electric wire is available with insulation of many colors which makes possible a system of color coding that identifies circuits at a glance. One such scheme is tabulated in Figure 7-20. Wiring already in place can be marked to conform to this system by tags bearing numbers that correspond to the colors. Specific circuits can be picked out

CONDUCTORS AND APPLICATIONS

TYPE	INSULATION	USE
RW (NEC)	Moisture resistant Rubber with Oil resistant Neoprene Jacket	General use except machinery spaces
RH (NEC)	Heat resistant Rubber with Oil resistant Neoprene Jacket	General use
RHW (NEC)	Moisture and Heat resistant Rubber with Oil resistant Neoprene Jacket	General use
TW (NEC)	Moisture resistant Thermoplastic Flame Retardant	General use except machinery spaces
THW (NEC)	Moisture and Heat resistant Thermoplastic Flame Retardant	General use
GPT (SAE)	General Purpose, Thermoplastic Insulated, Braidless	General use except machinery spaces
HDT (SAE)	Heavy Duty Thermoplastic Insulated, Braidless	General use
GPB (SAE)	General Purpose, Rubber or Thermoplastic Insulated, Single Braid	General use except machinery spaces
HDB (SAE)	Heavy Duty, Rubber or Thermoplastic Insulated, Single Braid	General use
HDB-X (SAE)	Extra Heavy Duty, Rubber or Thermoplastic Insulated, Double Braid	General use
SGT (SAE)	Starter or Ground, Thermoplastic Insulated, Braidless	General use
SGR (SAE)	Starter or Ground, Rubber or Synthetic Insulated, Braidless	General use
STS (SAE)	Standard Duty, Thermosetting Insulation, Braidless	General use except machinery spaces
HTS (SAE)	Heavy Duty, Thermosetting Insulation, Braidless	General use

Figure 7-17: This table identifies the code of each wire type with details of its insulation and suggestions for its safe use.

for inspection or trouble-shooting merely by looking for certain colors or numbers. This could be a heaven-sent convenience on that dreaded day when something goes haywire far from shore with a sea running.

Devices of widely different current ratings are normally fed by wires of different diameters. This, together with the code, further narrows the choice when seeking out a particular circuit. (The coding is not applied to shoreside 120-volt circuits, which on most boats are entirely separate.)

Wiring Diagrams

The negative lead in a negative ground system should *never* be broken for any fuse or any switch but must remain continuous. All fusing and switching is done in the positive lines from the battery. This guarantees that no device or appliance will have any potential difference

to ground after it is turned off, and this is a basic safety requirement.

The wiring diagram in Figure 7-21 gives all the electrical connections for a sail- or powerboat. The master battery switch, as close to the battery as possible, is an important safety consideration because opening it kills all juice in the entire system. The ideal location is outside the engine and battery space, but on a small boat this is not always possible.

Under certain conditions, if the master battery switch opened accidentally while the engine was running, serious damage or destruction could result for the generator or alternator. To avert this, the master switch should also open the field circuit of the generator or alternator, thus killing its charging ability and protecting it; this feature is also shown in the diagram. The master switch should be able to carry the total electrical load of the boat, includ-

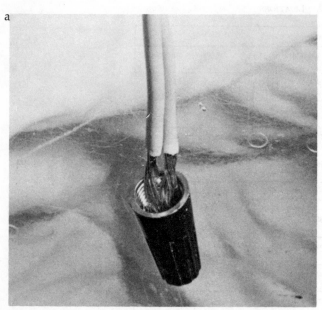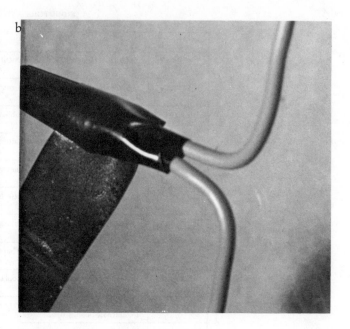

Figure 7-18: (a) Wire ends inserted in connector. (b) Rubber tape (optional) completes the connection and makes it weatherproof.

ing the starter, and this puts it into the heavy category. An open-knife switch is allowable if the location is not prone to hazardous vapors.

A switch which may be located anywhere, vapors or no, is shown in Figure 7-22. This device is explosion-proof and can handle up to 300 amperes. In addition to disconnecting the batteries entirely, as required for safety, it performs several other convenience functions. For instance, with two batteries aboard, either may be used separately or both may be tied together to help start a recalcitrant engine. Lights and other equipment may also be switched from one to the other or to both batteries together.

Some switches are available on the market that permit the two storage batteries to be connected in series for starting the engine, thus doubling the voltage. This doubled voltage is applied to the starter only (which can take it for a few moments) and not to the other electrical units aboard (which would burn out). This stunt approximately quadruples the starter's power and gives engines a whirl that they find hard to resist. Immediately after starting, the connections go back to standard.

An examination of the wiring diagrams shows that the

ammeter is connected into the main line of the battery so that it can indicate what goes in (charge) and what goes out (discharge). The standard procedure is to use a zero-center meter and let the pointer swing left for discharge and right for charge. When charging and discharging are occurring simultaneously, as with the engines running and lights or other appliances turned on, the ammeter subtracts and indicates the net current flow to or from the battery.

Heavy current drawing units, such as horns and starters, are not routed through the ammeter. These are in use only intermittently and normally do not have much effect on battery condition. Furthermore, an ammeter whose scale is adequate for indicating such large amperages would not be sensitive to the light currents taken by lamps and similar accessories.

WESTERN UNION SPLICE

Figure 7-19: The "Western Union splice" is a time-honored method of joining wires. It is a mechanically strong and electrically good connection, with or without solder.

Black	All ungrounded current carrying conductors	All return circuits
Red	All unprotected wires from battery and high-draw equipment such as spotlights, horns, lighters, etc.	Plus side of battery to fuse or protective devices, distribution panel and to high-draw equipment
Dk. Green	Non-current carrying ground conductors	Bonding system and hull ground plate
White	Navigation lights	Fuse or switch to lights
Dk. Blue	Cabin & panel lights	Do
Yellow	Spotlight, docking lights	Do
Brown	Pumps	Fuse or switch to pumps
Orange	Accessory common feeds, convenience outlets	Distribution panel to accessory switches
Purple	Instrumentation common feed	Distribution panel to electric instruments
Pink	Fuel level indicators	Fuse or switch to gauge
Lt. Green	Ventilation blowers	Fuse or switch to blowers

Figure 7-20: Inspection and trouble-shooting are greatly facilitated by adhering to color designations listed above. Circuit identification is easy with color-coded wiring.

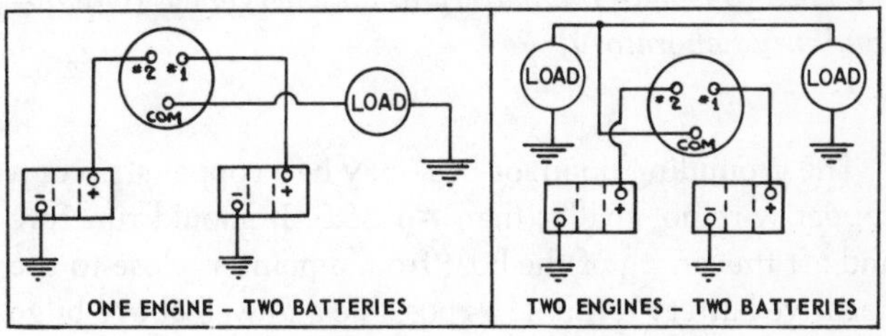

Figure 7-21: This vapor-proof, waterproof switch (a) can handle the full battery output (even to the starting motor) as well as switch from one battery to another; more importantly, it provides complete disconnection of the battery when the boat is unattended. (Note wiring diagram (b).) (Credit—Cole-Hersee Co.)

Ground Systems

Automobiles are wired with a one-wire grounded system; the wires feed the positive or "hot" side of each circuit and the negative return is through the chassis or "ground." Skippers who own metal-hulled boats may feel that they, too, could employ a similar one-wire scheme. It is *not* recommended.

It is all right, even advisable, to use the metal hull as a ground for everything electrical, including the radio, but the hull should *not* be a current carrier. All negative returns should be by actual insulated conductors. The bonds to the hull should merely maintain all portions of the circuit at ground potential but carry no current at all. (Under the color-coding system, these bonding wires would have green insulation.)

The fact that the starter, generator, and ignition circuits are grounded to the engine block forecloses any other choice but a grounded one, even for a wooden boat. The ideal would be a completely ungrounded, two-wire system. In such a wiring plan the connection from radio transmitter to the ground plate would be through a high-voltage capacitor and not by direct wire.

Figure 7-22: An explosion-proof switch which can handle heavy currents safely (including the starter current) can be used to isolate the battery in an emergency. (Credit—Sudbury Laboratory)

The grounding bond, or bus, may be a copper strip or a copper wire no smaller than #6 B&S. It should run fore and aft the length of the boat from a point as close to the negative battery terminal as possible and well above bilge contamination. A schematic arrangement is shown in Figure 7-23. Everything aboard that requires grounding—tanks, appliance covers, radio ground plates, and the engine block—should be connected to this bus with adequate wire, preferably green.

The safety test for a proper system is made with a sensitive meter, able to read in millivolts. It should indicate no potential difference between the ground bus and the case or grounded terminal of any operating appliance. Voltage indication is a sign that the ground bus is carrying current. This is a malfunction that should be traced down and corrected.

Grounding the cabinets of all electronic equipment that

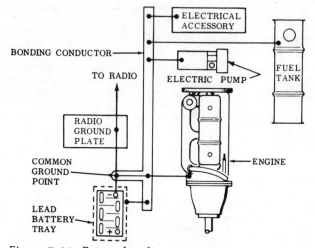

Figure 7-23: Proper bonding is a safety measure as well as a galvanic corrosion preventive. The main bonding conductor is a copper bus or a heavy copper wire; it should carry no current.

contains higher voltage (and most do) is a safety feature which prevents shock to personnel in the event of internal circuit trouble.

AC Voltage Regulation

Many devices are available for maintaining at a constant voltage the alternating current fed to radars, TV sets, and other sensitive equipment, even though the source of the AC fluctuates considerably. Such fluctuations could be caused by variations in the speed of the generating sets when the AC is manufactured abroad. At dockside it could result from too many customers on the lines of ill-equipped marinas.

These regulators fall into three types: vacuum tube or transistor, saturated transformer, and electromechanical. The first two are constructed without moving parts. The third is really a combination of the first two with a mechanical control added. All commercial regulators maintain the set voltage with a very small percentage of overshoot or undershoot.

AC Isolation

The ideal alternating-current installation on board is a completely separate system having no *direct* connection with the marina wiring that provides the energy. The connection is entirely inductive and not by wire. Such non-metallic connection is provided by an isolation transformer. Remember that in a transformer the primary (shore) and the secondary (boat) are connected only by magnetism.

Isolation transformers are relatively inexpensive, occupy little space, and have no moving parts. They thus can be relegated to space not usable for other purposes.

An isolation transformer eliminates the possibility of a "wrong polarity" connection to shore. It reduces one source of galvanic corrosion danger.

Shore Connections

The system for bringing shore electric power aboard the boat has been standardized so that the same approved components will function almost everywhere the craft is docked. The days when the plug and cord off an old floor lamp served as the connection are gone except on the oldest scows and at the most decrepit marinas.

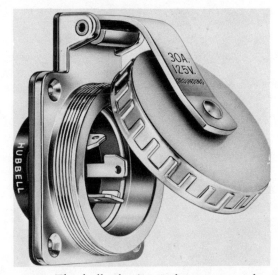

Figure 7-24: This hull inlet fixture has a watertight cover and accepts plugs intended for its current rating. The rating is stamped on the cover and is indicated by the prong configuration. (Credit—Harvey, Hubbell, Inc.)

Pictured in Figure 7-24 is a hull inlet fixture of a type found as standard equipment on most new boats. It is a three-wire system that provides a ground in addition to the neutral and hot lines. It has a twist-locking feature that prevents cable pullout and a waterproof screw cover for protection when not in use. The official capacity in amperes of each fixture is stamped on the cover.

Today, 30 amperes is considered a minimum capacity for a boat-to-shore line; in earlier days, the figure was 15 amperes. Even 30 amperes is not too generous an allowance when you consider the power-hungry nature of most appliances. A small-space heater will easily soak up 15 amperes and a toaster thinks nothing of taking 10.

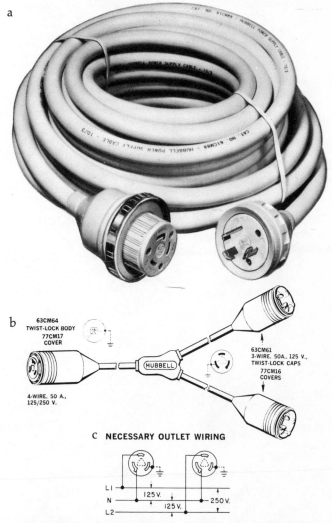

Figure 7-25: The heavy-duty cable (a) fits standard boat and pier fixtures designed for its ampere rating. A siamese connector (b) also is shown. A diagram of outlet wiring (c) also is given. (Credit—Harvey, Hubbell, Inc.)

The supply cable that fits into the hull inlet connection is shown in Figure 7-25. The hook-shaped slots that are part of the nonslipout design can be seen. The cable itself is covered heavily with insulation, to resist the normally strenuous usage.

Most small boats take 120-volt alternating current and this is available on the pier. Many very big boats, however, require a 240-volt supply, which may not be so easy to come by. Often 240 volts can be jury-rigged with a special Siamese connector that taps both sides of a three-wire shore line through two receptacles. Remember the cautions on voltage matching given earlier in this chapter.

8 Electronic Equipment

M OST boatmen are overawed and mystified by electronics. This need not be so. Electronics is *not* black magic that only the seventh son of a seventh son can comprehend.

No electronic circuit, no matter how complicated, contains more than five *different* kinds of units, or building blocks. There may be many or few of each kind, but there are never more than five kinds. Consequently, each circuit can be broken down for analysis on the basis of what each unit does. This removes some of the fog and makes understanding easier.

The five basic units from which all electronic circuits are assembled are: resistors, capacitors, inductors, vacuum tubes, and transistors. Don't let the names intimidate you. How and why each does what it does can be explained without difficulty, and without mathematics, so that it becomes as clear as the course you're steering. Perhaps a few liberties will be taken with the basic concepts of physics but only when they improve clarity with no detriment to the fundamental truths.

Examination of electronic circuits shows that the basic building-block units are generally found connected together in small combinations. Each individual unit of the combination contributes to a special overall result. You might think of the members of an orchestra; they play individual notes that blend into a complex tone. The ability to recognize these combinations and what they do is one of the milestones on the road to familiarity with electronic devices.

Resistors

If you have ever looked into a radio chassis, you can recall the multitude of little cylinders, each about the diameter of a soda straw and about half an inch long, encircled by colored bands and having a wire protruding from each end. These are the resistors. The colored bands are not decorations; they classify the resistors.

If you remember that resistors resist (reduce) the flow of electric current, the job of explanation is more than half done. A water pipeline into which a short length of very narrow tubing has been set could be an analogy. The restriction could be the "resistor" (as in Figure 8-1) and it can easily be seen how the flow of water would be reduced. How great the reduction is would depend upon the relative sizes of pipe and tube, in other words, upon

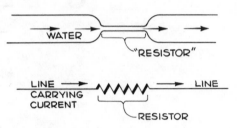

Figure 8-1: The resistor acts on the flow of electric current like a restricted pipe cuts down water flow. The symbol for a resistor is the zigzag shown.

the "value" of this resistor.

Actual resistors do not depend upon their small size or thin diameter to reduce the current flow. Their restrictive ability arises out of the material from which they are made. Some materials impede the passage of electric currents more than others—they have greater resistance. Carbon, for instance, has much greater specific resistance than silver.

To explain why some materials carry electric current with less facility than others, we must take a quick glance into the world of physics. Everyone knows by now that all materials are composed of atoms and that atoms in turn have electrons. Some materials, mostly the nonmetals, hold their electrons tightly and do not permit them to move about. By contrast, the metals allow their electrons to move freely under an electric influence. This unseen movement and flow of electrons is actually what we recognize as an electric current.

This concept of free and restricted electron movement makes possible the division of substances into two broad classes: the conductors of electricity (many free electrons) and the non-conductors or insulators of electricity (closely held electrons). Generally, metals conduct and nonmetals insulate. Recently an intermediate class was established whose properties are midway between the conductors and the insulators; these are the semi-conductors that make transistors possible.

The degree of electron freedom differs for various metals and this is called their resistivity. As shown in Figure 8-2, silver allows its electrons the greatest freedom and is therefore the best conductor. Lead is twelve times stricter with its electrons and therefore offers twelve times

Relative Electrical Conductivity of Metals at Ordinary Temperatures

(Based on Copper as 100)

Aluminum (2S; pure)	59	Iron (cast)	2–12
Aluminum (alloys):		Iron (wrought)	11.4
Soft-annealed	45–50	Lead	7
Heat-treated	30–45	Manganin	3.7
Brass	28	Mercury	1.66
Cadmium	19	Molybdenum	33.2
Chromium	55	Monel	4
Climax	1.83	Nichrome	1.45
Cobalt	16.3	Nickel	12–16
Constantin	3.24	Phosphor Bronze . . .	36
Copper (hard drawn) .	89.5	Platinum	15
Copper (annealed) . . .	100	Silver	106
Everdur	6	Steel	3–15
German Silver (18%)	5.3	Tin	13
Gold	65	Tungsten	28.9
Iron (pure)	17.7	Zinc	28.2

Figure 8-2: Metals vary in their ability to conduct electricity because some offer greater resistance to current flow than others. Silver is the best conductor, as the table shows.

the resistance to current flow. From this it follows, theoretically, that resistors could be made of lead; actually, they are composed of graphite, which has an even greater resistivity and thereby permits smaller size. Many large resistors are found with nichrome wire and a look at the table explains this also.

The energy apparently lost when an electric current is restricted by a resistor is turned into heat. The resistor must be of a shape and size to dissipate this heat or else it will quickly be destroyed. Hence the tiny resistors where the current flow is infinitesimal and the progressively larger ones as the current in the circuit is increased.

RESISTOR RATINGS.

Resistors are rated in ohms; the more ohms, the higher the resistance and the greater the obstruction to current flow. The letter *K* is often added to mean "thousand" and the letter *M* (or Meg) to indicate "million." Thus, three resistors marked on a diagram as 10 and 10K and 10M respectively would have individual resistances of 10 ohms, 10,000 ohms, and 10 million ohms.

Resistors are also rated in watts. This is a measure of the amount of heat the resistor can dissipate safely. The wattage rating is commensurable with the bulk of the resistor; the more watts, the heftier. (The tiny resistors seen most often in home radios are rated 1/4 watt.)

RESISTOR CONNECTIONS.

When several resistors are connected together, their

joining can be in either of two ways: series or parallel. Both are shown in Figure 8-3. In the series system, the tail of one is joined to the head of the next, elephant-line fashion. The parallel connection sets the resistors together, similar to the rungs of a ladder.

The series connection *increases* the total resistance. The parallel connection *decreases* the total resistance. These two facts are borne out by the numerical values in the

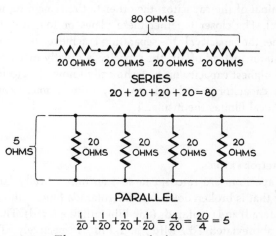

Figure 8-3: The manner in which resistors are connected determines their effect on current flow. A series connection increases the total resistance while a parallel connection reduces it.

illustration. The total series resistance is the simple sum of all the resistors. The total parallel resistance is the reciprocal of the sum of the reciprocals. (Recalling school arithmetic will convince you that this is not as difficult as it sounds.)

Capacitors

After resistors, the next most numerous item found in electronic circuits is the capacitor. The capacitor has the ability to store an electric charge. (It should not be confused with a storage battery which stores chemical energy and only indirectly an electric charge.) Whether a capacitor is miniature or large, it always has the same rudimentary construction: two or more metal plates or metal foils separated from each other by air or some other insulator.

Some very small capacitors are made in forms that closely resemble resistors and confusion, unfortunately, could result for even an experienced technician. Others are small plastic containers with two wires protruding. Still others are encased in short lengths of paper tubing and look like shotgun shells that have sprouted connecting wires. The largest capacitors are sealed into metal boxes or cans. An example of an air-insulated capacitor is the interleaving type that tunes AM radios.

One series of plates or length of foil is connected to one terminal of the capacitor, the other to the remaining terminal. The closer together these plates or foils are, the higher the capacity. If the separation is achieved by a good insulator instead of air, the capacity is greatly increased. The highest capacity units, technically known as electrolytic capacitors, reach this goal by using a microscopic chemical film as the insulator.

CAPACITOR RATINGS.

Capacitors are rated in farads, an impractically large unit that is broken down into microfarads (one-millionth of a farad) and picofarads (one-billionth of a farad). These are abbreviated Fd., Mfd., and Pfd., respectively. The greater the number, the higher the capacity.

In addition, capacitors have a voltage rating. This indicates the highest voltage that may prevail in the circuit before the capacitor is in danger of breaking down. The breakdown occurs because the overvoltage punctures the insulator and renders it useless. In contrast to the comparatively short life of a storage battery, a capacitor can last "forever" and repeated charging and discharging in no way deteriorates it. Capacitors are marked similar to resistors, as Figure 8-4 explains.

CAPACITOR CONNECTIONS.

Capacitors also can be connected either in series or in parallel. The results are directly opposite to what happens with resistors, however. Connecting capacitors in parallel *increases* the total capacity Connecting capacitors in series *decreases* the total capacity. Figure 8-5 substantiates this.

Capacitors are often connected into a circuit in order to separate alternating currents from direct currents. A capacitor acts as a full stop to a *direct* current; it permits an *alternating* current to flow through. (A squeamish physics student may object to the idea of "flowing through" as slightly oversimplified but it conveys the general idea.)

Color	A-B Signi-ficant Figure	C Dec-imal Multi-plier	More than 10 μμf. (in %)	Less than 10 μμf. (in μμf.)	Temp. Coeff. p.p.m. /deg. C.
			Capacitance Tolerance		
Black	0	1	± 20	2.0	0
Brown	1	10	± 1		—30
Red	2	100	± 2		—80
Orange	3	1000			—150
Yellow	4				—220
Green	5		± 5	0.5	—330
Blue	6				—470
Violet	7				—750
Gray	8	0.01		0.25	30
White	9	0.1	± 10	1.0	500

Figure 8-4: The colored bands which evaluate small capacitors are deciphered according to the table above.

Inductors

Chapter 7 showed that a magnetic field is created about a wire when current flows through it. If the wire is wound into a coil, the effect is multiplied and we have an inductor, in this case an air-core inductor. Inserting iron into the center of the coil still farther increases the magnetic effect and the result is an iron-core inductor. If two inductors are placed in magnetic relationship to each other, a transformer is formed, either air-core or iron-core. All this is depicted in Figure 8-6.

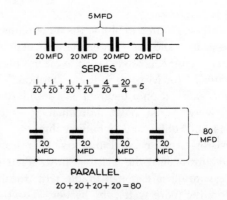

Figure 8-5: Capacitors can be connected in series or in parallel. The rule is the opposite of that for resistors: the series connection reduces the capacity while the parallel connection increases capacity.

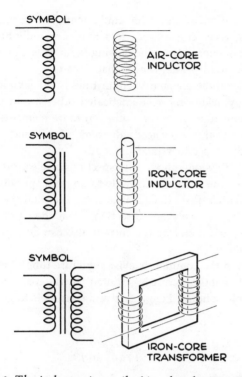

Figure 8-6: *The inductor is a coil of insulated wire with or without an iron core. Two such coils form a transformer. Remember that transformers operate only on alternating current.*

The most likely air-core inductors aboard are the helix-like coils in the radio telephone transmitter. Here they serve as tuning elements to get the transmission onto the correct frequency. The ignition coil on the gasoline propulsion engine is the most probable iron-core transformer familiar to the skipper.

INDUCTOR RATINGS.

An inductor is rated by its inductance; the more turns of wire, the more inductance. The unit of inductance is the henry. A millihenry is one-thousandth of a henry and a microhenry is one-millionth of a henry.

The inductors found in power supplies and battery-charging panels are usually of the henry sizes while those in radio receiver and transmitter-tuning circuits are in the millihenry and microhenry regions. Inductors are sometimes named for their uses in an electronic circuit. Thus we have "choke coils," "peaking coils," "tank coils," and "tuning coils," among others.

INDUCTOR CONNECTIONS.

It should not now be surprising that inductors also can be connected in series or in parallel. Inductors follow the style of resistors in the effects of these connections.

Placing inductors in series *increases* the total inductance. Connecting inductors in parallel *decreases* the total inductance. Figure 8-7 portrays this graphically.

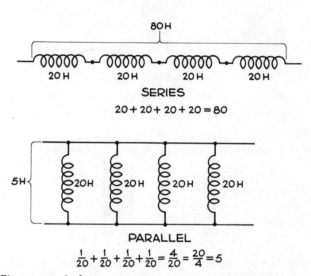

Figure 8-7: *Inductors in series increase inductance and in parallel decrease inductance; they follow the same rule as resistors.*

Vacuum Tubes

In England, vacuum tubes are called valves, a very descriptive name. In most cases, the action of a vacuum tube is exactly like that of a valve: A very small effort can control a much greater force. An analogy might be the slight pressure on the accelerator pedal of an automobile which controls many horsepower. In this case the linkage is mechanical; in the vacuum tube, the "linkage" is an invisible flow of electrons.

In its simplest form, a vacuum tube capable of valving or amplifying consists of three elements sealed in an evacuated bulb. These elements are the cathode, the grid, and the plate. The drawing in Figure 8-8 shows their relationship.

Another name for the vacuum tube is electron tube. This also is descriptive because its action is dependent entirely on the control of a flow of electrons. The cathode is the source of the electrons; it is heated electrically to a temperature high enough to cause electrons to "boil off" in a continuous flow. The electrons are made to travel to the plate because the plate is connected to the positive pole of the outside circuit. (Electrons, being negative, are

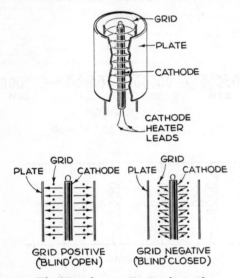

GRID

PLATE

CATHODE

CATHODE HEATER LEADS

PLATE   GRID   CATHODE   PLATE   GRID   CATHODE

GRID POSITIVE (BLIND OPEN)   GRID NEGATIVE (BLIND CLOSED)

Figure 8-8: The "inside story" of a three-element vacuum tube. The grid acts as an electronic "venetian blind" that cuts off electron flow or lets it through. (Of course the grid does not move; the action is purely electrostatic.)

strongly attracted to positive surfaces.) To get to the plate the electrons must pass through the grid—and this is the heart of the control action.

Imagine the grid to be a sort of electrostatic Venetian blind. When the grid has a positive potential, it is the equivalent of "open" and the electrons can sail through it to the plate without restraint. When the grid has a negative potential, the Venetian blind is "closed" and the electrons are completely blocked. The power necessary to put these potentials on the grid is negligible, yet the current and power in the electron flow can be heavy. There is your amplification—a small amount of power controlling a large amount of power.

It must be emphasized that nothing in the grid actually moves mechanically. All changes are invisible and electrical. The Venetian blind analogy is purely for simpler understanding.

The amplifying action of vacuum tubes is evident in

every piece of electronic equipment. The common home radio receiver picks up less than one-millionth of one watt of energy from the passing radio wave but the power at the loudspeaker can be many watts.

The three-element vacuum tube is the simplest in the family. Many more sophisticated tubes are in use; these contain four, five, six, and even more elements. But the action is always basically the same; if you understand the triode, you understand them all.

There is one important aspect of the electron flow that makes the vacuum tube able to do such specialized tasks as changing AC to DC. This is the fact that the electrons can flow in only one direction, from the cathode to the plate, and therefore the current also can flow in only one direction.

Even the common television picture tube is an electron tube. In it the picture is "painted" by the electrons striking the phosphorized front face and causing it to glow.

Transistors

Transistors are the latter-day marvels in the electronic world. They can do almost everything that vacuum tubes can do and they perform these tasks more efficiently and in much less space. They are cold performers, without need for the heated cathode of the tube. They have made tiny pocket radios possible and have gone on to miniaturize marine electronics.

Transistors, like vacuum tubes, depend upon electrons for their action. But in transistors the electrons move in solid materials and not in a vacuum, hence the designation "solid state." The materials that permit this specialized form of electron movement are few, principally silicon and germanium, and even they do this only after highly technical chemical treatment. They are the semi-conductors previously mentioned.

Transistors are of two general types: point contact and junction. The former were the original discovery and are now of historical interest only; the latter are a later and much more rugged development and the kind found in marine electronics.

Junction transistors are produced by making a sandwich of P type and N type germanium or silicon. The P and N conditions are achieved by various forms of chemical doping which create electron shortage and electron excess areas. These transistors are either PNP or NPN and the arrangement of the letters indicates the positions of the *P* and *N* materials in the sandwich. Figure 8-9 illustrates construction, but bear in mind that the actual internal assembly, the "sandwich," can almost fit on the head of a pin.

The electrical leads to the transistor are connected as shown and become the emitter, the base, and the collector. The approximately corresponding members in a vacuum tube would be cathode, grid, and plate, respectively, and there is a similarity in their functions. The transistor, too, is an amplifying device; very small amounts of power can control very large amounts of power.

The rudimentary comparison to the vacuum tube and the concept of the transistor as a valve will serve all the boatman's electronic needs. A complete explanation of the interior behavior of a transistor reaches up into the rarefied heights of atomic physics; it is an interesting study but not at all necessary for understanding the operation of a depth sounder, a radio telephone, or whatever.

It was stated earlier that transistor operation is devoid of heat. This is not strictly true, especially in the larger sizes that handle appreciable amounts of power. Heat is

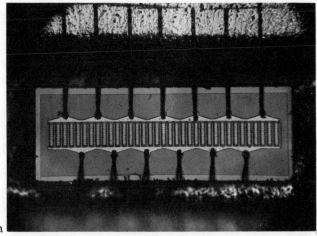

a

Figure 8-9: Transistors have revolutionized marine electronics: they are miniature, shock-resistant, reliable and consume minimal current. The stripline transistor (a) is a new development. Compare these transistors and integrated circuits (b) used in marine equipment with the coin to visualize the relative sizes. Overlay construction enables the transistor to handle greater power at high frequencies. (Credit—RCA Electronic Components)

developed, although it is not an intentional heat (such as the heated cathode of the vacuum tube) but rather an undesired heat resulting from current passing through a resistance. This heat could make the transistor self-destructive; it is therefore dissipated through the familiar ribbed aluminum "heat sinks."

One advantage of transistors in electronic equipment is their instant readiness to function when the switch is turned on. With vacuum tubes, time must be allowed for the heaters and cathodes to reach operating temperatures. Since transistors have no heaters, no such time lag exists with them. This means a great saving of battery current over such devices as vacuum tube radio transmitters which must "stand by" with tubes lit in order to be available at the touch of the microphone button.

The semi-conductor family also has its equivalent of the two-element vacuum tube. It, too, is called a diode and permits current flow in only one direction, hence its use to rectify alternating current to direct current for battery charging. The solid-state diode is not quite as perfect a one-way street for electric current as its vacuum-tube cousin; it permits a slight "leakage" current in the wrong direction. In most applications this does no harm because the leakage current is a tiny fraction of its forward capability. Solid-state diodes are found in many types of marine radio equipment and even in battery-charging alternators; they are the heart of most reverse polarity alarms.

Transformers

Two inductors in close relationship form a transformer. These transformers can take many shapes and sizes. In miniature transistor radios they could be housed in tiny one-quarter-inch-square metal cans while in husky commercial transmitters they could be heavy brutes weighing hundreds of pounds. The differences arise from the purposes for which they are intended and from the amounts of power which they must handle.

In Figure 8-6 (at bottom), one coil receives the input current and is called the primary. The other coil delivers the output current and is called the secondary. Either coil could be primary and the other secondary; the designation is determined by the manner in which it is connected into the circuit.

b

The output voltage bears approximately the same relationship to the input voltage as the number of turns of wire in the secondary bears to the number in the primary. (This explains the high-sparking voltage from the secondary of the ignition coil. The secondary has thousands of times more turns than the primary.)

Whether a transformer has an air core or an iron core is determined by the frequency of the alternating current it must handle. At high radio frequencies air is used, or sometimes a finely powdered iron. At low frequencies, such as the 60-cycle house current, iron is mandatory.

An important factor to remember about transformers is that the magnetic field created by the primary must be moving and must actually "cut" the secondary for output current to be induced. An alternating current provides this moving field while a direct current supplies only a steady magnetic condition. This is the reason why trans-

formers can not function on direct current and, if so connected, promptly burn up.

An examination of the diagram of a transformer reveals that there is no *electrical* connection between primary and secondary windings. Transformers can therefore be used to isolate two alternating current circuits from each other and to change their voltages. The step-up action of the ignition coil is countered by the transformers commonly seen on street poles which step-down the high-line voltage to the usual 120-volt, 60-cycle house current.

Frequency

Alternating current was mentioned in Chapter 7 and described as a condition in which each wire is alternately positive and then negative in polarity. The complete swing from zero to maximum positive, back to zero, then to

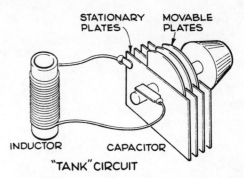

Figure 8-10: *The basic "tank" circuit. Turning the capacitor knob changes the resonant frequency; in other words, tunes the circuit.*

maximum negative, and finally back to zero constitutes one cycle. The number of such cycles per second is the frequency of the alternating current. For ease in expression, 1000 cycles becomes a kilocycle (Kcs.) and one million cycles is a megacycle (Mcs.) The alternating current available at home and from the marina outlets is supplied at a frequency of 60 cycles per second.

Recently, some scientific busybodies decided that Heinrich Herz, the discoverer of radio waves, needed commemoration. They made his name the unit of frequency in place of the term "cycles per second." Thus we have monstrosities like "kiloherz" (Khz.) to supplant kilocycle, "Megaherz" (Mhz.) in place of megacycle, and similar affectations in the latest technical literature.

This chapter retains the time-tested designation "cycle" in its explanations because it is easier for the boatman and every layman to understand.

Resonance

Everyone is familiar with tuning a radio set to get a desired program. What he really is doing is bringing the circuits of his receiver into resonance with the frequency of the transmitting station. This phenomenon is possible because of the singular property that an inductor and a capacitor exhibit when they are connected together into what the technicians call a tank circuit.

The simplicity of the tank circuit can be seen from the diagram in Figure 8-10. The arrangement would be the same for the tiny components in the tuner of a transistor radio or the huge tank of a major broadcast transmitter. Varying the inductance of the inductor or changing the capacity of the capacitor "tunes" the tank and thereby brings it into resonance at various frequencies.

Filter Circuits

It is often desirable to eliminate certain frequencies from the signals that are being passed through electronic equipment. Sometimes it is even legally mandatory: The Federal Communications Commission requires that all the highest pitches in the human voice (those above 3000 cycles per second) be eliminated from marine radio telephone transmissions. This reduces congestion and interference without reducing intelligibility.

The combinations of basic units that can remove undesired portions of the frequency spectrum are called filter circuits. They are generally interconnections of resistors and capacitors, although an inductor may be added to sharpen the action. Filters can be designed to pass only the lower frequencies or only the higher frequencies or just a slice from the middle. These are known respectively as low pass, high pass, and band pass. Similar combinations of basic units have the ability to change the shape of electronic pulses or to clip them all down to the same level. Such circuits are widely used in depth sounders and in radars.

Oscillators

Possibly the most important combination of basic units in the entire field of electronics is the one known as an oscillator circuit. Without it there would be no radio telephone transmitters, no radars, no depth sounders, no modern receiving sets. Yet, as shown in Figure 8-11, it

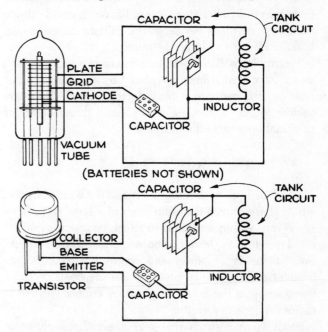

Figure 8-11: *This oscillator circuit is the heart of all radiotelephones, depth sounders, radars and most marine electronics. Note the similarity between vacuum tube and transistor (solid state) hookups.*

is a very simple and straightforward arrangement. The circuits are practically identical for vacuum tubes and for transistors. Note the importance of the tank circuit previously mentioned.

The oscillator circuit is made possible by the ability of the vacuum tube and the transistor to amplify, in other words, to put out more than is put in. (This is *not* a rebuff of nature's laws; the "more" comes from the batteries.)

To clarify the concept of oscillation, consider the ordinary clock pendulum. Its length determines how many times per minute it will swing and this could be equivalent to the tuning in the tank circuit. It is kept swinging continuously because the clock mechanism gives it a little push at just the right time during each pass. The energy from the battery, which the vacuum tube or transistor controls at a rate set by the tank circuit, gives the oscillator the "pushes" needed to keep it going.

The usable output from the oscillating circuit, an alternating current that changes its polarity from positive to negative many times per second, is the heart of most electronic equipment. Its strength might be very weak, as in a radio receiver, or it might pack thousands of horsepower, as in a military radar installation. It could vibrate thousands of times per second or billions of times—its basic character would be the same.

Electronic oscillator circuits also exist in which the tank as we have seen it here is replaced by a combination of resistors and capacitors. No inductor is used. These are seldom found in marine electronics and therefore are of marginal interest to the boatman.

Radiotelephones

The crashing spark, the huge coils and the odor of ozone, which characterized the radio room of a large ship, have given way within a lifetime to silent, compact, sophisticated panels with gleaming knobs and dials. This elimination of the large power and space requirements has brought radio communication to pleasure boats, even in many cases to the small runabout. A cruiser without a radiotelephone is a rarity.

Aside from basic marine gear, the radiotelephone is the single most necessary piece of safety equipment on board. It enables contact with other boats, with shore telephones and, when need arises, with Coast Guard rescuers. Modern equipment has been so simplified and fool-

proofed that no skill whatever is needed for its operation. The Federal Communications Commission recognizes this and issues licenses without technical examination. (See Chapter 25.) A typical marine telephone is shown in Figure 8-12.

Figure 8-12: The push-to-talk button on the microphone turns the transmitter of this radiofone on and off. A relay connects the antenna alternately to transmitting circuit and receiving circuit. (Credit—Apelco)

Also shown in Figure 8-12 is a typical citizen's band transceiver which combines reception, transmission and microphone in one unit. This system is known popularly as CB.

Many yacht clubs and marinas are installing CB base stations with which CB-equipped skippers can communicate for various kinds of service. CB is a short range system with minimal license requirements and equipment is widely available at attractive prices.

A radiotelephone transmission from one station to another entails a series of energy transformations. The power in the speaker's voice actuates the microphone, is transformed into an electric current, and this is amplified to a higher level. Meanwhile the oscillator is busily generating a strong alternating current at the transmission frequency known as the carrier. The two currents are brought together and the carrier is molded or modulated to a replica of the speech. This modulated current is fed to the antenna and causes the electromagnetic disturbance that affects the distant receiver.

At the receiving station the process is reversed. The antenna picks an infinitesimally small amount of energy from the passing wave and this is amplified through vacuum tubes or transistors. An electronic circuit known as the detector strips away the carrier and leaves only the voice currents. These in turn are amplified until they can operate a loudspeaker to re-create the sender's voice.

The various amplifiers in the radiotelephone are named after the function they perform: "radio frequency amplifiers," "intermediate frequency amplifiers," and "audio frequency amplifiers." They process the incoming signal in that order.

AM and FM

Two systems are presently in use for enabling the human voice to modulate the radio carrier. One is amplitude modulation (AM), the other is frequency modulation (FM). The names are almost self-explanatory.

In an amplitude-modulation system, the strength of the radio carrier is continuously being varied by the voice spoken into the microphone. The carrier frequency remains constant, although fringe frequencies known as side bands are generated. In the frequency-modulation system, the carrier remains at uniform strength but its frequency changes with each change in the voice. The FM type is reasonably immune to natural and man-made electric noises which would seriously interfere with the AM.

Radio Antennae

When an electromagnetic field or wave "cuts" a wire, a current is generated (see Chapter 7). This holds equally well at radio frequencies. Earlier installations suspended a long wire between the masts to act as the "antenna" or interceptor of the radio wave; modern powerboats have standardized on the vertical whip antenna. A great advantage of the whip is its omnidirectional character.

Theory and practice both prove that an antenna should be at least one-quarter wavelength long to be efficient. If you could actually see a radio wave, the distance from one crest to the next would be its wavelength. This is an unmanageable length; at the marine frequency of 2182 kilocycles, for instance, a one-quarter wavelength is 113 feet long! The length is therefore simulated electrically by a process known as loading.

Loading is accomplished by placing an inductor in the antenna circuit. This inductor, or coil, can be placed at the top of the whip (top loading), in the middle (center loading), or at the bottom (bottom loading). The presence of the coil tricks the radio wave into "seeing" the antenna

as being much longer than it actually is. The lead from some transmitters is a well-insulated coaxial cable that does not require any special care in its placement; from others it is a plain insulated wire.

The exposed position of a whip antenna automatically makes it a lightning rod. However, most whip antennas contain wires too small in diameter to carry lightning currents adequately and safely. The addition of a lightning arrester may help. (See page 479.)

Many sailboats use the backstay as the radio antenna. To accomplish this, the backstay (or other rigging) is well insulated at both ends or at a suitable length. The radio lead-in connects to the stay.

Quartz Crystals

The frequency of a transmitter (really of its oscillator) is set by the inductance and capacity in its circuit. These components are subject to change by temperature and vibration and consequently cannot maintain the constancy of frequency that the law requires. A quartz crystal is therefore added to the oscillator circuit and this maintains the desired frequency within very narrow limits. Such a crystal is shown in Figure 8-13.

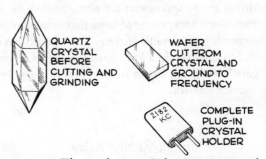

Figure 8-13: The evolution of the quartz crystal which stabilizes the frequency of an oscillating circuit.

A quartz crystal can act in this frequency-maintaining manner because it is "piezo-electric." This means that it will flex mechanically and vibrate when an alternating voltage is applied across its two faces. The remarkable thing is that it will vibrate only at the exact frequency determined by the thickness to which it has been ground and thus will hold the transmitter to that frequency. Radiotelephones usually have several crystals, each for a certain channel.

Overmodulation

In some radiotelephones it is possible for a loud voice in the microphone to overmodulate (overcontrol) the output of the transmitter with consequent distortion and interference to other stations. Such a condition is expressly prohibited by the FCC.

Most radiotelephones have some form of indicator by which the speaker can observe the amount of modulation his voice is causing. Generally this takes the form of a neon lamp, the glow of which is responsive to the microphone input; sometimes it is a meter. A few of the more advanced (and more expensive) radiotelephones incorporate automatic circuits that prevent overmodulation.

Noise Limiter and Squelch

The field surrounding an antenna is full of electrical disturbances caused by natural and man-made happenings. The stronger ones, shaped like spikes, are passed down to the receiver and would create annoying crackles and bangs if no preventive means were used. The noise limiter circuit eliminates these spikes of noise before they reach the loudspeaker.

In addition to the spikes that are eliminated there is a constant low-level background of noise that would quickly tire a listener for any length of time. The squelch circuit is intended to alleviate this. The squelch circuit is an electrical "gate" which can be set to any level of "opening" by the squelch control.

Transmit-Receive Relay

The transmitter and the receiver use the same antenna but obviously they cannot do so simultaneously; the heavy current from the transmitter would instantly burn out the delicate receiver. In earlier days, when transmitter and receiver were separate units, this situation was handled by a large switch thrown manually from sending to receiving.

Modern radiotelephones are single units and the large external switch has shrunk to a small relay inside the cabinet. This relay alternately connects and disconnects the antenna in response to the "push-to-talk" button on the microphone.

Single Side Band

Ordinary AM radiotelephone transmission is wasteful of precious space in the radio spectrum. Two side bands and the carrier are transmitted, although the intelligence resides entirely in each side band. You could visualize this transmission as a sandwich with the carrier frequency in the middle, an upper side band at the high end of the carrier, and a lower side band at the low end. An improved system has therefore evolved called single side band or SSB.

Only one side band is transmitted by an SSB radiotelephone. The carrier and the other side band are removed by the transmitter before the signal goes to the antenna. Unfortunately, SSB transmissions cannot be received properly by a standard AM receiver; both talker and listener must have SSB equipment. In an emergency, you can get rudimentary reception of SSB—sufficient to get the drift of the message—on an AM receiver by detuning it slightly.

Some modifications of SSB make reception possible by AM receivers. In one, a single side band is transmitted together with a full carrier (the FCC calls this A3H). In another the single side band is sent with a reduced carrier (the FCC calls this A3A). The full SSB transmission is labeled A3J while standard AM is known as A3.

FCC Rulings

From a purely technical standpoint, any of the types of modulation described could be used on any channel. There is a legal barrier to this freedom, however, because the FCC has laid down certain permissions and has made additional proposals. Transmitters operating in the 2–3 Mcs. band may use standard AM only until the end of 1976; thereafter, all such equipment must operate on SSB although the distress frequency of 2182 Kcs. must remain on AM. Transmitters in the high frequency (HF) band may use either AM or SSB. Transmitters in the very high frequency band (VHF) *must* employ FM *only*; this band is actually classified as marine mobile. Presently the FCC will not license 2–3 Mcs. equipment for a pleasure boat unless the craft also is equipped with VHF—although it will license the use of VHF alone.

The FCC sets a limit to the maximum permissible power *input* to the final amplifier of the transmitter. In the 2000 to 4000 Kcs. band this is 400 watts, in the 4-Mcs. to 25-

Mcs. range it is 1000 watts, and in the 156- to 162-Mcs. channel it is 25 watts with provision for reduction to 1 watt for nearby traffic. Equally subject to regulation is the extent to which this power is modulated. The leeway is between 75 and 100 percent. Under no circumstances may it exceed 100 percent; in other words, overmodulation is prohibited.

The power ratings given above correspond to the figures used by manufacturers in describing their instruments. It represents the power taken from the batteries during full operation and does *not* necessarily give a clue to the amount of this power that finally reaches the antenna to do useful work. The antenna power will vary between 50 and 80 percent of the input power.

Grounds

The ground connection is an important factor in obtaining good radiation and, fortunately, a good ground is easily secured on a boat. The FCC recommends a ground consisting of at least 12 square feet of copper sheet attached to the bottom. A VHF installation is an *apparent* though not an actual exception because no usual metallic ground is required. The peculiarities of VHF transmission in effect provide a ground equivalent.

Radio stations on shore connect with the ground directly whereas a boat must make this connection through the intervening water. Nevertheless, salt water is a good conductor of electricity and, from a radio standpoint, the surface of the sea is a continuation of the surface of the earth. Fresh water is a poor conductor and sometimes even a good insulator and therefore is much less effective as a ground.

A metal hull is obviously in good electrical contact with its surroundings and consequently provides a ready-made radio ground. Even if the hull is painted, this insulating layer is so thin with respect to the entire hull surface that a huge capacitor is formed which the radio currents traverse easily. Wooden and fiberglass hulls must add some direct provision for contact with the water, such as the copper sheet or any of the grounding gadgets available in marine catalogs. Some of these are very small yet claim the equivalent effect of the 12-square-foot contact legally recommended; whether or not they do is dubious. A grounding device is shown in Figure 8-14.

From a practical standpoint, the copper ground sheet presents some difficulties. It interferes with proper maintenance and inspection; rot and worms could have a field day behind its protective surface and remain hidden until too late. This seems to happen despite the fact that the metallic copper itself is toxic to marine organisms. The sheet could gradually work loose and cut boat speed until it finally broke away altogether and became a hazard to the propeller.

It is possible to put the copper sheet on the *inside* of the hull and still achieve a good radio ground. In this case, the action would be capacitive. Radiowise, this would

Figure 8-14: One form of radio ground. The fastening bolts also act as through-hull connections. The maker claims that this small unit is equivalent to the 12 square feet recommended by the FCC. (Credit—Layton Industries, Inc.)

function well but it would *not* be suitable as a lightning protection ground. Some builders of fiberglass boats embed the copper ground sheet within the hull thickness.

The mere fact that a ground makes a radio operative is no recommendation of its efficiency. The radio would put out *some* signal grounded only to the engine block—or even not grounded at all. The main question should be efficiency. Each little watt costs big money and should be made to provide maximum mileage.

Transmission Paths

The wave disturbance caused by the energy forced into a transmitting antenna can travel to the receiving station in any of several ways. It may get there by a ground wave or by a direct wave or by a sky wave. All three are diagrammed in Figure 8-15. Futhermore, its ability to get there or not and its strength when it arrives are affected by many conditions: the sun, the temperature, the season,

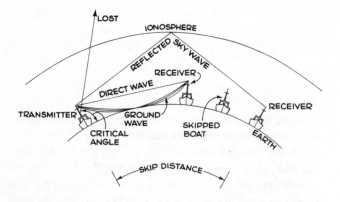

Figure 8-15: The signal from the transmitter can take various paths to the receiver: ground wave, direct wave or sky wave. Distance, season, time of day and transmission frequency all have an effect.

the time of day, the location, the transmission frequency, and others. Over *short* distances, however, the success of a transmission may depend only upon the transmitting power and the receiver sensitivity.

The earth is enclosed within a huge sphere of ionization called the ionosphere. The height from the earth to the inside of this shell varies with sun activity but may be considered to average seventy-five miles. The shell is composed of several layers and each reflects certain radio waves. It is these reflected waves that make long-distance radio communications possible. Whether a radio wave will be reflected or will simply penetrate and be lost in space is determined by its frequency and the angle at which it hits.

The "skip" phenomenon is known to every radio amateur and has been noted by many skippers. A comparatively nearby boat does not hear the transmission but a vessel farther away does clearly. The diagram in Figure 8-15 explains why.

Tips on Radio Installation

Almost complete instructions for making an efficient radiotelephone installation aboard any vessel can be given in three words: Keep connections short! This mandate applies specifically to the antenna and ground connections; it can be interpreted more freely when the power feed line is considered.

The ideal of short connections is best approached when the radiotelephone unit is in a direct, straight line between the antenna and the ground plate. Since the ground plate can be fastened almost anywhere along the bottom, it

becomes an easy choice to locate it directly below the radio cabinet.

The antenna location should give it a clear "view" all around the compass. Nearby metal structures absorb and waste power. Salt spray should not be able to reach the bottom insulator because of the danger of short-circuiting. Thought should be given to a location where the antenna will not become a handhold for guests coming aboard. The antenna must resist the wind, which tends to bend it, and the roll of the boat, which might snap it off.

The reason why short antenna and ground leads are so vital is their relationship to the frequency or wavelength at which the radiotelephone is operating. If these leads become an appreciable portion of a wavelength long, they act as miniature antennae. But the radiation from these unwanted antennae is not helpful; it dissipates part of the transmitter output into surrounding objects and actually lessens the effectiveness of the real antenna.

Remember that transmitter adjustments may be made only by holders of first- or second-grade radio licenses and not by boatmen licensed only to operate the equipment. (See Chapter 25.)

Depth Sounders

If you have ever whistled at a nearby hill and counted the seconds before the echo returned, you have done what a marine depth sounder does. It, too, sends out a sound and measures the time it takes the echo to bounce off the bottom and return.

The modern depth sounder sends out a tone whose pitch or frequency is far beyond the ability of humans to hear. It does this by means of a transducer fastened to the underside of the hull. The same transducer picks up the echo. The time for the round trip is then measured either electronically or by the displacement of a rotating arm. Since the speed with which sound travels through water is known, the depth is directly equivalent to one-half the round-trip time. The diagram in Figure 8-16 should clarify the concept.

An oscillator, previously described as the heart of much electronic equipment, is basic to the depth sounder too. It generates the tone that the transducer sends to the bottom. The balance of the depth sounder consists of amplifiers and timing circuits and a means of indicating the depth. This indicator can be a meter pointer moving

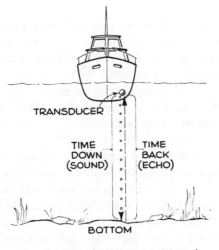

Figure 8-16: *The depth sounder measures the time it takes a sound to travel to the bottom and echo back and translates this into a depth reading.*

$$DEPTH = \tfrac{1}{2}\left(TIME\ DOWN + TIME\ BACK\right)$$

over a scale calibrated in feet or fathoms, or a rotating neon lamp whose flashes are read along a scale, or actual numerals projected on a screen, or even a chart recorder for making a permanent "picture" of the bottom. A typical unit is shown in Figure 8-17. (Digital readout, in which actual numerals take the place of a meter pointer, is making its entry into the marine instrument field from the world of computers where it is common.)

Figure 8-17: *This depth sounder uses a revolving flashing neon bulb to make its indications. (Credit—Sonar Radio Corp.)*

Fish in the path of the tone being directed at the bottom also send back an echo and give rise to an indication; this is why depth sounders are also dubbed fish finders. The nature of the bottom, whether rocky, sandy, muddy, or sharply inclined also affects the echo indication. This is borne out by Figure 8-18. Old-time sailors "armed" their lead with wax, tar, or other sticky substance to bring back a sample of the bottom for comparison with the chart; an experienced skipper can get almost as much information by watching his depth sounder carefully.

The depth sounder's transducer is a "loudspeaker" in the sense that it takes electrical energy and converts it to sound-wave energy in the adjacent water. The piezo-electric action which causes it to function has already been described. Many crystals, notably quartz, tourmaline, rochelle salt, and ammonium dihydrogen phosphate have this ability to flex when an electric current is applied. A ceramic, barium titanate, also has this piezo-electric ability and is much easier to manufacture; this is the material generally used for depth sounders.

Physicists long ago found that the speed of sound in water is 4794 feet per second under standard conditions. This is usually rounded off to 4800 feet per second in depth-sounder calculations. One fathom equals 6 feet, so the equivalent in fathoms would be 800. There is a slight difference between the sound velocities in fresh and salt water.

The rotating neon lamp performs its timing function very much as you would time an event in everyday life. You look at the position of a clock hand when the event begins and note the position when it ends; the distance the hand has traveled is the elapsed time. Similarly, the position of the indicating flash is determined by the distance the arm has traveled during the time the sound pulse has gone to the bottom and come back. Obviously the timing and the consequent accuracy of the depth reading are dependent entirely upon the ability of the driving motor to maintain its design speed. In some units, this is accomplished by centrifugal governors which open and close the contacts supplying current to the motor. In others, the driving motor is a synchronous type, like that used in clocks, and the frequency of the alternating current fed to it is controlled accurately by the nature of its circuit; this is the more accurate method.

The more elaborate depth sounders are recording instruments. They constantly draw a contour outline of the bottom on a moving strip of paper. A permanent record is thus established which can be compared with the chart or used merely to give a more comprehensive view of what lies under the hull. A depth recorder and a sample of the contour it provides are shown in Figure 8-19.

A further advancement in these instruments employs what is called white line recording. A narrow white space separates the tracing of the actual bottom from the echoes of any fish lying directly above. On standard recordings, such fish might blend into the bottom trace and not be noticeable.

DEPTH SOUNDER CAUTIONS.

The transducer is the only part of the depth-sounder installation that presents any problems, and these are minor. The location is important from two aspects: (1) it should be at a point on the hull that affords contact with smooth, solid water and (2) it should not be exposed

to damage from submerged objects. The first requirement is best met at a location just forward of amidships where there is minimum turbulence with its ingested air bubbles. A flush or nearly flush mount is the best protection against the second contingency. Many transducers are mounted on the side of the keel in a fairing block. This works well until there is an accidental grounding and then the transducer may join Davy Jones.

Some mechanics use a very clever maneuver to avoid hauling the boat when a depth-sounder transducer is being installed. They drill a hole in the bottom at the desired location. They then "shoot" a stick with a long string attached forcibly down through the hole. The stick floats to the surface at the side of the hull and the string it carries is fastened to the transducer neck or to its cable. Hauling back on the string then pops the transducer into place.

The face of the transducer must be level, that is, parallel with the waterline. Manufacturers caution against cutting

Figure 8-18: Figures (a) through (d) indicate a few typical Aqua-Probe readings. (a) A coral bottom at 50 feet with small blips between zero and bottom, indicating fish. (b) A weak flash, generally indicating a soft, muddy bottom. (c) A solid bottom, which is covered with vegetation or brush. (d) Sensitivity set too high at shallow water, making it difficult to read actual bottom.

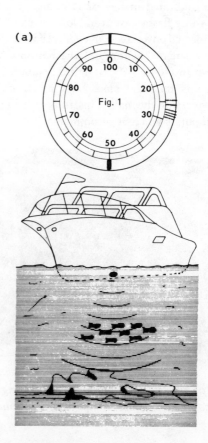

the cable connecting the transducer with the depth sounder; the instructions say to coil the excess and "leave it be." The transducer should be cleaned thoroughly with detergent and given a coat of bottom paint before launching. The paint is a necessary evil to prevent marine growth; it should be applied thinly to avoid desensitizing the instrument. (The anti-fouling paint must be non-metallic. Copper or other metallic paints act as barriers to the sound wave.) It is best to check manufacturer's recommendations.

Sailboats often present a problem for depth-sounder transducer installation because they seldom travel on an even keel. When the boat is heeled the transducer loses its desired vertical relation to the bottom. One palliative that has been tried is the installation of two transducers, one on each side, properly oriented, with a switch to cut in one or the other.

It seems redundant to mention that the indicator should be mounted near the helmsman's position so that he can

Figure 8-19: The depth recorder makes a permanent record of the bottom contour like the sample shown in the instrument window. (Credit—Triton Industry, Inc.)

read it conveniently underway and reach the controls without strain. The flasher types should be protected from sun glare; some have in-built sunshades for this purpose.

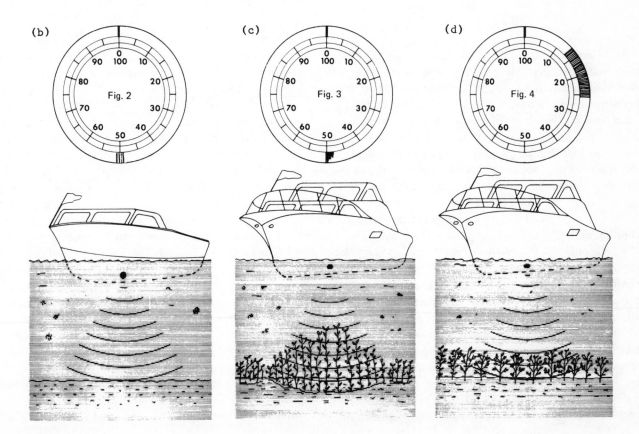

Since the transducer is mounted low down on the hull, the depth sounder reads the depth from this point and not the total water depth from the surface.

Radio Direction Finders (RDF)

The one-sided, peculiar reception characteristic of the loop antenna is the basis for the operation of all radio direction finders. A loop antenna receives signals very well from one direction and almost not at all from another. Because of this idiosyncrasy, the hand-held transistor radio is pointed toward the broadcast station and the direction finder above the pilot house is aimed at a radio beacon. Figure 8-20 shows an RDF in use.

The radio direction finder gives the skipper a "line of position"; it determines a line, radiating from the beacon like the spoke of a wheel, on which he is at that moment. The manner of making these determinations and the method by which they are combined into a "fix" are covered in Chapter 14.

LOOP ANTENNAS.

At its inception, the loop antenna was a loop or coil of wire. Many skippers can remember the loop, a foot or more in diameter, that fed early "antenna-less" radio sets; it was mounted in a bearing so that it could be rotated for best reception. The advent of powdered-iron cores changed all that. The loop (or loopstick) in a radio became a coil only an inch or two long wound on a powdered-iron core. Moderate-priced marine radio direction finders use a slightly larger version of this same loopstick. Professional equipment for large vessels employs a coil of wire encased in a protective ring which projects above the wheelhouse.

A loop antenna is shown in Figure 8-21. When the loop is pointed (edgewise) toward the transmitter, the arriving radio waves "cut" first one side and then, after an interval, the other. The induced voltages in the two sides are in phase and can add to form a strong signal. When the loop is pointed so that its plane, or flat side faces the transmitter, the same reasoning shows that the arriving waves strike both sides at exactly the same instant. The induced voltages in the two sides are now equal but opposite in phase and cancel each other; the output is zero. These two loop positions represent the

maximum and the null, respectively.

A further peculiarity of the loop is that the degree of maximizing and nulling are not equal for equal deflections from the best position. Simply stated, this means that the edgewise position can be varied considerably without apparently affecting the signal strength, whereas the flat side position is quite critical. A slight movement there brings a sharp transition from signal to null. Consequently, all radio direction finders use the null position for registering a bearing.

It could be inferred from the foregoing that a standard portable radio with its loop antenna could take the place of a direction finder and thus eliminate the need for the more expensive instrument. This is true only to a very rough and limited extent. The radio would give only a general idea of direction and certainly nothing that could be dignified by the term "bearing." This results because the loop in the radio is not balanced to ground, as is the direction finder antenna, and therefore does not hold strictly to the theory of maximum and null.

SENSE.

Figure 8-21 also shows one characteristic failing of the loop: It cannot distinguish from which side the radio wave is arriving and is therefore subject to an error of 180 degrees. It does not have "sense."

Radio direction finders acquire sense by adding a small whip antenna to the loop antenna. This whip is not permanently in the circuit but is under the control of a push button which activates it after the null has been found. The whip then reinforces the voltage on one side of the loop and cancels that on the other, thus establishing sense.

In the basic concept, the loop rotates so that its directional receiving characteristics can be utilized to give a null. The examples cited have actually, physically, turned the loop. It is also possible to leave the loop stationary and "rotate" it electronically by more advanced circuitry. Such a loop is called the Bellini-Tossi after its originators and is used in the more sophisticated RDF equipment.

The receiver in the RDF is standard. Often it is simply a counterpart of the radios built for broadcast and similar listening. The main addition is a meter for indicating the null more accurately than the ear can with the loudspeaker.

Radio direction finders are provided with an azimuth

Figure 8-20: The radio direction finder (RDF) will quickly provide a line of position (LOP). (Credit—Raytheon Company)

scale and a curser for reading the bearings. These can be either relative, magnetic, or true, as desired, and depend upon the curser setting.

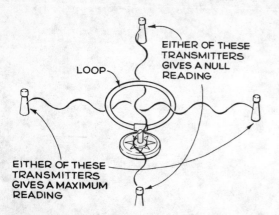

LOOP

EITHER OF THESE TRANSMITTERS GIVES A NULL READING

EITHER OF THESE TRANSMITTERS GIVES A MAXIMUM READING

Figure 8-21: The loop antenna has a null and a maximum determined by its position relative to the incoming radio wave. The loop antenna has a characteristic failing: It cannot distinguish by itself from which side a signal is arriving—and thus can be in error by 180 degrees.

Automatic Direction Finders (ADF)

The operations the skipper performs manually on the standard RDF are executed electrically or electronically by the automatic direction finder. A pointer on the indicator dial (or an electronic blip which acts as a pointer) continuously gives the heading of the received station. Proper setting of the curser on the dial can make this indication a relative, magnetic, or true bearing.

The loop antenna for the ADF, together with the necessary sensing whip, is mounted at the masthead usually in a protective plastic enclosure. Some manufacturers rotate this loop mechanically, others "rotate" it electronically and gain the advantage of removing motors and gears from the mast. In either case, once the skipper has tuned in the desired station, his part of the job is done and the instrument takes over.

Direction Finder Cautions

Since nearby metal objects degrade the readings of radio direction finders, it is only simple logic to choose the location of the instrument carefully. The chassis itself is shielded; it is the loop antenna that must be coddled. When the loop is a separate unit, it should be placed as high and as much in the clear as possible. The self-contained units which include the loop are of necessity mounted near the steering position but they must be kept as clear of nearby metal as this location allows. Once mounted and a deviation table made, they should not be moved.

When the RDF is near the helmsman, another consideration is its effect upon the compass. This could be considerable. The loudspeaker contains a powerful permanent magnet; so does the null meter. Other iron in transformer cores and loop is present as well. If a deviation chart already exists for the compass when the RDF is installed, it should be rechecked carefully. (How a deviation table is made for a radio direction finder is explained in Chapter 9.)

Many large ships have interlocking switches that disconnect and ground the radiotelephone antennas when the direction finder is being used; these antennas can act as spurious radiators of signals and thus confuse the bearing reading. This may be a point to consider in troublesome powerboat installations. Wire rope rigging on sailboats also can confuse the direction finder.

Loran

An electronic system for *long-range navigation* is known popularly by an acronym formed from the first letters of its intended use, namely, loran. Loran enables a skipper to pinpoint his location with a simple radio manipulation and practically no calculation, even when he is out of sight of land. It is useful and reliable over extreme ranges. It is free from the vagaries of transmission that afflict radio direction finder bearings taken over the longer spans. Loran is primarily an offshore aid and therefore found only on the more venturesome pleasure boats. A loran receiver is pictured in Figure 8-22.

Loran comprises two systems: Loran A and Loran C. The differences between these two lie in the transmission frequency and in the method of using the transmitted pulses. Loran A makes use of three channels: #1 is at 1950 Kcs., #2 is at 1850 Kcs., and #3 is at 1900 Kcs. A fourth channel at 1750 Kcs. is no longer in use. Loran C is transmitted at the extremely low frequency of 100 Kcs. and the characteristics of this long wavelength make it useful

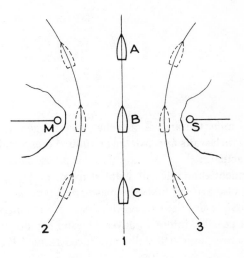

Figure 8-22: The delay indicated by the numerals above the lower knobs of this Loran receiver is referred to a Loran chart to establish a line of position. (Credit—Konel Corporation; Photo by Norton Pearl Photography)

at great distances.

The four channels that make up Loran A and Loran C are divided and then subdivided so that many stations can be fitted into the spectrum and thus provide position fixes almost everywhere. This ingenious system makes station identification relatively positive and largely removes the chances for error.

HOW LORAN WORKS.

The entire concept of loran is based on the fact that radio signals travel through space at a constant velocity, regardless of local conditions. This velocity is, in round numbers, 186,000 miles per second and the equivalent 300 million meters per second.

Two transmitters, hundreds of miles apart, send out related radio signals, and the distant ship that receives them measures the difference in their times of arrival. Considering the velocity of radio propagation, this difference in arrival time obviously will be in *millionths* of a second. Ordinary methods of timing, for instance, with stop watches, cannot be applied, but electronic circuits easily measure such unimaginably small increments of time.

Figure 8-23 shows a very elementary diagram of a loran situation in which the two transmitters are *M* and *S*. If the *M* and *S* signals are sent simultaneously, and if the ship receives them simultaneously, then it means that they have spent the same amount of time traveling and consequently have traveled equal distances. It can be proved

Figure 8-23: In this elementary loran situation, M and S are the master and slave transmitters. Lines of position are established by the differences in arrival time of M and S signals. Ships at A, B and C receive the signals simultaneously and therefore must be on line #1. A ship which receives M before S must be on a line like #2. Receiving S before M puts a ship on a line like #3.

by geometry that the ship must therefore be somewhere on line #1 (at *A*, *B*, or *C*), because this line contains all the points equally distant from *M* and from *S*. Line #1 would become a line of position, an LOP, and would serve to locate a fix if a crossing line could be found.

Had the ship received the signal from *M* much sooner than the signal from *S*, it would be at some point on a line like #2. Again this curved line could become an LOP. The same reasoning shows that the ship would be at some point on a line like #3 if the *S* signal had arrived prior to the *M* signal. The mathematical name for one of these unique curved lines is hyperbola; each contains all points that mark the same *difference* in distance (and therefore time) from *M* and from *S*.

Although this example serves nicely to illustrate the principle governing loran, it would not be feasible to operate an actual loran installation in this manner. The first problem would be trying to identify which signal arrived first. Then there would be many near-zero delay readings that would be almost impossible to measure exactly. A typical loran system therefore follows the principles explained but makes some practical changes in timing procedure.

First of all, the *M* and *S* signals are *not* sent out simultaneously. The *M* station, known as the master, originates a pulse. This pulse travels the distance to *S*, the slave, at the rate of 6.18 microseconds (millionths of a second) per nautical mile. On arrival at *S* the pulse triggers a delay circuit which waits approximately 1000 microseconds before it actuates the slave into its own pulse. This clever arrangement eliminates all doubt at the distant ship as to which pulse arrived first; the master pulse *always* must arrive first. It also does away with near-zero readings; the smallest possible interval between *M* and *S* pulses is the 1000 microseconds artificially introduced as the delay at *S*.

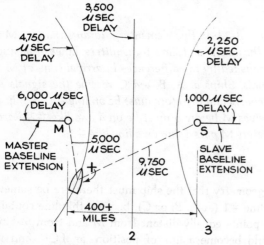

Figure 8-24: This simple numerical example should explain loran delays. A ship whose loran receiver indicates 3500 M's delay is on line #2; 4750 M's delay would place it on line #1; 2250 M's delay on line #3.

The numerical example in Figure 8-24 shows how easily the loran system can be understood. The master and the slave are slightly more than 400 nautical miles apart and simple multiplication shows that it takes *M's* pulse 2500 microseconds to reach *S*. Now *S* waits 1000 microseconds before sending its own pulse. A ship located anywhere along the slave baseline extension would therefore receive the *M* pulse and after a delay of 1000 microseconds would receive the *S* pulse. Contrariwise, if the loran receiver indicated a delay of 1000 microseconds, the navigator would know at once that his position was somewhere on the slave baseline.

Now imagine yourself on line #2, midway between the master and the slave. The *M* pulse has just been received but the pulse must take a further 1250 microseconds to cover the 200 miles to *S*. There it must wait 1000 microseconds before it can trigger *S*. Then the *S* pulse must consume 1250 microseconds to reach line #2. Adding 1250

and 1000 and 1250 gives a total delay of 3500 microseconds and this is what a loran receiver would indicate aboard a ship anywhere on line #2. The delay figures on the other lines are arrived at just as simply.

If the pulse from *M* required 5000 microseconds to reach a ship, and the pulse from *S* took 9750 microseconds, the difference would be 4750 microseconds and this would place the vessel on line #1. It's no more complicated than that!

LORAN EQUIPMENT.

The loran set has two functions to perform: to receive the radio signals and to measure microscopic time differences. The first job is taken care of without difficulty by a standard radio receiver designed for the loran frequencies. The second part of the task is accomplished with what amounts to the picture tube portion of a TV set.

The *M* and the *S* signals are projected as blips on the face of the cathode ray tube by a moving electron beam just as are the pictures on the TV. The *M* signal pulse arrives as the beam is beginning its trace to the right. The beam has made some definite headway before the *S* pulse arrives and thus this blip is some distance to the right. If you know how fast the beam travels, this distance becomes a measure of time.

It would be possible to measure the separation of the two blips on the face of the tube with some sort of gauge in order to arrive at the delay. It would be *possible* but certainly not very *accurate*. Instead, the measurement is made electronically by controls that move the *S* blip back and superimpose it on the *M* blip. These control knobs produce the digital reading of delay. (The most modern and most expensive lorans exhibit the delay reading automatically, without any manipulation of control knobs.)

LORAN CHARTS.

Loran lines are hyperbolas, the coordinates on Mercator charts are rectangular. A standard chart therefore is not of much help in loran plotting, although tables in Bowditch make the conversion possible. The normal procedure is to use charts with loran lines inscribed, such as the sample in Figure 8-25.

Each loran line on the chart is labeled with the delay in microseconds and sometimes also with the correction that must be applied for sky waves. Readings that fall between the lines are interpolated.

LORAN STATIONS.

Ground station installation costs are cut in modern loran practice by having one master function with two slaves. The practical effect is the same as though two masters and two slaves were in operation and the resultant crossing LOPs are used to establish a fix.

First of all, there must be a means of identification; it does the navigator no good to receive the signals unless he knows whence they come and can plot them accordingly. Identification is made possible by the frequency used (the four channels have already been listed) and by the pulse repetition rate, the PRR. This PRR is subdivided into two parts: the *basic* rate and the *specific* rate.

There are three basic rates. High (H) sends approximately 33⅓ pulses per second, low (L) approximately 25 pulses per second, and special (S) approximately 20 pulses per second. The word approximately is used because each rate is modified in steps of 100 microseconds to form 8 specific rates.

With this foolproof scheme, a loran station can be identified positively with a number and a letter and another number. Thus, 3H4 would be decoded to mean a loran pair transmitting on 1900 Kcs. and emitting pulses at intervals of 29,600 microseconds. (The pulses themselves are always about 40 microseconds long on all stations.)

Consolan and Consol

An electronic navigational aid whose development is an outgrowth of World War II, and attributable partly to the Germans and partly to the United States, is called either consolan or consol. The difference in nomenclature refers to the transmitting system, whether by two stations or three, and implies no difference in reception or use.

Consolan-consol does not provide a fix but only a line of position. These LOPs radiate like the spokes of a wheel from the only two stations now operating, one at San Francisco (SFI, 192 Kcs.) and the other at Nantucket (TUK, 194 Kcs.). The areas between spokes alternate as sectors in which dots are heard first at the beginning of each cycle of transmission, and in which dashes are heard first. The navigator identifies the radial on which his ship is located by counting dots or dashes in a simple formula and referring this to a special consolan-consol chart.

The consolan-consol signals are sent by continuous wave, a form of transmission not properly receivable by ordinary radio sets. A "beat frequency oscillator" is required and many marine radios include such a circuit for this purpose. The signals are not suitable for position finding in an area within a radius of about fifty miles from the station. They are also unusable in sectors on each side of a line through the transmitters, the baseline extension. A portion of a consolan-consol chart is shown in Figure 8-26.

Unfortunately, consolan-consol is not a positive location system in the sense that it will tell you in which sector you are; the readings would be the same for alternate sectors. It is therefore necessary that the skipper's calculated dead reckoning position identify the sector with the signals themselves picking only the exact radial.

The consolan-consol system is presently tottering on the brink of financial demise. Whether it will continue, expand or shut down depends upon government fiscal appropriations.

Radar

As everyone knows by now, radar is an acronym formed by the first letters of *radio detection and ranging*. Radar equipment, originally too heavy, complicated, and bulky for small-boat use, has now been engineered down to a size and cost that enable it to be found on many small vessels. Radar truly gives the skipper "eyes" to pierce the night and the fog.

Radar and depth sounders are alike in that both send out a pulse and then time the return of the echo. However, the similarity just about ends there. Whereas the depth sounders utilize a sound pulse, the radar units send out a radio pulse. The frequency of this radio wave is extremely high and its wavelength consequently extremely short. A representative figure is 9400 megacycles with a length of 3.2 centimeters. The sound pulse needs the medium of water in which to travel at fairly slow speed while the radio pulse ranges through free space at the velocity of light.

The relative difficulties in timing the return of the echo in depth sounders and in radar can be judged by looking at the numerical values involved. The sound pulse, in seawater, takes 1.26 seconds to travel one nautical mile. The radar pulse travels the same distance in 6.2 *millionths of one* second! It is evident from this tremendous speed

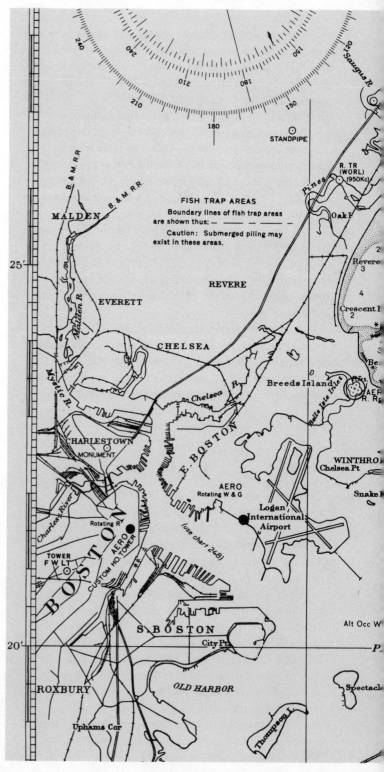

Figure 8-25: This section of a loran chart shows the hyperbolic lines of position, each marked with its delay in microseconds. (The lines actually are hyperbolas but appear straight over short lengths.)

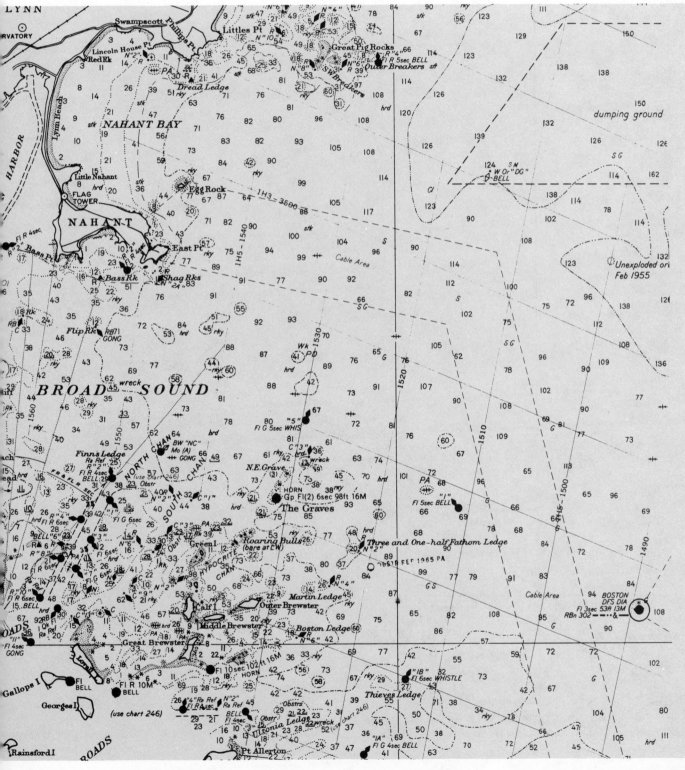

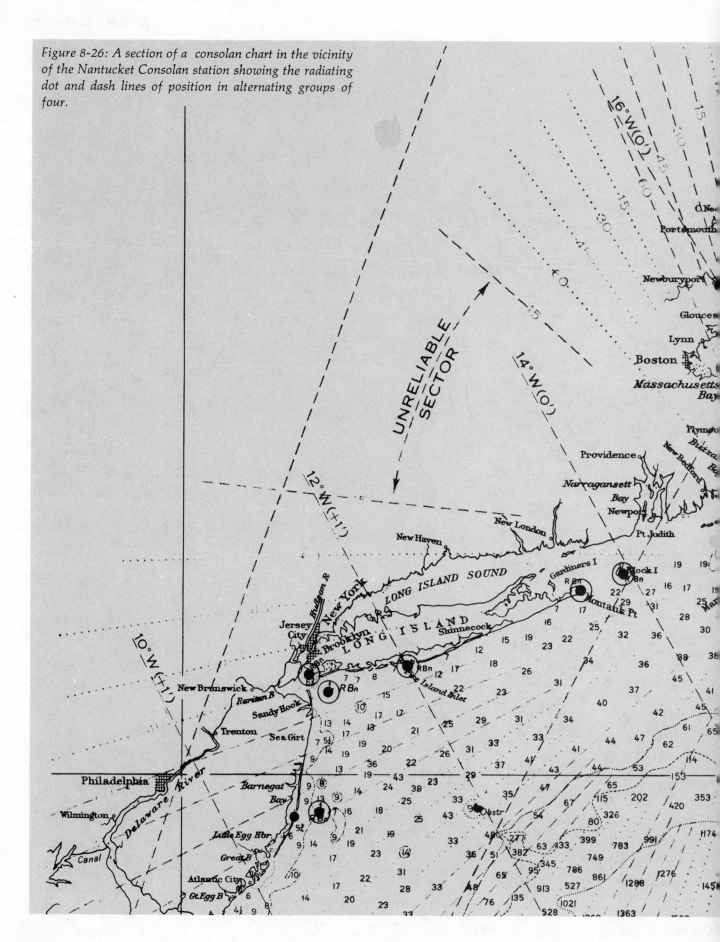

Figure 8-26: A section of a consolan chart in the vicinity of the Nantucket Consolan station showing the radiating dot and dash lines of position in alternating groups of four.

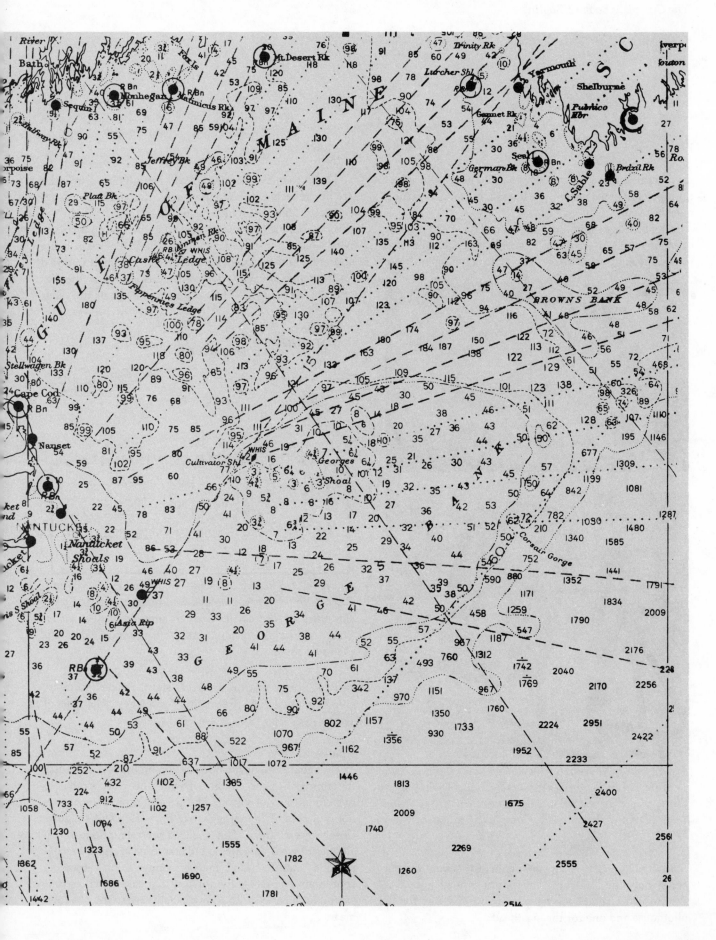

217

that no rotating-neon-lamp device could handle the job of timing; electronic means, such as a cathode ray tube, must be used.

In its broadest, simplified sense a radar system consists of a generator of a strong, very short radio pulse, a means for amplifying a very weak return echo, a timing indicator

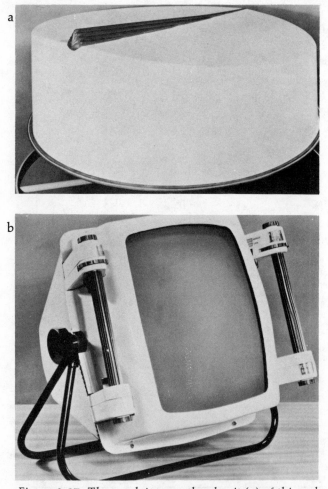

The extremely short radio wavelengths used in radar are not reflected by the ionosphere. Radar thus becomes a strictly "line of sight" apparatus, although "sight" in this case denotes a straight line and implies no comparison with what a human eye could see. The line of sight being straight and the earth being round, a limitation is imposed on the range of radar effectiveness, as shown in the diagram of Figure 8-28. The greater the height of the radar

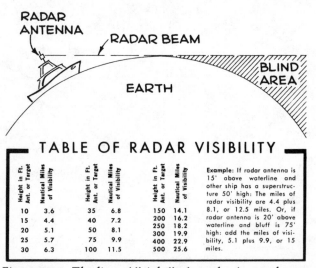

TABLE OF RADAR VISIBILITY

Height in Ft. Ant. or Target	Nautical Miles of Visibility	Height in Ft. Ant. or Target	Nautical Miles of Visibility	Height in Ft. Ant. or Target	Nautical Miles of Visibility
10	3.6	35	6.8	150	14.1
15	4.4	40	7.2	200	16.2
20	5.1	50	8.1	250	18.2
25	5.7	75	9.9	300	19.9
30	6.3	100	11.5	400	22.9
				500	25.6

Example: If radar antenna is 15' above waterline and other ship has a superstructure 50' high: The miles of radar visibility are 4.4 plus 8.1, or 12.5 miles. Or, if radar antenna is 20' above waterline and bluff is 75' high: add the miles of visibility, 5.1 plus 9.9, or 15 miles.

Figure 8-28: The line of "sight" of a radar (not to be confused with what a human eye could see) is limited by the curvature of the earth. Greater antenna height means greater "viewing" distance, as the diagram explains and the table shows.

antenna, the greater the range of "sight"; some figures are given in the table. (Refraction "stretches" the line of sight.)

INDICATOR UNITS.

The radar presents its information on the face of a tube, the appearance and circuits of which are very similar to the ubiquitous television. The presentation, however, is not a picture of the target range but a series of shadows closely resembling it. The idealized representations in catalogues of what appears on radar screens are easily recognized as familiar land masses; under actual seagoing conditions, the recognition is not that easy. It takes considerable experience to know exactly what the shadows mean.

Figure 8-27: The revolving masthead unit (a) of this radar is protected inside a plastic housing. The viewing screen (b) is placed in the pilothouse convenient to the helmsman. (Credit—Benmar Div. Computer Equipment Corp.)

calibrated in distance, and an antenna for aiming the outgoing pulse and catching the return echo. Figure 8-27 shows such a complete system in two parts, one for the pilothouse and one for the masthead.

The tube is known as the scope, derived from "oscilloscope," the instrument wherein it originated. The scope is an electron tube that functions because light is emitted when an electron strikes the phosphor coating on the inside of the face. As in all electron tubes, the source of the electrons is a heated cathode. How the electrons are controlled is explained in the section on vacuum tubes (see page 195). The spots of light are continually changing but the persistence of the phosphors and the persistence of human vision blends them into a picture.

A radar antenna at the masthead concentrates the radio wave into a beam, very much in the manner of a searchlight. This antenna revolves in synchronism with the beam in the scope so that what the antenna "sees" and what the scope shows are always in alignment. The position of each spot on the scope is determined by the time it took the pulse to hit that spot and be reflected back, in other words, by the distance from the ship.

The average diameter of the scopes used in radars suitable for pleasure boats is six or seven inches. This may seem small to television viewers with twenty-six-inch screens at home, but it is adequate for the purpose. Viewing hoods are supplied with some indicators to cover the scope and exclude ambient light, but a few radars have been able to achieve sufficient image brightness to make this pampering unnecessary. The lubber's line of the indicator is commonly parallel to that of the ship. The images seen then bear a proper relationship to actual port and starboard with "own ship" at the center.

RADAR CONTROLS.

Some of the controls on the panel of the radar set are familiar because of their kinship with a television receiver. Others are peculiar to the gadget. The sensitivity time control (STC) reduces the clutter during the viewing of close-in targets. Clutter is a term that can be considered synonymous with background noise and static in radio reception. Waves could be a source of clutter and could obscure a small boat or a protruding reef.

The fast time constant (FTC) control sharpens the target image on all ranges. It is also helpful in reducing the obscuring effect of rain. Although rain is composed of small, individual drops, a radar attempting to "look" through a mile or so of these randomly placed globules finds an almost impenetrable curtain.

TRUE-MOTION RADAR.

The standard radar exhibits on its indicator what is known as a relative-motion display. The forward motion of the boat and the persistence of the scope screen combine to smudge the outlines of stationary objects. A fixed buoy could appear like a moving vessel. A system called true-motion display corrects this. Course and speed information of the radar's own boat are fed automatically and continuously to special circuits which correct the indicator.

RADAR POWERS.

Since the *peak* power outputs of small-boat radars lie between 3 and 10 kilowatts, one would expect heavy current carrying components based on usual practice. The length of the radar pulse is so short that the *average* power is quite low, however. This explains the deceptively small sizes of the magnetron oscillators and other components. One manufacturer's specification lists peak transmitter power at 60 *kilo*watts and average power at 30 *watts!*

The impulse that goes from the transmitter is known colloquially as the "main bang." This main bang puts the mark at the center of the scope just as the outgoing pulse provided the zero mark for the depth sounder.

RADAR ANTENNAS.

The efficacy of the radar unit is determined largely by the narrowness of the radio beam; attaining this sharpness is the job of the radar antenna. Small boat radars currently are equipped with either of two antenna types: the slotted wave guide or the parabolic reflector. The latter is the radar equivalent of a searchlight.

Many radars employ the same antenna section for both transmitting and receiving. These must have special transmit-receive (TR) circuits to prevent the powerful pulse from destroying the receiver. Other makers avoid the TR complication by providing two antennas, one for transmit and one for receive, although both occupy a common housing.

The ideal beam is narrow in a horizontal direction and fairly wide vertically. This gives good horizontal definition of the scope picture but prevents the beam from hitting sea and sky alternately when the boat pitches.

Radar antennas are often housed in plastic radomes for

protection from wind and weather. The plastic is transparent to radio waves just as glass is transparent to light waves, although in both cases there is a slight loss.

Presently available marine radars operate in any one of three bands of frequencies: the *S* band, the *X* band, and the *Q* band. The *S* band centers around 10 centimeter waves, the *X* band around 3 cm. waves, and the *Q* band around ultra-miniature 8 *milli*meter waves. The *S* band has the greatest carrying power. The *Q* band gives excellent definition but over only short distances. The *X* band is a general compromise.

RACON.

A new navigational aid, "racon," has been developed which will prove highly beneficial to ships equipped with radar. This unique aid achieves positive identification of its own blip on a distant radar screen.

When the radar impulse from an approaching ship strikes a racon-equipped navigational aid, a transmitter is triggered which sends back a distinctive signal. This signal is displayed on that ship's radar in conjunction with the normal blip from that aid. Each racon is coded distinctly and uniquely so that the radar observer can have no doubt about the navigational aid he is approaching.

The value of the racon to navigators stems from the fact that many confusingly similar blips appear on the radar of a ship moving along a main fairway marked with numerous buoys and other aids.

OMNI RECEIVERS.

The visual omni-directional range receiver (VOR or OMNI) is an aircraft instrument that is finding increasing use on small boats. It is the simplest of all devices to operate and gives a direct reading in degrees of "to" or "from" the transmitter.

The omni receiver tunes to any one of more than eight hundred aircraft radio stations and the reading can be laid down on the chart as an LOP radiating from the transmitter. By reading a crossing bearing from another omni station, a fix is obtained. The system is usable up to about eighty miles from shore.

The antenna for the omni receiver is a simple dipole which is attached to the masthead and remains stationary. Connection is made to the receiver with a coaxial cable. Nearby metal objects do not degrade the readings as they would with an RDF.

A bonus feature obtained with the omni receiver is a weather report every thirty minutes. This report is intended for aircraft but certainly equally valuable for the small boat skipper when it includes his boating area.

Hailers

The combination of a simple amplifier circuit plus a loudspeaker and a microphone has been transformed into the "loud hailer" now seen more and more on pleasure craft. One such combination is shown in Figure 8-29.

Figure 8-29: The loud hailer fulfills several functions: It amplifies the pilot's voice for hailing, it "listens" for distant sounds, it acts as a ship's horn and foghorn. (Credit— Benmar Div. Computer Equipment Corp.)

A switch on the control box shifts the circuit to the various modes. In its normal state the unit projects through the loudspeaker whatever is said into the microphone when the button is pressed. The action then can be reversed into a listening device in which the loudspeaker becomes the sensitive pickup and the microphone becomes a speaker. A tone oscillator also is provided and its amplified sound is fed to the loudspeaker, thus permitting it to serve as the boat horn. Some units even automatically repeat this tone at the spaced intervals required by the Coast Guard for a fog signal.

9 Compasses and Instruments

Aт some point during the seven days it took the Lord to make the world, He did something that has been a great boon to the sailorman ever since: He made the earth magnetic. Man's ingenuity soon harnessed this phenomenon in order to give mariners a positive sense of direction, even when they are far out of sight of land.

Like all magnets, large or small, the earth has two poles at which the magnetic force is concentrated. These are the north magnetic pole and the south magnetic pole. These poles do *not* coincide with the geographic North and South Poles at the extremities of the earth's rotational axis. This disparity between the poles is apparently a little slipup that occurred during Creation; it has worried countless skippers ever since because it introduced the need for a correctional calculation in navigation.

The calculation corrects for the difference between the direction in which the compass points and the direction of the *true* North Pole. The error is in two parts so the calculation likewise must be in two parts. The first is for "variation," a natural phenomenon that differs with location on the earth and over which man has no control. The second is for "deviation," which is man-made and controllable. Both together are called somewhat ambiguously the compass error.

If some fine iron filings are sprinkled on a paper over a permanent bar magnet, a pattern will evolve, such as that shown in Figure 9-1. The filings align themselves along the invisible lines of magnetic flux that link the two poles and make them visible. Similar lines of invisible magnetic flux link the magnetic north pole with the magnetic south pole and surround the earth as shown. They are not as beautifully symmetrical as those on the paper because of the varying mineral content of the ground beneath, but they are what make magnetic compasses possible.

Man's first contact with magnetism came centuries before Christ in Asia Minor at a place called Magnesia. A ferrous ore found there and named magnetite after the place of its origin has the unusual property of attracting bits of iron. This mineral was the original permanent magnet; its popular name is lodestone.

Break a magnet in half and each piece nevertheless will have a north pole and a south pole. Break the halves again, still each smaller piece will possess a north and a south pole, ad infinitum. It is a peculiarity that a one-pole magnet cannot exist. Another peculiarity is that like poles repel each other while unlike poles attract. In other words,

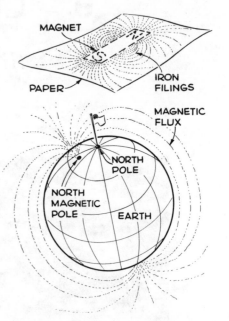

Figure 9-1: The earth, like every other magnet, has two poles: a north and a south. They are not *coincident with the geographic North and South Poles. (The iron filings on the paper make the lines of force of the magnet visible and demonstrate the linking of the two poles.)*

north repels north but attracts south; south repels south but attracts north. This explains why a compass needle never makes a mistake and points the opposite way.

The magnets for use in good compasses are made of special steel alloys which are mixtures of iron, aluminum, nickel, and cobalt and bear the trademark name of Alnico. This material has much higher coercive and retentive force than plain steel, and compass magnets made from it can truly be considered "permanent."

The Alnico bar can be magnetized by an arrangement such as shown in Figure 9-2. A heavy current passed through the coil produces a strong magnetic field which envelops the bar and induces magnetism in it by orienting all its molecules. Once magnetized, the molecules are prevented from returning to their neutral condition by the structure of the hard metal. In commercial practice, the magnetizing procedure is complicated by the many steps taken to insure permanency.

If a bar of this Alnico is balanced and suspended horizontally by a thread, it will align itself with the earth's magnetic flux and point approximately north and south. (Remember that the magnetic north and south poles of the earth do not coincide with the geographic poles, hence the "approximately".) The end of the bar that points north, actually the north-*seeking* end, is by custom called

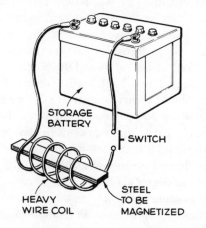

Figure 9-2: A steel bar can be made into a magnet with electric current. If it is hardened steel, the induced magnetism will be "permanent."

the north pole and is generally painted red. The south-*seeking* end or south pole is painted blue.

The Chinese were apparently the first to use a device for indicating north such as we today call a compass. They floated a cork in a bowl of water and placed a piece of lodestone on the cork. The lodestone slowly oriented itself to an approximate north and south position and maintained that direction regardless of how the bowl was turned. It is interesting to note that the modern idea of floating a compass card to reduce friction and curtail its gyrations is thus more than a thousand years old.

The intermediate improvement before the modern ship's compass came along was the single-needle type familiar to boy scouts and hunters. A light, magnetized steel pointer is balanced at its center on a sharp pivot so that it is free to swing horizontally. As can be expected from the foregoing discussion, the north-seeking end or north pole of the pointer points approximately north and gives the user a sense of orientation—provided of course that he is not careless enough to carry a large steel hunting

knife in a nearby pocket.

The directional markings of the pocket compass are printed on the base below the pivoted pointer. The user turns the case to bring the *N* under the head of the pointer and thereby establishes the proper relation of the markings to his surroundings. He then derives his desired direction by mentally extending the compass markings or perhaps even sighting over them. Obviously this is not a convenient way to navigate a ship.

Marine Compasses

The ship's compass reverses the construction of the hand compass. Its directional markings are printed on a card which is pivoted for free horizontal swinging. The magnet is affixed to the underside of this card and in aligning itself in a north-south direction maintains the card in that position regardless of the turning of the case. The reference mark, called a lubber's line, is on the case and in its movement around the card tells the direction in which the ship is heading.

During a change of course it always *appears* that the *card* is turning; the hardest thing for a newcomer to realize is that the card *never* turns with the ship. The case, fastened down, turns with the ship, and its lubber's line travels around the card a distance equivalent to the vessel's swing.

Great attention is paid in good compass design to the reduction of friction. The earth's magnetic field is weak, even though all-pervading, and thus exerts minimal force on the card. One method of reducing friction is a pivot of super-hard material and a rider of a hard jewel, such as sapphire. The case is then filled with liquid (generally kerosene) and the laws of buoyancy (see Chapter 1) take much of the card's and magnet's weight off the pivot. The liquid also has a damping or smoothing effect.

There is one further complication. The card is responsive only to horizontal magnetic forces because of the manner in which it is pivoted, yet the earth's field is horizontal only at the equator. Everywhere else it is the resultant of a horizontal and a vertical force, with the horizontal continuously becoming weaker until at the magnetic poles it is nonexistent and the compass becomes useless. A magnetic dip needle (pivoted to swing up and down) would behave as in Figure 9-3. Some compass manufacturers take this into consideration and balance

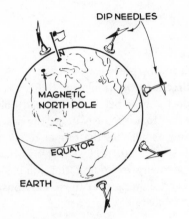

Figure 9-3: The earth's magnetic flux lines are parallel to the surface only at the equator and the force on a compass is greatest there, declining to zero at the magnetic poles.

their instruments differently for Northern Hemisphere and Southern Hemisphere use.

A cross section of a typical marine compass is shown in Figure 9-4. It is claimed that the spherical internal shape does more than merely facilitate reading because of its optical magnifying effect. Since the liquid is not forced to change its "shape" as the boat rolls and pitches (it is always ball-shaped), no swirls and eddies are generated

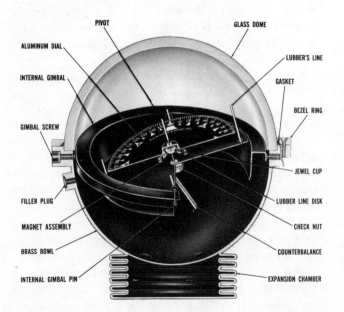

Figure 9-4: The components of an accurate compass are shown in this cutaway view. (In this model the lubber's line tilts for easy visibility.) (Credit—E. S. Ritchie & Sons, Inc.)

to affect the card. The liquid filling is under slight pressure to eliminate air bubbles and changes as expansion and contraction are absorbed by a bellows. The gimbals for maintaining a horizontal card are also within the sphere and thus subject to the damping action of the liquid, while a weight acts like a pendulum to steady the system.

The degree of gimbaling can be taken as one indication of compass quality. The moderately priced instruments rely on the tilting of the compass card to maintain readability. The finest compasses are suspended from bearings on crossed axes and the card remains horizontal regardless of the gyrations of the case—and the boat.

The traditional merchant marine compass card was divided into the 32 points familiar to old-time sailors; the Navy prefers the 360 degrees of the circle. Many small boat compasses carry both markings in concentric circles although the trend is to the 360-degree marks alone. Since courses are figured in degrees and given in degrees, the card marked in degrees is the best, most convenient, and least likely to cause misunderstandings. Samples of compass card markings are shown in Figure 9-5. A comparison table between degrees and points is given in Figure 9-6.

The shape of the compass card itself is either flat, dished, or cupped. The flat card is the conventional one and is read against a lubber's line forward of the edge. The dished card is a modification of the flat design and makes reading possible from a low line of sight. The cupped card carries the markings around the rim for front reading against a lubber's line aft of its edge. All three are shown in Figure 9-7. Many makers provide a high pin at the center of the compass card. This is a shadow pin used to project the sun's shadow onto the card; one useful purpose of this is compass compensation, described in Chapter 14.

A compass left quietly ashore would last "forever," and many skippers wonder why the durn thing goes to the dogs after a few seasons afloat. The answer is vibration. Vibration from the normal workings of the hull through the water and vibration from the engine; this is especially true on high-speed boats. The vibration has the effect of minutely bouncing the card on its pivot and this in turn acts like constant tiny hammer blows that blunt the point. The added friction from the dull bearing slows the card and sometimes stops it. Shock-mounting the compass on springs and rubber ameliorates the problem.

| 5° | 2° | 1° | 8"5° | NAVY |

Figure 9-5: Compass cards are available with a choice of markings from 5-degree intervals to 1 degree or smaller. Some cards also carry divisions marked in points.

Points	Direction Name	Degrees	Minutes	Seconds
0	north	000	00	00
1	north by east	011	15	00
2	north north east	022	30	00
3	northeast by north	033	45	00
4	northeast	045	00	00
5	northeast by east	056	15	00
6	east northeast	067	30	00
7	east by north	078	45	00
8	east	090	00	00
9	east by south	101	15	00
10	east southeast	112	30	00
11	southeast by east	123	45	00
12	southeast	135	00	00
13	southeast by east	146	15	00
14	south southeast	157	30	00
15	south by east	168	45	00
16	south	180	00	00
17	south by west	191	15	00
18	south southwest	202	30	00
19	southwest by south	213	45	00
20	southwest	225	00	00
21	southwest by west	236	15	00
22	west southwest	247	30	00
23	west by south	258	45	00
24	west	270	00	00
25	west by north	281	15	00
26	west northwest	292	30	00
27	northwest by west	303	45	00
28	northwest	315	00	00
29	northwest by north	326	15	00
30	north northwest	337	30	00
31	north by west	348	45	00
32	north	360	00	00

Figure 9-6: The relationship between the old point system and the currently used degree designations is given above.

Binnacles

The housing that encloses the compass on larger pleasure boats is called the binnacle. Binnacles, of course, are made of nonmagnetic materials such as brass or copper. They usually include an illuminating lamp and shutters to shield against glaring sunlight. Many sailboat binnacles are on beautiful free-standing columnar supports.

The Navy introduced red as the preferred color for lighting instrument panels. It was found that the eye underwent less strain adapting from red to the dark surroundings than from the previously used white light. Most manufacturers therefore now supply red lighting with their compasses. A further refinement is a dimming control, such as that found on automobile instrument panels.

Figure 9-7: A compass with conventional card and lubber's line is shown at (a) while the cupped card (b) makes front reading possible. The center pin (c) is a sun shadow pin. (Credit—E. S. Ritche & Sons, Inc.)

Deviation

To a compass card any magnetic field is a source of attraction, regardless of whether it be nature's or one made by man. The compass knows no discrimination and may even respond more strongly to a spurious field than to the earth's and may give an incorrect reading thereby. Foreign influences that deviate the compass from its correct alignment with the earth's magnetic field are very properly called deviation. Deviation is distinct from and must not be confused with "variation."

The false magnetic effects that cause deviation originate

on each boat from various sources. The most common cause is the proximity to the compass of iron or steel—and this includes the steel spokes inside a plastic steering wheel and even the "tin" cans that contain the skipper's beer. Loudspeakers are common offenders because they contain very powerful permanent magnets. Wires carrying direct current set up magnetic fields (see Chapter 7). Anything nearby that contains ferrous metal is suspect and sometimes even nickel plating has an effect. A steel hull would of course be highest on the list.

Compasses on sailboats are generally less affected by deviation problems than those on powerboats. This is because most sailing vessels carry fewer potentially disturbing electronic gadgets and have smaller engines whose iron masses generally are situated away from trouble.

A large steel-hulled boat in itself would be a huge floating magnet affecting not only its own compass but also those of any boats nearby. The hull becomes a magnet by being inductively magnetized by the earth. This may be hard to believe but it can be proved with a simple experiment. Hold a steel bar a couple of feet long in a north-south position, whack it with a mallet to help the molecules align themselves, and you will have made a long bar magnet inductively from the earth with a north pole and a south pole. The existence of the two poles can be verified easily with a pocket compass. The prevalence of earth-induced magnetism is so important in large steel steamships that the direction in which the hull is pointed while being built makes a difference in compass action when the vessel goes into service.

The inherent magnetism of a steel hull was used both offensively and defensively during World War II. Mines were laid that contained sensitive magnetic needles which fired them when a nearby hull caused a deflection. To counter this, ships were degaussed (de-magnetized) by hanging electric cables completely around the hull. Just enough current was sent through the cables to set up a counter field that neutralized the hull magnetism.

As can be expected from this tendency of the earth to cause induced magnetism, a steel hull presents special compass problems. Two of these are "quadrantal deviation" and "heeling deviation," and their respective errors. Although steel-hulled pleasure boats are a minority, these two conditions are discussed briefly for the benefit of "tin can" skippers—and other skippers with technical curiosity.

Figure 9-8: The iron spheres at the sides of the binnacle correct for quadrantal deviation encountered on a steel hull. (Credit—E. S. Ritche & Sons, Inc.)

Quadrantal Deviation

Granted that the steel hull has become a large magnet, it can be seen that the relationship of this magnet with the compass changes as the ship swings. In fact, these changes reverse themselves every 90 degrees, every quarter turn, and since a quarter of a circle is a quadrant, "quadrantal deviation" is a natural appellation.

Thanks to the thinking of some genius in the dim past, quadrantal deviation can be corrected very simply. It is done with two soft iron spheres or, in the newest installations, with two soft iron cylinders. These spheres are set at the compass level, one on each side athwartship, as shown in Figure 9-8. The direction of the magnetism induced in these spheres by the earth is always such as to counteract the effect of the hull on the compass. Without the spheres, there would be deviation on the intercardinal headings of northeast, southeast, southwest, and northwest. (On the cardinal headings of north, east, south, and west, the hull does not cause deviation but merely increases or decreases the earth's normal effect on the compass.)

It is imperative that the spheres be of dead soft iron that cannot retain magnetism. Sometimes these spheres harden through age and become retentive enough to retain some permanent magnetism. In that condition they will do more harm than good. The check is to rotate them (without moving them from their places) while watching the compass card; any swing makes them suspect. They can be brought back to the dead soft condition by being heated to red heat and allowed to cool slowly. (If a compass purchased for a wooden or other nonmetallic hull is equipped with quadrantal spheres, they should be removed.)

Flinders Bars

Quadrantal errors are caused by the equivalent of a magnet (the steel hull) lying horizontally parallel to the waterline. A portion of the hull also acts like a magnet standing vertically amidships; the compass errors this causes must also be corrected. This is done with Flinders bars.

Flinders bars are named after an English sea captain, Matthew Flinders, who introduced them about 150 years ago. They are short rods of soft iron (*not* permanent magnets) which are contained in a vertical brass tube just ahead of the compass. Enough pieces of rod are placed in this tube to cancel exactly the vertical magnetic effect of the hull and its machinery. Flinders bars derive their effect from earth-induced magnetism, just as quadrantal spheres do.

Heeling Deviation

When the steel-hulled ship is on an even keel, the center of the vessel's magnetic effect is directly below the compass and balances itself out symmetrically. When the ship heels to a considerable angle, this effect moves to one side or the other and deviates the compass. It causes the compass to oscillate annoyingly when the ship rolls. The remedy consists in placing a small heeling-error corrector permanent magnet directly under the compass. The height of this corrector magnet is varied until the undesired effects are neutralized.

The troubles just listed are specific errors that plague the compasses of tin-can skippers only. But all other small boat skippers, despite their nonmagnetic hulls, also have compass deviation problems to keep their lives from becoming too simple. In their case the deviation is caused by the engine and other ferrous masses in an otherwise nonmagnetic hull; for these problems there is no general correction and each manifestation must be treated separately.

Deviation Correction

Adjusting or compensating the compass on a small boat, in other words, eliminating the deviational errors caused by purely local influences aboard ship, is a convenience and not a necessity. An unadjusted compass could well be used for piloting if the amount of deviational error on each heading were known. These amounts would then be added or subtracted continually to arrive at the actual magnetic headings as the craft changed courses. This, however, is a tedious process and an unnecessary one if the errors can be eliminated and the compass then read directly.

Two phenomena of magnetism are utilized in correcting or adjusting the compass. The first is that the strength of the magnetic effect varies inversely as the square of the distance. Thus, a magnet three times as far away will have only one-ninth the effect, one five times as far only one-twenty-fifth the effect, and so forth. The second is that a magnetic field can be canceled by providing another field of the same strength but opposite polarity.

To put these phenomena into practice, small permanent magnets, called compensators, are placed near the compass in such a manner that they cancel the effects of the disturbing iron masses. These magnets must be placed with great precision both as to direction and distance from the compass. They must cancel undesired fields only and must not introduce errors of their own. (The mechanics of adjusting are described in Chapter 14.)

Deviational errors are divided into two classes and corrected in two steps, each with its own magnet. One correction is for deviation on the north-south heading, the other correction is for deviation on the east-west heading. How the corrective compensating magnets are arranged

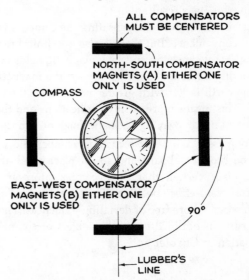

Figure 9-9: Small compensator magnets around the compass counteract the effects of deviation. (These are self-contained in the housing of some yacht compasses.) Magnets A have no effect when the boat is heading east or west; B do not affect north-south runs. (Only one A compensator and only one B compensator are used.)

with respect to the compass is shown in Figure 9-9. (Many commercial yacht compasses contain these two sets of magnets inside their housings and with these there is no need for outside compensators except in extreme cases.)

The axes that determine the locations of the compensators are drawn through the center of the compass, crossing directly under the compass pivot. One is exactly on or parallel to the lubber's line, the other at exactly 90 degrees to it. The distance of the compensators from the compass could vary from inches to feet; the directions of polarity are determined by trial and error. The compensators are adjusted separately, although there is some interaction between them.

Remember that the compass card is stationary and that the boat with its magnets swings around it. With this in mind, the action of the compensators can be understood more easily. When the boat is on a north-south heading, the compensator on the fore and aft line of the compass (the one that lies athwartship) is in the position of greatest influence. On an east-west heading, the compensator on the athwartship line (lying fore and aft) exerts greatest influence. On intercardinal headings, both compensators are in positions of partial influence and the effect on the compass is their resultant.

As already stated, compensating the compass is a matter of convenience. But there is also a technical reason for doing it. By canceling spurious magnetic fields and their detracting influences on the compass, the magnetic effect of the earth is left with greater power over the compass card. This means more positive indications and the elimination of much swaying back and forth or "hunting."

Compasses with self-contained compensators should not be brought aboard and set in place until after you have made certain that these compensators are in the neutral, zero-effect position. This is best done in some open space ashore free of deviating influences. The simple procedure is outlined under the subject of compass compensation in Chapter 14.

Deviation Tables

Theoretically it is possible to have a zero-deviation ship, either through construction or compensation; research vessels have been built with nary a piece of magnetic material, not even one steel bolt, and their compasses hug the magnetic meridians. As a practical matter, complete compensation may be too great a task; some small deviations are allowed to remain to assert themselves on certain headings. These are tabulated for the benefit of the helmsman into a deviation table.

The deviation table can be a simple listing of the more important compass headings and the amount of deviation to be added or subtracted at each. It could also be in the form of a so-called Napier diagram from which interpolated deviations can be taken for any compass heading. (See Figure 9-10.) The Napier looks complicated, yet it is simply a graph drawn to a system of coordinates slightly different from the usual rectangular ones. The Napier axes are at 60 degrees to each other; one is drawn in dotted lines and refers to compass heading, the other in solid lines for magnetic heading. Readings and interpolations are transferable back and forth by sighting parallel to the axes. (Making and using the tables and diagrams is explained in Chapter 14.)

Variation

Because the earth's north and south magnetic poles do not coincide with its north and south geographic poles, the magnetic meridians do not coincide with the geographic meridians. In simpler language, even a perfectly compensated compass does not point to true north except in a very few places on the globe. Instead, it aligns itself with the magnetic meridian and thus is generally at some angle with the meridian going to true north. This angle between the meridians at any location is the "variation" at that location.

Variation is a fact of nature and is beyond man's control. All man can do is record the amount of variation on his charts and then compute his navigational courses accordingly. Variation differs from one place to another and its value is not even permanent but changes slightly over the years. The rate of this change is also marked on the charts.

The magnetic north pole has been considered variously at 73 to 76 degrees north latitude and from 98 to 102 degrees west longitude within the period of recorded history. The differences in distance become less than 1000 miles from the true North Pole and are less than 4 percent of the distance around the globe. An assumption that the line between the magnetic poles goes through the center of the earth will slew the south magnetic pole over an

UNITED STATES POWER SQUADRONS

Compass Heading — Dotted Lines   **Magnetic Heading — Solid Lines**

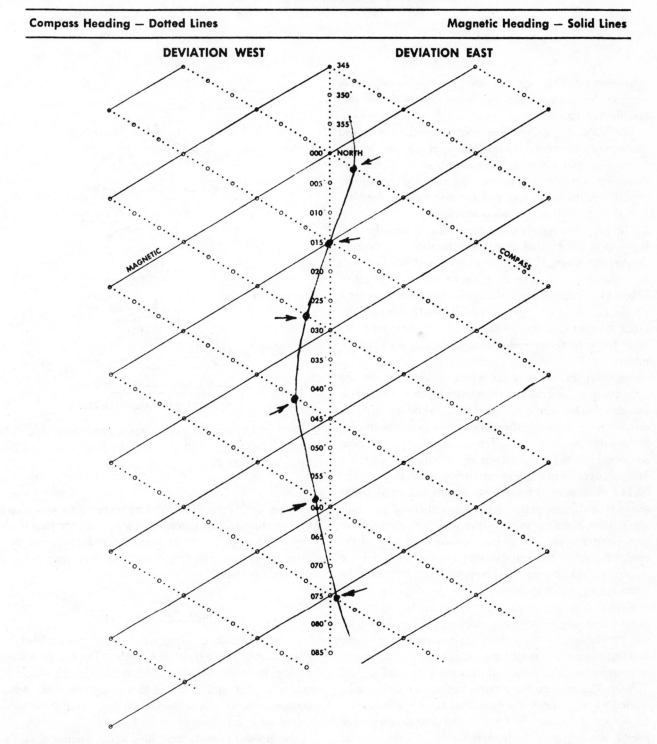

Figure 9-10: This deviation table and the Napier diagram convey identical deviation information, but the Napier enables interpolation for any heading. (The points on the Napier corresponding to the table are marked by arrows.) (Credit—U.S. Power Squadrons)

equal amount. This explains why magnetic meridians are not parallel to geographic meridians and is shown pictorially in Figure 9-1.

The lines of magnetic flux connecting the north and south magnetic poles are not segments of great circles but are considerably distorted in most areas of the globe. The distortions are caused by the varying nature of the mineral deposits in the earth and perhaps also by the electrical field conditions in surrounding space.

The variation figures sometimes bear an orderly relationship to one another in adjoining locations; sometimes they do not. Going down the Atlantic Coast, for instance, the variation varies from 20 degrees west off the coast of Maine to 15 degrees west off Cape Cod to 12 degrees west off New York to 10 degrees west off New Jersey to 7 degrees west off Chesapeake Bay and finally reaches 0 degrees (no variation) off Florida. (The figures are approximate.)

One way to visualize the effect of variation on the compass is to analyze exactly what happens to the card. Imagine first that there is no variation; the boat is heading directly true north and the lubber's line indicates this by being opposite 0 degrees. (Deviation, if any, has been neglected.) Now, continue on this straight course but bring 10 degrees of easterly variation into the picture. The lubber's line does not move but an unseen hand twists the card 10 degrees to the east (to the right) and the reading is now 350 degrees. Had the variation been 10 degrees westerly, the unseen hand would have twisted the card 10 degrees toward the west (to the left) and the reading would have become 10 degrees. Figure 9-11 illustrates the three examples.

Note that in each of the three foregoing situations the compass reading was different but the heading of the boat was the same. Obviously, then, if a true northerly course of 0 degrees is to be steered in a locality having 10 degrees of easterly variation, the compass must be held at 350 degrees. This proves that easterly variation must be subtracted when *uncorrecting* from true to compass (360 − 10 = 350). To make good the course of 0 degrees (true north) in a region of 10 degrees westerly variation, the compass was held at 10 degrees, which proves that westerly variation is added when *uncorrecting* (0 + 10 = 10). Zero degrees and 360 degrees are the selfsame point.

(A more thorough exploration of the three methods of describing courses—true, magnetic, and compass—is un-

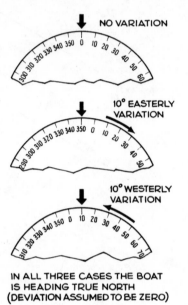

IN ALL THREE CASES THE BOAT IS HEADING TRUE NORTH (DEVIATION ASSUMED TO BE ZERO)

Figure 9-11: Three different compass readings which could ensue because of variation when the boat is heading due north are shown above.

dertaken in Chapter 17.) Working rules for correcting and *uncorrecting* are also given. An uncorrected compass reading includes the errors of variation and deviation; in a corrected compass reading these have been removed and the result is "true."

Total Compass Error

If compasses could talk they would surely sue for libel the writers who accuse them of "errors." The compass does not err; it merely reports what it feels to be the magnetic field around it, and is unable to discriminate. Still, it has become customary to call deviation and variation "errors" —and we will follow suit.

The amount of variation added to the amount of deviation equals the total compass error. But this is an *algebraic* addition. This mathematical description simply means that the minus or plus signs preceding the numbers must be taken into account when adding them together. (No sign preceding a number signifies that it is plus.)

When a +5 and a −5 are added, the sum is not 10 but 0; the positive amount cancels the negative amount. On the other hand, with different numbers either a positive or a negative could be in the majority. This is illustrated by the following simple examples: +20 added to +3 equals +23; −7 added to +4 equals −3; −6 added to −2 equals −8; +8 added to −12 equals −4.

The plus and minus signs before the degrees of variation and deviation are not found on the charts but must be supplied (at least mentally) by the skipper. When working from a true course to a compass course (*uncorrecting*), easterly variation and easterly deviation both take a minus sign; westerly variation and westerly deviation both take a plus sign. When correcting from a compass course to a true course, easterly variation and easterly deviation both take a plus sign; westerly variation and westerly deviation both take a minus sign. Correcting and uncorrecting are exactly opposite operations.

For a little mnemonic mental boost, think of the ship's cat helping you with the chart work and saying meeuuu (MEU). In this feline language *M* means minus, *E* means easterly, and *U* means uncorrecting—minus easterly uncorrecting. Ergo, both easterly variation and deviation take a minus sign when uncorrecting from the true course to the compass course. Westerly is opposite and that makes its sign plus when uncorrecting. Correcting is opposite from uncorrecting; thus, easterly takes a plus and westerly a minus. Listen to your cat and you can't go wrong.

Gyro Compass

At this writing, gyro compasses are found on few, and only the plushier, small boats. Similarly, a decade or so ago direction finders, loran, radars, and fathometers were not installed on modest pleasure craft, yet today the skipper of a yacht is surrounded by these electronic aids. It could well be that a gyro compass within the means of the average owner is just over the horizon. In that event the following information has educational interest in the present and will have practical value in the near future.

Despite its basic importance as a prime navigating tool, the magnetic compass has two flaws, one inherent (variation) and one peculiar to its location (deviation). The gyro compass has neither. A properly installed gyro points to the true north all the time that it is spinning. The earth's

magnetic variation does not affect it and any amount of local magnetism also does not affect it. The gyro, or "iron quartermaster" as World War II sailors learned to call it, does have an Achilles heel: When the electric power goes off, so does the compass.

Because the gyro compass is unaffected by its surroundings, it can be installed in any handy place on the average boat. Its directional indications are then relayed to the helmsman's position and to the flying bridge by compact slave units called repeaters. These repeaters can also perform other chores; they can orient peloruses, operate automatic course recorders or autopilots, and supply directional sense to radar screens.

You may not realize it, but you saw the working principle of the gyro compass every time you watched a child's spinning top or pivoted on your finger a toy gyroscope with its spinning flywheel in the wire cage. Both toys displayed the two attributes that make the iron quartermaster possible: precession and gyroscopic rigidity. All gyroscopes are governed by precession and rigidity, even that giant gyroscope upon which we live, the earth.

When the top of the spinning toy gyro moved in a small, slow circle, it was precessing; this was its reaction to the gravity that was trying to pull it down. It resisted the downward pull by moving sideways, and these constant little sideward motions became the circular path.

The toy gyro displayed gyroscopic rigidity by the way it kept pointing in one general direction while its flywheel was spinning fast. You may not have realized it, but that point was at some fixed spot in *space*; if you could have kept the flywheel spinning long enough, it would have maintained that point despite the turning of the earth. That little trick is the secret of its adaptability as a compass here on earth—it can be kept pointing at Polaris, the North Star. All this is pictured in Figure 9-12.

Of course, the commercial gyro compass for a ship is not all that simple, but what you have read is the basic principle underlying the complicated mechanism. The complication arises because the precession must be controlled with reference to the earth so that the point is always at Polaris. This is done by incorporating a pendulum weight and thus using gravity as an aligning force to take the place of magnetism. (A free-hanging pendulum anywhere on the globe always points to the center of the earth.) The mechanism must also be able to accept corrections for ship's courses other than the east and west which

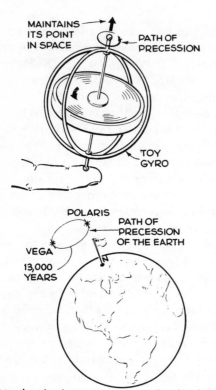

Figure 9-12: A spinning gyroscope maintains its point in space—hence its adaptability as a compass. The earth, itself, is a gyroscope and its axis points to Polaris, the North Star. In 13,000 years the axis will point to Vega because of precession.

lie in the earth's plane of rotation. (On a north-south heading the ship's speed and the earth's rotation are at right angles and the resultant is large enough to require compensation.) Iron quartermaster has no brain and cannot differentiate between ship speed and earth speed. Nor is iron quartermaster immune to little heading errors; these can be tabulated much like the deviations of a magnetic compass.

The foregoing schematic explanation assumed the gyroscope to be spinning with its axis parallel to the axis of the earth. Commercial makers of gyro compasses prefer to have this axis horizontal because then the gravitational effect of the pendulum is at a maximum and the north pointing more positive. (Technically this is known as the cosine effect.) They also use ingenious forms of damping which counteract the effect of roll and pitch and keep "hunting" down to a value too small for the helmsman to notice.

Figure 9-13: The gyro compass (a) does the direction sensing; it is not affected by nearby magnetic objects and can be located anywhere. The repeater (b) then displays this directional information at a remote point. (Credit— I.T.T. Decca Marine Corp.)

GYRO REPEATERS.

The "repeater" has no sensing ability of its own. It is simply an electrical indicating instrument which slavishly and accurately follows the movements of the master gyro. Figure 9-13 portrays a gyro compass and its repeater.

The electrical systems that actuate repeaters are of two types: step by step and continuous. The former is a direct-current system while the latter operates on alternating current and makes use of selsyn motors (see Chapter 7). In either case the operating current is low and the wiring simple.

Instruments

Modern technology has long since outstripped man's natural senses and he must therefore rely on instruments for information about the workings of the technical equipment surrounding him. The need for such information, and concomitant instrumentation, is especially acute on modern pleasure boats. In order to function safely and efficiently the skipper must have constant checks on the vital factors that govern his propulsion system, his electrical system, his navigation, and what might be called his "safety system" that wards off disaster from fire and flood.

METERS.

The most ubiquitous instrument in the electronic and electrical world is the simple meter. Its face can be calibrated in volts, amperes, gallons of fuel, degrees of rudder, or what have you—but at heart it is still the simple meter.

The type of meter considered to have the highest accuracy is built around what is known as the D'Arsonval movement; this is illustrated schematically in Figure 9-14.

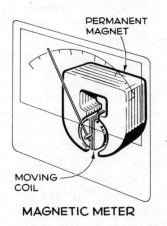

MAGNETIC METER

Figure 9-14: This D'Arsonval movement is the heart of the finest electric meters. Current flowing through the pivoted coil establishes a magnetic field which reacts with the permanent magnet and swings the needle.

A powerful permanent magnet surrounds a pivoted coil of wire. Current through the coil produces a magnetic field which interacts with that of the magnet and results in a movement of the needle. (It is named after Arsène D'Ar-

sonval, a scientist of the previous century.)

A simpler and less expensive movement is shown in Figure 9-15. Herein the current to be measured heats a

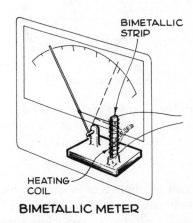

BIMETALLIC METER

Figure 9-15: This movement is simpler and cheaper than the D'Arsonval. Current through the heating coil heats and bends the bimetallic strip and moves the meter needle.

bimetallic strip whose flexure drives the indicating pointer. This device does not have the inherent accuracy of the D'Arsonval but is widely used by the automotive industry and is found on many boat instrument panels.

Although, strictly speaking, it is always the *current* through these meters that produces the reading, the devices can be calibrated in whatever units are appropriate for the circuit and sensor which operate them.

The greatest concentration of power in a boat is the propulsion engine. Its condition directly affects the safety and the pleasure of everyone on board. The engine's condition of well-being or malaise can be monitored continuously by measuring oil pressure, rotating speed, and temperature.

PRESSURE GAUGES.

Two forms of oil pressure gauge are available: the traditional mechanical and the newer electrical. The mechanical is the more accurate, the electrical is generally less expensive.

The so-called Bourdon spring is the heart and major constituent of the mechanical gauge. This spring is a

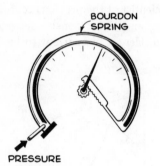

Figure 9-16: The Bourdon spring is a tube, elliptical in cross section. One end is closed and attached to a pointer. Pressure causes the tube to straighten and drive the pointer.

coiled brass tube of elliptical cross section which tends to straighten itself out when internal pressure is applied. This straightening effort is translated into a pointer moving over a dial by the connecting mechanism. The sketch in Figure 9-16 is self-explanatory.

The vacuum gauge, often called the power indicator, which measures intake manifold condition, is similar to the pressure gauge except for a much lighter Bourdon spring. The reduced pressure causes the spring to coil more instead of straightening.

The electrical pressure gauge operates on a totally different principle. It consists of a sensing unit and an indicator. The indicator is a simple voltmeter calibrated in pressure; the sensing unit permits more or less of the battery voltage to get to the indicator, depending upon the amount of pressure exerted upon it.

TACHOMETERS.

The speed at which the engine turns, in revolutions per minute, is measured by a tachometer. Tachometers are classified by their mode of operation as mechanical, electrical, or electronic. The simplest is the mechanical, the most complex is the electronic.

A common example of a mechanical tachometer is the speedometer on automobiles; it measures the revolutions per minute of the drive shaft but is calibrated in miles per hour. Except for calibration and the omission of the fancy dial face, powerboat mechanical tachometers are identical in construction with auto speedometers. Through a connecting flexible shaft the engine turns a small magnet inside a pivoted aluminum cup. The cup wants to follow the

magnet because of the induced currents (see Chapter 7) but is restrained by a light spring. Some models operate entirely by the air drag between two closely concentric cups. A pointer attached to the cup gives the reading on the dial. A schematic of this is shown in Figure 9-17.

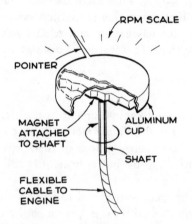

Figure 9-17: The mechanical tachometer is similar to an automobile speedometer. The internal magnet (or sometimes cup) exerts a drag on the aluminum cup in proportion to its speed of rotation.

The true electric tachometers are in effect a closed circuit consisting of a generator and a voltmeter. The generator is the sending unit on the engine and the meter is the speed-indicating unit on the instrument panel.

The electronic tachometer is the most complicated internally and yet, paradoxically, the simplest to install. It requires neither a flexible shaft nor a sensor at the engine and operates with an electric wire connection to the ignition system. (Obviously this precludes its use on a diesel engine, which has no ignition system, unless a special sensor is installed.)

The components of the electronic tachometer are connected to function as a counting circuit which counts the number of pulses (sparks) occurring in the ignition system. Since there is one spark per revolution in a two-stroke-cycle engine and one spark per *two* revolutions in a four-stroke-cycle engine in each cylinder, the dial can be calibrated easily.

TEMPERATURE GAUGES.

The simplest temperature gauge for an engine is a plain thermometer and, in fact, this ubiquitous motometer graced all automobile radiators a few decades ago. Admittedly this device would be a bit unhandy on a small boat where the skipper is removed from the engine by distance and closed hatches. Some form of remote indication is needed. Fluid systems and electric systems are available; the electric is the more common.

The indicating unit for the electric temperature gauge is again a simple voltmeter whose dial has been calibrated in degrees Fahrenheit. The sensor responds to the engine temperature by varying the current it permits to pass. Marine engines make provision for the sensor with a hole in the block tapped with standard pipe thread.

ENGINE-HOUR METERS.

Marine engines are always going "uphill," unlike an automobile, which coasts much of the time. This heavy duty makes regular maintenance mandatory. The surest way to accomplish this is by service based on hours of operation; the engine-hour meter keeps track of this.

The innards of the engine-hour meter consist of a clock movement geared to a digital counter. The clock is started and stopped in unison with the engine by a connection to the ignition circuit. On diesel engines a switch in the oil pressure line does the starting and stopping. A typical unit is shown in Figure 9-18.

Figure 9-18: The engine-hour meter records the hours actually run by the engine and aids in proper maintenance. It connects to the ignition system of a gasoline engine and to a sensor switch in the oil pressure line of a diesel. (Credit —Industrial Timer Corp.)

FUEL GAUGES.

Automotive and marine fuel gauges, which indicate the contents of the fuel tank, are practically identical except perhaps for slightly heavier and more corrosion-proof construction of the seagoing unit. The transmitter with its float located in the tank is shown in Figure 9-19.

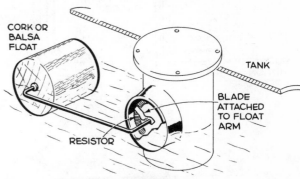

FUEL TANK SENDING UNIT

Figure 9-19: A float in the fuel tank sending unit varies a resistor that controls the current going to the fuel gauge on the bridge.

The indicator unit can be the usual simple voltmeter dependent upon magnetism for its action or, in some of the lower-priced units, a thermostatic type. In the latter, a thermostatic strip is caused to bend by a heating coil responsive to the current in the circuit, which in turn moves the indicating pointer.

SPEEDOMETERS.

Marine speedometers, no matter how accurate, never can measure speed over the *ground* except in the rare case of a current-less sea; they can only indicate speed through the *water*. The speedometer is the modern boatman's replacement for the historic heaving of the log over the taffrail.

Commercial marine speedometers are either mechanical, hydrostatic, or electrical. The mechanical type measures the rotation of a small impeller attached to the outer hull—just as the auto speedometer responds to the rotation of a gear in the transmission. Many of these units also include a mileage counter or odometer.

The hydrostatic marine speedometer takes its indications from the pressure generated in the water by the boat's forward motion. This pressure can be positive or negative (vacuum) and is determined by the design of the sensing head, or Pitot tube. Since pressure is the variable, the indicator is quite naturally a sensitive pressure gauge calibrated in speed. See Figure 9-20. One simple hydro-

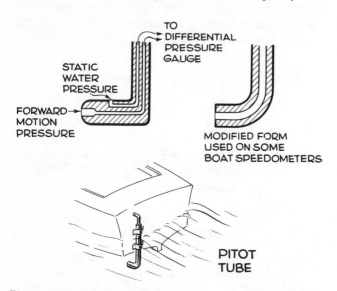

Figure 9-20: Marine speedometers can be operated mechanically, hydrostatically or electrically. Representative samples of each method are shown.

static speedometer is a self-contained tube that the skipper holds overboard.

The sending units of the electric marine speedometers vary in their methods of operation. Some actually are small propeller-driven alternators whose outputs vary in frequency and voltage, with the speed of the boat. Others use a little paddle wheel that sends pulses to a counting circuit which translates these into miles per hour. Still another dispenses with the rotating impeller and substitutes a light wand; the boat's movement pushes this back and varies the relationship of coils in an electronic circuit. All types of electric speedometers terminate in some form of voltmeter calibrated in miles per hour or knots.

The essential difference between speedometers for powerboats and for sailboats is sensitivity. Sailboats are slower and require speedometers able to function at minimal speeds.

RUDDER-ANGLE INDICATOR.

The man at the helm generally cannot tell from looking at the steering wheel what the position of his rudder is.

Except for the hard-over positions when the rudder hits the stops, the intermediate positions of the wheel give no clue to the steering direction unless the boat is in motion. The rudder-angle indicator eliminates this blind condition.

The rudder-angle indicator pictured in Figure 9-21 con-

Figure 9-21: Knowing the angle of the rudder can be important, especially when starting away from a pier. This equipment brings the information electrically. (Credit—Columbian Hydrosonics, Inc.)

tains its own actuating battery and is therefore independent of the boat's electrical system. The indicator at the helm is a simple voltmeter with a center zero and graduations right and left marked in degrees. Electrically the circuit is that of the Wheatstone bridge (see Chapter 7) with the meter as the null detector. Battery drain is so low that no switch is provided (the system is always on) yet one flashlight cell is claimed to last a whole season.

WIND INDICATORS.

The direction of the wind and its velocity are two characteristics of obvious importance to the sailboat skipper. The wind direction determines the courses he can maneuver and those he cannot; the velocity is his gauge of the safe point beyond which he should not venture. Understandably, therefore, there are many gadgets and instruments available to provide him with this information.

The more sophisticated instruments are electric in nature and give readings of both direction and speed. They do this by means of a wind vane at the masthead plus a wind-driven rotor. A connecting wire cable transmits the intelligence to the cockpit meter. A representative unit is shown in Fig. 9-22.

The meter, of course, reads true direction and true

velocity only when the boat is standing still. When the sailboat is underway, the readings become a .esultant of boat and wind motion and are known as the "relative wind" or the "apparent wind."

Deriving the true wind from the readings of apparent wind is a simple feat that makes use of a vector diagram in which boat speed and direction are the third leg. How this is done is taken up in Chapter 17. The illustration shows a sailboat wind indicator.

For many sailboat skippers a ribbon tied to a stay is indicator enough. They can get all the information they need from the ribbon's direction and the manner in which it flies.

Figure 9-22: The rotor and vane at the masthead transmit wind velocity and direction to the indicating unit below. (Credit—Airguide Instrument Company)

POLARITY INDICATOR.

One of the causes of electrolytic decomposition, as fully pointed out in Chapter 22, is a wrong polarity shore connection. This makes the underwater hardware of the boat act like the anodes in an electroplating tank and gradually dissolve into the sea. Aside from the economics of property protection, a reversed polarity shore connection could subject persons aboard to the hazard of dangerous shocks.

Polarity indicators give warning visually with a red light and audibly with a loud tone. The audible type lets the man making the connections on the pier know immediately of his error without waiting until he gets back to the boat and sees the light. A reversed connection causes current to flow through the indicator and sound the alarm.

FUME DETECTORS.

The most terrible disaster at sea is fire; even people who have been no nearer to such a holocaust than a movie will agree. The very idea of uncontrolled, searing flames in the midst of that universal extinguisher, water, is a frustration.

Fires on powerboats are almost without exception traceable to some mishap with the fuel aboard, either gasoline or propane; diesel hardly appears on the list of culprits. These fires invariably get a head start because they are initiated by explosions and, as if by immutable law, the blowups are set off in the bilge. The need for fume detectors that constantly monitor the bilge is therefore apparent. The bilge is the best monitoring place because the fumes from gasoline and propane are heavier than air and settle there.

The catalytic property of platinum is the principle on which most fume detectors function. (A catalyst is a substance that encourages chemical reactions without itself entering into them.) A self-heated platinum filament (a catalyst) is the heart of these detectors. Any combustible fumes impinging on the filament are "burned" harmlessly but the resultant heat changes the resistance of the wire and upsets the electric circuit of which it is a part. This sets off the alarm or registers an indication on a meter. Figure 9-23 shows a fume detector in detail.

Figure 9-23: Fume detectors continuously check the bilge for the presence of flammable vapors. Some detectors indicate the percentage of vapor present, others sound an alarm as soon as a potentially dangerous condition exists. (Credit—Pearce-Simpson)

One fume detector omits the complicated circuitry and instead makes direct use of the heat generated at the filament by the fumes. The increasing temperature bends a thermostatic element and closes a simple bell or lamp circuit.

Still another fume-detecting scheme takes an entirely original turn and makes use of a physical property known as adsorption. This is the ability certain materials have of entrapping (adsorbing) large quantities of the molecules of adjacent gases. In this fume detector, the change in electrical characteristics of the sensor, brought about by the adsorption, causes an electrical circuit to sound an alarm. One shortcoming of this method is that even non-combustible gases will trigger the warning; an advantage is that no current is drawn for standby.

FIRE DETECTORS.

Fires can of course start from sources other than explosive vapors. Fume detectors would give no warning of such occurrences and so the watching must be done by instruments sensitive to flames or rapidly increasing temperatures.

One marine fire detector has the added feature of automatically releasing a fire-existinguishing chemical. Photoelectric cells stand guard in this instrument and turn in the alarm when they "see" the light of flames or when an extraordinary rise in temperature occurs.

SMOKE DETECTORS.

A compact smoke detector is available for skippers who believe that where there's smoke, there's fire. This device employs a novel principle of physics known as the Tyndall effect.

A small electric light bulb and a photocell (electric eye) are placed at right angles to each other in a black tube. Light can reach the eye to set off the alarm only by being reflected from the smoke particles.

ENGINE SYNCHRONIZERS.

A twin-engine powerboat with two matched propellers runs most efficiently when the power plants are turning at identical speed. Any difference in revolutions per minute, and the consequent difference in thrust between port and starboard, requires rudder to be applied to maintain a straight course. This introduces wasteful drag. Another deleterious effect is the production of a "beat note" which

is annoying and can be destructive.

Tachometers are not sensitive enough to detect the small speed differences encountered in these situations. Engine synchronizers are the only answer.

The synchronizer takes the ignition pulses from both engines and feeds them to a comparison circuit whose output is the difference between them. In one such instrument these difference pulses fire a neon bulb. The frequency of the flashes indicates the magnitude of engine speed difference and a dark neon bulb means that the engines are in exact synchronism. Some devices present the indications on a meter instead of on a neon bulb, and this has the advantage of identifying the engine which must be corrected and by what amount. Figure 9-24 shows a typical unit.

Figure 9-24: These engine synchronism indicators enable twin engines to be held at identical speeds, thus avoiding annoying "beat notes" and lessening steering effort. (Credit—Airguide Instrument Company)

These synchronism detectors are not directly applicable to diesels (a diesel has no ignition) but adapters of various types are available.

THROTTLE SYNCHRONIZER.

The synchronizers just described bring the message of speed difference to the skipper but leave it to him to do the manual work of adjusting the throttles. An automatic gadget is available that takes over the whole job; it detects speed difference and corrects it without outside aid. Figure 9-25 shows it.

FUEL METERS.

Instruments for measuring the fuel consumption of gasoline engines are comparatively easy to construct because they are essentially flow meters. For diesel engines,

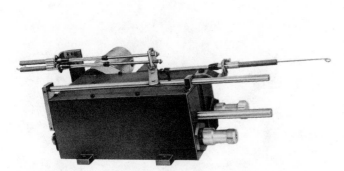

Figure 9-25: This synchronizer actually operates the throttles of twin engines to keep them at identical speed. It is automatic and requires no skipper participation. (Credit—Morse Controls)

Figure 9-26: The appetite of a diesel engine can be gauged accurately with this Fuel-O-Meter. The readout is digital in gallons. (Credit—Columbia Systems)

the problem becomes more difficult because a portion of the fuel flow is continually being rejected and returned to the tank.

Pictured in Figure 9-26 is a device which overcomes this hurdle by providing an intermediate tank which stores the rejected fuel and prevents it from being remeasured. Fuel consumption is registered digitally in gallons.

PELORUS.

The pelorus is sometimes called a dumb compass because it has a compass card and a lubber's line but has no magnetic-sensing ability. It is used for sighting and obtaining visual bearings. A good pelorus is set in gimbals to remain level in a sea.

The compass card is rotatable so that any point can be set against the lubber's line. This makes it possible to read bearings that are either true, relative, or magnetic, whichever are desired for the problem at hand. The sighting vanes are lined up on the target much like gunsights and their bearing is read from the concentric card below. A pelorus is shown in Figure 9-27.

A "pelorus" of sorts, helpful for practicing, can be made in a few minutes from an old chart. Cut one complete magnetic rose from the chart and mount it on cardboard. Cut only the inner rose from another section of the chart and also mount this on cardboard cut to its exact perimeter. A pin or thumbtack through the center of both roses so that the small one rotates concentrically on the large one plus a pin at 360° and at 180° of the small rose completes the "pelorus." You sight the instrument by lining the two

vertical pins up on the distant object and reading the angle on the large rose. The orientation of the large rose determines whether the readings are true or magnetic or relative. The "works" is shown in Figure 9-27 (b).

SEXTANT.

It is unlikely that the average small boat skipper will ever find it necessary to sight celestial bodies with a sextant to obtain a fix on his position. A familiarity with this instrument is a worthwhile skill that increases the pleasure of navigation, however. Furthermore, the sextant can be used to measure angles and distances in coastwise piloting.

The sextant is an optical angle measurer. Its name derives from its original shape which was a sixth (sextant) of a circle. It accomplishes its task by reason of basic optical laws, for instance, that the angle of reflection is equal to the angle of incidence, and that when two mirrors reflect a beam of light it is displaced twice the angle between them.

The battleship navigation officer's sextant is a beautifully precise and complex instrument but the small boat skipper can do with a much simpler and less expensive one. It's like the virtuoso's Stradivarius and the amateur's fiddle; both play music. As with the violins, the basic elements of all sextants are identical. A streamlined, low-cost, plastic model which could serve as the "practice fiddle" for new navigators is pictured in Figure 9-28. (The use of the sextant is covered in Chapter 17.)

a

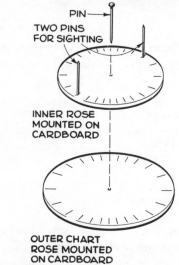

b

PIN

TWO PINS
FOR SIGHTING

INNER ROSE
MOUNTED ON
CARDBOARD

OUTER CHART
ROSE MOUNTED
ON CARDBOARD

Figure 9-27: The pelorus (a) (often called a dumb compass) is invaluable for many piloting tasks. Sighting is done through the vanes as through gunsights. A simple hand-made pelorus is illustrated in (b). (Credit—Davis Instruments)

Angles are laid down on a chart and measured with a protractor. Protractors for chart work appear more complex than the familiar half-circle of high school trigonometry. The three-arm protractor illustrated in Figure 9-29 is especially useful, as a perusal of Chapter 17 will show.

PARALLEL RULES.

The constant necessity when laying down courses for "walking" parallels from the compass rose to other sections of the chart has brought forth various gadgets. The

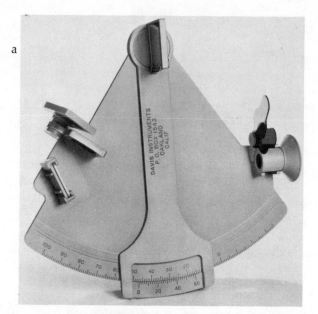

a

b

Figure 9-28: The low-cost streamlined plastic sextant (a) could serve as the beginning instrument for newcomers to navigation. The metal sextant (b) (it is really an octant) is a precision instrument with a micrometer drum that reads down to seconds of arc. (Credit—Davis Instruments and Weems & Plath Inc.)

time-honored one and still the favorite with the deep-sea boys is the parallel rule. Other devices are rollers and the more sophisticated course-plotting machine of Figure 9-30.

Figure 9-29: *The three-arm protractor can determine a fix by measuring the angles between three landmarks and transferring them to the chart. (Credit—Weems & Plath Inc.)*

TELESCOPES AND BINOCULARS.

Imaginative illustrations of old-time seafaring often show a telescope in the hands of a pegleg pirate standing at the rail searching the horizon. The telescope is seldom seen at sea today; the modern skipper prefers a good binocular.

A telescope of higher power than 10X has very little value on board a boat unless the sea is smooth as glass. The narrow field of view in the more powerful scopes magnifies the slightest motion of the deck until it becomes extremely difficult to gain any intelligence from the view. Since the usable magnification is so restricted, a good binocular of lower power and wider field is more serviceable.

Binoculars are of two types: the Galilean with straight-through light path and the prismatic, in which the light path is bent upon itself. The latter is the preferable kind and the more expensive. The surfaces of the lenses in good telescopes and binoculars are chemically coated to reduce image-degrading reflections.

Optical-viewing instruments are described technically by various characteristics: magnification, objective diameter, field of view, exit pupil, and relative brightness. These

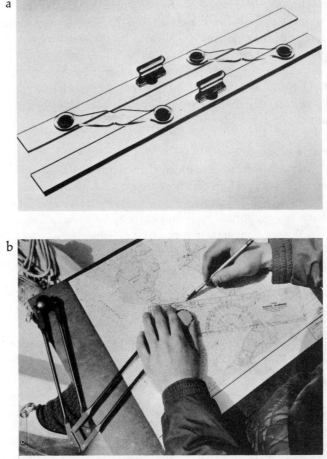

Figure 9-30: *The parallel rule (a) and the more sophisticated course-plotting machine (b) are both used in solving navigational problems. (Credit—Davis Instruments and Weems & Plath Inc.)*

do not necessarily indicate the high or low optical quality of the unit.

The magnification, listed as 6X, 10X, or whatever, tells how many times larger an object will appear than when viewed with the naked eye. The objective lens is the one farthest from the eye; its diameter is generally given in millimeters (25 to the inch). The field of view is the diameter of the distant scene observed through the instrument. The exit pupil is the diameter of the circle of light which is seen when the telescope or binocular is held at arm's length to the bright sky.

There are certain mathematical relationships between these measurement terms. For instance, the relative

243

brightness is the square of the exit pupil; the greater this brightness, the better the glass for night viewing. The diameter of the objective lens divided by the magnification gives the exit pupil. As an example, a 7 × 50 binocular, a favorite marine glass (7X magnification, 50-mm. objective), has an exit pupil of 7.1 (50 ÷ 7 = 7.1) and a relative brightness of 50.4 (7.1 × 7.1 = 50.4). This explains its popularity for marine work.

WATER TEMPERATURE.

Many "scientific" fishermen claim a direct relationship between temperature of the water and the quantity and species of fish caught. Knowing the temperature of the water is as important to them as type of bait and tackle.

A precise temperature-measuring system places a sensor in a through-hull fitting. The operation is electric and the indicator is a voltmeter calibrated in degrees Fahrenheit.

TIDE CLOCK.

A unique timepiece whose face is calibrated to the rising and falling of the tide is pictured in Figure 9-31. Once set for a particular locality, it is claimed to account for the succeeding intervals of time which mark the recurrence of the tides from day to day. (The hand makes a complete sweep in 12 hours 25 minutes instead of 12 hours and the indications apply in areas that have two tides per day.)

CALCULATORS.

Many skippers consider any mathematical calculation, however simple, as a needless chore and welcome any gadget that will free them of the task. Nomographs, calculators and disguised circular slide rules capable of answering navigational problems are available aplenty. Some figure out variation and deviation, others the resultant actions of current and wind, or fuel mileage, or speed. The calculator pictured in Figure 9-32 interrelates time, speed and distance.

Figure 9-31: Once set for a locality, this clock will keep track of the changes in time of the tides from day to day. (Credit—Time & Tides)

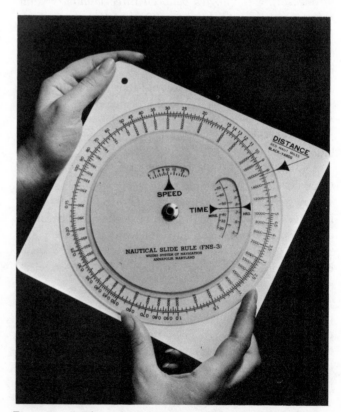

Figure 9-32: This calculator solves problems of speed, time and distance. (Credit—Weems & Plath Inc.)

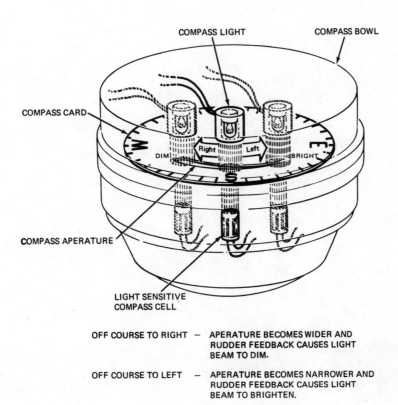

COMPASS LIGHT   COMPASS BOWL

COMPASS CARD

DIM   Right   Left   BRIGHT

COMPASS APERATURE

LIGHT SENSITIVE
COMPASS CELL

OFF COURSE TO RIGHT — APERATURE BECOMES WIDER AND
RUDDER FEEDBACK CAUSES LIGHT
BEAM TO DIM.

OFF COURSE TO LEFT — APERATURE BECOMES NARROWER AND
RUDDER FEEDBACK CAUSES LIGHT
BEAM TO BRIGHTEN.

10 *Heating, Refrigeration and Air-Conditioning*

Man is the only warm-blooded animal whom nature has not endowed with an in-built protection against a hostile environment. He has no fur and he has no feathers. He cannot maintain his bodily temperature in extremely cold or very hot surroundings without external aid. Since he cannot remain permanently encased in parkas when it is cold or in a cool bath when it is hot, he must be supplied mechanically with warmth and coolth. These basic needs of man do not change when he goes boating, hence the necessity for heating and cooling equipment on pleasure boats when the seasons require it.

Of course, heating is ever so much the simpler task than cooling. This is as true on a boat as it is in a home. Compare the simplicity of a stove or furnace with the complexity of even the smallest airconditioner. The laws of physics encourage the addition of heat to an object but seem to be stacked against any attempt to remove heat from it.

The sources from which heat can be derived for raising the temperature of a small boat cabin are four: basic fuels, propulsion engines, electricity, and reverse-cycle air-conditioning. The first requires the least equipment; a simple stove does the trick. The second is available only when underway. On most smaller boats, the third and fourth are usable primarily at dockside from shore power lines.

Since boating in northern climes is mostly a summer sport, this may lead to the quick thought that heating is unnecessary. But every skipper has memories of suddenly cold and rainy days, even in mid-season. At such times a heated cabin makes all the difference between acute discomfort and a cozy feeling of warm well-being. There is the added practical fact that cabin heating lengthens the boating season; cruising can begin earlier and continue longer before the winter shutdown. An added bonus from heating is the reduction of cabin dampness and the consequent lessening of mold and rot damage.

Heating Equipment

All heaters that use primary fuel, whether they are simple stoves or more elaborate furnaces, function through a process of combustion. The fuel is burned in a suitable chamber (the chemists call this "oxidation," or the chemical combination of the fuel with oxygen from the air) and

the locked-in energy is released as heat. How this heat is subsequently distributed, whether directly into the cabin or through an intermediate circulating fluid, constitutes the main difference between the systems.

SOLID FUELS.

The solid fuels such as wood, coal, and briquettes are burned on grates. The housing or enclosure that supports the grate serves the double purpose of providing a flow of air (oxygen) and acting as a radiator of the heat. The air movement is by gravity; the warmed air rises with a chimney effect and the surrounding cold air comes in to fill the void. Since the enclosure is soon at a much higher temperature than its surroundings, it radiates heat according to basic thermal laws. Figure 10-1 illustrates the principle.

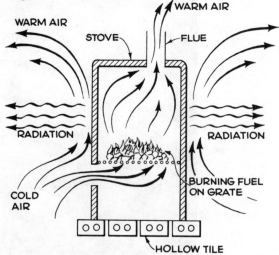

Figure 10-1: The oxygen needed for combustion in this basic stove is supplied by gravitational movement of air. Heat is produced and distributed by radiation and convection.

The burning of coal, wood, and charcoal creates undesired noxious gases, odors, and smoke in addition to the desired heat. These must be conducted to the outdoors without leakage; a smoke pipe leading through the deck does this. The smoke pipe must be installed in an approved and safe manner because it can become hot enough to ignite adjoining wood. In turn, the pipe must be capped with a smoke head to prevent the entry of rain or sea. Figure 10-2 shows a solid-fuel-burning stove.

Figure 10-2: Small stoves that burn coal or wood are a cabin comfort. The smoke pipe should end above decks in a smoke head, called a Charley Noble by old salts, which protects against the entry of rain and sea. (Credit— Fatsco Mfg. Co.)

One still finds powerboat skippers who snicker when mention is made of a fireplace aboard ship, yet sailormen have warmed many a cold body in front of them for many a year. The typical fireplace aboard small craft is designed for recessing into a bulkhead, has removable ash receiver, and stone tiles. It burns charcoal, coal, or wood.

LIQUID FUELS.

Alcohol is an approved fuel for shipboard use because its flame can be extinguished with water. The flame is smokeless and odorless; no ventpipe to the outdoors is required. Nevertheless, the danger always exists (as it does with all combustion) that the oxygen in a tightly closed cabin will be exhausted, thus preventing human respiration.

Other liquid fuels that can be used aboard are kerosene oil and fuel oil. Oil heat is especially apropos on a diesel cruiser because the burner takes its fuel from the same tank that supplies the propulsion engine.

The fuel oil can be burned with a wick, as in the old kerosene lamps and stoves, or it can be burned as a vapor without a wick. Modern deckhouse heating systems for all but the smallest cruisers follow the latter plan; in these the oil is extruded under pressure that changes it to a vapor or mist which, under proper conditions, allows complete, smokeless combustion. Home oil burners function in this manner. (The didactic physicists will explain, patiently, that it is always only the resultant *gas* that does the actual burning, regardless of the fuel or how it is fed to the flame.)

The conversion of fuel into heat is accomplished in an enclosed unit called the furnace. This furnace is composed of two parts, the boiler and the burner. In a steam system the boiler truly boils the contained water until steam is formed, but in a hot-water system the temperature is held to a lower value. The burner processes the fuel oil and makes it ready for combustion; its name is a misnomer

Figure 10-3: This oil heating unit is designed for marine use. It can be stowed in engine room or lazarette. Heat is brought to the cabins by steam or hot water piping. (Credit —Way-Wolff Corp., Inc.)

because the actual burning takes place only in the firebox section of the boiler and not in the mechanism itself.

A typical commercial unit consisting of burner and boiler designed for marine use is pictured in Figure 10-3. The mechanism at the top is the burner. A convection-type oil heater, which heats the air directly without an intermediate boiler, is shown in Figure 10-4.

OIL BURNERS.

The motive power for the burner is an electric motor which drives a pump and a blower. The pump draws the fuel oil from the tank and raises it to a pressure great enough to pass through the small hole in the nozzle at high velocity and emerge as a fine spray. The blower supplies air in sufficient excess to cause turbulence and assure good combustion. This excess has an optimum point beyond which it cools the flame and impairs efficiency, however.

The need for excess air becomes apparent when what happens at the instant of combustion is studied closely. Only one-fifth of our air is burnable oxygen, so that four-fifths of what the blower is providing does nothing to heat the boat. Actually, this interloping four-fifths is detracting from our heating purpose, but this is a fact of nature and cannot be avoided.

A spark jumping between two electrodes set in front of the nozzle ignites the oil spray. This spark is not just a single flash, such as occurs in an engine spark plug, but a continuous discharge that is maintained until combustion is well underway. Heat sensors detect the presence or absence of flame and shut the system down when combustion fails. Although safety is important in a home installation, it is doubly so in a pleasure boat.

The overall control of the burner could be a simple

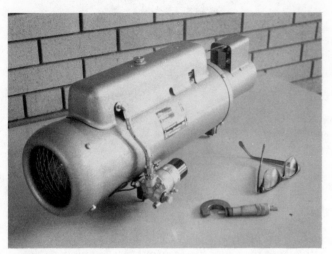

Figure 10-4: No boiler or pipes are needed with this oil heater; it warms the air directly and blows the hot air into the cabins.

switch handy to the skipper. This would be merely an on-off system taking no account of local conditions; if the old man forgot to turn it off, everyone would roast. A more sophisticated installation would be under the control of a thermostat, duplicating shoreside practice. The temperature element in the thermostat would then keep cycling the burner to maintain an even comfort in the cabin.

BOILERS.

A modern boiler is *not* simply a cylindrical tank with a flame playing over some portion of its outer surface like an oversize cooking kettle. Such a primitive construction would be highly wasteful of the heat available in the fuel cil. Instead, the internal configuration of the boiler is a series of tubes joined together at each end by "headers." A diagram of this is shown in Figure 10-5.

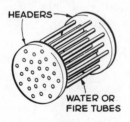

HEADERS

WATER OR
FIRE TUBES

Figure 10-5: A modern heating boiler is not just an oversize cooking kettle. It contains many tubes joined by headers. This construction increases efficiency.

The boiler is either "water tube" or "fire tube," depending upon whether the water to be heated or the hot gases that do the heating pass through the tubes. Each design has its adherents and its good points. Both aim at higher heating efficiency by promoting longer contact between the heat and the water and thus greater transfer of the heat. The ideal fire tube has a diameter just large enough to pass hot gases with minimum friction and is long enough to divest these gases of their heat.

The main effect of either design upon the boat owner could well be the ease (or difficulty) of cleaning. The combustion of the fuel oil is never perfect and the partially incomplete burning produces a soot deposit on the hot gas passages. This soot acts as an insulator and, as it gets thicker, less and less heat passes through to the water and more and more is wasted up the stack. Obviously, then, fire tubes that can pass a cleaning brush and are easily accessible have much to commend them when periodic cleaning is necessary.

Boilers for small boat heating are made of welded steel; the cast-iron construction often found at home is not a good sailor. An insulating jacket surrounds the boiler in order further to cut down heat loss. The space between boiler and jacket is filled with asbestos wool or a similar material that is an intentionally poor conductor of heat. The outside surface of a well-constructed unit never should be more than very warm to the touch when in full operation.

BOILER RATINGS.

Various methods of rating boilers are current, depending upon the industry in which they are used, but for good boat heating only two characteristics are important: the gallons of fuel consumed per hour and the BTU produced per hour. The first predicts the drain on the fuel tank during the heating period. The second makes it possible to approximate the size of boiler required for a particular boat.

BTU is the abbreviation for British thermal unit, as universal a measure of heat as the gallon is for liquids. By definition, it takes one BTU of heat to raise the temperature of one pound of water by one degree Fahrenheit. As an example of this method of calculation, theoretically it requires the same amount of heat (in this case 70 BTUs) to increase the temperature of 70 pounds of water by 1 degree or of 1 pound of water by 70 degrees.

The beauty of the BTU is that it can be employed in heating as well as in cooling calculations. For instance, if one pound of water were to be cooled one degree then one BTU would have to be extracted from it instead of added. The BTU-producing capability of a boiler sets the limit to the number and size of radiators and convectors which can be connected to it for cabin heating.

RADIATORS AND CONVECTORS.

The heat generated at the boiler is transferred to the cabin interiors by means of radiators and convectors. Speaking from a strictly technical and obvious standpoint, a radiator gives off heat by radiation, while a convector functions by convection. Most practical commercial units, however, operate in both ways and are neither entirely one or entirely the other.

Radiation is a static affair, while convection requires motion. A true radiator emits beams of invisible infrared energy because it is hotter than its surroundings; air need not be present for this to take place. On the other hand, a convector heats the air in contact with its hot surface. This heated air then moves away into the cabin, either by gravity or mechanical push, and new, cooler air moves in to be heated in a continuing movement or convection.

It is well known that warm air is lighter than cool air and that it therefore rises; in effect it "floats," and this is yet another facet of the buoyancy discussed in Chapter 1. Such motion is a simple gravity movement and requires no mechanical blowers or fans. Gravitational circulation is comparatively slow and may not always be adequate for the cabin requirements. In such cases, a small electric fan or blower is added to force air against the hot convector surfaces.

A convector depends for its effectiveness on the amount of heated surface it can expose to the passing air. The easiest way to increase this surface is to add fins to the pipes that carry the heating fluid. Copper fins and copper pipe are preferred in convectors; this metal is the best conductor of heat except for silver. Figure 10-6 shows the fins and pipe construction.

It is much more difficult to provide figures of required heat for a small boat than for a home. Compared to a room ashore, the average vessel's cabin has practically zero insulation from the outside temperature; the cabin sides (or ceiling) and the decks are generally a single layer of material or at best two layers, each too thin to be an effective insulator.

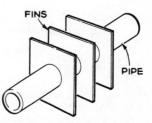

Figure 10-6: Fins increase the effective heat-radiating area of the pipe and raise the efficiency of heat transfer to the cabin air.

RADIATOR AND CONVECTOR RATINGS.

Experiments show that the usual radiator or convector gives off 1.6 BTU of heat energy per square foot of its surface for every degree of temperature difference higher than its surroundings. This factor is the basis for rating radiators and convectors on their ability to heat any boat cabins to comfortable levels.

The surface treatment of the radiator and convector is important; whether or not it is painted or polished has a great effect upon its heat-transferring ability. Curiously, the shinier it is, the worse its thermal efficiency. At one time it was common practice ashore to paint all radiators with a metallic aluminum coating and yet this drastically reduced their ability to heat the room. The best coating from a theoretical standpoint—although certainly not from the aesthetic—is dead black.

PIPING.

The connections between the boiler and the radiators and convectors can constitute a one-pipe system or a two-pipe system. In the one-pipe hookup using steam as the heating medium, the pipe delivers the steam to the radiator or convector and also returns the condensate to the boiler. Venting, when necessary, is to the atmosphere by means of small thermostatic valves which pass air but not steam or water. A two-pipe hot-water installation is shown in Figure 10-7; the tilt in the feed pipe is essential for return draining.

By using special fittings it is also possible to have a one-pipe system function adequately with hot-water heat. One fitting diverts a portion of the flow into the radiator or convector at its intake and a second creates a venturi (suc-

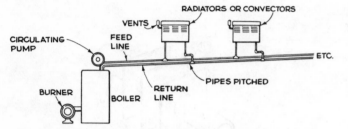

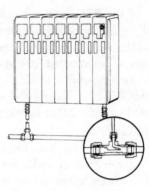

Figure 10-7: The feed lines of this two-pipe hot water heating system are pitched for easy draining. A pump forces the circulation. The vents relieve the system of entrapped air.

Figure 10-8: These special fittings (circle) permit a hot water heating system to be installed with only one pipe.

tion) effect at its exhaust. The drawing of Figure 10-8 illustrates this. The single pipe runs in a loop from and to the boiler and acts simultaneously as a supply and a return.

The recommended piping for a boat installation is copper tubing. The soft variety that is supplied in coils is more easily handled although the hard-drawn straight tubes may be convenient for long, straight runs. Connections can be made mechanically or by soldering.

Soldering (the so-called sweating) is widely used ashore but not particularly recommended for boat piping. The use of a soldering torch, with its open flame, is a great source of danger when working in the bilge and other enclosed spaces; it should be avoided if possible. Mechanical connectors can be equally leak-free when carefully installed and are perhaps less prone to eventual trouble from vibration.

The connecting tubing need not be insulated. This naturally means a heat loss, but since the lost heat is in the enclosed space of the boat, it is equivalent to an increase in radiation. On the other hand, there is nothing to prevent the meticulous installer from placing insulation around all tubing.

Copper-tube fittings are of two types: those which require flaring of the tube and those which hold the plain, straight, unflared tubing end; the latter is not recommended. A good flaring tool must be at hand when using the former type; the substitute practice of flaring the tube by hammering a steel ball against it does not produce satisfactory connections. Two wrenches (never just one) and a tubing cutter complete the tool kit. Figure 10-9 shows the fittings and the flaring tool. (These tools will become equally handy for engine fuel and oil lines.) Caution: Copper becomes hard from excessive working and

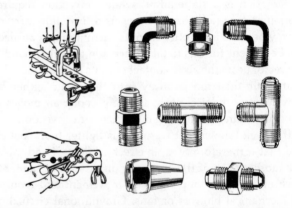

Figure 10-9: A flaring tool (above) should be used to make up copper tubing systems; makeshift flares leak. Some standard fittings are also shown.

then is prone to crack. (The copper can be brought back to normal by heating it red hot and allowing it to cool.)

BOILER TYPES.

Most small oil-burning hot-water or steam boat heaters are available for either horizontal or vertical installation, a choice that makes them adaptable to odd spaces. An ingenious installation in a forty-foot cruiser which uses space normally wasted in the lazarette is pictured in Figure 10-10. The necessary air intake and fuel exhaust are carried through the transom. The smoke pipe often required is thus eliminated, and the heating system becomes unobtrusive.

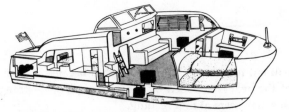

Figure 10-10: This complete oil heater fits snugly into the lazarette of an average cruiser; the hot water is piped to the convectors in the cabins.

Since the lightest of these units weighs over two hundred pounds, the fastenings must be sturdy enough to resist the effect of such mass when the boat pitches and rolls. The moorings should be to frames, stringers, and sturdy bulkheads and not to ordinary deckings.

SAFETY CONSIDERATIONS.

The stack from a properly operating oil burner does not get as hot as the smoke pipe from a coal stove, but the same precautions against fire should still be observed. A water iron (see page 142) should be used where the stack passes through a deck and the separation from all combustible material should be at least five inches, preferably with asbestos shielding as added insurance. A smoke head is required for prevention against downdraft and seawater; dampers are not permitted in the stack.

The Coast Guard requires inspection every three years of boilers on vessels licensed to carry passengers for hire. This, of course, is not mandatory on pleasure boats but it is a mighty good rule to follow voluntarily. Aside from any hazards, there are no plumbers at sea.

PROPULSION-ENGINE HEAT.

A goodly portion of every dollar spent for engine fuel is wasted as heat. This squandering of money and fuel is unavoidable because the laws of thermodynamics intervene to show that a perfect engine is impossible. During the cold season, however, a little of this waste can be retrieved to supply human comfort to the skipper and his passengers. The same thing is done in our automobiles.

The installation for using the engine as a source of warmth in the cabin is identical with the hot-water system already described, except that the oil burner and furnace are omitted. In their place is a heat exchanger. This heat exchanger is piped in series with the engine jacket so that the engine cooling water circulates through it and heats the entirely separate water flowing to the cabin radiators. For proper operation, the engine must have a thermostat to maintain its temperature at a high level.

For very small cabins, a standard automobile heater may be sufficient. This could be connected directly to the engine's cooling system by flexible hose without any additional piping. Depending upon engine size, several of these auto heaters could be connected in series. The only caution is not to slow the flow of engine coolant to the point where it is ineffective.

The best results with any of the systems using waste engine heat presuppose that the engine is fresh-water cooled. (See Chapter 2.) In other words, the engine-cooling water runs in a closed circuit of which the exchanger for cabin heating becomes a part. Raw seawater engine cooling presents problems when cabin heaters are to be added.

Since most boats are powered up to the limit, and even beyond, a great deal of waste heat is available but one obstacle is insurmountable: The heat is there only when the engine is running. Dockside heating must therefore be done with auxiliary means—or done without.

ELECTRIC HEAT.

Electricity is one of the hardest-working servants that man has at his beck and call but there is one thing this genie cannot do economically and that is heat living space. This is true afloat and even ashore, as attested by the comparatively small number of homes that are heated electrically.

True, the actual conversion of current to heat is efficient; all the "juice" goes directly into heat without waste. But the cost of the heating wattage is prohibitive because the original generating losses of converting fuel into electricity must be paid for. The high cost prevails regardless of whether the heating current comes from a dockside power line or from a shipboard generator. The only exceptions might be in locations close to immense sources of hydroelectric power, such as Niagara Falls.

Another deterrent to electric heating of small boat cabins is the heavy current needed to make a dent in even moderately cold weather. Only the largest cruisers are likely to have sufficient generating capacity aboard to run more than a small radiating unit because even this draws in excess of 1000 watts. Dockside operation of electric heaters is often disappointing because of the modest line capacity and the large number of customers—and often is discouraged by the marina owner. Running the electric heater off the boat batteries is, as the doctors say, contraindicated (meaning *don't!*).

The long and short of it, then, is that electric heating for small boats is at best a temporary assist to other heating installations. The plug-in type of portable electric heaters, whether radiant or convector, will ease an unseasonably cool night or warm a chilly corner. The radiant kind suffers the same drawback as fireplaces: They warm only what is directly in front of them. The convectors, especially those with fans, do a better job in spreading the warmth but it is still marginal.

REVERSE-CYCLE HEATING.

In this method an airconditioner is used in reverse to give off heat instead of absorbing it, hence the name. In essence this is a heat pump which pushes heat into the cabin instead of sucking it out as airconditioners normally do. (The concept of "pumping" heat back and forth as though it were a finite liquid will be understood easily after a study of the explanations of mechanical refrigeration and air-conditioning which follow.)

To a somewhat lesser extent, reverse-cycle heating meets the same problem that confronts electric heating; the lack of adequate sources of power. Still, an equal amount of electricity expended in the reverse-cycle system will put more warmth into the cabin because a large part of the heat is supplied by the cool outdoors—strange as this may seem at first reading.

The BTU output of an airconditioner operating on reverse cycle is greater than its BTU absorption when cooling. One reason is that all the mechanical losses which normally appear as waste become beneficial and add to the total heat output. The other reason is the one already stated, namely, that much of the heat is supplied by the outdoors and merely pumped in.

Mechanical Refrigeration

The old icebox, that instigator of corny jokes connecting wives and icemen, is disappearing from small boats almost as fast as it left homes a few years ago. Mechanical refrigeration adapted for marine use now comes in all sizes, some even small enough to permit a reasonable amount of operation off the storage batteries. Conversion units also are available for those skippers whose nostalgia wants the old box retained but the chore of lugging ice eliminated. (Figure 10-11 gives some hints on insulating the box properly.)

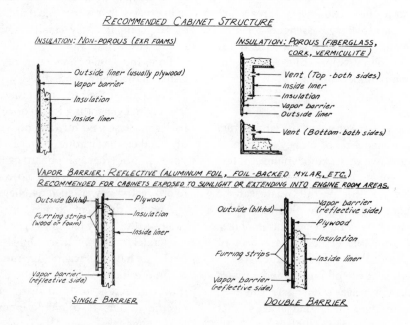

Figure 10-11: An icebox intended for conversion to mechanical refrigeration should be insulated properly. Here are some good guidelines which should be followed.

To understand mechanical refrigeration it is necessary first to clear up some physical misconceptions. The first has to do with "cold." Cold is not an entity, just as darkness is not; cold is the absence of heat as darkness is the absence of light. That can of beer in the fridge does not have cold put into it but rather has heat removed from it; this makes it cold.

Heat is a form of energy and the important characteristic to remember about it is that, of its own accord, it will flow only in one direction, from the hotter body to the colder body. To force it in the opposite direction requires power in the form of "pumping"; this situation is met in refrigeration, where the heat remaining in the cool food compartment must be pumped out into the much warmer cabin.

The movement of heat can be visualized as similar to the movement of water. Water will flow by gravity, without external aid, only downhill, from the higher location to the lower. If temperature be considered analogous to height, the similarity of heat flow becomes evident. To make water go uphill it must be pumped with an expenditure of energy determined by the distance it is lifted. This parallels what the refrigerator mechanism does with heat: It pumps heat from the cooler (lower) food compartment to the hotter (higher) cabin.

How does one go about "pumping heat"? Unfortunately, it is not as simple as pumping water. On the other hand, the process can be understood with little difficulty if the basic principles of physics which underlie it are explained. Of these the most important is the concept of latent heat.

Latent heat is hidden heat that must be added to a substance or taken from it in order to change its condition. A notable example is water. A thermometer in a pan of water over a flame will show a gradual rise in temperature until it reaches 212 degrees F. (at sea level) when the water boils. It will remain steady at this reading even though the flame continues to supply a great deal of heat. The heat added after boiling began was the latent heat needed to change the water from a liquid into a vapor, steam.

The same thing happens at the other end of the scale when the water is being frozen. The thermometer will drop to 32 degrees F. and remain there, despite the heat that is being extracted by the cooling apparatus, until all the water has become ice. This again was the latent heat needed to make the change from liquid to solid, from water to ice.

The second basic concept necessary to an understanding of mechanical refrigeration concerns boiling. We are used to having water boil at 212 degrees without realizing that this is true only at the normal air pressure found at sea level. Change the pressure and you change the boiling point. Thus the boiling point can be lowered by performing the operation in a vacuum. As a matter of fact, if the vacuum were good enough, the water could be made to boil by the heat given off by the hand! (This is a favorite demonstration in physics class.)

Mechanical refrigeration depends upon this ability to change the boiling temperature of a substance by varying the pressure upon it. It is equally dependent upon the phenomenon of latent heat. Many substances qualify under these two headings and could be used as refrigerants. However, the refrigerant in common use today is a chemical, "dichlorodifluoromethane," known to the trade as Freon 12. It is odorless, nonflammable, nontoxic, low in cost, and can be handled with comparatively simple equipment.

Freon 12 has replaced the sulphur dioxide formerly used in home- and boat-sized refrigerators. The sulphur compound is actually more efficient, but its noxious fumes are highly poisonous; its use entails a certain element of danger in the event of a leak. Ammonia is the best refrigerant of all and is found almost universally in large commercial plants; it is not suitable for small units because it is toxic and must be worked under great pressure.

Freon 12 is an oddity compared with ordinary liquids and gases. At atmospheric pressure it *boils* at *minus* 22 degrees F. (22 degrees *below* zero). Put it under a vacuum and the boiling point nosedives to an unbelievable 60 degrees below zero. Compress it to 160 pounds per square inch and the boiling point shoots up to 120 degrees F. This behavior is summarized by the graph shown in Figure 10-12 .

This wide spread of boiling points should expose the secret of Freon 12's adaptability to refrigeration. At one end of the scale the boiling point is lower than the temperature desired inside the refrigerator; at the other end it is higher than the temperature of the cabin into which the refrigerator heat must be pumped.

Freon *could* produce refrigeration without any equipment at all. An open dish of it left to evaporate (boil)

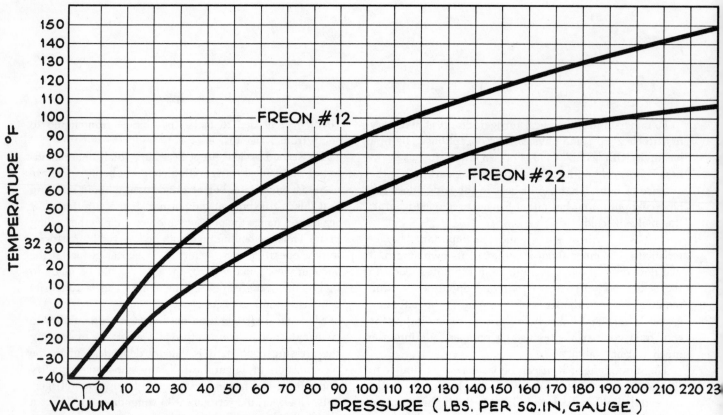

Figure 10-12: This graph shows how the boiling point of Freon used in refrigeration and air-conditioning varies with pressure. This characteristic is the secret of its popularity as a refrigerant.

would quickly reduce its immediate surroundings to minus 22 degrees F. But Freon is not free, nor is it found in the air, and this quaint method of refrigeration would be impractical even for a millionaire. To be practical, a small quantity of Freon must be used over and over again—and that is the purpose of the refrigeration machinery. Infinite continuous use is possible because Freon does not "wear out."

The Freon merry-go-round that provides the cooling is shown diagrammatically in Figure 10-13. Four units are needed in the circuit and these same four must be there whether it be a refrigerator or an airconditioner. The four are: compressor, condenser, expansion valve, and evaporator. (Some small units substitute a capillary tube for the expansion valve.) Of course the compressor must be driven by a motor of some kind, either gasoline, diesel, electric, or even the propulsion engine. Note that this is a completely closed circuit and that, if there is no leakage, the Freon will last "forever."

The compressor puts the Freon under high pressure and sends it into the condenser. The work done in compressing the gas puts heat into it and raises its temperature well above that of the surroundings. The condenser is thus

able to dissipate this heat to the adjacent air and cool the gas back to a liquid. The expansion valve permits only a controlled small quantity of the liquid to go to the evap-

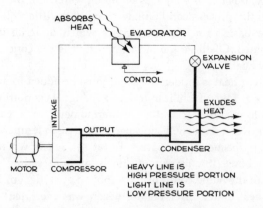

Figure 10-13: Refrigeration and air-conditioning are achieved by pumping Freon continuously around this circuit. Freon under low pressure in the evaporator boils and absorbs heat. It is then pumped under high pressure into the condensor where it gives up its heat. The expansion valve divides the high and low pressure circuits and controls the action.

orator. The evaporator is under low pressure (it is connected to the suction side of the compressor) and the Freon boils because of its previously explained characteristics. To boil it must have heat—and it takes this heat from the space around the evaporator, in other words, from the refrigerator interior. This goes on and on. The skipper has cold beer, the mate has fresh food, and nobody lugs ice.

For some reason, the theory of refrigeration has been clouded in an aura of mystery but the foregoing explanation should prove that this is undeserved. The whole business validly falls into the do-it-yourself realm and, in fact, many conversion units are available for installation by the skipper himself. One of these is shown in Figure 10-14; it is supplied charged with refrigerant so no Freon need be handled.

Refrigeration is held to a constant rate by the opening and closing of the expansion valve in response to signals from the evaporator. In addition, the motor driving the compressor is turned on and off, again in response to the signal. With the capillary tube (shown in the photos), the only control is the on and off of the motor; this is the system used in home boxes.

Small boat cabins are notoriously hot when the sun beats down on them and this makes it hard for the condenser to do its job. The more efficient installations therefore water-cool their condensers. Seawater is circulated around the condenser to take away the heat; the setup is similar to but smaller than the heat exchanger on an engine. The raw cooling water line requires its own pump and through-hull fittings.

HOLDOVER PLATES.

Some marine refrigerator manufacturers, realizing the exigencies of sailing, provide their units with so-called holdover plates. These retain some refrigerating ability without power after leaving the dock and will prevent food spoilage for a day or more. The holdover plates contain eutectic (chemical) solutions which freeze to a very low temperature while the unit is operating from dockside power. Their gradual "unfreezing" provides the refrigeration when power is removed. This does not imply something for nothing; nature just won't allow that. The secret lies in the additional power expended in freezing the plates originally.

Electronic Refrigeration

More than one hundred years ago, a scientist named Pierre Joseph Pelletier discovered that when an electric current is sent through the junction of two dissimilar metals heat is absorbed—in other words, the junction becomes cooler. This phenomenon remained a laboratory curiosity until the recent advent of certain semi-conductors which made it practicable.

The electronic cooling unit has no moving parts, consisting only of a small slab of semi-conductor material fastened to a large aluminum plate that acts as a heat sink. One commercial unit built on this principle is the size of a picnic basket and operates from the 12-volt boat battery; its makers claim that freezing temperature is reached after only an hour's operation of this completely electronic refrigerator.

Evaporative Refrigeration

The now familiar phenomenon of latent heat comes into the picture again with evaporative cooling. In this method the food compartment is surrounded or covered by a porous screen continuously kept wet. Air is blown through the screen, evaporates the water, and is cooled. (As should be clear from previous explanations, the water must absorb heat from its surroundings in order to become a vapor.)

The camper's porous jar that keeps drinking water cool is an example of evaporative refrigeration. The water constantly seeping through evaporates and cools the jar. For evaporation to take place, the humidity must be low. The humidity aboard a small boat is generally high. Ergo, evaporative refrigeration has little if any value on a pleasure craft except as a jury rig.

Absorptive Refrigeration

At one time, absorptive refrigeration was the most popular for home use. These refrigerators were marketed under the slogan, "The Flame That Cools." These were completely silent in operation because they had no moving parts.

The refrigerant in the absorptive system is a chemical, generally ammonia or lithium bromide, that has a high affinity for water. The chemical is alternately absorbed into the water (hence the name) and then boiled out of it

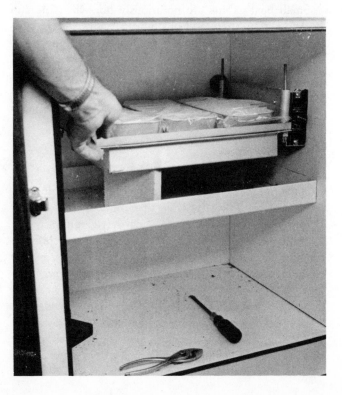

Figure 10-14: Conversion units turn iceboxes into mechanical refrigerators. The installation, shown in various stages above, can be a do-it-yourself project. (Credit—The Grunert Company; Photo by Gordon Manning)

in a continuous, closed-circuit process. The heat needed to change the chemical liquid into a chemical vapor (to boil it) in the evaporator is extracted from the food compartment, thus cooling its contents. This heat should not be confused with the flame-supplied heat that separates the chemical from the water by boiling. It is the same old latent heat merry-go-round, only with the compressor replaced by the silent flame or the equally silent electric heating coil. (If you heat a gas in a closed vessel, its pressure rises, it becomes compressed.)

The absorptive system is somewhat dependent upon steady gravity and that alone makes it unsuitable for small boats. In addition, the Coast Guard frowns upon gas devices that require pilot lights.

Fan Cooling

Fans are the old-time standby for keeping "cool" in a hot cabin. It is often hard to convince fan users that fans do not cool the cabin space (except insofar as they may pull in some cooler outside air) but only cool the occupants upon whom they blow. Each person in the fan's air path functions as an evaporative cooler for himself. The evaporation of his surface perspiration reduces his skin temperature—again by the application of the laws of latent heat.

The small, low-cost fans that abound on drugstore shelves are not suitable for marine use from the standpoint of either corrosion or durability. More sturdily constructed fans with a minimum of corrodible material are available from marine supply stores for all small boat voltages from 6 to 120. Fan motors that are to run on DC (direct current) must be of the commutator type (see Chapter 7); AC (alternating current) motors can have any construction.

Air-Conditioning

"Air-conditioning" is applied loosely to any cooling of air in a living space to make it more comfortable in hot weather. Strictly speaking, true conditioning of air may require not only cooling but heating, dehumidifying, humidifying, cleansing, or filtering as well. In other words, truly conditioned air can improve comfort and well-being in winter as well as in summer. Nevertheless, when the term "airconditioner" is used on small craft it signifies a cooling unit.

Small airconditioners are becoming commonplace in homes ashore for cooling individual rooms, especially bedrooms. They are also becoming more and more evident on small boats for cooling sleeping cabins. (Landlubbers believe that anything afloat is always cool; skippers know different.)

The underlying principles that govern refrigeration apply also to the cooling apparatus in airconditioners. The major difference in the mechanism is in its size and consequently in its cooling capacity. In addition, the evaporators in airconditioners are constructed so that fans or blowers can force air over their cool surfaces and into the space to be cooled. As with refrigeration, most marine airconditioners are two-unit affairs with the compressor and condenser placed in a convenient, remote location. Preferably, the condenser is water cooled.

As already stated, the smaller electric refrigerators can be run off the batteries for a reasonable (meaning short) time. Any airconditioner large enough to make a noticeable change in the temperature of even a small cabin *cannot* be run off the batteries for even a short time; its current drain is too heavy. This restricts airconditioners aboard either to dockside use or to pleasure boats with man-sized generating sets.

The industry rates airconditioners in "tons"—and this does not refer to their weight. An air-conditioning ton is the amount of coolth a ton of ice would provide if it melted within twenty-four hours. It so happens that the refrigeration ton and a horsepower almost coincide and a rough rule of thumb equates a one-ton airconditioner and a one-horsepower machine. This is a good thing for the skipper to bear in mind when he is shopping.

Experiment long ago disclosed that providing one ton of air-conditioning is equal to the absorption of 12,000 BTUs per hour. This leads to a much more scientific and more accurate manner of rating airconditioners, namely, in BTUs. Ethical manufacturers rate their units on the basis of BTU absorption capability and this enables the purchaser to know exactly what he is buying. Even more important, it gives him a means of specifying what he should buy for a particular installation.

The average small boat interior is difficult to air-condition because the ceiling and decks offer very little resistance to the entry of outside heat. They are either not insulated at all or else insulated in a very meager way. The automobile people ran into this same problem when they started air-conditioning the interiors of tin-can-bodied cars. A comparison will highlight the situation dramatically. The standard airconditioner for an ordinary bedroom is the *half*-ton size; the airconditioner in a sedan automobile is equivalent to the *three*-ton size.

Airconditioners, like refrigerators, are heat pumps that work against "gravity" by forcing heat from a lower temperature to a higher one. The fridge dumps the heat from the food compartment into the galley or the bilge or into the sea or wherever the condenser is located. The airconditioner in the cabin does a similar job; if it is a single-unit type, it must therefore be located with its condenser outside (usually not feasible) or with a seawater connection.

This may seem obvious but it wasn't so to a certain skipper who rated higher in his navigation than in his physics. He purchased a single-unit home airconditioner and proudly set it on a table in the middle of the cabin. He turned it on and happily sat down and waited for the place to cool. He may still be waiting.

The uninitiated often wonder why it is so much more difficult to cool a cabin than to heat it. Part of the answer can be found in the already explained manner in which heat travels, namely "downhill," from the hotter to the cooler. The steeper this "hill" (the greater the difference in temperature), the faster the movement. The heating surface of a radiator may be at 160 degrees F. or more with the cabin at 70 degrees F.—a "hill" of at least 90 degrees F. The evaporator of an airconditioner cannot go below about 35 degrees F. without frosting and usually is much warmer. The temperature difference here is at *most* 35 degrees. These figures emphasize the great difference in heat-transfer rates.

The water content of the air, its relative humidity, has a striking effect upon human comfort and upon air-conditioning. The relative humidity is the ratio between the amount of water vapor in the air at a given temperature and the maximum amount the air could hold at that same temperature. Zero percent is absolutely dry and 100 percent is fully saturated. Warm air can hold more moisture than cold air; at 70 degrees it holds sixteen times more than at 0 degrees.

High humidity affects humans because it interferes with evaporation of perspiration; the skin cannot cool itself by evaporating its surface sweat. High humidity affects airconditioners because the air must give up some of its moisture as it is cooled and the latent heat evolved as the vapor changes to water must be absorbed by the refrigerating unit. A portion of the cooling capacity is thus lost, although a beneficial dehumidifying action has automatically been performed.

One method of determining humidity is with a wet-bulb thermometer in conjunction with a standard or dry-bulb thermometer. Such a dual set is shown in Figure 10-15.

Evaporation from the wetted sleeve around the wet

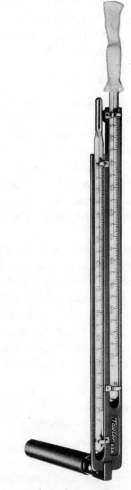

Figure 10-15: A regular thermometer and a wet bulb thermometer comprise this sling psychrometer. The difference between wet and dry readings when the instrument is whirled is referred to a table and determines relative humidity. (Credit—Robert E. White Instruments, Inc.)

bulb will cause this thermometer to read lower than the dry bulb. The amount of difference depends upon the relative humidity; when the relative humidity is 100 per-cent, or saturation, there will be no difference.

A representative marine airconditioner is shown in Figure 10-16.

Figure 10-16: This airconditioner fits nicely against a bulk-head in the cabin. Circulating seawater removes the heat from its condensor. (Credit—The Grunert Company)

CONDENSATE.

When moist air strikes the cold evaporator, the water it carries will condense. The amount of condensate that will collect on a humid day can be surprising.

Under no circumstance should this condensate be al-lowed to drain into the bilge. It is fresh water and would prove a sure accelerator for rot. (See Chapter 22.) The best disposal of the condensate is overside by means of a properly placed drain tube. Next best is a container to be emptied periodically, but this places dependence upon the human factor.

Combination Heating and Cooling

Admittedly, integrated systems for completely heating and cooling the entire interior are in the realm of the largest boats, those which unblushingly can be called yachts. A mouth-watering sample of one of these is shown in Figure 10-17. It is a target to shoot at for the average skipper because it may spark him into ideas for his own craft.

An interesting and ingenious facet of this installation is the single-pipe system. Cold water flows through it in summer and hot water in winter.

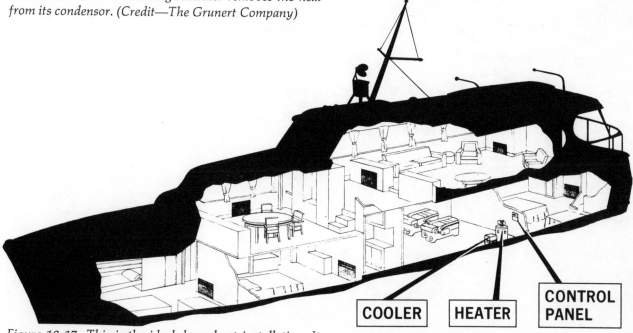

COOLER   HEATER   CONTROL PANEL

Figure 10-17: This is the ideal dreamboat installation. It cools in summer and heats in winter.

PART   III

THE WORLD OF SAIL

11 *Sailboats and Their Equipment*

Sailboat Mystique

WHEN you enter the world of sail you come into a realm as unique as the one Alice found when she stepped through the magic mirror. Everything is different from the normal way of life in the land of engines. The stinkpot skipper lusts after the newest technology while the sailboatman wants things to remain as simple as they once were. Even sail language and nomenclature are rife with ghosts of long ago.

It is not surprising then that sailors consider themselves a superior breed. There is a basis for this feeling and you cannot fault them; it does take more skill to sail than to power and there is more need to read nature's mind.

The driving force for the powerboat is always at the skipper's command. He turns a key and a wealth of power is ever-ready to whisk him where he wants to go at the speed he chooses. No such easy luxury is available to the sailboatman. Except on the rare occasions when his engine is in use, he must con uncooperative winds for his motive power and must lie becalmed when the breezes fail him altogether. These frustrations have hardened him and made him wily.

Not content to match wits with nature alone, the sailboatman constantly feels the urge to compete with his fellow sailors. He has a compulsive need to race.

The racing fever is endemic in the sailboat world. Be he in pram or 12-meter yacht, the sailor wants to race. He cannot meet another sailboat without subconsciously calculating how to skunk him out of the wind and beat him. His racing "speed" may be what the powerboatman would call trolling but to him the pace is exhilarating. Winning is a triumph to be remembered and recounted.

The sailboatman is content to use his muscle and often there is not a vestige of machinery aboard. An engine, if shipped, is a hidden stepchild so rarely run that it balks when its rest is disturbed. The true sailor gives in to mechanical aids only at the terminal point of physical ability. The winches on a larger sailboat represent this type of surrender and he keeps them highly polished, perhaps to mollify the gods into overlooking his fall from grace.

The aching of sailors for the long ago extends even to physical conveniences. Few heads are found on smaller sailboats; the bucket suffices. Electric lights and the accompanying messy battery with its need for charging? Who needs them; what's the matter with kerosene?

The hardware for sailboats also emphasizes the uniqueness of the sailing world. There are whisker poles and spinnaker poles and inclinometers and gadgets to measure the tension of the stays—names never heard around powerboats.

Tradition and the exigencies of sleek hull design have kept sailboat cabins minimal with hatchways and ladders designed for the springy muscles of youth. Most cabins are the trunk type (see Chapter 1) with the side spaces under the decks allocated for bunks. (Give a sailor a bunk with sideboards and safety straps and he will sleep securely with no thought that it is cramped.) Galleys are more often merely cooking spaces with a small alcohol or kerosene stove.

True, some of the foregoing description is becoming historical because the ladies are moving into sailing just as they have come aboard powerboats. And with them come these results: Cabin decor is receiving attention, galleys are sprouting and goodbye to this roughing-it stuff. Gimballed stoves are now taking the gymnastics out of cooking; the soup remains on an even keel even though the ship doesn't. Iceboxes and even mechanical refrigeration make good meals possible during a cruise.

Sailboat Types

Sailboats come in an almost infinite variety of sizes and styles, from the diminutive sailing dinghy to the gorgeous intercontinental racing machine. Some fulfill their purpose with a leisurely sail, others are meant for family cruising and still others have the stamina to battle for the America's Cup. All have one goal in mind: to make the best use of the wind within their individual capabilities.

Aircraft spotters during the war were taught to identify planes by certain salient and unique features. A similar scheme makes it easy to distinguish one type of sailboat from another. In this case, the salient feature is the placement of the mast or masts.

A single-masted hull becomes progressively a catboat, a sloop and a cutter as the mast moves from the bow toward the stern. The catboat has its mast directly at the bow and therefore cannot carry a jib; its motive power derives from a single mainsail. When the mast is stepped further aft, about one-third of the distance to the stern, the boat is a sloop; now it carries at least two sails: jib and mainsail. Place the mast still further aft, almost in the center of the boat, and you have a cutter which usually is rigged with a mainsail and two headsails.

Two-masted ships are either schooners, ketches or yawls. Again the placement and height of masts are the criteria. The schooner has its foremast shorter than its main mast. The ketch and the yawl both have a main mast forward and a shorter mizzenmast aft and the distinction hangs on the location of the mizzen. The ketch has its mizzen forward of the helm while the yawl carries its mizzen nearer the stern. The mizzen of a ketch usually is higher than the mizzen of a yawl. (A good memory gimmick is to bear in mind that *K* for ketch comes before *Y* for yawl.)

Each of the foregoing vessels is classified further by the nature of its suit of sails, its "rig." The ship is either gaff-headed or jib-headed in addition to its other designation. The four-sided, quadrilateral shape of the gaff-headed sail achieves its desired square footage with less height and thus this rig is lower than an equivalent jib-head.

As always there are advantages and disadvantages to each shape. The gaff sail can be raised and lowered by two halyards to its head, one at the peak and one at the throat. This allows two men to divide the effort needed for a large sail. On the other hand, only one halyard, that to the head of the sail, controls the triangular jib.

The difference in height of equivalent gaff and jib rigs can determine the boat's response to light airs. Sometimes a wind will be felt at a slight height yet be calm at the surface. Often the jib can reach up to tap such air movement that bypasses the gaff. All in all, the jib-headed rig is the more popular in pleasure boating.

The underlying motive in adding masts and several sails is to divide the sail pattern into smaller units that can be handled more easily by the crew. The individual sails also permit the skipper to have some control over the center of pressure. He can vary the canvas carried fore and aft to achieve the balance he wants for the weather he encounters. He can also reduce sail more effectively for extreme conditions.

Sailboat Design

The hulls of sailing vessels, like the hulls of all other ships, must obey the rules of buoyancy and hydrodynamics. These strictures are explained fully in Chapter 1. This obedience is as important for the sailing pram as for the huge three-masted coastal schooner because the sea makes no exceptions.

Once the dictates of buoyancy are met, wide choices are open to the designer. He has many patterns to follow, some with histories of success and acceptance that go back centuries. In much of his thinking, the designer must break from the accepted norms for powerboats and concentrate on the problems that come with wind power.

The restrictions grow out of the difference between the push supplied by nature and that derived from the oil companies. The forward thrust of a powerboat is applied by the propeller and shaft at or near the level of the center of gravity and in the direction of motion. The wind's thrust on a sailboat is applied in the sail area high above the center of gravity and usually at some angle to the course the ship is traveling. This means that on most headings a force is added which tends to heel the boat in addition to the force which propels it. No such condition ever exists on powerboats.

It was explained earlier that the forces of gravity and buoyancy can be considered as concentrated at finite points; the force of the wind can be thought of similarly. This point at which the full force of the wind can be imagined is called the "center of pressure" or the "center of effort." It is high up over the deck when the sails are fully flown.

Consider the wind abeam. The situation then becomes that shown in Figure 11-1. The wind is pushing to the left at the center of pressure while gravity is pulling down at the center of gravity. A torque couple has been formed (in addition to the force which propels the ship) and it is acting to heel the vessel over. Now it devolves upon the force of gravity to take the upper hand and keep the craft from capsizing. This explains the requirement for a heavy mass as far below the waterline as possible. This mass can be placed low within the hull or can even form part of the keel. On very small sailboats, human weight substitutes for the heavy mass but the principle is the same.

The human weight can, of course, be manipulated to

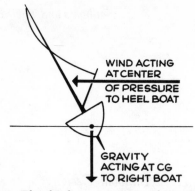

WIND ACTING
AT CENTER
OF PRESSURE
TO HEEL BOAT

GRAVITY
ACTING AT CG
TO RIGHT BOAT

Figure 11-1: The heeling torque is the twisting force exerted by the wind to heel the boat. The righting torque is the twisting force exerted by gravity to right the boat.

best advantage. The skipper and/or the crew can "hike out," lean far over the gunwale, to give their body mass the greatest leverage. The need for this gravitational assistance makes crew placement in the hull a major component of good sailing. Even on the largest boats, the crew will line up at the port or starboard rail, whichever is high, to help the ballast weight counteract heel.

Keels

A sailboat's keel will affect several aspects of its operation. The depth of water in which it can sail, the kind of weather it can master and the speed it will make are some of the characteristics influenced by this underwater appendage. A keel can be the traditional blade projecting down from the bottom of the hull or it can take the form of a centerboard or daggerboard. In all cases, its purpose is to counteract undesired sideward movement (leeway) of the ship and thus keep it on its intended course (headway). Some keels are shown in Figure 11-2.

Centerboards and daggerboards are alike in that both can be set for full engagement with the water or else fully retracted. The centerboard achieves this flexibility by virtue of the pin upon which it is hinged; the daggerboard slides up and down in a track or raceway. As their names imply, both are boards, thin slabs wide enough to be effective against the water. The leading and trailing edges of these boards are trimmed to aerodynamic shapes to reduce resistance or drag. (See Figure 11-3.)

Centerboards on racing craft are given special attention because their wetted surface can become a goodly percentage of the total wetted surface of the hull. The sides of these boards are sanded and polished to near perfect smoothness and the leading edge is sharp as a knife. This augments the beneficial effects of the aerodynamic treatment.

Obviously, the centerboard or daggerboard can be hauled up to reduce the boat's required draft but in this position the vessel's leeway may become excessive. Furthermore, sudden heeling from wind gusts will become more pronounced because some sideward resistance is

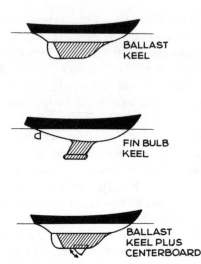

BALLAST
KEEL

FIN BULB
KEEL

BALLAST
KEEL PLUS
CENTERBOARD

Figure 11-2: The ballast keel performs the double function of lowering the center of gravity and increasing the lateral resistance of the hull. The lowered CG helps counteract heel; the increased lateral resistance helps resist leeway. Three types of ballast keel are shown. The fin bulb achieves the lowest CG.

removed. On the other hand, if the course can be held with the board up there will be a gain in speed. The sailboat skipper must always balance these bonuses against their costs.

The full keel of whatever type, especially if its weight is concentrated in its lowest portion, lowers the center of gravity. Thus, the sailboat will be able to carry more sail or else equal sail with less heel. Resistance to leeway is the greatest asset of the full keel. This factor is maximum when the boat is upright and decreases as the angle of heel increases because of the change in the projected effective area of the keel.

For sailboats in the trailerable class, there is another facet to keel choice: the effect of the keel in getting the ship onto a trailer. When the daggerboard or centerboard is withdrawn the vessel becomes keel-less and easily loaded. The hull with a deep keel remains a problem when it comes time to go on the road. Even on trailers with specially constructed deep beds the overall height may become troublesome. Launching and unlaunching these sailboats always requires the services of a crane or lift-truck.

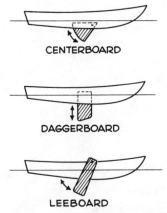

Figure 11-3: The centerboard is raised easily to clear obstructions. In the lowered position it provides lateral resistance.

Hard Chine? Soft Chine?

Many smaller sailboat hulls are built with a flat or slightly veed bottom which meets the sides at an acute angle: in other words, with a hard chine. Larger sailboats generally adopt the traditional round bottom with its soft (rounded) chine. What are the pros and cons?

The hard-chine boat, specifically one with a flat bottom, shows greater initial resistance to tipping. But as the angle of heel increases, this resistance is quickly lost and the craft becomes more easily capsized.

The soft-chine, round-bottom vessel does not exhibit this initial aversion to heeling. To the contrary, it maintains a continuous ability to right itself even in the extreme condition where the masts touch the water. To put it more technically, the round-bottom hull is characterized by a continuous stability curve while the curve for the hard-chine craft is discontinuous. (See Chapter 1.)

Another feature which marks these two types of hull must be considered in relation to sailing vessels. The immersed shape of the hard-chine hull changes drastically as the boat heels, which has an adverse effect on drag and therefore on speed. The immersed shape of many round-bottom hulls actually improves as it heels and the effect on drag and speed is beneficial.

Theoretically, the curved shape of the soft-chine hull is a much stronger engineering structure than the sharp-cornered hard chine. As a practical matter, this can be dis-

regarded. All good manufacturers build enough strength into their hulls, of whatever type, to be adequate for their intended service.

Ballast Weight vs. Boat Weight

The study of hulls in Chapter 1 disclosed that the righting torque of a ship, the twisting effort which returns it to an even keel from a heel, is derived from the forces of buoyancy and gravity. The major gravitational effect on a sailboat keel stems from the ballast weight of the keel.

A meaningful way to express the total effect is to give the ratio of keel and ballast weight to the displacement weight of the vessel, stated as a percentage. While this may sound mathematical, it isn't. Simply divide the weight of the ballast by the weight of the boat and multiply by 100. Naturally, the final answer must be less than 100 because any figure over 100 would imply all ballast and no boat.

The higher the percentage in the above calculation the greater the sail-carrying ability and the stiffer the boat. A vital assumption is that the ballast weight is carried as low in the hull as possible or in the keel itself.

Sail Cloth

Cotton and linen, once the exclusive materials from which sails were made, have been pushed out of the running by Dacron, a synthetic substance widely used for many purposes. This newcomer has many advantages; chief among them is its immunity to rot and mildew, two mortal enemies of the natural materials. Dacron is also much stronger which means that thinner cloth can be used at a great saving in weight. A further bonus with Dacron sails is that they can be stored without the usual prior careful drying—although this may prove harmful to a wooden sail locker.

The change from cotton and linen to Dacron for sail material had more far-reaching effects than one would suppose. The natural fibers are veritable sponges which soak up water from rain and even from moist air. This causes a great increase in weight which, carried so high above the waterline, raises the center of gravity. This in turn changes the metacenter and the period of roll. Thus the sailboat's response is altered. (See Chapter 1.) By contrast, neither Dacron nor nylon absorb any appreciable quantity of water, even when submerged, and thus no

undesired increase in weight takes place.

There are further advantages to these man-made fibers compared to the ones that nature provides. Dacron is practically stretchless whereas cotton and canvas have a great deal of "give" that must be taken into account by the sailmaker. His design must anticipate these changes.

Many super-pros among sailors heap even more praise upon the synthetics. They base their laudatory remarks upon experience in tough races when every iota of power must be squeezed from every square inch of sail. They claim that the minimal porosity of Dacron lets less wind escape before it has done its share of the work. They also claim that the smooth surface of synthetic sails reduces turbulence and thereby uses still another bit of power otherwise wasted. Furthermore, Dacron sails can be cut with wider individual panels because of the material's superior strength, resulting in fewer air-disturbing seams. Yes, all this is cutting things pretty fine—but that is the name of the game in sailing.

The various parts of a sail have names hallowed by time and as religiously held as the names of the deities. Woe to the would-be sailor who miscalls them. The illustration in Figures 11-4 and 5 show popular types of sails and label the various parts.

Sails on modern sailboats are almost universally triangular in shape and are called jib-headed or, less frequently, marconi-rigged. The four-sided, or gaff-headed, sail is rarely seen, although once it was quite common.

Cutting Sails

The cloth for the sails can be cut and laid in several ways. The method of cutting determines how the seams will run when the sail is sewed and this in turn can affect the sail's efficiency. The common procedure is to have the cloth run lengthwise at right angles to the leach; the seams then appear as shown in Figure 11-6a . It is claimed that this allows smoother passage of the wind and thus minimizes wasteful eddy currents caused by the seams.

Running the cloth and seams parallel to the leach (at right angles to the direction just described), results in a sail like that shown in Figure 11-6b. This style is peculiarly adapted to gaff-headed sails and consequently is in decline. Here the wind is obstructed by the seams and power-robbing eddies are generated.

The third method of cutting the cloth for sails is a combination of the previous two styles and is shown in

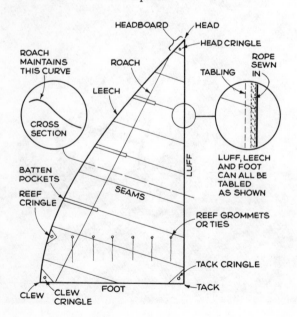

Figure 11-4: The correct names for each part of a sail are shown above.

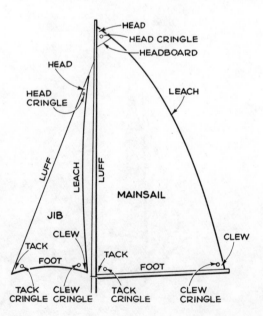

Figure 11-5: More parts of a sail are labeled in this illustration.

Figure 11-6c. The parallel and the right-angle runs meet in a line which originates at the clew and angles up to the luff. One advantage is the reinforced ability to take the stress imposed at the clew in a strong wind. (Tailors have long known that cutting and sewing cloth on the bias increases strength.)

a

Figure 11-6: Sails are cut in various ways as explained in the text and illustrated here: (a) cloth lengthened to leach; (b) parallel; (c) both.

Maintaining a Sail's Shape

The need for a sail to have an aerodynamic shape has been emphasized. One method of cutting and sewing helps assure this shape by producing what is called a "roach" (in no way connected with the crawling intruder) and is illustrated in the drawings. The roach is a fullness of the leach and adjoining area which facilitates the sail's assumption of the desired aerodynamic contour. The roach has a tendency to hang limp in light airs as well as in some directions of sailing; this can be prevented by battens.

Battens are reinforcing strips of wood, plastic or metal which fit into batten pockets in the sail. They are inserted and then tied securely in place to grommets with batten ties. (Some sailmakers provide batten pockets which do not require tying.)

The three corners of the jib-headed sail must be reinforced for the attachment of the halyard, the sheet and

b

the gooseneck shackle. This is done by sewing in what a landlubber would call a grommet but what the sailor insists are "cringles." These metal ring inserts distribute the stress and prevent tearing.

The luff is reinforced further with an integrally sewn luff rope. The foot likewise is strengthened by a bolt rope. Thus the edges of the sail along the mast and along the boom, the areas of greatest wear, are protected.

c

273

Travelers

The traveler is a horizontal track or bar running athwartship on the deck near the stern. Along it slides (travels) a block through which is rove the mainsheet. This movable feature allows the sheet to be led to the sail from the most favorable angle for a particular condition of wind.

In effect, the traveler makes possible improved control over the mainsail, more especially over the leach of the mainsail, by assigning freedom of movement to the lead block. The position of the lead block on the traveler is determined by the intensity of the wind. For light airs this position is close to amidships; as the wind increases, the position is moved leeward. The illustration in Figure 11-7 shows a traveler and its rigging.

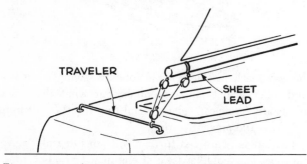

Figure 11-7: *The traveler at the stern allows the mainsheet to work from more effective angles.*

Halyards—Inside or Outside?

The advent of hollow masts, both wood and aluminum, has given the designer a choice of locations for mainsail and jib halyards: They can either run down the outside of the mast or inside a hollow mast. Aside from cleaning up the rigging, placing a halyard inside the mast removes one more source of wind resistance.

The only flaw in the idea of internal halyards is the difficulty of repair in the event of breakage. Replacing such a line takes neat "fishing."

Proponents of internal halyards cite the reliability of modern cordage, especially if the "cordage" is stainless steel wire rope. Even the new synthetics have such high breaking points that failure is rare.

There are other halyards which may or may not go inside. Among these are spinnaker, jib, signal and flag

halyards. All of these create drag for the racing sailor who is trying to squeeze the last ounce of push out of the wind.

Sailboat Winches

Standard winches, the type found on powerboats for raising the anchor, are discussed in Chapter 20. Sailboat winches are a different breed; they are never powered whereas most standard winches are.

Sailboat winches are available in many sizes from small to the powerful brutes found on the America's Cup contenders. Most winches are crank-operated. The drive from crank to spool can be direct or geared down as much as three or four to one. The purpose is to increase the mechanical advantage, to multiply human pull to a magnitude sufficient for controlling large sails. Spools on many models are free-wheeling, under the control of a brake, for rapid sheet-tending without the use of the crank.

Sheets, halyards and lines handled by the winch are "tailed" (wound several times around the spool or drum), which provides the friction needed for exerting traction. Some newer winches eliminate the need for manual tailing; one such self-tailing winch is shown in Figure 11-8.

While a powerboat has only one winch, a moderate or larger-size sailboat sometimes has many. They are dis-

Figure 11-8: *Sailboat winches are finely tuned mechanisms. Their purpose is to multiply the torque applied at the handle to several times human capability. Many models have several speeds selectable by direction of handle rotation; many feature overrunning clutches in the spool to permit fast tailing.*

tributed about the deck and mast at strategic locations for handling the various sheets and halyards. Some 12-meter yachts have their winches below in order to reduce the windage drag of crew members on deck. Obviously, the open space around a winch should be sufficient for un-impeded cranking. The line should approach the winch from a direction which will allow the drum to wind it on a level from bottom to top.

Roller-Reefing Gear

Not only winches differ from standard when they are intended for sailboats; much hardware does also. Some sailboat hardware has no equivalent on a powerboat; roller-reefing gear is an example.

Reefing sail (reducing its effective area) can be done by tying successive reef points around the boom. It is quicker and much easier to reef sails with roller-reefing devices. These function like the oldtime window shade roller except that a crank-operated gear supplies the rotation instead of a spring. The roller principle is also applied to furling the jib and for this purpose the crank is replaced by an actuating line wound around the furler's drum.

Blocks

A block is the assembly of the housing and its contained sheave or pulley. If it is intended for sailboat service, it is extremely strong and usually finished in high polish to help dress ship. The preferred material is stainless steel for the housing and one of the tough plastics for the sheave. The combination makes the block corrosion-free, easy-running and light in weight. The commercial models are single blocks (one sheave), double blocks (two sheaves) and triple blocks (three sheaves). The styles include deck blocks, cheek blocks and eyed blocks.

Cleats

Many sailboat cleats have a self-jamming feature which holds a sheet without the usual turns about the horns. This action derives either from eccentric jam-cams or from a veed opening into which the line is forced. The sheet or line is held securely against the pull from the sail yet can be released instantly by a short pull in the opposite direction. Handling sheets and lines on a sailboat must often be done with great speed and these quick-release gadgets help. (See Figure 11-9.)

Figure 11-9: This jamming cleat automatically secures a line or sheet, yet releases it instantly when desired. The two serrated cams grip the line and tension on the line only makes them hold tighter. A short pull on the inboard end of the line releases the grip.

Lifelines and Rails

It is seldom necessary for the powerboat crew to move about on the deck while underway in heavy weather; everyone can remain safely enclosed below. Things are different on a sailboat: sails require tending, heavy weather or no, and the crew *must* be on deck. Lifelines and rails thus assume a literally life-and-death importance.

The first requirement for lifelines and rails on a sailboat is that they must be strong and adequately fastened. The ticky-tacky (but highly polished) rails found on many powerboats just will not do. The sailboat rail must be able to sustain the weight of a man even when a sea has grabbed him and is trying to wash him overboard. (Wise and experienced crew members snap-hook themselves onto life-lines to eliminate the danger of losing their grip.)

Stanchions should be through-bolted without reliance on mere wood screws. The line itself should be stainless steel and turnbuckled for necessary slack takeup.

Motor Sailers

In response to popular demand there has been a wedding (perhaps with a shotgun) of the powerboat and the sail-boat, and the resultant offspring is the motor sailer. Now this is a difficult union at best because the paths of the two participants ordinarily lie in opposite directions. The best features of powerboat design are foreign to sailboats and vice versa.

The result, by its very nature, must be a compromise. The motor sailer does not sail as well as a true sailer of equal dimensions nor does it power as well as a comparable engine-driven craft. Still, the motor sailer has some excellent qualities especially in livability, and many skippers swear by it and will have no other deck under their feet.

Some general characteristics: The motor sailer may carry less sail than an equal-sized sailboat and much less power than an equal-sized powerboat. The hull will be heavier and beamier than that of its sailing peer and will exceed its power peer in keel and draft. The size of living quarters will be smaller than those of a powerboat and larger than those of a sailboat.

Auxiliaries

The dictionary defines an auxiliary as a helper and the true auxiliary sailboat makes use of its engine in just that way. Apart from its engine, the ship is a true sailboat and is rigged in sailboat fashion. The hull differs only in the provision for a propeller at the aft end of the keel. Often this prop space is borrowed equally from rudder and keel.

A standard three- or four-blade propeller would cause extreme drag with the ship under sail alone, therefore a two-blade wheel has been generally adopted. This propeller is preferably of the variable pitch type (see Chapter 3) and for sailing is set at infinite pitch with the blades in line with the direction of motion. Non-variable props are held with their blades behind the keel by means of a clamp or dog on the propeller shaft. (Allowing the prop to "windmill" can damage the reduction gears.)

Multihulls

Catamarans and trimarans, discussed in Chapter 1 and shown in Figure 11-10, are becoming popular sailing hulls. Their attraction is their superior speed plus their high resistance to capsizing under normal conditions.

An application of the principles of hydrodynamics and buoyancy explained in Chapter 1 leads to the direct conclusion that these multihulls are speedier and have greater stability than boats of equal size—and this conclusion is borne out in practice. The individual hulls are cigar-shaped, long and narrow with parallel sides and sharp entries. The total wetted surface is therefore minimum; drag is down and speed is up. The stability is a product of the wide stance; a boat of the same length with equal beam would be a tub. Refinements in the keeling and the use of the bridge as an airfoil lifting surface also help.

Rig-wise, the catamarans are generally sloops. Many trimarans make full use of the length of the center hull by rigging as ketches. As noted earlier, cabin accommodation is a problem; space is usually minimal.

Rigging

What on land would normally be termed guy wires are called stays and shrouds on a sailboat. They are made almost exclusively of stainless steel wire rope.

The guys for a mast ashore are anchored to the ground at equal distances from its base. This is not possible on a ship. The fore and aft guys (called forestay and backstay respectively) can take advantage of the hull length but the side guys (called shrouds) have only the beam of the boat for their major distance from the mast. These latter therefore rise at a steeper angle and in order to bear the load are often doubled or tripled.

When the boat heels, the shrouds on the windward side take on additional stress. On most points of sailing, the forestay carries a lighter load. When running with a spinnaker or balloon, the backstay is under greatest stress. However, the manner in which the stays are "tuned" (tensioned) has great bearing.

The shrouds and stays are the "standing rigging" because once brought to the correct tension they are left in place. (This assumes a non-trailered boat; the mast of a trailered sailboat is unstepped every time it hits the road, with consequent unsecuring of rigging.) The tensioning or tuning is done through turnbuckles, most of which are taped over in their set position to protect sails, to prevent unloosening and to inhibit corrosion "freezing."

Since the stays and shrouds are standing rigging, it is only natural that the sheets and halyards which hoist and control the sails be called "running rigging." The hoisting of sails and their subsequent control or trimming are two separate operations. The first job is taken on by the halyards, the second by the sheets. (Again, remember that "sheets" are lines or ropes and *not* sails.)

Figure 11-10: Because it has more than one hull, a trimaran
is a very stable boat. (Credit—Snark Products, Inc.)

The great strength of stainless steel wire rope and the tremendous mechanical advantage gained by turnbuckles make it quite easy to overtighten the rigging—even to the point of putting a bend in the mast. Tightening therefore should be done with caution and with a constant eye on the mast's fairness. (Sighting along the mast the way a carpenter sights a long board quickly reveals curves.) The mast should make a perfect right angle with the deck athwartship. Fore and aft, whether the mast makes a right angle or has a slight rake aft is a matter of design and balance. Aside from the undesired stress put on a mast that is being bent, sails are designed to fly from straight masts and will not be at their best unless this condition is met. (This is the majority view but it is pertinent to note that some successful racing sailors disagree.)

The relationships of shrouds, stays, halyards, sails and masts to each other and to the sailboat itself are shown graphically in Figure 11-11.

Very tall masts, which need additional support at the top section, are given extra strength by jumper struts, jumper stays and spreaders. The struts and spreaders increase the angle of effectiveness of the stays and allow them to function like the cables of a suspension bridge. It is important that spreaders and struts are rigged so that they bisect their angle with the stay; if this is not done, they will slip under pressure.

Bending on Sail

When you tread the deck of a sailboat you do not attach a sail—you "bend it on." The operation is made easy on modern sailboats by tracks or grooves on the mast and on the boom. The tracks are channels which function like the metal runways which suspend drapes at home windows. (Older practice depended on hoops which encircled the mast and to which the sails were fastened.)

Attached at intervals along the luff and the foot of sails are small slides which fit into openings in the tracks and are retained when they advance. These insertions are made progressively as the sail is bent on.

The mainsail is raised by a halyard rove through a block or sheave at the masthead and secured to the head cringle. The tack cringle is secured to the gooseneck which carries the boom at the mast while the clew cringle is fastened to the outhaul. This outhaul, with its outhaul line, keeps the foot of the sail stretched along the boom. On a small sailboat the outhaul line is a simple line; on larger vessels it may be a block and fall to multiply human effort.

The jib halyard on the other side of the mast also runs through a block or sheave at the masthead and then secures to the head cringle of the jib. (This cringle takes much punishment and is often reinforced with a "board" of metal or wood.) The headstay takes the place of a mast for the jib. The luff of the jib is snapped onto the headstay and slides along it the while the jib tack is secured to the headstay deck fitting. The jib clew secures to the jib sheet.

With all this discussion of sails and their rigging, perhaps it is wise to repeat that the mainsheet and the jibsheet are the lines which control these sails and are not the sails themselves.

Turning Center

Sailboat hulls, like all other hulls, have an imaginary vertical pivot somewhere along the centerline about which they turn when they are steered. When the rudder is

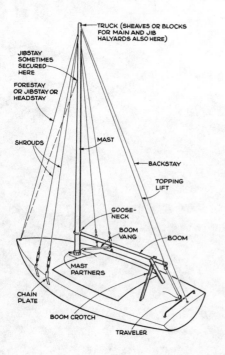

Figure 11-11: The basic running rigging and standing rigging are shown above.

swung, the bow will turn about this pivot in the desired direction and the stern will swing in the opposite direction. This center of turning or center of lateral resistance, and especially its relationship to the center of wind pressure on the sails, has an important bearing on the action of the boat when it is underway.

The center of turning is largely a result of boat design although the skipper has some control over its location by his manner of trimming ship. Shifting weight forward or aft affects it slightly; so does angle of heel.

The center of wind pressure shifts constantly with sail trim, amount of sail carried and relationship between course and direction of wind. Only the theoretical center of pressure, computed with full sail and a beam wind, remains "fixed" and moves only with changes in mast location or angle.

Technically, the situation again is the simple one of a torque couple, this time in the horizontal plane. Two forces are acting in opposite directions and are somewhat out of line, thus exerting a turning effort. The net result on a sailboat is either a lee helm or a weather helm when the forces are out of line and a neutral helm when they are directly opposed.

Lee Helm and Weather Helm

A sailboat is said to have a weather helm when it tends to point into the wind of its own accord. It has a lee helm when its tendency is to point out of the wind. Both cases require continuous steering correction in order to maintain a straight course.

The diagrams in Figure 11-12 are almost self-explanatory. They show clearly how the forces of wind and turning resistance swing the hull in one direction or the other—or have no swinging resultant when they are in line and neutralized.

Many sailboat skippers prefer their craft to have a small amount of weather helm as a safety measure. With this condition the boat will swing into the wind and stop if an emergency aboard causes the tiller to be left unattended.

Lee helm, on the other hand, can be a definite hazard. A vessel so afflicted will turn its stern into the wind when left to its own impulses. This is a dangerous condition which can lead to accidental jibing and even possible disaster.

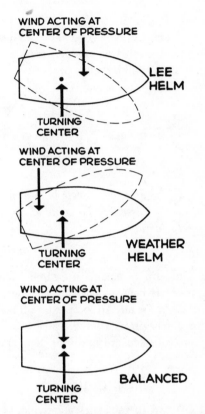

Figure 11-12: The weather helm is an automatic safety feature because the sailboat will head into the wind automatically and stop if the helm is unattended. The lee helm carries the danger of a possible jibe.

More than a slight amount of either helm is a drudgery for the helmsman attempting to steer a straight course. He must constantly fight the tiller in order to make good his intended track. With neutral helm all forces are in balance and the effort required at the tiller can be exerted almost with the fingers alone.

Heeling vs. Wind

If you assume that the wind is traveling parallel to the surface of the water, then when the boat is upright whatever sail area is flown is 100% effective. In other words, the projected area of the sails coincides with the actual area.

As the boat heels under the force of the wind, the projected area of the same amount of sail becomes less and less. For small angles of heel the percentage drop is negligible. As the heel goes beyond about 25 degrees, the reduction in effective sail area becomes marked. The diagram in Figure 11-13 will bear this out.

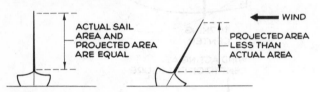

Figure 11-13: When a sailboat heels before the wind, its effective sail area is lessened. To some extent this is an automatic safety feature.

Since the wind force remains the same while the effective sail area has been reduced, less power naturally will be drawn from the air. To some extent this reduction in driving force may prove a safety valve because a sailboat in a greatly heeled attitude is in danger of being capsized.

Boom Control

The need for a sail to retain its aerodynamic shape in order to extract thrust from the wind has been stressed in Chapter 2. Sometimes, however, the very wind that supplies the thrust has a tendency to force the sail out of this airfoil contour.

When the sail is thus distorted, the boom to which it is attached is lifted. Preventing the boom from rising is therefore the obvious corrective measure. The boom vang does this; it is shown in Figure 11-14.

The boom vang can be a single line on light gear or a block and fall on heavier rigging. It runs from mid-boom to mast base or deck. Putting tension on the vang holds the boom down. The vang may sometimes exert a beneficial effect when jibing by helping to control the boom and preventing what are often wild and disastrous swings when the wind catches the sail. The boom vang is strictly a heavy-weather worker; in light airs it has little work to do, and it finds greatest use on broad reaches and runs.

Bernoulli Again

On most points of sailing the sail pulls the boat as well as pushes it. Often the effect of the pull is greater than that

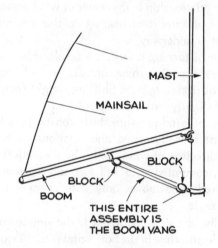

Figure 11-14: The boom vang controls the boom. It can be a single line or a complete block and tackle, as shown.

of the push. Why this happens should be clear from the discussion of the Bernoulli principle in Chapter 2 and it should be equally clear that this Bernoulli effect depends upon correct sail curvature. Although this curvature is built into the sail by every knowledgeable sailmaker, the final efficacy depends upon how the sail is flown. Hence one skipper can milk more thrust than another out of identical sails in equal winds.

Normally the wind expands the sail to the correct contour. However, there are times of light airs when the wind's power is just not sufficient. In such cases hiking out in reverse can come to the rescue. Whereas skipper and crew normally hike out on the windward side to counteract heel, now they hike out on the lee side to cause heel. The weight of the sail does the rest.

The expert sailboat skipper is a practicing aerodynamicist—whether or not he knows it. His trimming and adjusting of sails amount in reality to an expert control over the airflow upon which the complex behavior of a sail depends. As explained in Chapter 2, this flow, correctly applied, permits the Bernoulli principle to supply what the airplane technicians call "lift" and what the boat feels as a forward pull.

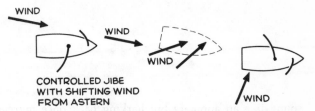

CONTROLLED JIBE
WITH SHIFTING WIND
FROM ASTERN

Figure 11-16: A jibe occurs when the wind from astern shifts from one side of the mainsail to the other. An uncontrolled, accidental jibe can be very dangerous. A controlled jibe in light or moderate wind is a useful maneuver. (A sailboat with a sail out on each side, as above, is running "wing and wing.")

Controlling the Slot

One of the critical points in this harnessing of air is the control of the "slot" between the jib and the mainsail. The width of this opening determines the velocity of the flow over the leeward side of the mainsail and therefore the amount of pull the sail exerts. It is much like a door through which a light breeze is blowing when it is wide open; as you gradually close the door, the "slot" becomes narrower and the air velocity increases without change in the original breeze. However, this beneficial effect ceases abruptly when the slot becomes so small that the mainsail is "backwinded" and loses its drive. The illustration in Figure 11-15 shows this and also explains why the flow

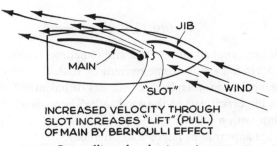

INCREASED VELOCITY THROUGH
SLOT INCREASES "LIFT" (PULL)
OF MAIN BY BERNOULLI EFFECT

Figure 11-15: Controlling the slot is an important part of sailing maneuvers. Too great a slot opening will "backwind" the main and destroy pulling power.

remains smooth, devoid of wasteful eddies, as long as the skipper gauges the opening correctly.

Running

The wind is a tricky worker who often turns out to be the master just when we think he is enslaved. Running before the wind, with the breeze aft and only pushing, would seem to be the simplest and fastest point of sailing—and yet it is not. The boat is slowest for a given wind velocity and the helmsman must stay alert and be sensitive to a change of wind direction because this point of sailing can bring trouble in any but mild winds.

This matter of wind direction when running is more important than might appear. The mainsail is swung far out over the beam and as long as the wind strikes it at close to 90 degrees you can laze along. But let the wind shift enough to grab the sail and all hell can break loose if you are not ready. A heavy boom swinging across the deck

with express train speed respects neither man nor rigging. That is why the helmsman must remain ever alert to counter incipient trouble by using his tiller.

A minor problem when running in this fashion with jib and mainsail out on the same side is that the smaller sail will be blanketed by the larger. The remedy is to swing the two sails out on opposite sides and run in what is picturesquely known as "wing and wing."

The trouble which awaits the inattentive helmsman while the sailboat is on a run is an uncontrolled jibe. This undesired jibe occurs when an astern wind shifts just enough to hit what had been the leeward side of the mainsail. Now the action becomes cumulative. As more and more sail is exposed in this fashion the boom gains momentum in its sweep over the deck to the other side. A swinging boom can destroy rigging and damage itself, can knock a person overboard and can even kill.

But there are useful jibes, controlled jibes, which are the opposite of tacking and almost as easy to execute. However, the controlled jibe is not a heavy weather maneuver and should be avoided in strong winds except by the most expert sailors. The path of the boat in relation to the wind and the trim of its sails is shown in Figure 11-16; in this example, the vessel is running wing and wing.

The main secret in executing the jibe is to control the boom closely. The mainsheet is hauled in tight, bringing the boom almost amidships before the course is changed just enough to let the wind swing the boom over (still under the tight leash of the mainsheet) and the jibsheet is released. All that is left to do now is paying out the mainsheet and trimming the jib to the new wing and wing position.

Tacking

The speed of a sailboat can exceed the speed of the wind which is driving it when the craft is tacking. This may sound like an anomaly but harking back once more to Bernoulli should explain it on the basis of the combined push and pull. Tacking therefore becomes a necessary and much-used method of sailing. Whether or not a sailboat is tacking is determined by its angle with the driving wind; this is illustrated in Figure 11-17.

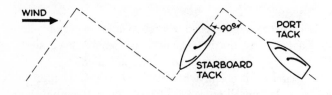

Figure 11-17: The side on which the wind strikes the boat determines the name of the tack.

Unlike jibing, tacking does not contain the seeds of inherent danger. The greatest danger is embarrassment for the skipper who is too slow in his swing from one heading to the other and thereby gets his ship stalled or, in the vernacular, "in irons."

Tacking is a sort of "stairway" which lets the sailboat climb up into the wind—although hardly ever closer than 45 degrees to it. By taking the wind first on one side and then on the other, a track upwind is made good. The side of the boat on which the wind blows, the weather side, gives its name to the tack: starboard wind, starboard tack, port wind, port tack. (This upwind sailing is called "beating" and tacking becomes a necessary part of beating when a directly upwind destination has to be reached.)

The port and starboard tacks can be uniformly short or uniformly long or one can be short and the other long. It is a helmsman's choice determined by the angle the wind makes with the desired effective track.

It is possible also to tack downwind. The difference between this maneuver and running is that the wind is kept on the quarter, more nearly abeam; actually, this becomes a series of broad reaches. Many sailors prefer this method in winds too strong for safe jibing.

It becomes clear that all these nuances of sailing require complete rapport between man and boat. The experienced sailor is acutely sensitive to the many messages the boat and the wind are constantly sending him. Even his fingers are receptors.

Tiller Sensitivity

This business of finger sensitivity is one of the secret ploys of the sailors who win races. These men tend the tiller with only a finger grip, preferably from underneath. They never rest their arms on the tiller because that would obliterate the "messages" from the rudder that constantly advise how well the craft is sailing. The slightest rudder drag is perceived as an omen that something is amiss.

The rudder also sends messages to the eye of the observant sailor. Drag is indicated by a string of tiny bubbles and eddies in the wake. Decoded, this means that some speed is being sacrificed. The avid sailor, especially the racing sailor, takes immediate steps.

Safety Considerations

Sailing is not all fair weather and sometimes cruises which start in fair are overcome en route by foul. The knowledge of what to do when the sea becomes turbulent is therefore an important part of the good sailor's armament. A tight ship with a knowledgeable man at its helm can survive what appear to be impossible situations.

One rule is never to have the sheets so tightly secured that they cannot be payed out on an instant's notice. Sudden gusts that can cause excessive heel can be spilled out of the sails by letting the mainsheet run out. (Quick action on the tiller can also accomplish this result and sometimes this is the preferable procedure because it does not kill headway as much as the spilling.)

Confirmed heavy-weather sailors carry a storm trysail and a storm jib which they set in place of the regular suit of sails when strong winds blow. The storm trysail takes the place of the mainsail; it is triangular in shape, has perhaps a third of the main's area and is used "loose-footed." The term loose-footed means that the lower edge of the sail is free and not held in the regular fashion by sliders along the boom. The storm jib is a diminutive jib made of heavy material and run up high enough on the headstay to be clear of the expected white water coming over the bow. How storm sails compare to regular sails is shown in Figure 11-18.

Earlier we examined the action of the wind and found that part of its force is exerted as headway while the balance causes heeling and leeway on many points of sailing. Obviously, leeway serves no useful purpose and will

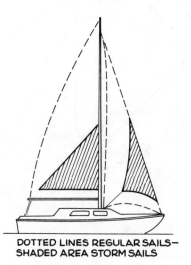

DOTTED LINES REGULAR SAILS—
SHADED AREA STORM SAILS

Figure 11-18: A skipper's response to heavy wind conditions can be to douse them and bend on smaller storm sails.

throw the ship off its mark unless continuous correction is made. This is done by easing the tiller to leeward (which swings the rudder to windward) thus pointing the boat enough higher on the wind to counteract the leeway.

Most sailboat hulls are faster when slightly heeled than when upright but beyond this point the heel detracts from performance. How to control the heel varies with the size of the boat. On the smallest craft, one-man hiking out is all that is needed; when the heel gets beyond his own ability to correct, it is high time to shorten sail, spill some wind and ease off.

Slightly larger boats that carry several crew members follow the same principle and simply have more human weight to work with. As boats get still larger the relative percentage of human weight to ship mass decreases to a point where even lining up the crew on the weather rail has little effect. At this point heeling control lies entirely in the realm of sail area manipulation and the relation of the course to the wind.

Sailboat Racing

Even the slightest acquaintance with the world of sailing removes all doubt that racing is endemic to sailing. As already stated, it is second nature for a sailing skipper sub-

consciously to plan the defeat of every sailboat he meets. This facet of his character reaches fever pitch in duly organized races.

Most organized races are conducted on a one-design basis. The one-design concept matches boats perhaps more alike than peas in a pod. All constructional details of the competing craft are as uniform as practical manufacturing can make them. Thus no boat has an inbuilt edge over another. As a consequence, one-design racing is a true pitting of one's skill against another's, of crew against crew, skipper against skipper. Knowing your boat and training your crew counts heavily toward success.

One-design racing has sprouted unbelievably throughout the world. There are more than 300 classes in this country alone and some of these contain several thousand boats.

The rules under which races are conducted are so precise and voluminous that they assume quasi-legal power. The NAYRU (North American Yacht Racing Union) racing rules alone cover more than 16 closely printed pages!

A Race Committee sets the course to be raced. The course can take many forms that require sailing ability of various degrees of expertness. It could be a simple statement of a definite starting point or line and a distant finish and would be considered a point-to-point race. On the other hand, the course could be closed, make one or more loops around specified markers and finish at or near the start. A complete description of the course would be published in advance for the competing skippers to study; the marks would be enumerated and instructions given as to whether they are to be rounded and on which side they are to be passed.

The closed courses often take the forms shown in Figure 11-19. The general purpose of each layout is to force the competitors into many points of sailing so that the race becomes a true test of overall skill.

Perhaps the mystique of sailing is highlighted best by what the bigwigs of sailboat racing do when they are not in hot competition: They sail dinghys! Between races you will find many of the names known world-wide for skippering the giant 12-meter ships at the helm of these tricky little boats. They claim this sharpens their skills because every little *faux pas* in a dinghy immediately takes its toll. In the language of the sailor, the dinghy is not as forgiving as the big boat—and that idiosyncrasy in itself adds to the mystique.

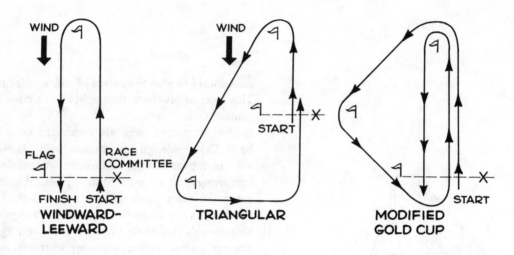

Figure 11-19: These three race course patterns are employed in addition to the point-to-point. Prior instructions inform the skippers how to round the marks, etc.

A Practice Sail

Doubtless you have watched on your television screen as our hero, pursued by a villain with gun blazing, races down the pier, takes a flying leap into a small boat and is off, safe. By all means leave the television in sole possession of this manner of boarding a boat. If you try it, either of two things will happen: You will go right on down through the bottom of the hull or else the boat will repay you for this indignity by capsizing and dumping you overboard.

So the first admonition on our practice sail is a lesson on how to board a small sailboat. Perhaps it should go back even further than that and say a word about the shoes to wear.

Shoes on board have the double purpose of protecting your safety and protecting the very vulnerable surface finish of the decks. This narrows down to rubber or cork or rope soles. All these materials are available on the market, none will mar the decks and all are reasonably non-slip on a wet surface.

So, properly shod, tread lightly. On boarding very small boats you must step as close to the center as possible; any foot placed on a gunwale is inviting disaster. Naturally, as boats get larger your weight has less and less effect and your leeway increases.

After reading the preceding sections, you are coming aboard reasonably knowledgeable. You know halyards from shrouds, you understand why and how sails work and you are aware that a sheet is a line. You will not give your skipper apoplexy (and yourself a skull fracture) by keeping your head up despite the call of "Hard alee."

The powerboatman starts his engines before casting off from his mooring because he wants power immediately at hand. Likewise the sailboatman raises his sails. The powerboatman has his clutch in neutral; the sailor leaves his sheets loose, which is the equivalent. In both cases motive power is available, in one by engaging the clutch, in the other by hauling in on the sheets (provided that there is a wind). Rudder and tiller are made operative.

Since the ship is secured, the next step is untying the knots that hold her. If these knots were correctly made, there is no problem because they will untie easily. So a knowledge of knots is an important part of the sailor's equipment and a study of Chapter 15 is well worthwhile. There are literally hundreds of knots, and whole books have been written solely on this subject, but a working familiarity with the basic four or five will see you through handily.

When making sail preliminary to getting underway, the sails must be raised and used in proper sequence. The reason for this is that the sailboat acts like a weathervane and this fact can be used to advantage. The correct order is for the aftermost sail to be put to work first. On a sloop this would be the main and on a ketch or yawl the mizzen.

The logic behind the procedure is quite simple: The center of pressure of these sails is aft of the natural turning point of the hull. This causes the boat to weathervane with its bow into the wind, an advantageous situation.

You now have sails up with battens, if any, inserted. The sails are providing no drive, but they are luffing, because the sheets are loose. If the boom crotch, or gallows, is removable it is out of the way; if not then the boom is raised clear of it. You are ready to cast off. The wind will drift you back to clear the mooring.

Unless you are hemmed in by other boats, you are now free to select any point of sailing. If you wish to go

boat cooperates happily and almost sails itself. If your boat has a centerboard, you will be using just enough of it to keep leeway and heel to a minimum.

It's time to pick up the mooring and the centerboard is down all the way for greater control as you come up into the wind. At this stage you will have to estimate how far your boat can shoot upwind after you loose the sheets and kill sail drive. The trick is to arrive dead in the water right at the mooring—and only after you become really

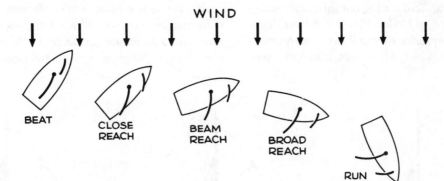

Figure 11-20: *The angle at which the wind strikes determines the name for the point of sailing.*

upwind, then a beat with sails close-hauled is in order.

Haul in on the mainsheet and the jibsheet to keep the sails close to amidships. Watch the "slot" between jib and main to get the greatest wind velocity over the back or lee side of the main, being careful not to make the slot so small as to backwind and kill the mainsail's drive. If your goal happens to be directly upwind you will have to make several tacks.

Coming home you may choose to run before the wind, being constantly alert to avoid an undesired, uncontrolled jibe.

Suppose that instead of the upwind beat when leaving your mooring you elected to start with a beat and then swing around through all the other points of sailing just for the fun of it. Your procedure is simple in the extreme and is diagrammed in Figure 11-20.

On the original beat your sails were close-hauled. As you swing around to a close reach, then a beam reach, then a broad reach and finally a run you successively ease the sheets out. The sails gradually swing out further from the center of the boat for each increase in reach angle. The

acquainted with your boat can you be letter-perfect in this maneuver. It makes a difference, too, whether the boat has a keel or a centerboard.

Once the boat is secured to the pennant, housekeeping begins on board. Sails are dropped by loosening the halyards and paying them out. Battens are removed as the sails come down. The sails are then either removed and bagged or furled. Furled sails are usually protected from wind and weather by sail covers.

The mainsail is furled by folding it accordion-fashion on the boom, then rolling all the folds into a neat bundle. This bundle in turn is tied neatly and securely to the boom with long strips of sail cloth called "stops." Square knots, easily reopened, secure the stops. The sail cover is the final enclosure.

Our imaginary boat for this imaginary sail was suited with standard sails, a mainsail and a jib. Figure 11-21 shows how she would look with a genoa jib, a standard jib and a spinnaker.

The genoa is an oversize jib. It is so large that it extends aft beyond the mast and must be set outside the shrouds.

When the boat comes about on a tack, the genoa cannot swing over as the standard jib does, and often must be walked around by a crew member. The advantage of using a genoa when winds permit derives from its larger size and its consequently greater power-delivering ability.

The spinnaker is another oversize sail, so large and billowy that it resembles a balloon and often is so called. The spinnaker is set well forward, is often kept open with a spinnaker pole, and is employed only for running before the wind.

Suppose you had capsized during our imaginary sail—what would you have done? What should you have done?

In the first place, capsizing in a sailboat in warm summer waters is not half as bad as it sounds. It happens very often and hardly ever results in even minor casualties. Members of the crew are in swim suits to start with, as a general rule, and the small boats which are the usual victims of capsizing can be righted without outside aid after the sails are taken off.

The admonitions are to don life preservers (or at least to hang on to them) and to stay with the boat. Small boats are either self-floating or have flotation added and make a safe rallying point until rescue comes.

Remember that often capsizing is not so much nature's fault as it is the helmsman's. He was not fast enough with tiller or sheet to spill wind and ease the heel. Sometimes, though, nature sneaks in a wild puff of wind that even the sprightliest man at the tiller cannot cope with.

(a) Genoa Jib   (b) Standard Jib   (c) Spinnaker

Figure 11-21: The genoa (a) is an oversized version of the standard jib (b). The huge balloon or spinnaker (c) adds pulling power in light airs.

PART IV

OUTBOARDS AND OUTBOARD EQUIPMENT

12 Outboard Boats and Motors

Boats propelled by outboard motors outnumber by at least ten to one all pleasure craft whose engines are inboard. This tremendous popularity is the outgrowth of a continuous revolution in the design and capability of outboard hulls and the motors and trailers which complement them.

The original outboard boats were simply flat-bottomed rowboats whose owners got tired of rowing. Today's outboard boats range from record-holding speedsters to small family cruisers that offer some simulation of the comforts of home. Centered in the lineup is the open runabout whose ample cushion space encourages bikini-clad lounging and whose speed is sufficient for good water skiing. Even some houseboats depend upon outboard motors for propulsion. Nor should it be overlooked that sailboats are not strangers to outboard motors. Many a windjammer relies on his putt-putt to move his love gently to a pier or precisely to a mooring.

The hulls intended for outboard power must follow the dictates of marine engineering discussed in Chapter 1, even as all hulls must. They are either displacement or planing, although planing is the more popular. But there are some differences in construction peculiar to the genre.

The outboard-powered hull is unusually well adapted to high-speed planing designs because it can change the angle of its propeller thrust to become optimum for each particular trim condition. The inboard-engined boat, with its fixed propeller shaft, cannot do this. Furthermore, the weight of the outboard engine so far aft helps planing. (Unfortunately, too much weight too far aft sometimes also induces "porpoising.")

Outboard Hull Types

No single hull can be called an outboard type. Perhaps the only feature common to all outboard hulls is that they are smaller—usually in the 14- to 20-foot range. This is smaller than the average inboard and the reduction has been brought about by the need for trailering and the limit on propulsive power available. (Highway regulations limit the trailered hull to a beam of 8 feet.)

RUNABOUTS.

The most popular hull is the runabout. This is an open hull which generally has enclosed storage space under the covered foredeck. Control is at an automobile-type steering wheel up forward behind a windshield. Often the windshield has a walk-through opening for convenience in handling lines on the deck. Seating is a combination of fore and aft and athwartships with cushions so arranged that they can be laid out flat to form a sun lounge.

Hull material is now predominantly fiberglass with some wood and a sprinkling of metal. Outside hull surfaces of the fiberglass boats are smooth, the equivalent of carvel. Wood hulls are either carvel or lapstrake. One aluminum hull maintains the surface ridges of lapstrake even though it is constructed of a single continuous sheet; this is done to add rigidity and strength, much like the grooves in the roofs of station wagons. (Chapter 1 details the forms of hull construction.)

Hull bottoms seem to follow the designers' fancies, but they can be classified as rounds, vees, gullwings, cathedrals, catamarans, and trimarans—the gamut of hull types. The fancier configurations are all in fiberglass because this material of construction is best adapted to complicated curves.

Many runabouts have adopted the folding top that characterizes the convertible sports car. These can become a most annoying sail when the wind kicks up—but then the runabout is not intended to be a foul-weather craft. The runabout is ideal for jazzing about on protected waters, for towing water skiers, for fishing in safe locations, and for just going out to lounge and swim. A typical runabout is shown in Figure 12-1.

In short, the runabout is a fun boat. Remember, however, fun or no, the runabout, like any powerboat, must conform to the legal requirements for its size and class. These are detailed in Chapter 25.

UTILITY.

It is begging the question somewhat to call the utility boat a separate class. Actually, the utility offered by any manufacturer is his identical runabout hull stripped of everything not absolutely necessary for the operation of the boat. It is something like the super-low-priced leader, advertised by some car dealers, which just about has the engine, wheels, and seats.

In other words, if the runabout is your cup of tea, then the utility can be your money-saving teabag. It will do everything the fancier runabout will do and you can bring it up in social status gradually as you are ready to spend the money for gadgets.

Material-wise and bottom-configuration-wise, the utility duplicates the runabout. It all simmers down to a matter of budget. (See Figure 12-2.)

Figure 12-1: The runabout is the seagoing version of the convertible automobile. It has ample power and speed for water skiing. Seat cushions slide together for sun lounging. (Credit—Starcraft Company)

Figure 12-2: The utility is generally a stripped-down runabout. It matches the performance capability of the equivalent runabout but is easier on the budget. (Credit—Boston Whaler, Inc.)

CRUISERS.

A cruiser is a boat in which you are able to cruise, and so even the *outboard* cruiser must have the minimum appurtenances for living afloat. These are sleeping accommodations, cooking facilities, a toilet, some lounging space, and storage tanks for enough fuel and water to enable a worthwhile overwater run. Of course, all these components are minimal in an outboard-powered craft because of the limitations imposed on length by trailering and on heft by available power.

The sales and advertising departments have subdivided outboard cruisers into "sedan," "express," and "day." It is difficult to fence these terms in because actually they are overlapping and indeed do not mean very much. Granted that the basics are there for the boat to qualify as a cruiser, then the sedan has more glass area, the express is faster, and the day squeaks by with the understanding that it will make few if any overnight runs.

The outboard cruiser usually sleeps two in forward vee bunks and possibly two more in a convertible bed arrangement in the cabin. Generally the head is hidden under a seat cushion—an idea doubtless borrowed from the potty in baby's high chair and affording equal privacy. The largest outboard cruisers, however, refine this into an enclosed toilet with head room.

The day cruiser devotes more of its length to a cockpit and this is a boon for the fisherman. Sleeping accommodations rarely go beyond the two vee bunks in the forepeak and toilet facilities may or may not include the enclosure. The outboard cruiser shown in Figure 12-3 illustrates the foregoing brief description. Obviously, any model can become an express if sufficient power and correct hull design give it the needed zip.

HOUSEBOATS.

Many of the smaller houseboats are designed for outboard engine power or are offered for sale with this option. The hulls of this newcomer to the field of boating encompass forms as varied as pontoons and trimarans.

These houseboat hulls have large flotation areas, which means that they require comparatively little immersion or draft. This makes them popular in shallow waters where standard powerboats of equal length cannot navigate.

The houseboat design tends toward large, flat topside

Figure 12-3: The outboard cruiser has some sleeping accommodations and cooking facilities.

surfaces and this exposes large sail area to the wind. The combination of large sail area and small underwater resisting area makes these craft more difficult to keep on course in a blow. Actually, an old-time sailor would not consider these vessels to be bad-weather boats, although the manufacturers claim full seaworthiness for them—and undoubtedly have made such claims only after thorough tests.

Design Factors

Several factors in the design of hulls are peculiarly important if outboard power is to be used in their propulsion. These are the height and rake of the transom, the size and extent of the keel, and the addition of a motor well.

TRANSOM HEIGHT.

Transom height becomes important because it determines the immersion depth of the propeller of the outboard engine. This depth, as explained in Chapter 3, has great bearing on the efficiency of the drive and on whether or not the prop will cavitate. The situation has virtually been standardized by agreement between the hull builders and the engine makers: Transoms will be either 15 inches or 20 inches high; outboard motors will be offered for those two heights.

The 20-inch height is recommended for the larger hulls,

especially if they are to use powers of 30 HP or more. Most engine manufacturers offer all their outboard motors with a choice of short (15 inch) or long (20 inch) shaft.

The ideal transom for outboard motor attachment is "plumb," meaning vertical. Any great amount of rake (slope) in the design complicates the attachment of the motor. Often, shimming or special brackets are required. Since the entire "push" is exerted against the transom, obviously it must be of sturdy construction.

MOTOR WELLS.

The low freeboard at the transom of outboard hulls could present a hazard in the form of seas coming aboard and swamping the boat. The motor well is a safety feature designed to prevent this. It isolates the passenger compartment and is self-draining so that any water shipped can flow out again.

The drawing and table in Figure 12-4 give all the pertinent dimensions for motor wells. Both single and twin installations are covered and shown. The span of the well fore and aft takes into account the added space needed to clear the power head when the motor is tipped way up.

The danger from swamping occurs not only from a following sea. A sudden stop from high-speed running can have the same effect; the wake keeps on coming, overtakes the boat, and rolls in over the transom.

Many commercial fishermen favor an unusual form of motor well for their dories. Their outboard motor is mounted just aft of the boat's center in a high box well. They claim two advantages: the stern is left clear for net hauling and these boats can streak along almost like a sea sled.

KEEL EFFECTS.

Outboard motor manufacturers stress that a heavy continuous keel can have a pronounced effect in downgrading the performance of a single-engine installation. This happens because the large area of the keel can obstruct the free flow of water to the propeller. The starved prop begins to churn air and, as detailed in Chapter 3, cavitation results with consequent increase of engine RPM and decrease of boat speed.

The general recommendation is that there be no, or a minimum, of keel for about four feet ahead of the transom. Any disturbance to the water caused by the forward

SINGLE MOTOR					
MOTOR H.P.	CUTOUT WIDTH A			MAX. RADII	
	X HT.	Y HT.	Z HT.	B	C
UNDER 5-1/2 H.P.	22"	22"	22"	5"	5"
5-1/2 H.P. to 12 H.P.	21"	23"	27"	5"	13"
12 H.P. THRU 50 H.P.	28"	34"	34"	8-1/2"	12"
OVER 50 H.P.	28"	35"	36"	9"	24"

TWIN MOTORS						
H.P. PER MOTOR	CUTOUT WIDTH A**			SPAC- ING S	MAX. RADII	
	X HT.	Y HT.	Z HT.		B	C
UNDER 12 H.P.	43"	45"	49"	22"	5"	13"
12 H.P. THRU 50 H.P.	50"	56"	58"	22"	8-1/2"	12"
OVER 50 H.P.	54"	61"	62"	26"	9"	24"

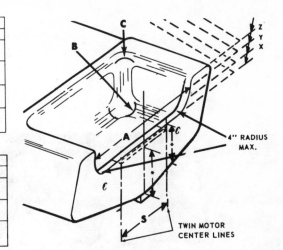

Figure 12-4: Motor wells are a safeguard against swamping by a following sea. The important dimensions are given above for single and twin installations.

section of the keel thus has a chance to be smoothed and eliminated before the propeller is reached.

If there must be some keel in this area, then it should fade gradually to nothing at the transom edge. Of course this keel treatment is not required for twin-engine installations; any keel disturbance would happen between them and not in their line of water approach.

Steering and Control

The very small outboard boats with engines of minimal horsepower generally are maneuvered directly at the motor with an integral steering handle that also contains the throttle control. This type of craft, except when it is the dinghy of a large boat, is a rugged way to go to sea and is confined mostly to the realm of the very young. Larger hulls with huskier motors are remote controlled from a forward steering position that includes forward-neutral-reverse shift, throttle, and ignition-starting key.

It is preferable that the steering position be on the starboard side. This serves a purpose in addition to the desirable one of enabling the helmsman better to see boats approaching in the danger angle in which his craft is burdened. The helmsman's weight in this position counteracts the torque reaction which the spinning propeller exerts on the hull.

The connection between steering wheel and motor is either a bowden cable or a system of pulleys and wire rope. The bowden cable installation has the advantage of simplicity because it can negotiate around obstructions and curves without the aid of pulleys and guides. The fittings must be sturdy and well anchored to the hull sides with through bolts because they withstand considerable stress when operating at high speed.

Two motors in a twin installation are connected together rigidly with a tie bar.

The smallest outboard motors are steered by someone sitting at the stern and swinging the motor arm either to right or left. As the motors get larger, the increased horsepower quite naturally imposes additional stress and the steering system consequently must be beefed up and made more elaborate.

Figure 12-5 shows one method of connecting the rope. The two springs actually are rope-tighteners that eliminate backlash and normally do not enter into the steering function.

The drawing also shows a section of flexible bowden cable. The inner cable slides freely in the outer housing and is able to transmit pushes as well as pulls. This is by far the simpler system to install and to maintain; most outboard boats use it.

Passenger Capacity

It is noted elsewhere that the drownings caused by overloading are a blot on recreational boating's safety record. These tragedies are the result of ignorance, yet it is hard to see how such ignorance can prevail in the face of all the publicity and all the manufacturers' efforts to set their customers on the path to safety.

Most outboard hulls, certainly all those built within the last five years, carry a factory-installed plate stating the number of passengers who can be carried. The reference assumes an average person of 150 pounds and allows for the weight of the motor.

The recommendation is based on a "static float line." This takes into account the height of the hull freeboard

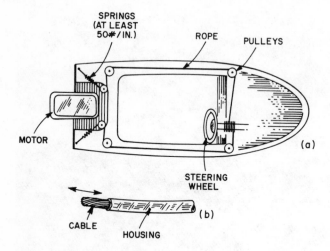

Figure 12-5: A two-spring rope assembly is shown at (a). A cross section of a bowden cable, sometimes used in place of a rope, is seen in (b).

at the lowest point, the one most vulnerable to hull flooding. The load capacity also can be calculated; the method is outlined in Coast Guard publication #340. The explanation of the procedure takes up a full page, so relying on the load plate for guidance is much the easier way.

The Coast Guard in addition gives a rough rule of thumb for determining a safe load: Multiply boat length by boat beam, both in feet, and divide the result by fifteen. The answer, taken to the nearest whole number, is the number of average persons who would constitute a maximum safe load. Remember, this is *maximum*.

Stability and Trim

The passengers aboard an outboard hull generally constitute a major portion of the total floating weight. Therefore they have a critical effect upon stability and trim.

The passengers should sit well down in the hull in order to keep the center of gravity as low as possible and favorable to the center of buoyancy. (See Chapter 1.) The fore and aft placement of the passengers should be such that the bow does not plow and the stern does not squat. Athwartship trim is achieved by keeping passenger weight symmetrical with the keel line.

It may prove necessary underway to have passengers move a bit forward to improve handling and control in

heavy wind and sea. Likewise, planing under good conditions may be improved by having them move slightly aft. Except in the larger and heavier outboard hulls, standing up and moving about should be done with utmost caution.

Outboard Handling

The general instructions for handling boats given in other chapters apply equally well to outboard craft. The sea is the sea and it is no respecter of status. Nevertheless, some added cautions are in order on the subjects of steering and speed in outboard boats.

The outboard hull steers with a quicker and sharper response to the wheel than the inboard. The reason is the nature of the propulsive force. The outboard does not rely on rudder reaction but instead directs the thrust of its propeller in the desired direction—and this is much more effective. As a consequence, the outboard can make almost right-angle turns.

The outboard also lacks the rudder reaction found in inboard steering when reversing. The outboard propeller pulls the hull astern directly in the desired direction; the inboard must depend entirely on the secondary effect of reaction on the rudder surface for astern steerage way. Then also, the very small outboard motors that have no reverse gear but instead swing the entire unit 180 degrees, actually *push* the boat when backing instead of pulling it.

The usual high speed at which outboard boats are operated brings with it the penalties associated with any fast traveling: All maneuvers require greater anticipation and more alertness. In addition, most hulls raise their noses when planing and this restricts the view of the course ahead; the prevalence of driftwood can make this a hazard.

Legalities

Outboard boats must comply with legal restrictions pretty much on a par with inboards; overall length determines the degree of compliance. The basics are spelled out in Chapter 25.

The main exceptions have to do with flame arresters, which are not required, and with extinguishers and ventilators, which may or may not be required.

The federal boating act mandates numbering for all

outboards of more than 10 horsepower. Some states supersede this with numbering requirements for *all* outboards, regardless of power plant size.

The passage of the Federal Safe Boating Act of 1971 portends changes in the numbering attitudes of many states. Sec. 17 of this Act reads as follows: "An undocumented vessel equipped with propulsion machinery of any type shall have a number issued by the proper issuing authority in the state in which the vessel is principally used."

Outboard Motors

The outboard motor started as a one-lung kicker that you carried to a rowboat and fastened to the transom. If you were lucky enough to get it going, it saved you the trouble of rowing. The overly loud putt-putts warned the fish of your coming and roused some shoreside listeners to murderous intent. None of its early devotees could guess how the contraption would blossom and grow.

Today's outboard motors are as reliable in performance as the automobile and are striving to become as quiet. Only the smallest require the skipper to yank a pull cord; most feature complete electric systems and start at the touch of a button or the turn of a key. Horsepower-wise, they have climbed well above the 100 mark and probably will go even higher in response to public demand.

The engines follow the modus operandi of all engines, which is clarified in Chapter 2. Their fuel is gasoline except for one import which runs on the diesel principle. Only one manufacturer espouses the four-stroke cycle; all others build their machines as two-cycle. The major difference from inboards is the very high speed at which the outboard engine's horsepower is rated.

The need for high RPM is explained easily. The *rate* at which work is done is part of the formula for horsepower. You can therefore boost the output from a small engine by increasing the number of times per minute its force is exerted. Whereas inboard engines are rated at somewhere around 3000 RPM, the outboards are designed for top speeds around 5000 RPM. That accounts for the beaucoup power in the mini package.

Engine Data

The standard arrangement for outboard engines is to have the cylinders horizontal. This makes the crankshaft vertical and thus easier to tie into the shafts and gears that eventually drive the propeller at the bottom. The clutch for remote-controlled forward and reverse rotation of the prop on the larger motors is in this lower section.

The small outboard motors do not have reverse gearing and the propeller always turns in one direction. Reverse motion of the boat is attained by swinging the entire motor around in a half circle. This requires the operator to sit in the stern, hugging the motor control lever. This is so low on the social scale nowadays, you'll hardly ever see anyone over sixteen doing it except in small fishing boats and dinghies. The photo in Figure 12-6 shows a standard power unit.

The two-cycle engines use their crankcases as part of the fuel injection system and thereby are robbed of an oil sump. The lubricating oil they need to keep going is fed to them as part of their fuel; the oil is mixed with the gasoline.

The ratio of oil to gasoline has steadily become smaller as lubricants were improved and engines became more efficient in their use of them. Some manufacturers have brought the figure down to 1 in 50, in other words, 1 ounce of oil to 50 ounces of gas or the equivalent of 1 pint for a 6-gallon tank. Some motors need more oil than this, but in each case the answer is in the owner's manual.

The oil-fuel mixture is critical because it affects the carburetor adjustment and it bears directly on the mechanical wear of the engine. The type of lubricant used also is important; here again, the owner's manual is the final word.

The oil in the gasoline, of course, eventually is burned —and when you burn oil, you get smoke. In the models of years gone by, when oil mixes were not as "lean" as they are today, this smoke was an admitted nuisance. Miserly use of oil in combination with underwater exhaust has all but banished smoke from the present outboard scene.

The oil in the gasoline lubricates only the internal parts of the engine itself; it does not reach the gearing and clutches. Lubrication of the gear case in the lower leg is accomplished separately through a grease fitting. The idea is the same on all motors, but each make has a slightly different method of doing the job. Step-by-step procedure is outlined in all owner's manuals.

Only a few outboard motors, and they are all of mini-

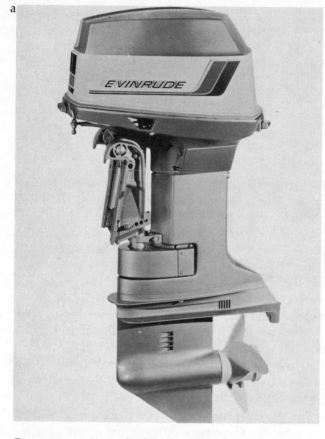

Figure 12-6: A standard outboard motor (a) is compared with a diminutive motor (b). (Credit—Evinrude Motors and Seaborne System, Inc.)

mal horsepower, rely on air cooling—and even these pump water through the exhaust as a safety measure. Water cooling is standard on all other outboard engines with force feed circulation via a pump. A drain hole usually permits visual check of the coolant flow.

Horsepower ratings start with a single cylinder 1½ and top out at 135, developed in six cylinders. Racing fans will find that high-speed lower units are available for some of the big horsepower models.

Any of the larger brutes places the transom under tremendous stress, not only from the great thrust but also from vibration and shock. The transom must be beefed up, of course, but this in itself does not remove these two damaging forces. The cure for the problem is accomplished by shock absorbers which are built into the assembly of most large units. The absorbers are constructed the same, and function the same, as their counterparts on automobiles.

The fuels recommended for outboard engines give the operator a wide choice. Any one of the following is adequate: white marine gas, hi-test automobile gas, standard automobile gas. As with automobiles, using the premium grade when the regular works all right benefits only the oil company. One manufacturer sums up his fuel recommendations by saying, "When in doubt, use any gasoline that is satisfactory for a car." (Outboards have come a long way since their forebears with the persnickety appetites for special gas.) The photograph in Figure 12-7 shows and labels the parts of a large outboard. (Latest directives from manufacturers specify the use *only* of leaded gas.)

Gear Shifting

The larger outboard motors feature automatic shifting which permits neutral, forward and reverse to be selected remotely from the helmsman's position. The methods of accomplishing this vary. One representative scheme does the actual mechanical work with oil under pressure; the oil in turn is controlled by a solenoid valve responsive to the remote switch. A clutch dog moving between the forward and reverse gears makes the final shift. The diagrams in Figure 12-8 show the various positions.

Engine Cooling

The great speed and high horsepower output of outboard engines make proper cooling a critical necessity. Over-

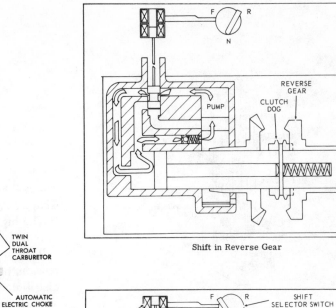

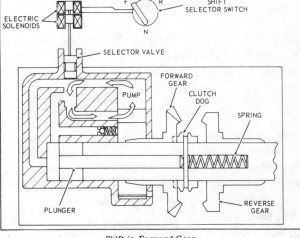

Shift in Reverse Gear

Shift in Forward Gear

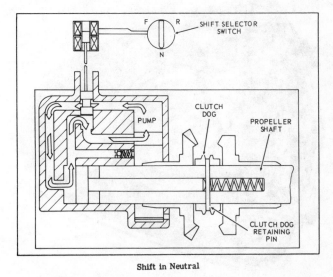

Shift in Neutral

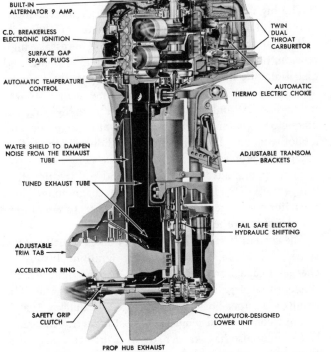

Figure 12-7: The major parts of an outboard motor are named above for easy identification. (Credit—Evinrude Motors)

cooling robs an engine of power and fuel efficiency while insufficient cooling obviously is destructive. The cooling circuit of an outboard engine is diagrammed in Figure 12-9. A thermostat maintains design temperatures. The circulation also cools the gear case.

Outboard Ignition

One- and two-cylinder outboard engines are fired by a type of flywheel magneto ignition system even more familiar on lawn mowers. The larger multi-cylinder models derive their ignition from battery and spark-coil systems which duplicate present automotive practice. Or else they use high-tension magnetos which were common on cars many years ago until cost tabooed them.

In the flywheel magneto type of ignition, permanent magnets are embedded in the rim of the engine flywheel.

Figure 12-8: Shifting from neutral to forward and reverse is accomplished by oil pressure controlled by a solenoid valve actuated by the remote switch. The three positions are diagramed.

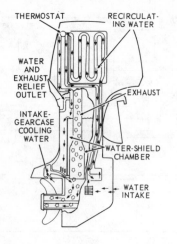

Figure 12-9: The thermostat in the cooling system re-circulates the jacket water until the design temperature is reached. The gear case is also cooled by circulating water.

These revolve past the cores of carefully placed coils and induce the spark voltage in them. The exact timing is obtained by a cam on the crankshaft which opens breaker points. Figure 12-10 is an overhead view showing a flywheel containing such an arrangement.

The battery and coil systems control the flow of battery current to the spark coil by means of standard breaker points. The battery voltage is raised to the high value

Figure 12-10: The flywheel containing the magneto is at the center of this overhead view. The high-tension cables leading from the flywheel to the spark plugs can be seen.

needed to jump the gap in the spark plug and a distributor routes this juice to the right plug at the right time. (See Chapter 7.)

The high-tension magneto combines all the functions in one unit. It generates the basic current, multiplies its voltage in an integral transformer to the necessary high tension, times the spark with its own breaker points and distributes it; there is *no* dependence upon the battery. This is the superior system. At one time, a fine car was not a fine car unless it had at least one high-tension magneto to guarantee a fat, hot spark at high speeds, and a pilot would not leave the ground without a high-tension "mag" (or preferably two) on his plane's engine.

There is one advance in battery and coil ignition that brings it up to the level of high-tension magneto ignition: capacitor discharge ignition. Many manufacturers of outboard motors are adopting it.

The current from the battery is *not* taken directly to the spark coil in capacitor discharge ignition. Instead it charges a capacitor. (See Chapter 8.) At the right instant, this entire charge is dumped into the coil en masse. The result is a super-hot spark generated so quickly that it can overcome fouled plugs. The most modern versions of this system also have dispensed with the breaker points; they have substituted an electromagnetic trigger that never wears out because it makes no physical contact. A complete hookup of such an ignition system is shown in Figure 12-11.

Various tricky forms of spark plugs have appeared on the market over the years and now some newcomers are offered to go hand in hand with these new systems of ignition. Many claims of superiority naturally are made for them. Whether any live up to these claims is problematical. Actually, all the gasoline mixture needs to set it off is a hot spark and the shape of this ignitor is of little consequence.

Outboard Electricals

The outboard more and more rivals the inboard in the completeness of its electrical system. The larger engines feature electric starting, electric chokes, electric sensing instruments, and they generate enough current to keep a battery charged and running lights lit.

These electrical units are smaller and more compact but otherwise do not differ from the basics discussed in

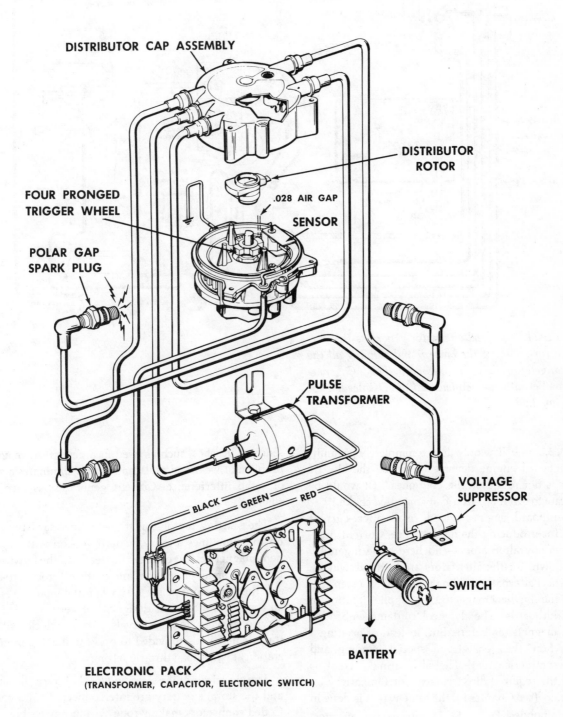

DISTRIBUTOR CAP ASSEMBLY

DISTRIBUTOR ROTOR

FOUR PRONGED TRIGGER WHEEL

.028 AIR GAP

SENSOR

POLAR GAP SPARK PLUG

PULSE TRANSFORMER

VOLTAGE SUPPRESSOR

BLACK   GREEN   RED

SWITCH

TO BATTERY

ELECTRONIC PACK
(TRANSFORMER, CAPACITOR, ELECTRONIC SWITCH)

Figure 12-11: This modern capacitor discharge ignition system eliminates the often troublesome breaker points. The spark is triggered by magnetic induction. (Credit— Evinrude Motors)

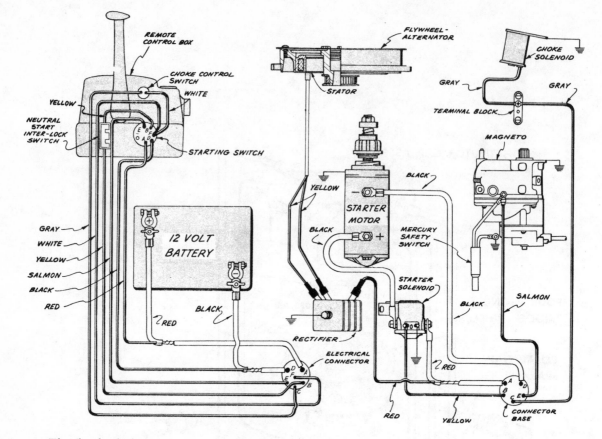

Figure 12-12: The flywheel alternator generates the current needed for charging the battery and running all the electrical gadgets on a modern outboard. The AC generated by the alternator is rectified into the DC needed for the battery by diodes.

Chapters 7, 8, and 9. The only device completely unfamiliar to an inboard engine devotee might be the electric choke; this is not found on the "big ones." (It would be more accurate to call it an electrically *operated* choke.)

Earlier outboard engines added small direct-current generators for producing the needed juice. Current practice is to employ alternators—and here some ingenuity has been shown, for the alternators are in the flywheels.

The flywheel alternator can be thought of as a step forward from the flywheel magneto that supplies ignition to the small outboards. The flywheel contains embedded permanent magnets, as before. But, instead of exciting a spark coil, here they energize a special winding and induce alternating current. The alternating current is rectified to the required direct current for the battery by diode rectifiers (see Chapter 8), the same way it is done in modern automobiles. Figure 12-12 depicts such an alternator together with the wiring for an entire electrical system.

In addition to the using of otherwise wasted space, the great advantage of this alternator is reliability. The ab-

sence of brushes, such as used in a generator, removes a problem of wear and replacement and eliminates a source of radio interference. Current generation is also more efficient.

The starting motor sometimes is standard but scaled down, sometimes a more modern version with a permanent magnet field. It engages the teeth on the flywheel rim through a small pinion that automatically goes into action and then spins out of the way when the motor fires. Like all starting motors, it is designed for very short duration service at very long intervals. An interlock with the throttle usually is provided to prevent starting motor operation at wide-open throttle settings.

The electricals at the steering wheel, those at the engine, and the storage battery are interconnected via a harness. Coded connectors make wrong wiring impossible.

Note from the wiring diagram in Figure 12-12 that a safety switch is provided in the magneto circuit. This is a gravity switch and shuts off the ignition in the event of a spill.

Outboard Propellers

Outboard motor propellers follow all the rules laid down in Chapter 3. The materials of which the props are made include bronze, aluminum, stainless steel, and plastic. Plastic is a late development and claims a durability and a freedom from accidental blade bending that should be very desirable.

The nature of much outboarding, which includes shoal-water cruising, increases the possibility that the fast-spinning blades will strike a rock or some other damaging object. This has been taken into account in the design of the driving system.

The underlying idea is to have some less costly component let go before the prop is harmed. Sometimes this is accomplished with an inexpensive shear pin which snaps (and must be replaced). Or else, the prop hub has a flexible core which absorbs shock and slips at the critical time. The latter requires no action by the operator but the former makes tools necessary.

The tools for changing shear pins should be mandatory to have on board because "you never know." The requirements are a wrench to fit the nuts which secure the prop and a pliers to handle the usual cotter pin which locks the nut.

Almost without exception the motors can be swung up high enough to permit shear pin change with a reasonable amount of convenience. The job of pin changing itself is simple but nevertheless requires considerable dexterity to perform in a bobbing boat.

A propeller whose pitch can be varied without removing it from the shaft is pictured in Figure 12-13. The blade angles of attack are changed easily with a special wrench which is supplied. This one propeller therefore can be left on the motor for all types of service from ski towing to trolling.

Another "propeller" innovation eliminates the prop entirely and substitutes an impeller in a housing, thus converting the unit into a jet drive. Among the advantages claimed is the safety achieved by elimination of the fast, unprotected whirring chopper.

Outboard Carburetors

Chapter 2 explained that the proportions of gasoline and air in the fuel mixture must remain within narrow limits in order to be acceptable for combustion in an engine.

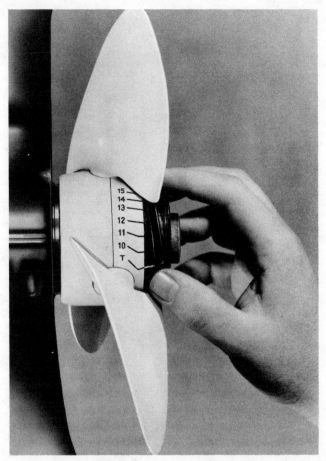

Figure 12-13: The pitch of this propeller can be changed in minutes without removing it from the motor to suit the type of boating to be done—skiing, cruising or trolling. (Credit—Lesnor-Maehr Marine Co., Inc.)

The fuel-to-air ratio of this mix may vary between 1 to 8 and 1 to 12, depending upon load and speed. However, the outboard motor is not called upon to deliver the sudden accelerations or the quick changes in power output common for an automobile, and consequently the maintenance of the right fuel mixture is not as difficult. Thus the outboard carburetor can be simpler.

The simplicity, in fact, can fall to the level of an ordinary mixing valve in the smallest engines. The higher horsepower models employ carburetors which are scaled down and simplified versions of automotive units; they often are devoid of the familiar accelerating pumps.

The high-speed fuel supply for these carburetors is usually metered throught a fixed jet, although variable orifices also are used. These factory-installed jets are of a size correct for optimum conditions; when the outboard motor is to be used on some lake at a high mountain elevation, the jet size is decreased.

In most outboard carburetors the only adjustment is for idling speed. This is a needle-valve screw which regulates the amount of air or the amount of fuel, depending

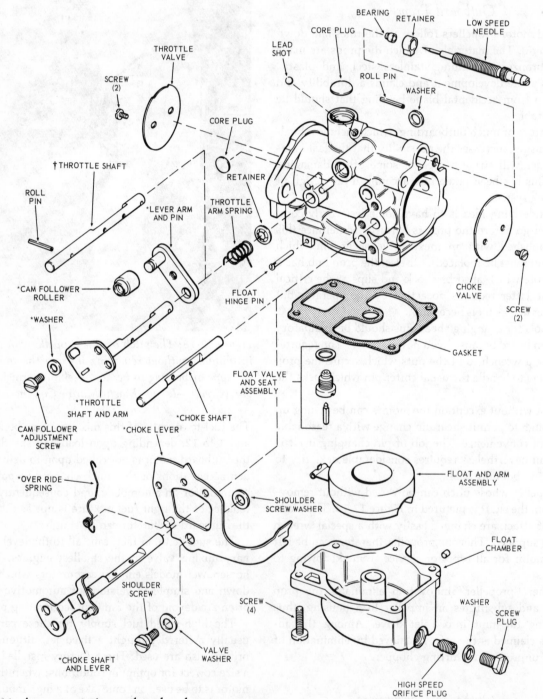

Figure 12-14: A representative outboard carburetor consists of many parts and the dotted lines show how they are assembled. The only adjustment on most outboard carburetors is the idle needle valve shown at top right.

upon design. As with all gasoline engines, starting is achieved by an enrichment of the fuel-air mixture through the closing of a choke. The parts which comprise a representative outboard carburetor are shown in Figure 12-14.

Like all carburetors, the outboard carb is finicky about having its fuel clean. The need for this lies in the small fuel passages and the closely fitted needle valves. The job of keeping the fuel free of particulate matter falls to the filter. The elements of such a fuel-filtering device are shown in Figure 12-15.

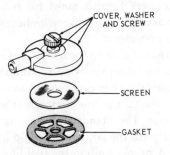

COVER, WASHER AND SCREW

SCREEN

GASKET

Figure 12-15: The fine passages in a carburetor and the close-fitting needle valve require that the fuel be free of particulate matter. The filter elements, above, see to this.

Permissible Horsepower

With outboard motors available whose outputs cover the whole range from 1½ horsepower to 135 horsepower, the problem arises of choosing the optimum size for any particular hull. The easiest and best guide is the maximum horsepower plate put into most outboard hulls by their manufacturers. The given figure should not be exceeded.

In the absence of such an information plate, it is possible to arrive at an approximation with a simple formula and the table in Figure 12-16. The boat length in feet is

multiplied by the transom width (also in feet), and the product is referred to the upper portion of the table. Directly below is the maximum permissible horsepower. Example: a 16-foot hull with a 3-foot wide transom (16 × 3 = 48). The number 48 entered into the table yields an answer of 15 horsepower. A further example: an 18-foot hull with a 4-foot transom (18 × 4 = 72). For this hull the maximum permissible horsepower would be 55 with remote steering and 35 without.

Outboard Steering

As already noted in Chapter 4, outboards steer by turning the entire engine unit so that the propeller thrust takes place in the desired direction. This is accomplished on low horsepower motors by sitting at the transom and moving the steering arm attached to the outboard's housing. Larger motors are remotely controlled from a forward steering position through tiller ropes or push-pull cables. The cable installation is simplicity itself.

The more complicated tiller rope installation is shown in Figure 12-17. Springs keep the tiller cable taut as it winds

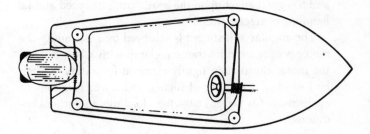

Figure 12-17: This schematic drawing shows how the cabling from steering wheel to outboard motor swings the motor and affects steering.

Overall Length (ft.) × Transom Width (ft.) = Factor						
Factor: Under 40	40–45	46–49	50–53	54–57	Remote Steering 20" Transom Over 57	No Remote; Lower Transom Over 57
Maximum HP Capacity: 5	10	15	20	25	2 × Factor − 90	3/4 Factor − 20
Gross Trailer Weight	up to 2000 #		2000 #–3500 #	3500 #–5000 #	Over 5000 #	
Minimum Ball Diameter	1-7/8 in.		2"	2" Best Higher Strength	Shall Conform to BIA Min. Strength Requirements	

Figure 12-16: Safe maximum horsepower for an outboard hull can be computed from the above tables.

and unwinds on the steering wheel drum. The rate of the springs (the effort in pounds required to stretch them) is specified by the manufacturer for each size of outboard motor. Sheaves, of course, must be located so that the cable moves freely.

Outboard Mounting

There are probably mighty few bodies of water frequented by outboard skippers that do not have at least one outboard motor on the bottom acting as an artificial reef for fish. Those motors belonged to owners who learned the costly way that proper transom mounting is important.

All outboard motors come with heavy-duty C clamps whose husky screws can clamp the transom tightly. These alone should never be relied upon, however, because of the strong effects of vibration. The forces set up by vibration actually can produce twisting effects powerful enough to turn and loosen the screws.

Safety chains on the lighter models will save the motors from a dunking if the unexpected happens. All manufacturers recommend that their large units be through-bolted to the transom and their brackets are drilled and slotted for this. Through-bolting is equivalent to a permanent mounting. This makes sense because these motors are far too heavy to be "portable" in the sense of easy transport to and from the boat for intermittent use.

One advantage which the outboard motor has over the inboard engine is the ability to change the angle of its propeller thrust. This angular setting is highly important and has great effect upon the boat's trim, its speed and its handling characteristics.

The angular adjustment is achieved by suspending the motor proper from its transom clamp with a hinge. Thus the motor can remain tightly clamped for safety yet can be locked in a number of higher and lower positions to compensate for various passenger loadings and other conditions.

The illustration in Figure 12-18 shows the effect of angles above and below the correct one. The effect of the incorrect settings is either to make the boat run with nose up or else to cause the bow to dig in. Both conditions are undesirable. The bow-up attitude makes the boat vulnerable to weathervaning in a cross wind. The bow-down posture makes for wet riding and robs speed.

Fuel Tanks

Except for the very smallest outboard motors, the so-called fishing motors, which have integral gasoline tanks, the manufacturers furnish tanks for remote placement. These are hooked to the engines with hoses equipped with quick-connect nozzles.

Devices are available on the market for hooking several remote tanks together to provide a continuous fuel supply. This eliminates the changing over of tanks as each goes dry and the resultant motor stoppage at an inconvenient or unsafe time. The standard remote tanks have a 6-gallon capacity for the large motors and half that for the small units. A primer bulb in the fuel line is a great convenience when starting or when changing tanks. A few squeezes does the job which old-timers used to do by sucking (and often gulping) gasoline. It is shown in Figure 12-19.

All makers stress the importance of proper mixing of oil and gas; they caution against pouring the oil first into an empty tank. The correct procedure is to place a gallon or so of gasoline in the tank, add the recommended amount of correct oil, mix thoroughly, and then complete the fuel fill. Oil poured into an empty tank probably will remain on the bottom and mix only slightly with subsequently added gasoline. (Many marina pumps dispense a gas-oil mixture.)

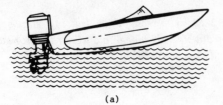

(a)

Figure 12-18: Fore and aft trim while underway is determined largely by the angle of the outboard motor; passenger weight distribution is also an important factor. Too open an angle (a) pushes the stern down and the bow up while too small an angle (c) keeps the stern up and the bow down. Correct motor angle (b) results in a level ride.

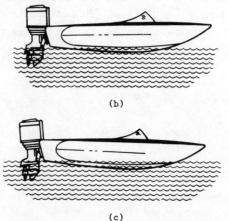

(b)

(c)

Outboard Care

Outboard motors, like any other metal objects on board, could become the victims of corrosion. (See Chapter 22.) The outboard has a positive method of protection not available to other immersed fixtures of the boat—it can be raised up out of the water when not in use.

The motor should be tilted down into the water only during its periods of actual use; at all other times it should be tilted up, clear. Of course no attempt to run the engine should be made in its raised position because this would rob it of its cooling water and destroy it quickly.

Before long periods of disuse, it is wise to unscrew the spark plugs and inject about a tablespoon of oil into each cylinder. Turning the engine over a few times before the plugs are replaced will distribute the lubricant over the cylinder walls. (Ground the spark plug wires while doing this to prevent voltage breakdown of the system.)

Water in its gasoline is no more acceptable to the outboard than to its larger inboard cousin, but the very nature of the situation makes it more likely that it be there. A very fine mesh metal screen or a chamois filter in the fuel-tank neck can be a good preventive; the gasoline goes through, the water separates out and remains behind. Additives (essentially an alcohol) can be added to the fuel mixture as another way to remove the water; these "soak" up the water chemically.

Outboard motors operated in salt water should be flushed with fresh water at the end of their duty. The spray on the outside of the motor, which evaporates and leaves salt crystals behind, also should be washed off.

Overspeeding is detrimental to the engine. A correctly chosen propeller automatically prevents the engine from revving beyond its designed optimum RPM (except during periods of cavitation already mentioned and explained in Chapter 3).

GALVANIC PROTECTION.

The deleterious effects of galvanic corrosion are detailed in Chapter 22. Outboard motors are as victimized by this evil as is any other seagoing metal. Fortunately, they are equally amenable to the anodic and cathodic protection measures described in that section.

All outboard motors are equipped with an anode. It may do double duty as a fin or stabilizer or it may simply be a slug of zinc attached to the housing. It must be replaced when it corrodes away in order to continue the protection.

As explained in Chapter 22, a more sophisticated defensive method is cathodic protection and this, too, is available for outboard motors. One commercial system that is installed easily at the transom is pictured in Figure 12-20.

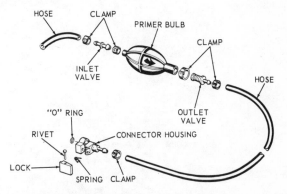

Figure 12-19: The primer bulb is a great convenience when starting and when changing fuel tanks.

Figure 12-20: Cathodic protection is the surest way to protect the outboard motor against the ravages of galvanic corrosion. The system takes a minimal current from the battery and with it counteracts the incipient deterioration of housing and propeller. (Credit—Kiekhaefer Corp.; Photo by Gordon Manning)

315

13   *Trailers*

One of the great attractions of outboarding is the ease with which the boats can be transported on trailers hitched to family automobiles. This gives the outboard skipper access within a few hours to many waters it would take days for an inboard boatman to reach, if he could get there at all.

Trailering is not limited to small, light runabouts. Some compact family cruisers have been designed to fit within the limits imposed by over-the-road hauling. In many cases, such cruisers are supplanting the campers in which families enjoyed previous vacations.

Trailering has not passed by the sailboatman, either. The smaller windjammers are seen increasingly on the highways. For centerboard sailboats trailering is no problem, only a bit more work because the mast must come down. Boats with deep keels require special trailer adaptation to assure proper hull support. These craft ride so high that thought must be given en route to trailer stability, especially on curves. Launching these high keelers also becomes more complex and generally devolves upon a crane or a travel lift with a sling.

It does take a little more doing to get a sailboat ready for the road than an outboard. The shrouds, stays, sheets and halyards all need proper stowage. The mast generally protrudes quite a bit aft of the hull and trailer and needs a red flag, at night preferably a red light. Sails can be left in their bags until the boat is overboard. It is important that the trailer arms and pads fit the hull for correct support.

Most trailerable sailboats are fiberglass and thus are not affected adversely by remaining for long periods on the trailer, out of water, as wooden craft are. Nor do they have the wooden boat's failing of soaking up water when immersed to cause an increase in weight when hauled out.

Trailering has boomed because of the wide availability of launching ramps or alternate mechanical launching facilities. Many waterfront towns and most marinas have them. The car with its trailered boat arrives, the craft is launched, the car is parked, and the skipper and his passengers are off for a cruise. The return is an easy reversal of these operations.

Present-day trailers can handle boats up to about 25 feet in length and weighing up to about 3000 pounds. The heavier units are equipped with winches, some electrically powered, for ease in launching and reloading their cargoes.

The use of trailers on public highways is subject to state laws and these often differ from state to state. The surest guide is an application to local authorities for up-to-date information. The laws relate to lights, to brakes, to methods of hitching, and to the maximum lengths, widths and weights permitted.

One of the most important points in the design of a trailer is its method of supporting the boat. A boat in its natural habitat, the water, is buoyed up uniformly along its entire submerged surface; any lesser means of support tends to distort the hull lines. A good trailer, therefore, should duplicate this uniform support as closely as possible. In an attempt to do this, trailers provide pads and rollers at various points along the bottom. These preferably are adjustable to conform to the many current hull shapes.

Trailer Choice

Several questions must be asked to help in choosing the correct trailer for an outboard boat, but the first of these concerns weight. What is the total weight the trailer must support?

Heaviest item on the list will be the hull itself and, if it is a wooden boat, from 10 to 20 percent should be added for the weight of water soaked up after a long cruise. To hull weight must be added the weight of all heavy gear aboard, such as anchors, and the weight of the motor with its tanks and battery. A safety margin should remain; it is not wise to load the trailer right up to the maximum specified by the manufacturer. (Family baggage often is hauled in the boat and this weight also should be taken into account.)

The next question is boat length. The trailer must be long enough to support the boat from bow to transom. The standard construction of outboard hulls makes the keel and the area directly below and ahead of the transom the main support points; the trailer should be adjustable accordingly. A suitable rollered vee should be provided at the front of the trailer to hold the bow central and to act as a forward jam point. Adjustable arms that carry rollers or pads should support the chine on each side. Obviously, rollers instead of pads make for less friction and thus easier boat loading and unloading. Rearranging arms and pads for a centerboard sailboat is little different from the procedure for an outboard but for a hull with a deep keel it is much more difficult.

A winch at the forward end of the trailer is an absolute necessity for handling the heavier boats. Hand power is cheaper but electric winching naturally is a great deal more convenient. (The power comes from the car battery.) The winch also serves to haul the boat's bow up tight into the receiving vee and to lock it there for safer transportation. The bow eye to which the winch rope is attached is standardized at 16 inches above the keel for hulls up to 16 feet and at 20 inches above for larger boats. This eye generally is *not* intended for lifting.

The trailer also should make provision for enough tie-downs to overcome the effects of running over a rough road. These fastenings should be located at several points along the boat length and especially should allow for athwartship hold-downs at the transom.

Trailers are made of steel as well as of aluminum. The aluminum manufacturers claim for their product that it is lighter for the identical carrying capacity and that it will not rust. The steel units often require sanding down of rust spots and subsequent protective painting.

Outboard trailers are two-wheeled for light loads and four-wheeled for large boats. The axles can be moved longitudinally to achieve the desired balance and the proper weight on the tongue. This tongue weight, or rather the correct percentage of the total weight, affects the road-worthiness of the trailer. Tongue weight also becomes important when the loaded trailer must be moved manually before it is hitched to the car.

Trailer Hitches

Trailer hitches are ball-and-socket affairs with the socket as part of the trailer and the ball attached to the towing automobile. Early connections were all "bumper hitches," meaning that the ball was simply clamped to the bumper. These are not satisfactory and in most cases are not even legal. Bumpers on modern automobiles are flimsy, more ornamental than useful, and should not be relied upon. A breakaway boat not only can destroy itself but is a grave danger to every other user of the highway.

The ball should be part of a structure attached directly to the frame system of the automobile. The size of the ball should conform to the size of the socket on the trailer and is usually specified by the manufacturer. (All standard

balls meet the strength requirements set by the Society of Automotive Engineers.) Safety chains always should be used as an adjunct to the ball and socket and in most states are legally required. Figure 13-1 shows an approved trailer hitch with safety chains.

Figure 13-1: A trailer hitch is shown with crossed safety chains.

Crossing the safety chains under the trailer tongue is a worthwhile extra precaution. When this is done it provides a support for the tongue in the event of ball and socket failure. Furthermore, whenever S hooks are used they should be inserted in from the bottom, not the top, to prevent their bouncing out.

Wheels, Tires and Brakes

Boat-trailer wheels are standardized at 8-, 9-, and 12-inch diameters. The tires to fit these wheels are made with from 2 to 10 plys. Tire inflation pressures are greater than those carried on passenger car tires; exact figures are set by each tire manufacturer but the table in Figure 13-2 gives close values.

The smaller wheels on the trailers mean higher RPM for them than for the car wheels at the same road speed. Lubrication and regular inspection of trailer wheel bearings therefore are critical factors in maintenance, especially when the constant possibility of immersion during launching is considered.

Some states require brakes on the wheels of trailers above a certain weight and/or length. Trailer makers provide brake backing plates on these units to facilitate the installation of optional brake systems. Since regulations change, it is best to inquire of the motor vehicle bureau of the state concerned.

BOAT TRAILER TIRES AT HIGHWAY SPEED TIRE LOAD CAPACITIES VS INFLATION

Tire Size	Ply Rating	Tire Load Capacity at Various Inflations														
		30	35	40	45	50	55	60	65	70	75	80	85	90	95	100
4.80/4.00 x 8	2	380														
4.80/4.00 x 8	4	380	420	450	485	515	545	575	600							
5.70/5.00 x 8	4		575	625	665	710										
5.70/5.00 x 8*	6		575	625	665	710	750	790	830	865	900					
5.70/5.00 x 8*	8		575	625	665	710	750	790	830	865	900	930	965	1000	1030	
6.90/6.00 x 9	4		785	850												
6.90/6.00 x 9	6		785	850	915	970	1030	1080								
6.90/6.00 x 9*	8		785	850	915	970	1030	1080	1125	1175	1225	1270				
6.90/6.00 x 9*	10		785	850	915	970	1030	1080	1125	1175	1225	1270	1320	1365	1410	1450
20x8.00-10	4	825	900													
20x8.00-10	6	825	900	965	1030	1100										
20x8.00-10	8	825	900	965	1030	1100	1155	1210	1270	1325						
20x8.00-10	10	825	900	965	1030	1100	1155	1210	1270	1325	1370	1420	1475			
4.80/4.00 x 12	4	545	550	595	635	680	715	755	790							
5.30/4.50 x 12	4	640	700	760	810	865	915									
5.30/4.50 x 12	6	640	700	760	810	865	915	960	1005	1045	1090	1135				
6.00 x 12	4	855	935	1010												
6.00 x 12	6	855	935	1010	1090	1160	1230	1290								

Single underscoring indicates maximum recommended loads published by Tire & Rim Association.
*not recommended for new design.

Figure 13-2: Exact tire pressures are set by each manufacturer for his product but this table gives general values that are close.

The simplest installation is electric brakes actuated by the stoplight switch of the towing car. These trailer brakes are energized every time the stoplight lights and this, of course, happens whenever the brake pedal is depressed.

Other braking systems also are available, notably hydraulic units that respond to the deceleration of the towing automobile. This makes trailer braking automatic. The more advanced installations automatically apply the brakes if the trailer breaks loose; this is a safety measure copied from the railroads.

Trailer Lighting

Boat trailers should be equipped with taillights, stop lights, directional signals, and license lights. In most states these, plus reflectors and clearance lights, are required equipment.

Figure 13-3 illustrates the correct wiring diagram for a boat trailer and shows the standard connector for coupling it to the automobile electrical system. The wires all should be of the stranded type to guard against vibration breaks and should be well insulated and protected from chafing.

The electrical demand on the towing automobile made by the boat trailer is not great. The tail, license, and possible marker lamps all take bulbs that consume low current. The directional and stop bulbs are high current consumers but they are lit only intermittently.

Trailer Handling

As already stated, trailer maneuverability is affected by the weight left on the tongue. Most manufacturers specify that the extreme forward end of the tongue at the hitch should carry from 5 to 7 percent of the total weight. The axle shift to achieve this is made easy by auxiliary slots and holes and is done with only a wrench.

Too little weight on the trailer hitch results in errant trailer behavior. Too much weight depresses the rear of the automobile, interferes with handling, and throws headlight beams up into the trees.

A very short period of familiarization puts most auto drivers at ease when handling a car-and-trailer combination. They realize and subconsciously compensate for more sluggish acceleration and extended stopping distances. They become more chary of passing other vehicles

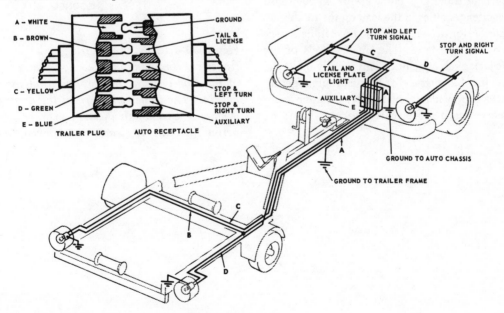

Figure 13-3: The wiring system of a trailer is connected to its tow car with a plug and receptacle for quick hitching and parting. Color-coded wires make the circuits easily identifiable.

and do so only when conditions are super-favorable. They overswing corners so that the trailer can turn them without ramming the curbs.

Only one facet of trailer handling remains to bother many drivers: backing up. (This is not strange because many drivers are bothered backing up a car without a trailer.) The difficulty is that the trailer always backs in a direction opposite to that in which the car is backing.

A simple gimmick that should solve trailer backing troubles is shown in Figure 13-4. When going ahead, steer with the *top* of the car steering wheel. When backing up, steer with the *bottom* of the steering wheel. The trailer will move in the direction in which your *hand* is moving. Incidentally, a truck-type rear-view mirror is highly preferable in place of the toy-type mirrors supplied with passenger cars.

Many outboarders add an auxiliary ball to the *front* bumper. They switch the trailer to this hitch when backing it down the launching ramp into the water. This avoids the possibility of the automobile's rear wheels and differential getting dunked or stuck in soft ground.

Some automobile manufacturers recommend overload springs or load levelers for the rear ends of their vehicles when used for boat trailering. These assure an even keel for the car, despite inequities in the load on the hitch.

Another caution for drivers who tow boat trailers concerns the matter of tire jacks. The small wheels of the trailer plus the lack of an attaching point usually make the car jack useless for changing trailer tires en route. Special, low trailer jacks are available. Naturally, a trailer spare tire and perhaps even a spare wheel bearing should be carried.

A gadget called a parking jack can be fitted to the tongue of a boat trailer. This keeps the boat level when the trailer is parked separated from its towing automobile. A caster wheel at the bottom of this jack facilitates moving the trailer manually.

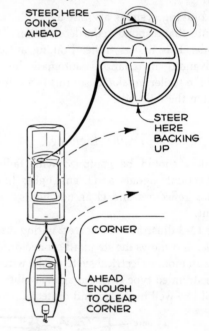

Figure 13-4: This simple trick will help in backing a trailer-car combination. Steer with your hand at the top *of the wheel when going forward, at the* bottom *when backing. The trailer will turn in the direction your* hand *is moving. Go enough ahead of a corner before turning to permit the trailer to clear the curb when running forward.*

PART   V

OPERATING A
POWERBOAT

14 *Operating Fundamentals and Seamanship*

THE creature of habit who rises, eats, and sleeps as though by a precise clock is often the butt of derisive jokes, yet the fact remains that humans do most reliably those tasks that they do instinctively. The newly "commissioned" skipper must acquire such instinctive reactions in relation to his boat, some pertaining to the general seaworthiness of the craft and others to its proper handling.

The engineering officer of an airliner arrives before takeoff time with a long list of items and functions to be checked. The rules require that each check be satisfactory before the ship flies. Similarly checking small craft before departure is equally to be recommended. Whether in the air or on the sea, priceless human life is still at stake, and checking the plane is no more important than checking the boat. A good skipper goes aboard with a checklist —if not actually in hand, then indelibly imprinted on his mind.

Checklist

The following list should be checked off routinely, item by item, immediately on coming aboard after an absence. No switch should be thrown, no power applied, until the results are affirmative. The steps are applicable to large powerboats as well as sailboats, although some items automatically can be omitted on, for instance, an open runabout with an outboard motor.

1. Open all hatches, doors, and perhaps even windows so that thorough natural ventilation can dispel any collected fumes.
2. Inspect the bilge for height of water and, even more important, sniff carefully for gasoline fumes. With diesel power, look for oil slicks. If gas fumes are present, use the hand bilge pump; do not turn on the electric pump until the fumes have been dissipated. This applies especially to the engine compartment.
3. Ventilate the battery compartment. Hydrogen gas, the explosive ingredient here, itself is odorless, but it always carries enough of the sulphuric acid odor to serve as a telltale.
4. When bilge, engine compartment, and battery compartment are free of fumes, throw main battery switch and switch on the exhaust blowers. Keep them running. The hatches and doors can now be closed to make the boat comfortable.
5. Make certain that all legally required equipment is on board. (See Chapter 25 for the list of preservers, extinguishers, etc.) Momentarily turn on running lights to check for burned-out bulbs and give the horn button or cord a touch to see whether the toot is still there. Turn each electronic gadget on long enough for its pilot light to assure you that no blown fuses or breakers will prevent its use when needed.
6. Check the fuel tanks for quantity on board. If this can be done other than by merely reading the instrument panel gauge, so much the better insurance. Check the water tank for quantity of aqua on board. If LP gas tanks serve the galley stove, check them.
7. Use the dipstick to inspect the level of lubricating oil in the crankcase of the propulsion engine. Do the same for the electric generating plant if you ship one. Ditto for the reduction gear box.
8. Start the engines after making sure that the clutches are in neutral. Let them run at idle to warm up while further inspection is carried on. Verify oil pressure, cooling water, and generator.
9. Have all ground tackle in place and available for use if needed during the cruise. Inspect deck lashings of the anchor, dinghy, and other heavyweights. Turn steering wheel from hard-over port to hard-over starboard to prove the rudder has not been jammed by flotsam.
10. The standing rigging and the running rigging on a sailboat present additional checkpoints. Shrouds and stays should be checked for tension and mast fairness. Sheets and halyards should run free. Sails should be readied for bending on. Battens should be ready at hand.
11. Unstow the charts, light lists, and other guides that will be needed on the cruise and clear all deviation-producing objects from the area of the compass. This is a good time to plot the courses to be steered or to refresh your memory of all the navigational aids on familiar courses.
12. Before getting under way with *any* boat, make certain that ground tackle is ready for instant use. Rode should be attached to an on-deck anchor and the line's bitter end should be secured. If the anchor is lashed down it should be in a manner that permits quick release.

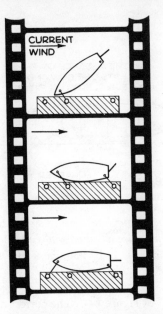

Figure 14-1: The sequence of maneuvers in coming to a pier: (1) With prop turning forward "kiss" pier gently with bow and fasten bowline. (2) With rudder hard over away from pier keep prop turning forward to push stern in. (3) Make fast. Bumpers are out, of course.

Sailboat Checklist

1. Open all hatches and portholes to dispel odors which may have collected from extended closure.
2. Inspect bilge for height of water and pump if necessary—manually if no electric pump is carried.
3. Make certain all halyards, sheets and lines are clear.
4. Attach the mainsail to boom and mast, and to halyard and sheet.
5. Attach the jib to jibstay or forestay and to halyard and sheet. Also attach mizzen if carried.
6. Attach service anchor to rode and have it ready on deck.
7. Make certain legally required equipment is on board.
8. Lower the centerboard if the boat is so equipped.
9. If rudder and tiller are not permanently attached, rig both in place.
10. If sailboat is equipped with inboard engine and fuel tanks, follow applicable items of the powerboat checklist.

Now that the immediate needs of Her Majesty, the boat, have been met, attention can be paid to the comfort of the human cargo. A baking-soda solution quickly will dispel the odors that often develop in an icebox or refrigerator from disuse; once cleaned, ice can be added or the switch thrown. All supplies brought aboard can now be stowed in their proper places. The guests can be shown the location of life preservers with a silent but fervent prayer that they will not be used. On the theory that a moment of embarrassment is better than an hour's tinkering with a clogged head, those newly aboard can be introduced to the landlubber's bogeyman.

The gods that watch o'er the sailorman by now hopefully have been appeased and it's time to head for the gas dock. This brings up the matter of the "dock" and the "pier." The dictionary insists that it is a pier but the average boatman persists in calling it a dock; it remains a Mexican stand-off and you can take your choice. At any rate, cast off and prepare to enrich the oil companies.

Gassing Up

Coming up to the gas dock, or to any pier, can be covered by a one-word instruction: SLOW. Any error or malfunction by man or machine is minimized and made easily correctible when the speed is kept slow. Don't ape the marine cowboys; they are identical twins of the auto drivers who leave rubber on the pavement at every stoplight—and usually sport bashed fenders.

Wind and current should be assessed. This is done by the natural senses and by observing how nearby boats and moorings lie to their anchors. In the beginning, such assessment is a conscious act but soon it becomes subconscious and second nature. The boat can be held motionless over the ground by heading it into wind and/or current and turning the propellers just fast enough forward to balance nature's forces.

If upstream approach to the dock is possible, choose it because it is the easier way. Often the relationship between dock, surrounding terrain, and nearby boats precludes a choice and forces either a downstream or a quartering approach. On the downstream run, way can be taken off the boat by keeping the props turning slowly in reverse. The quartering wind and/or current is more difficult and requires combinations of rudder plus forward and reverse propulsion.

Head for the dock at a slight angle so that the bow will touch first, and keep that touch as gentle as a kiss. Heave over a bow line for the dock attendant to fasten to a cleat or bollard or spile. Put the steering wheel hard-over away from the dock and keep the props turning forward. When the stern comes in, hold it fast with a stern line. The bow line will have moved aft and become an afterbow spring, so a new bow line should be laid before the engines are shut down. Of course, fenders and bumpers should have been put over the side.

The steps in the foregoing maneuver are shown clearly

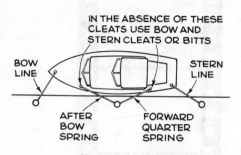

IN THE ABSENCE OF THESE
CLEATS USE BOW AND
STERN CLEATS OR BITTS

BOW
LINE

STERN
LINE

AFTER
BOW
SPRING

FORWARD
QUARTER
SPRING

Figure 14-2: These four lines should suffice to secure any boat except perhaps under abnormal conditions. Most of the time you will use only two: bow and stern. Don't forget bumpers!

in the "movies" of Figure 14-1. The correct names for the various mooring lines used in docking a powerboat are given in Figure 14-2; all of these would be used simultaneously only in extreme circumstances. Normally two would suffice: bow and stern lines. Find out about tide and allow for it if you are going to be tied up for any length of time.

The safety rule when taking on gasoline is to stop engines, shut off electric devices, extinguish galley flames, avoid smoking, and close all hatches. The rule is more often breached than observed, although engines at least are almost always shut down. The observance appears on a par with that paid the "No Smoking" signs at automobile filling stations. Diesel users are not bound by the same stringent rules because their fuel is so much less flammable, but the prudent will observe them anyhow, as added insurance.

Static electricity discharged from the gasoline nozzle to the boat's fill pipe was a bugaboo at one time. It is less so now because of provisions in the fuel pump equipment to eliminate it. Nevertheless, precautions are always in order. These consist of a good electrical connection between the filler-pipe deck flange and the boat's ground and also in maintaining contact between the gas nozzle and the flange during filling. (Static electricity is generated along the fabric-and-rubber gas hose by the motion of the gasoline and by atmospheric conditions.)

It is prudent to leave some space in the fuel tank for expansion; in other words, not to fill it to the top. Leaving five percent of the tank capacity empty should be enough based on fuel's average coefficient of expansion, but this is certainly nothing that must be calculated. Common sense can handle this matter.

LEAVING THE GAS DOCK.

Again, to quote the rules, five minutes should elapse, with exhaust blowers going, before the engines are started after gassing up. Admittedly, this procedure draws some coarse remarks at a busy gas dock and seldom finds actual application. But it is a goal to aim for; when it is missed, other precautions should be that much more thorough.

A motorist leaving a filling station "island" simply

turns his wheel away from it and gets going. A skipper who would try an equivalent maneuver would ram his stern into the dock. The reason, of course, is that boats do not steer like cars, as was pointed out in Chapter 4.

With plenty of room fore and aft and no wind or current problems, the boat could be run gently ahead along the dock until she is clear and then swung out into the stream. Heavy headwinds and/or currents plus lack of maneuvering space would require a slightly more complicated procedure like that in the "movies" of Figure 14-3. In this case, the boat's power and a forward quarter-

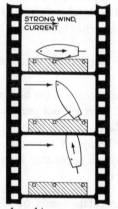

STRONG WIND,
CURRENT

Figure 14-3: Wind and/or current can aid you in leaving a pier. The forward quarterspring and slowly reversed props together with wind and current will get the bow out. Then run props forward, cast off the line and get away before the wind and current sweep you downstream. Watch the stern versus pier and have bumpers at the after quarter.

spring line work together. The natural forces actually help this maneuver, which is started with props reversed. When the boat has swung completely clear and is pointed bow out (as in the second frame of the movie films), the props are run forward and the line is hauled in. The gimmick is to watch the stern to avoid scraping it on the pier and to get forward way on before the spring is let go and before the boat is swept astern. Bumpers at the after quarter are good insurance.

An almost sure-fire method, which works under most conditions, is to leave the dock stern first. The rudder is set to a slight angle *away* from the dock and propellers are reversed. This takes the boat out at an angle and prevents the bow from scraping the pilings. Once far enough out to accommodate the turning circle of your boat, the rudder angle is increased to hard over, clutch is set to forward and you are on your way. The whole operation is simple in the extreme and makes a nice, professional big-ship maneuver.

In restricted space, the stern can best be gotten out by using an after-bow spring line, turning the rudder *toward* the dock and running engines *forward*. Once the stern is out, pull away in reverse.

All of the foregoing instructions apply as well to sailboats with auxiliary engines as they do to powerboats. The assumption is that the sailboat skipper will find horsepower more convenient than sailpower on his journey to the gas dock. Making it on sails alone puts you in the lap of the gods. (Of course, if you are wind-oriented through and through, and will not have a stinkpot aboard, you can smile tolerantly and pat yourself on the back for avoiding all this fuss—and expense.)

Getting Acquainted

There is a song in a famous Broadway musical which every new owner should sing to his new boat-love: "Getting to Know You." A skipper must know his own boat so well that there is perfect rapport between them and he can make it respond to his every command. The skipper of a sailboat must keep his sensibilities honed to an even finer edge because the nuances of sailing craft are more subtle.

Vessels constructed from the same plans and molds can vary in their reactions to command. They are like identical human twins, images of each other but nevertheless individual characters. This section explains the importance of knowing all the quirks and all the good points of your own boat. What follows is applicable equally to powerboats and to sailboats under motor power because a motoring sailboat is a powerboat.

The best place to get acquainted is a stretch of open water devoid of shoals, currents, and traffic—in other words, a locale that insures against getting into trouble with a wrong move. Put the rudder hard-over at moderate speed and ascertain the minimum turning circle. Try the same tactic at increasing speeds, to determine at what point the advance, sideslip, and heel become limiting factors. This will also reveal the point fore and aft on which the craft pivots, an important thing to know in many docking situations.

Simulate crash conditions in which you must go from forward to full reverse as fast as you can. (If there is no automatic control to assure this, make certain the engine is at idle when the clutch shifts to neutral.) Simulate a crowded marina situation in which you must make a fast forward recovery from reverse and note how much you overshoot.

On twin-screw boats, make turns with propellers alone, by running the outside prop forward and the inside one reverse. This is the turning-on-a-dime routine so valuable in marinas which provide fairway on the same miserly basis used by nightclubs to allot dancing space.

If your practice location has some means for measuring distance you are doubly lucky; this will enable you to make an "RPM versus MPH" table. Run back and forth over the measured course at various constant engine speeds and carefully check the running times. Take the averages and arrange them in a table. Your tachometer can now function as a speedometer. Always remember during future use that these speeds are through the water and not necessarily over the ground. (It is assumed that your speed trials were free of current and wind.)

A rough idea of boat speed can still be achieved without the measured mile. Mark a spot along the starboard or port rail exactly twenty feet aft of the bow. With the props running at constant speed, drop a small wad of paper into the water at the bow and count the seconds until it is exactly abreast of the mark. Refer this count to the table in Figure 14-4 to get the equivalent knots or nautical miles

Seconds to Reach Mark	Knots
1	12
2	6
3	4
4	3
5	2.4
6	2

Figure 14-4: In the absence of instrumentation, boat speed can be estimated by the time it takes a wad of paper to go by the 20-foot mark.

per hour. Then plot the results as shown. The curve will enable the translation of engine RPM into knots—but, as already admitted, it will certainly not win a prize for accuracy, although it will serve until you can do the thing right. (Speaking the words "one-hundred-one" without pause marks one second.)

Docking

Learning to dock the powerboat is the marine equivalent of those early days in your motoring experience when you had to learn bringing a car to the curb on the right side where your vision was obstructed. With the boat as with the auto, the only answer is continual practice.

To practice docking at an actual pier is the Spartan way. If you try it, your boat is certain to show the scars. It makes more sense to conduct at least the early attempts out in the already-mentioned practice location. Heave a large cardboard box overboard, steam away from it, and then come back alongside at various angles. If you bump the box, imagine your planking is nicked and feel as contrite as though it were. (*Don't* use a *wooden* box; it could get away from you and become a menace to another skipper.)

Few sailboat skippers will make their piers under sail alone and the even smaller minority who do it well are usually veterans who achieved battle scars on earlier hulls. The more common situation is for the sailboat to come to a mooring. (Many marinas prohibit *sail* approach to slips.)

The powerboatman's chore under similar circumstances is simplicity itself compared to what the windjammer has to do. Sheets must be loosed to kill the drive of the sails yet sufficient way must be left on the boat to assure reaching the mooring pennant against the wind. (The approach is made upwind.)

The first move when the distance left to go has been gauged is to drop the jib—but not on all boats. Some sailboats, because of their relationship between center of pressure and center of turning, will not handle with the jib down and only the mainsail up. Obviously, on these vessels the jib must stay on duty. Unless shallow water prohibits it, centerboards are left down on these mooring shoots to provide directive control.

Once the mooring pennant has been picked up, chocked and cleated, the chores of sail lowering and stowage start. The boom is secured in the boom crotch or gallows, sails are furled, rolled and tied or else removed and bagged. Some hulls require that centerboards be left partway down to deter severe rolling in heavy weather.

Compensating the Compass

It is an adage among experimental scientists that an in-accurate instrument is worse than none at all. It lulls you into a dangerously false sense of security. This is even more true of a compass upon which you depend for safety but which all the while is betraying your trust because of its errors. Assuming the compass to be in good condition, these errors are caused by deviation and must be removed or at least correctly ascertained.

The nature of and reason for deviation should be clear after a study of Chapter 9. Now we can zero in on the practical methods of compensating the compass to make it a reliable instrument. It should not be necessary to repeat the admonition to remove all magnetic offenders from the area of the compass and to have everything stowed in its proper cruising location before compensation begins. A further caution is that the compensators on compasses which contain them internally must be set to zero before any action is taken; screw-head aligning marks usually locate this condition.

Several methods are in general use for ascertaining the amount of deviation on each heading of the ship. (Note again that the deviation usually is *different* for each heading.) The job can be done by swinging the boat about a mooring and taking a series of bearing sights on a well-charted shore object with a pelorus or by sighting over the compass. Another procedure establishes a range of two objects on the chart and then measures the angle between this and the ship's lubber's line with a pelorus on various approaches; these readings are then compared with the simultaneous compass indications and reduced to deviations. Or the compass can be checked against the hourly azimuth of the sun, using its center pin together with almanac tables. All this must be done with due allowance for the variation shown on the chart.

For the powerboatman there is an easier way to arrive at his compass deviations—and to correct them—which does not even require a chart. It is done by making a few runs over reciprocal (exactly opposite) bearings on some open water. (Again, wind, current, and traffic should be absent.) The only "equipment" required consists of two floating markers which are easily constructed, as shown in Figure 14-5. (The construction is purposely flimsy to eliminate possible hazard to other skippers if the markers get away.) Two bar magnet compensators will also be required for compasses that are not self-compensating; these are available in any marine store. The exact measured center of each compensator should be marked.

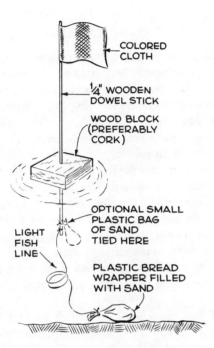

Figure 14-5: This marker float will help in running reciprocal courses for compass compensation.

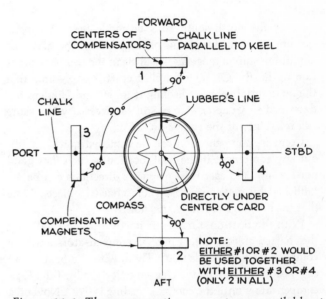

Figure 14-6: The compensating magnets are available at marine supply stores. Deviation is corrected as described in the text. (Many yacht compasses have internal compensators and may not require external magnets.) Only one fore and aft compensator and only one athwartship compensator are used.

Two chalk lines are drawn at the compass location so that their crossing point is directly under the pin at the center of the card. The fore and aft chalk line must be parallel to (or over) the keel and the compass' lubber's line must be immediately above it. The crossing line is athwartship at exactly 90 degrees to the first. The bar magnet compensators are placed with their centers on the chalk line as shown in Figure 14-6. (Note that these compensators may or may not be required with self-compensating compasses and that two at most will do the job on other compasses.) The bar magnets should be placed at the maximum distance from the compass at which they will still exert the desired effect; they deaden the instrument and slow the response of the card when they are too close.

The actual compass correction procedure is simplicity itself: Drop a marker overboard with enough fish line out to let the bag rest on the bottom and prevent drift. Swing the boat until the compass lubber's line is exactly at the north index on the compass card. Hold the course carefully for as far as you can still see the marker and at that point drop the second marker float overboard. Now

swing ship, pass hard by the second marker, pick it up, and point the bow at the first. Maintain this course by eye, the while reading the compass. Up to now, the compensators should be *well away* from the compass.

If the reading is exactly 180 degrees, there is no deviation and you are one of the very few favored by the gods. More likely the compass will indicate more or less than 180 degrees. Place magnet #1 or #2 centered on the chalk line and move it until the overage or underage has has been reduced by *only half*. Swing ship again, pass hard by the marker, and steer an exact compass north course as before. Drop the marker. Duplicate the entire procedure, running by eye back to the first marker, again reducing the error by *only half*. Repeat the job until the return-run compass reading is as close to 180 degrees as you can get it.

The east-west correction is carried out in an identical manner except that, this time, steering is exactly 90 degrees and the return by eye should read 270 degrees. Compensation is achieved by placing either #3 or #4 magnets centered on the 90 degree chalk line and moving it to cut the error in half. It is even immaterial whether the east-west or the north-south runs be made first. A careful execution of the foregoing on a wooden, fiberglass, or aluminum ship in most cases will clean the compass situation up neatly. On a steel-hulled craft it is possible that the quadrantal spheres, heeling magnet, and Flinders bar described in Chapter 9 may still be necessary to assure full reliability of the compass.

Compass compensation can be achieved quickly without any equipment if the boat location is such that good north-south and east-west magnetic directions can be established by means of observable charted objects. Note that the headings are *magnetic*, not true.

With the boat on a magnetic north heading (000°) by the charted objects, adjust the *N-S* compensators until the compass reading also is 000°. Then, with the boat on an east heading, again by the charted objects, adjust the *E-W* compensators until the compass reading is 090°. Now on a south heading by charted objects reduce the difference between 180° and the compass reading by only *one-half* with the *N-S* compensators. Next with the boat on a west heading by charted objects reduce the difference between 270° and the compass reading by only *one-half* with the *E-W* compensators.

After the foregoing has been done, repeat all steps but from now on reduce *all* errors by only one-half. This is continued until errors no longer can be lessened and must be noted in a deviation table.

It is theoretically possible to correct intercardinal deviation by carrying out the above-described program on the 45°–225° course and the 315°–135° course—but it is a tricky business. To accomplish this result both compensator magnets must be moved simultaneously for each correction; in non-expert hands, this surely would upset the good results already achieved. Discretion is the better part of compass adjustments. It is far safer and easier to live with the small amounts of deviation which remain after the cardinal corrections.

Sometimes a stymie is thrown into the adjustment program by some highly magnetic but unsuspected object in the compass vicinity. Such a miscreant can be ferreted out with a large soft-iron nail balanced on the finger. Bring the head near every suspect. The guilty one will topple the nail. If the offender cannot be dispensed with, perhaps it can be demagnetized in an auto repair shop with a "growler" or in a TV repair shop with a "degausser."

Charting Deviation

Rarely will a powerboat compass emerge from the compensation procedures entirely free of all deviations on all headings. In fact, were a compass to become so perfect, it would often be suspected of being overcompensated and deadened. The common practice is to find the residual deviation on various headings and then to tabulate these amounts for use in piloting.

The tabulation can take the form of a simple list showing the easterly or westerly deviations adjacent to the corresponding series of major compass headings. It can also be in the more sophisticated form of a Napier diagram which permits ready conversion from compass to magnetic and vice versa for any course. (The name is that of an English admiral who conceived this form of graphing more than 150 years ago; his method is explained later.)

A small bay surrounded by well-charted landmarks is an ideal place in which to measure the deviations remaining in a compensated compass. The only instrument required on board is a pelorus. If the compass is situated so that sights can be taken across it, then even the pelorus can be done without although the procedure will become a bit more complex. A chart of the bay obviously must also be at hand.

The deviation readings are made by swinging ship about a mooring whose location has been determined *accurately* on the *chart* by means of landmarks. If at all possible, the mooring should be on a range line through *two* landmarks.

Draw a line through the mooring and the landmark(s) and determine its *magnetic* bearing by transferring it to the inner, magnetic rose of the chart with a parallel rule. (Using the inner rose in preference to the outer eliminates the need for handling variation in the computations.) Set the pelorus lubber's line exactly parallel with the keel line of the boat and set the card's zero at this line; in this position, the instrument will read all sightings as relative. Figure 14-7 shows a hypothetical chart on which the landmark bears 330 degrees magnetic and which has been marked in the manner just described. If the mooring pennant is short and the distance to the landmark large, the errors from swinging will be inconsequential.

Swing ship until the compass reads exactly 000 (360), take a pelorus sight on the landmark, and enter the read-

Compass Heading	Pelorus Reading	Sum	− 360 (If Necessary)	Chart Bearing of Landmark	Positive or Negative Difference	Deviation for This Compass Heading
000	329	329	—	330	−1	1°E
015	317	332	—	"	+2	2°W
030	300	330	—	"	0	0°
045	290	335	—	"	+5	5°W
				"		
				"		
315	017	332	—	"	+2	2°W
330	358	688	328	"	−2	2°E
345	345	690	330	"	0	0°

Figure 14-8: The example above shows how readings are tabulated to arrive at the deviation on various headings.

ing in a table such as that given in Figure 14-8. Assume that this first pelorus reading is 329 degrees. The simple additions and subtractions leading to the last column reveal that, on this compass heading, the difference is 1 degree negative, equivalent to a deviation of 1 degree easterly. Several other hypothetical readings are also tabulated, further to illustrate the method.

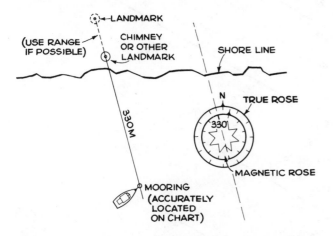

Figure 14-7: Residual deviations after compensation are found by selecting a well-charted landmark and swinging ship about an accurately charted mooring. The procedure is detailed in the text and the results of the example shown above are tabulated in Figure 14-8.

Readings and sightings are continued around the compass. The shorter the intervals between readings, the greater the final accuracy when the deviation values are put to use in actual piloting. Other methods of determining deviation are also available. For instance, the sun could be used either by shadow pin or by calculation from Bowditch tables. The swing-ship process described here is the easiest.

If you can determine exact high noon at your exact longitude, then the compass shadow pin becomes really handy. At that instant the sun's rays shine in a true North-South direction and the shadow bisects either 180° or 360° (plus or minus local variation), depending on latitude and season.

A watch set to accurate zone time is the basic tool for determining high noon but its reading is astronomically correct only for the center of the zone and therefore must be corrected. The correction is made on the basis of degrees of longitude east or west of the zone center. Each degree to the east is four minutes later, to the west four minutes earlier.

A few minutes either side of high noon introduces no appreciable error and this allows time for swinging ship while observing the shadow. Deviation determination on various headings can thus be made. Remember that the compass card should stand still while you swing and therefore any movement it makes is due to deviation.

NAPIER DIAGRAMS.

The Napier method of graphical representation owes its usefulness to the fact that a uniform scale of measurement can be applied in any direction. This is accomplished by abandoning the usual rectangular coordinates in favor of axes that cross each other at 60 degrees to form an infinite series of equilateral triangles. (An equilateral triangle is one whose three sides are equal in length.)

A blank Napier chart is reproduced in Figure 14-9; these are obtainable from many sources. In Figure 14-10 is an enlarged small section of a Napier chart bearing a portion of a curve of deviations for some certain boat. Point A is plotted from data stating that there is a deviation of 6°E on a compass heading of 260 degrees while point B shows a deviation of 6°E on a compass heading of 275 degrees. Since the dotted lines are used for compass heading, these points are established by counting six dots along the appropriately numbered courses. They are counted to the right because that is the established custom for easterly deviation. The entire curve was drawn through a whole series of points like A and B.

Suppose on this same ship you were steering a compass course of 270 degrees and wanted to know your magnetic course. You would put one point of your dividers at 270 degrees on the center scale (C) and stretch the other point to where the 270 degree dotted line intersected the curve (D). You would then swing the dividers back to the central scale with (C) as a pivot to (E). (The dividers are al-

CURVE OF DEVIATIONS

NAPIER DIAGRAM

UNITED STATES POWER SQUADRONS

Compass Heading — Dotted Lines

Magnetic Heading — Solid Lines

DEVIATION WEST

DEVIATION EAST

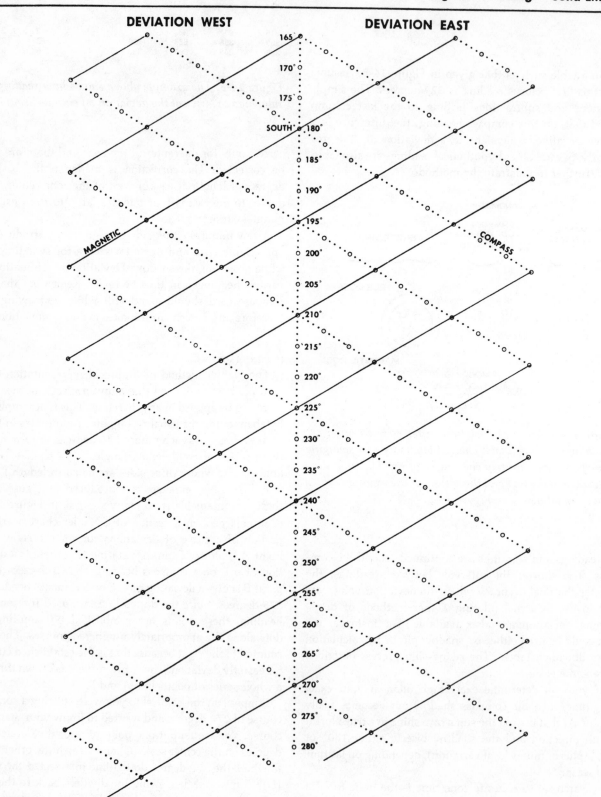

165°
170°
175°
SOUTH 180°
185°
190°
195°
200°
205°
210°
215°
220°
225°
230°
235°
240°
245°
250°
255°
260°
265°
270°
275°
280°

MAGNETIC

COMPASS

Figure 14-9: Blank Napier diagrams like this are available from many sources. Magnetic heading deviations are plotted along or parallel to solid lines, compass heading deviations along or parallel to dotted lines. (Memory aid: magnetic and solid both contain an i.) One side of each blank runs from 000° to 180° with overlap, and the other side from 180° to 360° with overlap. (Credit—U.S. Power Squadrons)

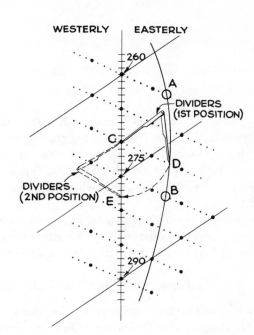

Figure 14-10: Compass courses are recorded along dotted lines, magnetic courses along solid lines in this Napier diagram. The dividers start from the central scale and swing back to it for solutions, always in a direction which completes an equilateral triangle. By swinging the dividers on this Napier diagram as shown above, the deviation on a compass course of 270° (C) is found to be 8° easterly (E). See text for complete explanation.

ways swung in a direction to complete an equilateral triangle.) The scale reading at (E) is 278 degrees, your magnetic course. The span of the dividers on the center scale, 8 degrees in this case, is the amount of deviation.

Suppose the case were reversed. You require a magnetic course of 278°. What is the compass course? Put one point of the dividers on 278 on the central scale. Keep the dividers parallel to the *solid* lines and place the second point on the curve. Swing dividers back to the central scale in a direction to complete an equilateral triangle (up) and the point will touch 270°, the required compass course.

It is not very practical to swing dividers on a Napier chart while doing a trick at the wheel. Consequently, a large number of solutions such as the one just illustrated would be made and tabulated for use at the helmsman's position. The utility of the Napier diagram lies in its ability to answer the deviation question for *any* point around the full 360 degrees simply by measuring magnetic courses along solid lines and compass courses along dotted lines. (Memory gimmick: Both *solid* and *magnetic* have an "i.")

Handling Singles and Twins

The foregoing maneuvering instructions have tacitly assumed that the boat has twin screws. This is a natural assumption because the overwhelming majority of inboard powerboats, small and large and many outboards, carry two engines. But single-screwers do exist in respectable numbers and a word should be said about them. Almost all sailboats with engines are single-screwers.

First of all, the turning on a dime, so valuable in close quarters, is beyond the ability of the craft equipped with only one propeller. This means that these craft must achieve their close turns with alternate, short fore and aft spurts, the while the rudder goes from hard-over to hard-over. Kicking the stern over with a very short fast engine burst while the rudder is at its extreme is of help here. (The stern moves sideward when kicked before the boat moves forward because of inertia.)

A single-screw vessel generally exhibits certain peculiarities that her skipper should bear in mind. A right-hand propeller often causes a boat to veer slightly to port when going ahead and this must be overcome with the necessary counter-helm. Steering may be a bit erratic, with a tendency to back to port when the propeller is reversing, until sufficient sternway is reached to enable the rudder to take solid control. These side effects are brought about by the various pressures generated by a revolving propeller, as explained fully in Chapter 3.

Narrow Channels

Skippers who must traverse narrow channels have found that unusual boat reactions occur in them, especially when they must hug one bank because of traffic. Under such conditions, the bow tends to be pushed away from the shore while the stern seems drawn to it.

The bow-away-stern-toward reaction is a natural result of the laws of hydraulics or, more directly, of the characteristics of fluids in motion. The action of the bow in cutting the water produces an increase in pressure; this forces the bow away. The water motion at the stern is more rapid and therefore the pressure is less, causing the stern to be sucked in.

The tendency to veer is corrected with counter-rudder. This is not an efficient method because it increases the hull resistance, but it is the only action which can be taken. Since narrow channels are (or should be) navigated at very moderate speed, the increase in hull resistance is not of great importance. The effects are greatest in channels with steep vertical sides and least in channels whose sides taper out into gradually shoaling flats. This is to be expected because of the manner in which hydraulic pressures act.

A powerboat in a shallow channel undergoes a noticeable sluggishness of rudder control. This ground reaction is a warning that there is not much water under the keel.

Handling Sea Conditions

Anyone who has been out in heavy weather can sympathize with the man who first wrote, "Oh God, Thy seas are so great and my boat is so small." When the wind blows and the waves kick up, even the most venturesome skipper gets a feeling of his own punyness.

The first thing to know about rough seas is to avoid them. This means to stay in the marina when the warning flags are up or when the marine weather broadcast predicts storm. Naturally, if you are already out when the trouble breaks, you have no choice but to match wits with nature —always remembering that it is *skill* and not bravado that will see you through. Nature is much more powerful than man's efforts ever can be.

Two aspects of a rough sea are of major importance, and a third ranks not far behind. The first two are wind and wave; the third is water depth. Depth is important because shallow water turns rolling waves into dangerous breakers. While wind and wave generally come from the same direction and can be fought as one, there are times when they do not and compromises must be made against each.

Depending upon course steered and storm direction, waves could be meeting the boat on the bow, on the quarters, on the beam, or at the stern. The point of impact can be changed by changing course. This may be good strategy; each evil also contains some alleviating good. The type of hull and her reaction to various seas are the determining factors, although it is almost a rule that beam seas are to be avoided.

It is possible to plow ahead, bow on. A generously flared bow is more adaptable to this maneuver than a straight side because the extra buoyancy will keep it on top and prevent diving. But the punishment to the hull could be severe and persons aboard will take a bad shellacking. The waves are hitting the boat at a velocity equaling the sum of boat speed and wave speed. The skipper, like a fighter's manager, must know when his charge has had enough.

The quartering course is usually the safest and yields the most comfort possible. Most powerboats take waves forward better than on the after quarters; this results from the standard wide-transom design. Unless luck permits an angular run to coincide with your intended course, you will have to tack from port to starboard repeatedly to make your landfall.

The sailboat skipper has less freedom of choice in heavy weather because his motive power, the wind, largely determines the directions in which he can steer or, to put it more precisely, the directions in which he *cannot* steer. Thus, when wind and wave are coming from the same direction, he cannot plow into them head-on even if he wants to; he *must* take them on an angle because his boat will not reach into the wind closer than 45 degrees.

Waves coming from the stern, "a following sea," are the most difficult for the unseasoned skipper and for many hulls as well. Most boats will "yaw" from side to side. (Generous deadwood aft reduces the tendency to yaw.) The dangers are seas coming over the transom and flooding the boat and waves grabbing the stern and flinging it broadside. This latter leaves the vessel in a trough and parallel to the oncoming wave, the most fearsome situation of all, a "broach." The broad transoms of stylish powerboats make them much more vulnerable than the old-fashioned double-enders, as discussed in Chapter 1. On the contrary, the classic sterns of sailboats afford good insurance against this mishap.

The trick in a following sea is to keep the boat ahead of the immediately astern wave. This is done by careful and constant manipulation of the throttles, assuming, of course, that boat speed and wave speed can be made equal. You stay off the forward slope of this wave so that you avoid pointing ominously at the bottom and you do not go fast enough to pitch over the crest of the wave ahead. Waves usually have a rhythm about them; studying this aids in assessing their danger and in formulating the strategy of defense.

To repeat what has been said in Chapter 11, skippers of sailboats running on a tailwind must be ever alert to avoid an undesired "jibe." A jibe occurs when the wind grabs the mainsail and slams it viciously from one side to the other. Aside from the dangers to personnel inherent in a wildly swinging boom, the sudden shock can tear sails and even wreck the ship because the power of the wind under such conditions is enormous.

Breaking out the life preservers and donning them is a wise move under any storm conditions. This may scare landlubbers, aboard as guests, into thinking their time has come, but it assures their floating in the unlikely event that they have to. Preservers also serve as good bumpers that prevent bodily injury when boats and people get tossed about.

A boat's silhouette (its sail area, as explained in Chapter 5), its pivot point, and the relative immersion at bow and stern all combine to determine how the craft will be affected by a strong wind. When the stern has the better "hold" on the water and the sail area is forward, she will tend to point with the wind; the popular term is weather-vaning. Keeping any other course will mean a struggle with engines and rudder.

Most rough sea conditions almost surely bring on a great deal of pitching, causing the propellers alternately to churn air. With their loads removed, the engines race into a dangerous speed range, which can disable them. The best preventive is a fast-acting automatic governor. Next best is instant skipper reaction on the throttles.

Sometimes the better part of valor in rough weather is to "heave to," wait and ride it out. Where the bottom and surrounding conditions are favorable, the hook can be dropped over with plenty of scope; often a "slow ahead on the engines" must be added to relieve the strain on the ground tackle and on the cleats and bitts. Alternatively, a sea anchor or drogue, pictured in Figure 14-11, can be put out, provided the lee shore does not present any dangers from drifting upon it. The sea "anchor" is not an anchor but a cone-shaped device for creating drag. ("Pouring oil upon the waters" to smooth them often works, and many sea anchors incorporate oil holders.)

Running in Fog

The only "good" thing about fog is that frequently it is accompanied by calm seas—a fortuitous condition because the lack of visibility is trouble enough. Human eyes are rendered impotent and the job of locating nearby ships must be taken over by human ears or by the electronic "eyes" of radar.

Since every skipper has ears but few have radar, the universal method of heralding a ship's presence is by making a noise. The type of this "noise" and the manner

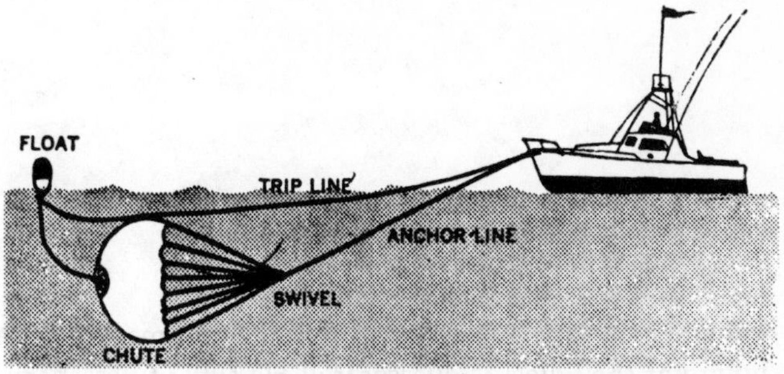

Figure 14-11: The sea anchor holds the bow into the wind. The trip line hauls the anchor in when it is no longer needed. Make certain there is plenty of good water to leeward.

in which it must be repeated are laid down by the rules of the road and are detailed in Chapter 16. Radar is used as an additional safeguard although, as accident records prove, it has often led to fatal overconfidence.

All rules emphasize the need for going slow in a fog and even for stopping dead in the water under certain circumstances. The great danger is that the unseen craft could be on a collision course. This is one condition that can be deduced easily from a radar screen: If the line through various successive positions of the target passes through the center of the scope, a collision will ensue; below center, the oncoming ship will pass astern; above center, ships *may* collide but most likely the oncoming ship will pass ahead.

"Conning" the Water

Surface indications can tell a great deal about the nature of the surrounding water. Many old-timers seem to be able to get more information just by looking around than an amateur can learn from a close study of the chart. This in no way negates the value of a chart; it simply affirms the cumulative benefits of experience.

Many of the telltales are elementary. Deep water is darker and smoother than shallow; thus, a change in color marks the shoal. Small areas of riffles are warnings that rocks or other obstructions are directly below the surface. A strong current running round a bend piles sand and silt up on the inside of the curve and reduces the depth there. Sand bars and mud flats often "grow" at the vees of river junctions. Heavy rains up-river can mean plenty of flotsam and jetsam intent on damaging your propeller. The way ships lie to their moorings and the inclinations of buoys and spars can show the set of the current and indicate its rate of drift. Smoke, pennants, flags are natural wind vanes. The high-water marks on piles and piers can show the relative height of tide.

Handling the Wheel

Whether on land or sea or in the air, one mark of the novice at the wheel is overcontrol. He substitutes sharp, jerky changes for the smooth, continuous, almost imperceptible control exercised by the expert.

One factor in the amount of response a boat makes to its rudder is the speed at which the craft is moving. When you think of it, this is equally true in an automobile: At turnpike speeds a very slight movement of the wheel takes you from lane to lane while a half-turn is needed for the same change when crawling in traffic.

Only experience instinctively tells the amount of rudder to apply to counteract any veering from course. The applications should be continuous and hardly noticeable, rather than a big correction for a large error. Unlike a car, a boat will overswing after the wheel has been returned to amidships. This tendency is anticipated and neutralized by applying counter-rudder; in the vernacular, this is "meeting her."

Steering a sailboat is more difficult than handling the wheel on a powerboat because the windjammer helmsman must keep an eye on the sails and a thought for the wind while he watches his course. He cannot devote his single-minded attention to the compass, the usual procedure when propellers do the pushing.

One trick that helps in steering a straight course is to watch the wake. If it runs straight out at right angles to the stern, you are right on the beam. If it angles to one side or the other, you are changing course and your compass should be showing this. Wiggles in the wake mean that you are overcontrolling and had better be a little less nervous at the wheel. One habit to acquire is to tune out your subconscious sense of what you are doing (often misleading) and rely on a good compass for the binding verdict.

Running Inlets

An inlet is a tricky stretch of water to navigate even under clear skies and in smooth water. It is the bottleneck through which water flows from one large body to another and, therefore, strong currents can be expected. The varying bottom prevents the flow from being laminar and smooth and causes the formation of complex waves and eddies. All this adds up to a trial for both ship and skipper.

It is a boon to some and a bane to others that inlets are distributed rather sparsely in comparison to the extent of navigable water. Thus, oldtime skippers may never have traversed an inlet in their entire boating experience while others must make it out and back on every cruise.

Going through an inlet is usually equivalent to running into a head sea or running with a following sea. Much that has already been said about these conditions will also apply here. Prudence should govern, as it should in any hazardous situation.

The danger of yawing and broaching in a following sea is even greater in an inlet than in open water because of the narrowness of the passage. Here again, synchronizing with the waves and adding a stern sea anchor for extreme cases are helpful moves. One serious thing about running an inlet: Once you start, you are committed; there is no stopping, no turning around and going back.

Each inlet is a case unto itself. The best founts of information about any particular inlet are the local fishermen who run it as a daily chore. The factors that shape it are the sizes of the bodies of water, the extent of the bars at the entrances, the channel depths and widths, and the character of the bottom. The inlet pictured in Figure 14-12 undoubtedly raises *no* desire to be there in any prudent skipper's mind.

ABCs of Cruising

Every new skipper with a new boat is like a kid with a Christmas bike: He can't wait to get going somewhere, anywhere with it. In truth, the instructions, explanations, and trial maneuvers covered in this book should make cruising safely possible, while the checklists should assure the seaworthiness of the vessel.

On board should be charts of the waters to be visited, the Coast Pilot for the area, and tables of tides and currents. (Coast Pilots for various areas are available from the Government Printing Office at low cost.) The more immediate needs of the ship herself already have been covered.

Even the rank novice skipper surely has heard of the "three Rs"—Red, Right, Returning. The implications of this little jingle and its application to the buoyage system on American waters is discussed at length in Chapter 17. For quick repetition, a summarization here would be "red buoys on your right when coming back and black buoys on your right when going out."

Figure 14-12: Inlets like these are obviously extremely bad medicine. The best advice is to stay out of them. If you are caught outside, heave to and wait for better conditions; if you are inside, stay there. (Credit—U.S. Coast Guard)

THINGS TO WATCH.

If the course be along tidal water, knowing the stand of the tide as well as the set (direction) and drift (speed) of the current can save time and fuel. Such information is taken from the tide and current tables.

It is possible that bridges must be passed under (or through). Whether it be "under" or "through" is determined by the relationship of clearance and mast height. Clearance shown on the chart is at mean high water; low-tide passage will add to this. Should opening of the bridge be required, the Coast Pilot spells out all the regulations governing this, including times of day and signals to be given.

Long tows can be encountered. These have entrapped hapless pleasure-boat skippers more than once. The error has been failure to see the partially submerged towline and running between tug and tow in the mistaken belief that they were separate. This is the marine version of the motorist who saw the lights of two approaching "motorcycles" and drove between them; at the hospital he learned that the two headlights were one car.

The wakes of passing craft can be a source of discom-

fort if they are not handled properly at the steering wheel. The most comfortable procedure for most boats is to meet the wake line at an angle, not head-on or parallel.

The roll from beam waves on the open water can become dangerous only if the heel approaches the critical angle. Chapter 1 explains the relationship of center of buoyancy, center of gravity, righting arm, and synchronous rolling. With this knowledge in the back of his head, the skipper should be awake to any possible danger and should be able to avoid it. Sailboats proceeding under power can cut down on rolling by raising enough sail to exert a steadying effect when wind direction permits.

Our coastal waters and rivers are so littered with flotsam and jetsam that the importance of constant vigilance cannot be overstated. No hull, save perhaps a naval craft built for fighting duty, can strike a heavy log at fifteen knots and come away from the collision unscathed—and no hull should be expected to be able to do this.

Two ships, passing each other close aboard, can create a zone of lowered pressure between them. This is the equivalent of a suction which acts to draw them toward each other. (The same effect often can be felt on the high-

way when a passenger car is passed by a speeding trailer truck.) When the two passing ships happen to be a large vessel and a small pleasure craft, the latter is in danger of being set over abruptly. The best preventive is to keep your distance. The same admonition applies which mothers give to youngsters: Don't fool around with the big boys!

LOCKING THROUGH.

The waters of coastal river mouths and bays are all at the one universal level of the connecting ocean. Inland lakes and rivers are at many levels and, for the purposes of navigation, they must be connected by locks. These locks are the "elevators" which raise or lower ships from one level to another.

Locks have sturdy, watertight gates at each end and large valves control the inflow and outflow of water. By admitting water from the higher level, ships in the lock are raised; by discharging it to the lower level, ships are lowered.

Entrance to locks is controlled by traffic lights, by VHF radio, and by loudspeakers. The details are found on local charts and in the many guides available from official and commercial sources. During the summer season the traffic jams in locks on popular routes can rival those on the highways. (More on locks and inland water in Chapter 17.)

AGROUND.

Even the most persnickety skipper may someday find himself aground. His immediate reaction can make the difference between small annoyance and large trouble.

It is pretty well agreed that the first and *immediate* action should be "full speed astern, all engines." The reverse should be of duration only long enough to stop all headway and (if you're lucky) pull the nose out of the clutches of the bottom. Whether or not reverse should again be applied depends upon the circumstances. If the initial *short* burst of reversed power does not free the ship, there is an even chance that additional reversing will only make matters worse by piling up silt, sand, and mud. Clogging engine-water intakes is an additional danger.

A sailboat, running under sail alone, lacks this ability to apply immediate reverse. Even with an auxiliary engine aboard, the time interval resulting from any attempt to start it negates whatever good it might have accom-

plished. However, with a light grounding, subsequent reverse engine may pull the sailboat off.

An incoming tide may solve your problem without any physical travail, simply by waiting. If the gods were mad enough at you to let you run aground at extreme high tide, then the only remaining solution is towing. This can be an actual tow from another boat to which you have passed a line or its equivalent with your own efforts, known as kedging.

Kedging is accomplished by taking an anchor and line out in the dinghy far enough to enable it to get a good purchase on the bottom. Backs are then bent to this line, with or without the aid of the reversed propellers. Shifting passengers and cargo to lighten the point of grounding is helpful.

A towline heavily loaded is under extreme stress and therefore can become a dangerous device. The line should be elastic to take up shocks but this very elasticity is what can make it lethal if it parts; the energy stored in it makes it snap back like a giant, overstretched rubber band. The danger of uprooting cleats and bitts is equally great.

Plotting the Course

A hypothetical cruise is plotted in Figure 14-13. The reasons for doing what is shown therein are explained carefully in Chapter 17, as are also the underlying theories. The purpose of this exercise is more closely to relate "book learnin'" with actual doing.

The cruise begins at (*A*) by following the channel and the marker buoys (black ones to right going out) to the point of departure (*B*), which is reached at a quarter past nine or 0915. Here the course is set to 300 degrees *magnetic* and the run is begun at a speed of 12 knots. The point (*B*) is fixed on the chart and is so labeled with time.

Note that the courses have all been laid down magnetic instead of true and consequently are taken from the inner rose. This simplifies the paperwork because it eliminates variation and leaves only deviation to be considered in setting a compass course. It is possible to take this liberty because the cruise is confined to an area with no changes in variation. Purists may object to this and insist that all plotting must be done with true bearings. The difference would simply be the use of the *outer* rose and the addition or subtraction of variation.

At 1025, on the basis of the originally prepared chart

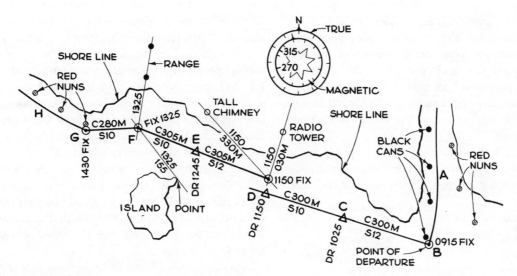

Figure 14-13: "Book learnin' " is reduced to actual practice on this hypothetical cruise. Note that time is always by the 24-hour clock. Details are in Chapter 17.

showing the equivalent distance for a certain speed and time, the navigator believes the boat to be at (C). He marks this as a dead reckoning with a little triangle to distinguish it from a fix and continues on the same course, although he has dropped his speed to 10 knots.

At 1150 he again marks his position to be at (D) but now he has an opportunity to make an actual fix by pelorus sighting on the chimney and by taking an RDF on the radio beacon. These sight lines are laid down and labeled; where they cross is circled as the fix. There is the usual slight discrepancy between the DR and the fix, but not enough to worry about; it is caused in part by the omission of wind and current when making the dead reckonings.

A new track is now taken up from the fix with a course of 305 degrees magnetic and a speed of 12 knots. At 1245 the position along the track is believed to be at (E); this is marked as a DR with a triangle and the course continued at a reduced speed of 10 knots. At (F) there is a range plus an opportunity to get a "kissing" sight on the island point with the pelorus and the 1325 fix is developed. The course is now 280 degrees magnetic to the buoy at (G), which establishes the 1430 fix. The finish of the cruise is now "downhill" at (H) with the channel buoys as guides (red right returning).

ETAs

By measuring the distances on the chart and computing the running times required at the different running speeds, the navigator easily arrives at the length of time needed for the cruise. Adding this elapsed time to the time of his departure would give him his Estimated Time of Arrival (ETA).

Skippers are wise to file their ETAs just as airplane pilots file their flight plans. The "filing" can be done with an official agency, with the marina, with the family, or even with friends at the destination. This is a valuable safety measure because it enables a search to be instituted without delay for boats too long overdue. (Remember to cancel the ETA promptly when it no longer is valid.)

Radiotelephone Usage

Shipboard radiotelephones are intended primarily as a safety feature. This becomes hard to believe when the loudspeaker disgorges the aimless chatter that clutters the bands. There are strict FCC rules to govern radio usage but these, too, are more often ignored than observed.

The standard procedure for making radiotelephone calls that are *not* distress is as follows: Listen on 2182 Kcs. (or on 156.8 Mcs. if using VHF) for a quiet period to avoid garbling a transmission already in progress. Then state clearly three times the name and call letters of the boat you wish to contact. Give an intermediate "this is" before following with your own boat name and call letters three times. Follow this sequence *exactly*, and repeat it two or three times for clarity, but restrict this entire transmission to one-half minute.

The call letters in these transmissions are spoken in the international phonetic code, as indicated in the accompanying table of Figure 14-14. Suppose, for instance,

A	alpha	N	november
B	bravo	O	oscar
C	charlie	P	papa
D	delta	Q	quebec
E	echo	R	romeo
F	foxtrot	S	sierra
G	golf	T	tango
H	hotel	U	uniform
I	india	V	victor
J	juliette	W	whiskey
K	kilo	X	x-ray
L	lima	Y	yankee
M	mike	Z	zulu

Figure 14-14: The letters of the alphabet are spoken by use of the code words listed above.

that you are calling the yacht *Mimi*, whose call letters are WM-1234, from your boat, the *Suzy*, with an assigned call of WD-4321. Your call would sound like this if you made it according to Hoyle (and the FCC): "*Mimi*, whiskey mike 1234, *Mimi*, whiskey mike 1234, *Mimi*, whiskey mike 1234, this is *Suzy*, whiskey delta 4321, *Suzy*, whiskey delta 4321, *Suzy*, whiskey delta 4321, over."

Listen on 2182 Kcs. (or on 156.8 Mcs. if using VHF). If the called station has heard you, it will so acknowledge on this frequency. Agree quickly on a working frequency and switch to it for your conversation. If you do not get a reply, wait a few minutes to give others a chance at the channel and then repeat the sequence. At the end of a conversation on a successful contact, repeat your assigned call and add the word "out!"—just the one word, "out," to indicate to others that you are through with the channel. *Don't* use any of the involved fancy terminating locutions so beloved by many skippers.

Under FCC rules, powerboats no longer are licensed to have 2000–3000 Kcs. radiotelephones unless they coincidentally are equipped with the VHF telephone. The rules now also prescribe that all contacts less than about 20 miles away must be made with the VHF, which means calling on 156.8 Mcs. Nearby calls made on 2182

Kcs. while these new rules are in effect will be certain to elicit a citation from the FCC. (See Chapter 25.)

It is quite natural to wonder, sometimes, whether the words spoken into the microphone actually are undergoing their electronic transformations and are being sent flying through space to far places. Many skippers have been in the habit of calling the Coast Guard for a radio check. Understandably, the CG did not like to be bothered with this and the new rules forbid the practice. All of these transmitters are equipped either with a light or a meter which flickers in response to modulation. (See Chapter 8.) Those flickers should be your reassurance of effectiveness—although, admittedly, some flicker would still be there even after the antenna were carried away in a storm.

As explained in Chapter 8, the transmitter is on the air only while the microphone button is depressed. The routine, therefore, is to press the button just prior to speaking and hold it down until that segment of talk is completed. The word "over" is spoken just before releasing the button and is the signal for the other party to go on the air and reply. At the completion of the conversation the call letters are repeated, plus the word "out." This button-and-over gimmick takes a bit of getting used to by people habituated to the home telephone. (Holding the button down when not talking obstructs the channel.)

A Mayday emergency message takes precedence over *everything* and should immediately sweep off the air all transmitters except those directly involved. (See Chapter 19.) This would seem to be dictated not only by law and common sense but by courtesy as well. Nevertheless, a fishing boat skipper, who tried to call the Coast Guard to report a capsizing in which several persons subsequently died, reported recently that he was jammed off the air by a powerboat's yak-yak. The legal requirements surrounding radiotelephones, such as licenses, logs, etc., are spelled out in Chapter 25.

Ship-to-Land Telephones

It is now possible for radiotelephones on small boats to be connected with any telephone in the United States or, for that matter, in the world. This has been brought about through a great number of transmitter-receiver stations on the coasts, on the Great Lakes, and on the Mississippi River maintained by the public telephone companies. The extent of these can be seen on the map of Figure 14-15,

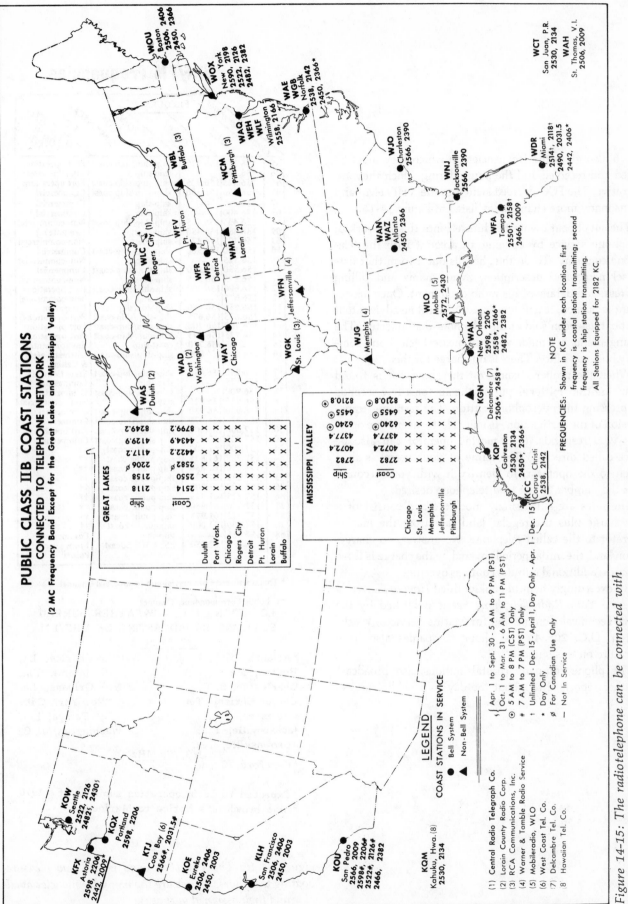

PUBLIC CLASS IIB COAST STATIONS
CONNECTED TO TELEPHONE NETWORK
(2 MC Frequency Band Except for the Great Lakes and Mississippi Valley)

WOU Boston 2506, 2406, 2450, 2366

WOX New York 2590, 2198, 2522, 2126, 2482, 2382

WAQ WEH WLF Wilmington 2558, 2166

WAE WGB Norfolk 2538, 2142, 2450, 2366*

WBL Buffalo (3)

WCM Pittsburgh (3)

WJO Charleston 2566, 2390

WAN WAZ Atlanta 2450, 2366

WNJ Jacksonville 2566, 2390

WDR Miami 2514†, 2118†, 2490, 2031.5, 2442, 2406*

WFA Tampa 25501, 2158†, 2466, 2009

WCT San Juan, P.R. 2530, 2134

WAH St. Thomas, V.I. 2506, 2009

WFV Pt. Huron

WLC Rogers City (1)

WFR WFS Detroit

WMI Lorain (2)

WFN Jeffersonville (4)

WAD Port (2) Washington

WAY Chicago

WGK St. Louis (3)

WJG Memphis (4)

WLO Mobile (5) 2572, 2430

WAK New Orleans 2598, 2206, 2558*, 2166*, 2482, 2382

WAS Duluth (2)

KGN Delcambre (7) 2506*, 2458*

KQP Galveston 2530, 2134, 2450*, 2366*

KCC Corpus Christi 2538, 2142

GREAT LAKES

	Ship	2118	2158	2206 Ø	2582 Ø	4117.2	4129.9	8249.2
Coast		2514	2550	2206 Ø	2582 Ø	4422.2	4434.9	8799.2
Duluth		×	×		×			×
Port Wash.		×	×		×			×
Chicago		×	×		×	×	×	×
Rogers City		×	×		×	×	×	×
Detroit		×	×		×	×	×	×
Pt. Huron		×	×		×			×
Lorain		×	×		×	×	×	×
Buffalo		×	×		×	×	×	×

MISSISSIPPI VALLEY

	Ship	2782	4072.4	4377.4	6240	6455	8210.8
Coast		2182	4072.4	4377.4	6240	6455	8210.8
Chicago		×	×	×	×	×	×
St. Louis		×	×	×	×	×	×
Memphis		×	×	×	×	×	×
Jeffersonville		×	×	×	×	×	×
Pittsburgh		×	×	×	×	×	×

NOTE

FREQUENCIES: Shown in KC under each location - first frequency is coastal station transmitting; second frequency is ship station transmitting.

All Stations Equipped for 2182 KC.

KOW Seattle 2522, 2126, 2482†, 2430₅

KQX Portland 2598, 2206

KFX Astoria 2598, 2206*, 2442, 2009*

KTJ Coos Bay (6) 2566#, 2031.5#

KOE Eureka 2506, 2406, 2450, 2003

KLH San Francisco 2506, 2406, 2450, 2003

KOU San Pedro 2566, 2009, 2598#, 2206#, 2522#, 2126#, 2466, 2382

KQM Kahuku, Hwa.(8) 2530, 2134

LEGEND

COAST STATIONS IN SERVICE

● Bell System

▲ Non-Bell System

(1) Central Radio Telegraph Co.
(2) Lorain County Radio Corp.
(3) RCA Communications, Inc.
(4) Warner & Tamble Radio Service
(5) Mobileradio, WLO
(6) West Coast Tel. Co.
(7) Delcambre Tel. Co.
(8) Hawaiian Tel. Co.

†{ Apr. 1 to Sept. 30 - 5 AM to 9 PM (PST)
   Oct. 1 to Mar. 31 - 6 AM to 11 PM (PST)
⊙ 5 AM to 8 PM (CST) Only
7 AM to 7 PM (PST) Only
† Unlimited - Dec. 15 - April 1, Day Only - Apr. 1 - Dec. 15
* Day Only
Ø For Canadian Use Only
− Not In Service

Figure 14-15: The radiotelephone can be connected with almost any phone in the world through these land stations maintained by the telephone companies.

which also gives the frequencies on which they must be called and received and the hours during which they are operative. The FCC-decreed switch to the VHF/FM band opens many more channels, as listed in Figure 14-16.

The small boat owner ties himself into this network of telephone service by opening an account with the telephone company. To do this, he fills out a form that lists vessel name and description, owner name and billing address, and details of his radio equipment. Once his account is opened, it will remain active until he advises that the boat has been sold or the telephone disconnected. The arrangements are made with the nearest telephone company business office. There is no charge for this.

When the proper channel on the above list is found clear, the transmitter is put on the air for a few seconds by pressing the microphone button. The resulting transmission of the carrier alone usually alerts the marine operator who responds. (The marine operator can also be voice-called directly.) The name of your vessel is then given to the operator, to identify it with your account, plus the number of the land telephone desired.

The rates are surprisingly moderate and consist of a flat charge plus the regular land rate from the marine operator to the called telephone. No answer, no charge. As on land, the initial period covered by the charge is three minutes; additional minutes count as overtime.

An exceedingly helpful booklet titled *How to Correctly Operate Your RadioTelephone Set* is published by the RadioTechnical Commission for Marine Services, Washington, D.C. 20554. The phone companies also have literature on this subject.

The phone company coastal stations also broadcast weather reports throughout the day as a public service.

VHF/FM Frequencies

Channel Designator	FREQUENCY		POINTS OF COMMUNICATIONS	AUTHORIZED COMMUNICATIONS
	SHIP	COAST		
65	156.275	156.275	ship-ship/ship-coast	Port operations
06	156.300		ship-ship	Intership safety
66	156.325	156.325	ship-ship/ship-coast	Port operations
07	156.350	156.350	ship-ship/ship-coast	Commercial
67	156.375	------	ship-ship	Commercial
08	156.400	------	ship-ship	Commercial
68	156.425	156.425	ship-ship/ship-coast	Non-commercial
09	156.450	156.450	ship-coast	(see note) †
69	156.475	156.475	ship-coast	Non-commercial
10	156.500	156.500	ship-ship/ship-coast	Commercial
70	156.525	------	ship-ship	Non-commercial
11	156.550	156.550	ship-ship/ship-coast	Commercial
71	156.575	156.575	ship-coast	Non-commercial
12	156.600	156.600	ship-ship/ship-coast	Port operations
72	156.625		ship-ship	Non-commercial
13	156.650	156.650	ship-ship/ship-coast	Navigation
73	156.675	156.675	ship-ship/ship-coast	Port operations
14	156.700	156.700	ship-ship/ship-coast	Port operations
74	156.725	156.725	ship-ship/ship-coast	Port operations
15	------	156.750	coast-ship	Environmental
16	156.800	156.800	ship-ship/ship-coast	Distress, Safety & Calling
17	156.850	156.850	ship-ship/ship-coast	State Control
77	156.875	------	ship-ship	Commercial
18	156.900	------	ship-ship/ship-coast	Commercial
78	156.925	156.925	ship-coast	Non-commercial
19	156.950	156.950	ship-ship/ship-coast	Commercial
79	156.975	156.975	ship-ship/ship-coast	Commercial
20	157.000	161.000	ship-ship/ship-coast	Port operations
80	157.025	157.025	ship-ship/ship-coast	Commercial
24	157.200	161.800	ship-public coast	††
84	157.225	161.825	ship-public coast	††
25	157.250	161.850	ship-public coast	††
85	157.275	161.875	ship-public coast	††
26	157.300	161.900	ship-public coast	††
86	157.325	161.925	ship-public coast	††
27	157.350	161.950	ship-public coast	††
87	157.375	161.975	ship-public coast	††
28	157.400	162.000	ship-public coast	††
88	157.425		ship-ship	Commercial
-	------	162.550	ESSA WX Bdcast	From selected Points

† This is a shared Commercial-non-commercial Channel

†† Public Correspondence Channel

LOCATION OF U.S. WEATHER BUREAU STATIONS BROADCASTING ON VHF/FM

162.55 MHz

*Atlantic City, N. J.	Lake Charles, La.
Boston, Mass.	Miami, Fla.
Charleston, S. C.	New Orleans, La.
Corpus Christi, Tex.	*New York City
Galveston, Tex.	Tampa, Fla.
Jacksonville, Fla.	Washington, D.C.
+Brownsville, Tex.	

163.275 MHz

*Hartford, Conn.

+Expected to be in operation summer of 1970
*Also broadcasts Notice to Mariners.

Figure 14-16: The VHF/FM band is the new pleasure-boating workhorse. These are the many frequencies available and their assigned purposes.

15 *Anchoring, Mooring and Ropes*

I N the Navy it is always a line. Among boatmen it is sometimes a line and sometimes a rope. Whatever it be called, there are occasions when it can become the most important link in the safety of life and ship.

Rope or some primitive equivalent has been identified with ships since earliest times. Wherever there were boats, there was need for securing them against the onslaughts of wind and current. In all this time the uses to which seagoing rope has been put have not changed, but the rope material has. The natural plant fibers, which once were the only raw material available to the rope maker, are rapidly being displaced by man-made synthetics that are stronger and longer-lived although not yet cheaper.

Rope is the intermediate link between the boat and the anchor or mooring or pier. This requires that it have special properties such as elasticity and the ability to absorb shock. Rope is exposed to the elements in the performance of its duty and must be able to resist them for reasonable periods of time. Rope is expendable and therefore its cost must be moderate. No known material can meet all these requirements fully, but the synthetics seem better able to do so than the naturals.

Rope Materials

Cordage can be made from most natural fibers. Hemp, cotton, sisal, linen, and manila are all commercially important, and it is likely that every other fibrous plant has also been made into cord by aboriginal civilizations. Of all these, manila is the only one that holds importance for the boatman, albeit a diminishing importance.

Manila, quite aptly, derives its name from the city of Manila in the Philippine Islands, which is the center of its growth area and the major shipping point. The manila plant is a perennial herb and a distant relative of the banana. The secret of its adaptability to cordage lies in its long, strong leaves, which may extend to twenty feet.

Modern machine methods have influenced the manufacturing process only slightly; the basic procedure is little different from that of the original native users. The long leaves are cut into strips. Drawing these strips over knife edges removes all clinging extraneous matter and leaves only the long, tough, course fibers which eventually become rope. Water has little effect on these fibers, hence their desirability for marine uses.

Synthetics are the products of the chemist's ability to juggle atoms into combinations unthought of by nature. These unusual atomic combinations result in unusual physical properties that easily excel nature's nearest competitors. Such inanimate creations are immune to the ills of living things; rot, fungus and bacterial growth cannot attack them. Fibers are produced that seem able to withstand everything except man's abuse.

You might say that chemists learned the art of making synthetic fibers by imitating the common spider. The spider exudes through its spinnerets a liquid that coagulates on striking the air and becomes the thread used in web making. Size for size, this is the strongest natural fiber known. The synthetic fibers for marine lines are also made by extrusion through spinnerets and they, too, excel in comparative strength.

Rayon was the first of the synthetic fibers; it was extruded from a solution of cellulose. Today, rayon is no longer found to any extent on boats and its interest for the pleasure boatman is purely historic.

Nylon has become the most popular synthetic material for boat lines and ropes. Nylon has greater comparative strength than manila, it has greater stretchability, and it has greater longevity. Only in lower cost does manila have the advantage—although even here the answer is unclear if increased length of service and smaller size requirement are considered together.

Nylon is a *poly*mer, which means that it is a molecular hookup of many *mono*mers, in this case groups known to the chemist as carboxyls and aminos. The importance to the boatman of this crossbreeding lies in the properties that evolve, primarily the imperviousness to water and many stronger solvents and the ability to recover from deformation, all in addition to great tensile strength.

Dacron is also a product of the art of polymerization. In this case the combining monomers are dialcohols and diacids and the final combination is technically a polyester.

Dacron has most of the desirable properties of nylon but differs sharply in one important characteristic: It does not stretch to any appreciable extent. Because of this, dacron cannot absorb shocks through elasticity as nylon can. This restricts it from some uses and recommends it for others.

POLYOLEFINS.

Olefin in chemical language means *oil forming* but the

significance of this term is lost by the time the end-product fiber is reached. The olefins that wind up in cordage after polymerization are ethylene and propylene; these are polymerized to polyethylene and polypropylene.

Polyethylene is an extruded fiber like nylon and dacron and is similar in appearance, but it has much less strength. Its specific gravity is less than unity and therefore this material will float.

Polypropylene differs chemically from polyethylene in that it contains an additional carbon-hydrogen group. It differs little in physical properties and appearance and the two are often used interchangeably and together. It too is a low-specific-gravity, floating material.

WIRE ROPE.

Metals in the form of wires are also used in "cordage" to make wire rope. Steel and phosphor-bronze are the metals for this purpose, the former being much the more common.

Wire rope is made from uncoated steel, from galvanized steel, and from stainless steel. Stainless is the best grade and the most expensive. Galvanized is the average grade found on shipboard, while the uncoated is not suited for marine duty.

Phosphor-bronze is of course nonmagnetic and is used where this characteristic is important. (Stainless is also nonmagnetic in certain alloys but can become magnetic from stresses and shocks.) The strength of phosphor-bronze, size for size, is less than that of steel.

Rope Construction

The initial stages in the manufacture of rope from either natural or synthetic fibers differ because the physical shapes of the raw materials differ. The natural fibers are of necessity short and uneven in length; the synthetic fibers are uniform and of any length desired. (The fisherman's light monofilament line, for instance, is a single extruded thread that can be thousands of feet long.) In both cases the purpose of the first stage is to twist the fibers into a yarn with strict control over the amount of twisting.

The yarns are formed into strands. This also includes a twisting process but this time the twist is in the reverse direction to that of the yarn. (Like plywood, adjacent layers are always crossed.)

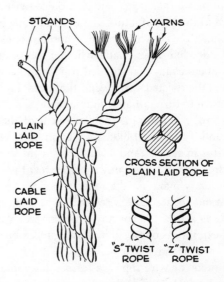

Figure 15-1: The anatomy (and the nomenclature) of a rope.

In rope-maker's parlance, the strands are *laid* into a rope, again with a counter twist. A rope can be *plain laid*, which means that it consists of three strands usually, although more are used occasionally. A rope can also be *cable laid*, in which case three of the plain-laid ropes have been twisted together into heavier stuff. The labeled sketch in Figure 15-1 shows the progressive growth of a rope.

The twist in the rope (or yarn or strand) is identified as *S* or *Z* by its direction. Holding the rope (or yarn or strand) vertically in front of you will cause the angle of twist to coincide with the central bar of either the letter *S* or the letter *Z*. This identification removes all ambiguity when describing cordage. The *Z* is also known as right-hand lay and the *S* as left-hand lay.

The strength and flexibility of the synthetic yarns allow the rope makers yet another manufacturing process: *braiding* the yarns instead of twisting them. The resulting braided rope has many desirable features, not the least of which is what the textile people call *hand*, which means pleasant to the touch.

Braided rope comes in single or double construction. The double actually is one braid inside of another. The advantage, in addition to added strength, is that different materials can be used in the two braids, thus achieving a balance of tensile, elasticity, and size. Since twisting is not employed in the manufacture, the finished rope itself has no tendency to twist when stored. Another bonus is flexibility; braided line stays pliable whether wet or dry.

The makers claim that braided rope is much easier to splice than the twisted variety and that even a novice can quickly learn to turn out a creditable job.

In wire rope, the wire is the equivalent of the yarn in cordage and it is twisted likewise into strands. The number of wires in each strand is specified in the description of the wire rope and this can vary from few to many. Six strands usually make up the rope. A 6-strand wire rope whose strands contain 19 wires each would therefore be cataloged as a 6 × 19. For any given size of wire rope, greater flexibility is obtained by having more but thinner wires in each strand.

The strands of wire rope are formed around a core of manila or hemp rope. This has a cushioning effect, as the strands tend to squeeze together when the rope is under heavy load. This central core is also the carrier of lubricant which increases flexibility and protects the steel. Fiber ropes are also impregnated during manufacture with lubricants and preservatives.

The commercial classifications consider the wire ropes in groups of equal strength and thus allow a certain latitude in makeup. The 6 × 19 classification, for instance, includes all 6-strand ropes with from 16 to 26 wires in each strand. Furthermore, the center core of a strand may be a wire; in this case, the 6 × 19 so constructed would in actuality be a 6 × 25.

Commercial Rope Sizes

To be simon-pure about it, custom decrees that fiber lines and ropes should be specified by their *circumference* and not by their diameter. This not only is misleading but is also hard to measure. As a consequence, a universal tendency has developed among boatmen and dealers to describe both wire and fiber rope by *diameter*.

Since the cross section of wire rope somewhat resembles a hexagon, mistakes could be made in measuring the diameter. Figure 15-2 shows the correct method and also illustrates the practice to avoid.

The diameter measurements found in tables are for new rope under no load. Loading has a tendency to reduce the

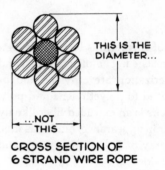

Figure 15-2: The correct way to measure the diameter of wire rope.

diameter, more so in some materials than in others. Furthermore, the sizes are nominal and may vary slightly one way or the other about the norm.

Rope Strength

In olden days, when manila was the only cordage available to the seaman, there was continuous relationship between the job to be done and the correct diameter rope to do it. Today, the extreme strength of synthetics has complicated the picture—and for the small boatman has improved it. The required ability to pull a given load can be had with much less heft and weight. For instance, the tensile strength of a 5/16-inch nylon line more than equals that of 1/2-inch manila; furthermore, a pound of the former yields 40 feet while only 13 feet can be had in a pound of the latter.

While this theoretical comparison is perfectly true, unfortunately actual use aboard ship introduces other factors of a practical nature. Chief among these is the "feel" of a line while it is being handled for a particular purpose; both too small and too large a diameter could cause discomfort in manipulation. The switch from one material to another is therefore generally a compromise that does not take full advantage of the relative tensile strengths. (One manufacturer recommends 3/4-inch nylon as interchangeable with 13/16-inch manila and 1-inch nylon with 1-1/4-inch manila. Admittedly, this is conservative.)

The tabulation in Figure 15-3 tells the rope story in comparative figures. The approximate length of line (in feet) per pound of weight is also indicated in this table so that the weight brought aboard can be calculated.

A glance at the numbers shows that nylon is almost three times as strong as manila of the same diameter. Dacron is only slightly less strong for its size. Polyethylene has the advantage over manila by about 1-1/2 times.

Wire rope, as could be expected, is far ahead in comparative tensile strength. The figures given in the tabulation are for a medium-grade steel not as good as stainless but better than the plain iron. Since wire rope is seldom found on powerboats, except perhaps the very largest, the comparison is of greater academic than practical interest to the average skipper. For many sailboatmen, however, wire rope is an ubiquitous shipmate.

Chain

Chain is generally thought of in connection with big ships, but it has a place in the anchoring equipment of even a modest pleasure craft, as later discussion will show. Chain is manufactured in cast and forged steel and with plain and stud-reinforced links.

Connecting links for joining lengths of chain are available with various ingenious closure means; one type is easily peened shut with a hammer, another makes use of an integral nut that tightly closes the opening. Chain is also supplied with all links fully rubber-coated as insurance against marring decks. Links and closures are shown in Figure 15-4.

A very rough comparison shows that chain weighs about forty times as much as rope. This weight can become an important factor in the trim of a small boat that carries its ground tackle in a forepeak chain locker. As a consequence, chain makes up only a small fraction of anchor rode footage aboard.

Light chain, especially if it is only a short section at the anchor end, can be handled manually. Heavier chain that constitutes the entire anchor rode requires deck equipment

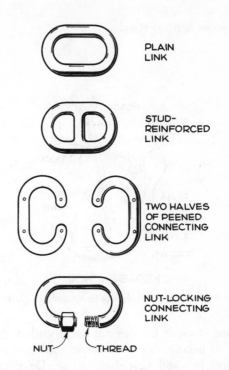

Figure 15-4: Standard chain links and their connecting links.

in the form of windlasses or capstans. These have wildcats of correct size to grip the chain and eliminate the need for snagging. The hoisting machinery is located directly over the chain locker so that the hauled rode can be passed through conveniently.

Anchors

Insuring the tensile strength of lines and chains in the ground tackle is all very well, but the final word in secure attachment to the ground is spoken by the anchor itself. It determines how much pull can be exerted by the boat without dragging.

Today's market offers pleasure skippers several styles of anchor and each has its good points and its bad. The daddy of them all is the common kedge, which is pictured in Figure 15-5 together with the proper nomenclature of its parts. It hasn't changed essentially in shape since the time of Christ; its only real improvement is that the stock has been made foldable.

									6×19		BBB gal.	
Diameter	Manila	ft/#	Nylon	ft/#	Dacron	ft/#	Poly	ft/#	Wire	ft/#	Chain	ft/#
3/16	450	68	1050	100	900	77	750	137				
1/4	600	51	1800	66	1725	47	1050	80	4300	1	2700	1.3
5/16	1000	35	2750	40	2600	30	1575	53	6700	.62	3700	.87
3/8	1350	25	4000	28	3650	21	2150	34	9600	.43	4600	.59
7/16	1750	19	5500	20	4850	15	3000	25	13000	.32	6200	.43
1/2	2650	13	7300	15	6200	12	3900	20	17000	.25	8200	.34
9/16	3450	10	9075	11	7700	9	4700	16	21000	.19	10200	.28
5/8	4400	7	10900	9	9300	7	6000	12	26000	.16	12500	.23
11/16			13300		11000							
3/4	5400	6	15600	6	13000	5	8000	9	37000	.11	17700	.16
13/16	6500		17700		15200							
7/8	7700	4	21400	5	17500	4	10500	6	50000	.08	24000	.12
1	9000	3	27000	3	22300	3	14000	5	66000	.06	31000	.95

Comparative Strengths

Figure 15-3: The comparative breaking strengths of various ropes and chains are given above.

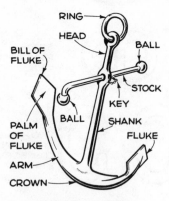

RING

HEAD

BALL

BILL OF
FLUKE

STOCK

KEY

BALL

SHANK

PALM
OF
FLUKE

FLUKE

ARM

CROWN

KEDGE ANCHOR

Figure 15-5: The kedge anchor is the daddy of them all.

The fixed stock of the original kedge anchor made it unwieldy to handle aboard and even with the present folding stock it is still a bit of a nuisance. Developments therefore were centered on eliminating the stock (or placing it out of the way down at the crown) in addition to improving the anchor's holding power. Some of these newer forms are the Navy stockless, the Northill, the Danforth, the plow, the Benson, the mushroom, and the grapnel. Some are pictured in Figure 15-6.

The Navy stockless is a favorite with big ships because it can be hauled right up into the hawse pipe; smaller versions are seen on pleasure boats. The Northill takes the stock from the head and moves it down to the crown. The Danforth also has its stock at the crown but turns it to be in line with the "arms"; in addition, it has sharp, welded steel flukes of large area for digging in. The Benson is similar but has a U-shaped shank which allows the ring to pull from either end; it is claimed this makes it unfoulable. All of these except the Northill have swiveled shanks.

The plow anchor is named for its shape; the makers claim that the harder the pull, the deeper it plows into the bottom yet always breaks out easily. The large mushroom anchor is the type chosen for permanent moorings although a small, light version is often used as a "lunch hook" on outboards. The grapnel is an all-purpose hook more often used for recovering sunken objects than anchoring boats. When used as an anchor the grapnel is almost guaranteed to foul and is practically unrecoverable without a separate trip line to the crown that permits it to be hauled up, business-end first from rocky bottom—and even then it may be a toss-up.

Anchor Holding Power

In thinking about anchoring, the newcomer often erroneously equates weight with holding power. This error has been brought home to everyone who has ever tried to make a permanent mooring with an old engine block.

Except under the luckiest conditions, the holding power of this couple hundred pounds of old iron is easily excelled by a good mushroom weighing less than half as much.

The most important thing to learn about an anchor is that its holding power is determined largely by the angle from which the pull on it is applied. When this pull is almost parallel to the ground, the holding power is maximum; when this pull is from directly above, the holding power is just about zero. This relationship is proportional to the cosine of the angle of pull and is illustrated by the diagram in Figure 15-7. (In anchor talk, the line or rope or chain to the anchor is the "rode" and its length is the "scope.")

At (a) the scope is approximately equal to the depth of the water; as a consequence, the rode is practically vertical and the anchor cannot hold. As a matter of fact, this is the position the boat would assume in order to weigh (recover) anchor when leaving the mooring.

At (b) the scope is assumed to be about seven times the depth. (The sketch is not drawn to scale.) The angle of pull is now perhaps 10 or 15 degrees off the bottom and the flukes can translate the pull of the boat into good digging action. The rode in this case is one of the fiber lines whose weight in the water is relatively light.

At (c) the scope is practically unchanged because the rode is about the same length, but the effectiveness of the anchor has been increased greatly. The reason is the lowered angle of pull, now almost parallel to the ground. This has been achieved by the length of heavy chain which has been inserted between the line and the anchor. This chain lying on the bottom not only improves holding power but also acts as a shock absorber. Any sudden increased pull by the boat, due to wind or current or whatever, will dissipate itself in the work of lifting the chain; line, chocks, and bitts, even the anchor, will receive protection. The elasticity of the line will also help.

The matter of scope rests largely on the experience of each skipper with his own individual boat and ground tackle, although seven times water depth is a pretty widely accepted figure. Storm conditions easily could double this length—and that's where the experience comes in and the rule goes out. The criterion is whether or not the anchor drags under load. Dragging calls for a longer scope or a heavier anchor or sometimes both. On tidal waters the high-water depth should be the one used in calculations.

A change in wind and current will cause the boat to

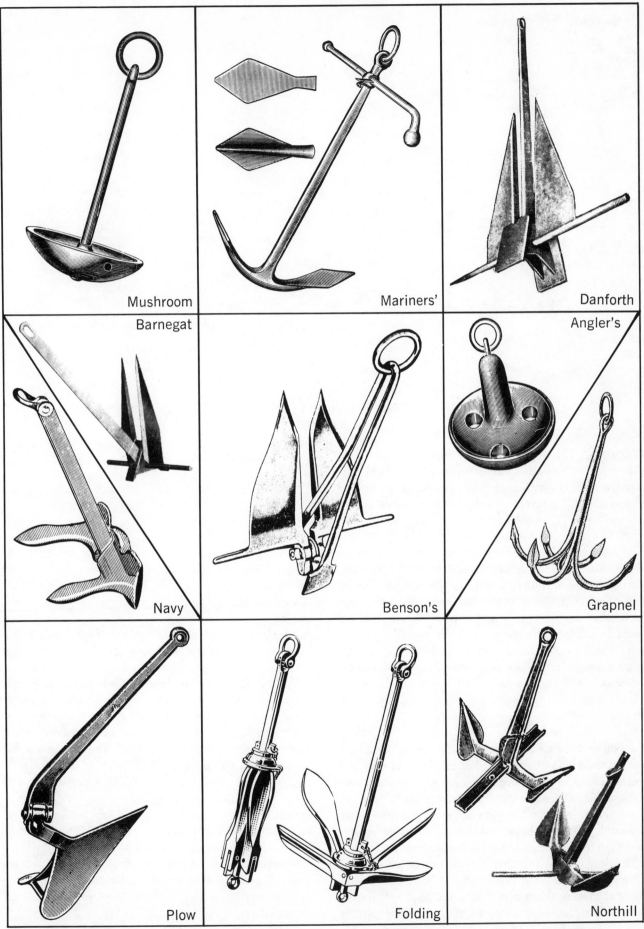

Figure 15-6: Anchors take many forms. Some types are especially suited for certain bottom conditions.

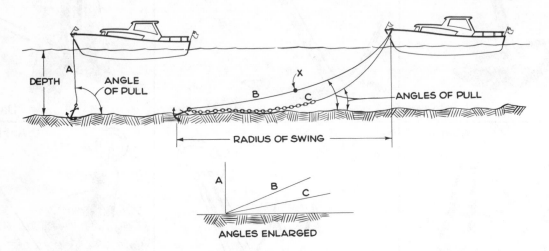

Figure 15-7: The secret of anchor holding power is to keep the pull at a low angle with generous scope. Angle "A" has practically no holding power; "B" has good holding power but "C" is better. A weight at X increases holding power.

swing in a circle whose radius is almost equal to the length of the rode. (Actually this radius will be equal to the distance from the anchor to a point on the bottom directly below the bow.) This swing could cover quite an area; in the discussion on scope, it was assumed that such space would be available. Sometimes it is not available because other boats are near. Under such conditions, shortened scope is the order; with a heavier anchor, even two anchors, each with its own rode.

Anchor Loads

The pull on the anchor is generated by the action of current on the hull and wind on the topsides. Yet the total breakout load is never the numerical sum of these two because the pull is never exactly parallel to the bottom but always at some angle. The forces of wind and current are also rarely in exactly the same direction. The actual anchor load therefore becomes the mathematical resultant.

The load imposed by the current can be understood more easily if the water is imagined to be stationary and the boat moving through it. If now the boat is propelled through the still water at the same speed as the current was moving before, then the mechanical conditions are equal. The force required to move the boat is the same as the force exerted by the current against the actual boat and therefore against the anchor. If you think of the horsepower required for boat propulsion even at slow speeds, you realize this force can be considerable. The force of a current is proportional to the *square* of its speed, thus a two-knot current exerts four times the force of a one-knot current.

Wind force cannot be gotten so easily but it can be calculated with an accuracy great enough for the purpose at hand. What is required is the area against which the wind acts (the sail area) and the force exerted against one square foot by winds of various velocities. The sail area is the same as total area *only* when the wind is acting directly at right angles to the surface. At all other angles it is the *projected* area (which is smaller), and the sketch in Figure 15-8 explains what this is; a graph of wind pressures is also given. The final force is found by simply multiplying the number of projected square feet by the force per square foot for a given wind velocity. (This assumes a form factor of 1.0 in the aerodynamic equation, a safe value.) Wind force also is proportional to the square of its velocity.

There is yet one more force to bedevil the troubled

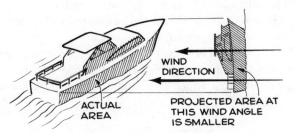

Figure 15-8: As the wind angles away from directly abeam, the projected area of the boat (the area upon which the wind exerts its force) becomes less than the actual area.

Boat Length (ft.)	Approx. Weight of Anchor (lbs.) for		
	Casual Stop	Overnight	Storm
15	8	10	15
20	10	20	30
25	10	20	30
30	10	30	50
35	10	30	50
40	15	50	85
45	20	50	85
50	25	60	120
60	30	80	150

Note: Anchors vary in their holding power and sea bottoms differ. These figures therefore can be only an approximate guide.

Figure 15-9: Some average recommended anchor weights are given above.

anchor—waves. The heaving, rolling, and pitching of a moored boat tossed by waves impart sudden, severe jerks to the anchor line. A portion of these impact surges will be absorbed by the elasticity of the anchor rode, another portion by the lifting of any heavy anchor chain. The force remaining will be added to the forces of wind and current already trying to uproot the anchor. It should be noted that the best antidote to the effects of wave action is added scope, especially when it consists in part of chain. The addition of a weight at the point *X* to a fiber line, as illustrated in Figure 15-7, makes an effective force absorber.

The tremendous force developed by a rapidly heaving ship can be explained by the laws of momentum. The large mass of many tons of the boat is accelerated in some direction by the waves and thus becomes a reservoir of energy. When this mass is suddenly decelerated to a stop by the tightening of the anchor rode, the entire energy is discharged almost instantaneously. The rode and the anchor are left with the job of absorbing it. (Where does this energy eventually go? Theoretically, into heat!)

Boat Versus Anchor

A rule of thumb for selecting the anchor to fit the boat is of value to the small boat skipper even though it must of necessity be only widely approximate. Such a rule is tabulated in Figure 15-9; it was compiled by averaging the preferences of experienced boatmen and the recommendations of anchor manufacturers.

Three choices are given for each boat length. The first is the lightest weight, used for short stops in good weather, the so-called lunch hook. The second is the weight for normal anchoring under average conditions. The third is the heaviest; this is the storm anchor for use when the elements get mad. In making a choice it is always best to err on the heavier side.

The anchor weight values given in the table must also be tempered with common sense. A small boat used on a quiet protected lake will certainly never need the holding power required for the safety of the same boat plying the coastal waters. A muddy, oozey bottom will never permit an anchor to develop the same holding power it displays in firm, hard sand. Of course the answers to these and similar situations are encompassed in the meaning of the word experience.

Earlier analysis of anchor holding power stressed that the pull should be applied as close to horizontally as possible in order to gain maximum benefit. The length of chain was added to achieve this result. An even greater boost in holding power can be obtained by utilizing this same principle and sending a "messenger" down the rode. This messenger can be a heavy weight or another smaller anchor.

Despite the blandishments of manufacturers, each anchor has its idiosyncrasies and works better on one bottom than on another. What the native boatmen of any locality find best is generally a good rule to follow.

Stowing Anchors Underway

Anchors should be stowed so that they can be broken out and over with a minimum of time and effort whenever any necessity suddenly arises. This automatically places them on the open foredeck. But the foredeck is a highly vulnerable location when the going gets rough, so the anchors must be lashed down securely. An anchor that

365

breaks loose in a sea is as dangerous as a shot from an enemy destroyer and will cause just about the same damage; it will then add insult to injury by waving bye-bye as it disappears overboard.

The time-honored method of securing the folding-stock kedge anchor is with wooden chocks that fit the flukes and the shank. The chocks are fastened to the deck permanently with bedding compound at the proper locations and provide the lashings that are tied around the anchor. This method is shown in Figure 15-10. Special fittings which

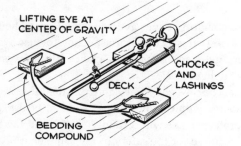

Figure 15-10: *The service anchor should be accessible but lashed securely when not in use. The eye at the center of gravity facilitates lifting.*

eliminate the individual chocks are also supplied by the various manufacturers for their own patent anchors. One of these is also shown in this figure; quick access and stowage are had without lashings.

Anchor Handling Equipment

The best equipment for manipulating light anchors is the human hand. It is versatile, can move in any direction, requires no maintenance, and lasts as long as the skipper. The only shortcoming of this equipment is its limited capacity, which seldom exceeds fifty pounds.

On larger boats, where heavier ground tackle must be used, mechanical aids are a necessity. These take the form of davits and winches or capstans driven manually or preferably electrically.

ANCHOR DAVITS.

The simplest anchor davit is a heavy vertical column rotatably fitted into a deck socket at the bow and bent sufficiently to be able to overhang the deck on either side. A hook or an eye at the top supports the block and tackle, or even a single block, for working the anchor. (The anchor

should have a lifting eye attached at its center of gravity, as in Figure 15-10, so that it can be swung in a horizontal position without gouging the deck.)

Most davits carry a cleat for fastening the lifting line; some are also equipped with a fairlead when the line has to be guided to a winch or capstan. Figure 15-11 shows

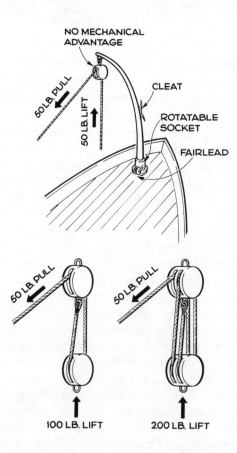

Figure 15-11: *A davit eases the handling of a heavy anchor; lifting tackle amplifies human force.*

a davit and also shows several forms of lifting tackle that could be used with it to increase lifting capacity. Certain arrangements of ropes and blocks afford a mechanical advantage. With a 3 to 1 advantage, for instance, a 50-pound pull will lift a 150-pound anchor. (The laws of physics are not being contraverted; no power is gotten for free. You are simply trading a longer, lighter pull for a shorter, heavier lift.)

Friction has been neglected in this simplified explanation, as have the weights of the blocks. It is safe to assume that in actual practice about two-thirds of the mechanical advantage will remain to do useful work. Note that a reciprocal of the mechanical advantage gives the relationship between distance pulled and distance lifted: mechanical advantage, 3; lift distance 1/3 of pull distance. The mechanical advantage is equal to the number of lines on the movable block when the pull is from the stationary block.

CAPSTANS AND WINDLASSES.

Although a capstan is generally vertical and a windlass horizontal, many boatmen (and many manufacturers' catalogs) use the terms interchangeably. Either name signifies a device for exerting a pull on a line, usually the anchor rode. Capstans and windlasses are available for manual operation as well as for hydraulic and electric operation. (See Figure 15-12.)

Figure 15-12: The motors for electric capstans can be above or below deck. The switches should be waterproof and easily accessible. Rope is hauled by the gypsy (right), the chain by the wildcat (left). (Credit—Ideal Windlass Co., Inc.)

The manual units provide mechanical advantages as high as 25 to 1. They do this through a crank and gearing or through a lever, ratchet, and gearing. Since all the power must be supplied by human muscle, there is cranking or levering aplenty to be done before the welcome sight of the anchor breaking the surface. (Several thousand years ago, those clever Chinese developed a capstan whose drum had two different diameters. The rope winding onto one and off the other gave a tremendous mechanical advantage. Present-day descendant of this idea is the differential chain hoist.)

There are two types of "working wheels" on a windlass and commercial units generally have both. One is the "gypsy," a smooth, spool-shaped drum. The rope is given a few turns around this drum and held reasonably taut. Friction then serves to transmit the pull from the machine to the work. The other is the "wildcat," a sheave with hollows around the circumference that fit chain links for slip-proof operation. A stripper finger prevents the chain from sticking and snarling. (The origin of the romantic terms, gypsy and wildcat, is obscure. A memory gimmick to tell the two apart: Both wildcat and chain contain a *c*.)

The electric capstans and windlasses are driven by electric motors fitted to the boat voltage. On low-voltage systems, such as 12 and even 32, these motors can draw an imposing number of amperes which most batteries can supply for only a very short time. (See Chapter 7.) Many of these units have an integral lever switch that can be thrown for forward or reverse. The handiest control is a foot-operated flush deck switch made waterproof with a securely fastened rubber gasket. Motors can be placed on deck or below deck.

Installation. The mechanical installation of capstans and windlasses must be sturdy enough to withstand the hefty pull of the unit plus the whiplashing of wind and wave. Sufficient falsework should be provided under the deck below the unit to distribute the stress of the fastening bolts over as wide an area as possible and preferably to a structural member.

Mounting the capstan or windlass directly over the rope locker makes for convenient rode handling. A deck pipe feeds the line or chain either to or from the gypsy and wildcat. (This presupposes either chain or nylon that can be stored wet; manila can*not* be stored wet.)

Automatic Anchoring

Several commercial devices are available that reduce the dropping and weighing of anchor to the mere flip of a switch. One of these is illustrated in Figure 15-13.

The electric control consists either of two buttons or a two-way switch for paying out and hauling in. This can be at the helmsman's position and makes one-man boat operation conveniently possible. The line is dogged tight when the unit is stopped and holds the anchored boat fast without additional belaying to cleat or bitt.

Figure 15-13: A flip of a remote switch by the skipper lowers or raises the anchor in this automatic anchoring unit and stows it securely. (Credit—Ideal Windlass Co., Inc.)

Figure 15-14: Certain anchors are designed to be stowed out of the way in special deck wells.

Anchor Wells

Arrangements such as the one illustrated in Figure 15-14 permit the anchor to be stowed for immediate accessibility yet without encumbering the deck and without lashings. The well opening is closed watertight by a gasketed door and lock. When the anchor is stowed it hangs down into the rope locker in space otherwise unused. This and other wells are adaptable only to anchors of specific design.

Sea Anchors

A sea anchor (or drogue) is not an anchor in the usual sense but rather a device to create drag in the water. It is used to retard the drift caused by wind of a boat with dead engines, or a boat hove-to in a storm, and to keep the bow headed into the wind and sea. The standard sea anchor is a large hollow cone and is dragged base first for maximum

resistance to its passage through the water. When resistance is no longer desired, it is hauled in, tip first, by a trip line.

A claimed improvement on a standard sea anchor is a series of small, specially shaped cones that replace the single large cone. The maker claims that these can be tripped by running a trip line through holes in the edges of the disks.

Bending Rode to Anchor

The simplest anchor connection is to run the line through the eye or ring and then complete the fisherman's bend, preferably adding an extra half-hitch for safety. This is the easiest and quickest to do but also the method with the least longevity; chafing soon takes its toll, and the end comes even sooner if there is any rusting.

The most seaman-like procedure is to make a tight eye splice about a thimble, then to connect thimble and anchor ring with a shackle. A swivel is sometimes interspersed but is generally unnecessary; with some types of rope lay, it is undesirable. The shackle allows a quick and easy disconnect if anchors are to be changed or if chain is to be inserted. Thimbles used with manila rope present no problem; with nylon, the stretch under load is sometimes sufficient to unship the thimble. (Some patent thimbles incorporate a retaining band.)

A quickee jury-rig anchor attachment can be made to a line with a large eye by passing the eye through the ring and then passing the whole anchor through the eye. Here again, watchfulness is indicated because chafing will soon reduce strength. The sketches in Figure 15-15 explain the various anchor and rode schemes.

How To Anchor

Anchoring seems a simple thing—and it is; nevertheless, there are techniques which show up the difference between the boatman and the lubber. They may also make the difference between safety and danger.

The importance of scope in guaranteeing anchor holding power has already been stressed. The need for a clear area in which the boat can swing on the chosen scope has also been cited. The main variables now are the character of the bottom, the depth of the water, and of course the weather. Each affects what you do and how you do it.

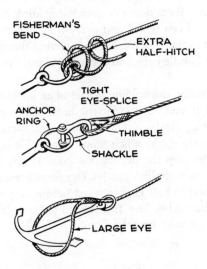

FISHERMAN'S
BEND

EXTRA
HALF-HITCH

TIGHT
EYE-SPLICE

ANCHOR
RING

THIMBLE

SHACKLE

LARGE EYE

Figure 15-15: A thimble and shackle make the best anchor attachment; a large eye in the rope can serve as a quickie.

The most reliable source of bottom and depth information is an up-to-date local chart; the skipper without this guide in his possession is taking an unnecessary gamble. Next in order is word-of-mouth description from an experienced local boatman, but here the human factor can be considerable. In the absence of both these sources, the depth indicator can give depth data and, to a very limited extent, a "look" at the bottom character. (See Chapter 8.) As a last resort, at least for today's electronically oriented skipper, there is the hand lead line for manual soundings.

Unless the indicated depth is safely greater than the boat draft, the effect of tides must be reckoned with. Local tide tables should be consulted. Many a skipper has anchored in "plenty" of water only to find himself high and dry a little later. This depth should be checked not only for the spot where the anchor is but also for the entire circle of swing. Check also for pipes and cables crossing; utility companies get peeved at skippers who haul up and break their lines. (One utility advises mariners that it will reimburse them if they cut fouled anchors loose rather than let them cause damage by hauling.)

The matter of weather means more than just the obvious condition of fair or foul. Wind becomes an important factor, especially with the large sail area presented by modern cabin powerboats. There are prevailing winds

and there are variable winds and often this knowledge is purely local and native. If there are many boats in a certain area, then going where the crowd goes is a good presumption of safety.

In gauging the wind, its probable effect on an accidentally drifting boat should be assessed. If the anchor broke loose, where would the wind drive the boat? To a shoal? Onto rocks? Into a jetty? Out to deeper water? The last eventuality is obviously the only acceptable one—provided you *had* to accept one.

Then there is the current to consider. (Often wind and current jockey with each other for control of your boat.) Current can be gauged by the inclination of buoys or the movement of floating objects with too little freeboard to be caught by the wind; in the Hudson River, driftwood goes by at a speed that makes you think it is motor-equipped.

The foregoing cautions are based on the premise that the competent skipper must be alert to every possibility of danger, no matter how remote. Carefulness is never wasted and the old saw about fools rushing in remains true. Of course there are some protected coves where anchoring is as safe as dropping the hook in a home bathtub and it is hard to get into trouble—but they are few.

Once the anchorage has been selected with all factors duly appraised, it should be approached properly. This approach is in a direction exactly opposite to that in which the dead boat would drift under the combined effects of wind and current. The boat is brought up to the anchorage *slowly*; don't imitate the marine cowboys. Headway is gauged so that the boat is dead in the water when the bow is directly over the chosen anchoring spot. At this instant the anchor is lowered.

A sailboat coming up to a desired anchoring spot follows the routine described earlier for coming up to a mooring. Once the anchor is down, the wind drifting the vessel back can be the force which embeds the flukes for a solid hold. If there is an engine aboard, it is well to use it in reverse for this purpose, just as the stinkpotter does.

The anchor is always *lowered*; it is never heaved out in a seeming attempt to achieve a distance mark. The make-believe Olympic discus thrower on the bow belongs on television or in the funny papers; he has no proper place on pleasure boats. (It seems superfluous to add that the bitter end of the anchor line should be fastened stoutly, just in case.)

The boat will have begun to fall back on wind and current as the anchor touches bottom. The anchor rode is then payed out just fast enough so that there is no load on the line. It should never be dumped overboard in coils. When the desired scope has been reached, the line is run through a chock and snubbed on a strong cleat or a mooring bitt. As the rode becomes taut, the anchor will dig in; its bite can be hastened by moderate use of reverse, now that there is no longer any danger of rope fouled on screws.

When there is no wind or current to aid in paying out the rode, slow reverse must be called upon from the instant the anchor touches bottom. It is now doubly important to keep the line going over without excess and thus to prevent loose rope from getting into the propeller suction current. Again, when the line is snubbed the anchor will dig in and it can be helped by an increase in reverse throttle.

The preferred methods of belaying the line to the cleat and the bitt are shown in Figure 15-16. The idea behind

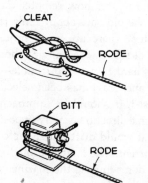

Figure 15-16: Note that the line goes around the base of cleat or bitt first *before being secured. This puts the strain directly on the fixture and not on the belayed part of the line. This method also prevents jamming and facilities unshipping.*

the proper tie is not only to secure the line (even a granny knot will do that) but also to make unfastening possible. The underlying principle is to leave the knot or hitch itself comparatively unstressed, and therefore removable, while the cleat or bitt surface takes the anchor load directly. This is especially important with manila, which swells when it gets wet.

The engines should be kept running throughout the anchoring maneuver even though the clutch be in neutral and the screws hopefully stopped. This takes care of any

contingency that might require way to be resumed. The time to shut them down is after the holding power of the anchor has been tested and everything is secure. That is when the captains of the big ships swing the engine room telegraph handle back and forth and signal "through with engines."

Incidentally, the holding power of an anchor can easily be tested if you have sufficient faith in the integrity of your chocks, cleats, bitts, and other gear—and they had better be strong. As much scope as possible is payed out in order to keep the pull on the hook nearly horizontal. Power is then applied gently. The service anchor should hold at least to half engine speed before dragging. (Keep clear of the anchor line. If it should fail, its elasticity will snap it back with brutal force.)

Safety Ranges

Checking the anchor intermittently to see if it is dragging becomes an important safety measure when the wind and sea kick up. This is done most conveniently by establishing some ranges and subsequently sighting them just by eye.

As soon as anchoring is completed and the boat has settled to its rode, pick out some easily recognizable landmarks and memorize their relationships. Objects in line that can become a range by sighting one in front of the other are best; several should be found around the compass. When noting any subsequent difference in the ranges, remember that the boat could also be swinging to wind and current without dragging its anchor.

Dragalarm

The big ships always have at least one crewman on watch while the others sleep. For about two dollars you can make a little electric robot who will watch while *you* sleep. This one will alert you when the boat moves but of course hasn't the brains to differentiate between a drag and a wide swing.

The construction of a dragalarm is detailed in Figure 15-17. The device is powered by a flashlight cell and needs no connection with the boat wiring. The base of the dragalarm is belayed to the deck or a stanchion or any other forward structure. The heavy fishing sinker at the end of the light cord is then heaved forward a good

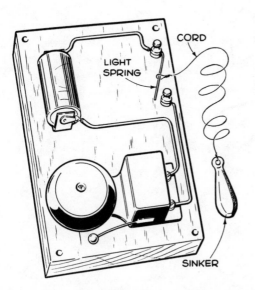

Figure 15-17: This simple dragalarm can be put together quickly and inexpensively. It will stand an "anchor watch" while you sleep.

distance and the line attached to the contact arm with very little slack. Any boat movement will drag the sinker along the bottom and the resistance to this motion will activate the unit.

Anti-fouling Measures

An anchor has an excellent chance of becoming fouled on a rocky bottom and defying all efforts to bring it up. The harder you pull, the more determined it seems to stay down there. The remedy must be applied before the anchor goes over because there is usually no cure once it is down.

The remedy is illustrated in Figure 15-18 and is called a trip line. A sturdy line is bent to the crown of the anchor with a scope slightly greater than the water depth. The far end of the line carries a buoy. Anchoring is accomplished in the normal manner. Weighing anchor is done by hauling in the rode to keep it from fouling but doing all the heavy heaving on the buoyed line. The hook comes up aft-end-to.

There are times, and this has happened to every seasoned sailor, when the anchor just will not come up—trip line or no trip line. There is only one final remedy and it is a sad one: Jettison the hook, cut it loose! (This remedy is sad only for the skipper and not for the marine supply store.)

Moorings

A mooring is a "permanent" anchorage. Since a mooring is intended to withstand the ravages of time and weather, its components are sturdier than those of the average anchoring; chain replaces rope.

The use of mushroom anchors for mooring is a fairly universal procedure except in locations where the bottom is hostile to this type of hook. A heavy mushroom has the ability to work itself farther and farther down into the ground to develop an increasingly tenacious hold.

The rode for permanent moorings is preferably chain. A husky buoy absorbs the chain weight. A pendant on this buoy then is used to secure the boat. This is shown in Figure 15-19 together with one manufacturer's suggestions of correct mushroom weight.

A mooring secured by only one anchor brings up the familiar problem of large area of boat swing. Where such freedom of space is not available, a multi-anchor mooring must be used. With several anchors properly placed, the mooring buoy becomes in effect a fixed point and the boat swings on a radius equivalent only to the length of its pendant. A three-point mooring of this nature is shown in Figure 15-20.

Many mooring and anchorage areas are officially designated, shown on charts, and under the control of the Coast Guard or Port Captains. The type and size of moorings may be specified by these authorities, and other legalities may also prevail. (See Chapter 25.) An unusually crowded anchorage may require separate moorings for bow and stern in order (almost) to eliminate swing.

Useful Knots

Myriad knots have been developed and dozens of books have been written on how and when to tie them. However, the small boat skipper is sufficiently well-equipped for his duties if he masters perhaps a half-dozen of the most useful ones. These are the ones that will tie him up safely and yet release him easily when he so desires.

Figure 15-21 shows clearly how to tie the most common

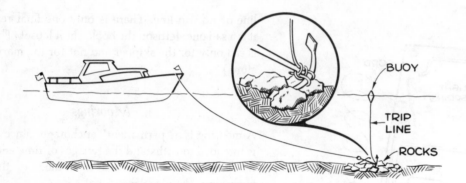

Figure 15-18: *A trip line should be attached to anchors used on bottoms likely to foul the hook.*

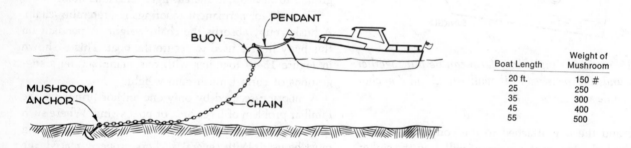

Boat Length	Weight of Mushroom
20 ft.	150 #
25	250
35	300
45	400
55	500

Figure 15-19: *Mushroom anchor and chain make a secure mooring. Suggested anchor weights are given in the table.*

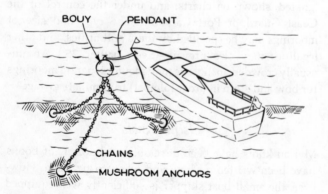

Figure 15-20: *This three-point mooring will restrict boat swing in anchorages where space is limited.*

utilitarian knots. It should be noted that all knots put great strain on the rope fibers and therefore reduce the ultimate breaking strength of the rope.

The illustrations clearly show the manipulations needed to achieve each knot. These are situations in which pictures are truly better than the proverbial thousand words; an attempt to reduce the required operations to verbiage surely would result in obfuscation rather than clarification.

A few cautions will help keep you on the road to good knot tying. The square knot should finish as two simple loops, one inside the other. Properly made, the square knot can be undone fairly easily by pushing these loops toward each other. If the direction of interleaving is reversed, the result is a "granny" almost impossible to undo once severe stress has been placed on it.

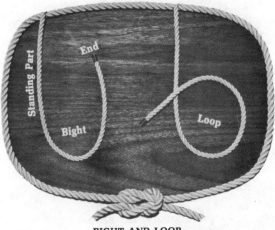

BIGHT AND LOOP

Like the earthworm, a rope has two indistinguishable Ends. Everything in between is the Standing Part. The simplest maneuver is a change of direction, called a Bight. A cross over or under is called a Loop. The end left hanging is called the Bitter End, a term you'll consider appropriate before you master all the following knots.

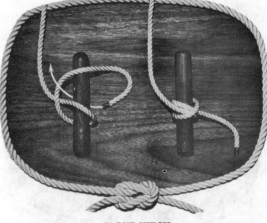

CLOVE HITCH

When a line has to be made fast to a pile or a spar quickly, the Clove Hitch is the simple, speedy answer. A simple loop around the pile, followed by a second, with the free end crossed under and pulled tight, results in a hitch that gets even tighter as tension increases on the standing part.

FIGURE-OF-EIGHT

Less complicated than the knot you put in your shoelaces, the Figure-Of-Eight is an ideal basic knot for use at the end of a line to prevent a sheet or line from slipping through a block. Make an underhand loop, then bring the free end over the standing part and bring it under and through the loop.

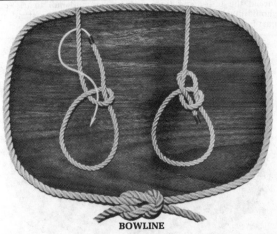

BOWLINE

For a simple running loop, the Bowline is the sailor's best friend. Begin with a small overhand loop, make a larger loop and bring the free end through the first loop, as shown at left. Now form a bight by bringing the free end under and over the standing part, then back through the loop. This won't slip or snarl under strain, yet unties easily with one tug on the bight.

(Credit—du Pont Co.)

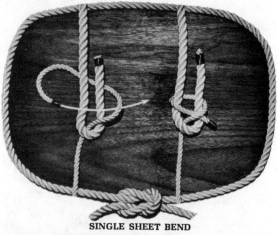

SINGLE SHEET BEND

The Sheet Bend, used to tie two ropes together, is at its best when things are complicated by ropes of unequal size. Form a bight in the larger line. Thread smaller line bitter end through the bight, around it, back through under itself, and out over on the same side as the large line's bitter end.

FISHERMAN'S BEND OR ANCHOR BEND

The two loops that swivel freely make the Anchor Bend perfect for making fast a line to an anchor, buoy or spar. Take two turns through the ring, followed by an underhand loop, then thread the bitter end through the turns and pull tight. You should give the bitter end an extra hitch around the standing part for greater strength.

DOUBLE SHEET BEND

When the strain on the two ropes you are joining is particularly great, tie the Single Sheet Bend, as above, leaving enough length in the small line bitter end for another loop around, under itself inside the bight and out over again. To prevent slipping and jamming, always make sure that both bitter ends are on the same side of the knot.

ROLLING HITCH

Two half-hitches, tied according to the book, have the appearance of uniform chain links. Here, again, the difference between right and wrong is the manner in which the bitter end (the loose end) is passed to make the second loop.

Leaving the Mooring

There is only one caution to observe in leaving (or even picking up) a mooring: Don't get the propeller fouled in the pennant or in the rode. If there is wind or current strain on the pennant, inch forward on "slow speed ahead" just enough to offset it and permit unhooking. Once free, back off until it is safe to maneuver.

The sailboat skipper leaving a mooring *under sail* follows a different program. (Should he choose to use his engine, he becomes a powerboat and uses powerboat procedure.) If the rudder has been detached, he fits pintles to gudgeons and gets it back in operative place. He then bends on (attaches) the mainsail and the jib, raises them but lets them fly with loosed sheets so that the wind imparts no forward motive force.

The mooring is now cast off and the boat allowed to drift back far enough to be clear. Hauling in on the jib sheet now swings the craft to the desired course and trimming the main sheet adds the necessary push.

This applies to stinkpotter and windjammer alike: The skipper's first instinctive action on coming aboard should be to pump or sop or bail the bilges dry. Remember the earlier admonition on the hazards of "free surface" water sloshing about.

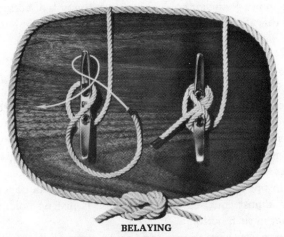

BELAYING

Endlessly winding rope around a cleat is not Belaying. Loop the line around the base, under the arms of the cleat, then bring it up and over diagonally, around and under one arm, then over, around and under the other, in a continuous figure-8, securing the bitter end by tucking it under the last crossover.

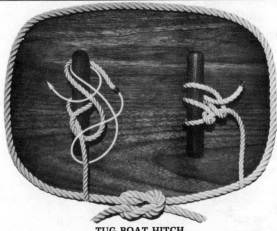

TUG BOAT HITCH

Ready for the final exam? The Tug Boat Hitch is ideal for heavy towing, yet can be released under great strain when necessary. Take one or two turns around the towing post, cross bight under, then drop bight over top. Now loop bight back around the standing part, drop bight over the top with half twist, and pull taut. Congratulations.

Chafing Gear

The fretting and mincing of a moored boat causes a continuous rubbing of the anchor line where it passes through a chock. This abrasion weakens the line and can in time destroy it. Adequate chafing gear is the preventive.

Chafing gear can consist of canvas wrapped around the line at the chock. Another form is a short length of rubber hose through which the line passes; sometimes this hose is split for ease of application. Matters can also be helped by seeing that the chock is burnished smooth.

The Complete Book of Boating

Fendering

The sides and edges of piers seem to lie in wait for the smoothly painted surfaces of a hull in order to inflict unsightly gouges and scratches. Fenders or bumpers properly placed are the preventive medicine.

Many types of fenders are available (see Chapter 20) but all have one purpose: To absorb shocks and to maintain a space between hull and adversary. Hull contour determines the most effective positions for fenders. Often fenders alone cannot give adequate protection and a fender board is added to widen the area of effectiveness. Figure 15-22 shows common fender and bumper applications.

An Anchoring Exercise

You have been cruising. The day is ending and it is time to plan snugging down for the night and to indulge in the ritual permitted when the sun is over the yardarm.

The chart should provide your first orientation. Study the available harbors in relation to the protection which they can offer from wind and weather. In such selections you are on your own but often the chart will indicate specific anchorages so marked; it is reasonable to assume that these have been selected to include as few hazards as possible. When such anchorages are marked "special" the added bonus is that boats under 65 feet need not maintain anchor lights.

Water depth is of controlling importance. All charts show depths in profusion; check to find whether the figures represent feet or fathoms, remembering that a fathom is equal to six feet. Next in importance, from the standpoint of anchor holding power, is the type of bottom, and this also is indicated on the chart by means of abbreviations. The chart sample reproduced in Figure 15-23 shows these two markings and the table decodes the abbreviations.

Modern anchors look so businesslike that you would expect them to do their appointed jobs no matter what the bottom coverage might be. Sadly, this is not so. Heavy greenery on the bottom, for instance, gives most anchors a sleigh ride and the flukes never get a chance to dig in. Slimy mud, by contrast, practically invites the flukes to dig in but that avails little; the flukes will pull out again with almost equal ease because there is just no holding power in such bottoms.

Rocks can have tremendous holding power. But it is a case of Russian roulette whether or not you get your anchor back. As already noted, the holding power may be so great that it will hold your hook until the end of time after you cut it loose—and this is true, often despite a rigged trip line.

The hazards of any anchorage are wind, current and shore terrain. Obviously, a gently sloping sandy beach will not offer the same danger if you are involuntarily swept upon it as a rocky promontory. Proximity to a traveled

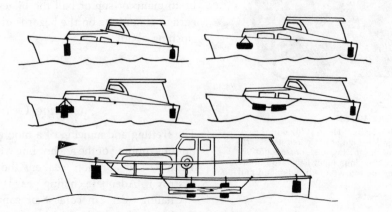

Figure 15-22: Proficiency in the art of fendering is good insurance against nicked hulls and other damage. Various methods of rigging fenders or bumpers are shown.

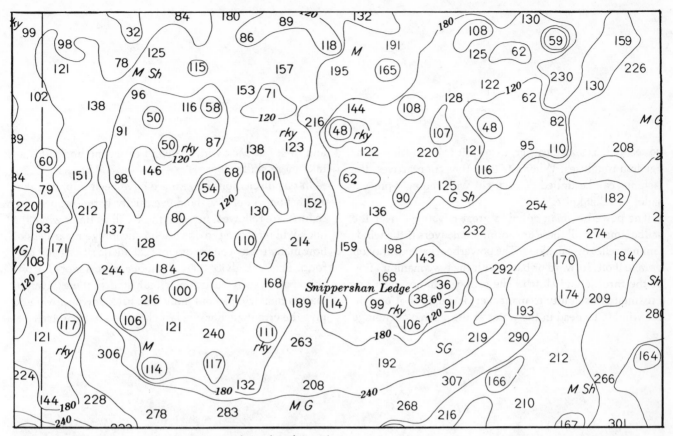

Figure 15-23: All charts are profuse in their detailing of water depths, either in feet or in fathoms. The many numbers on the chart section above show this.

channel can involve danger of being run down during a fog.

The very word "anchoring" implies a firm attachment to the ground, but every sailor knows that the situation can sometimes deteriorate to become very infirm indeed. Therefore it is essential, once the hook is down, to "mark" the position of the ship so that any drift can be noticed immediately. One way of marking the location is to take bearings on shore objects and to be alert to any change. Nothing can beat an alert human for such a watch but the dragalarm described on page 370 can become a close second.

An earlier discussion emphasized the need for adequate scope, but how can you know quickly how much line you have paid out? Many skippers have their own little gimmicks. Paint markings, plastic tabs, interleaved bits of colored cloth—all are in use with a fair amount of convenience and accuracy. Perhaps the simplest arrangement is to whip (bind) the rode with small stuff (light cord) every 25 or 30 feet in keeping with a predetermined code.

An anchor simply lowered to the bottom has no holding power until after it has dug itself in—and it will not dig in except under tension. The tension is supplied by backing down slowly until the boat is overpowered by the anchor's tenacity. This is called "setting the anchor" and is analogous to a fisherman's setting of his hook.

Paying out anchor line to attain the desired scope would seem to be simplicity itself and yet here, too, a bit of know-how comes in handy. The most important caution for inexperienced anchor handlers is to stay clear of the line. A boatman with his foot caught in the rode following the anchor overboard is a favorite subject for cartoonists, but it does happen in real life with sometimes tragic results. Coil the line so it can pay out without hitch or tangle and stay clear of it. And of course secure the bitter end so you won't lose your line, your anchor or your dignity.

Various methods of securing the anchor to the rode were mentioned earlier. The most convenient makes use of an eye in the line and a shackle as the connecting device to the anchor. With such an arrangement anchors can be changed with ease to suit conditions. The shackle pin should be screwed tight and then wired securely to prevent accidental opening and anchor loss.

Above all, a service anchor should be on deck at all times, ready for instant use. Many an emergency could be prevented by the immediate dropping of an anchor. Despite the need for instant availability, the anchor must be secured, as stated earlier, to keep it from causing damage in a rough sea. When the time for action arrives, the lashings can be untied or even cut with the ever-present sailor's pocket knife.

The powerboatman enjoys a great advantage over the sailboatman in all these anchoring maneuvers if the windjammer relies on sail alone. The powerboat can put way on or take it off, forward or back, with the easy manipulation of the throttle and clutch. The sailboat cannot even approximate this ability to maneuver; it must shoot up into the wind to be dead in the water at the desired anchorage

and then fall back with the wind to set the hook. It does take more skill.

In our discussion thus far we have been implying that an anchor will always hold eventually if the proper procedures are followed. In truth, there will be times when the hook will refuse to provide a solid anchorage regardless of how many tricks you try or what cabalistic rituals you perform. The best advice then is to move on to a more hospitable spot. In such frustrating circumstances it may avail to make a final try, pay out more line, back down slowly and give the errant anchor one last chance to redeem itself.

16 *Rules of the Road and Lights*

L AND vehicles travel clearly defined highways, make turns only at well-marked intersections, and in general proceed safely by obeying the simple rule of keeping to the right. Boats maneuver under more complicated conditions. Except in narrow channels, there are no lanes that must be followed and directional changes can be made wherever desired. These basic differences between land and water travel highlight the need for the specialized laws and rules that have been enacted to govern maritime traffic.

The original laws were agreed upon at a conference of maritime nations more than a century ago. Subsequent discussions and enactments by lawmaking bodies refined these into practical rules that mariners could follow. Autonomous governments, the United States among them, added rules of procedure that applied to their own specific waters. All of this national and international activity has one unified objective: safety at sea.

As with most laws, the navigation rules tended to lag behind technological developments even in nomenclature: The inland rules still referred to the propulsion machinery of a powerboat as "steam." Then, within this decade, revisions were made that brought much of the subject matter right up to date. Cognizance even was taken of the navigation of boats by radar under conditions of no visibility.

Insofar as they concern American pleasure boats, the laws affecting marine traffic are grouped into four categories: (1) International Rules of the road, (2) Inland Rules of the road, (3) Rules of the road for the Great Lakes, and (4) Rules of the road for the Western Rivers. The United States Coast Guard has the duty of administering and enforcing all of these rules and has issued comprehensive booklets which cover the subjects in full detail.

Copies of the *Rules* publications may be obtained upon request without charge from Coast Guard headquarters in Washington and from all Coast Guard Marine Inspection offices located in the major ports of the country. Pamphlet #CG-169 lists the International Rules and the Inland Rules. These two directives are printed side by side in juxtaposition on every page so that their similarities and differences can be seen at a glance. Pamphlet #CG-172 details the navigation requirements for the Great Lakes, while booklet #CG-184 lists all similar information pertaining to the Western Rivers.

The latest International Rules make provision for seaplanes that have landed upon the water and thus have become boats for all practical purposes. The rules specify how such seaplanes must be lighted and how they may be maneuvered. The Inland Rules do not do this but leave the matter to the regulations of the Federal Aviation Administration. The omission (or inclusion) has little or no effect on the average small boat operator because meeting seaplanes in boating areas certainly is not yet a common experience.

Since the rules, in effect, divide the nation's boating waters into various areas of differing authority, it is important to know what and where these lines of demarcation are. The International Rules apply to vessels on the "high seas." In this context, the high seas extend right to the coastal shores and "separate" themselves from inland waters by arbitrarily established lines at the entrances to rivers, harbors, bays, and sounds. The Commandant of the Coast Guard is empowered by law to fix these lines. He does this by relating them to lighthouses, buoys, lightships, coastal objects, or other chartable means that permit clarity.

A general rule is given for determining the line separating international waters from inland waters at locations where no specific Coast Guard definition exists. At such points a line is drawn approximately parallel with the shore and passing through the outermost buoys or other navigation aids. International Rules apply seaward of this line; Inland Rules apply landward of this line.

The Great Lakes category includes the five Great Lakes and also all their tributaries as well as the St. Lawrence River as far east as Montreal. The Western Rivers grouping includes the Mississippi River and its tributaries above the Huey P. Long Bridge at its mouth, the Red River, and the portion of the Atchafalaya River above its junction with the Plaquemine. The Department of the Army also has jurisdiction over some phases of navigation on the Great Lakes.

All of the rules concern themselves with the identifying lights and shapes, with the whistle signals, and with the legal and safe maneuvers applicable to the particular section of water covered by them. There are some variations and discrepancies between the requirements in one section and the corresponding ones in another, but these are gradually being reduced by continuing revisions. The small boat operator whose cruising range is great enough to take him from coastal water into the Great Lakes and the Mississippi could be affected adversely by the variations which remain and therefore should familiarize himself with them.

The rules that govern all vessels on the inland waters, the Great Lakes, and the western rivers are combinations of statutes enacted by Congress and pilot rules promulgated by the Commandant of the Coast Guard under the authority vested in him. Conflicts often have arisen in the interpretation of the rules in the light of the statutes and many of these have been resolved by the courts. Decisions are on file in the law books and in the normal course of legal procedure these undoubtedly will be cited in future litigations.

The rules apply to "all public and private United States vessels." Technically, this includes naval and Coast Guard craft, but special exemptions are made for these ships, especially in the matter of lights; standard lighting cannot be accomplished in many cases because of unusual hull or superstructure construction.

All the rules are mandatory: They must be obeyed. Obedience is not within the discretion of the skipper. Departure from the rules is permitted only in situations of extreme danger, for example, when disregarding the rules would be the only means of avoiding a collision.

The International and Inland Rules consider vessels on the water as being in one of three conditions, and this determines the application of the rulings. Boats are either 1) underway, 2) anchored or tied to the shore, or 3) aground. It becomes clear from these restrictive definitions that a boat adrift is considered as being underway and automatically incurs certain responsibilities under the rules.

A further classification applies to all boats underway when they are in situations that could result in collisions. In such cases, the vessels are either "privileged" or "burdened," depending upon their relative positions. As the names imply, one craft has a maneuvering advantage over the other but nevertheless the actions of both are strictly prescribed by the rules. The duties of each are outlined further along in the chapter.

Courts have held that there is a proper time for action under the rules of the road and that such time is "neither too early nor too late." It is incumbent upon skippers to make their moves while sufficient distance lies between the opposing boats to permit the required maneuvers. Yet the action must not be started when the craft are still so far apart that the movements could become confusing.

Since all the rules are promulgated with the sole purpose of preventing collision at sea, the question arises: When is collision imminent? The pilot rules state that this can be determined by watching the compass bearing of an approaching ship. If such a bearing remains constant and does not change for an appreciable length of time, then danger of collision can be deemed to exist.

This constancy of bearing can be simplified for the pleasure skipper steering his own craft. If the amount he must turn his head in order to look squarely at the approaching boat does not change as the two near each other, then they are on a collision course. Figure 16-1

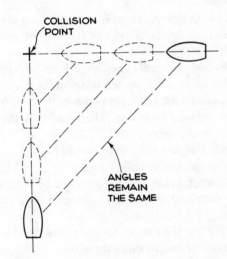

Figure 16-1: If the angle at which an approaching boat is viewed does not change, watch out! The two boats are on a collision course.

explains why this is so.

The International Rules are divided into six parts: A) definitions of terms, B) Lights and Shapes, C) Sound signals and Conduct in restricted visibility, D) Steering and sailing, E) Sound signals when in sight, and F) Miscellaneous rules. The Inland Rules follow this general pattern but are not directly subdivided.

Definitions

It is stipulated that the International Rules shall apply to all vessels (and seaplanes) upon the "high seas" and in all waters connected with such seas. Provision is made for local authority to set its own rules on the connecting waters, and this becomes the basis for the Inland, Great Lakes, and Western Rivers Rules. (The specifications in the International Rules are "rules," in the Inland Rules, they are "articles.")

A *vessel* includes every description of watercraft (other than seaplanes down on the water) capable of being used as a means of marine transportation.

Power-driven vessel means any vessel driven by machinery of any kind. A vessel with propulsion machinery that is being driven by *sail alone* is at that time considered to be a sailing vessel. However, a boat partially under sail and partially under power is considered to be a power-driven vessel.

Vessel not under command is a ship temporarily unable to maneuver normally but *not* in distress nor abandoned nor adrift.

Height above the hull is measured from the uppermost continuous deck, *not* from the waterline.

Length and breadth of a vessel means the length overall measured on the center line. The breadth is the widest dimension of the ship.

A *vessel-in-sight* condition is deemed to exist only when the other vessel can actually be seen.

Visible, when applied to the lights of a boat, means that they are visible at the required distance on a dark and *clear* night.

Short blast of the whistle (or horn) is defined as a continuous blast of one second's duration.

Prolonged blast is defined as a blast on the whistle (or horn) of from four- to six-seconds' duration.

Whistle (or horn) means any appliance capable of producing the short and prolonged blasts and capable of being heard for the legally required distance.

Steam vessel, when mentioned in the Inland Rules, means every vessel propelled by machinery of *any* kind.

Lights

Both the International Rules and the Inland Rules specify certain combinations and locations of white, red, and green lights by which the character of a vessel and her course may be distinguished at night. These legally required lights must be displayed from sunset to sunrise in all weathers. During this time, no other lights are per-

mitted that could lead to confusion or that could interfere with the keeping of a proper lookout.

The International Rules even permit using the prescribed lights betweens sunrise and sunset, when the visibility is restricted and when the skipper deems it necessary in the interest of safety. The Inland Rules are silent on this point; they neither forbid it nor recommend it.

The regulations concerning lights in the International Rules were promulgated initially with the large commercial vessels in mind and with little thought for the pleasure boatman. The provision for small pleasure boats is a sort of backtracking, a scaling-down of the requirements to make them usable on the smaller craft. Thus, the major specifications are first laid down, and then Rule 7 eases them for all vessels less than 65 feet in length, and again for boats less than 40 feet long.

Similarly, the Inland Rules concern themselves with the many types of commercial ships and then refer the matter of lights for powerboats under 65 feet in length to the Motorboat Act of 1940. Here, there is even greater subdivision on the basis of size than in the international rules; four classes are established and these determine the light requirements. (However, the first two are considered as one, and so are the last two.)

The Motorboat Act of 1940, as its name implies, concerns itself with vessels propelled by mechanical power. This excludes sailboats—but there is a hitch.

The hitch is that sailboats can lead a double life, so to speak, and most of them do. The majority carry engines of one kind or another and when these engines are propelling the boat, the sailboat is a powerboat within the meaning of the law. Therefore, when mechanically propelled, the sailboat must conform to the class rule to which its length consigns it.

MASTHEAD AND RANGE LIGHTS.

International Rule 2 and Inland Article 2 spell out the lights and placements required in order to achieve legal equipment. The dimensions alone are far too large to be applicable to the usual pleasure vessels. For instance, the forward range light is at least 20 feet above the deck and the after range light at least 35 feet!

Rule 7 scales these measurements down to practical sizes for all vessels under 65 feet long. Such boats must carry a white light in the forepart of the vessel where it can best be seen. This light must be at least 9 feet above the gun-

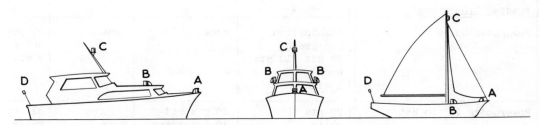

Figure 16-2: This composite diagram (a) shows the running lights required by the various jurisdictions. The table (b) is a composite and no boat carries all the lights shown. The table sorts out the correct combination for each type of vessel.

wale unless the craft is less than 40 feet long, whereupon the height may be reduced to 3 feet above the side lights.

The white forward light must be visible over an arc of 225 degrees (20 points) and this expanse must be divided equally on each side of the center line of the boat. (This is 2 points abaft the beam on both sides. There are 32 points to a full circle and a point therefore is 11.25 degrees.) The white light must be visible for a minimum distance of 3 miles.

The original Rule 2 specifies range lights fore and aft on the center line of the larger vessels, with the forward one always lower than the after one. These are of great aid to skippers at night in determining the course of distant oncoming ships. They are not required on powerboats under 150 feet long.

The Inland Rules do not require powerboats under 26 feet long (Classes A and 1) to carry bow lights. The Inland Rules do require powerboats between 26 feet and 65 feet, inclusive, in length (Classes 2 and 3) to display a bright white light as close to the bow as possible. This light must cover a forward arc of 20 points and must have a minimum visibility of 2 miles. (See Figure 16-2.)

SIDE LIGHTS.

The familiar red and green sidelights are mandatory under both the international and the inland rules for all vessels underway. The angular-visibility specification is the same under both jurisdictions and states that the angle of view must be 112.5 degrees, equivalent to 10 points. The minimum distance over which the side lights must be visible is 2 miles under the International Rules but only 1 mile under the Inland Rules. (The International Rules also drop this to 1 mile for small powerboats.)

The red light is on the port side (left, looking forward); the green light is on the starboard side (right, looking forward). The placement of the lights is such that the angle of visibility extends from dead ahead to 2 points abaft the beam. The lights are not to be visible across the bow (in other words, from the opposite side) and the International Rules assure this on large vessels by requiring a screen extending forward 3 feet. This requirement is not stated for the smaller craft. The Inland Rules also require 3-foot screens on large ships but omit the screen for boats less than 26 feet long. However, the inland rules do state that motorboats from 26 to 65 feet must have inboard screens so placed that the lights cannot be visible across the bow (only Western River Rules permit 1/2-point view across the bow.)

The Inland Rules Class A and Class 1 side lights may be of combination construction. This is a single lantern 10 points of whose lens area is red and 10 points green, with a dividing baffle between. The Class 2 and 3 side lights must be separated lanterns. Figure 16-3 illustrates the details of the viewing angles.

STERN LIGHTS.

All the jurisdictions agree that a boat underway must carry a bright white light at the stern. There is some disagreement as to the type of light, however.

The International Rules specify a 12-point light (135 degrees) set to show 6 points on each side of the stern center line and visible for at least 2 miles. There is no instruction as to height. (Light visible only from aft.)

The Inland Rules mandate the same type of light but add that, wherever practicable, it is to be placed on the same level with the side lights. The stern light visibility angle also is illustrated in Figure 16-3.

To complicate matters a bit for an already confused skipper, the Motorboat Act places the stern light higher

	RUNNING LIGHTS FOR	A	B	C	D
Inland, Western Rivers, Great Lakes	Powerboat under 26'	combination red-green 20 pts (10 pts each) 1 mile	none	none	32 pts white 2 miles
	Powerboats 26' to 65'	20 pts white 2 miles	10 pts red 10 pts green 1 mile	none	32 pts white 2 miles
	Yacht 65' or more	20 pts white 5 miles	red-green each 10 pts with screen 2 miles	32 pts white	12 pts 3 miles
	Anchoring (see text)	none	none	32 pts white	none
International Rules	Powerboat less than 40'	combination red-green 20 pts or separate 10 pts each 1 mile (at B)	none	20 pts white 3 miles	12 pts white 2 miles
	Powerboats 40' to less than 65'	none	red-green 10 pts each or 20 pts comb. 1 mile	20 pts white 3 miles	12 pts white 2 miles
	Yachts 65' or more	none	red-green each 10 pts with screen 2 miles	20 pts white 5 miles	12 pts white 2 miles
	Anchoring (see text)	none	none	32 pts white	none
Sailboats (All Rules)	Less than 40'	Combination red-green 20 pts or separate 10 pts (at B)	none	red over green optional	12 pts white 2 miles
	40' and longer	none	red & green each 10 pts with screen 2 miles	red over green optional	12 pts white 2 miles
	Anchoring	none	none	32 pts white	none

The drawing above is a composite and no boat carries <u>all</u> the lights

shown. The table sorts out the correct combination for each type

of vessel.

than the forward light and changes it to be visible "all around the horizon." This is a 32-point light. (The "higher than" applies only to Classes 2 and 3 because the Classes A and 1 do not carry a bow light.) (Permission is granted Class A and Class 1 boats to locate the aft light off the center line. This makes room for the usual outboard motor.)

COORDINATING AMENDMENT.

An easy way out of the maze has been provided for pleasure boat owners by an amendment enacted in 1956. This allows any motorboat of any size to carry lights in

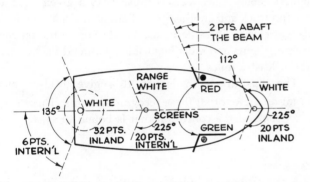

Figure 16-3: The required angular visibility of the range, side, bow and stern lights under the various jurisdictions is shown in this diagram. (Class A and class I boats may combine the two side lights into one red-green combination.)

accordance with the International Rules instead of in compliance with the Motorboat Act.

Every skipper would be wise to avail himself of the uniformity made possible by this coordinating amendment, more especially so if he cruises coastal rivers and waters. Under this system, his lights are legal in both jurisdictions. A future consideration is that the Inland Rules will undoubtedly be amended as time goes on to come more and more in line with the International, until the two are identical and devoid of disparity.

SEARCHLIGHTS.

Neither set of rules lays down any specifications for searchlights regarding size, number, or location. There

are provisions for the proper use of searchlights, however.

All searchlights or headlights that could interfere with an approaching skipper's handling of his vessel must be shielded to avoid such a situation. Expressly prohibited is the flashing of a searchlight into the pilothouse or onto the bridge of another ship.

LOWERING OF LIGHTS.

The mast lights may be lowered (by folding the mast) when such action is necessary in order to pass under a bridge or viaduct of limited clearance. The mast with its lights must be raised again immediately after clearing.

RECOGNITION LIGHTS.

Although his own vessel may never carry any of the lights intended to denote type of service and seagoing condition, the skipper often meets these signals during his cruises and should know what they mean. Day marks take over the identification duty when the lights relinquish it at sunrise and remain in force until the lights come on again at sunset. The various day marks are detailed on page 392.

The recognition lights (and the day marks) relate the vessel's mission to her seagoing condition, namely, whether she is underway, aground, anchored, or not under control. This knowledge is important to the oncoming skipper because it determines the amount and the manner by which he will keep clear.

SEAPLANES.

To all intents, a seaplane underway on the water looks like and is lighted like another boat. Its main difference is its inferior maneuverability and its greatly wider beam.

The International Rules are the only marine code that gives specifications on seaplane lights. The requirement is a white light in the forepart amidships where it can best be seen. It must be visible over an arc of 220 degrees (110 degrees on each side of the fore and aft center line) and able to reach at least 3 miles. On the wing tips are to be the usual red and green side lights, each of 110-degree arc (set to extend from directly forward to 20 degrees abaft the beam) and visible for at least 2 miles.

TOWING OR PUSHING (TUGBOATS).

A power-driven vessel engaged in towing or pushing is required by the International Rules to display 2 vertical white lights if the tow is less than 600 feet long, and 3 lights if it is longer. The arc of visibility of these white lights (20 points) is arranged symmetrically forward; one of them is to occupy the legal position for a masthead light. The separation between lights must be 6 feet and the lowest light must be at least 14 feet above the deck. In addition, the towing vessel must also carry a rearward-showing 12-point white stern light.

The Inland Rules are different. Two vertical white lights under this jurisdiction mean that the "towing" vessel has another craft *tied alongside* or else is *pushing* a craft. A *tow* of any length on inland waters requires 3 vertical white lights. The separation for these lights is a minimum of 3 feet. These towboats may also be required to carry 2 bright amber afterlights visible for 12 points from astern and set lower than the after range light. These amber lights are mandatory on western rivers.

Every night-cruising skipper should burn the tugboat light recognition pattern into his memory because these ships can be his greatest danger. Tugboats with heavy tows cannot maneuver easily. An unwary skipper mistakenly could attempt to cross between tug and tow. Plus—tugboat captains have never been known for kind hearts and gentle manners.

VESSEL NOT UNDER COMMAND.

Two bright red lights on the masthead, one directly over the other and separated at least 6 feet, designate a vessel not under command in the International Rules. These red lights replace the masthead lights; they must be capable of 2-mile visibility all around the horizon. (These are *not* requests for aid or signals of distress.)

The Inland Rules do not include a counterpart of these regulations for vessels not under command, that is, vessels temporarily unable to maneuver.

SPECIAL-DUTY VESSELS.

Vessels engaged in such special duties as laying or picking up submarine cable, marine surveying, or other duties that prevent them from getting out of the way of other craft also display special recognition lights under the International Rules. In these cases, the rules call for 3 lights, one directly above the other, and spaced at least 6 feet apart. The top and bottom lights are red, the center one is white. All must be visible around the horizon for at least 2 miles. These lights are in lieu of the regular white

masthead lights.

The Inland Rules break the recognition distinction down even further. A vessel towing a submerged or partly submerged object replaces the white towing lights with 4 vertical lights. The top and bottom lights are white and the 2 middle ones are red. Cable-laying vessels under these rules display 3 vertical red lights with the lowest one at least 15 feet above the deck. Active dredges carry 2 red lights under the forward masthead light and also 2 red lights at the stern pointing rearward over an arc of 12 points.

Recurring wartime conditions are reflected in the International Rules by a provision for recognition lights for minesweepers. Such vessels must carry a green light at the foretruck and another green light on the side on which danger exists. These lights are in addition to the regular running lights and must be visible all around the horizon for at least 2 miles.

The illustrations in Figure 16-4 give head-on and beam-on views of all these recognition lights. These may allay some of the confusion that is bound to exist.

SAILBOATS.

Since sailboats (under sail *without* power) have the right of way, the powerboat skipper must be able to recognize them even at night.

Rule 5 of the International Rules and Article 5 of the Inland Rules concern themselves with sailboats although, as is too often the case, these two authorities do not entirely agree. Both rules are clear on the requirement for red and green side lights on the port and starboard sides respectively. These are to be angled and screened just as for the power-driven vessels. Both rules also *prohibit* the carrying of white range lights or white masthead lights. A 12-point white light at the stern pointed symmetrically aft completes the legal lighting.

The International Rules permit a further method of clear identification. A sailing vessel under way *may* carry at the top of her foremast a red light over a green light. These colored lights are to have a 20-point viewing angle and must be visible for at least 2 miles. They are to be fixed showing symmetrically forward, in other words, the angle of visibility extends from dead ahead to 2 points abaft the beam on both sides. The Inland Rules do not mention these red and green masthead lights (not to be confused with the red and green side lights). (See Figure 16-5.)

FISHING VESSELS.

When fishing vessels are not actually engaged in fishing, they must show the proper lights required for any vessel of their class and size. The Inland Rules make an exception for fishing craft of less than 10 tons; these need not have permanently placed side lights but must have red and green lanterns ready for showing on the appropriate side to an approaching boat in time to avert a collision.

Confusion exists here again between inland and international light requirements during the time these fishing craft are actually plying their trade. The International Rules describe the fishing lights as a green over a white, both to be of 32-point visibility. The Inland Rules change this to a red light over a white light. The International Rules come into agreement with the Inland (by permitting a red light over a white light) only when the fishing is being done with lines and *not* by trawling; the Inland makes no distinction.

PILOT VESSELS.

Pilot boats are quite likely to be encountered by pleasure boat skippers whose cruising takes them to the mouths of rivers and tributaries that lead to the sea. When not engaged in piloting, these boats are lighted in keeping with their size and class.

The Inland Rules state that pilot boats, on station and engaged in piloting, "shall not show the lights required for other vessels." Instead, they are to show a 32-point white light at the masthead and in addition display a flare-up light at intervals not exceeding 15 minutes. On the approach to another vessel, the pilot boat is to flash its side lights as an indication of the direction in which it is moving. If the pilot boat is small and of the type that must go alongside a steamer in order to put a pilot aboard, she may merely show the white light instead of affixing it to the masthead.

The Inland Rules also specifically recognize the large, power-driven pilot boat which does not come alongside but sends a pilot over by tender. This vessel must add a 32-point red light to the mast 8 feet below the white light; she also carries the red and green side lights. When anchored at her station, this pilot boat douses the side lights but keeps the others.

The International Rules pick up at this point and require all pilot vessels to show the white-above-red lights in addition to standard side lights and a standard 12-point stern light. This vessel must also show a flare-up light at intervals not exceeding 10 minutes. (An intermittent white light visible over 32 points may be substituted.) When this pilot boat is anchored on station, she adds the regulation white anchor light and omits the side lights.

A skipper's recognition of a distant pilot boat should begin with the white masthead light. A red light below this will tell him that it is a large, power-driven craft. The flare-up or intermittent white light should be the clincher.

ANCHORED OR AGROUND.

The significant differentiation under International Rules between vessels anchored and vessels aground is the presence of two red lights in addition to white anchor lights on the grounded craft. These are the same red lights (as to position and type) which have already been mentioned for vessels not under command or temporarily unable to maneuver.

The distinction is not universal and shows up yet another disparity between the various rules that govern the boatman. The Inland Rules make no mention of the additional red lights for grounded craft. On the other hand, the red lights are required for all grounded vessels on the St. Mary's River but must be shown on the Great Lakes only when the ship aground is more than 65 feet long.

Vessels not aground but merely at anchor generally display a 32-point white light forward where it can best be seen. On ships more than 150 feet long a second white light is added abaft the first, near the stern, and hung at least 15 feet lower than the forward light. On the Great Lakes this same large ship must carry 2 lights forward placed 10 feet apart athwartship and a similar setup astern, making 4 lights in all; in addition, she shows white deck lights every 100 feet.

A clause that affects pleasure boat skippers refers to legally designated anchorage areas. In such zones, boats under 65 feet need not carry any anchor lights if the area is classed as "special."

The visibility requirement for the white anchor lights differs under the various rules. Under International Rules it is 2 miles (3 miles for the big ships). The Inland Rules

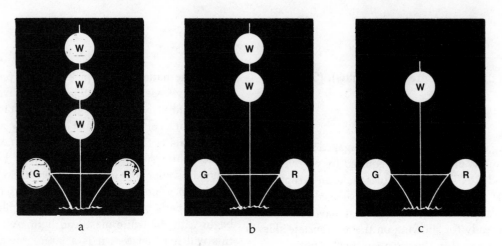

a   b   c

Figure 16-4: Boats approaching head-on at night signal their character by their light patterns: (a) a tugboat with a long tow astern, (b) a tugboat with a tow alongside, (c) a power vessel, (d) a vessel laying cable and unable to maneuver, (e) a sailboat and (f) a vessel at anchor.

also specify 2 miles. On the Great lakes it is 1 mile, on western rivers 2 miles. Anchor and aground lights are pictured in Figure 16-4.

FERRYBOATS.

The International Rules do not mention ferryboats (for obvious reasons, since there are no "ferries" in their areas) but the Inland Rules do and so also do the Western River and the Great Lakes Rules. All the rules are refreshingly uniform in their requirements.

A distinction is made between single-ended and double-ended ferryboats. The former is treated as simply another power-driven vessel and bears the standard lights for her class and size. The legal lighting for a double-ended ferryboat underway differs somewhat from the lighting of other routine vessels.

The double-ended ferryboat carries 2 range lights placed at equal heights above the deck and located on the keel line at equal distances fore and aft of amidships. These are white lights visible all around the horizon. Regulation colored side lights are carried, except that there are both red and green lights on each side so arranged that only the proper colors are illuminated for each direction of travel.

Where several different ferryboat lines operate in the same area, the Officer in Charge of Marine Inspection may designate a recognition light for each company to be carried midway between the range lights and higher; this light may be white or colored. (These recognition lights were a familiar sight on the Hudson River at New York City years ago when the ferry business was brisk.)

LAW-ENFORCEMENT VESSELS.

The Great Lakes Rules and the Western River Rules both authorize a special recognition light for law-enforcement vessels underway in the enforcement of their duties. This is a low-intensity blue light that rotates or appears to rotate by its mechanical construction. It is placed in the forepart of the law-enforcement boat where it can best be seen and is carried in addition to the legal lights.

The use of such a blue light is restricted to federal, state, or local governments. The situation is analagous to the familiar rotating red lights carried by police cars ashore.

BARGES BEING PUSHED.

On the Great Lakes and also on the western rivers, barges pushed ahead by a power-driven vessel show regulation green and red side lights. In addition, an amber light visible symmetrically ahead for 20 points over a distance of 2 miles is required on the western rivers. This amber light is optional on the Great Lakes.

The International Rules and the Inland Rules duplicate the requirement that barges being pushed by a power-driven vessel carry regulation colored side lights; the amber light is omitted. When several barges are grouped together, the international ruling is that they be lighted as one vessel. The inland ruling requires each barge of the

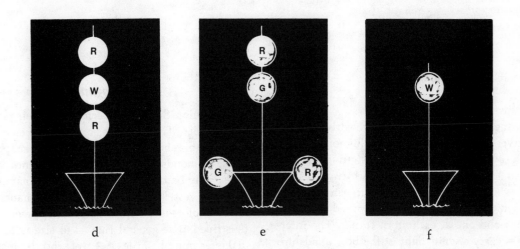

d   e   f

Figure 16-5: Sailboats have the right-of-way under most conditions (when under sail only) and can be recognized at night by lights such as the above.

group to carry its own side lights.

BARGES BEING TOWED.

A barge being towed astern of a power-driven vessel on western rivers must show 4 white lights, one at each corner. When several barges are towed astern in a string, the first shows 3 white lights, one at each forward corner and one at the stern amidships. The last barge in the string also shows 3 white lights but these are disposed one at the bow amidships and one at each stern corner. The intermediate barges carry a white light at the bow amidships and another at the stern amidships. All these are around-the-horizon lights visible for 2 miles.

The Great Lakes rules for barges being towed are different. Here each barge carries regulation colored side lights and in addition a "small, bright white light" aft which shall not be visible forward of the beam. When these barges are towed in tiers, only the outside barges are lighted and the small bright white light is carried by the centrally located last boat.

The Inland Rules on barges *exclude* the Hudson River and Lake Champlain and also Long Island Sound as far as Narragansett. They make special rules for these waters. On the remaining inland waters, barges carry regulation colored sidelights and a white stern light. On the last barge in a tow (or the only barge if it be a single tow) the single white amidships light is replaced by 2 white lights placed horizontally athwartship not less than 5 feet apart.

The special ruling for the Hudson River, Long Island Sound as far as Narragansett Bay, and Lake Champlain permits simplified lighting for barges being towed. A single barge in tow carries only a white light amidships at the bow and another white light amidships at the stern.

When a string of barges in these waters is separated from the towing vessel by less than 75 feet, the head barge carries a bow and stern light, the remaining barges only stern lights. When the separation is greater than 75 feet, each barge (except the last) carries amidships white bow and stern lights. The last barge replaces the single stern light with 2 athwartship white lights separated at least 5 feet horizontally.

Garbage barges and scows traversing the Hudson and the East River (New York) on their way to the high-seas dumping grounds carry special lights (for heaven knows what reason). These odoriferous carriers show regulation colored side lights and a regulation white stern light.

Day Recognition Shapes

The function that lights perform by their placement and color in identifying vessels at night is taken over by easily recognizable shapes in the daytime. The shapes in use are: balls, diamonds, cones, frustrums of cones, and baskets. These may be rigged singly or in combination depending upon the vessel and her situation. The shapes are painted in solid colors of black, white, red, or green, or they may be striped. The general rule as to size is that the major diameter must be at least 2 feet, and the instructions on placement generally state "in the forepart of the vessel where it can best be seen" from sunrise to sunset.

One diamond. A vessel being towed, when the length of its tow exceeds 600 feet, must display one black diamond shape. This is called for by the International Rules.

Single ball. A ship of any length, at anchor in international waters, hoists a black ball. Vessels anchored in the Great Lakes or in western rivers also hoist this day mark when anchored, if they are more than 65 feet in length. Under Inland Rules a black ball is shown by an auxiliary when she is under sail alone and not using her power.

Two balls. A vessel (or a seaplane down on the water) displays two black balls under International Rules when it is not under command, meaning when it is temporarily unable to maneuver. Under the Inland Rules and also under the Western Rivers Rules this same day mark signifies a dredge working the bottom. When the balls are red, the dredge is moored. When the balls are painted in orange-and-white vertical stripes, the vessel carrying them is a Coast Guard boat at work servicing aids to navigation. If the upper ball has black and white vertical stripes while the lower ball is red, the ship is a cable-layer.

Three balls. The arrangement of a hoist of three balls can be either one over the other in a vertical line or it can be in the shape of a triangle with the base horizontal. The vertical arrangement of black balls denotes a vessel aground under the International Rules. The same hoist is used on the Great Lakes for a grounded craft if she is over 65 feet long. The triangular pattern, also with black balls, signifies a minesweeper under International Rules.

Two cones. Two black cones hung vertically point-to-point is the recognition shape for a fishing vessel under the International Rules. She adds an additional single black cone to show the direction in which her nets are spread.

One cone. The International Rules require an auxiliary

that is using both sail and power simultaneously to hoist a black cone, hung with the point down.

Ball, diamond, ball. This combination of shapes is hung vertically, with the diamond between the upper and lower ball. On inland waters, when the balls are green and the diamond is white, the vessel showing the hoist is a Coast and Geodetic surveyor. Red balls with the white central diamond signify a cable-layer. Under International Rules this hoist, with black balls, marks a vessel engaged in launching or replenishing operations.

Cone frustrums. A cone frustrum is a cone with its tip cut off. A double frustrum consists of two of these mounted together, base-to-base. Care must be exercised in viewing these because from certain angles they can be mistaken for a diamond.

Two cone frustrums, hung one above the other with the top one striped horizontally in black and white and the bottom one red, marks a vessel towing a submerged object on all inland waters. When both frustrums are red, the vessel is a derrick working over a wreck.

Barrel. Except in international waters and in New York harbor, barrels are used to mark the anchors for a floating plant, for instance, a construction operation.

Basket. A basket in the rigging is the time-honored mark of a fishing vessel engaged in her trade on inland waters.

Red flag. On all inland waters, vessels handling dangerous cargoes such as explosives or highly flammable chemicals fly a red flag.

A full plate of all the day marks used to distinguish the various classes of vessels and services is shown in Figure 16-6. This, together with the foregoing itemization, should help skippers recognize what they are approaching or passing.

Whistle-synchronized lights. All the rules now permit a light to be carried at the masthead that is synchronized with the whistle. This light goes on when the whistle is blown, stays on for the duration of the sound, and goes out when the whistle stops. This device is a boon in crowded waters because it enables an approaching skipper to know for certain which vessel is signaling him. (In the days of steam, the white plume from the whistle performed this task automatically.)

Under the International and the Inland Rules the synchronized light is white. The Western Rivers and Great Lakes Rules order the light to be amber!

Sound Signals—Restricted Visibility

The International Rules, the Inland Rules, the Great Lakes Rules, and the Western Rivers Rules all recognize and define "restricted visibility" and prescribe signals that are different from those used in clear weather. (The Great Lakes Rules add fog signals to regular passing signals for inclement weather.) The aforementioned rules enumerate "fog, mist, falling snow, heavy rainstorms, or any other condition similarly restricting visibility, whether by day or night."

The sound-producing devices are whistles, foghorns, or bells. The legal requirements that these sound units must meet in order to be acceptable are detailed in Chapter 25 and are classified by boat size.

The distinction between the Great Lakes and all the other jurisdictions is that passing signals are given on the Great Lakes in *all* weather; in the other waters, restricted visibility calls for special fog signals, different from those used when vessels are in sight of each other.

The revised International Rules take cognizance for the first time of the increasing use of radar as a "visual" aid during periods of low visibility. Rule 16(c) mandates stopped engines and extreme caution when an approaching vessel is detected forward of the beam before it is heard or seen. An annex to the revision urges extreme care in the interpretation and use of radar information and cautions against making dangerous assumptions from scanty radar data.

The International Rules, the Inland Rules, the Great Lakes Rules, and the Western Rivers Rules all direct that the restricted visibility signals be given on the whistle by power-driven vessels and on the foghorn by sailing vessels. The rules consider a "prolonged" blast to have a duration of from four to six seconds, while a "short" blast lasts about one second.

BLASTS.

One prolonged blast. A prolonged blast repeated at intervals of not more than two minutes denotes, under the International Rules, a power-driven vessel underway. The Inland Rules reduce the interval to not more than one minute for the same power-driven vessel. When the prolonged blast is heard every minute on the *foghorn*, it signifies a sailboat on the starboard tack in all waters.

Two prolonged blasts. Two prolonged blasts with a one-

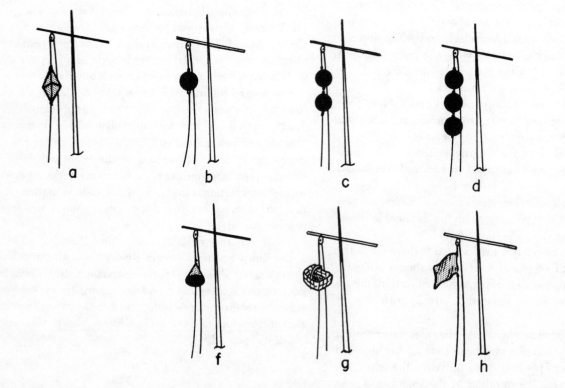

Figure 16-6: The various rules require certain vessels to announce their status during daylight hours by the display of easily recognized geometrical shapes. Some of these are shown above. (a) vessel on a long tow; (b) vessel at anchor; (c) vessel not under command; (d) vessel aground; (e) fishing vessel; (f) vessel making headway under both sail and power; (g) fishing vessel; (h) vessel carrying dangerous cargo.

second interval between them and repeated at least every two minutes are reserved under International Rules for vessels technically underway but not moving through the water. When the two blasts are sounded on the *foghorn* and repeated every minute, they indicate a sailing vessel on the port tack in all waters.

Three blasts. The triple-blast group conveys identification not only because of the number of blasts but also by the relative duration of the individual sounds. Thus, short and long blasts are sounded together in a definite code.

Three successive, equal-length blasts sounded on the foghorn denote a sailing craft running before the wind; this is true in all jurisdictions.

A vessel lying at anchor may (in addition to her prescribed bell signals) sound one short, one long, and one short blast in order more effectively to warn other ships approaching in the vicinity.

On the Great Lakes, a power-driven vessel underway sounds three "distinct" blasts on her whistle at intervals of not more than one minute. On western rivers, this identical series of blasts is the mark of a power-driven vessel towing another craft. Under International and Inland Rules this same vessel and its tow would sound one prolonged blast followed by two short blasts! This "long-two short" signal also indicates a fishing craft in these waters.

A power-driven vessel proceeding without a tow on western rivers sounds three blasts, the first two short, the last one prolonged.

Four blasts. Here, too, identification is made in part by the relative length and sequence of the four blasts.

A vessel at anchor or aground in the Great Lakes sounds (in addition to the bell signals itemized below) four blasts at least once every three minutes. The grouping is one short, two long, and one short.

A pilot boat on duty in international waters identifies herself with four short blasts. This is in addition to her regular fog signal.

A towed vessel, or the last vessel in a group of tows, is required under International Rules to sound four blasts at intervals of not more than one minute. The code here is one prolonged blast followed by three short blasts. Preferably this signal is given directly after the tug has given her signal.

BELLS.

A vessel at anchor is to ring a bell rapidly for about five seconds and this is repeated every minute during the period of fog. This is stipulated under International, Inland, and Western Rivers Rules. Exceptions are made for boats under 65 feet in length anchored in designated anchorages in western rivers; barges, scows, and canal boats are also excused. A boat under 65 feet long anchored in an anchorage under inland jurisdiction need not observe the bell-ringing rule.

On western rivers, a boat temporarily moored to the bank during thick weather indicates her position to approaching vessels with her bell. If she is on the right bank, the bell is tapped once; if on the left bank, twice. (Right and left are determined facing downstream with the current.)

A vessel in tow on the Great Lakes sounds four bells at intervals of not more than one minute. The striking is done in groups of two, much like the ding-ding, ding-ding of four bells on a ship's clock.

A ship aground in international waters rings the bell rapidly for about five seconds but precedes and follows this with three separate and distinct single strokes.

All nondescript craft underway or anchored during periods of impaired visibility are required to announce their presence by making some appropriately loud sound signal. Generally these signals must be made at intervals not to exceed one minute.

Sound Signals—Clear Visibility

When vessels are in sight of each other in clear weather, the signals sounded on the whistle pertain solely to the course each ship must steer and the action she must take. Here again, the criterion is whether risk of collision exists; ships that would keep clear of each other by continuing their previous course and speed do not exchange signals. (The only case that might be considered an exception is the ship that reverses her engines in sight of another and announces that fact by three blasts of her whistle.)

The International Rules combine a whistle signal together with a change of course; one is never given without the other. Under all other jurisdictions, the whistle signal indicates a compliance with the pilot rules and may or may not be accompanied by a course change.

The signals used are all short, distinct blasts of the whistle. Their significance depends on the number of blasts. There are no groups of long and short sounds such as are used in periods of restricted visibility.

BLASTS.

One blast. Under International Rules, one blast means "I am changing my course to starboard." Under the Inland, Great Lakes, and Western Rivers Rules a single blast means that vessels approaching each other bow to bow on directly opposite courses will pass port side to port side. When a vessel is overtaking another ahead of her and signals one blast, it means that she will pass on the overtaken boat's starboard side.

A boat leaving its pier or berth or emerging from its basin in an area where other slips are likely to pass is required to give a prolonged blast on her whistle as a warning, except on western rivers. (Once she is clear, the emerging vessel has no further rights and reverts to the applicable rules of the road and the accompanying signals.) A prolonged blast is also sounded when approaching a "blind" bend in a channel.

Two blasts. The International Rules direct that two short blasts on the whistle mean "I am changing my course to port." Two blasts under Inland, Great Lakes, and Western Rivers Rules indicate that two ships approaching each other bow to bow on directly opposite courses will pass starboard side to starboard side. When an overtaking boat blows two blasts, she is telling the craft ahead that she will pass on the overtaken boat's port side.

Three blasts. The International and the Inland Rules both recognize three short blasts on the whistle as an announcement by a vessel underway that her engines are running astern. This signal is tacitly understood to have the same meaning on the Great Lakes although not officially so recognized. On western rivers it is blown by a boat nearing a "blind" bend or leaving her berth.

Four (or more) blasts. This is a universally accepted danger signal. (It is five or more on international waters.) This signal is used when passing or crossing signals either are not understood or are considered unsafe by the recipient. A boat that is being overtaken and considers passing at that time unsafe gives this signal to the craft behind her. The overtaking boat must abandon her passing intention when she receives this signal; she must wait for a permissive signal of one or two blasts from the forward boat.

CROSS SIGNALS PROHIBITED.

It is forbidden under all rules to give a cross signal. By

"cross" is meant the answering of one blast with two blasts or of two blasts with one blast. Answer must always be given with the identical, acquiescent signal—or with the danger signal if to acquiesce is deemed dangerous. In the latter case engines on both craft are stopped and way is not resumed until signaling is understood.

It should be remembered that the International Rules have provision for only four underway whistle signals for *clear* weather: one blast, two blasts, three blasts, and five or more short blasts. As already noted, the first two indicate changes in course, the third announces an engine reversal, and the last sounds danger.

Steering Rules

The steering rules are tailored to meet the three situations in which a vessel underway can become involved with another craft: passing, crossing, or overtaking. In all of these, her proximity is assumed to be such that danger of collision exists. It is also assumed that the power-driven boat will give full right-of-way to any sailboat involved. That is the law. (The sailboat must be propelled by sail alone and must not be attempting to overtake the power-boat.)

PASSING.

A passing situation is deemed to exist when two vessels are approaching each other bow to bow on opposite courses which fall nearly on the same straight line. By day, a line through the bow and mast of one boat would very nearly pass through the bow and mast of the other. By night, each would see both the green and the red side lights of the other directly ahead. (It is *not* a passing situation if only one side light can be seen or if the two side lights can be seen elsewhere than directly ahead.)

Under International Rules, when two boats are in a passing situation each must alter its course to starboard so that the vessels can pass port side to port side. As already explained, this alteration of course requires a whistle signal of one blast. If it is safer to pass starboard side to starboard side, this can be indicated by two blasts and then carried out. If the bow-on courses of both boats are such that they would pass clear of each other without course change, then no action is required and no signals are given.

The Inland Rules achieve a similar result by slightly different means and make signals mandatory. Where the

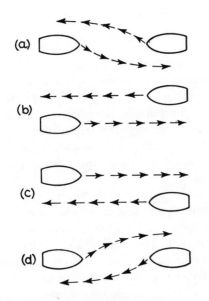

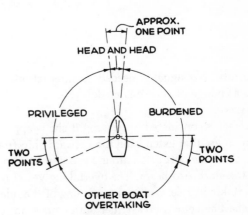

Figure 16-8: Your boat is the one at the center. A ship approaching in the segment marked burdened makes you the burdened boat. You are privileged if the approach is from the segment marked privileged. A vessel coming up from the overtaking segment is overtaking you. Head-on approach is from the narrow section at the top.

Figure 16-7: The situation at (a) requires one blast of the whistle under all rules. No signal is needed at (b) under International Rules, but Inland, Lake and Western Rules specify one blast. (c) calls for no signal under International, but two blasts under the other rules. All rules specify two blasts for (d).

boats are approaching each other bow-on, each is to alter course to starboard and pass port side to port side; this intention is announced by either craft with one blast which the other craft must answer with one blast. If the courses of the two boats lie to starboard of each other then the signal to be given and answered is two blasts and the passing is to be starboard side to starboard side.

The Great Lakes Rules state that vessels meeting bow-on shall pass port side to port side. If a course change is required to accomplish this, it must be announced with a proper whistle blast.

The Western Rivers Rule is almost identical with the Great Lakes, except for a special provision when boats are ascending or descending river currents. Under these circumstances, the descending ship is given both right of way and the choice of the better passing side. (In this instance the ascending ship gives the first signal but the descending ship may either accept it by repeating the signal or reject it by sounding the danger signal.) "Ascending" means going against the current.

The passing confrontations so far described are visualized in Figure 16-7. At (a) the ships are directly in line and give way to starboard in order to pass port side to port side; the signal under all rules is one blast. At (b) the ships

are to port of each other and can pass clear port side to port side without change of course; one blast is given under the Inland, Western Rivers, and Great Lakes Rules but no whistle signal is called for under International Rules. At (c) the courses of the meeting vessels lie to starboard of each other and they can pass clear starboard to starboard without changing course; no signal is called for under international rules but two blasts are mandated under all other rules. At (d) the vessels are meeting so that starboard side to starboard side passing is preferable; the signal is two blasts under all rules.

CROSSING.

A crossing situation is considered to exist when a ship has another vessel approaching on either side within an angle from one-half point off the bow to two points abaft the beam. The boat which has the other on her starboard side is the burdened boat; the boat which has the other on her port side is the privileged boat. It is the duty of the burdened boat to keep clear by whatever means, just as it is the duty of the privileged boat to hold her course and speed. A diagram of the crossing pattern is given in Figure 16-8.

The burdened vessel should cross *astern* of the privileged one; she is expected to stop, reverse, or take any other action to avoid crossing ahead.

All the rules except the International require one whistle blast from the privileged vessel verifying that she will hold her course and speed and one blast from the burdened craft acknowledging that she will keep clear and pass astern. No signal is needed on international waters unless a change of course is made.

OVERTAKING.

A vessel is considered overtaking if she is approaching within an arc that extends on the forward ship from two points abaft the port beam around the stern to two points abaft the starboard beam. The overtaking vessel remains an overtaking vessel within the meaning of the rules even after she has come abreast; her status does not change until after she has forged ahead and is completely clear. The area considered overtaking is pictured in the diagram of Figure 16-8.

A simple method by which a skipper can determine at night whether or not he is an overtaking vessel is to look for the colored side lights of the craft ahead. If he cannot see them, he is overtaking. (The International Rules admonish the skipper who is in doubt to consider himself as overtaking.)

In all jurisdictions except the international, the overtaking craft in effect requests permission to overtake. If she wishes to overtake on the forward vessel's starboard side, she blows one blast; if on the port side, two blasts. The forward vessel replies in kind if she believes the passing can be made safely; she sounds the danger signal if she does not believe so.

The danger signal mandates the rearward vessel to stay behind until the forward boat blows either one or two blasts as acquiescence for passing on the starboard or port side.

The International Rules do not go into these details of overtaking method. They simply require the overtaking vessel to "keep out of the way."

NARROW CHANNELS.

The original rules of the road considered all vessels large or small as equal in their rights and obligations. A basic early interpretation gave any sailboat the right of way over the largest steamboat and permitted a small motorboat to assert its privilege over an ocean liner—however foolhardy such action might have been. The latest amendments have taken more cognizance of the comparative maneuverabilities of the craft involved and have imposed restrictions.

Now a sailboat may *not* hamper the safe passage through a channel of a power-driven craft that can only maneuver within that channel. Nor can a sailboat hamper the safe passage of a large steam vessel that is ascending

or descending a river.

The amendments also recognize that a powerboat less than 65 feet long is more maneuverable than a much larger ship. Accordingly, the smaller powerboat may not hamper the safe passage of a large vessel passing through a channel or ascending or descending a river even though its privileged status under the rules might technically permit this.

All vessels must now keep to their starboard or right side of channels and fairways "when it is safe and practicable to do so." By implication, deviation from this rule would be permitted only when safety demands it.

The Western Rivers Rules are more stringent when two power-driven vessels are about to enter a narrow channel at the same time from opposite directions. In such cases, the ascending vessel must stop before the channel and wait until the descending boat has passed through. ("Ascending" means going against the current.) If they should both find themselves unavoidably together in the channel, the ascending craft must lie to at the bank and wait.

HELM ORDERS.

The lusty "Port your helm" so often heard in the romantic tales of the roaring deep is gone forever. All the new rules have banished it and substituted simple orders that cannot be misunderstood.

The only legally correct orders to the helmsman are now either "Right rudder" or "Left rudder." Right rudder means "direct the boat's bow to starboard." Left rudder means "direct the boat's bow to port."

The port-and-starboard-your-helms were doubly confusing because actually they did not refer to the direction the boat itself was going to turn, but rather to the movement of the tiller. On the sailboats where these helm orders originated, the direction of the tiller movement was opposite to that of the boat.

DISTRESS SIGNALS.

A skipper in distress notifies other boats and the shore that he needs assistance by standardized procedures understood by his fellow boatmen. All the rules specify these distress signals, some in greater detail than the others.

The Inland Rules are the least elaborate on this point. For daytime use they specify a continuous sounding of the foghorn or a repeated firing of a gun. These same signals may be used at night with the addition of flames in a tar barrel, oil barrel, or any other similar device at hand.

The Great Lakes Rules list as daytime distress signals the repeated firing of a gun, the hoisting of a square flag with a ball above or below it, the continuous sounding of the foghorn, or a person on deck slowly and repeatedly raising and lowering his arms outstretched at his sides. At night the gun may again be used, or flames in a barrel, or rockets may be fired into the sky, or the foghorn may be sounded continuously.

The Western Rivers Rules also recommend the continuous firing of a gun for daytime distress notification. In addition they specify the hoisting of the international code flags for N and C, a square flag hoisted with a ball above or below it, rockets fired into the sky, continuous sounding of any whistle or horn, or the raising and lowering of the arms outstretched to the side. At night, the gun, rocket, and continuous whistle are approved with the addition of the flaming barrel.

The International Rules contain the most complete list of means for attracting attention when in distress. Any of these may be used by day or by night, whichever the situation permits and the skipper thinks most effective. They may be used singly or in combination; the main purpose is to get help surely and fast.

The international list is as follows: a gun or explosive repeatedly fired, continuous sounding of the foghorn, rockets or shells fired into the sky, the SOS signal made by radio or any other signaling method, the spoken word "Mayday" on the radiotelephone, hoisting the two international code flags for the letters N and C, a square flag with a ball hoisted above or below it, a barrel of flames, red flares, an orange-colored smoke signal, and repeated raising and lowering of the arms outstretched to the side.

All these involved instructions on what to do when help is needed look very imposing in the rule books. But let's be practical! The small boat skipper has no tar barrel on board to kindle into a smoky fire. He does not normally carry a gun to fire at intervals, neither does his signaling equipment sport the code flags for N and for C.

The long and short of it is: When you are in true distress use any and all sensible methods to attract rescuers quickly. Of course orderly means within the capability of your boat are more effective than panic.

It should not be necessary to add that the giving of any distress signal when no distress exists is prohibited and punishable. This prohibition extends also to signals that might be confused with distress signals.

Regattas and Marine Parades

A permit from the District Commander of the Coast Guard is required for the holding of any marine show or marine sporting events on federally controlled waters. A permit may be required from local authorities for events on waters that are wholly within the jurisdiction of a state.

The authority of the Coast Guard derives from its duty to safeguard life and property at sea. The safety of the spectators, the participants, and the passers-by may be jeopardized by these sporting events in the absence of control because of the consequent heavier traffic in the area.

The permit granted by the Coast Guard may be for a single event or for a series of events. The latter might be in the case of a club that holds regular regattas in a fixed location throughout the boating season. (A permit cannot be issued for longer than one year.)

The application for a permit must be made to the local District Commander not less than thirty days prior to the event. Complete data must be submitted with the application, such as its nature, the number of participants, the expected number of spectators, the means provided for patrolling the event, and so forth. A section of local chart must accompany the application; on it must be clearly marked the area which the proposed event will occupy.

In some areas the Coast Guard has made arrangements with the state to police and regulate marine events. In such cases the state will make the final determination.

The holding without a permit of any marine event that requires a permit is prohibited and severely punishable. Licensed officers who transgress are subject to revocation of license. Others found guilty may be fined as much as $500.

"Rules" Aboard?

The Coast Guard rules require all boats over 65 feet long "when practicable" to keep on board copies of those "rules of the road" that apply to the waters they normally travel. Motorboats are specifically exempted from this requirement.

Despite this legal exception, the wise and cautious skipper should keep a pertinent copy of the rules on board, either CG#169 or CG#172 or CG#184, whichever applies. These little books can easily be kept safe by enclosing them in the small waterproof plastic enclosures now used for wrapping many grocery products.

Having a rule book handy makes a wonderful ready reference for checking on the many situations observed during cruising. Of course this means studying the rules during off-times; it certainly does not suggest a hurried look at the rules during the middle of a collision approach.

Coast Guard and Naval Exemptions

Many government boats, especially those in the service of the Navy and the Coast Guard, have superstructures so constructed that legal lighting is not possible. All the rules absolve these vessels of carrying the lights normal for craft of their size.

This may be of some direct interest to skippers of small boats who cruise in waters frequented by these

naval ships, and for them the rule books list the exempt vessels by name and number.

Submarines

Any skipper who has ever had a submarine pop up near his boat has a healthy respect for these monsters. Like icebergs, they show little above the surface; most of the "works" is either not visible or just awash, and the overall length is disturbingly surprising.

To ameliorate this situation, the Secretary of the Navy has authorized submarines to carry a distinctive light for recognition. This is an amber-colored rotating light. It is to be located about six feet above the masthead light, produce ninety flashes per minute, and be visible for three miles.

17 *Piloting and Navigation*

P

ILOTING and navigation serve a common purpose: to determine where you are and to show how to get from there to wherever you're going. A differentiation between the two terms might be that piloting is based upon the use of guides fixed to the land that can be seen and used directly or with electronic aid. By contrast, the celestial bodies used as guides in navigation give little or no position information until after they have been processed by mathematical computations.

A further broad division could be that piloting is the means by which a ship's course is directed when it is within sight of land, while navigation is needed when land is far over the horizon and invisible. The attempt to make a clear division invariably becomes semantic, however, because under some practical conditions the two methods meld into one.

Few sail- or powerboat skippers will ever find themselves, like Coleridge's Ancient Mariner, "alone, all alone, alone on a trackless sea." Piloting therefore assumes the greater importance for the owner of a pleasure boat. It is a skill he will need constantly unless his boating is confined to a small circular lake whose shores are like the walls of a swimming pool, devoid of shoals and dangers.

A cursory look at any chart might show that the start and destination of a cruise are connectable by a straight, overwater line. This could lead to the snap conclusion that the equivalent course could be steered in an equally direct manner. But closer inspection might show that such a simple approach would end only in disaster because of intervening shoals or other dangers. Thus the skipper follows what landlubbers would consider a zigzag path and puts to use the skill of piloting.

Since piloting depends upon visual objects (and visual in this sense includes "seeing" by radio and radar), it is a logical first step to become familiar with the various markers seen along the waters. These are the equivalent of the motorist's highway signs, although far less explicit; you will never come upon a buoy with a sign and arrow stating that it is only seven miles to Pookietown. Nor will you find a white line along the middle of a channel to separate the up and down traffic.

In some respects the marine "sign system" is more advanced than that along the highways. Only recently have road-sign shapes become standardized (for instance, the octagon of the stop marker), whereas the shapes of buoys have had a distinctive meaning from the beginning. Colors

also have a message for the mariner, and their use, whether in solids or in stripes, imparts further specific information.

The markers which guide the sailor consist of many things besides the familiar buoys. A glance at any chart (or an extended trip over any water) will show lighthouses, radio stations, day beacons, and, at the entrances to important tributaries, even lightships and "Texas" towers. All these are known by the collective, self-explanatory name, aids to navigation.

Aids to Navigation

The United States Coast Guard is entrusted with the management of all aids to navigation on the navigable waters of the United States. "Navigable" (as defined in greater detail in Chapter 25) includes all waters tributary to the sea as well as those bordering on two or more states or giving access to a foreign country.

The Coast Guard maintains and mans the aids, removes those that are no longer necessary, and provides new ones when safety so dictates. The regulations require that "any aid to navigation maintained and operated by the Coast Guard to serve the needs of commerce must be necessary for the safety of navigation, useful to commerce, of a substantial and permanent character and must be justified in terms of public benefit to be derived therefrom." Aids not meeting these criteria must be discontinued.

The most widely and systematically dispersed aids to navigation comprise the Buoyage of the United States. This is a *lateral* system, meaning that it designates the *side* on which a passage is to be made. The buoyage method is universal and a pleasure skipper who learns his buoys in Maine is equally at home when he gets to Florida.

LATERAL BUOYAGE SYSTEM.

Three types of buoys constitute the majority in the buoyage system. These are the can, the nun, and the spar. In addition there are whistle buoys, bell buoys, gong buoys, lighted buoys, and buoys for special purposes. The colors used are red, black, white, yellow, and green— sometimes in combination and always with uniform significance.

The can buoy is, like a can, cylindrical with a flat top. The nun buoy has the shape of a cone cut off slightly

Buoys and Beacons

No.	Symbol	Description		No.	Symbol	Description
1	•	Position of buoy		17	RB ⬥RB	Bifurcation buoy (RBHB)
2		Light buoy		18	RB ⬥RB	Junction buoy (RBHB)
3	BELL	Bell buoy		19	RB ⬥RB	Isolated danger buoy (RBHB)
3a	GONG	Gong buoy		20	RB ⬥G	Wreck buoy (RBHB or G)
4	WHIS	Whistle buoy		20a	RB ⬥G	Obstruction buoy (RBHB or G)
5	C	Can or Cylindrical buoy		21	Tel	Telegraph-cable buoy
6	N	Nun or Conical buoy		22		Mooring buoy (colors of mooring buoys never carried)
7	SP	Spherical buoy		22a		Mooring
8	S	Spar buoy		22b	Tel	Mooring buoy with telegraphic communications
†8a	P	Pillar or Spindle buoy		22c	T	Mooring buoy with telephonic communications
9		Buoy with topmark (ball) (see L-70)		23		Warping buoy
10		Barrel or Ton buoy		24	Y	Quarantine buoy
(La)		Color unknown		†24a		Practice area buoy
(Lb)	FLOAT	Float		25	Explos Anch	Explosive anchorage buoy
12	FLOAT	Lightfloat		25a	AERO	Aeronautical anchorage buoy
13		Outer or Landfall buoy		26	Deviation	Compass adjustment buoy
14	BW	Fairway buoy (BWVS)		27	BW	Fish trap (area) buoy (BWHB)
14a	BW	Mid-channel buoy (BWVS)		27a		Spoil ground buoy
†15	R "2"	Starboard-hand buoy (entering from seaward)		†28	W	Anchorage buoy (marks limits)
16	"1"	Port-hand buoy (entering from seaward)		†29	Priv maintd	Private aid to navigation (buoy) (maintained by private interests, use with caution)

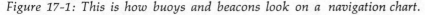

Figure 17-1: This is how buoys and beacons look on a navigation chart.

below the point (truncated); any relationship of its name to the religious order commonly so called is obscure. The spar is a long, narrow, slightly-tapered pole. All are securely anchored to the bottom with just sufficient scope to ride the tides.

All buoys, of whatever shape, are marked on charts as small diamonds. Beneath each diamond is a dot that shows the exact location of the buoy's anchor; when this dot is surrounded by rays or a magenta spot the buoy is lighted. (The latest revision replaces the diamond of a lighted buoy with an exclamation mark.) The diamond is black, red, or left blank; this indicates a black, red, or white coloring on the buoy, respectively. Each half of the diamond may be a different color and these halves may be split horizontally (to indicate horizontal stripes on the buoy) or vertically (to indicate vertical buoy striping). (See Figure 17-1.)

Daybeacons and daymarks are aids to navigation that supplement the buoys at many small harbor entrances and local channels; they are indicated on charts by small, solid triangles. The shapes of daybeacons are varied and intended to attract attention rather than to convey a standard meaning. They may consist of kegs atop poles, baskets on spars or dolphins, small latticed wooden towers, several spars lashed together as a pyramid, or even rock cairns. Some are illustrated in Figure 17-2. Daymarks atop daybeacons are colored to "lift" them out of their backgrounds, and when used as channel markers they follow the standard red and black of buoys in similar positions.

Buoys and Beacons (continued)

30			Temporary buoy (See K1,j,k,l)
30a			Winter buoy
31		HB	Horizontal stripes or bands
32		VS	Vertical stripes
33		Chec	Checkered
†*33a*		Diag	Diagonal bands
41		W	White
42		B	Black
43		R	Red
44		Y	Yellow
45		G	Green
46		Br	Brown
47		Gy	Gray
48		Bu	Blue
†*48a*		Am	Amber
†*48b*		Or	Orange
51			Floating beacon
52	△RW Bn △W Bn ▲R Bn		Fixed beacon (unlighted or daybeacon)
	▲ Bn		Black beacon
	△ Bn		Color unknown
†*(Lc)*	⊙MARKER ∘Marker		Private aid to navigation
53		Bn	Beacon, in general (See L-52)
54			Tower beacon

55		Cardinal marking system
56	△ Deviation Bn	Compass adjustment beacon
57		Topmarks (See L-9, 70)
58		Telegraph-cable (landing) beacon
†*59*	∘∘ Piles • Piles	Piles (See O-30, H-9)
	⊥ ⊥	Stakes
	∘• Stumps	Stumps (See O-30)
	⊥ ⊥	Perches
61	⊙CAIRN ∘Cairn	Cairn
62		Painted patches
63	⊙	Landmark (conspicuous object) (See D-2)
(Ld)	∘	Landmark (position approximate)
64	REF	Reflector
65	⊙MARKER	Range targets, markers
(Le)	W Or W Or	Special-purpose buoys
†*66*		Oil installation buoy
†*67*		Drilling platform (See O-0b, O-0c)
70	Note:	TOPMARKS on buoys and beacons may be shown on charts of foreign waters. The abbreviation for black is not shown adjacent to buoys or beacons.
(Lf)	Ra Ref	Radar reflector (See M-13)

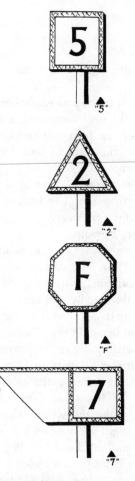

SHADED BORDERS ARE YELLOW ON THE "ICW"
(INTRACOASTAL WATERWAY)

Figure 17-2: Some day beacons are shown above together with their corresponding chart legends.

Meanings of lateral buoys. The basic rule that governs the color of buoys in the lateral buoyage system can be illustrated as follows: If you proceed from Maine to Florida along the coast, all the buoys that you must keep on your starboard or right side will be colored red and will bear even numbers. Along this stretch all the buoys that you must keep on your port or left side will be black, bearing odd numbers. This same relationship would hold true if you cruised along the Gulf Coast from Florida to Texas, and again along the Pacific Coast from California to Washington.

If you entered any harbor at any point along this circumnavigation you would remain safely in the channel as long as you kept the red buoys on your starboard and the black buoys on your port. The underlying idea is one of clockwise rotation: If you proceed clockwise around the perimeter of the country or if at any point you make a sharper clockwise turn *into* a harbor, you always have the *red* on your *right*. Obviously, if you were running up the Atlantic Coast or down the Pacific Coast (which would be counterclockwise in our concept) the situation would be reversed and the red buoys would be kept on your port side. Red would logically also be on your port side when coming *out* of a harbor *toward* the sea.

As already stated, the buoys bear numbers; these numbers run in sequence, but always with odd on the black and even on the red buoys. The numbers start at the entrance from the sea and increase into the harbor. Where the spacing of buoys is irregular, the numbers that would have been assigned to the missing positions are omitted. If a buoy is inserted into an existing series it is given the number of the preceding buoy and this is followed by a letter; the original buoys would not be renumbered. (On western rivers, lighted buoys only are numbered and these *not* sequentially.)

The buoyage for the harbors on the Great Lakes follows the now familiar pattern of red on the right and black on the left when entering from seaward; in this case, the lake is considered the "sea." On the Great Lakes themselves, travel in an approximately northerly direction, that is, from the lower ends to the upper, will find red on the starboard side and black on the port side of the ship. A look at a map of the United States will confirm that this remains within the idea of clockwise turning.

On the western rivers, of which the Mississippi is the major trunk, the overall rule still holds good if one considers them as being entered from the "sea," which in this case is the Gulf of Mexico. This is upstream and for greater clarity it is so designated in official publications. When cruising upstream, then, the red buoys are on the starboard side and the black buoys on the port side.

The standardized consistency of the lateral buoyage system fits it easily into the memory once a general mental picture has been acquired. Relying upon the reds and the blacks for guidance soon becomes second nature to the pleasure skipper. There are a few places where the geographical locations of adjacent harbors or branching waterways may make the layout of buoys appear inconsistent—but a look at the chart will reassure that it is not. The chart, of course, is always the final arbiter with an experienced skipper; it makes every buoy fall smoothly into place.

The buoys so far described mark the left and right boundaries of channels and fairways; there are also special buoys that will be found in mid-channel. These are striped or banded, again in accordance with an overriding plan; they are never numbered, but may be lettered.

The stripe colors are either black and white or black and red, and the stripes themselves run either vertically or horizontally. A memory gimmick could be that vertical stripes appear to pull you in closer while horizontal stripes appear to push you away—and this is the general idea.

The vertically-striped black-and-white buoys have no *shape* significance; this means that this coloring can be found on buoys of all shapes. These buoys are placed in exact mid-channel and, in accordance with the mnemonic trick just mentioned, should always be passed "close aboard," on either side.

The red-and-black horizontally-striped buoys are placed at channel junctions and also over wrecks or other obstructions that present a danger. They can be passed on either side but always with a generous berth. The method of coloring also tells the skipper which is the preferred side for passing.

When the top band of these red-and-black buoys is *black*, it is passed by keeping it on the port side when coming *from* seaward just as though it were a black buoy. When the top band is *red*, passing is done with the buoy kept to starboard again when the approach is from seaward (or the equivalent), just as though it were a red one. It can be seen once more that the consistency of the entire system is maintained, especially since a black top will be found on a can and a red top on a nun, although spars or other shapes can be of either pattern.

NON-LATERAL BUOYS.

Some buoys have no lateral meaning but are used to convey local, relevant information to the passing mariner. Such markers indicate anchorages, quarantine areas, fish net boundaries, dredging locations, or other special purposes. They are usually spars or cans.

The easiest to recognize, because yellow is also the color of the Q flag that requests pratique (see Chapter 25), is the yellow spar or can that marks a quarantine anchorage. Obviously it means keep out unless you have official business there.

A normal, open anchorage is marked by a plain white spar or can. The chart of the area will give the additional information regarding the extent and type of the anchorage.

A spar or can with black-and-white horizontal bands marks the limit of the area containing the fish nets of the commercial fishermen. Intrusion here generally brings its own "reward" in the form of fouled propellers and harsh words of wrath.

Dredging operations are indicated by a white spar or can with a bright-green top. The hazard is usually an immense steam dredge very noisy by day, very brightly lit by night, and very obvious.

The special purpose spars and cans are banded in orange and white. They take care of any urgency not covered in the list of usual marine hazards. Specific information is obtainable locally and sometimes also from the *Notice to Mariners* issued weekly by the Coast Guard.

Most of the lateral buoys in the Mississippi River system (except those horizontally striped) carry a white top. This does not signify any departure from the standard color coding described because the white top is not considered part of the "message." The meaning of the color is read by ignoring the white, which was added simply as an aid to night spotting with a searchlight.

In all waters an unlighted aid to navigation may be given special emphasis by the addition of a ball, a cage, or some other object to its top. The addition is intended to jog the skipper into extra attention and caution because of an imminent turn in the fairway or some similar need for careful maneuvering.

INTRACOASTAL AIDS.

The penchant that many small boat skippers have for migration, that inner compulsion which urges them to accompany the ducks southward, has led to the establishment of the Intracoastal Waterway, known as the ICW and even more familiarly as "the ditch." This is a protected, inside route that parallels the Atlantic and Gulf coasts and allows most of the run to be made without exposure to open ocean water.

The ICW has its own markings for buoys and aids to navigation, but these also dovetail neatly into the buoyage system of the rest of the country. As everywhere else, if you are going south you keep the red on the starboard side and the black on the port side. At some points the ICW route becomes identical with some local buoyage; confusion is cleverly avoided by combined markings.

Yellow is the distinguishing color chosen for ICW

identification. Every aid to navigation on the Intracoastal Waterway has a yellow band or a yellow border. Every buoy in a standard system that does double duty for the ICW (where the two routes coincide) carries a yellow triangle or a yellow square superimposed on its regular marking. (It may be only a coincidence that one of the airlines calls its southern flights the yellowbirds.)

The cans and nuns of an established buoyage that also serve as part of the ICW retain their standard local markings. Their ICW function is carried out by the addition of either a yellow triangle or a yellow square. When the triangle is added, that aid is to be considered a *nun* by the skipper *following the intracoastal*, regardless of its shape. When the additional marking is a square, the aid bearing it is considered a *can* for *ICW purposes only*. (The skipper following the local route disregards the yellow triangles and squares.) Since the triangle looks a little like the profile of a nun and the square resembles that of a can, the superimposed markings should be easy to remember.

SOUND BUOYS.

Buoys stand out so clearly in good weather that it is hard to realize how their visibility can shrink to zero when the conditions are bad. A skipper clawing through a pea-souper can be within a few feet of a desired buoy and never see it. Sound buoys alleviate this difficulty by transfering the search from the eye to the ear.

Sound buoys make use of a single bell, a set of multi-toned bells called a gong, a whistle, or a horn. The bell buoy is the simplest of all; it has a loose clapper that strikes the bell through the action of wind and wave. The gong action is the same except that there are four clappers and four vari-tuned bells; this is the eerie tolling for the souls in Davy Jones' locker that makes even old salts pine for hearth and home.

The older whistle and horn buoys developed the necessary air pressure as a result of their lifting and falling in the swells. Since the energy of the waves is always there to be tapped, these required no attention. But there are also periods of dead calm when no pumping takes place and tanks go empty. The more modern whistles and horns derive their tooting power from tanks of gas. These are more reliable and more regular in their soundings but of course the tanks require periodic replenishment.

The sounding buoys are identified on the chart by the usual diamond symbol but with the addition of a legend describing the type of sound. Their color conforms to the standard system of buoy marking. Their shape has no significance and is purely utilitarian.

Ranges

In many channels a skipper can remain safely in the fairway by steering his boat so that two markers or charted structures on shore remain in line, one above or behind the other. These markers delineate fixed courses known as ranges; they are found often along the Intracoastal Waterway and on western rivers, occasionally on eastern rivers.

When two especially placed markers or targets (not landmarks) determine the course line, it is known as an artificial range. An artificial range appears on the chart, whereas a natural range is selected by the skipper from landmarks in line with his own desired course.

One of the most important cautions about using a range is to know just how far to follow it. Such information is taken from the area chart; the skipper who lacks this knowledge may find that his actual, though undesired, destination is the beach.

Range marks for artificial ranges are round, oval, rectangular, or diamond in shape and colored black or red or striped as the buoyage system warrants. Often the round is the rearward mark, like a target. Many ranges, especially in heavily traveled areas, are lighted. Ranges on the ICW carry the yellow border in keeping with the plan already described.

Lighted Buoys

Since buoys are intended to guide the night-cruising mariner as well as the skipper who runs only by day, it is natural that many buoys should be lighted. The color of a light is allocated under a uniform system so that it, too, imparts some information. The colors used are red, green, and white.

A red light is found only on red buoys or on those red-and-black buoys whose top color band is red. A green light is found only on black buoys or on those black-and-red buoys whose topmost band is black. The white light is merely a visual aid and in itself carries no significance; the meaning is conveyed by the nature and color of the buoy on which it is placed.

LIGHT CHARACTERISTICS.

The light on a buoy can be a continuous, steady beam, which in nautical terms is "fixed." The light could be "flashing," which means that its percentage of time off is greater than its percentage of time on. It could be "occulting," which signifies that its percentage of time on is greater than its percentage of time off.

It is evident that lights which flash and occult on and off could be arranged into a recognizable code by varying the combination of the on and off periods. This is done. On all charts, next to each light symbol, there is a legend that describes the pattern of the light so that the skipper may identify it. For instance, "R "8" Fl R 3 sec" affixed to the dot-and-diamond symbol is decoded to mean "red buoy, #8, flashing red light, 3-second cycle." When no color abbreviation is given for the buoy, it is assumed to be black; lack of color code for the light assumes it to be white.

Whether a light is fixed or flashing also imparts information needed for cautious nighttime piloting. When the light is fixed, it tells the skipper that the buoy bearing it is *not* marking an obstruction or a junction or a channel fairway; it could be any other type of buoy. A light flashing at the standard rate of 30 flashes per minute will be found on nuns, cans, and special purpose buoys. When this flashing rate is doubled to 60 per minute (quick flashing or Qk Fl), it indicates special caution, perhaps an obstruction that must be passed only on the one side indicated by the color of the buoy. When such obstructions can be passed on *both* sides the light is "interrupted quick flashing" (I Qk Fl) and the buoy would have horizontal bands. (For "I Qk Fl" the quick flashing is interrupted every four seconds for four seconds of darkness.) A white short-long flashing light (S-L Fl) identifies a buoy with vertical black-and-white stripes which is passed close-to, as already explained. The chart in Figure 17-3 shows light phase characteristics.

The international Morse telegraph code lists the letter *A* as consisting of a dot and a dash, short followed by long. It is thus completely explanatory to characterize a light which repeats a cycle of a short flash followed by a long flash as "Morse A."

The Coast Guard is embarking on a long-range program to standardize the characteristics of all lighted minor aids to navigation including buoys. (Primary sea- and lake-coast lights will not be affected.) The purpose is two-fold: to provide a uniform, easily identifiable light code that will enable the mariner to distinguish one aid from another by simple clocking of the flash; to enable the Coast Guard to reduce the inventory of differing mechanisms and increase the time between service requirements.

Instead of the present large number of varied single-flashing light timings there will be only three: 2 1/2 seconds, 4 seconds, and 6 seconds. There will be only one flash in each time cycle. For instance, "Fl 2.5s" will signify that in a period of 2 1/2 seconds there will be one light flash. (This one timing alone will eliminate 9 present categories that have cycles from 2 to 3 seconds.)

Buoy Caution

Under ideal conditions, a floating aid to navigation is where the chart shows it to be. But conditions are not always ideal; weather and collisions with ships can move or sink buoys and spars. Calm seas can mute the sounding buoys. Mechanical failure can extinguish lights or change them. A buoy may remain where it was placed while the wreck or shoal it marks may have shifted.

All this leads to a warning that the cautious skipper observes: *Don't* consider floating aids to navigation as infallible. Their value is indisputable but they must always be used with caution and common sense—especially after heavy storms. The aids to navigation that never move are those on shore and these should be the mainstay of piloting.

Lighthouses

Lighthouses have been in use since ancient times by nations bordering on the seas. They act as a warning of hazards in the immediate area and form a target toward which to steer or to avoid. There have even been "bootleg lighthouses" erected by pirates to lure ships onto reefs where they could be pillaged.

Lighthouses are identified in daylight and correlated with the chart both by their shape and by their colors, and by night by the color and phase of their beams; all these data are given in the *Light List*. (The *Light List* is comprised of five volumes at $4 each, obtainable from most chart vendors.) Lightships are considered as

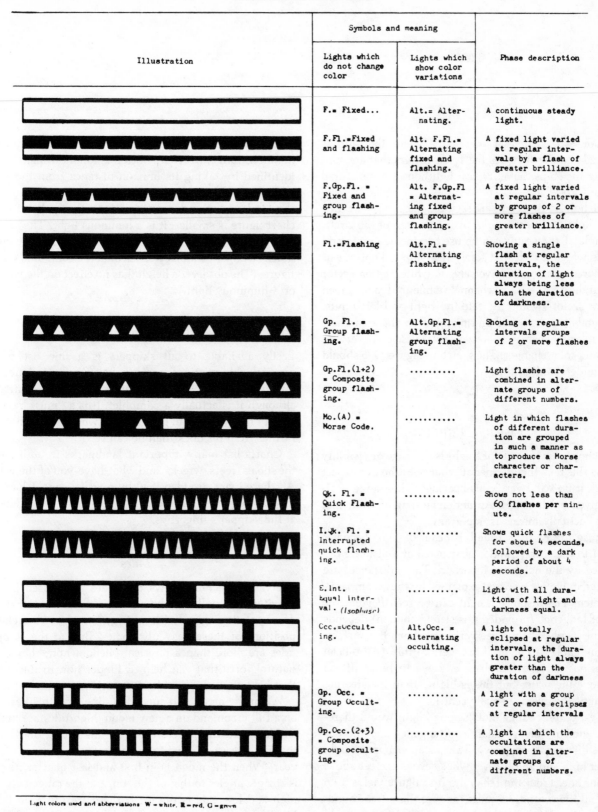

Illustration	Symbols and meaning		Phase description
	Lights which do not change color	Lights which show color variations	
	F.= Fixed...	Alt.= Alternating.	A continuous steady light.
	F.Fl.=Fixed and flashing	Alt. F.Fl.= Alternating fixed and flashing.	A fixed light varied at regular intervals by a flash of greater brilliance.
	F.Gp.Fl. = Fixed and group flashing.	Alt. F.Gp.Fl = Alternating fixed and group flashing.	A fixed light varied at regular intervals by groups of 2 or more flashes of greater brilliance.
	Fl.=Flashing	Alt.Fl.= Alternating flashing.	Showing a single flash at regular intervals, the duration of light always being less than the duration of darkness.
	Gp. Fl. = Group flashing.	Alt.Gp.Fl.= Alternating group flashing.	Showing at regular intervals groups of 2 or more flashes
	Gp.Fl.(1+2) = Composite group flashing.	....	Light flashes are combined in alternate groups of different numbers.
	Mo.(A) = Morse Code.	....	Light in which flashes of different duration are grouped in such a manner as to produce a Morse character or characters.
	Qk. Fl. = Quick Flashing.	....	Shows not less than 60 flashes per minute.
	I.Qk. Fl. = Interrupted quick flashing.	....	Shows quick flashes for about 4 seconds, followed by a dark period of about 4 seconds.
	E.Int. Equal interval. (Isophase)	....	Light with all durations of light and darkness equal.
	Occ.=Occulting.	Alt.Occ. = Alternating occulting.	A light totally eclipsed at regular intervals, the duration of light always greater than the duration of darkness
	Gp. Occ. = Group Occulting.	....	A light with a group of 2 or more eclipses at regular intervals
	Gp.Occ.(2+3) = Composite group occulting.	....	A light in which the occultations are combined in alternate groups of different numbers.

Light colors used and abbreviations W = white, R = red, G = green

Figure 17-3: Lights on aids to navigation are fixed (F), flashing (Fl), quick flashing (QFl), interrupted quick flashing (IQFl) and occulting (Occ). All these flashes are visualized in the above diagram.

413

"lighthouses" erected at the point where the ship is anchored and this includes the Texas towers that are supplanting the ships. Some typical lighthouses are pictured in Figure 17-4.

Some lighthouse beams are sectored, meaning that they show a light of different color over a portion of the circle. The angle of the sector can be used to include reefs and hazards which are cleared safely if a ship is kept out of the colored portion. Conversely, a white center sector could indicate the safe channel while red and green adjacent sectors would indicate the right and left limits. The details are described and pictured on the area chart and enable a helmsman to steer a safe course by observing colors and color changes. The sketch in Figure 17-5 should aid in understanding this.

Visibility Range

A most important feature of a light is its range of visibility because this tells the mariner at what point he can expect to "pick it up" and verify his bearings. This range is always given on the chart. An understanding of what that "range" actually means is important.

Because the earth is round, a beam of light becomes tangent to the surface and is obstructed at a distance determined by the height of its origin. These distances are tabulated in Figure 17-6 and explained by the accompanying sketch. The distance a light can be seen *beyond* the point of tangency (provided it is strong enough) depends upon the height of the observer's eye above the surface. The same table can be used to ascertain this. (All official publications assume the observer's eye to be at fifteen feet above the water but this is higher than the steering position of the average small yacht.)

The *geographic* range of a "strong" light would therefore be the sum of its distance to tangency and the observer's distance to tangency. Take as an example a light 120 feet high and an observer whose eye is 10 feet above the waterline. From the table, the first figure yields 12.6 miles and the second 3.6 miles; adding these two rounds off to 16 miles. With clear visibility, then, this light should hove into view for this skipper when he gets within 16 miles of it. (This would be the direct beam and not merely the loom which illumines the sky.)

Many lights are not strong enough to maintain a geo-graphic range (they are "weak") and can attain only a *luminous* range, which is shorter. A luminous light can be identified by taking its horizon distance from the table, adding 4.4 miles (for a 15-foot observer) and comparing the total with the distance printed on the chart. If the chart figure is smaller, it is a luminous light. The answer will always be very obvious because all lights are either much stronger or much weaker than the computed critical figure. (The observer's height has no effect on the viewing of a luminous light.)

Chart Symbols

Easily available to all skippers is a fine list of all nautical abbreviations and symbols used on American (and most foreign) charts. This is known as Chart #1 although it is actually a pamphlet. It is a "must have on board" for every small boat captain who intends to cruise farther from his dock than he can see it.

Charts list many important landmarks in addition to the shoals, reefs, wrecks, and what-have-you of the water. All these items are identified by a visual code. Chart #1 unscrambles this code nicely and puts all these guideposts at the skipper's fingertips.

Tides

Every school child knows that tides are caused by the gravitational pulls of the sun and moon and that the degree of the highs and lows is governed by the relative positions of these heavenly bodies. But, to the skipper, tides are more than a physical phenomenon; they are a natural force that can help or hinder him to the extent that his knowledge enables him to harness them.

When the moon and sun are in line, and this happens on a full moon and on a new moon, high tides are higher and low tides are lower. These are the spring tides; note that in this case "spring" does *not* refer to a season of the year. When the moon is in first and last quarter its pull is at right angles to that of the sun, and the range between high and low tide is the least; these are the neap tides. Neither the sun nor the moon has a constant, unvarying gravitational effect upon the earth and its waters; this introduces a further monthly and yearly variation in the tides. Figure 17-7 illustrates the sun-moon-earth relationship and shows that the line of gravitational pulls alter-

BOSTON, MASS.   ST. AUGUSTINE FLA.   CAPE HENRY, VA.   TYBEE, GA.

MASONRY STRUCTURE   CYLINDRICAL TOWER SQUARE HOUSE ON CYLINDRICAL BASE   OFFSHORE LIGHT STRUCTURE   SKELETON IRON STRUCTURE

Figure 17-4: Coastal lighthouses vary from time-worn classical structures to the modern offshore "Texas" towers.

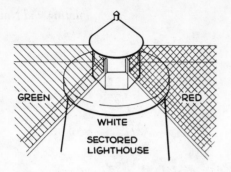

GREEN   RED

WHITE

SECTORED
LIGHTHOUSE

Figure 17-5: The colored sectors of a lighthouse beam mark danger zones or preferred approaches; these are clearly identified on the area chart.

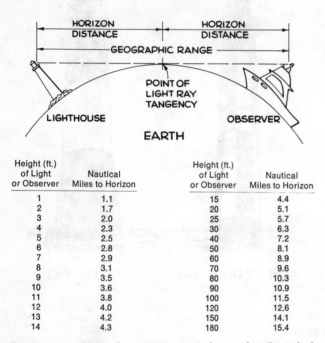

| HORIZON DISTANCE | HORIZON DISTANCE |
| GEOGRAPHIC RANGE | |

POINT OF
LIGHT RAY
TANGENCY

LIGHTHOUSE   OBSERVER

EARTH

Height (ft.) of Light or Observer	Nautical Miles to Horizon	Height (ft.) of Light or Observer	Nautical Miles to Horizon
1	1.1	15	4.4
2	1.7	20	5.1
3	2.0	25	5.7
4	2.3	30	6.3
5	2.5	40	7.2
6	2.8	50	8.1
7	2.9	60	8.9
8	3.1	70	9.6
9	3.5	80	10.3
10	3.6	90	10.9
11	3.8	100	11.5
12	4.0	120	12.6
13	4.2	150	14.1
14	4.3	180	15.4

Figure 17-6: How the curvature of the earth affects light range is shown above. The chart reduces this effect to actual miles of visibility.

nates above and below the equator.

The moon does not maintain a constant distance from the earth because its orbit is not concentric with the center of the earth. Since gravitational pull varies as the square of the distance, this unequal orbit has a considerable effect. When the moon is at its highest (and farthest) point, it is said to be in apogee; the resulting lessened tides are called apogee tides. The closest point of the moon is its perigee; the tidal effect is then the greatest and we have perigee tides.

The sun's varying effects are also caused by its changing distances from the earth, in this case due to the earth's noncircular orbit. The sun's pull on the waters is only 45 percent of the moon's but this is still a formidable quantity and cannot be neglected in reckoning tides. The resultant variations of tides from these gyrations of moon and sun (in addition to the spring and neap conditions, the earth's own gravity and centrifugal force) are higher and lower high water and higher and lower low water. The terms are self-explanatory.

There is a short period between the high and low tides when the water level is stationary, going neither up nor down; this is the "stand." "Mean low water" and "mean high water" are arrived at by averaging the lows and highs respectively. "Range" is the difference between high tide and low tide; it can vary from more than fifty feet to zero without dependence on geographical location. Some-

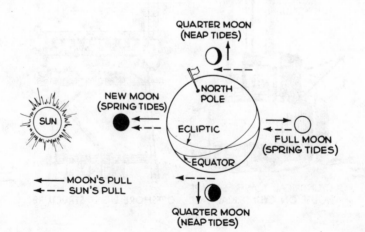

Figure 17-7: The relative directions of the moon's and the sun's gravitational pulls affect the heights of tides. ("Springs" are greater; "neaps" are lesser.) Earth's gravitation and earth's centrifugal force also play a part.

AIDS TO NAVIGATION ON NAVIGABLE WATERWAYS
except Western Rivers and Intracoastal Waterway

LATERAL SYSTEM AS SEEN ENTERING FROM SEAWARD

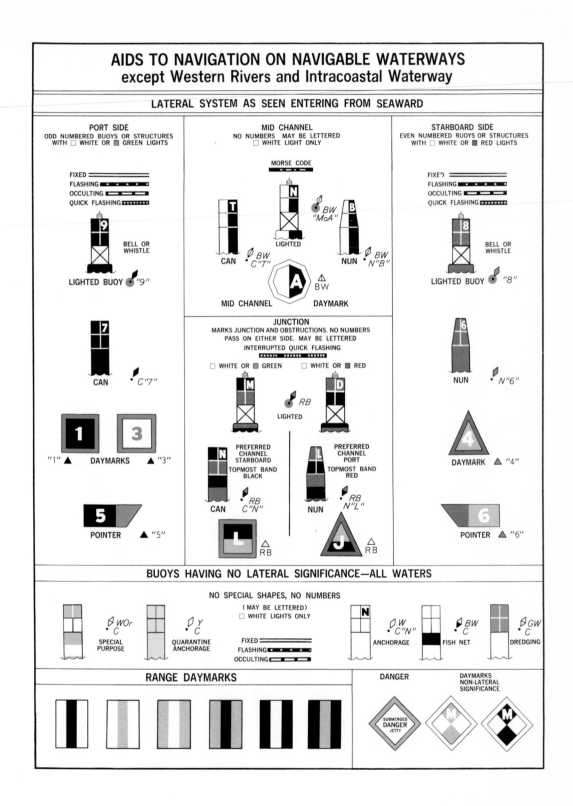

AIDS TO NAVIGATION ON THE INTRACOASTAL WATERWAY

AS SEEN ENTERING FROM NORTH AND EAST—PROCEEDING TO SOUTH AND WEST

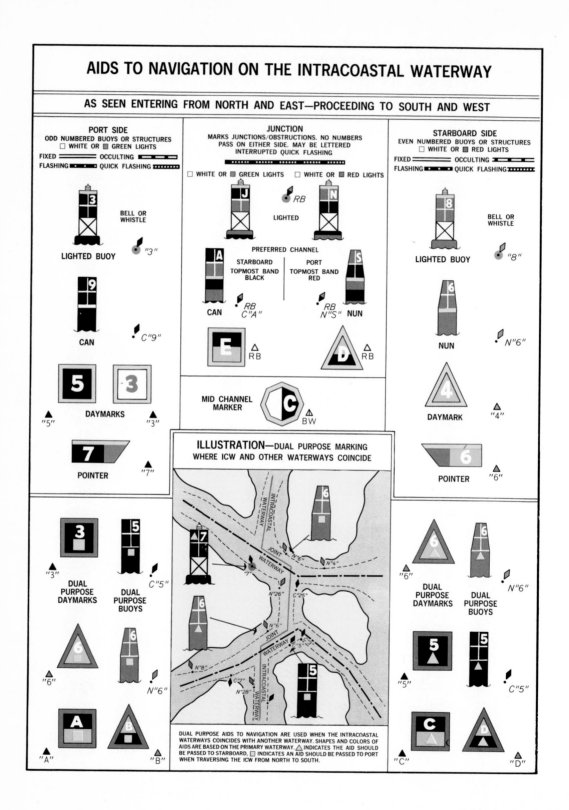

PORT SIDE
ODD NUMBERED BUOYS OR STRUCTURES
☐ WHITE OR ▨ GREEN LIGHTS
FIXED ═══════ OCCULTING ■■■ ■■■
FLASHING ■ ■ ■ QUICK FLASHING ▨▨▨▨▨

LIGHTED BUOY BELL OR WHISTLE "3"
CAN C"9"
DAYMARKS "5" "3"
POINTER "7"

DUAL PURPOSE DAYMARKS "3"
DUAL PURPOSE BUOYS C"5"
"6" N"6"
"A" "B"

JUNCTION
MARKS JUNCTIONS/OBSTRUCTIONS. NO NUMBERS
PASS ON EITHER SIDE. MAY BE LETTERED
INTERRUPTED QUICK FLASHING
☐ WHITE OR ▨ GREEN LIGHTS   ☐ WHITE OR ▨ RED LIGHTS

J RB LIGHTED N
PREFERRED CHANNEL
CAN STARBOARD TOPMOST BAND BLACK | PORT TOPMOST BAND RED NUN
RB C"A" RB N"S"
E RB D RB
MID CHANNEL MARKER C BW

ILLUSTRATION—DUAL PURPOSE MARKING
WHERE ICW AND OTHER WATERWAYS COINCIDE

DUAL PURPOSE AIDS TO NAVIGATION ARE USED WHEN THE INTRACOASTAL
WATERWAYS COINCIDES WITH ANOTHER WATERWAY. SHAPES AND COLORS OF
AIDS ARE BASED ON THE PRIMARY WATERWAY. △ INDICATES THE AID SHOULD
BE PASSED TO STARBOARD, ☐ INDICATES AN AID SHOULD BE PASSED TO PORT
WHEN TRAVERSING THE ICW FROM NORTH TO SOUTH.

STARBOARD SIDE
EVEN NUMBERED BUOYS OR STRUCTURES
☐ WHITE OR ▨ RED LIGHTS
FIXED ═══════ OCCULTING ■■■ ■■■
FLASHING ■ ■ ■ QUICK FLASHING ▨▨▨▨▨

LIGHTED BUOY BELL OR WHISTLE "8"
NUN N"6"
DAYMARK "4"
POINTER "6"

DUAL PURPOSE DAYMARKS "6"
DUAL PURPOSE BUOYS N"6"
"5" C"5"
"C" "D"

AIDS TO NAVIGATION ON WESTERN RIVERS

AS SEEN PROCEEDING IN THE DIRECTION (DESCENDING) OF RIVER FLOW

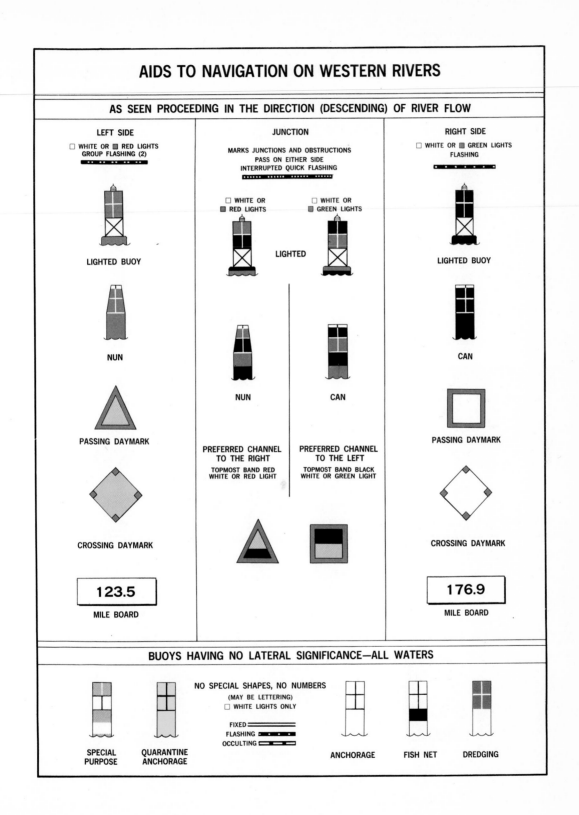

LEFT SIDE
☐ WHITE OR ■ RED LIGHTS
GROUP FLASHING (2)

LIGHTED BUOY

NUN

PASSING DAYMARK

CROSSING DAYMARK

123.5

MILE BOARD

JUNCTION

MARKS JUNCTIONS AND OBSTRUCTIONS
PASS ON EITHER SIDE
INTERRUPTED QUICK FLASHING

☐ WHITE OR ■ RED LIGHTS   ☐ WHITE OR ■ GREEN LIGHTS

LIGHTED

NUN   CAN

PREFERRED CHANNEL   PREFERRED CHANNEL
TO THE RIGHT   TO THE LEFT
TOPMOST BAND RED   TOPMOST BAND BLACK
WHITE OR RED LIGHT   WHITE OR GREEN LIGHT

RIGHT SIDE
☐ WHITE OR ■ GREEN LIGHTS
FLASHING

LIGHTED BUOY

CAN

PASSING DAYMARK

CROSSING DAYMARK

176.9

MILE BOARD

BUOYS HAVING NO LATERAL SIGNIFICANCE—ALL WATERS

SPECIAL
PURPOSE

QUARANTINE
ANCHORAGE

NO SPECIAL SHAPES, NO NUMBERS
(MAY BE LETTERING)
☐ WHITE LIGHTS ONLY

FIXED
FLASHING
OCCULTING

ANCHORAGE

FISH NET

DREDGING

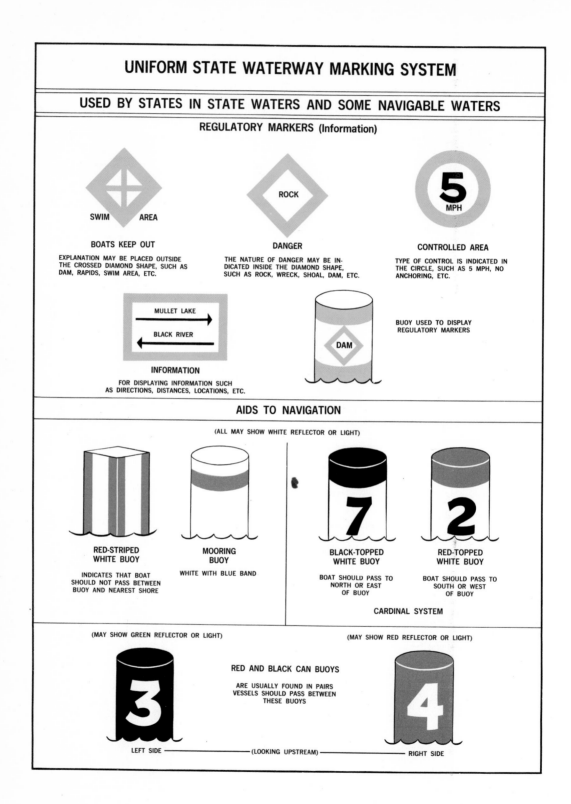

UNIFORM STATE WATERWAY MARKING SYSTEM

USED BY STATES IN STATE WATERS AND SOME NAVIGABLE WATERS

REGULATORY MARKERS (Information)

SWIM AREA

BOATS KEEP OUT

EXPLANATION MAY BE PLACED OUTSIDE THE CROSSED DIAMOND SHAPE, SUCH AS DAM, RAPIDS, SWIM AREA, ETC.

ROCK

DANGER

THE NATURE OF DANGER MAY BE INDICATED INSIDE THE DIAMOND SHAPE, SUCH AS ROCK, WRECK, SHOAL, DAM, ETC.

5 MPH

CONTROLLED AREA

TYPE OF CONTROL IS INDICATED IN THE CIRCLE, SUCH AS 5 MPH, NO ANCHORING, ETC.

MULLET LAKE →

← BLACK RIVER

INFORMATION

FOR DISPLAYING INFORMATION SUCH AS DIRECTIONS, DISTANCES, LOCATIONS, ETC.

DAM

BUOY USED TO DISPLAY REGULATORY MARKERS

AIDS TO NAVIGATION

(ALL MAY SHOW WHITE REFLECTOR OR LIGHT)

RED-STRIPED WHITE BUOY

INDICATES THAT BOAT SHOULD NOT PASS BETWEEN BUOY AND NEAREST SHORE

MOORING BUOY

WHITE WITH BLUE BAND

7

BLACK-TOPPED WHITE BUOY

BOAT SHOULD PASS TO NORTH OR EAST OF BUOY

2

RED-TOPPED WHITE BUOY

BOAT SHOULD PASS TO SOUTH OR WEST OF BUOY

CARDINAL SYSTEM

(MAY SHOW GREEN REFLECTOR OR LIGHT)

(MAY SHOW RED REFLECTOR OR LIGHT)

3

RED AND BLACK CAN BUOYS

ARE USUALLY FOUND IN PAIRS VESSELS SHOULD PASS BETWEEN THESE BUOYS

4

LEFT SIDE ——————— (LOOKING UPSTREAM) ——————— RIGHT SIDE

times the sun's gravitational pull takes effect before the moon's and advances or "primes" the normal time of the tide; at other times it may take effect later and "lag" the tide.

A glance at a tide table shows that the times of high and low tide gradually become later by approximately one hour each day and eventually lag right around the clock. Few people know why. The reason can be found in the moon's "day," which contains 24 hours and 50 minutes, versus an earth day of an even 24 hours. A tide cycle, which consists of a high tide and a low tide, therefore takes 12 hours and 25 minutes, since there are two cycles per lunar revolution. Theoretically, this would mean 6 hours and 12.5 minutes between high tide and low tide. Actually, this does not hold strictly true; the complex shape of the land masses and water cavities causes the deviation.

TIDE TABLES.

The National Ocean Survey publishes complete tide predictions in advance of each year. One volume covers the East Coast and another volume lists the data for the West Coast. Many newspapers and other publications excerpt some of the information pertinent to their own localities. From whatever source, tide values are of inestimable importance to every skipper who cruises tidal waters in any ship of greater draft than a rowboat.

The tide tables contain three sets of tabulations. The first gives the times and heights of tides at a long list of reference stations. The second calculates the tidal time difference between the reference stations and an even greater number of subordinate stations. The third is a complete set of interpolations with which tide conditions can be determined for any point on the coast for any day of the year. Portions of the tables are shown in Figure 17-8.

Currents

Perhaps the two most confused terms in the novice skipper's vocabulary are tide and current. They are often used interchangeably, when in fact their meanings are quite different.

A graphic way to note the difference is to remember that tide is a *vertical* movement of the water while current is a *horizontal* movement. Tide is, therefore, a change in

level and is expressed as a height in feet. Tide in itself affects any vessel only in the matter of having sufficient water under the keel.

Current, on the other hand, is an actual flow of water from one point to another and is expressed as a speed in miles per hour or knots plus a direction. Currents directly affect the movement of a boat. If they are in the same direction as the boat's course, the boat speed over the ground is increased; if they are running oppositely, the boat speed is decreased. If the current flow is at an angle to the course, the boat is moving over the ground at an angle to its desired direction. Note that in all these situations the boat's course *over the ground* is stressed because that is the factor which permits arrival at a destination which also is fixed to the ground.

Currents are an important ingredient in the calculations for a cruise. They will affect the length of time it takes, the amount of fuel consumed, the shoals avoided or struck. Currents can also preclude or prohibit certain courses, for instance, traversing a fast race that a slow boat could not buck.

There are tidal currents which, as the name implies, are caused by ocean water flowing into and out of rivers and bays. The narrower the entrance, the faster will be the current, because the time factor is always approximately the same. There are ocean currents caused by variations in pressure and temperature and ocean bottom topography and other reasons still unknown. Currents are also encountered in rivers and large bodies of open water.

The majority of skippers will have little to do with ocean currents but will find tidal currents of recurring importance in their cruises. The Coast & Geodetic Survey publishes annual charts and tables of tidal currents and ocean currents. (Heavy local weather occasionally offsets the predictions.)

The rise and fall of the tide, for instance, in a bay having a restricted connection with the sea, means that water has come in and water has gone out. When the water moves in from the sea, the current is "flood"; on the outward movement, it is "ebb." Flood and ebb currents are not necessarily in synchronism with the high and low tides. Generally, they are dependent upon the relative sizes of the channels and the bays or rivers and the general configuration of the surrounding shoreline. The condition between flood and ebb, when there is no

TABLE 1

WILLETS POINT, N.Y., 1969

TIMES AND HEIGHTS OF HIGH AND LOW WATERS

	JULY						AUGUST						SEPTEMBER				
DAY	TIME H.M.	HT. FT.	DAY	TIME H.M.	HT. FT.	DAY	TIME H.M.	HT. FT.	DAY	TIME H.M.	HT. FT.	DAY	TIME H.M.	HT. FT.	DAY	TIME H.M.	HT. FT.
1 TU	0630 1230 1842	-1.1 7.7 -0.4	16 W	0636 1218 1830	0.1 6.8 0.8	1 F	0124 0754 1354 2024	8.2 -0.8 8.1 -0.5	16 SA	0030 0642 1248 1906	7.5 0.0 7.7 0.2	1 M	0230 0854 1448 2142	7.1 0.3 7.6 0.2	16 TU	0124 0730 1348 2006	7.3 0.2 8.1 0.0
2 W	0042 0730 1324 1948	8.5 -1.0 7.7 -0.3	17 TH	0018 0654 1248 1854	7.4 0.1 7.0 0.7	2 SA	0218 0848 1448 2124	7.8 -0.4 8.0 -0.2	17 SU	0106 0718 1330 1942	7.4 0.1 7.8 0.2	2 TU	0318 0948 1536 2242	6.5 0.8 7.2 0.6	17 W	0212 0818 1436 2100	7.0 0.5 7.9 0.3
3 TH	0142 0824 1424 2048	8.2 -0.8 7.7 -0.2	18 F	0054 0712 1318 1930	7.3 0.2 7.2 0.6	3 SU	0312 0942 1542 2224	7.3 0.0 7.7 0.1	18 M	0148 0754 1412 2030	7.3 0.2 7.8 0.2	3 W	0424 1048 1636 2348	6.1 1.2 6.8 0.9	18 TH	0306 0912 1530 2206	6.6 0.8 7.5 0.6
4 F	0242 0918 1524 2154	7.8 -0.5 7.7 -0.1	19 SA	0136 0748 1400 2012	7.3 0.2 7.3 0.6	4 M	0412 1036 1642 2324	6.7 0.5 7.4 0.3	19 TU	0236 0842 1500 2124	7.0 0.4 7.8 0.4	4 TH	0542 1200 1800	5.8 1.5 6.6	19 F	0412 1018 1636 2348	6.3 1.1 7.3 0.7

TABLE 2

TIDAL DIFFERENCES AND OTHER CONSTANTS

No.	PLACE	POSITION		DIFFERENCES				RANGES		Mean Tide Level
		Lat.	Long.	Time		Height		Mean	Spring	
				High water	Low water	High water	Low water			
		° ' N.	° ' W.	h. m.	h. m.	feet	feet	feet	feet	feet
	NEW YORK Long Island Sound, North Side			on WILLETS POINT, p.58						
				Time meridian, 75°W.						
1253	Port Chester-------------------------	41 00	73 40	-0 09	-0 12	+0.1	0.0	7.2	8.5	3.6
1254	Rye Beach----------------------------	40 58	73 40	-0 28	-0 29	+0.1	0.0	7.2	8.4	3.6
1255	Mamaroneck---------------------------	40 56	73 44	-0 08	-0 11	+0.2	0.0	7.3	8.6	3.6
1257	New Rochelle-------------------------	40 54	73 47	-0 24	-0 17	+0.1	0.0	7.2	8.6	3.6
1259	Davids Island------------------------	40 53	73 46	-0 02	-0 07	+0.1	0.0	7.2	8.5	3.6
1261	City Island--------------------------	40 51	73 47	-0 03	-0 03	+0.1	0.0	7.2	8.5	3.6
1263	Throgs Neck--------------------------	40 48	73 48	+0 02	+0 14	-0.1	0.0	7.0	8.2	3.5
	East River									
1265	Whitestone---------------------------	40 48	73 49	+0 02	+0 14	0.0	0.0	7.1	8.3	3.5
1267	Old Ferry Point----------------------	40 48	73 50	+0 04	+0 16	0.0	0.0	7.1	8.3	3.5
1269	College Point, Flushing Bay---------	40 47	73 51	+0 20	+0 28	-0.6	0.0	6.5	7.6	3.2
1271	Northern Blvd. Bridge, Flushing Cr--	40 46	73 50	+0 23	+0 37	-0.3	0.0	6.8	8.0	3.4

Figure 17-8: With an up-to-date tide table you can figure the state of the tide at any point at any time of day. Excerpts from the tables above are: Table (1), tide data for a full year for each reference station; Table (2), tidal differences from the reference for all subordinate stations; Table (3), state of tide for any intermediate time.

TABLE 3

HEIGHT OF TIDE AT ANY TIME

Time from the nearest high water or low water

Duration of rise or fall, see footnote (h. m.)	h. m.	h. m.	h. m.	h. m.	h. m.	h. m.	h. m.	h. m.	h. m.	h. m.	h. m.	h. m.	h. m.	h. m.	h. m.
4 00	0 08	0 16	0 24	0 32	0 40	0 48	0 56	1 04	1 12	1 20	1 28	1 36	1 44	1 52	2 00
4 20	0 09	0 17	0 26	0 35	0 43	0 52	1 01	1 09	1 18	1 27	1 35	1 44	1 53	2 01	2 10
4 40	0 09	0 19	0 28	0 37	0 47	0 56	1 05	1 15	1 24	1 33	1 43	1 52	2 01	2 11	2 20
5 00	0 10	0 20	0 30	0 40	0 50	1 00	1 10	1 20	1 30	1 40	1 50	2 00	2 10	2 20	2 30
5 20	0 11	0 21	0 32	0 43	0 53	1 04	1 15	1 25	1 36	1 47	1 57	2 08	2 19	2 29	2 40
5 40	0 11	0 23	0 34	0 45	0 57	1 08	1 19	1 31	1 42	1 53	2 05	2 16	2 27	2 39	2 50
6 00	0 12	0 24	0 36	0 48	1 00	1 12	1 24	1 36	1 48	2 00	2 12	2 24	2 36	2 48	3 00
6 20	0 13	0 25	0 38	0 51	1 03	1 16	1 29	1 41	1 54	2 07	2 19	2 32	2 45	2 57	3 10
6 40	0 13	0 27	0 40	0 53	1 07	1 20	1 33	1 47	2 00	2 13	2 27	2 40	2 53	3 07	3 20
7 00	0 14	0 28	0 42	0 56	1 10	1 24	1 38	1 52	2 06	2 20	2 34	2 48	3 02	3 16	3 30
7 20	0 15	0 29	0 44	0 59	1 13	1 28	1 43	1 57	2 12	2 27	2 41	2 56	3 11	3 25	3 40
7 40	0 15	0 31	0 46	1 01	1 17	1 32	1 47	2 03	2 18	2 33	2 49	3 04	3 19	3 35	3 50
8 00	0 16	0 32	0 48	1 04	1 20	1 36	1 52	2 08	2 24	2 40	2 56	3 12	3 28	3 44	4 00
8 20	0 17	0 33	0 50	1 07	1 23	1 40	1 57	2 13	2 30	2 47	3 03	3 20	3 37	3 53	4 10
8 40	0 17	0 35	0 52	1 09	1 27	1 44	2 01	2 19	2 36	2 53	3 11	3 28	3 45	4 03	4 20
9 00	0 18	0 36	0 54	1 12	1 30	1 48	2 06	2 24	2 42	3 00	3 18	3 36	3 54	4 12	4 30
9 20	0 19	0 37	0 56	1 15	1 33	1 52	2 11	2 29	2 48	3 07	3 25	3 44	4 03	4 21	4 40
9 40	0 19	0 39	0 58	1 17	1 37	1 56	2 15	2 35	2 54	3 13	3 33	3 52	4 11	4 31	4 50
10 00	0 20	0 40	1 00	1 20	1 40	2 00	2 20	2 40	3 00	3 20	3 40	4 00	4 20	4 40	5 00
10 20	0 21	0 41	1 02	1 23	1 43	2 04	2 25	2 45	3 06	3 27	3 47	4 08	4 29	4 49	5 10
10 40	0 21	0 43	1 04	1 25	1 47	2 08	2 29	2 51	3 12	3 33	3 55	4 16	4 37	4 59	5 20

Correction to height

Range of tide, see footnote (Ft.)	Ft.	Ft.	Ft.	Ft.	Ft.	Ft.	Ft.	Ft.	Ft.	Ft.	Ft.	Ft.	Ft.	Ft.	Ft.
0.5	0.0	0.0	0.0	0.0	0.0	0.0	0.1	0.1	0.1	0.1	0.1	0.2	0.2	0.2	0.2
1.0	0.0	0.0	0.0	0.0	0.1	0.1	0.1	0.2	0.2	0.2	0.3	0.3	0.4	0.4	0.5
1.5	0.0	0.0	0.0	0.1	0.1	0.1	0.2	0.2	0.3	0.4	0.4	0.5	0.6	0.7	0.8
2.0	0.0	0.0	0.0	0.1	0.1	0.2	0.3	0.3	0.4	0.5	0.6	0.7	0.8	0.9	1.0
2.5	0.0	0.0	0.1	0.1	0.2	0.2	0.3	0.4	0.5	0.6	0.7	0.9	1.0	1.1	1.2
3.0	0.0	0.0	0.1	0.1	0.2	0.3	0.4	0.5	0.6	0.8	0.9	1.0	1.2	1.3	1.5
3.5	0.0	0.0	0.1	0.2	0.2	0.3	0.4	0.6	0.7	0.9	1.0	1.2	1.4	1.6	1.8
4.0	0.0	0.0	0.1	0.2	0.3	0.4	0.5	0.7	0.8	1.0	1.2	1.4	1.6	1.8	2.0
4.5	0.0	0.0	0.1	0.2	0.3	0.4	0.6	0.7	0.9	1.1	1.3	1.6	1.8	2.0	2.2
5.0	0.0	0.1	0.1	0.2	0.3	0.5	0.6	0.8	1.0	1.2	1.5	1.7	2.0	2.2	2.5
5.5	0.0	0.1	0.1	0.2	0.4	0.5	0.7	0.9	1.1	1.4	1.6	1.9	2.2	2.5	2.8
6.0	0.0	0.1	0.1	0.3	0.4	0.6	0.8	1.0	1.2	1.5	1.8	2.1	2.4	2.7	3.0
6.5	0.0	0.1	0.2	0.3	0.4	0.6	0.8	1.1	1.3	1.6	1.9	2.2	2.6	2.9	3.2
7.0	0.0	0.1	0.2	0.3	0.5	0.7	0.9	1.2	1.4	1.8	2.1	2.4	2.8	3.1	3.5
7.5	0.0	0.1	0.2	0.3	0.5	0.7	1.0	1.2	1.5	1.9	2.2	2.6	3.0	3.4	3.8
8.0	0.0	0.1	0.2	0.3	0.5	0.8	1.0	1.3	1.6	2.0	2.4	2.8	3.2	3.6	4.0
8.5	0.0	0.1	0.2	0.4	0.6	0.8	1.1	1.4	1.8	2.1	2.5	2.9	3.4	3.8	4.2
9.0	0.0	0.1	0.2	0.4	0.6	0.9	1.2	1.5	1.9	2.2	2.7	3.1	3.6	4.0	4.5
9.5	0.0	0.1	0.2	0.4	0.6	0.9	1.2	1.6	2.0	2.4	2.8	3.3	3.8	4.3	4.8
10.0	0.0	0.1	0.2	0.4	0.7	1.0	1.3	1.7	2.1	2.5	3.0	3.5	4.0	4.5	5.0
10.5	0.0	0.1	0.3	0.5	0.7	1.0	1.3	1.7	2.2	2.6	3.1	3.6	4.2	4.7	5.2
11.0	0.0	0.1	0.3	0.5	0.7	1.1	1.4	1.8	2.3	2.8	3.3	3.8	4.4	4.9	5.5
11.5	0.0	0.1	0.3	0.5	0.8	1.1	1.5	1.9	2.4	2.9	3.4	4.0	4.6	5.1	5.8
12.0	0.0	0.1	0.3	0.5	0.8	1.1	1.5	2.0	2.5	3.0	3.6	4.1	4.8	5.4	6.0
12.5	0.0	0.1	0.3	0.5	0.8	1.2	1.6	2.1	2.6	3.1	3.7	4.3	5.0	5.6	6.2
13.0	0.0	0.1	0.3	0.6	0.9	1.2	1.7	2.2	2.7	3.2	3.9	4.5	5.1	5.8	6.5
13.5	0.0	0.1	0.3	0.6	0.9	1.3	1.7	2.2	2.8	3.4	4.0	4.7	5.3	6.0	6.8
14.0	0.0	0.2	0.3	0.6	0.9	1.3	1.8	2.3	2.9	3.5	4.2	4.8	5.5	6.3	7.0
14.5	0.0	0.2	0.4	0.6	1.0	1.4	1.9	2.4	3.0	3.6	4.3	5.0	5.7	6.5	7.2
15.0	0.0	0.2	0.4	0.6	1.0	1.4	1.9	2.5	3.1	3.8	4.4	5.2	5.9	6.7	7.5
15.5	0.0	0.2	0.4	0.7	1.0	1.5	2.0	2.6	3.2	3.9	4.6	5.4	6.1	6.9	7.8
16.0	0.0	0.2	0.4	0.7	1.1	1.5	2.1	2.6	3.3	4.0	4.7	5.5	6.3	7.2	8.0
16.5	0.0	0.2	0.4	0.7	1.1	1.6	2.1	2.7	3.4	4.1	4.9	5.7	6.5	7.4	8.2
17.0	0.0	0.2	0.4	0.7	1.1	1.6	2.2	2.8	3.5	4.2	5.0	5.9	6.7	7.6	8.5
17.5	0.0	0.2	0.4	0.8	1.2	1.7	2.2	2.9	3.6	4.4	5.2	6.0	6.9	7.8	8.8
18.0	0.0	0.2	0.4	0.8	1.2	1.7	2.3	3.0	3.7	4.5	5.3	6.2	7.1	8.1	9.0
18.5	0.1	0.2	0.5	0.8	1.2	1.8	2.4	3.1	3.8	4.6	5.5	6.4	7.3	8.3	9.2
19.0	0.1	0.2	0.5	0.8	1.3	1.8	2.4	3.1	3.9	4.8	5.6	6.6	7.5	8.5	9.5
19.5	0.1	0.2	0.5	0.8	1.3	1.9	2.5	3.2	4.0	4.9	5.8	6.7	7.7	8.7	9.8
20.0	0.1	0.2	0.5	0.9	1.3	1.9	2.6	3.3	4.1	5.0	5.9	6.9	7.9	9.0	10.0

Obtain from the predictions the high water and low water, one of which is before and the other after the time for which the height is required. The difference between the times of occurrence of these tides is the duration of rise or fall, and the difference between their heights is the range of tide for the above table. Find the difference between the nearest high or low water and the time for which the height is required.

Enter the table with the duration of rise or fall, printed in heavy-faced type, which most nearly agrees with the actual value, and on that horizontal line find the time from the nearest high or low water which agrees most nearly with the corresponding actual difference. The correction sought is in the column directly below, on the line with the range of tide.

When the nearest tide is high water, subtract the correction.

When the nearest tide is low water, add the correction.

horizontal movement of the water, is "slack." "Set" is the direction *toward* which current flows and "drift" is its velocity in miles per hour or knots.

Currents, like tides, can be calculated for any place and any time with up-to-date current tables, also published yearly by the Coast & Geodetic Survey.

The only ocean current with which East Coast American small boat skippers are likely to become familiar is the Gulf Stream. It has been called a "river within the ocean." It parallels most of the Atlantic Coast, becomes a major ingredient in the fogs of the Grand Banks, and then swings over to the British Isles to help the Britons forget the fact that they are actually as far north on the globe as Labrador.

The Gulf Stream flows only a short distance offshore and many skippers have taken game fish from its warm waters. The more adventurous returnees north from Florida who take the outside route are able to add up to three knots to their speed by staying in the Gulf Stream.

The rotation of the earth produces a "coriolis effect." This causes the generally clockwise rotation of ocean currents in the Northern Hemisphere. Coriolis also affects the major wind patterns.

Charts

When a map goes to sea it becomes a chart and calling it a map around boatmen leads to sure ostracism. Charts are the result of many years of survey which is continuously in progress and, considering the difficulty of probing into the myriads of square miles of deep water, are remarkably accurate.

Charts are classified by the Coast & Geodetic Survey as harbor charts, coast charts, general charts, and sailing charts. The differences lie in the amount of detail, the area covered, and the scale to which it is drawn. The harbor chart, as is to be expected, contains the most details.

Harbor charts are to a scale of 1:50,000 or less, which corresponds to about 7/10 nautical miles of distance to 1 inch of chart. Coast charts run to a scale of from 1:50,000 to 1:100,000, or a maximum of 1 4/10 nautical miles per inch. The scale of general charts lies between 1:100,000 and 1:600,000 (a maximum of 8 2/10 miles per inch), while sailing charts are drawn to a still smaller scale. The underlying principle is that the closer you are to shore, the greater the requirement for detailed infor-

mation to insure safe piloting. The table in Figure 17-9 shows the continuous relationship between scale and miles.

A chart is revised and published in a new edition whenever the changes which have taken place in the area are important enough to warrant this. The edition number and the date of printing are carried in the lower left-hand corner. When this new edition is subsequently revised, the revision date is printed to the right of the original edition date. Changes which occurred after the latest revision were formerly entered on the chart by hand but this has been discontinued. Information taken from all issues of the *Notice to Mariners* published since the date of the last chart revision (stamped in the lower left-hand corner) can be used to bring a chart up-to-date. The meticulous system under which all drafting is done is the reason why such great dependence can be placed on the charts; it also emphasizes the wisdom of discarding out-of-date charts.

Chart Scale 1 to	Nautical Miles per Inch
5000	.069
10000	0.137
15000	0.206
20000	0.274
25000	0.341
30000	0.412
35000	0.480
40000	0.550
45000	0.618
50000	0.686
55000	0.755
60000	0.823
65000	0.890
70000	0.960
75000	1.028

Figure 17-9: The actual linear measurement on a chart for a charted mile at various scales is given above.

A recent development is the small-craft chart designated by the "SC" following the chart number. This resulted from the official realization that most small boat skippers are not blessed with the large chart tables without which the regulation charts become unhandy to use. The SCs are somewhat along the line of motorists' maps from the standpoint of handiness, but quality-wise the charts are far above comparison. The small-craft charts also list service and repair facilities in addition to suggested courses and tidal and other marine data, information of great value to the pleasure skipper in a strange harbor.

The National Oceanic and Atmospheric Administration (NOAA) of the Department of Commerce issues free catalogues in two volumes of the available charts, tide tables, coast pilots, and current tables. One "volume" (it is a large, folded sheet) lists the Atlantic and Gulf coasts plus Puerto Rico and the Virgin Islands. Volume 2 lists the Pacific Coast including Hawaii, Guam, and Samoa.

The United States Lake Survey of Detroit, Michigan, issues a catalogue of charts covering the Great Lakes and their connections. Charts for the western rivers are issued by the United States Army Engineers from the various Army District Offices in which the rivers lie.

CHART-MAKING METHODS.

The chart-maker's problems arise because the earth is round while a chart is flat. It is therefore impossible to transfer terrain outlines from one to the other with absolute accuracy; distortions must result. The various methods of chart making were devised to minimize or equalize these distortions, each in its own way and for its own special purpose.

Four principal methods have been developed for charting the surface of the earth: the Mercator, the gnomonic, the polyconic, and the Lambert. Most small boat skippers, except possibly those cruising on the Great Lakes, will find that their entire experience is with charts made by Mercator projection. The Army feels that polyconic projection is better suited to the comparatively smaller individual areas of the Great Lakes. Neither gnomonic projection nor Lambert projection is likely to be found in the chart rack; both of these types are valuable in deep water and great-circle sailing, and the Lambert is favored by aircraft.

Since gnomonic and Lambert are not the pleasure skipper's best friends, only a few quick glances will be given them for purposes of orientation. Polyconic will be treated a little less curtly since understanding it can be of service to many, and then the emphasis will go onto Mercator's method.

GNOMONIC CHARTS.

The gnomonic chart has great value for long-distance sailing because great circles plot out on it as straight lines. Since a great-circle route is the shortest distance between two points on the surface of the earth, the value of this feature is obvious. (A great circle is formed when a plane cuts the earth and passes through its center; the equator is a great circle, so are the meridians of longitude.)

Technically, a gnomonic chart is made by projecting the features of the earth by rays emanating from the center (or some other agreed point) on to a plane tangent to the surface. You can unravel this language by looking at the illustration in Figure 17-10. Imagine the globe to be trans-

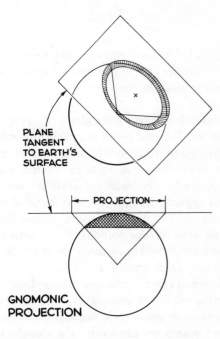

Figure 17-10: The gnomic projection utilizes a plane tangent to the earth at the center of the area of interest.

parent and the light coming from a beam at the center. The shadow on the flat plate will be a gnomonic projection for the area around that point on the globe. It is evident that the distortion for areas away from the point of tangency will be great. These charts are also known as great-circle charts. The familiar and helpful compass rose cannot be shown on them.

LAMBERT CHART.

The various land masses of the earth retain their relative areas when shown on a Lambert chart; this is *not* true of the Mercator method. The concept of the Lambert projection is a little more difficult than the gnomonic but the illustration in Figure 17-11 should clarify it.

As shown in the sketch, a cone with its apex in line with the earth's axis is imagined to have cut through the

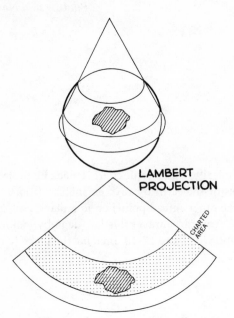

Figure 17-11: The Lambert projection makes use of a cone cutting under the area of interest; subsequently unrolling the cone produces the chart.

surface so that it leaves a doughnut-like ring parallel to the latitudes. The land patterns on this ring are then projected through to the outside of the cone. The cone is then slit from apex straight down to the bottom and laid out flat (developed). The resulting chart is shown; it will doubtless appear unfamiliar because the usual square grid of latitude and longitude is missing. Instead the parallels of latitude have become portions of concentric circles and the meridians of longitude converge to the polar center, much as they do in actual life.

The Lambert chart is preferred in long-distance aviation because the fidelity to area makes the land masses easier to recognize. A great-circle track between two widely separated points on the earth is a straight line when plotted on a Lambert chart.

POLYCONIC CHART.

The polyconic projection, as its name implies, also uses cones as the receiving surface but it does this in a different manner. A separate cone is used at each parallel of latitude (or other selected interval). Each cone is tangent to the surface of the earth at the point (or more truly, ring) of contact and this automatically places the apex of the cone in line with the earth's axis. The cones are considered transparent and the features of the earth are projected through them onto the outer surfaces. The unrolled cone, developed and flattened, becomes the chart. Figure 17-12 illustrates this.

The polyconic projection shows land areas with the least amount of distortion although, strictly speaking, this no longer holds true when the distances covered are very large. This high degree of fidelity over compact sections undoubtedly led the Army to adopt polyconic pro-

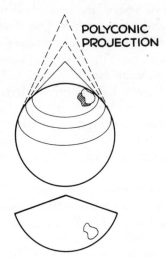

Figure 17-12: The polyconic projection also is made onto cones, but these are tangent to parallels of latitude. The cones are then unrolled (developed.)

jection for the Great Lakes charts.

The parallels of latitude become portions of concentric circles when shown on a polyconic chart, and the meridians of longitude are radii emanating from the pole. An advantage is that the distances in all directions can be measured with good accuracy with a common scale. A disadvantage is that the rhumb line of a course becomes a curve when laid down on the chart—although this becomes apparent only on very long runs.

MERCATOR CHART.

In the sixteenth century, Gerard Mercator, then cartographer to King Charles V, was seeking a method of portraying the land areas of the earth on a flat chart having a rectangular grid of latitudes and longitudes. His goal was to lay rhumb lines down as straight lines and to specify locations by reference to rectangular coordinates. He developed the Mercator projection, the most widely used charting method in the world today.

Nearly all the charts that come to hand on small craft will have been made by Mercator projection. The simplicity and advantage of locating a point on the earth by specifying merely a horizontal distance and a vertical distance are obvious. To this is added the convenience of being able to lay out a course by connecting the desired points with a straight line and then reading the required bearing from the chart rose.

Bearing can be read by such easy manipulation because on a Mercator chart any given rhumb line crosses all meridians and parallels at a constant angle. This is not true with the other systems of chart projection. Distance measurements also can be made along the rhumb line by taking the length of a unit from the nearest grid.

Of course some distortions result from the Mercator method. The earth's surface is in three dimensions while the chart drawing is only in two. It is impossible to lay the surface of a sphere out flat except by first serrating it into sections, and distortion is therefore unavoidable. The classic example is the relative sizes of Greenland and the United States on a globe and their disproportionate representation on a large Mercator chart.

To the small craft skipper the technical shortcomings of the Mercator projection are purely rhetorical and he can forget them. The land areas on the charts he uses are comparatively small and the projection errors negligible. He is safe in considering his chart his cruising bible, his magic talisman to lead him through the next maze of buoys and shoals and channels.

A Mercator chart is made by imagining the earth to be inside a tight-fitting transparent cylinder tangent all around the equator. The surface of the earth is slit (from the equator up and down) along each of the meridians of longitude. These orange-like sections are then lifted up against the inside of the cylinder. The pointed ends are now stretched sideways until they have the same width as at the equator, in other words, until the normally converging meridians have become parallel lines. To minimize distortion, one further stretch is made, this time lengthwise in the direction of each pole. What now is seen through the transparent cylinder becomes the chart when it is rolled out flat.

RHUMB LINE.

Much use has been made of the term rhumb line in the discussion of charts, and more will be made in relation to the plotting of courses. It is therefore wise to fix in mind exactly what a rhumb line is.

The dictionary defines rhumb line as a line crossing successive meridians at a constant angle. More exactly, a rhumb line on the surface of the earth is a curve whose tangents make a constant angle with every crossed me-

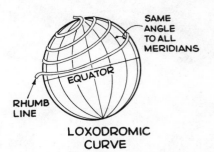

Figure 17-13: A true rhumb line (other than 0° and 90°) is a loxodromic curve whose tangents meet all meridians at a constant angle and which spirals to the pole.

ridian. When this angle is either 0 degrees or 90 degrees, the resulting course becomes a circumnavigation of the globe; with any intermediate angle the course becomes a loxodromic curve that ends at the pole. (A loxodromic curve looks like the skin of an apple that has been pared by keeping the peel in one continuous piece; it is illustrated in Figure 17-13.

To the small boat skipper, the rhumb line is the straight line depicting the course of his craft on a Mercator chart. He lays this line down either by establishing fixes of his positions which determine it or by connecting certain points of departure with equivalent destinations. It is customary practice to write the course direction above the line and the speed below it. As already explained, the shortest distance between two points on the earth is a great-circle route and this would appear as a curve on a Mercator chart; for short distances the disparity between the rhumb line and the curve would not be noticeable.

CHART MEANINGS.

Charts are based on data from two simultaneous surveys: topographic (the land) and hydrographic (the water). These data can be distinguished on the chart by observing the nature of the printing used to describe them. Printing that is erect refers to topographic elements; printing that is italic (slanting) refers to hydrographic conditions.

Space on even the largest-scale charts is cramped and at a premium. Abbreviations must therefore be used. These are listed in detail in Chart #1 (a pamphlet) obtainable from the Government Printing Office, Washington, D.C., as well as from many local outlets. Conformity with the editorial code is fairly uniform throughout the

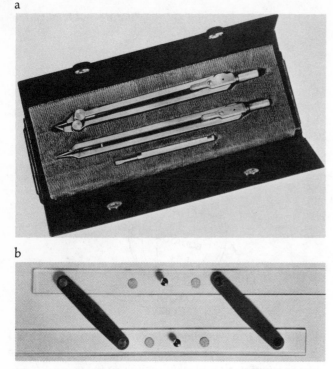

a

b

Figure 17-14: The bare essentials of a navigator's equipment, in addition to pencil and eraser, are compass and dividers (a), parallel rule (b) and hand-held compass (c). (Credit—Weems & Plath Inc.)

charts. Chart #1 also illustrates the significance of all colors, shadings, and pictograms used by cartographers. Depths are given as at mean low water and the units could be either feet or fathoms (one fathom equals six feet) depending upon the chart legend. Heights of landmarks are in feet, generally above mean high water. Since this is not necessarily true on *all* charts, always check the chart legend for proper datum.

Navigator's Equipment

The pilot-navigator (on most sail- and powerboats he will be the skipper) should have the following equipment and materials at hand before attempting a cruise: plotting devices such as protractors, parallel rules and dividers, perhaps even a hand-held compass to substitute for a pelorus (see Figure 17-14), plus soft lead pencil and eraser and an accurate watch or clock, even a stopwatch if possible. It is assumed that the necessary instrumentation, described in Chapter 9, is aboard. A table or other flat surface on which the charts can be spread and worked is a convenience that approaches a necessity.

For coastal cruising, the printed materials should include: tide tables, tidal current tables, the appropriate volume of the *Coastal Pilot*, the latest issue of the weekly *Notices to Mariners* for that particular district, the applicable volume of the *List of Lights and Other Marine Aids*, a copy of the *Rules of the Road* for the area and, perhaps most important of all, enough charts to cover every intended course adequately. If the compass has not been

c

entirely compensated, a deviation table must of course be available to the helmsman. The compilation of such a table is explained in Chapter 14: so also is the making of an rpm vs. speed table.

All the oil companies that cater to the marine trade issue charts free for the asking and all navigable areas of the United States are covered. These charts are helpful as an overall guide to a cruise, especially for their complete details of available facilities and their listing of points of interest. Although they show most buoys and other aids to navigation, they are *not* suitable for plotting a course. These charts are not (and are not intended to be) a substitute for the official C&GS charts.

From Theory to Practice

All the aids to navigation a small boat skipper will meet underway have now been examined in detail and should have become familiar; the compass and other instruments of navigation were studied with equal care in Chapter 9. The situation is now akin to that of the trainee in boot

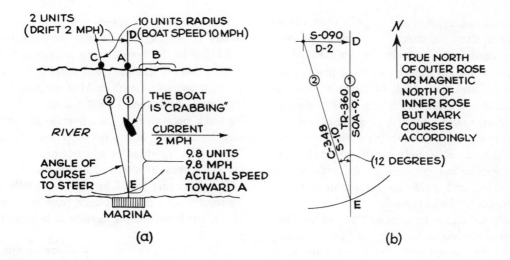

Figure 17-15: The illustration at (a) is a descriptive rendering of the problem given in the text. In actual practice, the problem is worked out as shown at (b) by drawing vectors and completing the vector triangle. It is important to identify each vector with its correct markings.

camp who has studied the pictures and components of a rifle ad nauseam and is itching to get his fingers on a trigger and take a potshot at something.

Looking over the shoulder of an experienced skipper-navigator is an excellent way to correlate theory and practice; items remembered from various chapters fall smoothly into place. Accordingly we will go along on several short runs and cruises and observe how easily a boat is taken from point *A* to point *B* by the best route and with the greatest safety. (Old salts claim that seamanship cannot be learned from a book but they fail to differentiate between the science and the art.)

Effects of Current

One of the simplest runs to make would be from the marina in Figure 17-15 directly across the river to point *A*. If there were no current, there would indeed be nothing to it. The helmsman would merely keep the bow headed for point *A* until he arrived there.

But suppose a current to be running up the river in the direction of the arrow. The water is carrying the boat upstream, despite its apparent straight-across course, and

the destination will no longer be *A* but must become some point around *B*.

The problem now is to find what course to steer from the marina in order to get to *A* without back-tracking. The basis for the solution is trigonometry but the solution itself is graphic and requires no mathematical knowledge. Common sense says that the current must be counteracted, in other words, we must steer for some point like *C*, and this is the underlying idea of the method.

The solution could be worked out right on the chart as follows: A line of indeterminate length (marked #1) is drawn from our point of departure at the marina through our desired destination, *A*. This is the path over the ground we would like our vessel to follow as it contends successfully with the current. At some convenient point *D* on line #1, near our destination, a line is drawn at right angles because the current is at right angles to our path. The length of this line is two units because the current has a drift (velocity) of two miles per hour.

The units can be any convenient length provided only that they are maintained uniformly. As an example, if the unit be 1/4-inch, then this current line will be drawn 1/2-inch long. Incidentally, this current line has now become a vector. The criterion for a vector is that its length be an exact indication of the *magnitude* of a force and its orientation show the *direction* in which that force is acting. These conditions obviously now are satisfied.

Note that the vector portraying current is placed near the destination end and on that side of the path line from which the force of the current is acting. This is slightly unorthodox and may raise a murmur of dissent from old-timers who dot their *i*'s and cross their *t*'s religiously. But this method is chosen deliberately because it emphasizes the idea of counteracting current, greatly reduces the possibility of error, and yields an answer most easily understood because it "looks right."

A radius is chosen that is 10 units or 2 1/2 inches (because the speed of the boat is 10 mph.) and this is swung from the end of the current vector to intersect the path line #1 at E. This is line #2, the resultant of the vector diagram, and it points in the direction the boat must be steered. The solution to the problem was made rather picturesquely at (a) for ease of understanding; in actual practice the work would take on the appearance of (b). The lines preferably are penciled in a clear space on the chart rather than through the landmarks; the compass rose provides a convenient means of reading and laying down angles with a parallel rule. Either the inside or the outside compass rose can be employed, although using the outer rose for true bearings is considered standard. However, the inside magnetic rose generally is simpler for the shorter runs of the average small boat because it eliminates the calculations for variations and lets the solution be applied directly to the steering compass with only deviation to be taken into account. (If the graphic solution is worked on a separate paper instead of on the chart, it is wise to draw a reference north line.)

The graphic solution has yielded one additional answer which can be of great importance on a cruise: the *actual* speed made by the vessel along its intended path from start to destination. (This should not be confused with the 10-mph speed of the boat through the water along line #2.) Measuring the length of line (now vector) #1 from the intersection E to the point D shows that it is 9.8 units long; the speed along #1 therefore is 9.8 mph. If the river were 4 miles wide, it would take exactly 24.5 minutes to cross even though the boat is traveling at 10 mph. (4 ÷ 9.8 × 60 = 24.5 minutes). Transferring the direction line #2 to the compass rose shows that the course should be 12 degrees.

These two diverse speeds bring the need for the terminology with which the lines in (b) are marked. Line #2 is labeled in the normal way with course C above and speed S below. The course is identified in degrees from the compass rose (mark it M if magnetic), the speed is the speed of the boat. Line #1 is marked above with TR for track because it is the direction the vessel is taking even though this is not the direction steered. Below the line is SOA for speed of advance or SOG for speed over ground because this is the answer found in the solution.

The procedure just illustrated is equally applicable to the solution of currents coming from *any* angle. In Figure 17-16, for instance, the current is helping the boat and

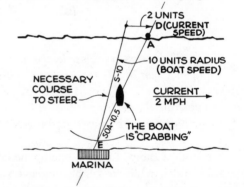

Figure 17-16: The graphic solution follows the same procedure as that in Figure 17-15 for currents from any angle. Again, the length from D to E is the speed the boat will make over the ground.

SOA is greater than S. There are only two exceptions that make a graphic solution unnecessary. These are a current going in *exactly* the *same* direction as the boat and a current going in *exactly* the *opposite* direction as the boat. In the former case, the speed of the current is added to the boat speed; in the latter case, it is subtracted. The reasons for all the graphics, additions, and subtractions is that our interest is in the speed and course of the craft over the *ground* and not just through the water. (Remember, the point of departure and the destination are both fixed to the ground.)

Solutions could of course be made trigonometrically to much greater exactitude, but for all practical purposes the graphic errors can be neglected. As the old-time Navy captain said to the newly-aboard ensign who complained about a half-degree error in the compass: "You try and steer that close!"

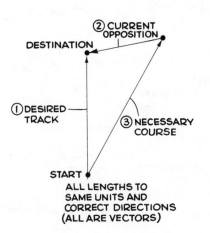

Figure 17-17: The basic vector triangle solves for the third side whenever two sides are known. Each side is a vector and must be drawn to exact length and direction.

The diagram in Figure 17-17 is the basic vector triangle and it should be committed to memory. With any two of its sides known and drawn to correct angles and lengths, the third can be found instantly simply by drawing the completing line. This line then is read for direction and length. For instance, if the course steered and the time at speed is known (side #3), and a fix from landmarks or other means determines the actual track made good (side #1), then the set and drift of the current or wind which was acting on the boat is side #2.

The current with which we have been dealing in these examples presumably is merely the actual motion of the water over the ground. The professional navigator has a much broader definition of "current" when he makes these computations, however. Under the heading of current he lumps everything that causes his ship to move over the ground in a direction and speed at variance with the course he is steering and the RPM of his engines. Thus "current" for him includes winds, waves, unintended changes in RPM, lapses in exact steering, and even a fouled bottom whose added hull resistance cuts down speed.

One further very important piece of information for the skipper is yielded by the simple vector triangle: It tells the number of miles, or the speed, which must be run in order to make good the desired number of miles or speed. This could be more or less, depending on the direction of the current relative to the direction of the destina-

tion. The answer is given by the relative lengths of sides #1 and #3. In Figure 17-15 the boat has made way *through the water* for more miles than the actual distance straight across the river. In Figure 17-16 the boat has made way for fewer miles *through the water* than the direct straight line to the destination.

The vector relationship is in use routinely in the navigation of commercial and naval ships. They usually must complete a certain track in a definite time at a definite speed. To accomplish this they vary their speed on the steered course. This does not apply as widely to pleasure craft because small boat skippers generally cruise their vessels at a constant, optimal speed—and they need not meet the exigencies of a schedule—while strict windjammers are at nature's mercy.

Chart Work

All professional courses in navigation lay great stress on clean, clear, businesslike chart work. A medium-soft lead pencil sharpened to a good point is the preferred marking tool because its lines can be erased without undue damage to the chart.

As in any technical computation or diagram, every line should be marked for later identification and understanding. A set of symbols for this purpose is suggested. These should be memorized and used until they become habitual. The shapes chosen should provide immediate visual identification on first glance at a chart bearing them. For example, a circle denotes a "fix." A half-circle shows a "running fix." A square identifies an "estimated position." A triangle marks a "dead reckoning."

POSITION FINDING.

The souse who wakes up the next morning and mutters "Where am I?" is no more baffled than many novice skippers on their first cruise. Yet, it isn't as difficult as all that —as further glances over the shoulder of our experienced skipper-navigator will show.

Position to the landlubber is generally a very finite thing: He is at the corner of such a street and such an avenue. To the navigator, his position may be only a line and the knowledge that his ship is somewhere on it. (A similarity in motoring might be driving down a known avenue but being unable to identify the cross streets because they are not marked.) Such a line is a "line of position" and abbreviated by professionals into LOP.

This is a timely point to urge every small boat skipper to acquire a beneficial habit—the habit of labeling every line he puts down on a chart. Nothing is more conducive to error than a conglomeration of lines on a chart whose individual imports have been forgotten, and whose distinction between tracks and LOPs has been lost.

There is an accepted standard convention of marking and labeling the lines drawn on a chart while working out a ship's position. Above the line is placed the time the observation was made; it is preferably noted in the four digits of the twenty-four-hour system. Below the line (and directly under the time) is written either the bearing in degrees for a straight line or the radius in miles for the arc. The foregoing is for *LOPs*. Track lines, the lines depicting the paths of the boat, are labeled slightly differently. On these the course in degrees (followed by *M* if magnetic) is preceded by a *C* and placed above the line; directly below is the speed, preceded by an *S*. Illustrations of these markings are given in Figure 17-18.

RANGE.

The easiest line of position is the range, and here range does *not* mean distance. A line is drawn on the chart through the two range marks that are seen directly in line from the boat. (See the description of ranges given on page 411 in this chapter.) This line becomes an LOP. It is labeled above with the time but *no* bearing is written below because its position is a fixed-chart function, always the same whether or not the boat is there. The range line is observed by sighting without instrumentation.

As with all lines of position, this LOP tells the skipper only that his boat is on that line; it does *not* tell him *where* on that line. Such precise information is obtained by methods explained on page 429 in this chapter. The range LOP is pictured at (a) in Figure 17-18.

BEARING.

The pelorus is used for obtaining a bearing line of position. To do this, the pelorus is sighted on a charted shore object of known position. (The pelorus is described in Chapter 9.)

Pelorus bearings can be taken either as true, magnetic, or relative. The time-honored method is true and for this

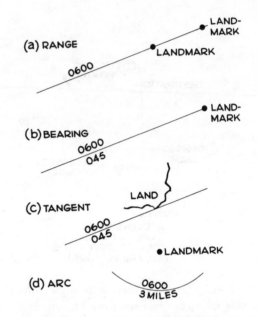

Figure 17-18: (a) A range line of position laid down on a chart is marked only with the time above the line. (b) A bearing line of position is marked with the time above and the direction in degrees below. (c) A line of position laid down as a tangent to a land promontory is marked with the time above and the bearing below. (d) An arc of position is marked with the time inside and the radius distance outside. (All times are noted in the 24-hour system. All bearings are assumed to be true unless marked as magnetic.)

the pelorus card is set to its lubber's line so that its reading corresponds to the compass heading plus or minus any deviation and plus or minus any variation. This aligns the pelorus card with true north. The charted object is then sighted, as with gunsights, and the pelorus card reading under the sight vane is noted. A line drawn from the charted object at the reciprocal of this angle on the chart becomes the bearing LOP. (The reciprocal of an angle is found by adding or subtracting 180 degrees.) The result is shown at (b).

The foregoing operation assumes a calm sea and absolutely steady steering, two fortunate conditions that do not always obtain. Under less benign circumstances the pelorus card is set with its zero at the lubber's line. At the command "Mark" the helmsman notes the exact compass heading and the man at the pelorus takes his sight and reading. This is a relative bearing and is easily converted to true for application to the chart by addition or subtraction of compass bearing, deviation, and variation.

TANGENT.

Sometimes the only visible, fixed charted object is a promontory which is much too large to be considered as a single-point target for a sighting. In such cases a sight is taken that just "kisses" the extreme edge, in other words, a tangent. Again, the pelorus is used. (This sight can be tricky because the promontory often does not look as clearly defined as it appears on the chart.)

As before, the pelorus card is set to the corrected heading and the sight taken therefore becomes true. (The rough weather technique can also be used, of course.) The bearing laid down on the chart is the reciprocal of the pelorus reading. The line, an LOP, is labeled with time and bearing as shown at (c).

CIRCLE.

In some situations only an "island" object like a lightship or a Texas tower may be seen without any visible correlating land mass. The distance to this object can be found either by timing the difference in arrival between its radio signal and its sound, by checking a radar screen, or by measuring the angle subtended by its known height with a sextant and referring to Bowditch tables. This distance, translated into chart miles, is used as the radius of a circle with the object as the center. This circle is the LOP at that particular time and is so inscribed, as at (d). The boat is somewhere on that circle. (The identical technique can be used with a prominent landmark such as a tower or a tall chimney.)

FIX.

A fix is a mark on a chart that shows the "exact" position of the boat at that exact indicated time. A fix is arrived at by having two or preferably three or more LOPs cross; the crossing point is the fix. It is only the meticulous (and lucky) skipper whose LOPs cross at a point; most of the time the crossing will be a small triangle. The boat is within that triangle, and generally this is accurate enough for practical purposes. A fix is always labeled with the time of its determination, the time being given in four digits (e.g., 1425). A fix is emphasized with a small circle around the intersection. (The four-digit system of noting time starts at one minute after midnight, 0001, and continues to the next midnight, 2400.)

Any of the four enumerated lines of position may be combined with any other in obtaining a fix. The only

requirement is that there be an intersection. The closer this angle of intersection is to 90 degrees, the more accurate the fix is likely to be, because the effect of slight sighting errors is reduced. For this reason two bearing LOPs which are close together should be avoided if possible because the errors are magnified. Some typical fixes are illustrated in Figure 17-19.

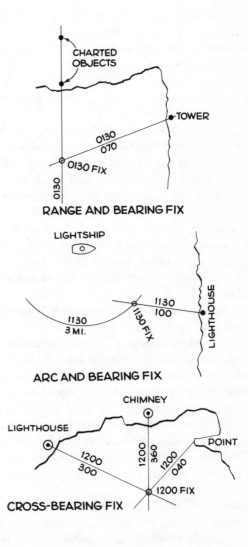

Figure 17-19: How LOPs are combined to make a fix is illustrated above for various combinations.

THREE-ARM FIX.

The three-arm protractor, described in Chapter 9, makes possible what might be described as an "automatic" simultaneously two-bearing fix. The three-arm method provides a reasonably accurate fix except under a special condition called the "monkey loop." When the boat is on this monkey loop, the three-arm no longer affords a fix but only a circular line of position which has little if any value.

Three objects, clearly marked on the chart and visible at the same time, are selected. The angle between the center and the one on the right is measured with a pelorus or a sextant. This angle is set on the right arm of the three-arm protractor. The angle between the center and the left object is measured and set on the left arm of the protractor.

The protractor is now placed on the chart with the central arm's datum line directly on the central object and the marking hole at the approximate location of the boat. The protractor is now moved about until the left and right arms simultaneously bisect the left and right objects. A pencil mark through the hole now provides the fix.

Theoretically, the two measurements of angles should be made at exactly the same instant. Practically, on a boat of moderate speed, or no speed at all if it is stopped, the error caused by viewing the angles in quick succession is negligible.

As to that monkey loop: Geometry tells us that any three points not in a straight line determine a circle. Thus, if the boat happens to be on the circle determined by the three sighted objects, it is on the monkey loop and its position is indeterminate. The best preventive is to select three objects on, or nearly on, a straight line. Then the determined circle is so large that it will not affect the fix because it will be off the chart. Another safeguard is to select a central landmark nearer than the right and left ones. Then the monkey loop curves landward, away from you, and leaves you safe from it.

ELECTRONIC NAVIGATION.

The radio direction-finding devices described in Chapter 8 can greatly simplify and expedite position finding. In one sense, these are visual aids, although their "eyes" can see through night and fog.

The laying down of an LOP with the data obtained from a radio direction finder is not much different from the same operation when the information derives from a pelorus. In both cases an angle is given and drawn from a fixed landmark on the chart. Two radio LOPs can be crossed to make a fix or a radio line can be crossed with any of the other lines.

Radar has the additional advantage that it supplies distance information as well as angle information. These in themselves constitute a fix—although generally not one of great accuracy.

Loran is the fastest method of obtaining LOPs and fixes once the technique of instrument operation has been mastered. Either loran charts or loran tables are required to be on board in addition to the loran equipment. (Loran is explained in Chapter 8.)

The proper loran radio station pair is selected by referring the approximate or DR position of the boat to the loran chart. The receiver is then set to the controls indicated for that station pair. The time differences in the received signals, determined manually (or automatically in the more elaborate equipment), indicate which of the charted loran curves are applicable. As in all other methods, a single loran curve is an LOP and the intersection of two loran lines is the fix.

It should be remembered that radio waves, for all their magic, are not infallible. They are affected by sun and atmospheric conditions, they are refracted by the different mediums through which they pass, they fade, and they skip.

DEAD RECKONING.

The logbooks of years ago had a column headed "deduced reckoning." Entered under this heading were those data not collected by actual sightings and fixes. This became shortened to "ded. reckoning" and phonetically evolved into the dead reckoning of today. The history of the term makes its definition obvious. In chart work the dead reckoning is abbreviated DR and a DR position is suggested to be marked with a triangle.

The DR track on a chart could be defined as nautical wishful-thinking because it marks the path the navigator hopes the ship will take. Currents, and here the word is used in the all-inclusive sense already defined, may throw the boat off course or slow it down and discredit the navigator's estimate. Dead reckoning is the only resort when the weather closes off the landmarks and misfortune eliminates other position-finding means. While the DR track rarely is an exact trace of the boat's path over the ground, it is valuable nevertheless, as an indication of proximity to or safety from danger.

A DR track is laid down from a well-defined fix. Above the line is the course and below it the speed. The line continues straight as long as the course remains unchanged and for a distance determined by the speed of the boat and the scale of the chart. At regular intervals distance traveled is computed and the line is marked with a triangle and labeled with the time followed by DR. A change in speed is noted between two DRs. A change in course changes the direction of the line appropriately and the point of change is marked with a timed DR. An illustration of a DR track is given in Figure 17-20.

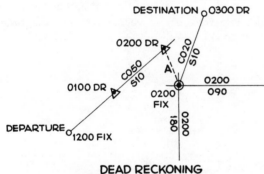

**DEAD RECKONING
& COURSE CORRECTION**

Figure 17-20: This dead reckoning plot was given a course correction by an 0200 fix (A) and a new DR plot was made from the fix to the destination.

The prudent skipper lays down his DR track on the chart before he leaves the dock. It does for him what a carefully itemized touring instruction does for the motorist; it alerts him to the maneuvers needed to reach his destination safely and expeditiously. Of course, if conditions permit en route, the skipper "updates" his DR track at every opportunity with a fix. These fixes almost never fall right on the DR track but with luck fall near it. The DR track is terminated at such an occurrence and a new track started with the fix as its origin. The process is repeated throughout the cruise. This track renewal is also depicted in Figure 17-20.

RUNNING FIX.

Since the small boat skipper is almost always his own

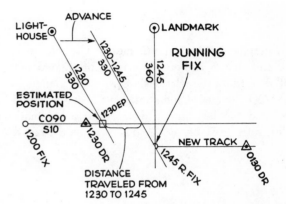

Figure 17-21: The LOP from the lighthouse at 1230 is advanced to 1245 with a parallel line moved forward for the distance traveled in 15 minutes. Crossing with another LOP makes a running fix. (The original 1230 LOP crossing with the track yields an Estimated Position EP.)

navigator, this puts a premium on his time at the chart and the pelorus. Often he gets only one "shot" at a landmark for a line of position before the target vanishes. With the "running fix" routine, he can advance this LOP to a further forward position on the chart.

Suppose the interval to be fifteen minutes. The skipper assumes that during this quarter-hour period the boat maintained its course and speed and therefore covered a predicted amount of ground in a predicted direction. He thereupon draws a parallel LOP as far forward as the number of miles traversed reduced to the scale of the chart. Figure 17-21 explains this. (The new LOP bears both times.)

ESTIMATED POSITION.

Often the data compiled to determine a ship's whereabouts are not sufficiently trustworthy to generate a fix but nevertheless have some validity. Such information can be used for an estimated position EP. Figure 17-21 shows an EP determined by an LOP and a DR track. An EP is marked with a surrounding square and labeled with time followed by the designation EP.

DISTANCES.

Distance is an important parameter to the skipper—not so much the total distance run as the distance from a shoal or other danger. This distance can be measured by optical-mechanical means, as for instance the stadimeter or the range finder shown in Chapter 9. But more often these distances are not measured directly but rather are deduced by graphic or trigonometric means. The solutions are by rule of thumb without knowledge of trigonometry, but all depend on the relationships within a triangle.

Most famous of the stratagems is the bow-and-beam method for determining distance off a landmark; it is illustrated in Figure 17-22. It is based on the fact that the

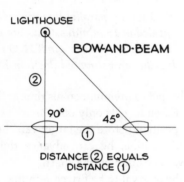

LIGHTHOUSE

BOW-AND-BEAM

②

90° 45°

①

DISTANCE ② EQUALS
DISTANCE ①

Figure 17-22: When the lighthouse bears exactly 90° the boat is as far from it as the distance run since the 45° bearing.

two sides of a 45-degree right triangle are equal. A landmark ahead is sighted on the pelorus. When it is bearing 45 degrees timekeeping is begun. Course and speed are maintained and the landmark is kept in sight; when it bears 90 degrees the elapsed time is computed and turned into miles by reference to the RPM-speed chart. At that moment the boat is exactly as far from the landmark as the distance run.

It is obvious that other innate relationships of the angles and sides of a triangle could be used for distance measurement, not merely the 45-degree case. Many such are listed in the table and more are found in Bowditch.

AVOIDING DANGER.

Often in coastal running it is important to keep a certain distance offshore to avoid shoals. Visual judgment is

easily fooled by the monotony of sea- and landscapes; the prudent skipper wants a more reliable warning. Common methods are danger bearings and danger angles.

The methods are simple. The danger area, usually one that lies submerged and therefore cannot be seen directly, is outlined on the chart. The outline is correlated with one or more landmarks and those bearings noted beyond which the boat will stand into the danger. The skipper then takes constant sight bearings underway and makes certain that none of them approaches the critical angle. These would all be horizontal angles.

Vertical angles can also be employed, usually in connection with Bowditch table #9. The angle subtended by a landmark of known height is computed from the edge of the danger outline. Subsequent sightings of the vertical angle are made with a sextant and if any approaches the critical angle the boat is veered off. The diagrams in Figure 17-23 show both vertical and horizontal methods.

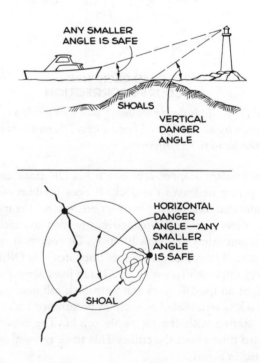

ANY SMALLER
ANGLE IS SAFE

SHOALS

VERTICAL
DANGER
ANGLE

HORIZONTAL
DANGER
ANGLE—ANY
SMALLER
ANGLE
IS SAFE

SHOAL

Figure 17-23: Both horizontal and vertical angles can be used to stay out of danger areas. The vertical angle method requires landmarks of known height.

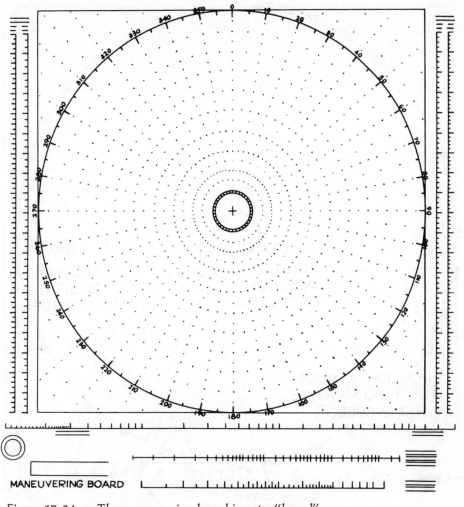

*Figure 17-24-a: The maneuvering board is not a "board"
but rather a sheet of paper almost a foot square printed as
shown above. These sheets come in pads of 50 and were
originated by the Hydrographic Office (now the U.S.
Oceanographic Office); they bear the number H.O. 2665
and are available at most chart outlets. They make it easy
to solve relative motion problems graphically.*

MANEUVERING BOARD.

Figure 17-24 is a reproduction of an extremely handy navigating gadget called a Maneuvering Board put out by the U.S. Navy Oceanographic Office and available at nominal cost from the Government Printing Office or, more conveniently, from chart vendors. The maneuvering board is not a "board" at all but rather a printed sheet of heavy paper about a foot square. The imprints consist of a large, centrally located circle divided accurately into degrees, a speed-time-distance nomograph and several ratio scales. The only "tools" needed for solving navigation problems with this device are a pencil and a straight edge although the addition of a parallel rule and a pair of dividers enables the retrieval of additional information.

The simplest navigation problem, and the one most often requiring solution by the pleasure boatman, involves distance traveled, elapsed time and the resultant speed.

The maneuvering board provides the answer either with a dividers or with a pencil and straight edge. Figure 17-24b shows both methods.

The divider solution involves the long logarithmic scale directly below the large circle. Assume that you have run three miles and it took you 20 minutes to do it. Place one point of the divider on 20 and open the second point to 3. Now without changing the divider spread, move the first point to 60 and the second point will rest on 9, the desired answer (9 miles per hour).

The straight edge solution of this same problem is even simpler and uses the three-scale nomograph. With the straight edge on 20 (time scale) and also on 3 (distance scale) draw a line. This will intersect 9 on the speed scale.

The advantage of the divider method is the ability to constantly reuse the same sheet for successive problems because no drawing is required. Such drawing soon would

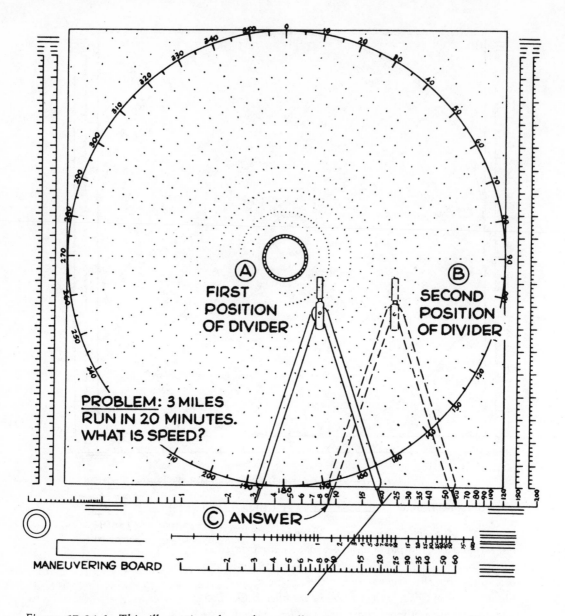

Figure 17-24-b: This illustration shows how walking a divider along the logarithmic scale of a maneuvering board immediately solves time-distance-speed problems without computation.

fill the nomograph with lines that create confusion. (Of course you could avert this by reading the answer directly from the straight edge without actually drawing the line.)

The foregoing are elementary, kindergarten uses of the maneuvering board. The board really comes into its own when it is employed for the solution of the more sophisticated problems involving the relative motions of your ship and another or the effects of wind and current on your course. Figure 17-24c explains a sample operation. The basic instruction to remember is that in all solutions your ship is at the exact center of the circle and is the reference ship (R) while the other boat is the maneuverer (M). Standard practice is to designate the points of a *relative plot* with capital letters and the points of a *speed triangle* with lower case letters. The common abbreviations are

DRM (direction of relative motion) and CPA (closest point of approach).

The concept of relative motion is fundamental in naval maneuvers but nevertheless also useful to the serious pleasure boatman. Your own boat is considered to have no movement of its own, to be stationary, with the other boat, the maneuverer, constantly changes its position relative to yours. To fix this idea in your mind, think of driving down a highway at 50 miles per hour when another car going at 60 miles per hour passes you. If you imagine yourself standing still during this passage then the other car has a relative motion of 10 miles per hour away from you. In maneuvering board problems, likewise, your boat always is standing still at the center.

The first sighting of the maneuver in Figure 17-24c oc-

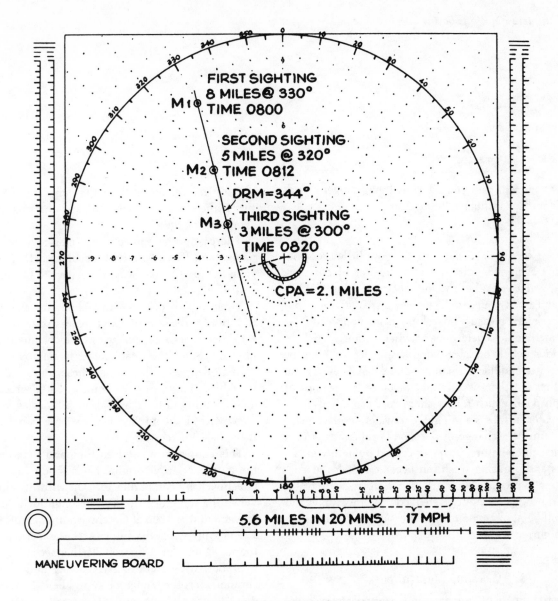

FIRST SIGHTING
8 MILES @ 330°
M1 ⊙ TIME 0800

SECOND SIGHTING
5 MILES @ 320°
M2 ⊙ TIME 0812

DRM=344°

THIRD SIGHTING
M3 ⊙ 3 MILES @ 300°
TIME 0820

CPA=2.1 MILES

5.6 MILES IN 20 MINS.   17 MPH

MANEUVERING BOARD

*Figure 17-24-c : Plotting three sightings of an approaching
vessel on the maneuvering board leads to a graphical solution of that vessel's speed and its closest point of approach
(CPA). The above plot proves that there is no danger of
collision because the other vessel will pass astern.*

curred at 0800 and was found to be 8 miles at 330 degrees; this becomes the point M-1. Second sighting is 5
miles at 320 degrees and 0812 noted at point M-2. Third
sighting is 3 miles at 300 degrees, time 0820 for point M-3.
Plotting these and connecting them with a straight line
gives the DRM; transferring the line to the center with a
parallel rule shows the direction of relative motion to be
344 degrees. A perpendicular from the center to this line
(a perpendicular is the shortest distance) becomes the CPA
and the distance circle at this point shows that the closest
point of approach of the maneuver will be 2.1 miles, if
both ships maintain course and speed, and she will pass
astern.

The only drawback to the foregoing on a small boat is
that distance must be measured or closely estimated and

the equipment for this often is not at hand. In this connection, radar shines because it reads distance automatically. One method of "guesstimating" distance is to check
the horizon distance for your height of eye in a Bowditch
table and to use this as a "unit."

Further information can be gleaned from the plot in
Figure 17-24c. Placing a dividers from point M-1 to point
M-3 and using the measuring circles shows this distance
to be 5.6 miles made in 20 minutes. The logorithmic scale
solves this as being 17 miles per hour. Now you know
that the ship you have been observing is running on a
course of 344 degrees at a speed of 17 MPH. (Unless you
intend to torpedo her, this is not very valuable information, but you cannot dispute the fascination of being able
to perform these navigational tricks. However, the knowl-

edge that she will pass you astern without danger of collision definitely is valuable information.)

EYEBALL TECHNIQUES.

Many experienced boatmen develop little personal tricks for estimating distance offshore, set of currents, depth of water and other routine aspects of piloting. Dot-your-*i* and cross-your-*t* sailors often disparage these but they serve many pleasure boat skippers in good stead.

One method is to determine at what distances offshore the various details on land (windows, signs, etc.) can be distinguished and then to maintain these distances. As you get further out there is the sight distance to the tops of telegraph poles which follow shore roads.

The water surface is a fair guide to water depth. The indication can be a change in color on windless days or a difference in the nature of ripples caused by light winds.

Wake and propeller wash can become telltales of current acting to produce leeway. When such sideward offset occurs during a straight-steered course, the wake and wash will be at an angle toward the side from which the wind or current is acting.

Celestial Navigation

For most skippers of sailboats and powerboats, celestial navigation is a hobby rather than a necessity. Accordingly, it will be dealt with here only fleetingly, more with the intention of inducing future study than of turning out practitioners. It often has been said facetiously that if you are on the Atlantic Ocean and remember where the sun sets, you can always steer your way home—and therefore that's all the celestial navigation you need to know.

The most important factor in celestial navigation is time. The art of determining precise locations on the globe by means of the heavenly bodies did not come of age until the chronometer was invented. In latter years, the chronometer has lost its importance because super-accurate time is available all over the earth by radio.

Our conception of time derives from the rotation of the earth. This is *solar* time; it is not as unvarying as we commonly believe. Depending upon the earth's position in its orbit around the sun, our day is sometimes a little more and sometimes a little less than twenty-four hours in length. Since clocks cannot follow such variations, they work on an even twenty-four-hour cycle and consequently

develop discrepancies with the sun. The difference between the clock or mean time and the solar time is the "equation of time."

There is another kind of time that is met with in celestial navigation. This is *sidereal* time. Sidereal time is computed from the rotation of the earth relative to the stars. ("Sidereal" denotes stars.)

Time actually differs with each minute change in longitude but for the sake of convenience arbitrary hourly time zones have been established in which time is considered uniform. Since the total change in time is one hour for each 15 degrees of longitude, these zones are 15 degrees in width (15 degrees $\times$ 24 hours = 360 degrees). By common consent, all time, and all longitudes as well, start at Greenwich, England, and Greenwich Mean Time (GMT) is the basis of reckoning.

This equivalence between time and longitude enables the navigator to determine his position east or west of Greenwich by comparing the sun with his chronometer. When the sun crosses 0 degrees longitude in its *apparent* movement it is 1200 at Greenwich. By definition it is also 1200 locally when the sun crosses the meridian on which the navigator finds himself. If this second event occurs five hours after the first, which fact he learns from his chronometer, the navigator knows he is 5 $\times$ 15 or 75 degrees west of Greenwich. (The small correction for the equation of time has been neglected.)

As in terrestrial navigation or piloting, this knowledge affords only a line of position (the longitude), and some other data must provide a crossing line in order to get a fix. A suitable crossing coordinate would be the latitude; this, too, can be found with the sextant.

Since the earth's axis is inclined, the apparent path of the sun around the earth (actually the earth's path around the sun), called the ecliptic, is also inclined to the equator. The inclination is 23.5 degrees and the sun thus oscillates from this value above the equator (the summer solstice) to this amount below the equator (the winter solstice). The two crossings of the equator that occur during this path are the vernal equinox and the autumnal equinox. (See Figure 17-25).

The reason these ecliptic movements of the sun have importance in celestial navigation is that they have been minutely computed and tabled for every day and every time. By reading the sun's altitude with his sextant and referring this to date and time, the navigator can deter-

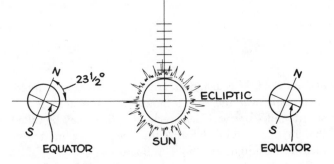

Figure 17-25: The earth experiences summer and winter because its axis is inclined to the plane of the ecliptic. The sun's most northerly "position" occurs at the summer solstice, the most southerly at the winter solstice. The sun's two "crossings" of the equator are the vernal equinox and the autumnal equinox.

mine a line of position.

The stars also are useful to the celestial navigator. The stars, like all celestial bodies, have an *apparent* movement across the sky. In consequence, each has a continually changing ground position (GP) which is the point on the earth directly beneath it. (The sun also has a GP.) This GP is the center of an imaginary circle on the earth from every point on which an observer would see the celestial body at the same angle of elevation. The celestial triangle is formed by connecting the GP, the observer's assumed position, and the nearer pole. The solution of this triangle leads to the determination of the navigator's line of position. Although this triangle is in the realm of spherical trigonometry, it can be unraveled without mathematical skill by using the Bowditch tables. (See Figure 17-26.)

The foregoing is an academic procedure. Today's navigator opens his H.O.214 or H.O.229 and works his

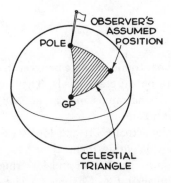

Figure 17-26: The celestial triangle is in the realm of spherical trigonometry but it can be solved for the observer's position with the aid of Bowditch tables.

solutions from the tables contained therein.

POLARIS.

One star in the firmament supplies approximate information from a simple sighting without further tables or computation. This star is Polaris, the North Star. This is true because it is almost exactly 90 degrees from the equator.

Directly reading the declination of Polaris with a sextant gives the latitude of the observer. Depending upon the time of night, the error could vary from zero to about fifty miles. Even this error can be eliminated, if need be, by simple computations with the aid of Bowditch tables.

The Inland Boatman—
Boating on Lakes and Rivers

The myriad lakes and rivers of America have lured boatmen as effectively as have the coastal waters. No inland lake large enough to float a hull is without its quota of pleasure boats, no river runs its course without passing marinas. Thus the landlocked flotillas are comprised of every type of vessel from the smallest sailboats and outboards to the most majestic yachts.

The basic skills of handling a boat properly are the same regardless of where the cruise may lead but there are nuances peculiar to inland waters. Some lakes are veritable oceans and often produce ocean-like storms, but Nature expresses herself in a voice different from the one she uses on the coasts. Many inland rivers technically are without tides but their rise and fall, caused by rain and land drainage, can assume tidal proportions without tidal regularity.

Perhaps the greatest variance between inland and coastal boating has to do with water levels. All rivers, bays and sounds that flow into the ocean have their confluence at sea level.

By contrast, inland rivers of any great length often flow through topography of widely varying elevations. They went their way via raging rapids and even waterfalls that made boating impossible until man arrived with his locks and dams. Knowing how to traverse these locks ("locking through") therefore becomes a necessary skill for the inland boatman.

It is part of Nature's scheme that rivers carry silt. But accumulations of silt rob channels of their depth and confound man's efforts to maintain accurate charts. Thus the inland chart is not as reliable as one for coastal waters—and the inland skipper must be able to surmount the discrepancy by his ability to "read" the waters.

Except on the largest lakes, the inland boatman's cruising area does not take him out of sight of land in fair weather. On most rivers his courses are restricted to the channels, which may be tortuous. This puts the emphasis on manual steering and makes autopilots excess baggage, but the ever-changing shoreside scene turns the watch at the wheel into a bonus instead of a drudgery. The landscape reeks with history and runs the gamut from the poorest to the richest. Some showboats have even defied time to give an inkling of what it was like to live on the river early in the century. (Figure 17-27.)

A major facility for pleasure boating in the eastern central portion of the country is the complex of dams, lakes, reservoirs and locks built by the Tennessee Valley Authority (TVA). From beginning to end, this man-made or man-improved waterway stretches for 650 miles, every inch suitable for sail and power. The extent of the development is shown in Figure 17-28.

The Mississippi Valley is another treasure trove for the pleasure-boatman. The mighty Mississippi River and its tributaries provide thousands of miles of cruising and myriads of natural coves and safe harbors for pleasant overnight mooring. Here, too, the river was tamed and shorn of most of its dangers by locks, dams and canals around the bad spots. The intricacy of some of this massive engineering is shown in Figure 17-29.

CHARTS.

Charts for lakes and rivers differ in their technical construction (and often in their general appearance) from the charts of coastal waters. The Corps of Engineers, which is responsible for charting inland waterways, prefers the polyconic projection (see Chapter 422) to the Mercator projection which is standard for the coastal delineations.

Since river depth (or height) is largely dependent upon seasonal and weather conditions, and consequently can vary drastically and uncyclically, this factor is given great importance on river maps and charts. Bulletin boards which list the water stage are placed prominently at intervals along the shore.

Navigational aids such as lights are labeled with name and mileage. The distances are computed from a reference point near the river's mouth and are measured in statute miles upriver. Dead reckoning (if it may be called that in this simplified form) thus becomes a matter of identifying a light or a bulletin board.

Rivers tend to drop their ingested silt on the inside of a curve where the water velocity is lower. This places the deeper, desirable channel on the outside of the curve and necessitates some crossing over. Navigational aids line the crossover path and the charts show these in detail. Arrows indicate the direction of river current; this is very helpful when only small sections of the water are shown in detail. Coastal skippers will be familiar with the shades of blue that indicate shoal water because it is similar to the coloring on coastal charts.

Bodies of water that connect with the ocean are subject to tidal changes. Long rivers, such as the Mississippi, whose mountain headwaters are thousands of miles removed from its ocean or gulf mouth are subject to two sometimes opposing forces. One is the flow from the head of the river which is always down. The other, the tidal flow at the mouth, is both down and up in cyclic rotation, which often causes confused and choppy water.

Charts of lakes and rivers can be purchased from many of the marine suppliers in the specific area. Less conveniently, they can be ordered from the authorities who are in charge of the bodies of water. In most cases this would be the U.S. Army Corps of Engineers at the various regional headquarters. The Tennessee Valley Authority is the source for information about the waters which it controls. (These are shown in Figure 17-28.)

LOCKS.

Locks make boat traffic possible between two bodies of water which are on different levels. They route vessels around waterfalls and rapids and can act as the entrance gate for ships at a dam.

Although locks actually lift and lower vessels of any tonnage that can fit within them, they have no hoisting mechanism as such. The lifting and lowering is entirely the result of buoyancy. (See Chapter 1.) The ships in the lock simply continue to float as the water level therein goes up or goes down. The sketch in Figure 17-30 should help explain this.

Figure 17-27: Resplendent showboats like this were common on the inland rivers earlier in the century.

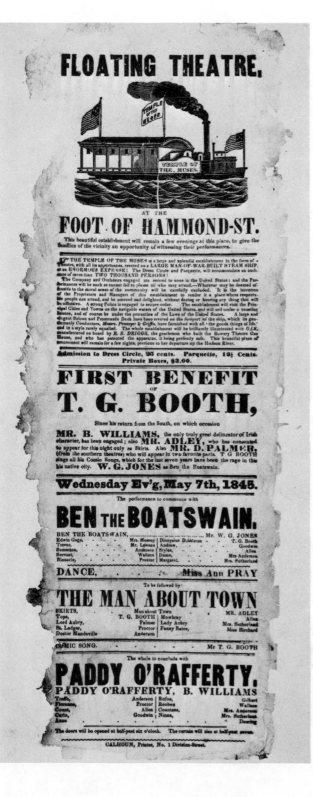

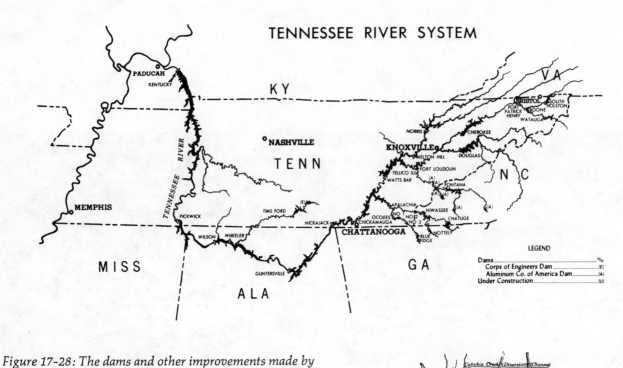

TENNESSEE RIVER SYSTEM

Figure 17-28: The dams and other improvements made by the Tennessee Valley Authority (TVA) have made 650 miles of water available to the pleasure-boatman.

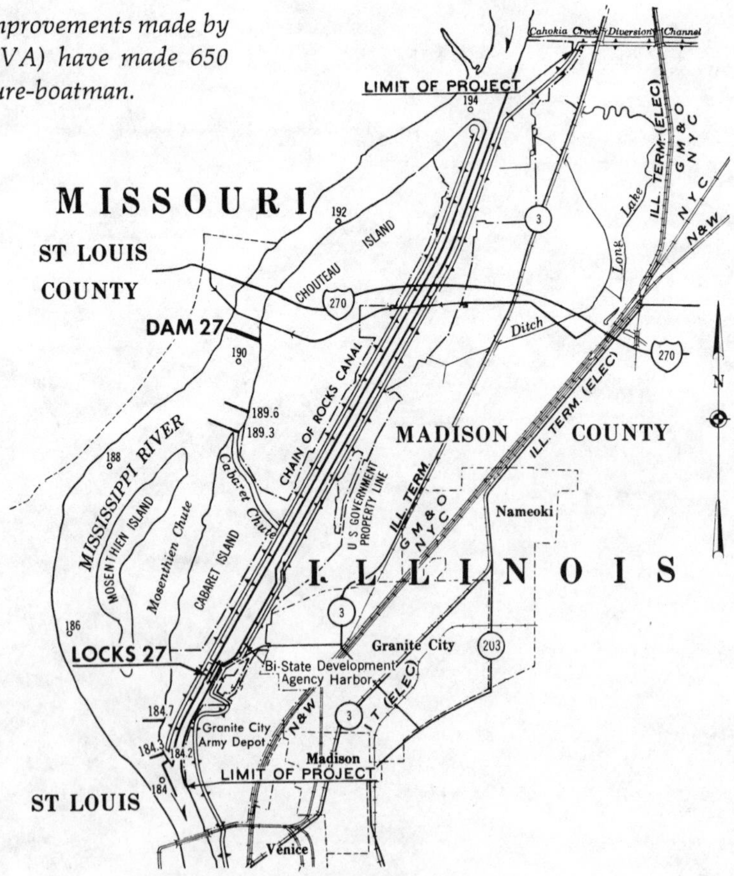

Figure 17-29: This map of a section of the Mississippi Valley shows the complicated constructions which have made this portion of the river navigable.

When Lock A is open and Lock B is closed, the water level within the lock is the same as that of the lower body of water. Vessels from this body enter. Lock A is then closed.

Water from the higher body is then allowed to enter the lock through sluiceways or pipes controlled by valves. This flow is caused entirely by gravity and ceases when the level within the lock is equal to the level of the higher body of water. Gate B is now opened and the vessels in the lock proceed out onto the higher body. Going from the higher to the lower is merely a reverse of the procedure just explained.

Another facet of the traffic problem is the fact that many boats are often in the lock simultaneously. This requires adequate fendering for self and neighbor protection.

Tying up in the lock while waiting for the ascent or descent also requires a bit of special attention. A boat may be level with the top of the lock upon entering and find itself perhaps twenty feet (or more) lower before leaving, or vice versa. This difference must be allowed for in the mooring lines. The best method is to loop the lines with one end under continuous manual control. Lines completely secured to cleats are simply asking for trouble.

Boats placed directly against a lock wall are most in need of adequate fendering because most walls are rough. Allowing the boat to rub against such surfaces on the way up and down is like subjecting the hull to the action of a huge rasp.

The time required to "lock through" (the interval between the closing of one gate, water level change and the opening of the other gate) is only a few minutes, always less than ten. Although this requires a tremendous amount of water to be transferred, the system is so well-conceived that currents are not a problem.

The gates of locks are of several types. One design is similar to huge doors that swing on hinges and make a watertight closure. Another slides up and down. Still another functions in a manner similar to garage doors. All are under complex electrical control; no major lock has manually operated gates.

DAMS.

Man has emulated the beaver in his zeal to dam up water. But while the beaver's dams are marvels of trees and brush, modern dams are highly engineered structures erected after long study of the ecological and commercial after-effects.

The hydrostatic forces exerted against a large dam are astronomical. Dam walls are so thick at the bottom that, despite the fact that they taper as they rise, the top is still wide enough for a multi-lane highway. Another form of dam has its top flush with the desired water level and acts as a spillway to maintain it. This latter form of dam can be a hazard to navigation for the unwary.

The hazard exists because the water spilling over the top looks like a horizon to an approaching boat, and the skipper cannot see beyond it. It is easy to get too close and be swept over—and boats have done this. Such mishaps are inherent to the upper level but the lower level has dangers too in the currents arising from spillover and spillway.

PILOTING IN RIVER, LAKE AND LOCK.

Earlier it was stated that the inland skipper must learn to "read" the water. He must not only learn, he must develop this skill to a high order if he wishes to keep from grounding on bars and scraping his bottom on obstructions. In many areas he cannot rely implicitly on charts; Nature's whimsical changes are too rapid for the cartographer.

The fluctuations from the charts occur most often on rivers with many bends and narrows and consequently many changes in velocity. Local knowledge, if it can be obtained, is a valuable addition to charts and skippers' skill. After all, the big ships take pilots aboard for upriver runs without any deflation of the captain's ego.

The eddy on the downstream side of buoys, spiles, spars and other fixed objects is a clue to current. The length and turbulence of this disturbance is a measure of water velocity and its point is in the direction of current flow. Objects just below the surface are revealed by lesser changes in the water plane; these partially hidden obstructions are the devils that lie in wait to rip propeller blades. (See Figure 17-31.)

Waves on the surface of a body of water are a visual evidence of hydrostatic pressures at work. There are also unseen pressure effects whose action is downward. When the water is deep enough for the uninhibited release of the forces peculiar to a certain wave height, the waves proceed smoothly. When the water is not deep enough, the

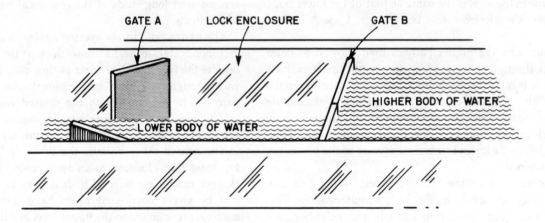

GATE A   LOCK ENCLOSURE   GATE B

HIGHER BODY OF WATER

LOWER BODY OF WATER

NOTE: BOTH GATES WOULD NOT BE OPEN SIMULTANEOUSLY

Figure 17-30: Locks harness the force of gravity to raise
and lower ships from one river level to another.

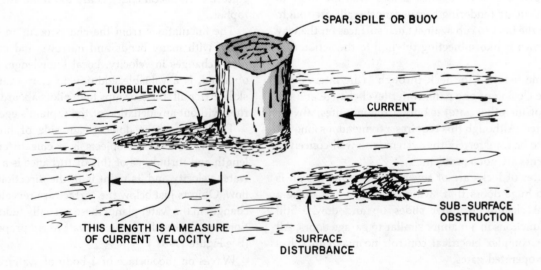

SPAR, SPILE OR BUOY

TURBULENCE

CURRENT

SUB-SURFACE
OBSTRUCTION

THIS LENGTH IS A MEASURE
OF CURRENT VELOCITY

SURFACE
DISTURBANCE

Figure 17-31: Many telltale signs advise the pleasure-
boatman about currents. Some are shown above.

forces are unbalanced, the wave tilts forward and the top breaks. This is the reason for breakers as the waves approach the shore.

Remembering this phenomenon can be of great use to the river and inland lake pilot. By watching the action of his bow wave and the waves in his wake he can get a warning when the depth becomes too shallow for comfort and safety.

The stretch of water between dams is referred to as a "pool" and the depth of this water determines the "pool stage" which is posted on bulletin boards along the way. There are frequent bulletin boards; chart notations alert the skipper where to look for one.

On many stretches of rivers the surrounding landscape abounds with identifiable landmarks which can be referred to on the chart. These, plus mileage markers, make it relatively easy to do "dead reckoning."

Commercial traffic has the edge on inland waters just as it seems to have on the coasts. Sometimes this is by legal decree but often it occurs only because the commercial boats are big enough and husky enough to take it. At any rate, it is wise for pleasure skippers to stay out of the way. Bear in mind the inscription on a certain gravestone: "He had the right of way and he took it."

18 *Weather Signs and Forecasting*

WHEN nature concocts our weather she seems to taunt man on his impotence. Fair weather or foul, rain or shine, whatever she decides to send, man can alter it not one whit.

All the energy locked in all the hydrogen bombs pugnacious man has stockpiled is dwarfed by the power nature unleashes in the first few minutes of a hurricane. A lightning storm carelessly dissipates more kilowatts than the largest central stations can generate. The force in the winds alone is greater than any which man's combined ingenuity has ever been able to produce.

The small boatman, like all his fellow creatures on this earth, must protect himself against nature's whims and learn to take advantage of her largesse. For every weather condition that endangers him, there are many that can add to his boating pleasure. The secret lies in knowing whether a good or a bad day is coming over the horizon. This depends on forecasting.

Weather Forecasting

The sailorman no longer needs the fanciful interpretations of "a red sun at dawning, a blazing ball at eve"; more scientific methods now are available to him. International agreements have spread a weather information-gathering network around the world. Weather satellites continuously circle the globe. Meteorologists and computers digest the resulting mountains of data into frequent terse statements of what we can expect.

The careful skipper can get daily, even hourly, weather forecasts from many sources. The radio broadcasting station is the most ubiquitous and perhaps the most widely used. In addition there are the TV, the newspapers, aircraft radio stations, the telephone companies, and the transmitters operated directly by the Weather Bureau. The Bureau offices also can be telephoned for last minute forecasts.

WEATHER MAPS.

The many factors needed to describe a weather condition precisely at any given place would become unwieldy and impossible to handle without a specialized shorthand notation. Such shorthand is used on weather maps. Like the squiggles in a stenographer's notebook, each line portrays a meaning.

A weather map is reproduced in Figure 18-1. If the mass of detail it carries is overwhelming at first inspection, this is a natural reaction for the uninitiated. But, as you get the hang of it, decoding becomes a simple, almost subconscious procedure, and the amount of information gained is surprising.

Two types of information coding are found on the map. The first refers to a general condition prevailing over a large area; examples of these would be isobars, frontal lines, isotherms, and precipitation shadings. The second type gives the exact weather conditions at one of the more than three hundred observation stations in the United States. This station information or report is grouped about the observatory's geographical location on the map and follows an exact pattern which is uniform throughout the world.

STATION REPORTS.

Illustrated in Figure 18-2 is a reproduction of a complete station report from a major Weather Bureau office. Information is given under *sixteen* categories; these items are lettered (only in this explanation, not in the original) and will now be explained. The central dot or circle (tagged X) locates the station on the map and by the solidity of its inking tells the total cloud cover at the time of observation. The code under which this inking is carried out is also shown. The circle in the example is completely inked and reference to the code reveals this to mean "sky completely overcast."

Item A. This symbol reports the type of *high* cloud cover which existed at that location at the time of observation. These symbols are decoded by Table A. The symbol in the example means "dense cirrus clouds in patches or twisted sheaves."

Item B. This symbol reports the clouds found at *middle* level and is decoded in accordance with Table B. The example conveys "altocumulus clouds in a chaotic sky."

Item C. This three-digit figure states the barometric pressure in millibars reduced to sea level so that pressures at various points may be compared. The first part of the numeral, a 9 or a 10, is omitted to save space because there is no practical possibility of confusion. In the example, 247 is read as 1024.7 millibars. The standard comparison pressure is 1000 millibars and this is equivalent to 29.53 inches of mercury. (The millibar is a unit in the CGS or centimeter-gram-second system.) Table C

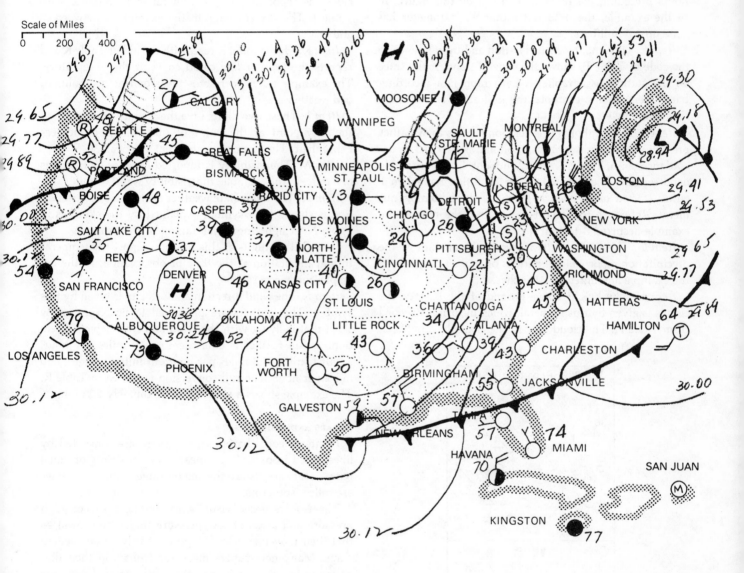

Figure 18-1: A daily weather map like this will be found in most big city newspapers. Decoding the wealth of information is not at all difficult.

compares millibars with inches of mercury.

Item D. The change in barometric pressure in the three hours preceding the reading is shown by this figure. In In the example, the +28 states that the barometer has gone up 2.8 millibars.

Item E. This line, by its inclination and by reference to the code in Table E, shows the general trend of the trace on the station barograph. (A barograph is a recording barometer.) In the example, the indication is a steadily rising barometer.

Item F. The symbol at this position reports the weather prevailing at the observing station and is decoded in accordance with Table F. The solid dot in the example denotes rain. The time when the condition named in F either started or stopped is given by the adjoining numeral. Reference to Table F shows that the rain in the example occurred 3 to four hours ago.

Item G. These two digits represent the amount of the precipitation reported in *hundreths* of an *inch*. The rain in the example amounted to .45 inches.

Item H. The height above ground of the base of the clouds is given by this numeral, which in turn is decoded from Table H. The cloud base in the example is between

300 and 599 feet high.

Item J. The portion of the sky covered by middle or low clouds is reported by this numeral in accordance with Table J. The sky coverage in the example is between .7 and .8

Item K. This symbol is read with the aid of Table K and reports the *type* of *low* cloud cover at the observatory. The example refers to fractostratus or fractocumulus of bad weather.

Item L. These two digits give the actual temperature of the dew point at the point of observation in degrees Fahrenheit. The example states that this was 30°F.

Item M. The visibility is reported in miles or fractions of a mile. In the example, the visibility was 3/4-mile.

Item N. The immediate weather at the time of observation is shown by a symbol explained by the sketches in Table N. A light snow was falling in the example.

Item P. Two digits at this position report the temperature at the station at the time of observation. In the example, this was 31°F.

Item R. The wind direction and velocity is given by this symbol. The feathers are presumed to be on an arrow shaft that is flying with the wind and thus depicts direction. A full feather is equivalent to 10 miles per hour, a half feather to 5 miles per hour, an initial wedge to 50 miles per hour. The full conversion is shown in Table R. The example shows a wind of approximately 20 mph.

ISOBARS AND ISOTHERMS.

Points of equal barometric pressure are connected by lines called isobars ("iso" means equal). Points of equal temperature are also connected on some maps; these lines are called isotherms.

The isobars serve visually to confine areas of high pressure and areas of low pressure (highs and lows) so that their movement can be spotted easily on succeeding maps. Many newspapers mark the isobars in their diagrams in inches of mercury; the official maps follow the international convention and mark in millibars. (See the conversion table.)

FRONTS.

The advancing edge of an air mass is called a front. Four types of fronts are indicated on weather maps: the cold front, the warm front, the occluded front, and the stationary front. The names are self-explanatory; the

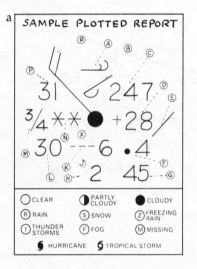

Figure 18-2: A complete sample station report (a) is located around every major reporting station on the large weather maps issued by the Weather Bureau. An explanation of the codes can be found by referring to (b) and (c). The central dot (marked X) is decoded by the table above.

b   PRESENT WEATHER (Descriptions Abridged from W. M. O. Code)

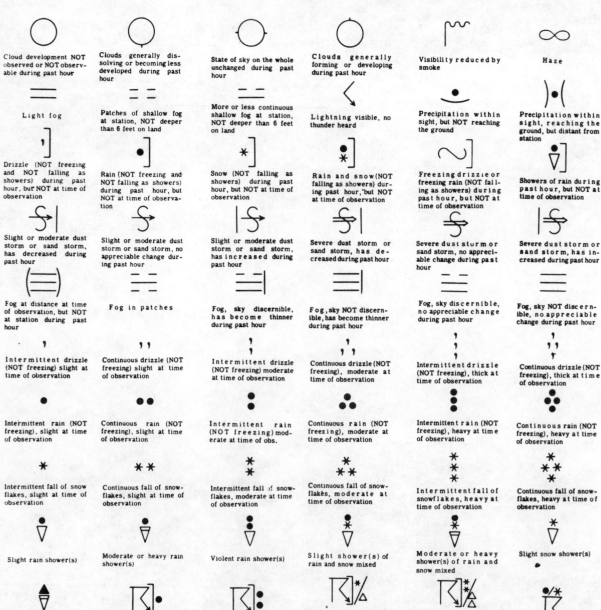

Cloud development NOT observed or NOT observable during past hour

Clouds generally dissolving or becoming less developed during past hour

State of sky on the whole unchanged during past hour

Clouds generally forming or developing during past hour

Visibility reduced by smoke

Haze

Light fog

Patches of shallow fog at station, NOT deeper than 6 feet on land

More or less continuous shallow fog at station, NOT deeper than 6 feet on land

Lightning visible, no thunder heard

Precipitation within sight, but NOT reaching the ground

Precipitation within sight, reaching the ground, but distant from station

Drizzle (NOT freezing and NOT falling as showers) during past hour, but NOT at time of observation

Rain (NOT freezing and NOT falling as showers) during past hour, but NOT at time of observation

Snow (NOT falling as showers) during past hour, but NOT at time of observation

Rain and snow (NOT falling as showers) during past hour, but NOT at time of observation

Freezing drizzle or freezing rain (NOT falling as showers) during past hour, but NOT at time of observation

Showers of rain during past hour, but NOT at time of observation

Slight or moderate dust storm or sand storm, has decreased during past hour

Slight or moderate dust storm or sand storm, no appreciable change during past hour

Slight or moderate dust storm or sand storm, has increased during past hour

Severe dust storm or sand storm, has decreased during past hour

Severe dust storm or sand storm, no appreciable change during past hour

Severe dust storm or sand storm, has increased during past hour

Fog at distance at time of observation, but NOT at station during past hour

Fog in patches

Fog, sky discernible, has become thinner during past hour

Fog, sky NOT discernible, has become thinner during past hour

Fog, sky discernible, no appreciable change during past hour

Fog, sky NOT discernible, no appreciable change during past hour

Intermittent drizzle (NOT freezing) slight at time of observation

Continuous drizzle (NOT freezing) slight at time of observation

Intermittent drizzle (NOT freezing) moderate at time of observation

Continuous drizzle (NOT freezing), moderate at time of observation

Intermittent drizzle (NOT freezing), thick at time of observation

Continuous drizzle (NOT freezing), thick at time of observation

Intermittent rain (NOT freezing), slight at time of observation

Continuous rain (NOT freezing), slight at time of observation

Intermittent rain (NOT freezing) moderate at time of obs.

Continuous rain (NOT freezing), moderate at time of observation

Intermittent rain (NOT freezing), heavy at time of observation

Continuous rain (NOT freezing), heavy at time of observation

Intermittent fall of snow flakes, slight at time of observation

Continuous fall of snow-flakes, slight at time of observation

Intermittent fall of snow-flakes, moderate at time of observation

Continuous fall of snow-flakes, moderate at time of observation

Intermittent fall of snowflakes, heavy at time of observation

Continuous fall of snow-flakes, heavy at time of observation

Slight rain shower(s)

Moderate or heavy rain shower(s)

Violent rain shower(s)

Slight shower(s) of rain and snow mixed

Moderate or heavy shower(s) of rain and snow mixed

Slight snow shower(s)

Moderate or heavy shower(s) of hail, with or without rain or rain and snow mixed, not associated with thunder

Slight rain at time of observation; thunderstorm during past hour, but NOT at time of observation

Moderate or heavy rain at time of observation; thunderstorm during past hour, but NOT at time of observation

Slight snow or rain and snow mixed or hail at time of observation; thunderstorm during past hour, but not at time of observation

Moderate or heavy snow, or rain and snow mixed or hail at time of observation; thunderstorm during past hour, but NOT at time of obs.

Slight or moderate thunderstorm without hail, but with rain and/or snow at time of obs.

456

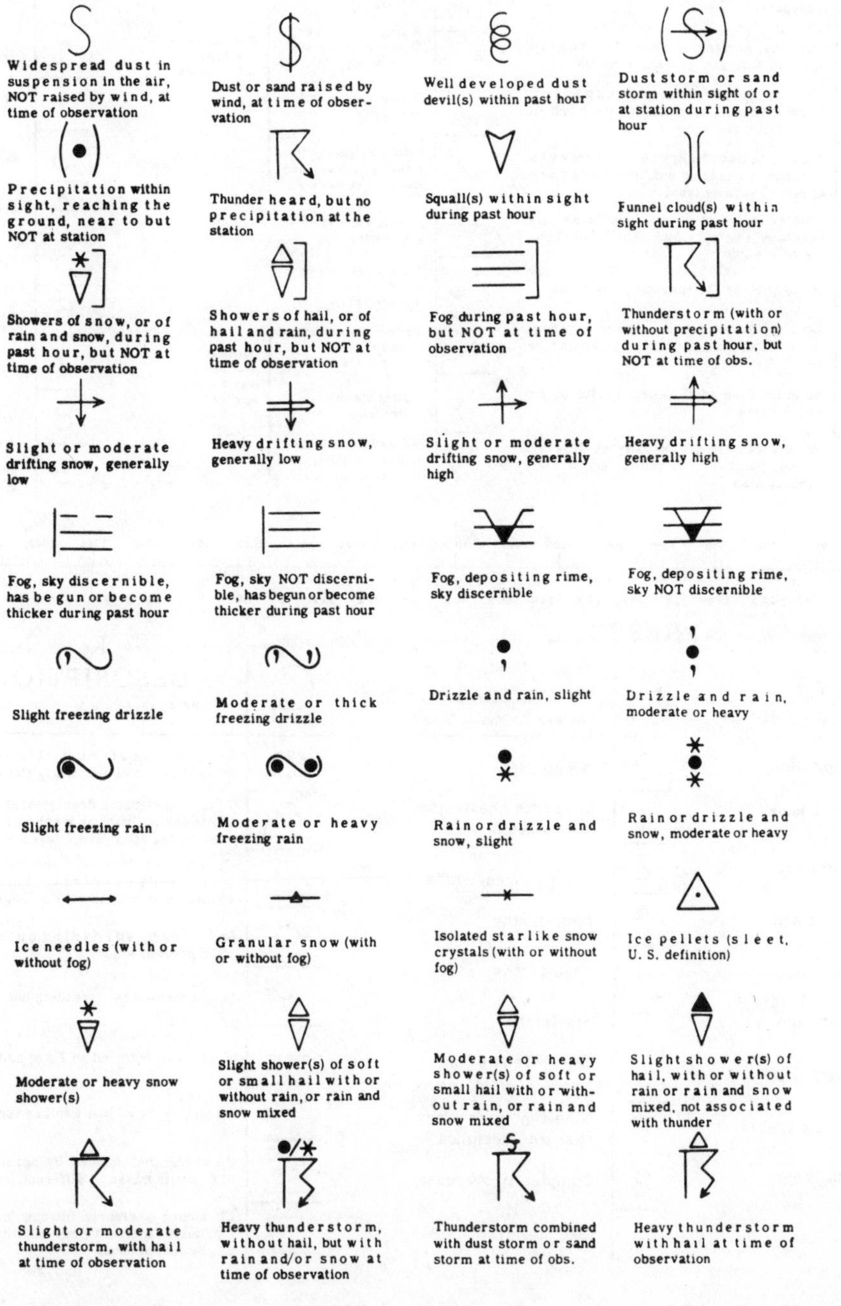

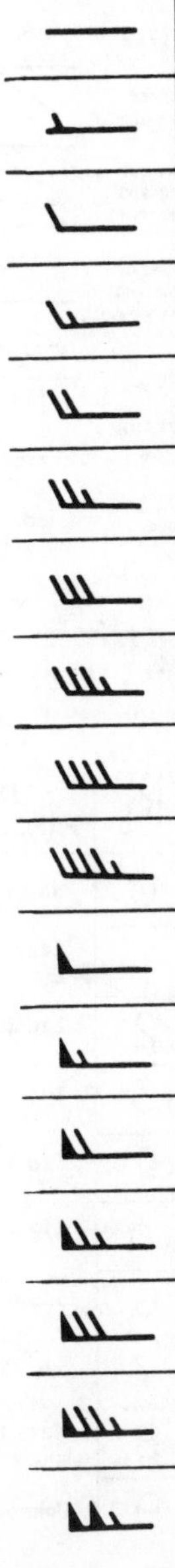

ff	MILES (Statute) Per Hour	KNOTS
⊚	Calm	Calm
	1 - 2	1 - 2
	3 - 8	3 - 7
	9 - 14	8 - 12
	15 - 20	13 - 17
	21 - 25	18 - 22
	26 - 31	23 - 27
	32 - 37	28 - 32
	38 - 43	33 - 37
	44 - 49	38 - 42
	50 - 54	43 - 47
	55 - 60	48 - 52
	61 - 66	53 - 57
	67 - 71	58 - 62
	72 - 77	63 - 67
	78 - 83	68 - 72
	84 - 89	73 - 77
	119 - 123	103 - 107

Widespread dust in suspension in the air, NOT raised by wind, at time of observation

Precipitation within sight, reaching the ground, near to but NOT at station

Showers of snow, or of rain and snow, during past hour, but NOT at time of observation

Slight or moderate drifting snow, generally low

Fog, sky discernible, has begun or become thicker during past hour

Slight freezing drizzle

Slight freezing rain

Ice needles (with or without fog)

Moderate or heavy snow shower(s)

Slight or moderate thunderstorm, with hail at time of observation

Dust or sand raised by wind, at time of observation

Thunder heard, but no precipitation at the station

Showers of hail, or of hail and rain, during past hour, but NOT at time of observation

Heavy drifting snow, generally low

Fog, sky NOT discernible, has begun or become thicker during past hour

Moderate or thick freezing drizzle

Moderate or heavy freezing rain

Granular snow (with or without fog)

Slight shower(s) of soft or small hail with or without rain, or rain and snow mixed

Heavy thunderstorm, without hail, but with rain and/or snow at time of observation

Well developed dust devil(s) within past hour

Squall(s) within sight during past hour

Fog during past hour, but NOT at time of observation

Slight or moderate drifting snow, generally high

Fog, depositing rime, sky discernible

Drizzle and rain, slight

Rain or drizzle and snow, slight

Isolated starlike snow crystals (with or without fog)

Moderate or heavy shower(s) of soft or small hail with or without rain, or rain and snow mixed

Thunderstorm combined with dust storm or sand storm at time of obs.

Dust storm or sand storm within sight of or at station during past hour

Funnel cloud(s) within sight during past hour

Thunderstorm (with or without precipitation) during past hour, but NOT at time of obs.

Heavy drifting snow, generally high

Fog, depositing rime, sky NOT discernible

Drizzle and rain, moderate or heavy

Rain or drizzle and snow, moderate or heavy

Ice pellets (sleet, U.S. definition)

Slight shower(s) of hail, with or without rain or rain and snow mixed, not associated with thunder

Heavy thunderstorm with hail at time of observation

c

A

C_H DESCRIPTION
(Abridged From W.M.O. Code)

- Filaments of Ci, or "mares tails," scattered and not increasing
- Dense Ci in patches or twisted sheaves, usually not increasing, sometimes like remains of Cb; or towers or tufts
- Dense Ci, often anvil-shaped, derived from or associated with Cb
- Ci, often hook-shaped, gradually spreading over the sky and usually thickening as a whole
- Ci and Cs, often in converging bands, or Cs alone; generally overspreading and growing denser; the continuous layer not reaching 45° altitude
- Ci and Cs, often in converging bands, or Cs alone; generally overspreading and growing denser; the continuous layer exceeding 45° altitude
- Veil of Cs covering the entire sky
- Cs not increasing and not covering entire sky
- Cc alone or Cc with some Ci or Cs, but the Cc being the main cirriform cloud

B

C_M DESCRIPTION
(Abridged From W.M.O. Code)

- Thin As (most of cloud layer semi-transparent)
- Thick As, greater part sufficiently dense to hide sun (or moon), or Ns
- Thin Ac, mostly semi-transparent; cloud elements not changing much and at a single level
- Thin Ac in patches; cloud elements continually changing and/or occurring at more than one level
- Thin Ac in bands or in a layer gradually spreading over sky and usually thickening as a whole
- Ac formed by the spreading out of Cu
- Double-layered Ac, or a thick layer of Ac, not increasing; or Ac with As and/or Ns
- Ac in the form of Cu-shaped tufts or Ac with turrets
- Ac of a chaotic sky, usually at different levels; patches of dense Ci are usually present also

E

BAROMETRIC TENDENCY

- Rising, then falling
- Rising, then steady; or rising, then rising more slowly — Barometer now higher than 3 hours ago
- Rising steadily, or unsteadily
- Falling or steady, then rising; or rising, then rising more quickly
- Steady, same as 3 hours ago
- Falling, then rising, same or lower than 3 hours ago
- Falling, then steady; or falling, then falling more slowly — Barometer now lower than 3 hours ago
- Falling steadily, or unsteadily
- Steady or rising, then falling; or falling, then falling more quickly

H

h HEIGHT IN FEET (Rounded)

0	0 - 149
1	150 - 299
2	300 - 599
3	600 - 999
4	1,000 - 1,
5	2,000 - 3,
6	3,500 - 4
7	5,000 - 6
8	6,500 - 7
9	At or abo 8,000, or clouds

C PRESSURE

MILLIBARS → 956 960 964 968 972 976 980 984 988 992 996 1000 1004 1008 1012 1016 1020 1024 1028 1032 1036 1040 1044 1048 1052 10

INCHES → 28.2 28.3 28.4 28.5 28.6 28.7 28.8 28.9 29.0 29.1 29.2 29.3 29.4 29.5 29.6 29.7 29.8 29.9 30.0 30.1 30.2 30.3 30.4 30.5 30.6 30.7 30.8 30.9 31.0 31.1

F

PAST WEATHER

- Clear or few clouds ⎫
- Partly cloudy (scattered) or variable sky ⎬ Not Plotted
- Cloudy (broken) or overcast ⎭
- Sandstorm or duststorm, or drifting or blowing snow
- Fog, or smoke, or thick dust haze
- Drizzle
- Rain
- Snow, or rain and snow mixed, or ice pellets (sleet)
- Shower(s)
- Thunderstorm, with or without precipitation

F

R_t TIME OF PRECIPITATION

0	No Precipitation
1	Less than 1 hour ago
2	1 to 2 hours ago
3	2 to 3 hours ago
4	3 to 4 hours ago
5	4 to 5 hours ago
6	5 to 6 hours ago
7	6 to 12 hours ago
8	More than 12 hours ago
9	Unknown

J

N_h SKY COVERAGE
(Low And/Or Middle Clouds)

0	No clouds
1	Less than one-tenth or one-tenth
2	Two-tenths or three-tenths
3	Four-tenths
4	Five-tenths
5	Six-tenths
6	Seven-tenths or eight-tenths
7	Nine-tenths or overcast with openings
8	Completely overcast
9	Sky obscured

K

C_L DESCRIPTION
(Abridged From W.M.O. Code)

- Cu of fair weather, little vertical development and seemingly flattened
- Cu of considerable development, generally towering, with or without other Cu or Sc bases all at same level
- Cb with tops lacking clear-cut outlines, but distinctly not cirriform or anvil-shaped; with or without Cu, Sc, or St
- Sc formed by spreading out of Cu; Cu often present also
- Sc not formed by spreading out of Cu
- St or Fs or both, but no Fs of bad weather
- Fs and/or Fc of bad weather (scud)
- Cu and Sc (not formed by spreading out of Cu) with bases at different levels
- Cb having a clearly fibrous (cirriform) top, often anvil-shaped, with or without Cu, Sc, St, or scud

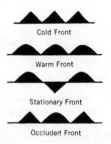

Figure 18-3: *The advancing edge of an air mass, the "front," can take four forms: cold front, warm front, occluded front and stationary front: The symbol for each is shown here.*

symbols used are depicted in Figure 18-3. When two fronts meet they do not immediately mix, as might be expected, but retain many of their original characteristics. The subsequent interaction has a profound influence upon our weather.

Barometric Pressure

Air, like any other mass, is acted upon by gravity and therefore has weight. The total weight of the "pile" of air overlying any point on the earth is the cause of the barometric pressure at that point and is measured by a barometer. (See Chapter 9.)

The barometer "weighs" the air. It could be calibrated in pounds; in fact, this might lead to a better understanding of the function of this instrument. Actually, the barometer is calibrated in inches of mercury or in millibars, but this in no way changes its basic purpose.

It should be easy to understand that the "pile" of air resting on a mountain top is not as high as that upon a sea-level location and that therefore the barometric pressures between these two places would vary accordingly. For forecasting use, such diverse pressures are brought to a common basis by adding to the mountain reading the weight of a column of air exactly as high as the mountain. This in no way changes the effectiveness or meaning of the reading.

Winds

It is not difficult to visualize that air from an area of high pressure would flow to an area of lower pressure. The many pressure differences in turn are caused by strong thermal currents produced by unequal heating from the sun. The rotation of the earth is still another cause.

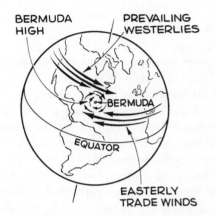

Figure 18-4: *The "Bermuda high" is formed by a confluence of the prevailing westerlies and the easterly trade winds.*

Winds can be warm or cold or dry or moist, depending upon the place of their origin. This in turn becomes a factor in determining whether the approaching weather will be warm or cold or dry or moist.

Winds are not the simple direct currents shown by the arrows in diagrams. They are influenced by the contour of the earth over which they flow and are deflected and concentrated by mountains and mountain passes. The rotation of the earth also deflects them from a straight path by what is known as the coriolis effect.

Highs and Lows

The winds which go to lows and come from highs follow a circular pattern. In the Northern Hemisphere this rotation is counterclockwise in a low-pressure area (looking down upon the map) and clockwise in a high-pressure area.

The counterclockwise motion in the low is inward toward the center and then up, chimney fashion. This causes warm moist air to condense as it reaches the colder heights and explains why lows often bring wet weather.

The clockwise rotation in the high is downward in the center and then outward. The colder and drier upper air thus provides the fair weather usually associated with highs.

One high-pressure area that has an almost continuous effect upon our weather is centered in the Bermuda vicinity and is called a Bermuda high. The diagram in Figure 18-4 shows how this high is born from a confluence of the prevailing westerlies and the easterly trade winds.

Moisture

There is a never-ending interchange of moisture between the oceans and the lands. It is well that this is so because the lives of all living things depend upon it.

Evaporation and the passing of the winds take moisture from the oceans. Eventually, this moisture is dropped upon the earth in the form of rain or snow or dew. It sinks into the earth to the water table or else it runs off the slopes into the rivers. At long last, the moisture finds its way back to the oceans for a repetition of the cycle.

When and where the moisture will be dropped is influenced greatly by the earth's topography. A mountain may rob a wind of all its moisture on the up slope and allow only dry air to pass over the top to the other side. The lush fields on the west side of the Sierras and the desert sands on the east side are the products of such a phenomenon.

Clouds

Clouds are vast accumulations of moisture in the form of water droplets or ice crystals. They are one of the few signs the careful skipper can use directly without instruments in his weather prognostication.

Clouds can tell the direction of the wind and its velocity. The moisture content of a cloud and its effect upon approaching weather can be gleaned to some extent from its appearance. Clouds can be an advance warning of imminent and dangerous conditions which cautious mariners should avoid.

Clouds are *not* formed in supernatural and permanent molds and therefore are never exactly identical. But, their general forms are sufficiently similar so that they can be classified and named. For example, see the illustrations in Figure 18-5. Between 16,500 feet and 45,000 feet clouds are "high." Between 6500 feet and 16,500 feet they are "middle." Below 6500 feet they are "low." Some clouds are vertical in development and do not extend horizontally.

Three general descriptions extend to all cloud classes. These are the "cumulus," which means billowy or arranged in successive piles, "stratus," which means spread out in a layer, and "cirrus," meaning filmy. "Nimbus" is added to these descriptions to indicate rain-bearing, and "fractus" shows that the cloud is broken up.

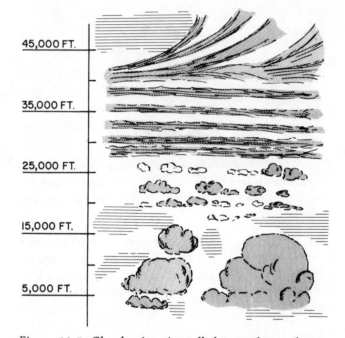

Figure 18-5: Clouds often foretell the weather and training your eye to the sky is part of good seamanship. The standard cloud shapes are illustrated above and described in the text.

Fog

Fog is the torturer of the sailorman and it may be some comfort to know what the critter is and why it exists. The bare fact that fog is composed of moisture is well known. The aviator has one great advantage over the mariner—he can climb over the fog and travel in the clear weather invariably above it.

Fog is a cloud of moisture that remains close to the ground or sea surface. It is formed of tiny droplets numerous enough to obstruct visibility. These droplets generally have cores about which to form; such cores are available in dust and in the pollutants normally in the air. The formation takes place when the temperature of the air falls to the dew point and causes condensation; this cooling can be caused by passage of the air over cold ground or cold sea or by other local causes.

Since fog depends upon condensation and this in turn upon cooling, it is evident that heating should be a curative. The sun does this when it "burns" away a fog.

Hurricanes

Anyone who has watched a sturdy vessel smashed in a few minutes, or a concrete breakwater reduced to rubble, can attest to the awesome power of a hurricane. The en-

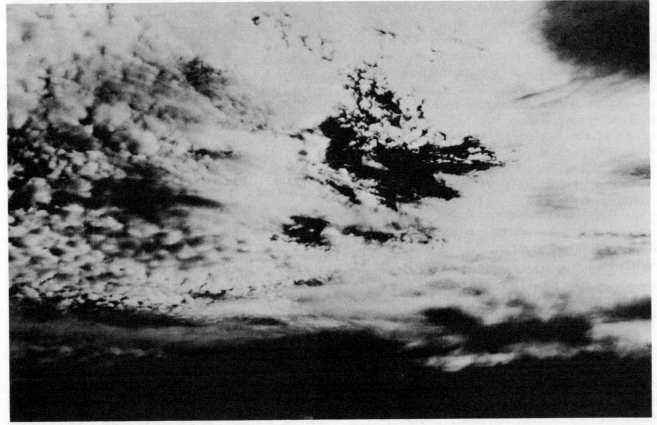

gineering sciences tell us that power cannot be developed from nothing; it must be generated from some finite source. What is the source of the hurricane's apparently limitless power?

The hurricane is a vast "heat engine." It transforms heat energy into mechanical energy. It extracts this heat energy from the water vapor upon which it feeds. This appetite explains why the hurricane is always born in tropical ocean areas where warmth and moisture are plentiful.

When water is vaporized it imprisons large amounts of energy. These are released when the vapor subsequently is condensed. This explains why steam, for instance, makes such a nasty burn: It condenses on the skin and discharges great energy as it reverts to its original water.

If the hurricane be called by its technical name, tropical cyclone, which implies a rotating air mass, some of its actions will be understood immediately. In keeping with other low-pressure systems, the rotation of this cyclone or hurricane is counterclockwise. As the ingested moisture condenses, heat is released, rotation is accelerated, air pressure is lowered, and ever more moisture is drawn in. The process thus becomes regenerative, cumulative, and steadily more powerful. Only when the hurricane exhausts its fuel (moisture) by passing over land does it lose its zing.

The hurricane mass is a huge wheel of wind at whose hub, called the eye, an unexpected and unbelievable calm prevails. Mariners lucky enough to have lived through a hurricane they could not avoid at sea tell of this awesome experience: screeching winds and mountainous seas, then comparatively fair weather with almost clear skies, then screeching winds from the opposite direction as the full system passed over.

Four lists of names, all feminine in apparent defiance of woman's liberation, have been prepared by the Weather Bureau for tagging hurricanes and these are used in yearly rotation. However, the name placed on a particularly destructive hurricane is not used again for ten years.

Precipitation

When the moisture in clouds agglomerates into particles too heavy to remain in suspension, precipitation takes place in the form of rain or hail or sleet or snow. Among the conditions which can bring this about are temperature, wind, and proximity to low- and high-pressure areas. Clouds are a necessary condition because there can be no precipitation without clouds.

Precipitation may leave clouds in one form but intervening conditions can change it to another form before it reaches the ground. Thus, what is originally snow may pass through a warm layer and arrive as rain, while rain could well freeze during its descent and become sleet.

Lightning and Thunder

Thunderstorms are purely local manifestations connected with cumulonimbus clouds. Lightning always accompanies a thunderstorm because the generation of vast amounts of electricity takes place as part of the process of storm formation. Thunder, of course, is the audible result of a lightning stroke. The thunderstorm is a vertical rather than a horizontal cloud activity and the high, anvil-shaped cloud is one of its hallmarks.

Thunderstorms are essentially a summer phenomenon although they do occur in spring, fall, and winter in that order of declining frequency. The thunderstorm is a short-lived disturbance. Its average time of existence is perhaps an hour, but several storms may follow in succession and give the appearance of one continuous occurrence.

The electricity in lightning is a static charge unlike the useful kinetic forms discussed in Chapter 7. It is generated by frictional means and by heat-energy transformations, many of which are not entirely understood. A rather rudimentary illustration of the frictional effect might be walking on a carpet and then having a spark jump to a doorknob from a fingertip on a cold dry day.

Immense static charges build up on the portion of one cloud near another or near the earth. These induce opposite charges on the adjacent surfaces. When the "tension" becomes great enough to break down the intervening air, a flash takes place. Actually, each stroke is preceded by a smaller pilot stroke that serves to ionize the air and improve the conductive path.

The feeling of electric tension in the air, the odor of ozone, and the crashing noise are familiar appurtenances of the thunderstorm. It may be less familiar to learn that thunderstorms are in progress continuously on some portion or another of the globe. It has been estimated

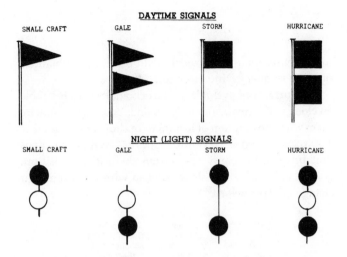

Figure 18-6: Wise skippers heed the small craft warnings displayed at Coast Guard stations and elsewhere.

that thousands are taking place somewhere at all times and that the number of lightning strokes which strike the earth is many each second.

Weather Signs

The most ubiquitous and the most reliable weather signs for the pleasure boat skipper to heed are the small-craft warnings displayed at official stations as well as at yacht clubs and marinas. This combination of pennants and flags or lights, illustrated in Figure 18-6, should be the final arbiter of whether or not to go when the weather is doubtful.

The radio receiver is a good detector of nearby thunderstorms. Increasingly loud crashes of static caused by lightning mean that the storm is not far away and approaching. When the lightning flashes finally are seen, an estimate of the distance to the storm can be made by timing the interval between the stroke and the thunder, allowing five seconds to the mile. A good *FM* radio receiver may prove *useless* as a storm detector because its circuits are designed to ignore the lightning bursts.

A rapidly falling barometer, especially with easterly winds, is a sign of an approaching storm. It must be emphasized again that the fanciful markings of "storm-rain-change-fair" on commercial barometers have no real significance and should be disregarded. The actual position of the barometer needle is relatively unimportant; what counts is how rapidly it got there and whether the movement was up or down.

Incidentally, birds, waterfowl, and various assorted animals are lousy weather forecasters despite the many myths about their prowess. The action of birds is not a prognostication but a reaction to the immediate air density. They remain "grounded" during extremely low barometric pressure because it is harder for them to fly for the same reason that an airplane finds it more difficult: wing loadings become more critical in the rarified air.

Three main factors determine weather: the wind, the temperature, and the moisture content of the air. Consequently, measurements of any of these factors will aid in forecasting. But when all is said and done, and despite the sophisticated instrumentation, weather forecasting is still more art than science—which is another way of saying that experience is the most important ingredient.

Weather Forecasts

A series of publications called "Coastal Warning Facilities Charts" is available from the Superintendent of Documents in Washington, D.C., for a nominal charge. These cover the entire coastlines by sections and should be near the helm of every cruiser. Listed on each chart are the following: (1) charted location of every public and private facility that displays small-craft and gale warnings; (2) telephone numbers of Weather Bureau stations that can be called directly for current information; (3) program time and frequency of every broadcast, FM, TV, and marine radio station, in the area that transmits weather data.

The Weather Bureau has discontinued sending daily weather maps on individual subscription. Essentially the same map, however, can be found in newspapers in most large cities. Such a map, plus the information contained in this chapter and a bit of practice, should make a dedicated skipper a reasonably good self-service forecaster. In the beginning you will merely correlate your findings with the information from official sources. As you gain proficiency, your solutions to the weather problem will become more and more reliable and the increased knowledge of natural forces will prove helpful in many phases of boat handling.

A cardinal principle is to take into account the characteristics of the area from which the wind has come. It is reasonable to assume that a wind off a desert will be drier than a wind from the Gulf of Mexico. Air from the north can safely be considered colder than air from the south. Furthermore, changes in weather invariably travel from west to east across the country.

The Weather Bureau has one great advantage that the individual is not likely to be able to duplicate: knowledge of upper air conditions gathered by many weather balloons across the country. In addition, the major stations locate area storm conditions by radar and can base predictions on the actual movements of these disturbances. Such information is also circulated to the other Bureau offices either by code or by facsimile.

Sea Conditions

Adverse weather underway affects the small boat skipper and his craft in two ways. The wind hits the above-water frontal area of the boat directly and the waves caused by the wind buffet the hull. The combination is always uncomfortable and can be serious.

Sea conditions can vary from a simple wave or swell to a confused chop caused by wind and current meeting at incompatible angles. The "swell" is a reaction from a distant storm and is marked by the "elastic" surface that conforms to hill and dale without breaking. The "wave" crests and breaks.

How a wave breaks is determined in deep water primarily by the force of the wind and in shoal water additionally by the contour of the sea bottom. The wind forces water into "hills"; when the height of the hill reaches gravitational instability, its top breaks over. This action is accelerated in water of gradually decreasing depth by the forward leaning of the wave as its lower portion is impeded.

In all wave motion there is a mathematical relationship between the number of waves that occur per second (frequency), the distance between wave peaks (wavelength), and the velocity of forward wave travel. The knowledge gained from this can be helpful to a skipper whose boat is making way in a following sea. If he can estimate the distance between waves, the table in Figure 18-7 will tell him approximately how fast the waves are approaching. This in turn will tell him what RPMs the engines should deliver in order to keep the craft on the back of a wave, going neither fast enough to pitch over the crest of the wave ahead nor slow enough to be pooped by the wave astern.

Waves are either of trochoidal or of cycloidal form. As explained in Chapter 1, certain sizes and shapes of

hull may resonate disastrously with certain combinations of wave frequency and strength.

The surfaces of cycloidal and trochoidal waves resemble an elongated letter *S* laid upon its side. You might compare them with the diagram of a sine curve shown in Chapter 8. The rises can be very gentle slopes or even sharp cusps that break into foamy sea. Often there is a transition, going landward, from slope to cusp with a concomitant change in wave velocity.

Distance Crest to Crest (Feet)	Approximate Speed of Wave Advance (Knots)	Time for Crests to Pass Stationary Point (Seconds)
25	6	2
50	10	3.3
75	12	4
100	13	4.3
125	14	4.6
150	16	5.3
175	18	6
200	19	6.2
300	23	7.6
400	27	9

Figure 18-7: The relationship between the length of a wave and the speed of its advance is shown above.

Winds

The chief culprit responsible for adverse sea conditions is the wind; consequently, it should be watched carefully. The instruments for doing this are the weather vane and the anemometer (see Chapter 9) but a great deal of information can be obtained by eye and ear without mechanical help.

The surface condition of the sea is a good wind gauge. The table in Figure 18-8 correlates the observations of

Wind Velocity in Knots	Approximate Wave Height (Feet)	Beaufort Scale Number	Designation
None	0	0	calm
1–3	.27	1	light air
4–6	.75	2	light breeze
7–10	1.8	3	gentle breeze
11–16	2.6	4	moderate breeze
17–21	3.5	5	fresh breeze
22–27	5.0	6	strong breeze
28–33	6.0	7	moderate gale
34–40	7.3	8	fresh gale
41–47	8.0	9	strong gale
48–55	10.0	10	whole gale
56–63	13	11	storm
64–71	15	12	hurricane

Figure 18-8: The velocity of the wind has a direct effect on the height of the generated waves. The Beaufort scale numbers also are correlated above with wind velocity and common description.

wave height with the corresponding Beaufort number of wind velocity.

The gentle zephyrs which often waft about can blind us to the strong force in even a moderate wind. If you hold a flat square plate 1 foot on a side directly before a 30-mile-per-hour breeze, you will feel a force of 3 pounds pushing against it. This may not seem like anything startling until you realize that a powerboat with a sail area of 350 square feet (nothing unusual) would find more than half a ton of force to battle in the same wind. Consider, then, what a sailboat with more than that square footage of spread sail is up against.

19 *Safety, Emergency and Fire Protection*

STATISTICS show that pleasure boating is one of the safest family participation sports. But the record is not perfect and many accidents do occur. Most of these marring incidents could be avoided by a more intense application of simple common sense.

One example is the matter of boat overloading. Certainly it should require no more than observation and ordinary judgment to determine when a craft is carrying excessive load. Nevertheless, drownings attributable to overloading are a major blot on the record. This is the more remarkable when one considers that most small boats now carry manufacturer's plates clearly stating the maximum capacity.

Accidents deriving from the flammability of fuel are high on the list, too. This includes the supply for the galley as well as that for the engines. The proper routine for "gassing up" is discussed in Chapter 14 and the legally required extinguishing equipment is listed in Chapter 25. The wise skipper is not content with the bare minimum quota of extinguishers but will increase the number so that one is at hand in any part of the boat during an emergency.

Injuries to swimmers are often listed. These accidents are of two types: those involving members of the boat party and those inflicted on casual swimmers in swimming areas. A precaution against the former is to stop engines dead when a swimming party is over the side. The obvious preventive for the latter is to keep well off swimming beaches; if such waters must be entered, it should be done slowly and with extreme watchfulness. Injuries resulting from being struck by the hull are usually subordinate to those inflicted by the whirring "knives" of the propeller.

Just one caution if you have children aboard, although it applies also to adults. It has to do with passengers riding out on the bow. This is a dangerous (and often illegal) position.

Children have an especial liking for straddling the bow with legs dangling over the side. A collision, even a very minor one, can cause serious injury to anyone riding in this position. Furthermore, a sudden stop can slide the bow rider into the water.

Exhaust fumes are an insidious poison; the victim is overcome with slight warning or with no warning at all. The lethal ingredient is carbon monoxide which has *no* telltale odor. It can leak into cabins through faulty exhaust lines. It can also be blown back at cockpit occupants by a strong following wind that picks up the transom exhaust. In this matter of poisoning, a well-run diesel is very much safer than a gasoline engine because the excess air in its cylinders makes its exhaust almost devoid of carbon monoxide.

The Coast Guard often reports boat accidents in which drownings occur despite the presence aboard of the required life preservers. In these instances either the preservers were stored in places that could not be reached in emergency or else the guests aboard were not instructed about location and use of the aids. Life preservers are no things of beauty and trying to keep them from sight is understandable—but foolhardy. A caution about preservers is not to jump into the water from any height with one on; the sudden buoyant reaction could break a neck or smash a jaw.

The cry of "man overboard" has always sent a chill into the heart of every sailor. Two dangers immediately arise when a person is lost over the side of a powerboat: (1) he can be lost sight of and lost and (2) he can be chopped up by the prop in the close maneuvering needed to get into position to fish him out. The person in the water is completely at the mercy of the skipper's skill. Any large buoyant object should be dumped over immediately to help mark the spot; hopefully a life ring has also been tossed. Failure to rescue the lost person must be reported to the Coast Guard immediately.

An ever-present danger in the man-overboard situation is the impulse for someone aboard to jump in after him as a means of rescue. The skipper must prevent this. Invariably, this innately heroic act results in *two* persons to fish out instead of one—and the tragic possibility of *two* drownings instead of one. Good seamanship and calm heads combine as the best rescue formula.

Accidents happen through ignorance of the rules of the road and through willful disobedience of them. The rules are detailed in Chapter 16. They are easy to learn and should be learned.

High-speed planing hulls, and the reduction of vision which their bow-up attitude brings about, have fostered a seeming contempt for the basic precaution of seeing that the course ahead is clear. "Clear" means not only free of other craft but free also of dangerous driftwood. Few hulls can weather a high-speed impact.

The movies and TV have dramatized the "abandon

ship" order on large liners and war vessels and have fo-
cused on the attendant mock heroics. The need suddenly
to abandon ship can strike any pleasure boat as well. A
flare-up fire can send skipper and others aboard over the
side within minutes or even within seconds. When this
happens, it is most advisable for those in the water to
stay near the boat; this makes a target for rescuers.

The uninitiated may snicker at an order for donning
life preservers when the going gets really rough, but
it should be done anyway, with insistence on all aboard
doing it. This is the time when prudence proves to be
the better part of boldness and daring.

No matter how many fancy bilge pumps with their
automatic starters and stoppers are hooked into the electrical system, never cruise without having aboard a plain,
ordinary, hand-operated bilge pump. Electric power could
go dead; while you're alive, muscle power is always available.

Drownproofing is a new system of emergency survival
in the water for long periods without great effort. It is
being sponsored by private and federal agencies. A leaflet
describing the method and giving instruction in it is available from the Superintendent of Documents, Washington, for a few cents per copy. In drownproofing the body
is allowed to float just below the surface with its natural
buoyancy; the head is raised above the surface only at
breathing intervals. It is claimed that this system enables
anyone to remain afloat for hours without tiring, as long
as he does not panic. It would seem to take a bit of getting
used to plus iron nerves.

Distress Signals

Distress signals should be sent in any dangerous situation
as soon as the skipper realizes that the dire conditions are
too great for him and his crew to overcome. The most
obvious method of transmission is the "Mayday" on
radio. With radio out of commission or not aboard,
numerous other methods can be used.

Mayday is the international radiotelephone code word
for extreme distress. It is the phonetic for *m'aidez* which
means "help me" in French and is the spoken equivalent
of the well-known SOS used in radio telegraphy.

The official Coast Guard chart (#CG-3892) reproduced
in Figure 19-1 gives detailed information on the procedure
to follow in placing a Mayday call. Following an estab-

lished routine most likely will hasten understanding and
speed the requested succor. However, don't lose sight of
the prime purpose—to get help fast; if the rules hinder,
abandon the rules. Under true emergency conditions, *any*
procedure which can attract the needed help automatically
becomes legal.

With 2–3 Mcs. (2000–3000 Kcs.) radiotelephones, the
distress call initially is made on 2182 Kcs.; on VHF the
call is made on 156.8 Mcs. If conditions permit, the entire
communication back and forth will be carried out on
these frequencies (on ordinary contacts only the initial call
is made on them) although the Coast Guard may shift the
transmission of vital information to another channel. The
CG will want to know the exact nature of the trouble,
positive position by coordinates or landmarks, number of
people on board, exact description of vessel appearance,
and what form of assistance would be best.

Assuming that you and your boat *Suzy* (call number
WD-4321) are in dire straits, your Mayday should sound
like this: "Mayday, Mayday, Mayday, *this is Suzy*, whiskey delta 4321, *Suzy*, whiskey delta 4321, *Suzy*, whiskey
delta 4321, over." If the distress channel is unavailing,
switch to any and all other channels. Blast away until you
are heard; this is one time the FCC won't tag you. It is wise
to keep the transmitter on the air as much as possible to
enable radio direction finders to pinpoint your location.

The basic rule in true distress is that all rules may be
disregarded in favor of any action that brings the needed
relief and rescue. Nevertheless, certain forms are prescribed for distress communications and if they can be followed the chance of being understood is that much better.

The classic distress signal is the flag upside down on its
staff. Frankly, this is not particularly effective because it
requires keen observation on the part of the observer to
note this actually small change in general appearance.

Standing on a top deck and waving both arms to the
side from overhead to straight down is a good attention-
getter for distances up to perhaps two miles. Holding a red
flag while doing this increases range and effectiveness.

Newly recognized by the Coast Guard as a distress signal is a red cloth, 6 feet by 4 feet in size, along the center
of whose long dimension are sewed or painted an 18-inch
black circle and an 18-inch black square. A craft in distress
is to lay this "flag" out on the top deck where it can be
seen by airplanes. (Perhaps a Betsy Ross aboard is expected to whip up this flag with needle and thread when

MARINE EMERGENCY AND DISTRESS INFORMATION SHEET
U. S. COAST GUARD

SPEAK SLOWLY AND CLEARLY
CALL:

1. If you are in DISTRESS, (*i.e. when threatened by grave and imminent danger*) transmit the International Distress Call on 2182 kc/s - "MAYDAY MAYDAY MAYDAY THIS IS (*Your vessel's call and name repeated THREE times*)".*

2. If you need INFORMATION OR ASSISTANCE FROM THE COAST GUARD (*other than in a distress*), call COAST GUARD on 2182 kc/s, (*the International Distress and Calling Frequency*).

* The Radiotelephone Alarm Signal (*if available*) should be transmitted prior to the Distress Call for approximately one minute. The Radiotelephone Alarm Signal consists of two audio tones, of different pitch, transmitted alternately. Its purpose is to attract the attention of persons on watch and shall only be used to announce that a distress call or message is about to follow.

IF ABOARD VESSEL IN TROUBLE - give:

1. WHO you are (*your vessel's call and name*).

2. WHERE you are (*your vessel's position in latitude/longitude or true bearing and distance in nautical miles from a widely known geographical point - local names known only in the immediate vicinity are confusing*).

3. WHAT is wrong (*nature of distress or difficulty, if not in distress*).

4. Kind of assistance desired.

5. Number of persons aboard and condition of any injured.

6. Present seaworthiness of your vessel.

7. Description of your vessel - length, type, cabin, masts, power, color of hull, superstructure, and trim.

8. Your listening frequency and schedule.

IF OBSERVING ANOTHER VESSEL IN DIFFICULTY - give:

1. Your position and the bearing and distance of the vessel in difficulty.

2. Nature of distress or difficulty, if not in distress.

3. Description of the vessel in distress or difficulty, if not in distress (*see Item 7 above*).

4. Your intentions, course, and speed, etc.

5. Your radio call sign, name of your vessel, listening frequency, and schedule.

NOTE: The international signal for an aircraft that wants to direct a surface craft to a distress is: Circling the surface craft, opening and closing the throttle or changing propeller pitch (noticeable by change in sound) while crossing ahead of the surface craft, and proceeding in the direction of the distress. If you receive such a signal, you should follow the aircraft. If you cannot do so, try to inform the aircraft by any available means. If your assistance is no longer needed, the aircraft will cross your wake, opening and closing the throttle or changing propeller pitch. If you are radio equipped, you should attempt to communicate with the aircraft on 2182 kc/s when the aircraft makes the above signals or makes any obvious attempt to attract your attention. In the event that you cannot communicate by radio, be alert for a message block dropped from the aircraft.

NOTIFY THE COAST GUARD PROMPTLY AS SOON AS THE EMERGENCY TERMINATES

POST NEAR YOUR RADIO FOR READY REFERENCE

TREAS. DEPT., USCG, CG-3892 (Rev. 1-62)
PREVIOUS EDITIONS ARE OBSOLETE

GPO 963061

GPO : 1962 O - 632444

Figure 19-1: This is the official procedure for emergency use of radiotelephones. (Credit—U.S. Coast Guard)

danger threatens?)

The firing of a gun or other explosive sound at regular intervals of about one minute is also recognized as a distress signal. Since guns do not form a part of the standard equipment of pleasure boats, this form of signaling is unlikely to prove of practical value. It seems in the same category with the creation of a smoke cloud by burning a tar barrel, which also is listed often in the literature, but never found on a pleasure boat.

Rockets fired from a hand-held rocket-launching pistol produce an effective distress signal that can be seen for many miles even in daylight. These rocket sets are for sale by most marine suppliers, are not too expensive, and should form part of the emergency equipment of all cruising small boats. (An irony is that the sinking *Titanic* fired many rockets that presumably were seen by a distant ship not yet over the horizon—and they were ignored.)

The simplest form of distress signal is a continuous sounding of the horn. The peewee nature of most pleasure boat horns (despite legal requirements for loudness) relegates this method to fairly crowded waters, however.

An old martinet of a commander once insisted that the best distress signal was the one that was never sent. Good seamanship made it unnecessary.

Water Skiing

Water skiing has sprouted into the most popular aquatic sport in the country today. Aside from the exhilaration of the sport itself, one reason for its rapid growth is the availability of fast boats, both inboard and outboard, at comparatively moderate cost.

To the onlooker, water skiing seems difficult but the experts assure us that learning the game is easy and beginner after beginner is quickly able to ski with no apparent trouble. Skiing becomes still another source of pleasure for the boat owner and his family.

However, the fact that water skiing is easy and fun does not mean that it should be done haphazardly. There are rules which will reduce or possibly even eliminate the chance of accident. The first of these is that it is preferable to have two people in the towing boat: one to skipper and the second to keep the skier under constant watch. (Many jurisdictions permit a rear view mirror to take the place of the second person.) The skier in turn communicates his requests by the use of standardized hand signals. These

are depicted in the drawings of Figure 19-2.

Many of the rules governing skiing are simple common sense. It should be obvious that heavily traveled waters are no place for skiers. Skiers should not intrude on areas frequented by swimmers, nor impede traffic through narrow channels, nor slalom around buoys.

Elsewhere it is stated that swimmers should not approach a boat whose engine is running because of the ever-present danger that an accidentally thrown or defective clutch could turn the propellers into chopping knives. The same caution applies to skiers being picked up. The safest manner of getting a skier back on board a small boat is over the transom after the engine has been stopped.

And finally a rule which is more often breached than observed: The skier should wear an approved life preserver. The best swimmers can get cramps or become incapacitated.

Skin Diving

The skipper of a powerboat or a sailboat is affected by skin diving only as a hazard from which he must keep clear. And it is *his* responsibility to keep clear; in any injury caused by his boat, the presumption of guilt will be on him.

For his part, the skin diver is expected to announce his presence with an orange flag bearing a diagonal white stripe. This flag could be flying from a boat, from a stake or from a float but in every case it literally means "stay away!" The wider the berth, the better.

Skin diving is so popular today that the orange flag can be encountered almost anywhere there is clear water suitable for diving. For the skipper it is a case of "look sharp."

If skin divers are operating from the skipper's own boat, then the admonition to stop engines is even more imperative than it is for recovering water skiers. In this case the skipper's boat would fly the proper flag and all other vessels would be expected to keep clear.

First Aid

Custom permits a skipper to perform weddings even though the marriage may be "legal" for that voyage only,

FASTER

SLOWER

SPEED O.K.

RIGHT TURN

LEFT TURN

BACK TO DROP-OFF AREA

CUT MOTOR

STOP

SKIER O.K. AFTER FALL

PICK ME UP OR
FALLEN SKIER — WATCH OUT

Standardized hand signals bring added safety to water skiing.
Credit: United States Coast Guard

Figure 19-2

but no justification exists for a skipper to become a surgeon when he administers first aid. In other words, first aid should be *just* first aid and not a usurpation of a medical doctor's functions.

The marine environment is a strange one for most guests that come aboard. The rolling upsets the natural working of their bodily organs and the frequent absence of a firm footing can lead to falls and hurts. First aid is therefore a valid knowledge for the skipper to possess.

FIRST-AID SUPPLIES.

First-aid kits are available from most marine suppliers in a variety of sizes and prices. The better ones take account of the environment in which they will be stored and make use of corrosion-resistant cabinets or boxes.

The bare essentials of equipment are: Band-Aids, gauze bandages, absorbent cotton, gauze pads, adhesive plasters, splints, tweezers, and scissors. The chemical contents should include: iodine or similar antiseptic, spirits of ammonia, essence of pepperment, petrolatum, toothache drops, aspirin, and seasick pills. A quick reference chart of instructions should be posted near the kit or contained in its inside cover.

SEASICKNESS.

There are old wives' tales about an *empty* stomach being proof against seasickness—and there are as many stories claiming this magic for a *full* stomach. The truth of the matter is that seasickness can hit the best of men—and does on occasion.

Several pharmaceutical houses produce seasick pills under several proprietary names. These help some people and not others. It is a case of individual trial and error.

It has been well established that the combined balancing mechanisms of the ear and the eye are a prime factor in seasickness. Consequently, watching a horizon that is alternately diving and soaring can add the final push to a bodily system already whoozy from the gyrations of the middle ear. It helps to keep eyes closed and it helps even more to be involved in a task that requires full concentration, such as steering. The tendency to seasickness shows queer quirks; some old dogs in the Navy who can take anything on the bridge get the whoopses when they go below and get a whiff of the engine room.

FOOD POISONING.

Boating often exposes picnic food to warm weather and this can lead to spoilage and food poisoning. Mixtures containing mayonnaise and chicken as well as desserts made with cream are notable offenders. The best course is to avoid these, the next best is to pack them in ice so that they are under continuous refrigeration in transit.

Nature brings forth her own defenses against food poisoning and in the milder cases these may prove sufficient. Her method is to induce diarrhea and vomiting and thus clear the offenders from the alimentary tract. An additional dose of a saline cathartic will help free the intestines but this could be hazardous ground and caution is required.

There are many types of food poisoning and none should be taken lightly. The end result could be mere discomfort or it could be death. Between these two extreme effects of food poisoning lie other symptoms and manifestations: double vision, respiratory paralysis, and speech impairment. One source of immediate medical advice via the radiotelephone is the Coast Guard, who will switch a doctor into the circuit.

The onslaughts on the human system caused by so-called "spoiled" food are the direct result of bacterial action. These organisms multiply at geometric rates when not held in check by refrigeration or destroyed by heating.

Refrigeration is effective only if it can keep the food below 40°F. Heating does not begin its destructive effect on bacterial growth unless it goes beyond a minimum of 120°F. (There is no maximum other than the temperature at which texture and flavor are destroyed.)

Clostridium perfringeus, staphylococcus aureus, clostridium botulimum, and salmonella constitute the danger in spoiled food. None of these is compatible with the human alimentary tract. Extreme care in food handling is the price of keeping them out.

SHELLFISH.

Oysters and clams are often found in cruising areas and may therefore be included on the menu. These shellfish can cause hepatitis and typhoid when taken from polluted water.

Public health authorities are vigilant in posting areas from which shellfish should not be taken for food. These signs should be heeded strictly. The best safeguard in unfamiliar localities is to abstain.

SUNSTROKE.

True heat stroke or sunstroke is an extremely dangerous condition for which medical aid should be sought at once. Complete stoppage of perspiration is one phase of heat stroke, hence the victim's skin is dry and very hot; this serves as a telltale sign.

Emergency treatment until a doctor arrives or can be consulted via radio is to get the patient's skin temperature down to near normal. This is done with cold-water baths and by wrapping him in sheets soaked in cold or ice water. The safest position is half-sitting. Whether or not subsequent hospital treatment is successful depends largely on how quickly first-aid measures reduced the original excessive skin temperatures.

HEAT EXHAUSTION.

The symptoms of heat exhaustion are opposite to those of heat stroke; this condition is less serious and should not be confused. The victim of heat exhaustion perspires profusely and his skin is clammy. His condition is usually brought about by overexertion in the sun, which has caused him to lose too much salt from his system.

The patient may faint. This indicates the use of spirits of ammonia to revive him; application is by inhalation of the fumes followed by giving a few drops in water by mouth as soon as he can swallow. Strong coffee will help once the patient approaches normal.

Many authorities advocate the ingestion of salt tablets by persons who perspire heavily because of strenuous work performed in a hot climate.

BURNS.

The two areas on a powerboat in which burns usually occur are the galley and the engine room. In the galley, hot food spilled by a passing wake is the culprit, while accidental contact with a hot manifold does the business with the engines. Even a sailboat may present these two hazards.

The science of treating burns has changed greatly in the past few years; methods once thought adequate are now in disfavor. The application of greases ranging from butter to petrolatum was once recommended; this now is considered taboo. Tannic acid and picric acid were favorites also; they are used no longer.

A burn is a destruction of the skin by excessive heat. The depth to which this destruction takes place deter-

mines the classification of the burn into first class, second class, or third class. The severity and danger are in that same order.

Mild sunburn is a first-degree burn, as is the red skin caused by momentary contact with scalding water in the galley. Despite the pain, this form of injury is usually taken care of by the body itself, without external aid, although any of several sprays containing a local anesthetic will relieve the discomfort. Cold water run over the affected area reduces the skin temperature and therefore also the pain.

A deep sunburn characterized by blistering is a second-degree burn. This form of skin injury is a common summer affliction and in most instances also heals normally with nothing more than soothing lotion or spray application. Nevertheless, a second-degree burn is on the borderline between self-ministration and hospital care. Where the burn is extensive, it is safer to seek professional medical attention.

Third-degree burns go deeply enough into the layers of the skin to present immediate dangers of infection, shock, and dangerous side effects. Immediate professional medical attention is imperative.

Third-degree burns often are not as painful as lesser burns because a portion of the nervous system that senses pain has been destroyed. Third-degree burns often require surgery and skin grafting.

As already stated, greases are no longer in favor because, among other reasons, they present a messy cleanup problem which adds to the patient's trauma. Modern burn ointments are emulsions of a kind which chemists describe as having "water in the outer phase." This means that the emollients, oils, unguents, or other medicaments are so suspended that the ointment can be washed off with plain water. These ointments give the impression of being greases but they are not.

The aerosols are even easier to use in relieving the pain and discomfort of sunburn or other minor burns. They are sprayed on the affected areas of the skin from pressurized cans. They form a protective, healing, and soothing cover without the prior irritation of surface application. The cooling induced by the evaporation of the aerosol propellant also acts to reduce pain.

FISHHOOKS.

A fishhook embedded in a finger is an unfortunately

common ailment aboard. The remedy most often proposed in the literature is a spartan procedure. It consists in snipping off the shank eye, pushing the hook on through the flesh until it exits, and thus removing it. This eliminates the tearing of flesh by the barb which would accompany any attempt to back it out. The entire operation requires a metal-cutting snipper, copious application of iodine to prevent infection (especially from a contaminated hook), and, above all, a steely nervous system for both victim and first-aider.

A more practical course for the skipper who has not been conditioned to blood by battle scenes on color TV is to take the victim back ashore for regular medical treatment. In most cases, the doctor will also include tetanus shots.

POISONOUS PLANTS.

Infections from contact with poison oak, poison sumach, and poison ivy have become common in boating circles; formerly these ailments bothered only the camping fraternity. The explanation lies in the picnic party to strange islands, one of the lures of cruising.

Few people are immune to the red rashes, blisters, and painful itching brought on by contact with these poisonous plants. No immunizing serum has yet brought any notable success in avoiding the usual results of contact. Some proprietary medicaments are on the market which claim to provide relief.

The insult to the skin is made by an oil that these plants secrete. This oil is so powerful that microscopic droplets carried by the smoke when the plants are burned can cause infection. Obviously, touching infected clothes, pets, or skin areas will also impart the irritation.

Since the noxious factor is an oil, it should be removed by washing with a strong soap that will emulsify it and render it harmless. Applying any solvent (this includes greases, oils, alcohols, cleaning fluids) dissolves the poisonous oil and helps spread it.

BUMPS.

The cramped condition of a boat makes it more likely that a fall will involve striking some protruding object and raising a consequent bump. A cold compress will control the swelling of the rank-and-file bump.

The important points to check after a severe fall are these: Is the victim conscious or unconscious? Has he suffered a concussion? The indications are: Is he rational? Is the pupil of one eye larger than the other? Is he vomiting? If any question exists of the severity of the injury, the victim should be kept quiet and given professional attention as quickly as possible.

LACERATIONS.

Small accidental cuts are just as common on a boat as they are on land. Most require no more than thorough washing with soap and water and perhaps the application of a local antiseptic like iodine before applying sterile covering. The initial bleeding serves a useful purpose in cleansing the wound of foreign matter.

Severe cuts require medical attention competent to bring the wound edges together by suturing, to accelerate healing. Professional aid will also assure correct dressings and tetanus shots, if indicated.

BRUISES.

Bruises (including the black eyes that sometimes result from skipper-crew-passenger relationships) are marked by bleeding in the tissues without external laceration. The time-honored steak that is used as medicament benefits only the butcher and not the eye.

Alternate cold and warm compresses bring some relief but do not inhibit the rainbow-like stages during recovery.

RESUSCITATION.

Mouth-to-mouth resuscitation is the most approved method today for reviving persons whose regular breathing has failed. The correct positions and actions for this rescue method are shown in Figure 19-3.

Plastic breather tubes are available for those who are squeamish about the mouth-to-mouth or mouth-to-nose process. They are included in some first-aid kits or can be bought separately.

FRACTURES.

A simple fracture is one in which the ends of the broken bone do *not* penetrate the skin; a compound fracture is one in which they do. In either case, the victim should be moved as little and as carefully as possible.

Diagnosing or treating a fracture is beyond the realm of first aid. Simple splinting to keep the fractured member immobilized is the limit to which amateur treatment should go.

ARTIFICIAL RESPIRATION
MOUTH-TO-MOUTH (MOUTH-TO-NOSE) METHOD

If there is foreign matter visible in the mouth, wipe it out quickly with your fingers or a cloth wrapped around your fingers.

①

Tilt the head back so the chin is pointing upward.

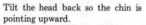

⬆ Pull or push ⬇ the jaw into a jutting-out position.

②

③

④

Open your mouth wide and place it tightly over victim's mouth. At same time pinch victim's nostrils shut.

⑤

Or close the nostrils with your cheek.

Or close the victim's mouth and place your mouth over the nose.

⑥

Blow into the victim's mouth or nose. If you are not getting air exchange, recheck the head and jaw position (see drawings above at left).

⑦

If you still do not get air exchange, quickly turn the victim on his side and administer several sharp blows between the shoulder blades in the hope of dislodging foreign matter.

Resume breathing procedure.

Figure 19-3: Mouth-to-mouth resuscitation is the approved method for restoring breathing. (Credit—American National Red Cross)

TOOTHACHE.

When toothache is caused by a cavity, the best first aid is the application of the proprietary toothache drops as directed on the label. When the pain derives from some malaise in the gums, application of hot or cold compresses, or alternations of both, are the best source of relief. Aspirin may help relieve pain.

PROFESSIONAL ADVICE.

A radio call to the nearest Coast Guard is an ever-present source of professional advice for the skipper puzzled by an accident aboard. The CG will get a medical doctor on the line who will discuss and evaluate the symptoms relayed by the skipper.

The medic will advise the proper procedure for treating the patient. If in his opinion the situation is sufficiently grave, the doctor will arrange for a pickup of the incapacitated person by Coast Guard helicopter.

This availability of medical advice and help is a wonderful service of which many skippers are unaware.

Fire Protection

Many fires on unattended boats are listed as "mysterious" when in fact their origin has no element of mystery. The cause of the fire is spontaneous combustion.

One example of spontaneous combustion is a dark, unventilated locker into which oily rags have been thrown and left for a period of time. Unnoticed chemical reactions gradually raise the temperature until the combustion point of the rags or of the surrounding material is reached. A full-fledged fire is in the making.

The insurance against spontaneous combustion is to make an inflexible rule that no oily rags are to be stored and that those which must currently be used are to be kept in closed metal containers. Paint rags are just as dangerous as oil rags.

The galley is a potent source of fires aboard by the very nature of the activities which take place there. The key fire prevention measures for the galley concern the proper installation of the stove and its fuel supply; these are discussed in Chapter 6.

Flammable cleaning fluids, spot removers, and paint removers should never be used aboard. Carbon tetrachloride, although nonflammable, also should not be used. The reason for the exclusion of this material is the toxicity of its fumes; these are heavier than air, collect from the bilge up, and can easily reach fatal concentration. A feeling of being light and airborne is an advance warning of carbontet poisoning and should be the signal for immediate exposure to fresh air. Prompt medical examination is imperative because the vapor inhalation may have damaged the kidneys. (This plus the fact that carbon tetrachloride in contact with flame makes a lethal war gas was the reason for the banning of this material in fire extinguishers.)

Eternal vigilance is the price of fire protection. This vigilance is exerted much more efficiently by bilge sniffers than by human noses. Sniffers that automatically sound an alarm when dangerous levels are reached (see Chapter 9) are preferable.

Portable Fire Fighters

The familiar small, wall-hung extinguishers comprise the portable fire fighters. The earlier models which required hand pumping for activation are now passé and all modern extinguishers are self-propelling either through the use of a contained gas or by means of two chemicals which generate a gas when mixed. (Extinguishers are described in greater detail in Chapter 25.)

In most cases the legal requirements for fire extinguishers aboard a boat are minimal and the wise skipper provides more units than the law demands. The additional money spent is in fact cheap insurance for life and property. At least one fire extinguisher in every cabin enclosure is not too many.

Fire extinguishers so rarely come into use that few people would know how to use one properly at a moment's notice. So it pays to read the label carefully long before an emergency arises, to take the unit down from its holder, to grasp it in a businesslike way, to get the "feel" of the thing.

As noted earlier, common table salt is an effective extinguisher for frying pan flareups—but this means salt in liberal quantities, not just a sprinkle from a little shaker.

Fixed Fire Fighters

Fire-extinguishing systems which are permanently and adequately installed give the most reliable protection on any vessel. (They also reduce insurance premiums.) Such systems make use of carbon dioxide gas to smother the fire by robbing it of its necessary oxygen. Carbon dioxide (CO_2) is contained in our exhaled breath and comprises the bubbles in soda water and in champagne.

The system functions by releasing CO_2 from storage tanks into the areas where the fire is raging through permanently installed nozzles. The release is made either manually or automatically in response to a sensor which has detected the fire.

The carbon dioxide must never be discharged into areas containing humans; they as well as the fire would be smothered. The size of the CO_2 installation should follow manufacturer's recommendations.

Fire Extinguisher Maintenance

It is a tribute to the safety of boating that fire extinguishers are so rarely put to use. However, that does not lessen the need for maintaining all extinguishers aboard in a ready-to-shoot condition.

Skippers should make frequent checks to see that all fire extinguishers are where they are supposed to be and that they show no sign of mishandling, especially units with hoses that can deteriorate.

Most extinguishers dependent upon pressurized gas are equipped with pressure gauges and these are marked at the correct operating limits. Daily visual inspection should verify that each unit conforms.

Some general recommendations for fire extinguisher maintenance follow:

Foam-type extinguishers should be discharged and recharged approximately once every year. A tag showing the date of this service should be attached to the unit.

Dry chemical fire extinguishers that are equipped with gauges should be checked to see that pressure is within allowed limits. In addition, each unit should be weighed as a means of verifying powder content. Seals should be intact and there should be no sign of recent use in the nozzle. It is wise occasionally to turn these extinguishers upside down and shake them to break up any caked powder. Tag the unit with the date of inspection.

Dry chemical extinguishers not equipped with gauges can be checked only by weighing. A loss of weight as great as a fraction of an ounce from the stamped weight makes recharging mandatory. The date of recharging should be marked on a tag.

Carbon dioxide (CO_2) and Freon fire extinguishers are also checked by weighing and here, too, any weight loss calls for recharging. Seals should be intact. Most of these units have some form of safety pin under the operating lever; check to see that this pin is removable and not corroded in place. If recharging is needed and done, the date of this service should be marked on a tag.

Most skippers will find fire extinguisher service better left to the specialists. Most marinas can arrange for a local contractor to perform the required work and certify it.

Lightning Protection

The mast tip of any vessel, even though it reaches to no great height, nevertheless is the highest point in its vicinity and thus becomes a lightning attractant in a storm. This vulnerability can be reversed into protection by very simple procedures.

The degree of protection any mast height will afford can be gauged from Figure 19-4. (When the whip antenna of the radiotelephone is higher than the mast, *it* takes over the protective functions *provided* it meets the criterion given on page 479.)

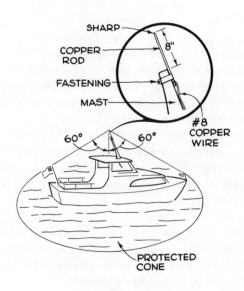

Figure 19-4: A properly installed lightning rod provides a "cone of protection" against lightning. Certain radio antennas also afford protection.

A copper rod with a pointed tip is securely fastened to the mast top so that it extends at least eight inches above it. The rod is connected as straightforwardly as possible to a submerged hull plate or to the radio ground plate or to a metal hull with #8 copper wire. Any *large* interior metal objects such as engines, cabinets, tanks and controls that are within six feet of the grounding wire should also be connected to it. This is done to prevent flash-overs which these objects would attract during a heavy lightning stroke. Exterior metal such as spotlights, stacks, scoops, and rails also should be connected.

As seen from the illustration, the protected area becomes a cone with its base on the water and its apex at the sharp point. The volume of this cone is found by rotating an imaginary line extending from the tip at 60 degrees from the vertical. Obviously this cone should include all parts of the boat; if it does not, the point can be raised until it does.

That lightning can strike a boat protected in this way and yet cause no damage is indicated by the photo in Figure 19-5. This test was carried out at a high-voltage laboratory under completely scalar conditions that duplicated actual situations in the real world.

When the radio antenna is *higher* than the mast, it can take over the job of lightning protection and eliminate the need for the pointed rod. To be able to do this, the antenna must first of all be a single metal rod unbroken by a central loading coil. Furthermore, it must be grounded with a switch or with an approved lightning arrestor; a switch which completely disconnects the radio is preferable. (Fiberglass whip antennas with spirally molded wire are *not* adequate lightning protectors.)

Long powerboats with a low profile can rig more than one elevated rod for overall protection. In such case, several cones would overlap and enshroud the vessel. The high masts of sailboats can become excellent protection when grounded as described. Wire rope stays and shrouds should also be grounded.

The safest personal action during a lightning storm underway is to avoid contact or proximity with any of the metal objects in the protection line. All aboard should stay off decks and remain in the enclosed cabin space.

Lightning currents are so large and the attendant magnetic fields so strong that compasses and electronic instruments aboard could well be affected (even though not destroyed) by them. If there is reason to suppose that a lightning stroke has been absorbed by the protective system, all instruments should be checked, especially the compass.

Fire at Sea

The literature abounds with instructions to skippers whose vessels are afire at sea. These advise turning the bow into the wind when the stern is afire and turning the stern into the wind when the bow is afire. At best, such modes of action apply only to large steamers; at worst, they are not very effective even then, as newspaper accounts testify.

The safest and smartest thing a small boat skipper can do when any *extensive* fire breaks out on his boat is to abandon ship. A hasty "Mayday" on the telephone, the dinghy alongside, everybody in it, and away! The chance of explosion is so great on the average powerboat using gasoline as fuel that staying aboard to fight any *large* fire is foolhardy. It is better that the weeping be done by the insurance company rather than by the skipper's widow.

Coast Guard search patterns cover a designated section thoroughly. Coast Guard aircraft can scan large areas in all but the worst weather. The chances of being picked up quickly by the Coast Guard or by other boats that respond to the Mayday are therefore excellent.

Figure 19-5: This test, conducted under exact scalar conditions, showed that lightning can strike a properly protected boat repeatedly without causing damage. (However, the compass should be rechecked.) (Credit—General Electric)

The best advice can be given succinctly: Keep your wits about you and don't panic!

Assess the extent of the fire quickly: Is it within the scope of the extinguishers on board or is it clearly beyond sensible effort? Is everyone aboard accounted for and out of the immediate fire zone? Have life preservers been donned?

Buoyant Clothes

A trend that serves fashion and safety at the same time is the advent of buoyant clothes. Jackets and other garments of this type have the flotation ability to keep the wearer from sinking yet look attractive enough for normal wear. These clothes may *not* be substituted for legally required life preservers, however.

Float Plan

The Coast Guard has devised and is recommending a novel and useful printed form illustrated in Figure 19-6 and called a Float Plan. The idea is an offshoot of the flight plans filed by aircraft pilots. The CG does *not* distribute these forms at present but hopes that yacht clubs, marinas, and others will make them available for the good of the sport.

The Float Plan is filled out by the skipper prior to departure and is left with some responsible person or agency. Should his boat become alarmingly overdue at its destination, all the facts the Coast Guard needs for an efficient search are quickly at hand. (An important factor in successful Float Plan use is to cancel them immediately once they no longer are applicable.)

A "Backup"

The technological philosophy of the armed services requires that a "backup" be provided for every piece of important equipment. In the event of failure of the unit on line, another is instantly available. To borrow this thinking, the skipper of a pleasure boat certainly is an "important piece of equipment" and a backup therefore should be provided if he is disabled for any cause.

The wise skipper arranges his backup by instructing someone aboard in the intricacies of running the boat. This person could be a guest but preferably is the mate or someone already familiar with the vessel. The idea is like fire insurance and fire extinguishers: You certainly do not expect a fire but you are ready just in case.

FLOAT PLAN

of _____
(name of boat owner)

{ **IF TROUBLE OCCURS** while you're cruising on your boat, help will come faster if the Coast Guard or other rescue agencies know *where to look for you*. For your safety and your family's peace of mind complete this form— leave it with a responsible person whom you can depend upon to notify authorities if you're overdue. }

IF OVERDUE, CONTACT ➤ _____
(name, phone number of nearest Coast Guard Rescue Coordination Center or other rescue agency)

BOAT: Name of vessel_____ Length overall_____

Registry number_____ Color of hull_____
(white hull, blue top, etc.)

Power_____
(inboard, outboard, sail)

Radio aboard { (transmit frequency) _____

NUMBER OF PERSONS ABOARD_____ { (receive frequency) _____

DEPARTURE FROM_____ DATE & TIME DEPART_____

DESTINATION_____ DATE & EST. TIME RETURN_____

ROUTE OR CRUISING PLANS_____

Figure 19-6: The Coast Guard recommends that a Float Plan such as this one be filed by every skipper leaving for a cruise. (The CG does not *distribute these forms but hopes that others will.)*

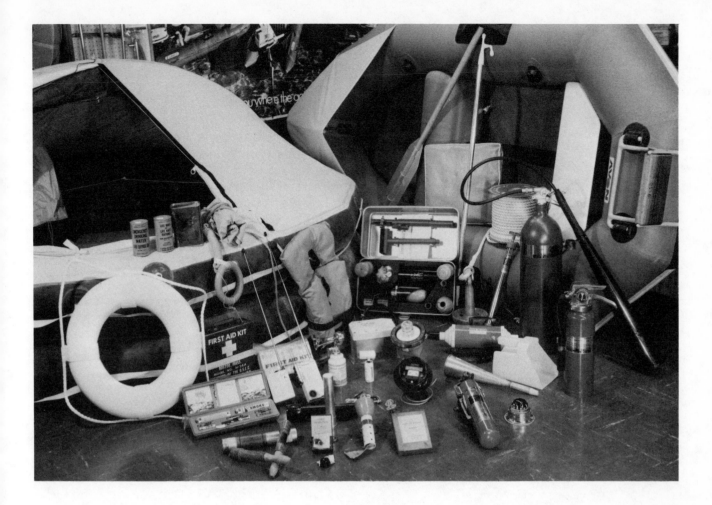

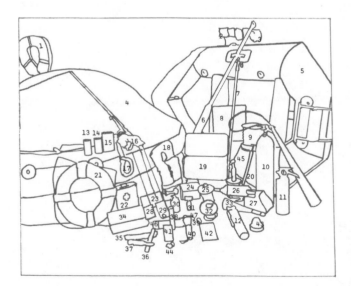

SURVIVAL PRODUCTS

1	Horseshoe Ring Buoy	4	Inflatable Life Raft
2	Running Lights	5	Inflatable Boat
3	Compass	6	Paddle or Oar

7 Boat Pole
8 U.S.C.G. App'd Cushion
9 Anchor Rope
10 15 Lb. Carbon Dioxide Fire Extinguisher
11 5 Lb. Dry Chemical Fire Extinguisher
12 2¾ Lb. Dry Chemical Fire Extinguisher
13 U.S.C.G. App'd Emergency Drinking Water
14 U.S.C.G. App'd Food Biscuits
15 U.S.C.G. App'd Combination Ration
16 Nylon Sea Anchor
17 Rescue Quoit and Line
18 U.S.C.G. App'd Life Jacket
19 U.S.C.G. App'd Line Throwing Device
20 Hand Pump
21 U.S.C.G. App'd Life Ring
22 U.S.C.G. App'd Lifeboat First Aid Kit
23 U.S.C.G. App'd Life Raft First Aid Kit
24 Bilge Pump
25 Distress Markerlight
26 Revere Inflator

27 Bailer (Hand)
28 Radio Locater Beacon
29 Pocket Transceiver
30 Falcon Freon Air Horn
31 Falcon 2″ Freon Air Horn
32 Bilge Sniffer (Gasoline Vapor Dector)
33 Manual Fog Horn
34 Penguin Rescue Kit
35 U.S.C.G. App'd Hand Held Rocket Parachute Flare
36 U.S.C.G. App'd Red Hand Flare
37 U.S.C.G. App'd Orange Hand Smoke Flare
38 U.S.C.G. App'd 37 mm Pistol Parachute Flare
39 Water-Activated (Personal) Rescue Light
40 Man Overboard Light (Water Activated)
41 U.S.C.G. App'd Fishing Kit
42 U.S.C.G. App'd Signaling Mirror
43 Emergency Compass
44 U.S.C.G. App'd Whistle
45 Anchor
46 U.S.C.G. App'd Flashlight
47 U.S.C.G. App'd Jackknife

PART VI

MAINTAINING
AND REPAIRING
PLEASURE BOATS

20 Hardware and Accessories

T HE marine hardware industry has done a great deal to further the safety and increase the comfort of the modern boatman. It has placed upon the market devices able to perform tasks that range from automatically opening and closing the windshield to keeping a drink spill-proof at the helmsman's side.

Marine hardware differs from its shoreside counterpart primarily in the material of which it is constructed but also in the sturdiness of its design. The marine environment is deadly to many substances that can lead a long life ashore. Protective finishes are more important at sea and very often become the determining factor in the longevity of the article they cover.

Preferred Materials

"Hardware" generally connotes an article made of metal, although plastics are making some encroachments into the field. The long list of metals used commercially shrinks to a very few when the article is intended for a boat. Even a leading structural metal on land, steel, for example, becomes marginal or unacceptable at sea because of its vulnerability to the environment.

Two metallic elements form the basis for most successful marine metals: copper and nickel. Neither commonly finds utilization in its pure form; both universally serve as the major constituent of the recommended seagoing alloys.

The magic of alloy chemistry makes strange partners and subdues the character of the individuals. An unsuitable metal such as iron can join in an alloy with copper and nickel and help rather than hinder the final qualities. Other unlikely elements—chromium, manganese, silicon, and molybdenum—join in the mix and improve the alloy, some for reasons that can be explained and some for reasons that are a mystery.

A glance at a catalogue of marine hardware items shows that the favored materials for cleats, chocks, bitts, and bollards are bronze and stainless steel. A choice is offered between plain bronze and chrome-plated bronze at increased cost. Galvanized iron and brass are available but considered of lower quality.

High-strength bronzes, and especially several patented and trademarked bronze-type alloys, are preferred for fasteners such as screws, nails, and bolts. Here, also, galvanized steel can be had at a lower cost—and with lower

life expectancy.

Bronze. Copper is the majority element in the alloy called bronze, with tin as the other major constituent. Various hardnesses and tensile strengths of bronze are obtained by the addition of zinc and tiny quantities of other elements to the melt. These mixtures have special names such as admiralty bronze, marine bronze, and so on. The trademarked, bronzelike alloys make nickel the major element and copper the balance; this combination yields extreme strength plus toughness.

Brass. Copper is the main element in brass with the remainder zinc. Small additions of other elements are used here also in order to attain special qualities for special purposes. Brass is not recommended because of its tendency to de-zincify in the marine environment.

Iron. The extremely high tensile strength of iron in the form of wrought iron or steel has dictated its use for hardware that must operate under stress. Since this bare material is almost defenseless under marine conditions, it is always galvanized or otherwise protected by plating. (Galvanizing is the application of a coating of zinc by hot dipping or electric means.)

Stainless steel. The addition to steel of chromium and silicon coupled with other changes in the mix makes the metal highly resistant to corrosion and chemical deterioration. This has led quite naturally to the name stainless. Many alloys of stainless are available commercially, each identified by a number, which in turn is part of a series with similar properties. Some stainless steels are magnetic, others nonmagnetic; some of the nonmagnetic types become magnetic from hammering and other cold-working.

Aluminum. Aluminum weighs approximately one-third as much as steel. This light metal has the unique property of forming an oxide protective coating when exposed to the atmosphere and this accounts for its wide structural use. Only a few alloys of aluminum are suitable for marine service; the others deteriorate rapidly when exposed to seawater.

Plastics. Many marine items formerly made only of metal are now to be had in plastic, at a saving in weight and sometimes also in cost. Plastics can be divided into two general classes: thermoplastic and thermosetting. The former softens with heat, the latter is permanent and does not. The number of plastic formulations is legion, each with some special claimed advantage.

Plating. Many metals fare better on sea duty when they

are protected by an electroplated surface layer, and chromium is usually chosen for this purpose. Technical reasons prevent the chromium from being plated on directly; the standard process is to plate first copper, then nickel, and then chromium over this. Chromium is an exceedingly hard element and therefore protects against abrasion also.

Bolts, Screws and Nails

The threaded fastenings are divided into bolts and screws mainly on the basis of relative size; the larger ones being known as bolts and the smaller as screws. Further classification is determined by the shape and style of head and by intended use, whether for wood or metal. The metal fasteners are placed either in holes large enough for clearance or else in holes with preformed threads. The wood fasteners draw themselves in like an augur and in a sense cut their own threads. Some metal fasteners also do this; they are known as self-tapping or sheet metal screws.

The nails have a point which aids penetration into the wood. This point is cold-formed on stock nails and not particularly sharp; the really sharp points, such as on tacks, are cut. Some boat nails have serrations along their length which act like the barbs of a fishhook to hold them securely in place.

Grommets and Fasteners

A tie passed through a plain hole, for instance in a curtain, would soon tear and become useless. Such damage is avoided by what is called a grommet. A grommet becomes in effect a metal lining for the hole. Grommets can be purchased in many standard sizes and each easily is fastened in place with an inexpensive appropriate tool.

Various twist and snap fasteners are especially handy for securing curtains and covers. Attachment is generally by prongs that pierce the materials and then are set by a special tool.

Chocks, Cleats and Bitts

The material of which chocks, cleats and bitts are made is important, but even more important is the security of the fastening that holds them to the deck. The main stress on chocks, cleats and bitts is lateral but some vertical component of stress usually is present as well. This means that merely screwing these items down with wood screws is a marginal method not to be recommended. They should be secured with bolts that go through to fish plates or large washers that can distribute the load under the deck. The choice of materials is largely a pocketbook matter with full realization of the effect quality has on longevity. Figure 20-1 identifies these hardware items.

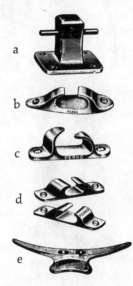

Figure 20-1: Smoothly polished surfaces of chocks, cleats and bitts are an important aid to rope longevity. (a) bitt, (b, c, d) chocks, (e) cleat. (Credit—Perko Marine Lamp & Hardware Corp.)

Bilge Pumps

If you disregard its physical effect upon the skipper, the most efficient bilge pump is probably an empty tin can. With the skipper's comfort in mind, the choice narrows down to an electric bilge pump, with a hand-operated type for emergencies. Both are shown in Figure 20-2.

Many electric bilge pumps are not submersible and must be located above the bilge; this seems strange but is a fact. The vulnerability to water damage arises from the electric motor and not from the pump. The few submersible electric bilge pumps achieve this feature either by thoroughly gasketing the motor against water intrusion or by locating the motor in the equivalent of a "diving bell" with its protective air bubble to prevent water entry. Some pumps employ a flexible impeller. This permits the passage of

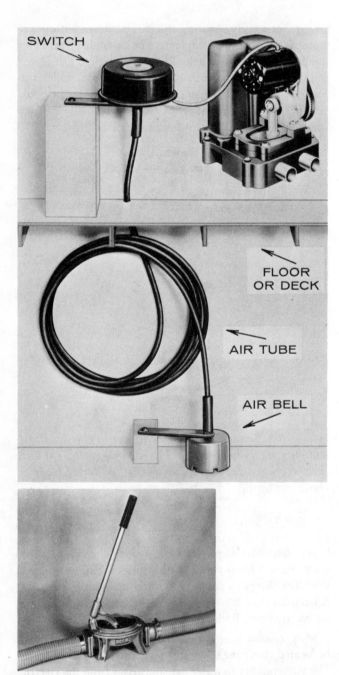

small solid matter picked up in the bilge without damage to the pump and often also allows the pump to run dry without harm.

The electric bilge pump can be made automatic by the addition of a switch responsive to water level. Such switches function either by means of a float which rises with the water or by entrapping air whose pressure increases as the bilge fills. One of the latter is also shown.

Ventilators

The job of ventilating the interior of pleasure boats can be left to nature, which is generally a bit laggard, or it can be expedited with electric power. The power devices take the form of centrifugal blowers such as the one shown in Figure 20-3. These blowers can move a considerable

Figure 20-3: Squirrel cage blowers are highly efficient air movers for ventilating galleys or motor compartments. The self-powered turbine-type is also a good galley ventilator. The funnel-type swivels to catch prevailing winds. (Credit—Peters & Russell)

amount of air and are able to buck the back pressure caused by ducting. The ordinary exhaust fan with standard radial fan blades is not of much value.

A wind-powered mechanical ventilator known as the turbine type is also shown. The rotating head creates a light suction which brings up the air from below. The funnel type has no moving parts and depends for its action on the rush of wind past its mouth, a venturi effect.

Figure 20-2: An electric bilge pump with its automatic switch gives a skipper ease of mind. The manual pump is a standby in case of power failure. (Credit—Peters & Russell and Dart Union Corp.)

The transparent plastic ventilator brings in light while it takes out stale air and is especially valuable for the forepeak.

The subject of ventilation should consider the lazarette. This area deteriorates quickly from dry rot if it is kept closed up. Adequate ventilation is usually accomplished by substituting a grating for the solid cover when the weather is good. Engine compartment ventilation is a legal requirement and is covered in Chapter 25.

Davits

The trailing dinghy, a common appendage of most boats a few years ago, has virtually disappeared; dinghies, where carried, are now stowed on board or hung from davits. The dinghies are raised, lowered, and secured by davits located either on deck or on the transom. This is an ideal method for the lighter fiberglass dinghies; the wooden dinghies are not as adaptable because they become waterlogged and heavy and open their seams when stored out of water.

Some davits contain their own block and fall and some incorporate electric winches. Stern davits fit into slides so that they can be removed without undoing the holding bolts. Dinghies are lifted either by two davits or by one davit and a sling between fore and aft lifting rings. (See Figure 20-4.

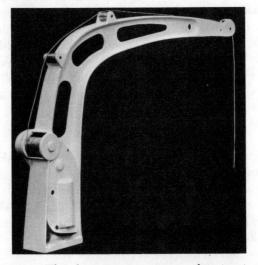

Figure 20-4: This davit incorporates an electric winch and spares the skipper's elbow grease. (Credit—Hummel Manufacturing Co., Inc.)

Bumpers, Fenders, Buoys

Old auto tires served as bumpers long before boating got classy; today no self-respecting skipper would use any but the fancy, store-bought kind. An example of the latter is shown in Figure 20-5. The resilient material that ab-

Figure 20-5: Functional bumpers have replaced the old auto tires that did this duty in days of yore. (Credit—Nelson A. Taylor Co., Inc.)

sorbs the bumps ranges from air to plastic foam and all have provision for horizontal or vertical mounting.

Buoys for marking and holding mooring lines can be anything from a homemade block of wood to a gaily colored metal or plastic sphere complete with eyes and swivels. The only technical requirement for a buoy is that its buoyancy be sufficient to hold up the cable or chain below it and that it maintain this buoyancy for a reasonable length of time.

Horns

A horn is a legal requirement; Chapter 25 discusses the law's specifications. Power horns driven by Freon from small replaceable cans fulfill the need on small boats without electrical systems. Beefed-up versions of electric automobile horns are available for larger boats and full-throated blasters that operate with compressed air can be had for still larger vessels. Some horns can be set to sound fog signals automatically.

The Freon horns are hand-held and require no installation. The electric horns draw a comparatively heavy current and are therefore activated by relays; this is standard automobile practice. The air horns are of two types: those which operate off regular pressurized air tanks fed from separate compressors, and those which have instant-starting compressors that can supply immediate air without tanks. Horn shapes vary all the way from long trumpets to small hemispheres. Figure 20-6 shows one unit.

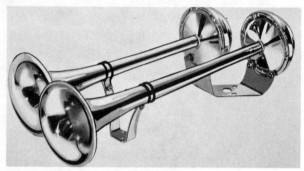

Figure 20-6: Horns are a legal requirement, but the type and shape to some extent are subject to the skipper's whim. (Credit—Sparton Corporation)

Searchlights

Searchlights are not required equipment but nevertheless almost a must for skippers who must pick up moorings after dark. The law governs searchlights only insofar as it specifies how they are *not* to be used.

Some lower-priced searchlights are built around standard automobile sealed-beam lamps. This is in no sense detrimental because these units have benefited from the experience of millions of users and are widely available; it does restrict the power to the automotive standard. The large searchlights are built with separate bulbs, many with projection-type filaments. A representative unit is shown in Figure 20-7.

Control of searchlight direction, laterally and vertically, is by handwheels and levers or, in some cases, simply by a handle on the back of the housing. One manufacturer is marketing an electric remote control.

Windshield Wipers

The standard powerboat windshield wiper is a heavy-duty

Figure 20-7: This search light has controls inside the pilot-house, a convenience. The law does not require search-lights; it merely specifies how they are not to be used. (Credit—Perko Marine Lamp & Hardware Corp.)

version of the automobile electric wiper. Some larger craft, which carry a compressed-air tank for the horn, have air wipers; these are similar to the vacuum wipers on cars, except that the activating pressure is positive instead of negative.

A form of windshield cleaner which is not a wiper is now being marketed for sail and powerboats; heretofore it has been used by large commercial and government vessels. This device cuts a round hole in the windshield and covers it with a circular disk of glass that is revolved by an electric motor. Centrifugal force throws off all rain and snow and keeps it clear. It is shown in Figure 20-8.

Boarding Ladders

The boarding ladder is a convenience for getting aboard high-freeboard small craft from a dinghy or from a low finger pier. These ladders hook into sockets at the gunwale and are removable. Many fold to half length. These or similar ladders are often installed at the transom for access to a low-placed swimming platform. Material is mahogany, aluminum, stainless and even plastic.

One ingeniously designed ladder continually adjusts itself to varying pier heights yet always keeps its steps horizontal. Its principle is that of the parallelogram.

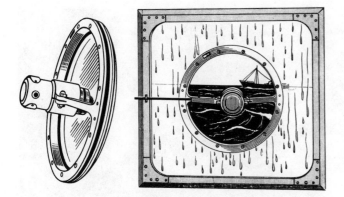

Figure 20-8: The whirling insert in the pilothouse wind-shield keeps itself clean by centrifugal action.

Accessories

A boat hook should be on every vessel for fending off, for picking up a mooring, and for many other routine uses. Some innovations have been added to the standard hook; one has two hooks and two points to aid in casting off and another incorporates a latch that holds a line in the hook once it has been snared. Clips and clamps are available for stowing the boat hook securely and neatly without marline ties.

The skipper who finds opening and closing the wind-shield too great a physical exertion can have the job done by electricity. A kit that can be adapted to most wind-shields includes an electric motor and the necessary gear-ing; a touch on the switch opens or closes to any degree. The same manufacturer provides a similar kit for raising or lowering outriggers and radio antennae; this is claimed to be a great convenience for skippers whose course takes them under low bridges.

A radar reflector hoisted to the mast or yardarm of any boat will increase its visibility in sticky weather to the radars of large vessels. Store-bought reflectors are usually of aluminum and made foldable for stowing. A jury-rig reflector can be made up in an emergency with large metal pans from the galley.

Most automobiles today carry no tools, and many skippers have carried this habit over into their marine touring. It is a bad habit that could lead at the least to inconvenience and at the worst to danger. A boat does not travel along turnpikes lined with service stations. At least minimum tools therefore should be aboard, housed in a convenient and serviceable box. The selection of these tools is covered in Chapter 23.

Gimmicks and Gadgets

The marine hardware shelves are replete with gimmicks and gadgets that claim to improve the life of the yachts-man. The more useful of these include rod holders, chart holders, window anti-rattlers, gimbaled drinking-glass holders, and emergency lanterns.

Stuffed predators such as eagles and owls are even being sold for mounting at the masthead. Hopefully, these will scare the seagulls into staying away from that nice, clean, inviting deck and depositing their "calling cards."

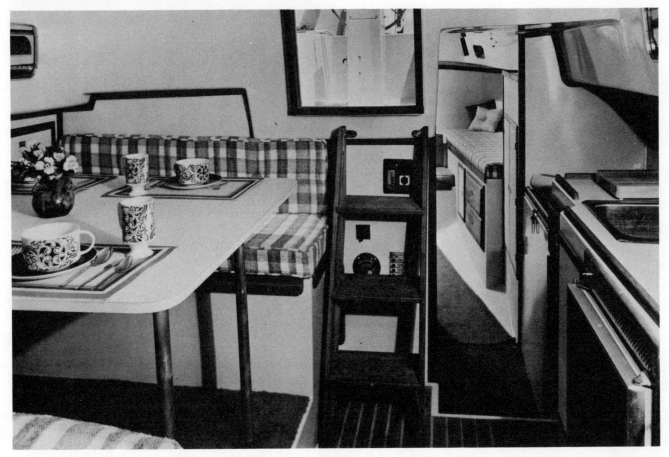

21 *Paints and Protective Coatings*

A WIDELY advertised slogan once promised that you would save the entire object if you protected its surface. Like all selling spiels, it was a slight exaggeration. Yet the advice was basically good; the surface of any object is its first line of defense against its environment. When the surface is exposed to marine conditions, the defense must be strong enough to cope with the severe punishment inflicted by wind, sea, sun and weather.

The most common surface protection is an applied adherent film described by the loosely defined word, paint. All marine materials of construction such as wood, fiberglass, and metal are generally painted. In some applications, the paint is purely protective; in others, it is decorative; in still others, it performs both functions.

Paint has a long history and it is therefore reasonable to expect that many varieties have been developed. Modern technology has been able to zero in on the various specialized requirements and has produced unique formulations to do each type of job. In fact the choice has become so wide that the layman is confused and even many professionals have joined in his bewilderment.

Types of Paint

The paints used in marine work, and paints generally, fall into three categories. One is varnish, a material that imparts a transparent or translucent film without adding color. The second is any coating comprised of varnish plus a pigment which hides or colors the surface on which it is placed; many paints and enamels fall into this category. The third is lacquer which is a clear or pigmented solution of resin in a solvent.

Each of the foregoing types of coatings is composed of some or all of the following basic constituents: drying oils, resins, solvents, diluents, pigments, extenders, driers, and fillers. Variation in the proportions in which these ingredients are mixed together determines not only the type of coating but often also its quality and price level.

DRYING OILS.

The concept of an oil that dries to a hard film may be hard to imagine for a boatman whose only experience with oil has been derived from the engine kind that never dries. The natural chemical reasons why one oil dries and another does not are derived from its molecular structure.

All oils contain a number of carbon atoms in each mole-

cule of their makeup. These carbons are either free to take up oxygen, in which case they are "unsaturated," or they are completely bound and "saturated." An oil must be unsaturated in order to have the property of drying to a hard film.

Use of the word dry to describe the action that takes place is a misconception. The drying oil actually oxidizes because its carbons take oxygen from the air when the paint containing it is applied. This oxidation is a heatless and flameless "burning" that "cooks" the liquid into the coating we know as dried paint.

The most common drying oil is linseed oil. This has been used since biblical times; it is pressed from the flax family of plants. Another widely-used drying oil is tung oil; it is even faster in its film-forming effect than linseed. Drying oils have also been pressed from some fish, but these are malodorous and will be found only in paints of a lower quality.

RESINS.

Many resins are found in nature but the resins incorporated in modern paints invariably are synthetics born in the chemist's laboratories. The natural resins are substances exuded by plants and trees mainly as a protective covering when wounded. Pine trees are a notable source of resin; this material, called pitch, was employed by the earliest sailors as a protection for the wood in their ships. Some of the best resins (called copals) are found in fossil form in the ground, from trees long disappeared.

Synthetic resins have pushed the natural ones almost out of the picture. Their list is endless. They are produced by processes which the chemists call polymerization and esterification. Polymerization occurs when similar molecules of a substance combine themselves into chains of much higher molecular weight. Esterification takes place when certain acids react with certain alcohols.

Among the synthetic resins important in marine paints are epoxy, alkyd, vinyl, polyurethane, phenolics, rubbers, and bitumins. These constitute only a small percentage of the synthetic resins used by the paint industry in general and new developments are being announced constantly. The universal purpose of the researchers is to produce a resin that will impart to the applied paint film greater strength, increased resistance to abrasion, and longer life under adverse weather conditions.

Epoxy resin is one of the newcomers that has achieved

popularity for marine use. This resin is the chemical outcome of a condensation reaction between epichlorohydrin and bisphenol. The epoxies are incompatible with the celluloses and most alkyds.

The alkyd resins are widely incorporated in modern paints and have developed a history of excellent serviceability. They are formed by the reaction of certain *alc*ohols with certain a*cid*s, hence the acronym, alkyd, with a slight change of spelling. Typical of the process is the reaction between glycerol (an alcohol) and phthalic acid.

Vinyl resins are an offshoot of the acetylene family. The forms used in paints are vinyl chloride, vinyl acetate, and vinylidene chloride, among others.

The synthetic rubbers and the bituminous resins are practically immune to the action of acids and alkalis. They are the principal ingredients in seam fillers and bedding compounds.

SOLVENTS.

The time-honored solvent for the classical formulations of paint is turpentine, a terpene derived from the pine family. Turpentine is not effective on the newer varieties of coatings, however; these require special chemical mixes.

Other solvents used in paints are alcohols, esters, acetates, ketones, and mineral spirits, the last usually as a substitute for turpentine. The greatest solvent in nature is water. This, too, finds a place in paint although such "water paint" is not used in marine work.

Solvents can be classified as true solvents, which actually dissolve the resin; latent solvents, which first swell the material and then work much more slowly; and diluents, which have no direct solvent action. Most commercial thinners are combinations of these three types.

PIGMENTS.

Pigments added to the paint mix give it color and hiding power; they also add desirable properties to the coating film. Pigments are available from natural sources and are also manufactured. Myriads of colors and shades can be had between the two extremes of white and black.

The most efficient white pigment is titanium dioxide; it has ten times the hiding power of white lead and zinc oxide, other popular whites. Each of these is relatively expensive and the amount found in any can is in ratio to the cost of the paint. The high cost of pigment makes it economically necessary in cheaper paints to supply a por-

tion of the required pigment in the form of extenders.

A common extender is magnesium silicate. It does not add any hiding power to the paint containing it but does add bulk and workability. Extenders can also control gloss.

Certain pigments are added to paints for the utilitarian purpose of inhibiting corrosion, toughening the film, killing fouling organisms, or others. Zinc oxide, for instance, gives paint great mildew resistance.

DRIERS.

As already pointed out, the "drying" of a paint is almost entirely an oxidation (except in lacquers). Certain chemicals can hasten this oxidizing action by acting as catalysts. They assist the drying oil in its capture of oxygen and thus hasten film forming. Chief among the driers are the heavy metal elements: cobalt, manganese, and lead.

Ready-to-use paints contain the amount of drier considered optimum by the manufacturer. When more rapid drying is required, driers can be added; since they reduce the time needed for a film to form they inadvertently also reduce brushability.

Varnishes

The earliest "varnishes," those used by the ancients, were simply raw or boiled linseed oil. It was applied to the wood and, when finally dry, left a film which, while adequate for the times, certainly would not be acceptable commercially today. Nevertheless, such a film has good protective power. (Incidentally, "boiled" linseed oil is just heated, not boiled.)

The subsequent improvement in varnish has carried over to the present day. It consists of combining natural or synthetic resins with the oil, together with stabilizing chemicals, and heating these together. This product dries rapidly and forms a tough, transparent, weather-resistant varnish coating.

Varnishes are "long" or "short," a rating made on the basis of the amount of oil they contain in the original formulation. When there is less than 15 gallons of oil to every 100 pounds of resin, the varnish is "short"; when the oil content exceeds 30 gallons, the varnish is "long." In-between, the varnish is "medium."

A formulation known as a spirit varnish is entirely different from the foregoing. In this type, a resin is dissolved in a solvent and no drying oil is included; the drying action is one of evaporation in which the solvent disappears and leaves the resin film. Shellac would be an example. (Shellac is not recommended for marine use.)

Paints

As already noted, paints, with the exception of lacquer, consist of a varnish to which pigments have been added. The category of paints for small boats includes enamels, flats, undercoaters, surfacers, sealers, fillers, primers and anti-foulants. The differences lie in the types and percentages of ingredients.

The varnish base is the "vehicle"—quite appropriately named since it carries the added materials. The type of thinner is determined largely by the type of vehicle.

EXTERIOR PAINT.

The traditional exterior paint consisted of linseed oil, white lead, and turpentine. This formulation is still a favorite with the old-time housepainters who "mix their own," although it is inferior to modern paints in color retention.

The nemesis of the traditional paint was the hydrogen sulphide belched into the air by chimneys; this reacted with its white lead. It turned the original pristine white color into a grayish hue within a few years. As far as the film itself is concerned, without regard to color, the longevity and weather resistance are good. This standard exterior white is not recommended for marine use, however.

TOPSIDE ENAMELS.

Enamels yield smooth, hard and glossy coatings. Most are self-leveling, meaning that their innate surface tensions will smooth out the applied film and eliminate brush marks.

The favored vehicles for topsides enamels are based on epoxy, alkyd, acrylic, and phenolic resins. All have their good points, dependent largely on the integrity of manufacture, and there seems no justification for picking any one out as superior.

BOTTOM PAINTS.

Bottom paints differ from other marine varnish-pigment combinations in two respects: (1) the pigment has the added function of destroying marine organisms and (2) the paint is designed to leach or lose this poisonous pigment at a controlled rate while in service.

The most effective poisons for keeping the bottoms clear are the heavy metals, lead and mercury, and the lighter metals, copper and arsenic; a form of tin also has been used successfully in the latest bottom paints. But effectiveness alone cannot be the deciding factor because government regulations have stepped in: Arsenic and mercury are virulent poisons to man and have been banned. This leaves lead, copper and tin for commercial use, with copper dominant. Some bottom paints must be launched wet because they lose their effectiveness if a surface film forms in the air.

UNDERCOATERS.

Modern painting technology thinks in terms of a "system" of coatings rather than repeated random applications. The system consists of two or more compatible formulations each of which assists the other to do its job.

An undercoater forms part of such a system. It adheres to the surface better than the topcoat could and in turn provides a proper base for the topcoat.

PRIMER.

"Primer" and "undercoater" are often used synonymously, although in the case of a metal surface the primer could be a third unit in the system which precedes the undercoater. The primer in metal painting has the primary job of preventing corrosion; it must also dry with sufficient adhesion and "tooth" to give the following coats a good hold.

SEALERS.

Sealers are placed on porous surfaces as a first coat in order to stop the suction which otherwise would absorb the topcoat and prevent a good finish. Sealers are generally thin varnishes that sink into all the pores of the surface and seal them. Sometimes additives are included in the varnish to increase this sinking-sealing action.

SURFACERS.

When a smooth, glossy top coat is to be placed on a surface that is inherently rough or pitted, a surfacer is applied first. The surfacer is a vehicle containing a high percentage of an easily sandable filler, such as a carbonate or a silicate.

When a relatively thick coat of surfacer has dried, the peaks can be sanded down even with the valleys to make a completely smooth and level base for subsequent painting.

LACQUERS.

Lacquers differ from ordinary paints in two ways: (1) they are actual solutions and not several ingredients in suspension and (2) they thus dry by evaporation and not by oxidation. Lacquers are popular because they dry extremely fast (sometimes too fast for brush application unless a retarder is added) and because their solubility makes it easy to patch them.

The original lacquers were solutions of nitrocellulose but the lacquers now on the market run the gamut from vinyls to acrylics. All are easily thinnable by the addition of more solvent and hence easily sprayable; all are characterized by high gloss and good elasticity of film. The nature of their solvents makes most lacquers very flammable in use.

Paint Removers

Paint can be removed from a painted surface by mechanically abrading it with sandpaper and a wire brush, by burning it with a torch, or by applying chemical paint removers. The first method requires tremendous work for any but the smallest surfaces. The second is hazardous in the hands of any but the expert. The danger is not only to the boat, which can be damaged, but also to the yard, which can be burned down. The third method, the use of a chemical remover, is most suitable for the average pleasure boat owner.

Chemical removers work by being incompatible with the paint film and attacking it. The coating becomes a soft mass easily removable with a paint scraper.

The remover must remain in contact with the paint coating until the action is completed. For this reason the liquid removers are useful only for horizontal surfaces; vertical surfaces require a paste remover that can be daubed on and will stay in place. Most removers contain a wax which increases their effectiveness. This wax must be washed off completely before repainting.

Brushes

The old adage about a workman and his tools applies strongly to painting; it is practically impossible to produce a good paint job with poor brushes.

The best brushes are made with hog bristles properly balanced between long and short. Synthetic bristles of various plastics have moved in strongly but, according to the old-time painters, the hog is still preeminent. The ideal brush is not square-ended but rather is tapered, as shown in Figure 21-1. The various shapes of brushes and related tools used in boat work are shown in Figure 21-2.

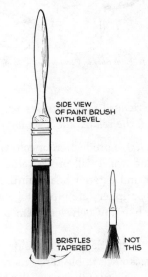

Figure 21-1: Good painting can be done only with a brush which has properly shaped bristles.

Colors

It is well known that white light contains all the colors; a prism held to sunlight proves this by forming a rainbow. The eye perceives color because each hue is on a different wavelength and causes its own unique stimulation of the optic nerves.

A painted surface shows its particular color by means of reflection and absorption. For instance, white light falling on red paint has its red component reflected but all its other hues absorbed; therefore the paint gives to the eye the sensation we call red. If blue and yellow paints are mixed, between them they will absorb almost all colors except green and hence the mixture will look green. (This

Sash Brush—3" Paint Brush—Duster—Wirebrush—Sanding Block—Scraper

Putty Knife, Broad Knife, Paint Bucket, Varnish Cup, Cup and Mask in use

Figure 21-2: Experienced boat painters use brushes like these together with the related tools shown.

is known as subtractive production of color.)

A common color wheel will prove valuable in mixing colors for interior and exterior boat painting. When any two colors on the periphery are mixed together the result will be the shade halfway between them by the shorter route.

The important properties of any color used in boat painting are its resistance to bleeding, its fastness under sunlight, and its intensity. Of course, the pigment must also be compatible with the vehicle and the other additives. The lighter versions of colors are called tints; the darker ones are shades.

Practical Boat Painting

It seems almost unnecessary to emphasize that the surface to be painted must be clean, dry, smooth, and completely devoid of loose particles of the previous coating. The chief tool for achieving this condition is the abrasive called sandpaper. (The steel wool normally used by cabinet makers is not recommended for amateurs.)

SANDPAPERS.

Sandpapers have not used sand as the abrasive since very early times; modern papers are made with garnet or aluminum oxide and some with carbides. The type of adhesive that holds the abrasive determines whether the paper can be used wet or must be used dry.

The number on the paper indicates the fineness of the abrasive particles; and the higher the number, the finer. A 200 paper, for instance, means that every particle has passed through the holes in a 200-mesh screen (200 holes to the square inch). Coarse cutting down is done with the low numbers and this rough surface is then smoothed with the higher numbers up to about 320, which yields a glass-smooth surface.

An ultra-fine grade of abrasive paper (or cloth) is called "pouncing paper." Its abrasive action is so light that the result of its use is a high polish.

The approved way to sand is to hold a small section of paper on a block, never in free hand. Sanding is always done with the grain of wood, never across.

POWER SANDING.

Power sanders can save a great deal of elbow grease but they can also ruin the work if inexpertly used. The machines are built to cut in either of three fashions: circular, orbital and straight. All will cut right down through the paint and gouge into the surface if left stationary in one spot for more than a minute. Hand-finish sanding invariably is required after the power tools do the heavy work.

Face masks always should be worn when sanding. The dust from any surface is irritating; the dust from bottom paints is poisonous.

SURFACE PREPARATION.

Many amateur painters have the mistaken idea that paint hides surface irregularities. It does not. Actually it magnifies them. The most important step in painting is therefore the preparation of the surface.

Seams should be inspected. Any seam caulking that appears doubtful should be removed and replaced with any of the compounds recommended by the manufacturers. (The tang of a file bent into a hook is as good a tool as any for clearing seams.) Cuts, dents, scratches, and other imperfections should be filled and sanded smooth. Make certain that the caulking and filling compounds are compatible with the paints that will follow. (Priming the seams is recommended before applying compounds.)

Any bare wood spots and all fillings should be primed to reduce their suction. Bare metal should be primed as a corrosion barrier. All primers, of course, also must be compatible with subsequent coatings.

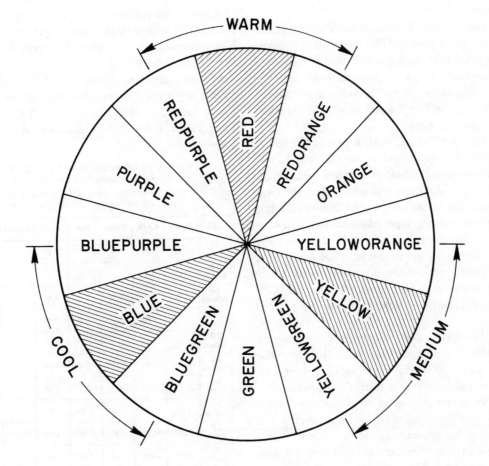

PAINT SELECTION.

Modern technology, as already explained, applies paints in systems that work together for maximum effect. The easiest way to choose a correct system for any job is to stay with one manufacturer and use his products in the rotation he directs. There is then no worry about compatibility, either immediate or latent. A system could be as simple as a single coat of an all-purpose paint or else it could start with a sealer and then proceed through primer, undercoater, and several finish coats. Corrosion must be guarded against whenever an anti-fouling paint is used over metal. (See Chapter 22.)

Paints are available ready-mixed to a catalogue color and ready to apply; those requiring a hardener or catalyzer are packed in two cans and mixed on the job. The more expert painters with a unique color in mind can buy a basic white and add the required compatible colors from tubes. The colors should be checked for fastness.

An important point to remember with any undercoat (and for that matter with any original surface) is that it must supply "tooth" for the coating that follows. This tooth or microscopic roughness is usually obtained by light sanding.

PAINTING PROCEDURE.

Since paint drips, common sense dictates that all painting be done from the top down. This means that topsides and decks be coated first, then the hull, and last the bottom. It is even an excellent idea to paint the cabin interiors before any outside work; this eliminates the dragging back and forth of spillable paint and paint-covered shoes across a newly painted boat.

Laying out the waterline is a ticklish part of the job. If the waterline can be established while the boat is still afloat, that is the easiest and best way. After hauling, the dirt and oil-slick line along the hull often gives the clue. The experts paint the waterline division free-hand while the less handy use masking tape. Masking tape can be a great help but it also can ruin a paint job: If it is loosely applied, paint will run behind it; if it is left on too long, it will take some paint with it when it is pulled away. Wide boot-tops are often used to fake unsure waterlines. (Colored tape is available which takes the place of a painted boot-top.)

Brightwork, beautiful wood showing its grain through transparent coats of high-gloss clear varnish, adds éclat to every boat—but it also adds much work. Brightwork must be revarnished often if it is to retain its distinction.

Brightwork in reasonably good condition can be revarnished with little preparation beside light sanding and thorough cleaning. No attempt should be made to revarnish brightwork in bad condition without first sanding right down to the wood. The steps then are the same as for new wood. Any discolored spots left by weathering can be bleached out with a saturated solution of oxalic acid. (Caution: Use rubber gloves.) Immediately the spot disappears the acid action is arrested with a borax neutralizer. Varnish is as skittish about the weather as a hypochondriac with a cold. Never attempt a varnish job on a cold, damp day.

The pores in such woods as mahogany and oak can be filled by daubing on any of the prepared wood fillers. The material is then rubbed off across the grain with a cloth; this leaves the pores filled but removes the filler from the surface. Less noble woods such as pine need no filler but are usually improved with a rub-on of stain.

Canvas decks can be painted with the formulations offered by many manufacturers for this purpose. New canvas is first primed by thinning the deck paint down according to label directions so that it can soak through.

Old, worn, and cracked canvas decks can be sanded before painting, if care is taken not to cut into the cloth. The better decision on canvas that is very badly cracked is often to replace it.

Marine paints are expensive and there is little point in purchasing more than required for a given job. The question is just how much to buy without risking a shortage. The table in Figure 21-3 should aid in obtaining a working answer.

ESTIMATES OF AVERAGE PAINT REQUIREMENTS
For Two Coats Over Existing Finish
Over *bare wood* quantities shown will be about double.
Less will be required on fiber-glass or metal.

SIZE	Topside	Bottom	Boottop	Deck	Varnish	Flybridge	Interior	Engine
10' Dinghy	1 qt.	1 pt.	—	—	1 qt.	—	—	—
14' Rowboat	2 qts.	1 qt.	—	—	—	—	—	—
14' Outboard	1 qt.	1 qt.	½ pt.	1 pt.	1 qt.	—	—	Single aerosol
18' Runabout	1 qt.	3 qts.	½ pt.	1 pt.	1 qt.	—	—	Single aerosol
20' Sailboat	2 qts.	3 qts.	½ pt.	3 qts.	2 qts.	—	—	—
24' Runabout	2 qts.	3 qts.	½ pt.	1½ qts.	2 qts.	—	—	Single aerosol
24' Utility	2 qts.	3 qts.	½ pt.	1½ qts.	1 qt.	—	—	Single aerosol
25' Cruiser	3 qts.	3 qts.	1 pt.	2 qts.	2 qts.	—	2 qts.	Single aerosol
32' Cruiser	2 gals.	1½ gals.	1 pt.	2 qts.	3 qts.	1 pt.	2 qts.	2* aerosols
36' Sailboat	2 gals.	2 gals.	1 pt.	1 gal.	1 gal.	—	3 qts.	Single aerosol
40' Cruiser	2½ gals.	2 gals.	1 pt.	1½ gals.	1 gal.	1 qt.	1 gal.	2* aerosols
60' Yacht	4 gals.	5 gals.	1 qt.	3½ gals.	2½ gals.	2 qts.	2½ gals.	4* aerosols

Requirements for twin-engine installation. Halve quantities for single engine.

Figure 21-3: Buying enough paint to do the job without having too much left over is a prudent goal. This table is a valuable guide.

Hints to Painters

Varnishes and other paints of honey-type consistency which do not contain suspended ingredients should not be stirred. Stirring entraps air bubbles which take a long time to rise and break because of the viscosity of the liquid. Such bubbles could be carried on the brush and mar the work. Paints "stirred" in high-speed mechanical shakers should also be inspected for bubbles.

Most paints are brushed out to an even film; varnish is not. Varnish should be flowed on and not rebrushed.

"Flowing" can be overdone to the point of sags, however.

Although paint is strained at the factory, careful painters always restrain it on the job. This is especially important for paints from partly used cans. Paper-disposable funnels containing strainers are available in all supply stores at low cost.

Lacquer applied on damp, cold days will show a blush or whitening when dry. This can be removed by a light spray of clear thinner. The blush can be prevented by adding retarders to the lacquer.

Removing all hardware when painting decks makes the work easier and eliminates the chore of scraping paint splashes off the metal or the equal chore of masking with tape. Reinstalling the hardware in bedding compound is insurance against leaks.

Miscellaneous Coatings

Heat resistant enamels, "engine enamels," are ideal for sprucing up the motive power. The preferred color is a business-like battleship gray. The metal surface must be completely free of grease. This is best achieved with an alkali-type cleaner such as trisodium phosphate (found in many proprietary soil removers). All trace of TSP must be removed with a water wash before painting.

Hand creams, variously described as "liquid gloves" and "gloves in a jar," are useful by making wash-up easier after painting. However, they are not substitutes for protective gloves when handling corrosives.

Seam compounds are available in single-can formulations (self-curing) and in two-can types (added catalyzer). Their content of tar, other resins, or synthetic rubbers lets them set into an elastic never-completely-hard, impervious filling.

The Navy coats the bare metal parts of the ships it mothballs with a liquid plastic as a long-time protection against corrosion. The film is stripped easily, like the skin off a banana, when the ships go back into service. Similar formulations are available to the careful boatman for winter lay-up.

A substitute for deck canvasing and painting can be found in the vinyl sheets sold in rolls for this purpose. The top surface is imprinted and colored to simulate various deck woods and decking styles. For application notes, see Chapter 23.

Beautiful, glass-smooth, glistening decks admired by landlubbers are known as arm-and-leg breakers by old-time sailors. Cellulose powders are available for mixing with deck paints; on drying these present a microscopically gritty surface which prevents slipping. Tight-fisted oystermen used to make slip-proof decks by sprinkling fine sand on new paint, but this is hardly a finish for a nice sailboat or powerboat.

Electroplating

A chrome surface deposited by electroplating is the universal protection afforded metals other than stainless when intended for marine use.

Chrome has a tendency to pit when exposed to salt atmosphere. Many prudent skippers counter this by coatings of clear plastic lacquer. Wax is also a protective but requires constant reapplication.

Hardware stores sell plating kits intended for repair of electroplated surfaces. They use the current from a dry-cell battery to apply a coating of the metal from a paste containing the metal salt.

22 Corrosion and Infestation

ALL metals have a natural tendency to deteriorate into the primeval state in which man finds them in the earth. Iron, for instance, is mined as iron oxide, is refined to become commercial iron and steel, and then, unless man prevents it, rusts back to its original iron oxide. Copper, aluminum, magnesium, zinc, other metallic elements—all follow the same circuit, although perhaps by slightly different paths. In short, all corrode.

Nor is wood immune to a cycle of deterioration, albeit the destruction here is biological. Wood is the natural food of certain marine organisms and is their chosen habitat. They destroy wood by boring, chewing, and "rot," in other words by infestation.

Hence corrosion and infestation become the sworn enemies of the small boat owner; they work day and night to destroy his property. But the battle to prevent loss no longer ends in a draw; indeed, results constantly are becoming more optimistic. Modern technology has provided the knowledge and the tools for safeguarding metal and wood in a marine environment. It requires only an understanding of why and how to apply them.

Wooden boat hulls that have metal fittings, still the predominant combination, require simultaneous protection against both corrosion and infestation. Hulls made of fiberglass are immune to biological damage and only the metallic protection is needed for them. Aluminum and steel hulls also are beyond the domain of organic deterioration but here the need for anti-corrosion measures is intensified.

What Is Corrosion?

The dictionary defines corrosion as a "gradual eating away by chemical action as if by gnawing." This description is accurate, as many small boat skippers know to their sorrow. But it does not give any clue to the kind of intelligent understanding that must precede adequate counter-measures. It becomes necessary to use the teachings of chemistry and physics.

The development of our modern view of how and why steel rusts is a good illustration. The old thinking considered the rusting of ferrous material as a simple process of oxidation, a sort of slow "burning" in which the oxygen in the air combined with the iron, without flame and with no appreciable heat. This idea resulted from the fact that rust is iron oxide, a combination of iron and oxygen.

Then it was discovered that iron did *not* rust when immersed in purified water from which all impurities had been distilled, thus making it a poor conductor of electricity. This upset all previous theories. Clearly, there was plenty of oxygen suffused with the water and in contact with the metal. A new line of reasoning was needed and it evolved in the form of the electrochemical theory.

ELECTROCHEMICAL ACTION.

It is now generally accepted that an electric current is the prime mover in all forms of metallic corrosion. When conditions exist for such a flow of electricity, the metals concerned waste away; when these conditions are absent, the metals are stable. The tremendously important corollary of this is that the conditions can be manipulated to *oppose* corrosion and thus provide planned protection.

Four factors must be present before the destructive current can flow: (1) water, even minimally in the form of moisture; (2) chemical elements, such as salts, alkalis, or acids, which will change the water into an electrolyte capable of carrying current; (3) dissimilar metals, often even a single metal having differing surface properties; and (4) an electrical connection between the dissimilar metal areas. Oxygen plays an important role in this quadrangle. The strength of the current that will flow (and consequently its destructive effect) is partially determined by the amount of oxygen available at the site of the electrochemical action.

Offhand it would seem that the laws of chance would operate to prevent the necessary four factors from being present simultaneously, in other words, that luck would be on the side of the boat owner. The contrary is true and an illustration will show why. Take a metal fitting on an upper deck, high above the waterline and presumably dry. Examine it in the light of the new knowledge.

A tiny salt crystal has dried on the fitting when the sun evaporated the spray that put it there. The salt, being hygroscopic, attracts moisture from the air and soon becomes a salt solution, a drop of electrolyte. Although the metal of the fitting is considered homogeneous, imperceptible differences caused by manufacture or by strain exist within it; the area where the drop rests becomes the equivalent of dissimilar metals. So *three* of the conditions necessary for corrosion already have been met. The fourth is easy: The current flow between the dissimilar areas has an easy path through the parent metal. Corrosion has begun and will continue because the favorable conditions are now self-generating.

GENERAL CORROSION.

The foregoing is called general corrosion and explains why a single metal, unconnected to any other, corrodes when immersed in seawater. The drop of peripatetic electrolyte has been replaced by an ocean full. The light contact between electrolyte and metal is now the continuous washing of the waves to provide agitation. The slightly dramatized, microscopic illustration of Figure 22-1 depicts

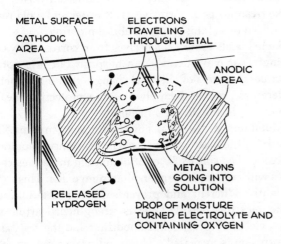

Figure 22-1: Two nearby areas on a metal surface can have microscopic differences which would make one an anode and the other a cathode. Add a drop of electrolyte and the metal will pit and corrode by electrochemical action.

what happens. Ions of the metal are dissolving into the electrolyte. The electrons left behind travel through the metal to the dissimilar area where they recombine with other ions to form and release hydrogen molecules. The metal wastes merrily away.

GALVANIC CORROSION.

"Galvanic" or "voltaic" corrosion is applied to those cases involving two actually dissimilar metals. Galvani

and Volta were two eighteenth-century Italian scientists who first noticed the electric effects of two dissimilar metals and an electrolyte in mutual contact. Their work underlies our modern primary electric cells such as flashlights batteries (see Chapter 7). The small, stacked-construction 9-volt transistor battery is actually an updated version of Volta's historic "pile."

Mention of the electric primary cell is apt because this is the best analogy of galvanic corrosion. The two dissimilar metals are functioning like the two electrodes in the cell and are generating an electric current in exactly the same manner. The magnitude of this current, and its corrosive effect, are determined in part by the areas involved, in part by the kinds of metal and the resulting voltage.

Electrochemical Series

In Figure 22-2 is a list of metals and alloys arranged in a very special order, the "electrochemical series." The more advanced textbooks also refer to this compilation as the

THE ELECTROCHEMICAL SERIES

magnesium and its alloys	manganese bronze
CB-75 aluminum anode alloy	naval brass
zinc	nickel (active)
B-605 aluminum anode alloy	inconel (active)
galvanized steel	yellow brass
aluminum 7072	admiralty brass
aluminum 5456	aluminum bronze
aluminum 5086	red brass
aluminum 5052	copper
aluminum 3003, 1100, 6061, 356	silicon bronze
cadmium	bronze (75% cu–20% ni–5% zn)
2117 aluminum rivet alloy	bronze (90% cu–10% ni)
mild steel	bronze (70% cu–30% ni)
wrought iron	bronze G
cast iron	bronze M
ni-resist	nickel (passive)
stainless steel 410	inconel (passive)
lead-tin solder (50-50)	bronze (30% cu)
stainless steel 304 (active)	stainless steel 304 (passive)
stainless steel 316 (active)	stainless steel 316 (passive)
lead	hasteloy C
tin	titanium
muntz metal	platinum

Figure 22-2: Metals immersed in an electrolyte develop electric potentials in progression from most active (magnesium) to most stable (platinum) in the order shown.

magnesium	+2.450 volts
aluminum	+1.712 "
zinc	+0.758 "
iron	+0.441 "
cadmium	+0.398 "
nickel	+0.231 "
tin	+0.136 "
lead	+0.122 "
hydrogen	−0.0 "
copper	−0.345 "
titanium	−0.370 "
silver	−0.800 "
gold	−1.360 "

Figure 22-3: Finite values in volts for the potentials developed by some metals immersed in an electrolyte are listed above.

"single electrode potential series." A simple explanation will clarify both terms. (The listing is also a good guide to practical applications.)

When a metal is immersed in a solution of its own salt (for instance, copper in copper sulphate, zinc in zinc sulphate, aluminum in aluminum chloride, or any similar electrolyte), an electrical voltage or potential is developed at the interface where liquid and solid come together. The number after each metal in the table of Figure 22-3 is the magnitude of this voltage. Each metal develops a very definite and a very individual potential as attested by the minuteness of the decimal figures.

The list is called *single* electrode potential because only one electrode (the metal) is being measured. Some of the figures are preceded by a minus sign, some by a plus. When two of the listed metals are placed together in a galvanic corrosion couple, or in a primary electric cell, the electrode potentials are combined with due regard for whether they are on the same or opposite sides of the center zero. Were the couple to consist of zinc (0:758 volt) and copper (0.345 volt), the developed potential would amount to 1.103 volt because one is above and the other below center zero. (If both were on the same side the resulting potential would be only 0.413 volt.)

Even the amount of metal that will be removed while this couple is active can be calculated, thanks to laws developed by Michael Faraday in the early nineteenth century. This quantity is called the "electrochemical equivalent." It is interesting to note that a given amount of current liberates more silver than copper and more copper than aluminum.

Mechanics of Corrosion

Metals have their individual vulnerabilities and immunities. Aluminum is not affected by mild acids but soon fails under the onslaught of alkalis. Copper withstands both the mild acids and the mild alkalis without appreciable damage. Lead can stand up against such strong acids as hydrochloric and sulphuric but gives up the ghost when faced with much weaker ones. An encasing material can protect a vulnerable metal: Embedding steel girders in concrete (an alkaline substance), as is the practice in heavy buildings and in concrete boats, prevents their corrosion.

It should not be surprising to learn that the acidity or alkalinity of the water in which a boat is moored directly affects the rate at which underwater metal will corrode if left to itself. The water condition, described technically by a "pH number," can run from 0 to 14. In this scale pH-7 is neutral; lower numbers signify acidity, and higher numbers indicate alkalinity. Some industrial wastes can make fresh water as corrosive as seawater and a pH reading would reveal this at any doubtful mooring.

Some metals protect themselves from corrosion by corroding. That may sound like a misprint but it is not; it describes a process of chemical changes that many metals undergo to provide themselves with a protective sheath. Aluminum is one of these metals.

Aluminum has a great affinity for oxygen; this "romance" is the basis for its excellent resistance to outdoor exposure. The surface layer of aluminum molecules combines with oxygen to form an aluminum oxide. This oxide is tightly adherent and prevents further deterioration. Sometimes this outside layer is strengthened artificially by an electric process called anodizing and the resistance to corrosion is increased. (This anodic layer can be dyed to various colors for decoration.)

An opposite condition exists with steel, although the first steps in the process are similar. The outer surface of steel also combines with oxygen to form an oxide, in this case called rust. But this oxide has minimal adherence to the parent metal; it flakes and washes off continuously to expose new steel to corrosion. In addition, the rust is cathodic to the underlying steel. Thus, the oxidation of steel accelerates its destruction, while a similar chemical change preserves aluminum. Metals that have this ability to form impervious external shields are selected for exposed services.

Corrosion Protection

It should be clear now that galvanic corrosion requires

the flow of a current of electricity. It is therefore no more than reasonable that galvanic corrosion can be controlled by reducing or preventing or reversing this current. This is the basis for protective measures.

Metal can be painted. Provided the paint forms a tightly clinging, impervious layer, the metal is denied access to electrolyte and oxygen; current cannot flow; galvanic action cannot take place. Of course, the paint must not itself contain corrosive or incompatible substances. The main shortcoming of paints and similar films is that it is difficult to prevent microscopic holes; time and abrasion supply them; periodic replacement is required to sustain the anticorrosion condition. The deleterious action is magnified greatly at any pinhole in the paint.

ANODIC PROTECTION.

By following the dictates of the electrochemical series, metal combinations can be chosen that will control or reverse the flow of current. By this means, a desired metal becomes a cathode and is held secure from deterioration while another metal, an anode, purposely chosen to be sacrificed, is destroyed. This is called anodic protection. (Current flows *from* the anode into the electrolyte and from there *into* the cathode.)

The sacrificial metal is more active and comes from the upper or anodic end of the list. Magnesium would be a first choice, but it is expensive and for some purposes even too active; zinc usually substitutes with adequate protection. The distance between zinc on the list and the copper alloys standard for marine use is an indication of its effectiveness. Since it is above aluminum, it also affords protection for this metal.

Zinc sacrificial anodes are available in various shapes to suit the particular job. Split collars can be attached easily to propeller shafts, flats and bumps are adaptable for rudder protection. The bolts that hold these halves together are of bronze or Monel and therefore are protected also. Figure 22-4 shows some of the forms in which zinc sacrificial anodes are available.

The tale of the disappointed skipper, who dutifully attached a zinc anode to the wooden hull but found his rudder and his prop wasting away nevertheless, may serve to illustrate the most important point about sacrificial anodes. *They must be connected electrically* to the metal they are to protect. Our sad example simply

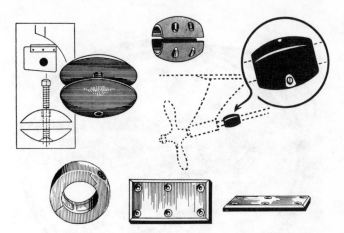

Figure 22-4: *Some of the forms in which sacrificial anodes are available for protecting underwater boat metal are shown above together with methods of use.*

fastened the zinc to the hull, no other connections. In effect, he was adding only so much ballast, devoid of all protective power. What he omitted was a good copper-wire connection to the underwater metal part needing protection or at least to the common ground system of the boat, to which these parts also were attached. (The zinc anodes on propeller shaft and rudder must make good, clean, electrical contact with the parent metal.)

Painting the sacrificial anodes is another error often made; the skippers who do this are happy to note that the zinc "is lasting a long time." Of course; this is exactly opposite to what should be happening; the zinc should be wasting away. Only by sacrificing itself can the anode protect its charges. This also points up the need for occasional hauling to verify the presence of some remaining zinc.

The similarity of all metallic corrosion, whether of a single independent piece or of a connected couple, should become evident. The single piece will deteriorate at many small points on its surface where dissimilarities exist; there will be an infinite number of microscopic anodes and cathodes. In the protected metal of a galvanic couple, these points will be electrically overcome by the voltage generated and the entire piece will become a cathode. (A cathode is the opposite polarity of an anode.) The metal ions of the cathode are repelled by the electrolyte and thus protected; while the ions of the anode are forced to dissolve until there are no more.

The galvanic current will be concentrated at the zinc anode when this area is very small compared to the area needing protection. Within limits, this generally does no harm although, as expected, it will hurry the demise of the zinc. In rare cases the paint around the zinc may be "burned" by this hyperactivity.

Available on the market is a heavy zinc anode shaped like a fish on a long flexible wire terminating in a clip. The anode is hung overboard when the boat is moored and the clip attaches to the boat ground circuit. (See Figure 22-5.)

Figure 22-5: This anode is hung overboard and its wire is clipped to the boat's negative line for corrosion protection while moored. (The "fish" is zinc.) (Credit—FMD)

CATHODIC PROTECTION.

The cathodic system differs from the anodic system in that the required current of electricity is impressed from external sources and not self-generated. This method is more flexible although much more costly; it also has the inherent possibility of *over*protection.

Cathodic-impressed-current protection systems consist essentially of four electrically interconnected parts: (1) a reference electrode below the waterline (one form is a combination of silver and silver chloride); (2) a control unit that determines the amount of current required to maintain protection; (3) a source for this current, usually the main boat battery, although it can be a separate battery reserved for this duty; (4) an anode electrode below the waterline from which this current is sent into the water. An illustration of representative equipment is shown in Figure 22-6.

The silver electrode immersed in the seawater becomes part of a galvanic cell whose other electrode is the underwater metal to be protected. That this should generate a voltage is readily provable with the table in Figure 22-3. The magnitude of this voltage is directly proportional to the corrosion tendency of the metal and indicates the amount of protection required. The silver electrode thus becomes the "brain" of the system.

The control unit acts as a variable "gate" in the path of the current supplied by the battery. When the corrosion conditions are bad, the gate is wide open and more current is allowed to pass to do its protective job. When conditions are good, for instance, at a mooring in a pure, fresh-water stream, the gate is almost closed. In the units designed for powerboats this control is usually exercised by so-called solid-state circuits containing transistors (see Chapter 8).

The current drawn from the battery under ordinary

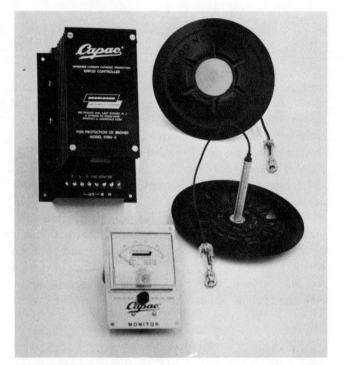

Figure 22-6: The components of an impressed current system for cathodic protection of underwater metals are shown. (The necessary current is drawn from the boat battery.) (Credit—Englehard Instruments & Systems)

circumstances is in milliamperes (thousandths of one ampere) and should go unnoticed in any properly operating electrical system. Separate batteries can be used but this seems an unnecessary precaution.

The current-emitting anode is also mounted below the waterline. It is common practice to plate this electrode with platinum in order to prevent its dissolution into the seawater in a short time. (Note that platinum is at the bottom of the single electrode potential series, hence least attacked.) An important point about a cathodic protection installation, often overlooked, is that the system and all metal parts it is to protect must be connected to a common ground.

Corrosion Cautions

All underwater metal parts should be bonded to a common ground as shown in Figure 22-7. All electric and electronic equipment aboard should also be bonded to this ground, but this ground circuit should *not* be a carrier of any current. (See Chapter 7.)

The use of dissimilar metals should be avoided. Or, at least, the choice should be confined to metals that are close together in the table of Figure 22-2. When a dissimilar

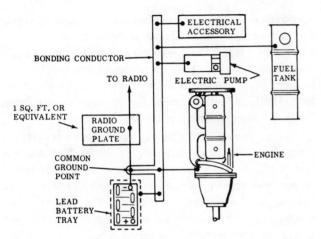

Figure 22-7: All metallic units aboard and underneath should be properly bonded to a common ground. This is of prime importance in preventing corrosion.

metal cannot be avoided, it is important to have complete bonding *plus* anodic or cathodic protection. Theoretically, the dissimilar metal can be insulated and thereby prevented from forming a galvanic couple which would lead to corrosion. Practically, it is extremely difficult to attain such perfect isolation in seawater.

The screws holding a metal unit should always be of the same composition as the unit or, better still, of a composition *lower* in the table. If this condition is reversed, the screws will disappear quickly.

Metallic paints should not be applied to metal parts indiscriminately. Their composition should be determined to verify that the metal they contain will not cause corrosion. Again, this means that both metals must be close together in the table. This caution is applicable particularly to the painting of metal hulls. For example, do not cover galvanized iron with bronze paint; the zinc coating will vanish, and the iron along with it.

When several boats at a marina simultaneously are taking power from the shore lines, they are in effect connected together electrically. This easily could set up galvanic cells between boats and cause corrosion. Such a situation points up the value of isolation transformers. (See Chapter 7.)

Overprotection in a cathodic system can cause excessive liberation of hydrogen at the protected cathodic areas. This in turn may cause paint to lift and blister and show "burns."

"Dry" Rot

The first thing to learn about "dry" rot is that it is *not* dry. Completely dry wood will never rot. The deteriorations we lump under the name of rot require very finite conditions for their existence. Chief among these is moisture. Yet there is an anomaly here; a great excess of moisture, meaning complete submersion, also prevents rot.

The progenitor of rot is a fungus, or rather any one of several fungi. ("Fungus" comes from the Latin and means a mushroom; often a mushroom-like growth can be seen in acute cases of rot.) The fungi are plants but, unlike most plants, they contain no chlorophyll and therefore cannot photosynthesize. This turns their feeding habits into a direction most unfortunate for owners of wood boats: They can digest cellulose.

Wood is composed primarily of cellulose with lignin as a binder. When the cellulose is gone, nothing but powder or mush remains and the structural strength of wood has vanished. An initially strong hull timber cannot support even its own weight after a complete ravage by rot. Adding to the danger is the fact that rot is generally internal and unseen; it comes to the surface only at the terminal stages of destruction. At this stage the infected wood becomes brownish to whitish in color.

Although the fungi that infect wood are almost universal, the latitude of conditions that foster fungal growth is relatively narrow. The optimum moisture content of the wood for fungal propagation is between 20 and 30 percent; below and above this range rot is minimal or nonexistent. The optimum temperature for rot growth is about 75 degrees; below 45 degrees rot fungi become dormant and above 130 degrees they are boiled to a deserved death. Fresh water, especially rain water, is the ideal ambience for the rot fungus; it has a doubtful survival rate in salt water and the old-time sailors who salted their bilges were not entirely wrong. The absence of chlorophyll makes the fungus independent of sunlight, but it does require some oxygen.

Spores are to fungi what seeds are to plants. These spores can be airborne or waterborne or distributed simply by contact. A source of concentrated infection, such as a pile of rotting logs, can therefore spread the malady to sound wood over a wide area. This is one of the strong incentives for policing boatyards and keeping them clean.

Rot Prevention

The surest way to protect wood against rot is to treat it with a fungicide that kills any fungus present by poisoning it and makes the conditions inhospitable for fungal spores. Many such fungicides are available, from the time-honored creosote to the more sophisticated (and perhaps more effective) chemicals and proprietary formulas. Creosote has the disadvantage of being incompatible with paint, a shortcoming happily not present in the other chemicals.

Standbys in the fungicide arsenal are various concoctions based on the poisonous qualities of copper, mercury, arsenic, zinc, lead, and the phenols. Lately these have been joined, and in many cases displaced, by a form of tin.

Methods for use of the fungicide vary from pretreatment of the wood before its incorporation into the hull (a Navy specification) to periodic applications to boats in service. The pre-construction applications are made by immersing the wood in a tank of fungicide; often this is done under pressure to force the liquid into the pores. In-service applications of necessity merely are brushed on like paint. The surface tension of the fungicidal liquid, which determines how well it will soak in, has much to do with its effectiveness.

Rot Cautions

The fresh-water seepage that facilitates rot generally gets into a boat from two sources: rain and the "hosing down" ritual now in wide observance because of the presence of hose outlets on all marina piers. Aside from actual leaks in decks, most water seeps in from places where it can accumulate, such as the crevices in windows, ports, and other openings.

High humidity can also provide attractive homesites for rot fungi without the contact of actual water. Such conditions prevail when the boat interior is tightly closed and denied ventilation. The water vapor "exhaled" by the boat is then held and concentrated; very soon, the conditions become optimal for fungal growth. A similar condition exists on boats that are hauled and tightly encased in winter canvas. The prophylaxis in these cases is to leave openings that permit the entry of air without the intrusion of rain. Judicious placement of these will coax Mother Nature into supplying forced ventilation.

Winter covers bring to mind the specter of contamination. Frugal yachtsmen often build the supporting frame for winter canvas from old odds and ends of lumber found around the yard. If these are contaminated (and there is a good chance that they are), the homesteading fungi will be brought aboard to spend a happy winter in the promised land. The fungi's disregard of family planning will bring the boat owner anything but a happy spring.

The places aboard to check carefully are such normally damp locations as the rope locker in the bow and the lazarette in the stern. The advent of synthetic ropes, which do not in themselves rot and can therefore be stored wet, has increased the dampness hazard in the forepeak. Lazarettes are uninviting to anyone on pleasure bent and understandably receive little inspection.

Marine Pests

Nature has provided several forms of marine animal and vegetable pests to add to the cross the small boatman already bears with rot. Some of these animals actually destroy his investment, while the others do no physical damage but force the periodic trouble and expense of their removal.

Highest on the marine criminal list are shipworms and limnoria; slightly lower, because they are less common, are several other destructive members of the crustaceans and molluscs. These are followed by a number of animal and vegetable species that have no desire to destroy but become a costly nuisance when they attach themselves to the hull. The drawings in Figure 22-8 show these various enemies; if they were larger in size, they would be hair-raising to meet.

TEREDOS.

The shipworm causing the most anguish to owners of wooden boats is the teredo. Despite its name, this is actually a mollusc or clam. It enters the planking as a tiny animalcule through an almost invisible hole which it promptly plugs from the inside to assure its protection. It uses its bivalve structure as an efficient, high-speed boring apparatus.

Once comfortably housed inside the plank, it spends its time boring, eating, and growing. It can digest the cellulose of wood, and thus its food supply is limitless—or at least it is limitless until the plank is gone. Teredos have been found fat and more than a foot long.

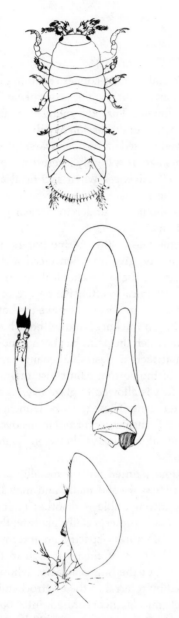

a

b

c

Figure 22-8: Illustrated here are some of the animal and vegetable pests which plague a boatman and destroy his investment. Shown are the gribble (a), the teredo (b) and the barnacle (c).

Unlike rot, teredos do not affect the strength of the remaining wood; the wood surrounding their burrows is normal. The difficulty lies in the amount of wood consumed over a period of time, which is so great that soon the plank is a hollow shell.

The presence of teredos can be discovered by probing with a sharp point, an ice pick or, better still, a steel darn-ing needle, encased in a handle. It can also be done by tapping and listening for the telltale hollow sound. This is akin to tapping a wall in a house in order to find the studs; it takes a practiced ear.

GRIBBLES.

These are tiny crustaceans of the family of limnoria. They bore very shallow runways which make the surface of the plank peal off and thereby reveal their presence.

PUTTY BUGS.

These borers make their entry into the hull by way of the seams between the planking. As soon as they arrive at an internal unpainted surface, they tunnel in.

SESSILE ANIMALS.

The sessile forms of marine life, those which attach themselves to a hull for life, comprise the barnacles, the mussels, the hydroids, and the bryozoans. These do not destroy the wood. They are obnoxious because they build a rough outer contour of the hull which reduces speed and increases fuel consumption.

The secreted cement these various animals use to fasten themselves to the hull is impervious to everything but the mechanical force needed to knock them off. That is why preventive measures, to be successful, must overcome these creatures before they have made their permanent attachment.

All the sessile forms of marine life are indigenous to shallow coastal salt water. They grow best in warmer climates; protection against them is much more difficult to achieve in tropical climes. As a comparison, boats in Maine waters are subject to sessile attachment only between about May and October; craft in Florida require preventive measures throughout the year. Even at that, the Maine situation becomes acute only during midsummer while southern waters remain "condition red" continuously.

The sessiles also need quiet water in order to make their attachment. Boats moored where there is a continual strong current are relatively immune; so are vessels continuously underway.

Marine Grasses

Algae and other marine grasses form the long green

"whiskers" so common on neglected bottoms. The algae seeds or spores have a specific gravity equal to that of water. They are therefore in suspension and able to drift about at various levels, responsive to every tidal current. They adhere to hulls on contact and then grow to many inches of length.

The grasses, like the sessiles, do no damage to the wood or other material of the hull. They are objectionable because their presence adds great hull resistance which cuts down speed and adds to fuel bills. Aside from economics, the bushy green whiskers undulating from the hull are an eyesore to a sailor. These grasses contain chlorophyll and need sunlight to carry on their synthesis, hence they cluster near the surface and are never found down under the turn of the bilges.

When it comes to sessile flora and fauna, wood, fiberglass, and metal hulls all have one thing in common: All are attacked (or should we say attached) with equal facility. It has been said that a man-made adhesive with the tenacity of the cement used by these hull clingers would be far ahead of any stickum available commercially today.

Defensive Measures

The boat owner has only one defensive weapon with which to combat all the borers and hangers-on that plague him: paint. This weapon's effectiveness depends upon its two characteristics of imperviousness and lethal chemical content.

BOTTOM PAINTS.

The purpose of a bottom paint is literally to poison the immediately adjacent water. The paint does this by containing a lethal chemical and then leaching or losing this at a controlled rate. Attempts to discourage attachment by keeping the surface smooth fail because the offending organisms seem able to anchor firmly to anything.

Copper in excess is abhorrent and fatal to aquatic life. The salts of this metal are therefore a predominant ingredient in bottom paints. Arsenic and mercury are even more poisonous but not used because of their toxicity to

man. (See Chapter 21.)

Even metallic sheet-copper sheathing leaches or ionizes into the surrounding water at a rate sufficient to discourage attachment. That the metal does this should be no surprise after our discussion of galvanic corrosion. Copper bottoms were used on wooden warships perhaps two hundred years ago. It is highly interesting to note that copper loses its effectiveness when sacrificial anodes are added because the reversal of current flow stops the leaching; this also should be understood clearly from the earlier explanations.

For some reason the marine borers, which drill wood with impunity, give up when faced with a coat of paint. This seems to be a mechanical reaction entirely aside from the chemically offensive nature of the coating. For this reason it is important to have the bottom-paint application of even thickness and without breaks. Even a tiny spot from which the paint has been removed by accidental abrasion attracts undesirable tenants immediately.

Many of the bottom paints lose their ability to leach if their surface is allowed to glaze over as a result of oxidation from the air. These must be launched while the paint is still wet. Some newer formulations overcome this drawback and allow delays between painting and being launched.

A bottom painted with a metallic paint takes on the characteristics of solid metal and may then become galvanically incompatible with other underwater metal fittings. This can be especially acute with metal hulls; all paint manufacturers specify an intermediate insulating coating. The type of chemical used in the paint relative to the metal of the hull is a factor whose importance can be gauged by referral to the electrochemical series.

The chemicals incorporated into bottom paints are harmful also to man. They should be applied with minimum contact with the skin and should be sanded with minimum inhalation of the dust.

Fouling conditions differ in various parts of the country, even in adjacent sections of the same bay. Paints that are terrific in one locality may be poor or bad performers elsewhere. The best guide is local experience. Local seasonal fouling characteristics also are the guide for best application time.

23   *Maintenance and Repair*

MANY skippers, from sad experience, equate "robber" with "boatyard"; in truth, it *does* cost the well-known arm and leg to have any work done. The fact is that the yards are pilloried unfairly. Wages have skyrocketed while workmanship has plummeted, taxes have soared, and in northern regions nature has called two strikes on the marinas by amputating the boating season.

Justified or not, the high prices are a burden to many boat owners. They have only one ameliorating solution: Do it yourself.

It would be foolish to believe that every boat owner can do *all* of the needed work on his craft. Some operations will always be beyond his skill or beyond his equipment or both. However, there is much maintenance and repair that every skipper *can* do himself, and the savings from this could make the inevitable yard bills more palatable.

The work aboard, the husbandry, can be divided into several departments on the basis of work similarity. Convenient classifications: hull, machinery, electrics, electronics, and marine gear. Of course, this is only one man's opinion; every skipper can regroup his chores to his own satisfaction.

Tools

There is that old adage about a workman being known by his tools, but the quality of tools has a much more basic purpose than praising the possessor. If you ever have put your muscle to a cheap wrench while trying to persuade a stuck nut, only to have the dang thing let go and smash your hand against an obstruction—well, you got the message loud and clear.

"Tools" (the quotation marks are intentional) are for sale in almost every five-and-ten-cent store for the fools who blissfully buy them. Good tools cost money to manufacture and, therefore, cost money to buy. Purchasing inferiors is not a saving, but in the end a waste of money.

TOOL KITS.

A tool kit that should prove adequate for most of the contingencies that can arise aboard should contain at least the following:

Wrenches, open-end or box or both, to fit every nut and bolt on board; also a pipe wrench.

Screwdrivers to fit the varying slots of all the screws on board. (Don't forget Philips.)

Pliers, electrician's side-cutting, slip, or groove joint, needle nose, angle cutting, vise grip.

Hacksaw and blades, fine tooth and coarse tooth.

Hammers, small and large ball peen.

Soldering iron, electric, and rosin core solder. If you can find one for boat battery voltage, so much the better.

Sockets in standard sizes and for spark plugs (for gasoline powered boats).

Drill, electric; also, hand drill and set of assorted-size drill bits.

Chisels for wood and metal.

Grommets and grommet-setting tool.

Keys, assorted sizes for socket-head screws.

Files, coarse, fine, and wood rasp.

Tubing cutter and tubing flaring tool.

Wire brush.

Selecting the right box to keep these tools in is important. Steel tool boxes soon become rust buckets. Sturdy wooden or plastic is preferable. All tools should have a generous coating of kerosene and grease.

Junkbox. Every tinkerer knows the value of a junkbox. In fact, marine tragedies have been averted by repair parts taken or improvised from this haven of odds and ends. The recommendation relative to a box (just discussed for tools) applies here also.

The boatman's junkbox should start off its useful career with the following contents:

Screws, metal and wood, a good conglomeration.

Washers, ditto.

Nuts, ditto.

Nails, ditto.

Tape, plain insulating and rubber.

Marine putty.

Plastic wood.

Bedding compound.

Cement, waterproof.

Epoxy filler.

Oil, penetrating and rust-releasing.

Wire, bailing and insulated electric.

The sailboatman's junkbox can profitably contain all of the foregoing (especially if he ships an auxiliary motor) plus the following:

Sailmaker's palm, a leather or plastic hand protector which enables heavy needles to be pushed through sails and ropes.

Needles, straight and curved including heavy triangular for penetrating several thicknesses of sail cloth.

Bench hook, for holding sails in position for easier sewing of long seams.

Beeswax, for waxing needle and twine to aid penetration through sail cloth and strengthen the twine.

Sail cloth, small pieces for patching.

Marline, assorted small stuff for sizing.

Awl or spike, this can be in combination with a folding knife.

Knife, heavy enough to be serviceable.

Once the junkbox is on duty, never discard any part or mechanical piece; squirrel away everything that could have any conceivable future use. The inconsequential thing you throw away has a fiendish ability to become indispensable just about ten minutes later. Even an old spark plug, otherwise intact, can replace an accidentally broken one on the engine and get you home.

The prudent skipper insists on instruction books, parts lists and service manuals for every piece of mechanical, electrical and electronic equipment on board, from the engine on up. There should be a wiring diagram on board for each electrical or electronic gadget; an apparently hopeless maze of wiring can become crystal clear after reference to a diagram showing which wire goes where.

Hulls

Hulls are wood, fiberglass, aluminum, concrete or steel. The techniques of maintenance and repair must suit themselves uniquely to the characteristics of each material. Some hull ailments are democratic and can plague any boat, while others are more snobbish in their selection and confine their mischief to one certain type.

One general item of hull maintenance applicable to all craft is the avoidance of salt encrustation. Fresh-water swabbing or hosing is important after any salt water cruise, with special attention to brightwork and to metal. The residual salt layer can even cripple the radiotelephone by shorting out the antenna insulator. An oily rag for wiping down all the exposed metal parts is a good final touch. (Fresh-water seepage to the bilge *must* be guarded against strenuously, as explained in Chapter 22.)

WOOD HULLS.

One recurring need of most wooden boats is caulking, not only of the hull but also of the decks. Theoretically, caulking is a simple procedure: You fill the bottom of the seam by ramming home some oakum or treated cotton, then add caulking compound until the seam is level with the planking. Actually the appearance is deceiving; it is not that simple at all. It requires a practiced hand; an unskilled person can do more harm than good. This is one of the jobs best left to the yard.

This does not mean that minor seam repairs in hull or deck need go to the professionals. Many seam compounds are available and can be used with or without cotton. Most do-it-yourselfers will do a better job with the no-cotton routines described in the instructions that come with the materials.

The photo in Figure 23-1 may inspire the small boat

Figure 23-1: Minor caulking repair of hull and deck seams can be a do-it-yourself job with compounds formulated for that purpose. Masking tape used as shown saves cleanup later. Total caulking is best left to professionals. (Credit —Tarp Seal Adhesives)

skipper willing to tackle a minor hull or deck caulking job himself. The masking tape along both sides of the seam to be caulked saves a great deal of cleanup work caused by not-too-steady beginner's hands.

Often the best cure for a really leaky sieve of a wooden hull is complete fiberglassing. One step in such a process, which conveys the general idea, is pictured in Figure 23-2.

Dry rot is an ailment that wood unfortunately is heir to. Small spots can be "cured" with epoxy-type liquids

*Figure 23-2: When the faithful old tub no longer responds to caulking, she may be a good candidate for fiberglassing. The photo shows one step in the process of rejuvenation. (Credit—*Motor Boating *magazine)*

made for this purpose. They seep into the rotted portion by capillary attraction; there they act as a fungicide and then harden to replace the lost wood. The cost of the liquids relegates them to only small repairs. Extensive damage requires surgery and replacement by professional labor. (See Chapter 22.)

Bilges should be kept clean. A sloppy bilge is a fire hazard when it contains floating oil and gasoline and a spawning ground for rot and mildew when it consists of fresh-water seepage. Various proprietary compounds are sold for adding to the bilge so that the roll of the boat can help in the cleanup process. Limber holes, in the frames at the keel, where provided, can be kept open to do their work by threading a limber chain through them. (This is standard equipment on many popular makes of boats.) Dirty bilges pose the constant threat of plugged-up bilge pumps; pump strainers should be inspected and cleared regularly.

Proper painting is a continuous hull requirement; it is covered fully in Chapter 21. Maintenance procedures can take care of scrapes and other small hull-surface casualties. It is an excellent idea to retain in tightly closed containers small samples of all the coatings applied at painting time. With these it is possible to repair later damages with the identical material for both color and chemical compatibility. Most repairs can be made from the deck

by hanging over the side; the low-down tricky ones are handled from a dinghy, while those below the waterline mean a haulout or, for a small boat, beaching.

Minor seam leaks and small holes can be patched from the inside to avert immediate repair. The jury rig by which this is accomplished is shown in Figure 23-3. Canvas or

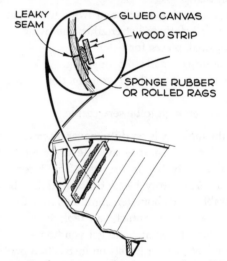

Figure 23-3: Leaky spots in the seams and small holes can be patched from inside without interrupting the cruise with this jury rig.

rags liberally coated with cement are spread over the leak area after it has been dried as much as possible. Strips of foam rubber, rolled rags, or other springy materials to apply constant pressure are then overlaid quickly and held in place by strips of wood nailed to the hull.

Many books and magazine articles recount the details of placing crash mats on the outside of a hull after a collision has smashed a large opening. This is standard practice in the Navy and applicable to ships divided into watertight compartments. These procedures, however, are of merely rhetorical interest to the average yachtsman. When *his* hull is holed through that badly, he has had it; he had better go about the process of abandoning ship, after sending out what distress calls he can.

A hull exposed to the hot midsummer sun for long periods of time will shrink and warp its planking sufficiently to show its seams above the waterline. While this presents no navigating danger, it is ugly. Many skippers have found that a prolonged hosing-down of the hull sides, administered daily, retards this.

FIBERGLASS HULLS.

Fiberglass hulls have been sold to the public as requiring *no* maintenance. This is an overly optimistic statement although truly the maintenance required is only a fraction of that needed for wood. But even in a matter so unrelated to fiberglass originally as paint—many fiberglass owners now paint their hulls to hide patches, crazes, and other time-developed flaws.

The maintenance for fiberglass hulls in good condition is elementary: Scrub it clean, then wax it. This is parallel to the care required for automobile bodies, which also have high-gloss finishes.

Fiberglass has an innate flexibility which enables it to come unscathed from an impact that could hole hulls of other materials; like a fighter, it can "roll with the punches." When fiberglass does get holed, the repair is within the ability of almost any skipper willing to take the trouble.

The steps taken to repair a hole in a fiberglass hull are detailed in Figure 23-4. The repair can be made from the outside or from the inside with almost equal ease. It is quite possible to make a hull patch of this nature while on a cruise and suffer no more than a few hours' delay. (This presupposes a fiberglass repair kit carried in the maintenance locker.)

ALUMINUM HULLS.

Two maintenance problems that occur frequently on aluminum hulls are scrapes and dents. On unpainted hulls, the scrapes are merely unsightly; on painted hulls, the scrapes down to bare metal can start serious corrosion, as explained in Chapter 22. Dents are unsightly; in addition, they increase the possibility of corrosion because of the highly-stressed condition of the deformed metal.

Scrapes on bare metal can be fudged out by starting with #100 grit paper, then using progressively finer grits, and finishing with #300 grit. The finer grits can be eliminated when repairing scrapes on painted hulls. On these, the abrasion is carried only to the point where a completely clean metal surface is reached. This is then primed and repainted with a duplicate of the original coating.

Do-it-yourself dent removal is possible only on the hulls made with light-gauge metal. Undenting a large aluminum vessel's hull constructed with plates of comparatively heavy gauge is for the professionals who have the necessary hydraulic equipment.

The tools for taking the dents out of light-gauge metal are a bumping hammer and a dolly. These are common tools in automobile body shops and can be bought in auto supply stores. The hammer has a large, square, slightly convexed face; the dolly is a polished piece of heavy steel which is held against the metal on the side opposite the hammering and directly under the blows. (The dolly acts as an anvil.) Repeated light taps do the trick rather than a few heavy hits. The hammering is from the outside of the dent gradually toward the center. Stretching the metal must be avoided because it causes wrinkles.

Sometimes the stretching caused by hammering is unavoidable. The added metal can then be removed by drilling a hole at its center which subsequently is filled by welding, further bumping, or otherwise. The sketches in Figure 23-5 show the various techniques. They also illustrate how a crack can be prevented from spreading by drilling a small hole at each end. These, and the crack, can then be filled if desired.

Aluminum hulls should be examined for such signs of corrosion as pitting and also for fine, hairline stress cracks. These are often found around stuffing boxes, skegs, and other vibration points.

STEEL HULLS.

Rust is the principal enemy of steel hulls and it is fought with elbow grease. Large vessels clear rust with chipping hammers; small boats, with coarse grit abrasive papers. When bare metal is reached, the scrape is repainted after first being primed.

Large dents from heavy impacts should be left to professional craftsmen. Small dents in light gauges of steel can be bumped out with bumping hammer and dolly, as mentioned for aluminum. They can also be filled with epoxy body putty made for this purpose and then faired smooth with the rest of the adjoining surface. These putties are similar to the ones automobile body shops use.

Decks

The universal complaint about decks is leakage. Most dry-rot areas in cabins are attributable to rainwater that got through the deck. Narrow-strip decks are the worst offenders simply because they have the greatest number of locations for possible leaks.

Localized leaks are best corrected with caulking compound which is packaged in convenient spouted tubes.

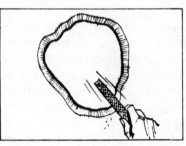

1. Saw out all damaged parts including delaminated fiberglass...after cleaning the area and sanding away all paint, inside and out.

2. Bevel or scarf both inside and out with a coarse rasp or disc sander. The bevel length determines the patch strength.

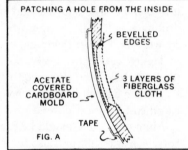

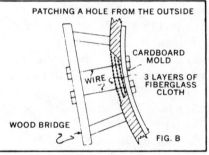

3. Make a mold of cardboard, or sheet metal covered with acetate film. Where possible, fasten mold to outside of hull with tape and make repair from inside

(Fig. A) If you can't reach repair from inside, or boat is double shell filled with foam, make repair from outside. (Fig. B)

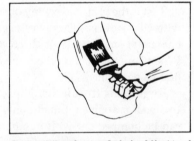

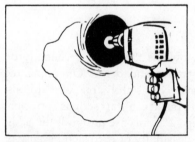

4. Cut Fiberglass to fit hole. Mix ¼ of Kwik resin with catalyst, as per instructions on can, and coat mold, using clean brush. Lay fiberglass in and wet it out with balance of already mixed resin.

5. Cut Fiberglass larger than first cut. Mix more resin and recoat first layer. Put in second layer, wet out thoroughly. Repeat complete procedure for third layer. Let resin cure 30 minutes before recoating last layer of cloth with remaining resin.

Figure 23-4: Repairing a hole in a fiberglass hull is not difficult if these instructions are followed—and if you carry a fiberglass repair kit in the maintenance locker.

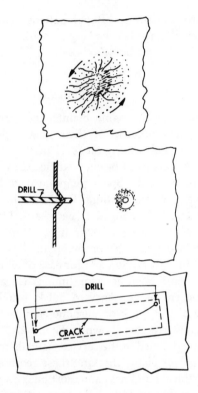

a

b

DRILL

c

DRILL

CRACK

Figure 23-5: Dents in light metal hulls can be removed with a bumping hammer and a dolly (obtainable from auto supply stores). The dent is hammered in a circular pattern (a). Unavoidably stretched metal can be relieved by drilling a hole (b). A crack can be prevented from spreading by drilling a hole at each end (c).

The leaky seam is cleaned out so that the adhesive in the compound can take good hold when it is forced into place.

Decks that leak in a discouraging number of places are best cured by being canvased. The "canvas" can be the real thing or one of the synthetic materials that are printed and grained to simulate wooden decking. If canvas is chosen, it should be the *preshrunk* type. (Raw canvas must be shrunk by soaking in water for several hours. It must be absolutely dry when it is applied.)

Canvasing a deck is not difficult; care and patience will produce a good-looking job. All deck fittings including the toe rail are removed first. The canvas then is folded in half to mark its center and this is tacked lightly and temporarily directly over the center line of the deck, in order to place the material for cutting. The cut to shape is made with several inches of overlap all around. The

canvas is now rolled from both sides toward the middle (as shown in Figure 23-6) in order to make room for the cement application to the deck. The cement is put down one strip at a time, alternating from one side to the other. The canvas is pushed down and out into each cement strip immediately upon its completion, with care taken to squeeze out all air bubbles. (The tacks, of course, were first removed and the center line was cemented down.) Deck fittings are reinstalled in bedding compound, as is the toe rail. The final step is the painting of the canvas with any material recommended as suitable by the manufacturer.

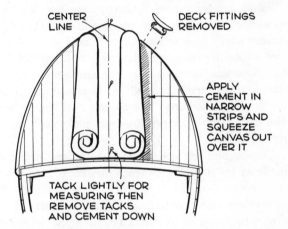

CENTER LINE

DECK FITTINGS REMOVED

APPLY CEMENT IN NARROW STRIPS AND SQUEEZE CANVAS OUT OVER IT

TACK LIGHTLY FOR MEASURING THEN REMOVE TACKS AND CEMENT DOWN

Figure 23-6: Preshrunk canvas or one of the synthetic materials printed to simulate wood can make a deck "new" again. It's not hard to do if you follow the sketched instructions.

Sailboat Maintenance

The type of maintenance required by a hull is determined by its material and is not affected by whether it derives its motive power from fuel or from wind. But above the hull the windjammer has many unique requirements for attention not shared by the stinkpotter. These center around masts, booms, rigging, winches, sails and other items foreign to engine-driven boats.

Masts are either of wood or extruded aluminum tubing. An outer protective coating is mandatory with wood masts but only elective with aluminum. Careful sanding to achieve super-smoothness followed by one or preferably several coats of varnish is the norm for wood.

Unpainted aluminum masts are made smooth and glistening with pouncing paper and are subsequently waxed. Longer-lasting protection can be achieved by painting the mast. Prime and finish coats can be applied in any desired color although aluminum color hides scratches and mars most effectively.

What has been said for masts applies equally well to all other spars. Like the proverbial little woman at home, a sailor's work is never done. Wooden masts are subject to cracks and dry rot in spots where fittings can accumulate rain water. Aluminum masts may also develop cracks but they are hairline in size and are the result of stress and fatigue. Careful examination, like a monkey going over another's fur, constantly is in order.

Standing rigging needs frequent inspection too. Where wire rope is used there always is the likelihood of broken strands which pose an immediate hazard to handlers and a possible future danger to the safety of the vessel. When the inspection divulges only one broken strand, some frugal sailors tape it carefully to disarm it and consider the balance of the rope still equal to all calls made upon it. The truly careful skipper, however, junks such rope and replaces it.

Turnbuckles left at one setting for a long time have a tendency to "freeze" even when they are of stainless steel and despite thorough taping. It is wise to untape them, squirt them with penetrating oil and then work the screw thread back and forth before resetting and retaping. At this time it is also wise to examine the areas where thimbles and stainless wire rope are in close contact because crevice corrosion is common at such interfaces. A bit of grease here helps keep water out.

Sail maintenance is a sort of magnified laundry job. The sails should be washed of all salt residue and scrubbed glistening clean with a brush and detergent. Inspect for tears, loosened stitching and cringles working their way out. Sun-drying of canvas is beneficial and has a bleaching effect; for Dacron the sun is not so beneficial.

Sailboat winches are finely tuned, expensive mechanisms and the prudent skipper will do well to remain within the bounds of the manufacturer's instructions as far as maintenance is concerned. Taking them apart and repairing them should be the province of the skilled mechanic.

It goes without saying that all sheaves, wherever located, should be checked for smoothly oiled free running. Sheaves whose working surface has become worn or corroded to the point of abrading the rope should be replaced.

Battens, especially wooden ones, require occasional in-

spection for smoothness. Rough battens soon cut through sail pockets. Remember the king who lost his kingdom for want of a nail in his horse's shoe.

Engine Maintenance

The basic steps in engine maintenance are familiar to most skippers because of their long experience with automobiles. Lubricating-oil level in the engine and in the reverse gears must be checked periodically and necessary additions made. Spark plugs must be inspected for soundness, gap, and fouling. Fuel and oil filters should be inspected and changed if necessary. Linkages from the throttle to the carburetor in gasoline engines and to the injectors or injector pump in diesels should be inspected for lost motion and for ease of actuation.

Proper ignition or injector timing has an important bearing on engine efficiency. A quick, rough test of the adequacy of the spark on gasoline engines can be made with a screwdriver as shown in Figure 23-7. The proper settings are detailed in the service manuals for each make and size power plant; checking these requires only average mechanical handiness and most boat owners will find themselves able to follow the instructions. Always remember that nuts are removed with *wrenches, not* with pliers.

Drive belts to generators, water pumps and/or alternators should be tightened to the degree stated in the manuals. Generally this means taut enough so that good pressure at the midpoint deflects the belt inward only very slightly. Loose belts wear quickly, prevent the driven unit from reaching its full capacity, and generate static electricity which can be heard as crackles in the radio receivers. (*Overly* tight belts are ruinous to bearings.)

The constant vibration and movement of the boat hull puts a severe strain on fuel tubing and its connectors. Policing these connectors for absolute tightness is a worthwhile safety precaution. Note that these connectors always should be tightened with *two* wrenches as shown in Figure 23-8 and never with one wrench or one wrench and a pliers.

One ill affecting old engines is wornout threads in spark-plug holes; it is the result of innumerable installations and removals of plugs, some done not too carefully. In olden days this was a serious problem, curable only by drilling and re-threading for a much larger size spark

Figure 23-7: The "screwdriver test" is a quick check on spark plugs. Be sure to use a driver with an insulating handle to avoid shock. With the screwdriver shank touched to the plug terminal and the tip held about ¼ inch from the block (engine running) a spark should jump. No spark—fouled plug. (Credit—Ray Krantz Photographic Illustrations)

Figure 23-8: Tubing fittings should always be worked with two wrenches, never with one wrench alone or with one wrench and a pliers. (Credit—Motor Boating magazine)

a   b   c   d

Figure 23-9: Worn spark plug holes in blocks can be repaired so that they continue to accept standard plugs. Three simple steps do the trick: Drilling to specified size (a), threading the hold (b), turning in the insert (c). How the insert looks is shown at (d).

plug. Today, inserts can be fitted as shown in Figure 23-9. These permit the continued use of standard plugs.

Spark plugs are the Achilles heel of gasoline engines, usually through no shortcoming of their own but rather through such other malfunctions as improper fuel mixture, worn piston rings, defective cooling and overloading. Luckily, plugs are easily accessible and the appearance of their business ends can give much pertinent information to the experienced eye. Even a tyro can make a valid diagnosis by using the photos in Figure 23-10 as a standard of comparison. Manufacturers of engines specify the torque (tightness) with which spark plugs should be installed; it is wise to heed this whenever available equipment makes it possible.

ENGINE STARTING TROUBLES.

Since an engine requires electricity, fuel, and air in order to start and run, it is logical to look into these three departments when a push on the starting button or a turn of the starting key brings no results. First comes electricity.

If the starting motor turns the engine over at normal speed, this is evidence that sufficient electric current is available. On gasoline engines the current must also provide ignition and the presence of a spark at the plugs should be verified by shorting with a screwdriver. (See Figure 23-7.)

If the starter does not respond, it may mean a dead battery. It could also mean a faulty starter solenoid or a broken connection. One way to differentiate is to turn on a cabin or instrument light. When the starter button is pressed the light will go out with a low battery, will remain on with the other causes. (Of course this presupposes that lights and starter are on the same battery.)

Fuel is the next item to inspect. Is there fuel in the tank?

Is the fuel getting through strainers and piping and reaching the engine? Is air passing through possibly clogged flame arresters and silencers? The remedy in each case is obvious.

A very important caution in starting balky engines is to listen carefully for unusual clanking or knocking. Broken pistons, piston rings, and connecting rods are not unusual; they will let their presence be known by these sounds. Every additional revolution can make matters worse. Do *not* attempt to start.

Engines on sailboats are mere auxiliaries and as such are used much less often than their counterparts in powerboats. This comparative disuse often affects the ease (or lack of it) with which they start. So turning the key on a sailboat engine normally may elicit a slower response and this in itself may not be a harbinger of trouble. An ancillary problem arises with the batteries; they seldom are fully charged because of the shorter engine running time. It may be prudent to run the engines periodically just to keep them limber.

One overriding aspect of marine engine maintenance is the necessity for eliminating the automobile-conditioned feeling that repair stations are only minutes away and consequently there is no need to carry spare parts. Spare parts on a boat are a prime safety requirement; there is no mechanic out near buoy #1.

Electric Maintenance

As pointed out in Chapter 7, the storage battery is the "sun" about which everything else electrical revolves. About the only service and maintenance operations possible with a battery are to see that its electrolyte level is maintained by the addition of water, that it is kept charged, and that corrosion is removed from the terminals. Vent holes must not be clogged.

Lead Fouling   Fuel Fouling

Insulator Erosion   Normal   Wrong Heat Range

Oil & Carbon Fouling   Engine Overheating

Figure 23-10: Removing a spark plug and comparing its appearance with the photos above often can lead to a diagnosis of engine malaise. (Credit—Kuhman Photographic)

A type of meter the radio service technicians call a VOM (Volt-OhmMeter) is a very handy gadget to have on board. It need not be a fancy one, or even very accurate. Low-priced models are for sale in all radio supply stores. Reading the instructions plus a little practice will make this instrument locate that bugaboo of all electric equipment: broken wires in a circuit. It will also measure the voltages in the system, although this value as a battery *condition* indicator is not very satisfactory.

One difficulty with electric equipment in a marine atmosphere is the green chloride that forms on copper contact surfaces and interferes with proper current conduction. Abrasion with fine sandpaper is the only method of removal. All contacts should be down to the shiny copper or silver.

Most modern, small motorized equipment is built with sealed bearings. These are generally lubricated for life and require no further attention except at eventual overhaul. Other motors need lubrication either with grease or with oil. An inspection provides the proper answer by turning up either grease cups or fittings or oil holes or neither.

Electronic Maintenance

When transistors replaced vacuum tubes in much of the electronic equipment aboard, the job of electronic maintenance was greatly reduced. Most of this work had always consisted of taking tubes out to check them and often to replace them.

The first place to look when trying to sleuth out the cause of any electronic failure is the fuse. Simply replacing the fuse blindly is *bad* practice; at best, it could result in another ruined fuse, at worst, in ruined equipment. The cause of fuse failure should first be found and corrected. A handy wiring diagram here is the difference between being lost in a labyrinth and threading a straight path from one component to another.

The only legal restriction on do-it-yourselfing the electronic equipment applies to the radio transmitter and the radar transmitter. As pointed out in Chapter 25, the internals of these black boxes is no-man's land to all except the duly licensed technician. Fuse changing is among the permitted operations, however.

The output power actually being sent to the antenna can be gauged roughly by having it light a standard 110-volt house bulb and estimating its relative brightness.

Either 50-, 100-, 150-, or 200-watt bulbs would be used depending on the transmitter power. The increased brightness when the microphone is spoken into is an indication of the modulation effectiveness.

Fume detectors can be checked by holding the sensor in a tin can which contains a few *drops* of gasoline; this should cause the instrument to indicate "dangerous." Direction finders and depth sounders are checked by training them on known objects and depths.

Battery chargers should be set to deliver an amperage one-twentieth the ampere-hour capacity of the storage battery. Thus a 200 AH battery installation would normally be charged on a continuous basis at 10 amperes. Most chargers have meters which facilitate the setting. Emergency charging at much higher rates can be done if care is taken to avoid battery overheating and if electrolyte level is watched.

Electrical noises from ignition and other equipment can make radio reception difficult and sometimes impossible; depth sounders can also be affected adversely.

Ignition interference is eliminated with resistance-type spark plugs and with resistance-type ignition cable. Extreme cases which refuse to yield to this treatment may require an airplane-type metal harness to shield the entire ignition system.

Generators are also offenders. Their contribution is recognized as a whine whose pitch varies with engine speed. The correction is made by connecting a low-loss *coaxial* capacitor from the armature terminal to ground. Do *not* connect it to the field terminal.

Alternators rarely produce noise. When they do, the cure is similar to that used with generators: a capacitor connected from *output* terminal to ground, *never* from the field terminal.

The clicking of voltage regulators can also make an annoying sound in radio receivers. This, too, is corrected with coaxial capacitors.

The capacitors employed to overcome very low levels of electrical interference, the so-called static, may be of the ordinary metal-encased type commonly used in automobile work. Where the static is heavy, these simple capacitors are not sufficiently effective and the more efficient type, called a coaxial, is needed. These latter must be purchased with a rating sufficient to carry whatever current is involved.

Marine Gear

At the head of the list of troublemakers is the head. This human necessity is cantankerous in the extreme, although most of the vexation it causes is traceable to the users.

Manufacturers supply an instruction sheet showing the valving and giving maintenance instructions. The usual trouble is clogging; invariably this is caused by some object thrown or fallen in. It is therefore good practice to avoid locating shelves and racks directly over heads; this eliminates the accidental drop-ins.

Each maker also supplies head repair kits that contain those parts needing periodic replacements, such as flapper and joker valves. Any skipper who has ever taken apart a clogged head will never fail to give his guests explicit instructions as soon as they come aboard. Nonmetallic heads should be cleaned with detergents, not scouring powders.

Running lights, stern and bow lights, and anchor lights should be checked before getting underway. Spare bulbs in the various sizes should be on board together with a flashlight.

Propeller pullers are the only tools recommended for removing props from shafts. Hammering them off is definitely taboo. (A good time to clean all strainers on through-hull fittings is during propeller servicing.)

Rope ladders with wooden steps often make nuisances of themselves by floating. This can be cured by attaching a weight underneath the bottom step. Rubber bumpers (the kind with nails embedded) are affixed to the back edges of all steps for hull protection.

PART   VII

OWNERSHIP
AND
RESPONSIBILITY

24 *Boatyards, Yacht Clubs and Marinas*

THE boat owner has a problem similar to that of the man in a big city who owns a car: where to put the durn thing when it is not in use. The solution for the auto is simpler than for the boat. The automobile can be parked free in the front yard or at innumerable curbs, often without time limit. There are no "curbs" for boats and "front yards" exist only for those few skippers who reside in waterfront homes. Most pleasure boat owners, excepting only those whose craft are trailered, find "parking" a complicated and expensive process.

The total cost of parking a boat is directly proportionate to the ease of access and the convenience of use. The municipal mooring provided by many waterfront towns is the cheapest; most towns make no charge or only a nominal one for registration and assignment of location but require the user to supply his own ground tackle. Although cheapest, this is also the least convenient. In the absence of a public pier, the dinghy has to make its run from and to a private boatyard with commensurate payment and consequent elimination of some of the economy.

A marina is considerably more convenient and of course considerably more expensive. Boarding and disembarking are done easily at the finger pier without the usually uncomfortable dinghy trip. Supplies can be loaded without trouble. Even a mooring at a marina is rented with included launch service to and from the boat.

At the highest point on the scale, both status- and comfort-wise, is the yacht club; quite naturally, it is often at the top in cost. Some yacht clubs have only moorings for their members; others have both piers and moorings. The breadth of the club's services is determined by its size, wealth, and geographical location.

Marinas

Marinas are as new on the American scene as the word which designates them. The word was coined by the National Association of Engine and Boat Manufacturers to describe a sort of nautical garage in which boats could be berthed permanently or on a transient basis. The original modest concept has sprouted and expanded, often in a grandiose manner, as every skipper knows.

The marina is a service establishment and should be judged on the basis of the diversity and efficiency of the services it renders. The marinas along the country's coasts, rivers, and lakes run the gamut from small enclaves with a few rickety piers to the super-gorgeous creations first found in Florida but now appearing widely. One of these is shown in Figure 24-1.

MARINA SERVICES.

First and most important, the marina supplies the skipper with a berth at a pier. On this pier, usually of the floating finger type, there will be electric outlets for city current and hose connections for city water. Somewhere on the premises will be receptacles for garbage disposal and pumps for fuel. The foregoing is the minimum. The electric outlets, similar to the one shown in Figure 24-2, will be placed conveniently at each slip for easy boat cable connection. (See Chapter 7.)

The plush marinas of course will add to this. The amount of addition is limited only by the inventiveness and wealth of the owners. Telephones are provided at every berth for use aboard and these are connected to a central switchboard which places calls and takes messages. Within the grounds are swimming pools, bath and toilet facilities, laundries, valets, shopping centers, movie theaters, and even supervised playrooms in which to park the kids while Momma and Poppa enjoy a quiet cruise.

MARINA COSTS.

The charge for the plain or fancy marina service is on a per foot, per diem basis for transients and on a monthly or seasonal scale for the permanent boats. Charges vary with location and poshness, just as they do with hotels, motels, and other accommodations. An average would seem to be around 20 cents per foot of boat length per day for transients. "Permanent" dockage, meaning for a full season of six or seven months, averages out at about $15 per foot of boat length.

The above approximate costs are for active use in the boating season. Out-of-season rates, for instance, for in-the-water layover in the winter in the north, are lower and include protection against icing where necessary. The guard against icing applies only to the water in which the craft lies and does not include the so-called winterizing of the boat itself or the snow covers.

*Figure 24-1: Marinas have come a long way since their
introduction into pleasure boating. Here is one of the
super-gorgeous creations. (Credit—Pier 66)*

Figure 24-2: This weatherproof outlet, found at each slip in most modern marinas, will take standard ship-to-shore cables. Current capabilities are marked and should be observed. (Credit—Hubbell)

RENTING SPACE.

A "slip contract" is entered into between the marina and the prospective tenant. The summer season usually is considered to extend from May 1 to November 1. The contract describes the boat by registration and size, establishes the cost and method of payment, and spells out the rules by which the tenant or lessee agrees to abide. It also limits the liability of the management for any loss.

Perhaps the first item to affect the marina's rating in a skipper's mind is the quality of the attendants. Spry and cheerful dock boys, who perform their duties with dexterity and a smile, have given many a marina a rating higher than its physical plant deserves. Conversely, good marinas have been beclouded by surly employees.

Boatyards

The original boatyards were places devoted only to building, storage, and repair, but most contemporary yards have added some amount of marina service. Nevertheless, the average small boat skipper shows up at a yard with his craft only when he needs repairs or out-of-season storage.

Boatyards generally have not taken the glamour route that has brought marinas to their present state. The usual picture is an unimproved, unpaved plot of waterfront property in an undesirable part of town. The major portion of the land is devoted to boats blocked up for dead storage. Some sheds house the mechanical operations. A marine railway does the hauling in yards equipped for large boats and a travelling crane or lift does the job in the others. The yard is often run by the local nautical seer.

RESERVING DEAD STORAGE.

A reservation for and subsequent occupancy of dead storage space entails a certain amount of paperwork. In signing the storage contract the skipper agrees to accept the "terms and conditions" of the yard and states that he has read them. These terms and conditions are printed on the back of the contract. The dead storage "season" commonly is considered to extend from October 1 to June 1. The storage contract identifies the boat and owner and specifies the cost and terms of payment.

The conditions delineate exactly what the yard can do and what the skipper cannot do on his own boat while in storage. If the boat is housed inside one of the closed sheds, then the answer for the skipper is zero; he is permitted to do no work at all, except possibly fool around inside a cabin. All improvements, maintenance, and repair are the exclusive province of the yard at prevailing yard rates of pay. If the needed work is of a technical nature that the yard's personnel cannot perform, they will hire outside technicians and add a commission to their charges.

Some boatyards do have a self-service arrangement for boats stored in the open. Under this plan, the owner can be his own maintenance man with only a few restrictions; for instance, he may not use a torch for burning paint and this is certainly understandable from the standpoint of general safety. Nor can he employ outside artisans. If the do-it-yourselfer gets tired or beyond his depth he can call on the yard facilities at the usual rates.

Neither the boat nor its content is insured by the yard and no responsibility is assumed for loss. The insurance must derive from the owner's own policies. The yard reserves the right to act as its own judge and jury to determine whether any damage caused to the boat while being handled is its responsibility; if the verdict is against itself, the yard sets the amount of compensation. Nor does the boatyard guarantee either hauling date or launching date. Calling these conditions "one-sided" is being

charitable; they give hardly a toehold to the owner whose valuable property is being stored for a hefty consideration. Nevertheless, these restrictions will be no surprise to anyone who has ever signed a lease for an apartment. (It is possible that admiralty courts could be called into the picture for certain causes of dispute. See Chapter 25.)

BOATYARD COSTS.

The charges for out-of-season or dead storage in a boatyard traditionally have been made on the basis of boat length. There is a tendency to change this to a consideration of the square footage occupied by the vessel (length × beam) or even to the cubage (length × beam × height). This is not unreasonable; commercial space is always rented with a charge based on the square feet given over to the renter.

The storage charge covers the usual nonboating period in the locality, which could be as long as nine months. One hauling, one moving to the final location, and one launching are incorporated in the cost; additional movings for the convenience of the owner or for preferential launchings are extra. Sometimes a bottom wash is thrown in free.

It is difficult to enumerate an average charge made for dead storage because this, as with all rentals, varies with location, status and demand. Perhaps a figure of 20 percent less than in-season live rates might give a representative idea; this would be for outside storage, with extras for boats inside a closed shed. The entire rent is payable on hauling. There is universal agreement among all boatyards on one point: No boats leave until everything is paid. In some storage agreements the owner acquiesces to a lien on the boat for all charges incurred. (See Chapter 25.)

Those yards that also perform a brokerage service place restrictions on the owner who wishes to sell his boat. They will permit no direct "For Sale" signs on their property; all inquiries must be routed through the brokerage department, which will extract a commission in the event of sale.

YARD WORK ORDERS.

Orders by the owner for work to be done on the boat are handled very much in the style common to automobile service stations. A detailed checklist is presented and marked with the items that are to be given attention. However, there is less flat-rating than there is with cars;

operation is on a time-and-material basis.

The charge made for work done can be approximated as at least twice the local going rate of hourly pay for the mechanics. Thus, if a worker gets $3 per hour, the charge to the boat owner for the labor will be at *least* $6 per hour and possibly even as high as $10 per hour. This is not necessarily exorbitant; to the actual wages paid out in cash, the employer must add the many fringe benefits, the several insurances, the extensive overhead, and the other monetary annoyances. A handling charge is also added to material used. The trade association claims that the boatyard owner who gets rich is a rare bird, indeed; going broke is more common.

Yacht Clubs

For the boat owner who has social desires and the wherewithal to pay for them, a good yacht club is the ultimate answer to the problems of berthing and storage. Yacht clubs, too, come in many varieties but, strangely, the cost is not necessarily in direct ratio to facilities and status. Some of the swankiest clubs have the lowest initiation fees and dues; the catch is that the membership lists are closed until deaths or resignations reopen them.

Most yacht clubs have limited pier facilities and rely on moorings in a reserved anchorage for their members. Service to and from boats is given by private launches that respond to toots, flags, lights, or radiotelephones, whichever has been prearranged. This and the other services are included in the membership dues, but prudent skippers add occasional tips to insure continuation of friendly attention.

Many owners value the social aspects of a yacht club more than the utilitarian. The usual appurtenances are a bar, lockers, and dining and dressing rooms. The social additions are dances and other functions, boat races, cruises, many diversions for members' kids, and the opportunity to wear full yachting regalia on the clubhouse grounds.

YACHT CLUB COSTS.

There is no meaningful way to estimate the costs of belonging to a yacht club. Initiation fees run all the way from nothing to $1500 and more. Membership dues start from a bottom of $10 annually and top out above $750 per year. But, as already stated, the appearance of a club is often not an index to its price level.

The usual procedure for joining a club applies to yacht clubs as well. An applicant is sponsored by one or more members who certify to his desirability. The membership committee or sometimes the entire membership then votes on his acceptance.

Icing Protection

Keeping berths clear of ice is now a common winter procedure in northern marinas. The usual method is to pump a continuous supply of air through an arrangement of porous hose laid on the bottom.

The explanation given by the makers of these ice-elimination systems is that the air changes the specific gravity of the warmer water on the bottom and causes it to rise to the top. This seems somehow to contravene some laws of physics. It is more likely that freezing is prevented by the continual motion; running brooks never freeze. Whatever the modus operandi, experience has proved that

the scheme works. However, a protected berthing location is still required because the anti-ice devices do not guard against floating ice floes. The diagrams in Figure 24-3 show the placement of the porous hoses and the photograph depicts the results.

Boat-handling Equipment

Traveling hoists are replacing marine railways for handling most pleasure boats weighing up to about 30 tons; this would normally mean up to about 55 feet. These machines pick the boat out of the water with slings and then transport it around the yard. They are an adaptation of the hoists long used in lumber yards. One is pictured in Figure 24-4.

Preventing boats from banging against each other is sometimes a problem when craft are berthed perpendicular to a long pier without intervening finger piers. A vee-shaped holding device which is claimed to do away

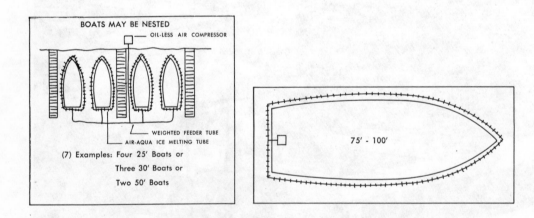

Figure 24-3: (a) Air bubbling systems keep water ice-free around boats. (The notched lines show the location of the porous hoses laid on the bottom.) (b) The photograph depicts the results. (Credit—Hinde Engineering Co.)

with this nuisance replaces the usual crossed bowlines.

A dock wheel could be a comfort to skippers who wear down their rub rails everytime they berth their boats. It is attached to project over the pier and engage the hull as it "rolls" in.

Air tanks are no longer used to float finger and other piers. Modern flotation is in the form of slabs of plastic foam cut to shape. This innovation also makes it easier and cheaper for those boat owners living at shorefront locations who want private piers. The pier itself can be of wood or aluminum. The flotation material is fastened underneath; it is rot- and mold-proof and requires no attention. The specific gravity of the flotation materials is so low their buoyant lifting power approaches the theoretical maximum of 65 pounds per cubic foot. Spiles may be driven into the bottom to hold the piers in position.

b

Figure 24-4: Traveling cranes have simplified the moving of boats around a yard. (No more foot-by-foot moves on rollers.)

25 *Legal Aspects of Boating*

IN this crowded world everyone's freedom is circumscribed by some privileges and many responsibilities. The owner of a pleasure boat is no exception. To acquire the privilege of operating his craft on public waters he must assume responsibility to various governmental agencies ranging down from the federal to the local.

The boat owner's responsibilities do not end with his obligations to these departments of government. He bears a responsibility toward all other boatmen who share the waters with him and even to all owners of property along his route whom he might damage. As if to add woe upon woe, the skipper is also responsible for the safety of all persons on his boat.

In order to understand the boat owner's responsibilities more clearly, this chapter divides them into their various channels of authority and then studies each separately. First, most important, and perhaps most pervasive, is the authority of the federal government. Next in line is the authority of the state. Finally, there is the authority of the immediate local town or city. Each government entity exercises its authority with an existing law enforcement arm, generally with a department especially empowered to do the job at hand.

The overall "umbrella" under which the law enforcement structure exists, insofar as it concerns powerboats, is the federal Motorboat Act of 1940. Further coverage and delegation of authority was provided by the federal Boating Act of 1958. The 1940 law divided powerboats into designated classes by reason of size and also stipulated certain basic equipment requirements. The 1958 law delegated certain phases of control and enforcement to the individual states but outlined the areas of their jurisdiction.

Briefly summarized, the federal government concerned itself with overall safety while the states (with a few exceptions) went about the task of identifying and recording powerboats much as they did motor vehicles. The purely local jurisdictions confined their rules and taxes to their immediate environs, such as anchorages and harbors.

A rundown of the federal laws which most directly affect the pleasure boat skipper is as follows: the Refuse Act of 1899, the Oil Pollution Act of 1924, the Motor Boat Act of 1940, the Federal Boating Act of 1958, the Oil Pollution Act of 1961 and the Boating Safety Act of 1971. These run the gamut from protecting the purity of navigable waters to enforcing safe operation of boats.

Federal Authority

Five federal departments exercise control in varying degree over the owner of a small boat: the Bureau of Customs, the Federal Communications Commission, the Coast Guard, the Public Health Service, and the Immigration Department. Every boatman is subject to Customs if he makes trips to foreign countries; in this event, he also comes within the ken of the Public Health Service and the Immigration Department. The Federal Communications Commission controls his use of radio and radar. The Coast Guard checks his equipment for safety and monitors his conduct underway. Of all these, the Coast Guard is by far the most influential.

Powerboat Classes

Safety afloat was the main objective of the Motorboat Act of 1940. It aimed at this target by prescribing in minute detail the safety equipment every powerboat must carry. Since it is obvious that a large boat and a small one should not be required to have identical installations, the Act divided all powerboats into four classes; overall length is the criterion for classification.

Class A is composed of all motorboats under 16 feet long.

Class 1 contains all motorboats 16 feet or more long but less than 26 feet long.

Class 2 starts with 26-footers and includes all larger motorboats less than 40 feet long.

Class 3 is made up of motorboats 40 feet long and longer but not more than 65 feet long.

In the above measurements length is the straight-line distance in feet, parallel to the center line and excluding sheer, from the forwardmost bow to the aftermost stern. It is the overall distance but *excepts* bowsprits, bumpkins, rudders, outboard motors, and similar projections not considered part of the hull proper.

The apparent loophole for larger vessels created by limiting the classified sizes to 65 feet was plugged by a further section of the Act. This made the requirements for safety equipment applicable to *all* craft more than 65 feet long propelled by machinery. The word "machinery" was held to mean all forms of self-propulsion other than steam—and steam was covered separately. (An interesting nuance in Coast Guard nomenclature considers a motor "boat" as under 65 feet long and a motor "vessel" as over that length.)

The classification makes no distinction between methods of mounting the propulsion machine, whether permanently installed or temporarily attached. Outboard motors are thus lumped together with inboard engines. In short, if any mechanical device propels the craft it is either a motor boat or a motor vessel in the eyes of the federal law—and subject to regulation.

Legal Equipment Covered

The federal jurisdiction concerns itself with specifically named pieces of safety equipment (legal equipment) and makes the Coast Guard the judge of their fitness. The items covered are: life-saving devices, fire extinguishers, running lights, whistles, foghorns, bells, backfire flame arrestors, and ventilation of dangerous spaces. Certain of these devices must bear Coast Guard approval numbers and cannot legally be used without such markings. (It is possible to use substitute equipment but only after the Commandant of the Coast Guard shall have been satisfied by suitable trials that it is as efficacious as the specified device.)

Some of the specified safety equipment is required in different type or size or quantity, depending upon the class of powerboat on which it is to be used. The underlying inference is that the larger the boat, the more likely it is to carry more people. The table in Figure 25-1 tabulates the requirements by classes for ready reference. Detailed descriptions of some of this equipment follow.

LIFESAVING DEVICES.

Flotation devices which prevent people thrown into the water from drowning are the most important pieces of legal equipment. These may take the form of jackets, vests, ring buoys, or cushions. Their use is not interchangeable in all classes of small boats, as will be noted from the table. In each case, however, the intention is the carrying of at least one approved lifesaving device for each person aboard.

In many cases the buoyancy of the lifesaving device

is obtained by the use of kapok and fibrous-glass flotation material. Such materials must be confined in heat-sealed plastic bags to be acceptable to the Coast Guard. This specification was not enforced until January 1, 1965, but is now mandatory.

Life Jackets are of complete wrap-around design found most effective in keeping the wearer's head above water. They are manufactured in two sizes, adult and child, and must be so marked. The prescribed color is "Indian orange"; this shade is visually arresting and is found more and more on all safety equipment both ashore and afloat.

Life jackets which have been approved must bear two markings: (1) the manufacturer's stamp giving his name and address and showing the official approval number; (2) the Coast Guard inspector's stamp indicating approval of the particular piece.

Life Vests are of the horse-collar design which keeps the wearer's face out of the water. The specifications for these buoyant vests are slightly less stringent and their approved use is consequently more restricted; they are approved for use only on powerboats of Classes A, 1, and 2 and in no case for boats carrying passengers for hire. They are made in two child sizes and one adult size and may be of any color. The standard label shows the size, the manufacturer's name, address, and approval number, and also directions for storage care.

Ring Buoys are approved in three sizes: 30 inches, 24 inches, and 20 inches in overall diameter. All must be fitted with grab lines; the color may be either white or orange. The construction may be of cork or balsa wood with a canvas cover, or else of plastic foam with a special surface as the cover.

When the flotation material is cork or balsa wood, the ring buoy must bear two markings: the manufacturer's stamp with its details and the Coast Guard inspector's stamp. The plastic rings need bear only a metal plate listing the manufacturer's name and address and the Coast Guard approval number.

Buoyant Cushions contain the standard flotation materials and may be covered with various fabrics, coated upholstery cloth, or vinyl-dipped cloth. There is no restriction on size, shape, or color other than that grab straps must be provided. The approval label lists the name and address of the manufacturer, the amount of

EQUIPMENT REQUIREMENTS

Minimum Required Equipment

EQUIPMENT	CLASS A (Less than 16 feet)	CLASS 1 (16 feet to less than 26 feet)	CLASS 2 (26 feet to less than 40 feet)	CLASS 3 (40 feet to not more than 65 feet)
BACK-FIRE FLAME ARRESTOR	One approved device on each carburetor of all gasoline engines installed after April 25, 1940, except outboard motors.			
VENTILATION	At least two ventilator ducts fitted with cowls or their equivalent for the purpose of properly an efficiently ventilating the bilges of every engine and fuel-tank compartment of boats constructed or decked over after April 25, 1940, using gasoline or other fuel of a flashpoint less than 110°F.			
BELL	None.*	None.*	One, which when struck, produces a clear, bell-like tone of full round characteristics.	
LIFESAVING DEVICES	One approved life preserver, buoyant vest, ring buoy, special purpose water safety buoyant device, or buoyant cushion for each person on board or being towed on water skis, etc.			One approved life preserver or ring buoy for each person on board.
WHISTLE	None.*	One hand, mouth, or power operated, audible at least ½ mile.	One hand or power operated, audible at least 1 mile.	One power operated, audible at least 1 mile.
FIRE EXTINGUISHER— PORTABLE When NO fixed fire extinguishing system is installed in machinery space(s).	At least One B–1 type approved hand portable fire extinguisher. (Not required on outboard motorboat less than 26 feet in length and not carrying passengers for hire if the construction of such motorboats will not permit the entrapment of explosive or flammable gases or vapors.)		At least Two B–1 type approved hand portable fire extinguishers; OR At least One B–11 type approved hand portable fire extinguisher.	At least Three B–1 type approved hand portable fire extinguishers; OR At least One B–1 type *Plus* One B–11 type approved hand portable fire extinguisher.
When fixed fire extinguishing system is installed in machinery space(s).	None.	None.	At least One B–1 type approved hand portable fire extinguisher.	At least Two B–1 type approved hand portable fire extinguishers; OR At least One B–11 type approved hand portable fire extinguisher.

Fire extinguishers manufactured after 1 January 1965 will be marked, "Marine Type USCG Type ——— Size ——— Approval No. 162–028. . . ."

*NOTE.—Not required by the Motorboat Act of 1940; however, the "Rules of the Road" require these vessels to sound proper signals.
**NOTE.—Toxic vaporizing-liquid type fire extinguishers, such as those containing carbon tetrachloride or chlorobromomethane, are not accepted as required approved extinguishers on uninspected vessels (private pleasure craft).

Figure 25-1: Motorboats are divided by law into four classes. The legally required equipment for each class is tabulated above.

flotation, the Coast Guard approval number, and a warning against wearing the cushion on one's back because of danger of face immersion.

There is no prohibition of unapproved lifesaving equipment being present on a boat used only for pleasure and not for hire. However, such flotation devices are considered to be merely the owner's personal property and do *not* count toward fulfillment of legal requirements. The legally required lifesaving equipment must be on board *in addition.*

Photographs of approved life jackets, life vests, ring buoys, and buoyant cushions are shown in Figure 25-2. These should aid the new boat owner in recognizing the spurious from the real. It is important to remember that a device is no longer considered approved if its label of approval has become illegible—regardless of its good condition. The Coast Guard publishes a complete list of manufacturers of approved equipment and their products in booklet CG#190.

FIRE EXTINGUISHERS.

The legal equipment next in personal importance to the lifesaving devices is the fire extinguisher. There is no running to the corner and pulling the hook in the lamppost fire alarm box when flames break out in a boat underway. Fighting fire at sea is a grim business; for the skipper it means act quickly and conquer or else go overboard.

Units are classified into three general types and subclassified on the basis of size. The designation is by one of three letters (*A*, *B*, or *C*) indicating type and by a Roman numeral (I, II, etc.) showing the size.

The *A* fire extinguisher is intended for fires in ordinary combustible materials such as paper, cloth, and wood. The *B* fire extinguisher is designed to fight fires in gasoline, oil, grease, and fats. The *C* fire extinguisher will put out

fires in electrical equipment without subjecting the user to danger of electrical shock. The fire extinguishers approved by the Coast Guard for legal use on powerboats are either B-I or B-II; both are hand portable.

A Coast Guard-approved fire extinguisher can be identified by any one of the following means: the manufacturer and model number can be checked against the listing in CG#190, the booklet already mentioned; the Underwriters' Laboratories label has the addition "marine type USCG"; the name plate bears a Coast Guard approval number.

The chemicals contained in the approved fire extinguishers can be liquid, foam, or dry. However, two chemicals once popular as fire fighters—carbon tetrachloride and chlorobromomethane—are now banned; their vapors when exposed to flames are so toxic that they could kill the fireman as well as the fire.

A restriction has been applied to dry chemical fire extinguishers since January 1, 1965. This requires the use of a visual pressure gauge on all models that have the propellant gas and the extinguishing powder stored in the same bottle. Leniency is permitted toward older models without gauges if they have been weight-checked within six months, if the seal is intact, and if they show no evidence of use or leakage.

The table in Figure 25-1 breaks the requirements for fire extinguishers down into classes. An overall governing factor is whether or not a permanent fire-fighting system is installed in the boat. (This consists of cylinders of carbon dioxide connected by piping to nozzles in various critical areas of the boat.) Outboard motorboats less than 26 feet long, which have no compartments in which flammable gases can collect, are offered an exception. Approved types of fire extinguishers are pictured in Figure 25-3.

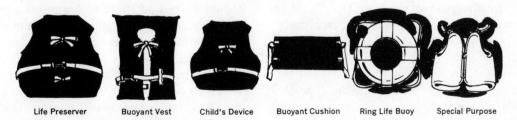

Life Preserver   Buoyant Vest   Child's Device   Buoyant Cushion   Ring Life Buoy   Special Purpose

Figure 25-2: An approved lifesaving device must be carried for every person on board. For regulations governing type, see text.

Figure 25-3: Fire extinguishers must be Coast Guard approved for marine use. Various types are shown above.

FLAME ARRESTORS.

These are required by the Coast Guard on all gasoline engines except outboards; they are of course not necessary on diesel engines. There are two technical exceptions which, because of age limitation, affect very few powerboat owners: Arrestors may be absent on all engines installed before April 25, 1940, and arrestors not currently approved may be used if installed before November 19, 1952. Except for the foregoing deviations, no gasoline engine may be used without a flame arrestor unless it bears a label from the Coast Guard expressly permitting its arrestor-less operation or is so installed that any back-fire flame would be directed into the open air and clear of the boat.

Flame arrestors must be connected to the carburetor by a flame-tight connection. The grid elements must be tight in the housing so that no flame can escape, and the internal construction must be clean and not in itself a fire hazard. The air cleaners and "flame arrestors" used on automobile engines are definitely *not* acceptable; these contain either steel wool or cloth or paper filters, in themselves a fire hazard.

LIGHTS.

Lights are an important part of the legal equipment required for conformity with the Motorboat Acts. The law states that every motorboat must exhibit the proper running lights according to its class at all times when under way between sunset and sunrise. (At present, no light equipment is required for purely daytime running.) It adds further that no confusing lights are to be shown. The placement of the running lights varies slightly with the size of the powerboat, as is adequately shown by the sketches in Figure 25-4. Sailboats, too, must carry adequate lights for nighttime running.

The act prescribes that every white light must be visible at a distance of at least two miles (masthead lights, three miles), and every colored light must be visible for at least one mile. "Visible" is defined to mean capable of being seen on a dark night with a clear atmosphere. The port light (red) and the starboard light (green) must each show unbrokenly for an arc of ten points. Each must be affixed to shine from dead ahead to two points abaft the beam on its respective side and suitable screens must prevent its being seen across the bow. (Remember that one point is equal to 11.25 degrees.)

On the matter of visibility of lights it is well not to skimp. To paraphrase a well-known safety slogan, the protection you insure may be your own. The first protection against collision is making yourself seen by the other fellow. A little larger bulb in each of the running lights than absolutely necessary to comply with the law equals watts well spent.

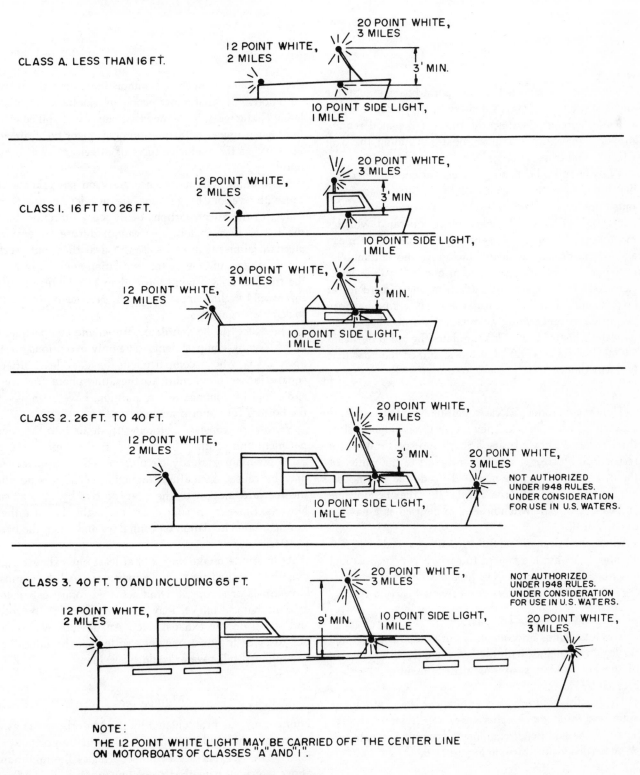

INTERNATIONAL RULE LIGHTS FOR MOTORBOATS INBOARD OR OUTBOARD

MAY BE SHOWN ON THE HIGH SEAS AND ALL U.S. WATERS EXCEPT WHERE CONTROLLED BY A STATE WHICH HAS NOT GIVEN APPROVAL

PREFERRED ARRANGEMENTS

CLASS A. LESS THAN 16 FT.

20 POINT WHITE, 3 MILES
12 POINT WHITE, 2 MILES
3' MIN.
10 POINT SIDE LIGHT, 1 MILE

CLASS 1. 16 FT TO 26 FT.

20 POINT WHITE, 3 MILES
12 POINT WHITE, 2 MILES
3' MIN
10 POINT SIDE LIGHT, 1 MILE

20 POINT WHITE, 3 MILES
12 POINT WHITE, 2 MILES
3' MIN.
10 POINT SIDE LIGHT, 1 MILE

CLASS 2. 26 FT. TO 40 FT.

20 POINT WHITE, 3 MILES
12 POINT WHITE, 2 MILES
3' MIN.
20 POINT WHITE, 3 MILES
NOT AUTHORIZED UNDER 1948 RULES. UNDER CONSIDERATION FOR USE IN U.S. WATERS.
10 POINT SIDE LIGHT, 1 MILE

CLASS 3. 40 FT. TO AND INCLUDING 65 FT.

20 POINT WHITE, 3 MILES
NOT AUTHORIZED UNDER 1948 RULES. UNDER CONSIDERATION FOR USE IN U.S. WATERS.
12 POINT WHITE, 2 MILES
9' MIN.
10 POINT SIDE LIGHT, 1 MILE
20 POINT WHITE, 3 MILES

NOTE:
THE 12 POINT WHITE LIGHT MAY BE CARRIED OFF THE CENTER LINE ON MOTORBOATS OF CLASSES "A" AND "1".

Figure 25-4: A boat owner can avoid much of the present confusion of rules by adopting the lights diagramed above which are legal in all waters.

WHISTLES.

Whistles are required on all powerboats except the smallest, those in Class A. However, this exception provides an anomaly because the rules of the road require proper signals from *all* powerboats, including those in Class A, and from sailboats.

Whistles may be hand-, power-, or mouth-operated, depending upon the classification of the boat. Class I permits any type, Class II excludes the mouth-operated whistles, and Class III makes power-operated whistles mandatory. "Whistle" is generally interpreted to mean any sound-producing device including the automobile-type horns. An audibility range of one-half mile is sufficient for Class I; Classes II and III must be heard for at least one mile. Boat owners who want to be really sharp are permitted to synchronize automatically a masthead light with the whistle blasts. This simulates the old-time steam whistles where the puff of steam identified the boat that was whistling.

BELLS.

They must produce a "clear, bell-like tone of full characteristics" when struck. They are required only on Class II and Class III powerboats. There is no specification (or restriction) on size; this is evidently left to the vanity of the owner. Bells may be mounted inside the pilothouse, but the Coast Guard "recommends" that they be movable and carried outside when needed to be used as a navigational warning.

Under the International Rules, a sailing vessel of 40 feet or more in length is required to carry a bell such as just described for powerboats. The Inland Rules state that sailing vessels of 20 tons gross or more must carry a bell.

LEGAL EQUIPMENT VERSUS BOAT SIZE.

The total kinds and quantities of equipment required for legal compliance with the law are tailored to the size of the boat and this size, as already mentioned, is expressed by classes.

The legally required safety equipment is the bare minimum and prudent skippers carry much more aboard. Some of the additional equipment generally accepted as being needed is illustrated in Figure 25-5.

Ventilation

Probably the most important aspect of individual boat safety covered in the Motorboat Acts concerns ventila-

tion. Gasoline is such a common ingredient in today's automotive life that many people overlook its potentially lethal character. It is claimed that one cup of spilled gasoline, when mixed with the optimum quantity of air and ignited, has the explosive force of fifteen sticks of dynamite!

Ventilation systems are necessary on powerboats because the vapors of gasoline are heavier than air and collect in the lower portions of the boat's interior. Since the fumes in such locations cannot diffuse by gravity, mechanical means must be used to clear them out. Technically, the requirements for ventilation apply only when the fuel has a flash point lower than 110 degrees F., and this would exclude most diesel oil; practically, it is wise to comply, regardless.

The spaces to be ventilated are engine compartments and fuel tank compartments. The only exceptions are in open boats whose compartments have at least fifteen square inches of opening to the atmosphere for every cubic foot of volume and, in addition, have openings at the bottom for vapor drainage.

Ventilation consists of forcing fresh air into the compartment and venting this air back to the atmosphere so as to maintain a steady circulation. The air movement may be caused by natural induction such as wind and the forward motion of the boat, or else by mechanical blowers. Blowers, of course, are preferable because they can maintain circulation on calm days and when the boat is at rest.

At least one intake duct and at least one exhaust duct must be provided for each compartment. All ducts must have cowls or scoops; a wind-actuated rotary exhauster or a mechanical blower may be substituted for the cowl and scoop on the exhaust duct. An obvious caution is not to place the duct openings so low in the bilge that accumulated bilge water could block them.

Numbering

Numbering was promulgated by the Motorboat Act as a means of census, identification, and regulation of powerboats. The Act specifies 10 horsepower as the minimum above which all powerboats *must* be numbered. The Federal Boat Safety Act of 1971 specifies no minimum. Further, it turned over to the states the actual numbering and registration, provided the states had compatible laws

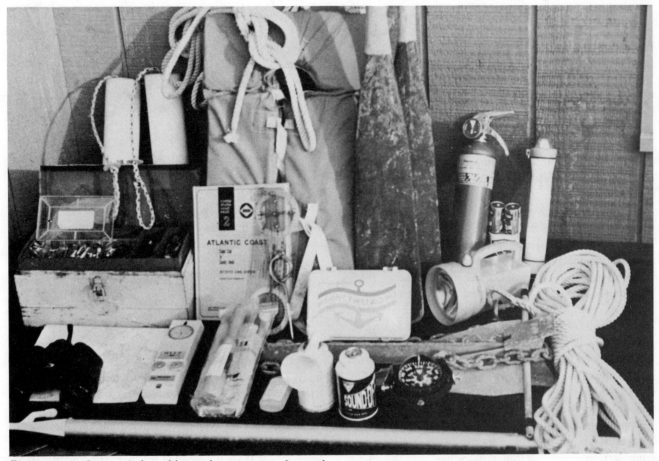

Figure 25-5: Some of the additional equipment, beyond the legal requirement, which a prudent skipper should carry and which is required for Courtesy Inspection Approval.

and extended reciprocity to each other. The Act permitted a fee for the registration but did not set its amount; as a consequence, each state charges the boat owner what its conscience and the demand will bear—and the fees keep getting higher. The Act did limit the validity of a registration to a maximum of three years (but permitted subsequent renewals) and required all states to recognize each other's registrations for a period of at least sixty days.

At this writing, all states of the continental United States with the exception of Alaska, New Hampshire, Washington, and the District of Columbia, have compatible boating laws on their books and have taken over the task of numbering the boats of their residents. (It is

quite likely that the four dissenters will enact numbering laws in the near future.) There are considerable differences between the states in the details of fees and duration of validity of registrations. The "State Authority" section of this chapter gives excerpts of the pertinent facts regarding numbering in each of the registering states.

A Certificate of Number is issued as proof of registration by the state (or by the Coast Guard in states that do not number). This certificate is pocket size and must be on board whenever the boat is in use. The number the certificate shows and the number the boat bears must be identical. Reissues are made on lost or destroyed certificates for a small fee.

The Application for Number procedures vary in different states and may change. Where application must be made to the Coast Guard (as in the four dissident states previously listed), forms are available at Post Offices and Coast Guard installations. After execution, the forms and the accompanying $6 fee must be mailed to Coast Guard headquarters in Washington, D.C.

Some states require documentary proof of ownership and title as a prerequisite to number issuance. The Coast Guard does not; however, the applicant must declare, under penalty for false certification, that he is the lawful owner.

All awarded numbers consist of three parts. The first part consists of two letters which are a code for the state of issuance or residence. The second portion of the awarded number consists of a maximum of four digits. These are registration numbers. When this number *begins* with one or more zeros, these need not be shown on the boat. For instance, 0032 can be shown on the bow simply as 32. The third part of the assigned number again consists of two letters but these do *not* refer to the state. They are a code which amplifies the numbering system so that more than 9999 boats can be accommodated. (One style permits three letters when the preceding group contains only three digits.)

The Coast Guard regulation is that the awarded number must be borne on both sides of the bow. It must read from left to right. No other markings may be in the vicinity, except for validation stickers in states that require them. The letters and numbers must be at least three inches high, straight up-and-down block (not italic or script), and of a contrasting color. The spacing must be exactly as shown in Figure 25-6, and the letters *I, O,* and *Q* are not to be used.

Where a widely-flared bow might obscure the visibility of the numbers, they may be placed on an appropriately visible portion of the superstructure forward of amidships. It has been held that attached letters securely fastened or decalcomanias well varnished-over are acceptable. Numbers stay with the boat even when the owner doesn't; to wit, a sale or transfer for use in the same state.

The Coast Guard makes a semantic distinction between "official number" and "awarded number." The former is the official number granted to a documented vessel and carved on her main beam. The awarded number is the one issued persuant to the Motorboat Act of 1958.

Figure 25-6: Boat identification letters and numbers must conform to these standards.

Accident Reports

These reports form an integral part of the safety program promulgated by the Motorboat Act. The requirements for reporting boating accidents (and the definition of an accident) vary with the different states and are listed in the excerpts which follow later. An accident occurring on navigable waters within the jurisdiction of a state that does not have a federally-approved numbering system must be reported directly to the Coast Guard. A federal form, CG #3865, is provided for this. The line of demarcation for reporting is based on the severity of the mishap: An accident that caused death must be reported within 48 hours; a lapse of 5 days is permitted if any person is incapacitated for more than 72 hours or if the property damage is $100 or more. More minor accidents than these are not reportable federally but may require a state report.

A glance at a boating accident report (CG #3865) will show how complete is the information requested from the participating skippers. The contents of individual reports are not disclosed publicly but are used in the preparation of statistics concerning boating safety.

Basically, a "boating accident" in the nomenclature of the Coast Guard occurs whenever there is damage by or to the vessel or its equipment, when any person in the situation is injured, loses his life, or is lost overboard. Boating accidents include capsizing, collision, foundering, flooding, fire, explosion, and loss of the vessel other than by theft. These definitions present a very finely meshed net through which little can go unnoticed and unreported.

The owner of a powerboat must also look to the Coast Guard if he wishes to document his craft as a yacht or if he intends to become engaged commercially in trade or fishing. To qualify in either category his boat must be five net tons in size or larger. The many steps that must be taken to achieve documentation must be followed strictly. In all government departments, you get there eventually if you follow the red tape—and you run into an impenetrable wall if you don't. (Documentation formerly was under the jurisdiction of the Customs Bureau.)

Net Tonnage

Net tonnage has been cited as the unit of measurement with which is determined the eligibility of any vessel for documentation. It is well to understand this term and to realize that the ton so used does *not* refer to weight. This ton denotes the volume of a closed space; by agreement, the amount of this space per ton is 100 cubic feet. (An enclosed space in a hull 2 feet wide, 10 feet long, and 5 feet high would be considered a ton—$2 \times 10 \times 5 = 100$.)

The *net* tonnage is the space actually available for the carrying of passengers and cargo, what the airplane people would call payload. It is determined by first calculating the *gross* tonnage; this is the total cubeage of *all* enclosed volume aboard. From the gross tonnage is deducted the total of all volumes needed for operating the boat such as crew quarters, engine room, tank room, chain locker, and so forth. What remains is the net tonnage; as already stated, this must amount to five or more if the small boat is to be eligible for documentation as a yacht. (By accepted rule of thumb, a cruiser 32 feet long with 8-foot beam and 2 1/2-foot draft would squeak by as 5 net tons.)

Documentation

This removes these craft from the state and Coast Guard numbering systems and places it under direct federal control. It truly becomes a "vessel of the United States." Several advantages and privileges ensue and, as usual, some responsibilities are acquired. First of all, the documented yacht has the legal authority to fly the yacht

ensign. In the present day this is a privilege of questionable value because many documented yachts fly the *national* ensign and contrarily many undocumented boats fly the *yacht* ensign. The difference between the national ensign (the standard national flag) and the yacht ensign is illustrated in Figure 25-7.

NATIONAL ENSIGN

YACHT ENSIGN

Figure 25-7: "According to the book," the documented yacht flies the yacht ensign; other boats fly the national ensign.

A more tangible advantage of documentation is the privilege of having mortgages, bills of sale, and some other legal instruments recorded with the Documentation Officer of the Coast Guard at the yacht's home port. This ability to keep at one official fixed location the deeds pertaining to a property as movable as a boat can prove of great help in determining legal ownership and encumbrance. Clarity of ownership in turn can facilitate financing, sale, or other transfer of title. Under the previous system, when the Bureau of Customs had jurisdiction, all legal papers in connection with documentation were filed at the Custom House. All these earlier filings are now under the care of the Documentation Officer.

A further benefit from documentation accrues to skippers who contemplate voyages to foreign countries. At first glance this might conjure up transoceanic trips, but actually some foreign shores are easily within the cruising range of more adventurous skippers: Canada, Mexico, the Bahamas, and Bermuda are all foreign ports.

The documented yacht need not "clear" and "enter" when she goes from port to port nor formally clear any United States port when heading for a foreign destination. When returning from such a trip, she need not make formal entry but is permitted a simple Report of Arrival. This report is accomplished when the skipper telephones the nearest Custom House within twenty-four hours after reaching his berth. He reports the presence or absence of dutiable merchandise. The customs officer will send an inspector to check the dutiable goods and assess duty—he may even be sent to check the accuracy of any report that *no* dutiable material has been brought in.

If a powerboat of five net tons or larger is to be put into commercial fishing, or trade, or commercial transportation, then documentation is mandatory. Heavy penalties are imposed for noncompliance. Documentation in this instance amounts to a federal permission to engage in the desired marine business and a notice of the fees which will be incurred. Such vessels must make Formal Entry (in place of the Report of Arrival) and must pay tonnage taxes and navigational, harbor and light fees. Under Formal Entry no one may leave the ship and no merchandise may be discharged until an inspector boards.

OFFICIAL NUMBER.

The number received from the Documentation Officer upon documentation is an official number and stays with the boat as long as she remains in use. Accordingly, this number must be imprinted permanently. In the eyes of the law permanent imprinting would be carving into a wooden main beam or prick-punching into a steel beam. The official net tonnage is shown with the official number. Where needed for visibility, the indenture is outlined with paint of a contrasting color. Technically, the main beam is the beam at the forward end of the largest hatch; on a powerboat it can be a main structural member integral with the hull. The plain, arabic numerals must be at least four inches in height.

The documented yacht must have its name and home

port or hailing port properly marked on some conspicuous part of the hull, generally taken to mean the stern. Powerboats documented for trade or commercial fishing must in addition carry their name on each bow. The letters must be straight, upright roman and at least four inches high. They may be painted on or transferred on by decalcomania, in both cases varnished over for permanence. Cutout letters permanently fastened are also acceptable.

Fines are assessed for failure to comply with the naming and numbering dictum. Originally compliance was ascertained and certified by an inspector who filled out Form #1322, if he was satisfied with what he saw. More recently, the situation has been eased somewhat by permitting the owner himself, or his agent, to make the certification on Form #10-170, when an inspector is not available.

INSTRUMENTS OF DOCUMENTATION.

"Documents" is a generic term that describes all the legal forms with which documentation of a boat is accomplished. These legal forms are: Certificate of Registry, Consolidated Certificate of Enrollment and License, License of Vessel under 20 Tons, and Consolidated Certificate of Enrollment and Yacht License. By striking out a headline, the latter instrument may also be issued as a License of Yacht under 20 Tons.

The Certificate of Registry will probably be of least interest to the average small boatman because it is issued to vessels in the foreign trade. It is the only one of the documents that need not be renewed periodically; all the others contain a license valid for one year only but subject to renewal.

The distinction between whether a craft is to be "enrolled" or "licensed" when it is documented is determined by its size. Vessels under 20 tons (but at least 5 tons) are licensed; larger than that, they are enrolled. There is no practical difference to the boat owner. Actually, all documented vessels (except those registered for foreign trade only) need a license which states their permissible mode of operation. For the larger boats, this license is combined with the enrollment in the Consolidated Certificate of Enrollment and License. The license spells out the exact nature of the commercial activity or the type of commercial fishing permitted; in the case of a yacht, the license restricts the boat use to "pleasure exclusively."

In each license, the master, having duly sworn that he is

a citizen of the United States, swears that the vessel will not engage in any prohibited action nor violate the revenue laws of the United States. Further, he agrees to comply with the laws in all other respects and agrees that the license will be valid for exactly one year and no longer. (As already stated, it can be renewed.)

In a copy of a Consolidated Certificate of Enrollment and Yacht License, the first part of the title is struck out for a yacht of under 20 net tons. The details of measurement for tonnage can be seen from the various items listed. The granted license is within the lower portion directly before the seal and signature of the Documentation Officer.

Documentation Procedure

The steps toward obtaining documentation for a small boat are legally hidebound and therefore somewhat complicated. The first is the application for admeasurement.

Admeasurement is the proper determination of the net tonnage of the vessel under consideration. The measurement (or the admeasurement, the dictionary does not show any difference in meaning) is performed under the jurisdiction of the Coast Guard Officer in charge of marine inspection.

The recent simplification in the admeasurement procedure is a real boon to the pleasure-boatman who wishes to document his craft. In place of the previous waiting for an official admeasurer to come to the boat with his measuring tapes, the owner now can do the job himself—and entirely by mail and free. An application for simplified admeasurement is filed with the Officer in Charge of Marine Inspection in the local district Coast Guard office. The owner does his own measuring of length, breadth, and depth, and the net tonnage is computed from these. The information required by the Officer in Charge of Marine Inspection under this simplified system is listed in Figure 25-8.

One peculiarity of the *old* Bureau of Customs procedure had caused some well-founded gripes among boat owners. This was the rule governing charging or not charging for the admeasurement services. The admeasurement was free to the vessel located in the immediate district of the Customs office to which application was made; there was a charge for time and travel if outside that district. In an

---

The application for simplified measurement should contain the following information:

Owner's name, address, and telephone number.
Name of the yacht.
Rig (that is, propulsion machinery or equipment, as "gasoline engine," "diesel," or if no motor is used for propulsion, "sail," "houseboat," or other).
OVERALL length, breadth and depth stated in feet and inches or in feet and decimal fractions of feet.
Builder's name and address, and place and year of build.
Material of hull.
Model, serial, official number, and other identifying numbers.
Whether or not the vessel is designed for sailing.
Whether or not the propelling machinery is wholly or in part within the hull.
Rough dimensioned sketches of the hull if it approximates a regular geometric solid.
Rough dimensioned sketches of the deckhouse if the volume of the deckhouse is disproportionate to the volume of the hull.
A request for the forms necessary for documentation, i.e.:
    Application for Official Number, Form No. 1320
    Designation of Home Port, Form No. 1319
    Oath on Registry, License, or Enrollment and License of Vessel, Form Nos. 1258 (individual) or 1259 (corporation).

Figure 25-8: The information listed above must be given for a yacht desiring documentation under the simplified admeasurement procedure.

---

exaggerated case, a local ocean liner could be measured free while the owner of a small boat located further away could be given a substantial bill for expenses of the admeasurer. (Of course, the small boat owner could have brought his vessel into the district and then he, too, would have received the same free service.) Anyway, the new system eliminates the old irritation.

An official number is applied for next. The form provided for this is #1320 and is entitled Application of Owner for and Notice of Award of Official Number and Signal Letters. Another form, #1319, must be submitted simultaneously; this one is the Designation of Home Port of Vessel.

The official number, as previously stated, is the number that must be marked permanently into the main beam of the boat. Signal letters are issued routinely to vessels of 100 net tons and over but may be had for smaller craft upon special application. Their use is shown in Figure 25-9; they are international code letters flown in a single hoist below an international code pennant. They are generally identified with the radio call letters and enable distant ships visually to learn the call sign and make radio contact. The serious cruising skipper *might* find it advantageous to fly his visual call on his signal mast when in foreign waters—although this *does* sound like heady

Figure 25-9: Signal letters are issued routinely to vessels over 100 tons but can be had for smaller boats on application.

medicine.

Designation of home port is an application to the Documentation Officer of the Coast Guard to approve the choice of "home port" selected by the owner or his agent. A common layman's misconception considers the home port to be the usual berthing place of the vessel; this is entirely wrong—although the two places may be identical by coincidence. The home port of any area is the place where the Marine Inspection Officer of the Coast Guard for that area is located. The area itself must contain the location where the business of the *boat* is transacted (meaning where its bills are received and paid).

The hailing port can be the home port, or the place where the boat was built (provided it lies within the home port district), or the place where the owner resides (again provided it lies within the home port district). The hailing port on the stern can therefore differ from the home port shown in the documents—but only within the limitations just mentioned.

Declaration of citizenship is the next step in the documentation procedure. The declaration covers all who are in ownership relation to the boat, whether this be as individuals, partners, or corporation officers. An individual uses Form #MA-4558; the members of a partnership, co-ownership, or unincorporated owner association use #MA-4559; an incorporated owner uses Form #MA-4557.

In all of these declarations the purpose is the same: to certify to the United States citizenship of all persons connected with vessel ownership and to prohibit more than 25 percent of control of the craft ever to be exercised by any non-citizen. Where the individual concerned is native

born, a declaration of citizenship is sufficient; a naturalized citizen must produce his certificate of naturalization.

Master carpenter's certificate (Form #1261) is the next completed legal form that must be submitted in the process of obtaining documentation for all vessels. "Master carpenter" is a generic term and refers to the builder of the boat or an authorized official of the builder. He certifies that the name on the boat is exactly identical with the name given in the certificate and adds a complete description of the craft and her motive power together with the name and address of the person for whom she was built.

In the case of an older boat originally built for someone other than the present applicant for documentation, there must be filed a complete chain of bills of sale so that title can be traced consecutively. Admittedly, such a complete legal series is often impossible to obtain and an alternative is offered in the form of a waiver.

The application for this waiver must state the usual pertinent data such as the owner's and boat's names and proposed new name for the boat. In addition, the applicant must state how long he has owned the boat and detail the efforts he has made to obtain the builder's certificate and the chain of title. Any former state motorboat number must also be given if there has been one. Finally, the applicant must certify that to the best of his knowledge and belief all previous owners of the vessel in question were citizens of the United States.

If the owner's nervous system, stamina and available time have been able to survive the foregoing necessary legal steps, and if the examining officials are satisfied with the results, a document will duly be issued to the vessel. Happily, the annual renewals are devoid of most of this involved original procedure.

Since many purchasers are now buying vessels built in foreign countries and exported to the United States, they should be warned that the steps for documenting these are even more involved. Duty is collected if the imported boat is to be used exclusively as a pleasure yacht. The payment is at the rate of 4 percent of the appraised value if valued at $15,000 or less; the rate jumps to 10 percent for valuations in excess of $15,000.

Furthermore, the purchaser of a vessel whose documentation is unencumbered and in order can obtain continuation of the documentation in his own name with very little paperwork.

MASTER'S ENDORSEMENT.

All of the marine documents mentioned above require the identification and signature of the current master of the vessel. When a new master takes over he must sign and endorse the document. (The owner may of course double as the master.)

Federal Communications Commission

If any vessel carries and intends to use any "apparatus designed for the radiation of electromagnetic energy," then the jurisdiction of the Federal Communications Commission is invoked, and proper licensing of the equipment is required. A radiotelephone transmitter is such apparatus, and so is a radar installation. Radio receivers of whatever kind are passive devices, do *not* radiate energy if of correct construction, and consequently do *not* concern the FCC. Whether the receiver is for broadcast reception, for communication, for direction finding, or for any other purpose—it is immune from regulation.

Radio Licensing

Persons who operate the radiotelephone transmitters on small boats must themselves also be licensed, although there are exceptions. The major exception grants permission for an unlicensed person to talk into the microphone and in effect (by manipulating the push-to-talk button on the mike) to operate the transmitter. However, the unlicensed "operator" must be under the supervision of the duly licensed operator—and the latter retains all responsibility for the proper conduct of the transmission.

A further exception permits an unlicensed person to operate the radar unit. There is no restriction on who uses the equipment but any repairs and adjustment must be made by duly licensed personnel. Furthermore, the radar set must have been manufactured to FCC approval and must be licensed for use on the particular boat. (When you analyze these grandiose "exceptions" it seems that the elephant labored and brought forth a mouse.)

RESTRICTED RADIOTELEPHONE OPERATOR PERMIT.

Since most small boats already have radiotelephones, and the balance undoubtedly eventually will also be so equipped, it is advisable for *all* skippers to get an FCC

"ticket." Form #753A, which is illustrated in Figure 25-10, offers a painless procedure; no exam, no technical knowledge, no personal appearance. The few simple questions are answered and the form together with a check for $8 is mailed to the FCC at Gettysburg, Pennsylvania. Within a short time the applicant is rewarded with a Restricted Radiotelephone Operator's Permit Form 753B (also illustrated), which remains valid for his lifetime. (United States citizenship is a requirement.)

The FCC designation for the restricted permit is RP, for the third-class telephone license is P-3, for the second class is P-2, and for the first class is P-1. The RP does *not* permit operation of transmitters more powerful than 100 watts. For powers up to 250 watts, a P-3 is required, and for higher power than this, the rules call for a P-2.

SUPERIOR RADIO OPERATOR LICENSES.

The restricted permit just mentioned (RP) is adequate for the skipper of a cruising pleasure craft, but it is the lowest on the totem pole. No adjustments, installations, or repairs to radiotelephones may be made with it; it is not sufficient for the master of any boat that takes out more than six people for hire. The man who operates such a party boat must have a third-class radio license. The examination which precedes the issuance of this ticket goes into rules and regulations of operation but does not encompass any technical radio matters. It also does *not* permit tinkering with the innards of the transmitters but, as already noted, allows control of higher power.

The radio operator licenses which permit repair and adjustment of small boat transmitters are the first class and the second class. Applicants for these must pass a thorough examination in radio theory and practice and must be well grounded in rules and regulations. If either of these licenses bears a "radar endorsement," earned after further examination, the holder may also tinker with radar sets aboard. (The *operator* of the radar does *not* need a license. He may also replace fuses and rectifier tubes *only*.)

TRANSMITTER APPROVAL.

No radio transmitter, either telephone or radar, may be used on any vessel until it has officially met FCC requirements. This will be indicated by either a "type approved" or a "type accepted" designation. Type ap-

FCC FORM 753-A
MAY 1965

FEDERAL COMMUNICATIONS COMMISSION
GETTYSBURG, PA. 17325

FORM APPROVED
BUDGET BUREAU NO. 52-R146.7

APPLICATION FOR RESTRICTED RADIOTELEPHONE OPERATOR PERMIT BY DECLARATION

A. USE TYPEWRITER OR PRINT IN INK. Signatures must be handwritten. Be sure to Complete all items including 7, 8, 9, and 10.

B. Enclose $2.00 fee with application. DO NOT SEND CASH. Make check or money order payable to Federal Communications Commission. See Part 13, Volume I of FCC Rules.

C. No oral or written examination is required. Applicant must be at least 14 years of age.

D. U.S. NATIONALS AND U.S. CITIZENS Submit one application to FCC, Gettysburg, Pa. 17325. U.S. Nationals who are not U.S. Citizens must attach a copy of certificate of identity.

E. ALIEN PILOTS Submit one application to FCC, Washington, D.C., 20554. ALSO complete and attach FCC FORM 755.

DO NOT WRITE IN THIS BLOCK

1. REASON FOR APPLICATION
   [ ] NEW PERMIT
   [ ] NAME CHANGE (*Attach Present Permit*)
   [ ] REPLACE PRESENT PERMIT DUE TO ITS CONDITION (*Attach Present Permit*)
   [ ] ORIGINAL PERMIT IS LOST OR DESTROYED. IF FOUND I WILL RETURN IT TO FCC. A REASONABLE SEARCH HAS BEEN MADE FOR THE PERMIT
   [ ] OTHER (*Specify*) _____

2. NAME (*Last*) | (*First*) | (*Middle Initial*)
   PERMANENT ADDRESS (*No. & Street*)
   (*City*) | (*State*) | (*ZIP Code*)

Figure 25-10: Getting a restricted radio operator "ticket" is painless. Application is made on the upper part of the form. The lower part is the license itself.

FCC FORM 753-B   UNITED STATES OF AMERICA
MAY 1965   FEDERAL COMMUNICATIONS COMMISSION
This PERMIT, when countersigned by the Secretary of FCC, authorizes

JOHN DOE

to operate licensed radio stations for which this

RESTRICTED RADIOTELEPHONE OPERATOR PERMIT

is valid under Rules and Regulations of the Commission and for the lifetime of the holder subject to suspension pursuant to the provisions of Section 303(m) (1) of the Communications Act and the Commission's Rules and Regulations. This Permit issued in conformity with Paragraph 903, International Radio Regulations, Geneva 1959.

PERMITEE SIGNATURE _John Doe_

proval is the more stringent; the equipment which gains it has been submitted to the FCC laboratories and tested by FCC engineers and found satisfactory. Type-accepted equipment has gained that marking on the basis of an affidavit which the manufacturer sends to the FCC listing the results of his own tests.

SHIP RADIO LICENSE.

As already stated, shipboard radio transmitters and radars must be licensed by the FCC. Application is made by filling out Form #502 and mailing it, together with $20, to the FCC office at Gettysburg, Pennsylvania. The Commission is unique among government departments in that it will *not* return the remittance if the license is not granted; the money goes into the kitty (presumably for the common good) just the same.

An interim license for immediate operation may be obtained by presenting the completed form and $25 in person at the nearest field office of the FCC or at the Washington, D.C., main office. Such permission is valid for six months; during this period, the regular license valid for five years will be sent by the Commission. Station license renewals, at the termination of the five-year period, entail a fee of $20.

The license application places stress upon the citizenship of the owner of the vessel and radio equipment; he must be a citizen of the United States. Even if a corporation or an association is the owner, its principal officers must be United States nationals. This insistence upon citizenship parallels that when documentation is sought. Otherwise, the questions on the form are straightforward and routine; they should present no problems to the boat owner. Incidentally, radiotelephone transmitters may be "type accepted" while radar units must be "type approved."

The Federal Communications Commission rules require that provision be made to prevent unauthorized operation of the radiotelephone transmitter on board. Such provision could take several forms: a locked cabinet containing the radio unit, a hidden master switch, or a key-operated switch on the radio panel. Such guardians should not be self-defeating in the event of an emergency, however.

POSTING LICENSES.

The license for the radio and radar equipment must be posted conspicuously at the main transmitter location. The preferred method is to place it under glass or transparent plastic to achieve visibility and protection. This does *not* preclude the operation of the radiotelephone from other than the main location, for instance, with remote-control units.

First-, second-, and third-class radio operator licenses must similarly be posted. Posting is optional for the restricted operator license. However, in lieu of being posted, the holder of the restricted ticket must keep it on his person for presentation when required.

LOGBOOK.

The keeping of a radio logbook is mandatory. The rules of the FCC (Section #83) specify the type of entries which must be made and the manner of making them. The logbook should be able to account for the entire consecutive time that the craft is actually in service. The pages must be numbered (to disclose the removal of any page) and each page must be headed with the name and radio call letters of the vessel; loose leaf is not acceptable.

Every radio transmission on a *pleasure* craft need *not* be entered and signed by the licensed operator—only those which have a bearing on disaster or safety. Nor is it mandatory to keep a watch on the distress frequency,

although such watching is a mighty good habit to acquire. All time notations in the log must be by twenty-four-hour-clock, starting at midnight. All distress, urgency, or safety signals heard must be entered completely.

The first- or second-class operator who makes repairs or adjustments to the radio transmitter or the radar must enter into the logbook the nature of his work. He must also sign his name and give the class and serial number of his license as well as its expiration date and his home address.

The logbook should be retained by the powerboat owner for a period of at least one year from the last entry. If any entries relate to distress or disaster, then the log must be retained for three years. If the entries relate to an FCC investigation of which the owner has been advised, then the retention is indefinite until authority is given to discard. A sample page from a correctly kept radio logbook is shown in Figure 25-11.

NOTICES OF VIOLATION.

The Federal Communications Commission is empowered to assess penalties and revoke licenses for infractions of applicable rules and regulations, but before doing this it sends a notice of violation setting forth details of the misdeed. Such notices must be answered within ten days of receipt; any unavoidable delay in meeting this time allowance must be explained fully at the earliest possible moment.

The answer to the notice of violation must contain a full account of measures taken to remedy the malfunction (if that is the complaint) plus the name and license number of the operator on duty if the violation was one of

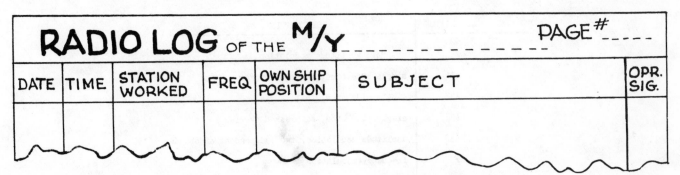

Figure 25-11: This is a sample of the correct form for a radio logbook.

operational procedure.

It should be borne in mind that the use of profanity on the air is prohibited and so are false or misleading calls of distress.

PERMITTED EMISSIONS.

Radio transmitters are technically capable of several modes of emission. The type to which they are restricted by the FCC for each service is shown in the table in Figure 25-12.

The continuous wave form and the modulated continuous wave are of little interest to pleasure skippers since they are for Morse code telegraphy. The form generally found in pleasure boat equipment is the A3, although the A3H and the F3 are coming into use more and more. The PO type is restricted to radar at present.

CITIZEN'S BAND (CB) RADIO.

The boating fraternity is beginning to show active inter-

est in a comparatively new form of two-way radio communication called Citizen's Band or CB. Many marinas and yacht clubs have equipped CB base stations and calls can be made to them for tender service, accommodation reservations and such.

The whole activity was made possible when the Federal Communications Commission set aside 23 frequencies around 27 Mcs. for a so-called Citizen's Radio Service. At the same time the commission imposed certain restrictions on the equipment which could be used for transmission but took an ultra-liberal stand on the operators and ruled that they need not be licensed. A pro forma, almost automatic license is necessary for the transmitting station, however.

The power of the transmitter is restricted to 5 watts. This is not the power going to the antenna but the power fed to the transmitting tube or transistor. (The actual antenna power would be only a fraction of this.) This, of course, is infinitesimal power when you compare it to the 100 or more watts output of some 2-3 Mcs. marine radio-

FREQUENCY RANGE	DESIGNATION OF EMISSION PERMITTED
2KHz to 3KHz	A-3 until Jan. 1, 1977 (installation permitted to Jan. 1, 1972)
but 2182 KHz	A-3 or A3H until Jan. 1, 1977 and A3H after Jan. 1, 1977
156.275 MHz to 157.425 MHz	F3
other than 2-3 KHz (special application)	A3, A3A, A3B, A3H, A3J

DESIGNATION	EXPLANATION
A3	standard amplitude modulation
A3A	single side band, reduced carrier
A3H	single side band, full carrier
A3J	single side band, suppressed carrier
A3B	amplitude modulation, two independent sidebands
F3	frequency modulation

Figure 25-12: This table lists the permitted type of emission for radio transmitters, as well as the cutoff dates.

telephones and naturally its range is minimal. The system is intended purely as a local, short distance link.

CB equipment comprises hand-held portable units and cabinet-type base stations. Circuits run from the bare minimum required to generate an acceptable signal to highly sophisticated instruments which squeeze every last bit of distance out of every watt. Prices vary accordingly.

The table in Figure 25-13 lists the actual frequencies of the 23 channels set aside for CB.

Channel		
1	26.965	Mcs.
2	26.975	
3	26.985	
4	27.000	
5	27.015	
6	27.025	
7	27.035	
8	27.055	
9	27.065	
10	27.075	
11	27.085	
12	27.105	
13	27.115	
14	27.125	
15	27.135	
16	27.155	
17	27.165	
18	27.175	
19	27.185	
20	27.205	
21	27.215	
22	27.225	
23	27.255	

Figure 25-13: The exact frequencies of the 23 channels open to the Citizen's Radio Service by the FCC are enumerated above.

United States Coast Guard

The marine inspection and enforcement arm of the federal government is the Coast Guard. The authority of the Coast Guard extends throughout all the "navigable waters" of the United States and its powers are far-reaching. In addition to its job of marine policeman, the Coast Guard is also entrusted with the duty to safeguard and rescue life and property. As already noted, the Coast Guard was given the chores of documentation previously carried on by Customs. All in all, the CG has quite an assignment!

Navigable Waters

"Navigable water" may be misleading. Merely being deep enough to float a bottom does not make the body of water "navigable" within the legal sense of conferring jurisdiction upon the Coast Guard; it must be tidewater or else contiguous to two or more states or to a foreign country so that water-borne commerce could be carried on between them. Even an inland "ocean" completely within the borders of one state is not "navigable" as far as the Coast Guard is concerned; consequently, it has *no* authority upon it.

However, a water like the New York State Barge Canal, which connects navigable waters, has itself been declared "navigable" and under CG control.

Since the Coast Guard is responsible for enforcing the safety provisions of the federal boating acts, it must have means for inspecting the equipment carried by boats within its jurisdiction. It does this by its authority to go aboard any and all vessels on the waters it patrols.

Boarding

The Coast Guard boards boats by right of federal law and has done this for more than 175 years. It is the legal duty of every skipper to heave-to and be helpful whenever a Coast Guard patrol signals that it intends to send a boarding party. Failure to do this results in penalties which have been upheld by the courts.

Stringent rules fix the conduct of the boarding officer and his boarding party. The patrol boat must fly the national ensign and the Coast Guard ensign so as to be readily identifiable by the skipper of the craft about to be boarded. The boarding officer and his party must be presentable, must wear identifying arm brassards, and must wear clean, unfrayed uniforms of the day. They must wear soft-soled shoes which will not injure the decks of the boarded boat. They must refuse graciously all offers of sociability other than the courteous conversation necessary for the job at hand.

Coast Guard boats that come alongside must be adequately fendered with clean fenders that will not mar the boarded boat. The boarding party's boat must be handled in an efficient and seaman-like manner that will bring credit to the Coast Guard. Sidearms are *not* to be worn by the party unless a dangerously illegal situation warrants them. The boarding officer must be at least of Petty Officer rating, although his party may be nonrated men.

BOARDING ROUTINE.

The purpose of boarding by the Coast Guard falls into four categories: enforcement of motorboat and navigation laws, enforcement of the Customs laws, general federal law enforcement, and general security. The overall purpose is safety at sea.

The boarding officer will have available a kit of necessary tools and a weighing scale for checking fire extinguishers. In addition, he will have all pertinent Coast Guard manuals for reference, plus copies of CG-#290, which latter he will leave with the skipper. He will make his observations and reports on proper Coast Guard forms and will leave copies of these when so required.

The states with approved numbering systems have also been delegated the right to inspect boats, but their inspection centers on the observance of state law. This does *not* preclude the Coast Guard from inspecting if the state water be "navigable" within the meaning already explained.

Boarding officers have authority under the United States Code simply to go aboard, without asking permission, any unnumbered, numbered, or documented vessel in United States navigable waters and all United States vessels on the high seas. They may use force if resisted and may arrest the resisting person. The regulations do enjoin the boarding officer to cause as little hindrance as possible to the business or pleasure of the boarded boat.

One stringent new power given the Coast Guard Officer under the boating safety act can have a mandatory effect on the negligent or careless skipper. The officer can order a pleasure boat back to its mooring or pier. Such an order can be given if the officer finds the boat overloaded, if insufficient legal safety equipment is aboard, if he considers the vessel unsafe or if he considers the boat being operated in an unsafe negligent manner. It goes without saying that such an order must be obeyed under pain of arrest for refusal.

Incidentally, the officer's authority to order a return includes weather situations. If he thinks the prevailing weather is beyond the safe capability of the boat, he can order it back!

BOARDING REPORT.

The Coast Guard officer will make his report of the boarding inspection on Form CG #4100A, which is reproduced in Figure 25-14. (State reports differ with each state.) This boarding form consists of a white original and a two colored duplicate; one of these pages is given to the skipper of the boarded vessel.

A boarding officer who finds a skipper in possession of only the white CG #4100 knows at once that violations were found on the previous inspection. (The colored duplicate is not given when violations exist.) Likewise, a colored CG #4100 presented by a skipper indicates a satisfactory inspection.

The boarding officer has the right to require identification from those on board, especially the skipper and owner. He will examine for expiration date and authenticity the certificate of number or the document, whichever the craft carries, and will verify the numbers on bow or main beam. He will verify the presence (or absence) of the legal safety equipment. He will record any observed infractions of the rules of the road. He will advise the skipper of any potentially dangerous conditions which are not legal violations but should be corrected.

Penalties for violations are not set or indicated by the boarding officer. These are determined by the local commander on the basis of what he reads in the report. Penalties may be appealed and it is within the discretion of the commanding officer (not the boarding officer) to mitigate or remit penalties. The appeal must be made within thirty days. The penalty remains in force during the appeal until or unless it is revoked.

NOTICE OF VIOLATION				**REPORT NUMBER**	

VESSEL NUMBER   **VESSEL NAME**

VESSEL DATA

FUEL COMPARTMENT
☐ OPEN
☐ CLOSED

ENG. COMPARTMENT
☐ OPEN
☐ CLOSED

MAKE AND MODEL   **P.O.B.**

HULL MATERIAL   **LENGTH**   **NET TONS**   **G.R.T.**

USE
☐ PLEASURE   ☐ PASSENGERS FOR HIRE
☐ FISHING (*Commercial*)   ☐ FREIGHT

PROPULSION ☐ INBOARD ☐ OUTBOARD (*CONSTR:* ☐ OPEN ☐ CLOSED) **H.P.**
☐ OTHER (*Specify*):   ☐ OIL ☐ GAS

NAME AND ADDRESS OF OWNER (*First, Middle, Last*) ☐ MR. ☐ MRS. ☐ MISS

- -

- -

- -

NAME AND ADDRESS OF OPERATOR OR MASTER ☐ MR. ☐ MRS. ☐ MISS

- -

- -

AGE (*Minors*):

OBSERVED UNDERWAY AT THE FOLLOWING:

DATE (Mo., day, year)	TIME, A.M. P.M.	ZONE	LOCATION

YES	NO	RESULT OF EXAMINATION (Check only applicable items and explain all details in remarks)			NONE
		ITEM	YES	NO	**ITEM**
		Valid Certificate of Numbers			Horn or whistle adequate
		Numbers properly displayed			Bell adequate
		Required lights (Night only)			Ventilation adequate
		Flame arrestor properly installed			Engine Compartment
		Lifesaving devices adequate			Fuel Tank Compartment
		Number of approved acceptable lifesaving devices on board			Fire extinguishers adequate
		Number of non-approved or not serviceable lifesaving devices			Number of approved serviceable fire extinguishers on board
		Reckless or negligent operation (Explain)			Number of non-approved or not serviceable fire extinguishers

REMARKS (*Describe details of violations, continue on reverse if necessary*)

UNIT TO WHICH ATTACHED   **BOARDING OFFICER'S SIGNATURE**

Violations are listed above. Correct discrepancy as soon as possible.

See reverse side for further information.

EDITION 10-64 MAY BE USED   DEPT. OF TRANSP., USCG, CG-4100A (Rev. 5-67)

Figure 25-14: The Coast Guard boarding officer will make his report on this form. If he presents you with a white copy—take heed! Violations! (Credit—U.S. Coast Guard)

Operator Licensing

One of the functions of the Coast Guard is the examination of applicants for operating licenses and issuance of such licenses to qualified persons. Every pleasure boat carrying passengers for hire must be under the charge of a licensed operator. *No* license is required by the operator of a pleasure boat whose passengers are guests and carried free. Boats more than 65 feet long carrying freight for hire also must be in the charge of licensed personnel.

The category of "passengers for hire" has become subject to stringent interpretation. Simply because a person does not come openly to buy a ticket does not necessarily relieve him of his status as a passenger for hire. If in *advance* he has agreed to contribute any valuable consideration for his passage (paying a share of the fuel, for instance, or paying dockage or tolls) the craft on which he is riding is carrying a passenger for hire. As a result, the skipper must be licensed and other requirements must now be met.

Note that "advance" was emphasized alone; it holds the key to the decision regarding a paying or a nonpaying passenger. If no advance decision has been made but, during the trip, one of the guests voluntarily and on an impulse of friendly gratitude pays an item of expense, he does *not* become a paying passenger. (Yes, this whole question *is* treading on eggshells.)

Nevertheless, there is a way for a group of friends on a cruise to share expenses without running into the sticky morass of "carrying passengers for hire." They must enter into a binding legal agreement which makes each one responsible for his proportionate share of any liability that the boat may incur under Admiralty law during the cruise. (In effect, each signer assumes the responsibilities of a proportionate owner without acquiring any actual ownership.)

It is believed that bona fide guests on a pleasure boat who bring the owner gifts such as would normally be given a host are *not* passengers for hire. The language of the previous statement is purposely cautious. The caution has been engendered by recent court decisions. One such decision held that a salesman demonstrating a powerboat for a prospective customer was in fact carrying a passenger for hire, and therefore should have been a licensed operator. (The court held that there was an indirect, valuable consideration.) Interestingly, the Act of 1971 does not require a license in this case "unless necessary for boating safety."

In all fairness it should be stated that the Coast Guard is not the instigator of this nit-picking to determine when and when not a person aboard any vessel is a passenger for hire. The fine-toothed comb of semantics was introduced by insurance companies going to court seeking means to slough off losses incurred by accidents to policyholders. In the case of the demonstrating salesman (he had a bad accident), the court decision voided the policy and absolved the insurance company from a heavy payment. The court held that the boat was operated illegally (without a licensed operator) and therefore beyond the coverage agreed to by the insurance company. Settlement thus became the liability of the owner. The warning to an owner is obvious.

One aspect of pseudo-commercial activity that, under the law, requires a licensed skipper is often overlooked. This is the carrying of *freight* for hire. To many people this designation conjures up a tramp steamer laden down with cargo—but it could as easily be a small powerboat. Consider an owner about to take his boat south. He has a friend in the airconditioner business. As a favor, plus a contribution toward the costs of fuel and dockage en route, the owner stacks cartons of airconditioners wherever he has room for them. He is happy to be able to save his friend some of the heavy cost of normal trucking and is on his way. The boat is carrying freight for hire and the skipper must be licensed, but only if his boat is more than 65 feet long.

GRADES OF LICENSES.

The Coast Guard, under authority of two separate acts of the law, issues three grades of licenses to skippers of powerboats. Under the Motorboat Act of 1940 it issued licenses to operate motorboats carrying passengers for hire; the Coast Guard *no longer does this*. Under the Act of 1956, it issues two grades of licenses to operate mechanically propelled vessels carrying passengers for hire.

The Act of 1956 permits holders of its licenses to skipper vessels up to 100 gross tons and carry passengers up to the licensed load limit of the craft. The licenses may be restricted by limits on gross tonnage and by scope of the waters in which operation is permitted.

The licenses are issued for a period of five years and

may be renewed during the fifty-ninth month of their tenure or within one year of their expiration. Whether or not an examination is given before renewal depends upon the holder's service record in the immediately preceding period.

Licensed operators may skipper any vessel requiring a lower grade than that for which they are licensed; an ocean operator could legally run a yacht club tender but certainly not vice versa. The holder of a "third-mate" ticket has the equivalence of any license issued under the Act and may therefore legally operate any craft covered by the Act.

INLAND OPERATOR, MECHANICALLY PROPELLED VESSEL.

The licenses issued under this title are of two types: the launch tender, whose waters are restricted to the immediate vicinity of the marina or yacht club that employs him; and the inland operator, who has wider latitude but must nevertheless stay inside the headlands of the coast. (The line of the "headlands" does not always coincide with the demarcation between "inland" and "international.")

The launch tender may not legally operate a boat more than thirty feet long. An applicant for this classification need not be a citizen of the United States but he must be at least eighteen years old. His physical examination must be passed and his nautical examination will include: (1) the rules and regulations dealing with inspected vessels, (2) forty lifesaving and fire-fighting questions, and (3) sixty questions on general subjects. The first twenty questions on rules of the road (inland) must be answered with 90 percent accuracy with the bars let down to 70 percent for the balance of the question.

Experience-wise the launch tender has it easy. He need have only one full season of actual tender operation (under the guidance of a licensed operator) or four months in any powerboat larger than Class A. In either case, his experience must be attested to by a responsible person other than himself.

The full inland operator license application requires experience of at least one year but the minimum age is still only eighteen. All other prerequisites and even the nautical examination are the same as for launch tender license. The size of vessel (gross tonnage) for which this license is endorsed is based on the judgment of the examining officer, who reaches his decision on the basis of

examination result and caliber of experience. The maximum allowable tonnage is one hundred.

OCEAN OPERATOR, MECHANICALLY PROPELLED VESSEL.

This is the top grade of license and the requirements are commensurately tough. First of all, the applicant must be an American citizen at least twenty-one years old. He must be able to prove his citizenship documentarily with a birth certificate or a naturalization certificate or the equivalent. He must pass a physical and visual examination, including a color test.

The ocean operator applicant has several options for the fulfillment of his necessary experience record. He can qualify with two years' experience in running a motorboat carrying passengers for hire with at least one-half of the time spent in ocean or coastwise operation. Alternately he can have had three years' experience in the deck department of a coastwise or ocean vessel; he can cut this time to two years if he held a motorboat license during the period. His last option is to show one year's service as able seaman on an ocean or coastwise vessel plus one year's service in the deck department, all the while holding a ticket as "able seaman." As with all other license applications, he cannot attest to his own service but must have documentary evidence from the proper reputable people.

The nautical examination is a toughie! First come twenty questions on rules of the road (inland and international), then ten questions on chart navigation, plus ten questions on the compass and ten queries on signals. All of these must be passed with a rating of at least 90 percent. These are followed by seventy-five questions covering seamanship, aids to navigation, first aid, weather, lifesaving, fire fighting, rules and regulations of inspected vessels, engines, and a general knowledge of his local marine area. The passing grade on these is 70 percent.

The applicant for an ocean operator's license must now demonstrate his practical knowledge by an actual demonstration of his use of tide tables and current tables. Finally, he is given a chart problem and must work out the actual solution on a chart.

The lucky applicant who comes through this barrage of questions unscathed and receives a license as ocean operator is now ready to skipper a passenger-carrying vessel almost anywhere. He is, however, restricted to 100 gross tons and to the number of passengers for hire which the craft's certificate of inspection permits.

All applications for operator licenses (or for their renewal) are made on Form CG #866. By strike-outs and insertions this license is adapted to the various grades awarded under the 1956 act. The bodies of water to which the validity of the license is restricted are also inserted.

OCMI

The Officer in Charge, Marine Inspection is the division of the Coast Guard with the duty and responsibility of inspecting all vessels not more than 65 feet long which carry more than 6 passengers for hire and all vessels more than 65 feet long which carry *any* passengers for hire. This division issues a certificate of inspection without which no boat may legally carry more than 6 persons who pay for any part of their passage either directly or indirectly.

All vessels carrying freight for hire must be inspected. This rule holds regardless of vessel size.

The owner of any vessel (or his agent) who wishes his craft inspected and certificated makes a written application on Form CG #375A to the OCMI at the controlling district office of the Coast Guard. Thereupon a marine inspector is assigned to visit the vessel at a mutually agreed time and place. The owner or someone representing him must be present during the inspection.

The preferred routine is to submit complete blueprints of the boat prior to the initial inspection. Such plans include profiles, sections, machinery, electrical, piping and fuel locations and arrangement of decks. However, the OCMI has the discretion to permit the omission of any or all of this material or to accept photographs and descriptions instead.

No charge is made at present for the inspection or for the issuance of the certificate if the work be done within the port area by the regular personnel. The owner must reimburse travel expenses if the inspector must go beyond his normal radius. Heavy penalties are meted out to inspectors found accepting illegal payments.

INITIAL INSPECTION.

On his initial visit, the inspector thoroughly examines all aspects of the internal and external construction of the boat. His criteria of adequacy or inadequacy are the specifications laid down in CG #323 (Rules and Regulations for Small Passenger Vessels). These rules list detailed standards for hull construction and bulkheading, machinery installation, electric wiring, safety equipment, stability, and even the cooking and heating devices.

Those vessels covered by the CG #323 regulations are divided into two groups: those not more than 65 feet long, and those longer, up to 100 gross tons. The smaller of these two are called *S* vessels, while the larger are called *L* vessels. There are some differences in the application of the rules to the *S*'s and the *L*'s.

Should the marine inspector find deficiencies that prevent certifications, he lists these and discusses their correction with the owner or his agent. More happily, if every item of inspection proves to be in acceptable condition, a "certificate of inspection" is issued for the boat.

CERTIFICATE OF INSPECTION.

The rules state that the certificate of inspection shall be framed under glass or other transparent material and posted in a conspicuous place.

The certificate, CG #3753, completely describes the craft for which it is issued. In addition, it outlines the routes she may travel and the crew that must be aboard to man her. The maximum number of persons (passenger or other) that may be carried is also fixed, on the basis of deck area, rail length, and other criteria. The certificate of *S* boats is valid for a term of three years, but the one for *L* vessels for only one year.

PERIODIC REINSPECTION.

Certificated vessels must be hauled out for inspection at least every eighteen months if they have been operating in salt water during one-half of the preceding eighteen-month period. The hauling intervals can be increased to thirty-six months for correspondingly shorter salt-water operation and stretched to a maximum of sixty months if the boat was used exclusively in fresh water.

Annual inspections are made primarily to check on the adequacy of safety equipment. These are generally made without regard to the hauling cycle, although it is possible that the two may coincide.

The Coast Guard OCMI must be informed whenever the boat is hauled out for repairs which could affect the safety of the ship. Such a report can be made verbally or in writing. Hauling out for a simple propeller change or for scraping or painting need not be reported.

United States Immigration Department

Only the skipper coming back with his boat from a foreign country has occasion to meet the Immigration Department officially. The return from a foreign country could be the result of a transocean run (for those top-echelon yachts capable of making such a trip) or the cruise from a "contiguous territory" which is well within the range of many pleasure boats. Canada, Bermuda, Nassau, the Virgin Islands are among those classed as contiguous territories by the Immigration Department.

The procedure is simple and unusually devoid of the expected red tape. For instance, the skipper returning to New York Harbor would pull into one of the slips at Rosebank Quarantine Station on his way through the Narrows. Here he would be boarded by an Immigration officer, a Public Health officer, and perhaps even a Customs inspector. On the other hand, the craft could proceed to its moorings or marina without stopping, then notify the authorities of its arrival and wait for the inspection team. In the interim, no one could legally leave the boat. This latter method would be used by any vessel returning to one of the smaller harbors along the coast that do not have inspection stations; the nearest station would be contacted by radio, by land phone, or otherwise. Every person aboard must be listed on a manifest (Form #1-418).

The Immigration inspector requires proof of citizenship in the form of birth certificates or naturalization papers from returning citizens. Other passengers need proper passports. Under present rulings any visitors from countries in the Western Hemisphere (except Cuba) need not have passports, only proper identification.

United States Public Health Service

This department has the duty of guarding the country against the invasion of epidemics and disease. The inspectors accomplish this by examining travelers from foreign countries to whatever extent is necessary to establish their freedom from contagion. Those coming from areas known to be free of epidemic are looked over more leniently.

The best document for easy passage through the Public Health exam is the international certificate of immunization. This can be had from any reputable physician who administers the immunizing serums. It is valid for three years and is recognized in most of the countries of the world.

PRATIQUE.

Attainment of a clean bill of health from the Public Health Service entitles the boat to pratique. Webster defines pratique as "permission to hold intercourse with a port."

In many harbors the vessel seeking pratique goes to a designated quarantine anchorage, drops the hook, and hoists the international yellow Q flag. She then waits for the inspectors to come aboard. Any skipper who has tried this in foreign ports will appreciate by contrast the alacrity of the United States Public Health Service.

State Authority

The Federal Boating Act of 1958 delegated to the individual states the power to regulate pleasure boats by licensing, numbering, and other means. Although the general numbering system is uniform between the states—and must be so in order to get federal approval—many other differences exist. These mainly take the form of license fee amount, length of time of validity, requirements for accident reporting, and some operating restrictions.

The states that have federally approved numbering systems and use them also have been given the right to inspect boats. This inspection can be made by boarding exactly as described earlier under "Coast Guard." The state officers must be properly identified and will check for state law compliance. This does not abrogate any authority the Coast Guard might have over the same boat.

The money flowing to the states from the licensing fees has been a new source of revenue. Some have succumbed to the temptation and are adding a large portion of this money to the routine state budget. Others, more farsighted, earmark these dollars for exclusive boating use to affect improvements that will inure to the benefit of the boat owners who pay the money. Judged by present monetary values, for instance, the cost of registering automobiles, the licensing fees for boats are still very moderate.

The pleasure boatman who cruises from one state to another, and especially the skipper of a trailered boat, runs into a morass of conflicting regulations. Although the numbering requirements are, of federal necessity, uniform, wide differences exist in other areas.

These differences are so numerous that collating them into a country-wide ready-reference table of practical size is impossible. As an example, the Outboard Boating Club of America devotes 4 booklets, each of more than 100 pages, to an explication of the state laws governing boating. (These booklets, which divide state laws into Southern States, Western States, North Central States and New England States, are available from the Outboard Boating Club of America, 333 North Michigan Boulevard, Chicago, Ill.)

The phases of pleasure boating into which the states intrude their varying authorities include such items as toilets and their connected holding tanks or purifiers, safety equipment required to be carried, how water skiing may be conducted and definitions of proper and improper boating conduct. The regulations affecting trailering are even more pervasive and refer to the height, width, length and weight of the trailer as well as the necessary brakes and lights. There are even restrictions on the sizes of boats which may be car-topped.

Local Authority

The towns and villages along the navigable waters exert their authority over the powerboatman by their control over speed limits in adjacent areas, by their regulation of anchorages and launching ramps, and sometimes even by local taxation. The usual practice is the appointment of a harbor master, port captain, or dock master to whom application must be made and who doles out the requested mooring sites or ramp privileges. In most cases eligibility is restricted to local residents and often even to local property owners.

The tax structures of many states permit the towns to levy personal property taxes; automobiles, boats, and trailers come within the meaning of personal possessions and are taxed at figures derived by subtracting depreciation from original cost. A fine, snazzy boat can slice a nice chunk of tax off the owner's bank account. It is well to figure this item (if it exists in your locality) into the total cost of a proposed boat.

Surprisingly, most communities make no charge for the assignment of a mooring space although the boatman, of course, must provide the necessary ground tackle at his own expense. The allotments, in the order of their de-

sirability, are made on a first-come or seniority basis with political influence perhaps sneaking in occasionally. The shape of some harbors places the least desirable, outermost moorings so far from the dock that it is almost a cruise in itself to get to them.

The catch in the mooring problem is how to make shore contact with the dinghy. The mooring may be free, but where do you keep the dinghy and where do you load and unload your passengers? The answer in most cases is a payment to a local marina or boatyard. (See Chapter 24.) The actual placing of the ground tackle also is often restricted to licensed or favored contractors whose charges are unfettered by competitive bidding.

Local regulations generally govern the relation of tackle weight to boat size. A usual requirement where icing winter conditions prevail is that the mooring be hauled up at the end of the season. Homemade substitutes for mushroom anchors, such as engine blocks and concrete slabs, do not always meet with official approval, especially in crowded moorings where dragging could cause much damage.

NEW YORK CITY.

An exception to the conditions just described exists in New York City and its environs. There the Coast Guard has jurisdiction over mooring and anchoring. Its control extends from the lower Long Island Sound all the way around the city and up the lower Hudson River.

The points in the Sound at which the Coast Guard takes over are at Huntington Harbor on the east coast and New Rochelle on the west coast. The city government, through its police, retains control of speed limits and water pollution but permanent moorings and temporary anchorings are under federal authority.

Any pleasure skipper is at liberty to come into a designated anchorage and drop his hook wherever he does not interfere with an authorized mooring. His temporary anchoring privilege is good for thirty days from his first appearance. This is a continuous calendar period and is not lengthened by any absence during that time. In other words, he may come and go as much as he likes (provided he finds the space each time) but after thirty days from his first visit he becomes persona non grata.

Permanent moorings are assigned on the basis of application to the Coast Guard headquarters of the Third District. There is no charge for a permit but a $100 penalty is levied for putting down an unauthorized mooring. The permit is valid for one year, expiring on April 30; it will be renewed if a new application is made before that date.

The Coast Guard regulations provide that the floating buoy must be removed before winter icing because a breakaway could cause a hazard to navigation. The entire mooring can be removed or merely the buoy, with the chain dropped flat on the bottom; the chains are retrieved by grappling in the spring. In any case the moorings must be hauled periodically for inspection. The Coast Guard also sends divers down to check the situation whenever it is deemed necessary because suspicion exists.

Here, again, arises the problem of contact with the shore for the loading and unloading of passengers and supplies. As before, it is generally solved by payment for dinghy privileges to a nearby boatyard or marina. It is true that public city docks could be used, but considering their size and height this often is impractical.

WATER POLLUTION LAWS.

The prevention of water pollution is more than just a good deed under the golden rule; it is required by law. Three federal statutes (passed in 1899, 1961, and 1971, respectively) are aimed at maintaining the purity of coastal and inland navigable waters and these give the Coast Guard and the Army Engineers the duty of acting under them, the former being the enforcing arm.

The Refuse Act of 1899 is the one that basically affects all users of the navigable waterways. It prohibits the "discharge, deposit or throwing of any refuse matter of any kind from vessels into the navigable waters of the United States." (Certain matter "passing from a sewer in a liquid state" is excepted.)

The 1971 federal law will set up standards of performance anti-pollution devices must meet. These undoubtedly will be tough (you could even say unrealistic) and any contraption other than a holding tank will have a hard time squeaking through. The main good feature will be that the federal statute supersedes the varying and often antagonistic ideas of the separate states.

The federal act of 1961 deals primarily with the discharge of oil from vessels. This hardly is pertinent to powerboatmen; at today's fuel prices, who would dump oil? But there is another factor: oil in the bilge. "Any visible sheen of oil" in the discharge from the bilge can result in penalties as high as $20,000 under the 1971 act.

The act of 1971 is the stinger! When fully fleshed it will have the greatest impact so far on the design, installation and use of marine toilets.

Of great present importance is the fact that many states are becoming even stricter on the matter of pollution of their waters and are looking with a severe eye at marine toilets. Some already bar every device except holding tanks; a few grudgingly permit macerator-chlorinators. (The mechanics of these devices are detailed in Chapter 6.)

Legal Responsibilities

Maritime law is largely a thing unto itself and the small boat owner's contact with it frequently leads to results quite different from those in comparable situations ashore. This affects him in two ways: in the judgments and penalties for his transgressions and in the security of his investment in his boat. On most pleasure boats the owner is simultaneously acting as skipper, and this accentuates his situation before the law. As with all laws, ignorance of them is not accepted as an excuse.

First and foremost, the skipper is responsible for the safety of his passengers, his crew, and his vessel. Should he endanger these, or any other person or property, because of his reckless or negligent operation he will upon conviction become subject to a fine of $2000, a year in prison, or both. The court interpretation of "negligent" may take many forms other than his direct, personal act; his failure to have a vital component repaired could be a negligence. Incompetent navigation without any taint of recklessness could be negligence; being under the influence of alcohol or permitting overloading could be negligence.

A skipper's prime responsibility is to assure the operation of his boat in full conformity with the applicable rules of the road. This includes his cooperation in the avoidance of collision even when he technically has the right of way. This is emphasized by Rule #27, the general prudential rule, which could even mandate a *departure* from the rules. The rules themselves are discussed fully in Chapter 16.

All life is a balance between privileges and responsibilities. The skipper has the privilege of supreme command; in return, he is responsible for everything that happens on his vessel, or to it, or by it.

Admiralty Courts

Cases of legal action arising out of incidents connected with vessels on the navigable waters of the United States are heard in Admiralty Courts. These are subdivisions of the federal District Courts. The authority of an Admiralty Court supersedes that of a state court whenever the two are coincidentally concerned with the same case.

The Admiralty Court has no jurisdiction over cases arising from nonnavigable, purely state waters; these are adjudicated in state or local courts under standard legal procedure.

The practice of admiralty law is a specialized field and most "land" lawyers leave this branch of practice to members of the legal profession especially trained for it. In turn, it is not unusual to find admiralty lawyers who are good seamen in their own right and consequently handle their cases against a practical, nautical background.

Before any case or any discussion can be carried on fairly and intelligently key words and situations must be clarified by explicit definitions. Following are a few such definitions:

Underway. A vessel is considered underway if it is not anchored, not made fast to a shore or its extension, and not aground. A boat that has broken away from its mooring is underway, so is a boat that is dragging its anchor. In both cases, the rules of the road apply, whether to the benefit or to the detriment of the underway craft.

Inland waters. The means of demarcation between the offshore and the inland waters of the United States is a line drawn approximately parallel to the shore line and going through the outermost aids to navigation such as buoys or other marker systems. All waters landward of this line are "inland waters." (An exception to this definition occurs in the endorsements on Operator Licenses. Therein the divider is a line farther inward connecting the outermost land points.)

International waters. Based on the foregoing description of inland waters, international waters are easily defined: waters lying to seaward of the line defining inland waters. *Exceptions:* There are some exceptions to the basic definitions for inland and international waters. These are detailed, harbor for harbor, in "Title 33, Navigable Waters, Chapter 1, Subchapter D, Part 82, Sections 82.5 to 82.275," Coast Guard publication CG #169.

Passenger for hire. As already explained, any person who pays for all or part of his passage directly or indirectly with any valuable consideration to the owner or agent is a passenger for hire within the meaning of the Coast Guard regulations.

Arrest. Any empowered officer may make an arrest with or without process for a violation. However, an arrest without process may be made only for a violation which has actually been observed by the officer.

Charter

The owner of any vessel or his agent may rent or lease the use of the craft to someone, just as equipment or property or automobiles can be rented or leased ashore; this is a charter. There are two forms of charter and they are defined below.

CHARTER PARTY.

Contrary to general belief, the charter party is not the group of people that comes aboard but the contract or legal paper which sets forth all the terms of the charter. ("Party" derives from the original "partita," a document.) It must be carried aboard to be shown in the event of Coast Guard boarding.

TIME OR VOYAGE CHARTER.

In this form of charter the owner retains legal control of his boat and continues in his responsibility because he supplies the vessel complete with its operating crew. The charter party will state clearly the time-span of the boat use or else the destination or even both. Nevertheless, the charterer can decide the details of the voyage for which he is paying. Incidentally, this develops into a case of carrying passengers for hire in which the skipper must be properly licensed.

DEMISE CHARTER.

In a demise charter, also known as a bareboat charter, the owner turns over to the charterer a legally equipped boat in good running condition. That is all; *no* crew. The charterer hires his own crew and acts as, and assumes the responsibilities of, an owner.

The advantages of a demise charter to the actual owner are several: He sloughs off responsibility for the operation of the boat (although the boat itself can still become liable as explained below); the craft is *not* carrying passengers for hire and therefore no licensed operator is required; the charterer has no right to charge any indebtedness, incurred en route, to the boat. Clandestinely, the owner usually retains some unseen, extralegal control of his property by "suggesting" to the charterer which skipper he is to employ. Obviously, such a suggested skipper is one on whom the owner feels he can rely.

Contributory Negligence

A skipper may be held responsible for a mishap even though his own negligence was only partly the cause and the accident was abetted by the laxity of someone else. Thus, a skipper who does not warn a guest against a potentially dangerous position from which he could be swept overboard becomes liable if that person subsequently goes over.

It is the skipper's duty to look out for the safety of his boat and the safety of every person who is legitimately on board. This thinking recurs continually and is the basis of all marine command psychology; the underlying idea is that anyone who bears full responsibility must be given full control to exercise it.

Compulsory Aid

It is the duty of a captain to go to the aid of any vessel or person in marine distress. This broad command has a mitigating clause: He need do so only to the extent that it does not unduly endanger his own ship; he is not expected to involve himself, vessel, and crew in a self-sacrificing situation. Nevertheless, the succoring tradition of the sea is so deeply rooted that a skipper would not use the escape clause except in extraordinary circumstances.

This humanitarian precept is strongly bolstered by an article in the United States Code which reads in part: "Every master of a U.S. vessel who fails without reasonable cause to render such assistance shall be deemed guilty of a misdemeanor and subject to penalty of $1000 or imprisonment for two years. The monetary penalty is collectible against the *boat*." (Incidentally, one-half the fine goes to the informer.)

The Federal Safe Boating Act of 1971 removes one source of fear for the good samaritan boatman. Heretofore he was apt to be involved in a suit for recovery of damages for any harm done by his completely goodwill rendering of assistance. The Act puts a stop to this. Under Section 16, any person who "gratuitously and in good faith renders assistance" without objection from the person assisted "shall *not* be held liable for any civil damages as a result of that rendering of assistance."

Wake

The owner and skipper are responsible for any damage caused by the wake from their boat. This is generally held to apply only to a damaging wake resulting from excessive speed. The damage could be to a shore installation or to a boat in an anchorage or to a person aboard such a boat. An instance of the latter could be a mate in a galley who scalds herself because of the sudden and unexpected lurching of the boat caused by an excessive wake.

Liens

In admiralty law the vessel is considered a "personality"; a lien against the boat requires the *boat* to pay, regardless of the owner's financial capability. The boat pays (if the owner doesn't pay in its behalf) by being sold at a marshal's auction if necessary. This situation differs from the usual practice on land; there the debtor is sued for a debt and his ability to pay is gauged by the property he owns, although this cannot be seized without further process.

A lien is a claim on a boat. Certain limitations hedge the placing of the lien but in return it also affords the holder some privileges.

To have standing in an Admiralty Court, the lien must have originated from a situation arising on navigable waters; these are defined on page 563. The lien must be the result of indebtedness incurred for service or repairs or supplies required to keep or make the boat navigable. As a contrary example, a person lending an owner a sum of money for personal use is not entitled to a valid lien on the borrower's boat to cover it. However, a boatyard hauling the craft and replacing the propeller has a lien automatically if the work is not paid for. Similarly, a marina has the basis for a lien if its dockage charges remain unpaid for an unreasonable time after the owner has been dunned.

One advantage of a maritime lien for the creditor is that

the sale of the boat to a new owner does not invalidate it. The craft may be in another person's possession but the boat still owes the money. Another advantage to the holder of the lien is that his claim in the Admiralty Court supersedes all claims in state courts and only the federal court can order a foreclosure. Furthermore, the order in which the liens are valued, when there are more than one, is not in accordance with their dates of inception but the reverse. In other words, the last comes first.

A lien is not necessarily bombproof, despite the foregoing safeguards; it could be faulty or even not available to a vendor. For instance, a person not the owner and not authorized by the owner could order supplies at a distant port. The purveyor who delivers them would not be entitled to a lien on the boat; he would have to get his money there and then or else be in an unprotected position.

The holder of a lien on a vessel who wishes to use the facilities of the law for collecting his money must first find the boat. Considering the mobility of the craft and the vastness of the waterways, this could be a problem in itself. Assuming he is lucky, he then files suit (a libel) in the nearest Admiralty Court which has jurisdiction. If the ensuing hearings end in favor of the lien holder, a notice of arrest is issued *against the boat*. A United States Marshal, acting under this arrest order, next takes the *boat* into custody and safeguards it until the sale at auction. The lien holder is paid from the proceeds of the sale and the balance, if any remains after court costs, goes to the late owner.

The attitude of the Coast Guard toward liens is interesting. Under Subchapter S, Part 171.35-5, the regulations state that "liens of all kinds, including transfers of title to secure debts or claims, will be disregarded in determining ownership." The certified statement of ownership on the original numbering application is considered proof. Anyone who becomes the actual owner through subsequent lien action must certify this fact in detail when applying for the new number.

Chattel Mortgage

The proliferation of boats has created a financing situation very similar to the installment buying of automobiles and has brought with it the well-known chattel mortgage. Under this method the purchaser gets title to his boat but concurrently gives a mortgage on it to the bank (or other) that lent him the money to buy it. This beclouds his title until such time as he has repaid the borrowed money in full and the mortgage is canceled.

Banks generally look askance at the chattel mortgage because the very nature of maritime law makes for mortgage insecurity. A partial exception is the documented boat; its mortgages may be filed for reference with the Documentation Officer of the Coast Guard at the port of registry.

Conditional Sale

When a boat is purchased with deferred payments under a conditional sale agreement the buyer gets physical possession and use of the craft but does not get the title to it. The title remains in the hands of the bank, the dealer, or other lender of the purchase money. When the debt is completely satisfied, the title is given to the purchaser, who then becomes the actual owner.

Limitation of Personal Liability

Although many monetary claims in maritime law are filed directly against the vessel, it is easily possible for an assessment to be so large that it exceeds the value of the boat and spills over as a debt against the owner. A damage award resulting from a bad accident could be in this category. Admiralty law allows an escape clause for such a harried owner, of which he can avail himself under certain conditions; it is the "limitation of liability."

Limitation of liability is a uniquely marine concept and has no direct parallel in shoreside law. The closest thing to it on land would be the incorporated organization whose liabilities are limited to its corporate assets—and, even here, situations arise that make officers and directors personally liable.

Limitation of liability is available only by a petition to the United States District Court and then only for cases which arose out of a happening on navigable waters, these waters again being defined as on page 563. A major requirement for obtaining limitation is that the negligence or the defect or whatever it was that formed the basis of the claim must have been completely beyond the owner's knowledge or that of his agent. The petition can be made to the United States court even though the action concerned is being carried on in a state court; if the petition is granted the state actions are transferred to the federal court.

Limitation of liability restricts the owner's liability for the total of all actions against him to the value of his boat. No matter how large the claims and how small the value of the vessel, the owner thus favored need turn over only the boat itself or its equivalent value in money.

Limitation of liability is considered by many to be an unfair hardship on legitimate claimants and, truly, it has deprived many victims of just compensation. The device has been adopted by large steamship companies after severe loss of life on one of their vessels and by owners of small powerboats after a bad or fatal accident. The recovery for the litigants has often been less than the cost of bringing suit. When there are several suits and a number of awards, the value of the boat is still the top limit for their total and this is divided pro rata. It could well be that the vessel in question became a total loss with zero value—zero would then be the total amount the claimants could recover!

Collision

The owner's or skipper's liability in a collision could be one of four degrees: (1) the onus could be entirely on him because the accident was caused by his infraction of the rules or his incompetent seamanship; (2) he shares the blame to some adjudicated degree with the colliding skipper because both were at fault; (3) he is completely in the clear because the accident was caused by the other skipper's incompetence or infraction of the rules; or (4) he is not at fault and neither is the other skipper because the accident was just what the name implies, an accidental happening not traceable to culpability.

Awards by the Admiralty Court in the foregoing cases are based on the degree of guilt as illustrated by the four possibilities above.

Owner/Skipper versus Law

The danger that a skipper or owner could become an unconscious law violator arises from changes in his geographical location. Some rules and regulations change as he crosses the unseen boundary between inland and international waters, others differ from state to state. Un-

fortunately, laws are not uniform except for some basic requirements. As an example, most states insist that two persons be in the powerboat that tows water skiers.

Owner Liability to Seamen and Workers

The relationship of a boat owner to the people working for him aboard his craft is complicated—much more so than that of a boss to his workers ashore. The complication arises from the Jones Act, which considers seagoing workers as seamen and compels a paternalistic, protective care for them by the owner. Here again, the small boatman's interest is academic because his insurance company agrees to assume the burden in a full-coverage policy.

Owner Liability to Guests

The guest who subsequently sues his host to recover for injury in an accident has become a common occurrence in automobile damage actions. A parallel situation exists afloat. Persons injured while guests on a small boat can (and do) bring actions against the owner-host for monetary compensation.

The lawyers' maneuvers in these accident-plus-injury cases generally lead through a legal maze, in these instances further obfuscated by the oddities of maritime law. It is all generally beyond a layman's understanding. The best safety "equipment" against these happenings is insurance.

Every owner is wise to shift the burden to an insurance company by means of a full-coverage policy. The owner is then absolved of all claims up to the limit of his policy.

Salvage

The dictionary defines salvage as the "act of saving a vessel from great danger such as perils of the sea." The definition contains the major necessary ingredient to qualify a situation as salvage, namely, great danger. The danger may take many forms but it must be present in such degree as to constitute an obvious threat to the survival of the ship. However, the danger need not be a full-scale, technicolor storm with falling rigging illuminated by lightning flashes. Many calmer-appearing scenes could still contain the needed element of "great danger."

The act of salvage automatically creates the salvor, the

person or group that performs the rescue. Maritime law outlines the qualifications for a salvor and, if he meets them, rewards him handsomely. The amount of his reward is determined by the value of what he has salved and by the danger to which his own vessel became exposed; human life is never considered one of the evaluating items. Salvage cases are heard only in Admiralty Court and must therefore have originated on those oft-mentioned navigable waters.

To qualify as salvage, the rescue must have been performed voluntarily by someone who had no duty to do so other than his humanitarian instincts and, perhaps faintly, the thought of the ensuing reward. This automatically cuts out the skipper and crew of the foundering vessel; they are paid to do their utmost to see their craft through hazards encountered en route. There are borderline cases where a member of the crew of a thoroughly abandoned vessel could make his way back and save it. The same duty requirement prevents Navy, Coast Guard, and other official personnel from claiming salvage.

The foregoing are the broad delineations of salvage. As it concerns the average small boatman, salvage is construed along much narrower lines, more in keeping with the experiences to which he might become subject. For instance: The weather and his position are bad when the skipper's motor conks out and he feels himself being swept into a dangerous situation unless he gets a tow. Luckily, another powerboat happens along; he asks for a tow and gets it. Is this salvage? In a limited legal sense, yes. Still, 99.9 percent of his fellow powerboatmen would never think of asking the unfortunate skipper for more than a thank you and perhaps a drink. But, on a larger scale, were two steamships involved, the owner of the towing vessel would certainly make a claim for salvage.

A cruising skipper who comes upon an abandoned, adrift boat and brings it safely to harbor is entitled to salvage. The amount of salvage in this, as in all cases, would be determined by the value of the goods salved. It is quite possible that his efforts would not be worth while if his salvage operation involved a broken-down old hooker. Also, he would get nothing if he failed to bring his salvage safely into port, regardless of how much effort he expended; salvage is paid only for success.

It is possible to perform salvage under a contractual agreement. Again considering the unfortunate skipper in need of a tow, he could arrange the price of the service with his tower before accepting the tow. If the tower took advantage of the dire situation and forced a usurious price, this could later be taken in account by an Admiralty Court.

Presumably, boatmen will have only an academic interest in salvage because their insurance companies see to the operational details when the necessity arises. Full-coverage insurance policies take the possible need for salvage into account and detail the owner's responsibilities and the actions required of him.

26 *Purchase, Charter,*
Sale and Insurance

A WISECRACK that has fastened itself on pleasure boating is now so old and hoary its whiskers are thick as seaweed. It goes: "The two happiest days in a boatman's life are the day he buys his boat and the day he sells it." Don't believe it!

Most boats represent sizable investments. A person who has chosen a bad boat or a wrong boat has made a poor investment and it is only natural that he is unhappy about it. But this has nothing to do with boats per se; he would be unhappy with a bad car or a bad home or a bad anything that cost a great deal of money.

A boat often is a highly specialized piece of equipment and it takes an expert, or at the very least someone with experience, to judge its worth. Human nature universally is less than perfect, and a seller's description and claims should be viewed with some degree of skepticism. The neophyte buyer goes awry in his estimate of how much to believe and how much to doubt. The expert disregards the sales talk and makes his own appraisal.

Since most boat buyers are not experts and many are uninitiated newcomers, the question is how they should proceed with a purchase. The answer is that the necessary experience can be had vicariously. A friend, a broker, or a surveyor can supply it.

The least likely source of valuable vicarious experience is probably a friend impressed into service by the buyer. Even a friend with ample boating knowledge may find his judgment swayed by the friendly relationship; he may be anxious to please or at least not to offend. It is free advice and free advice often is worth exactly what you pay for it.

An important consideration also enters here—that of money or, more correctly, whether full value is received in return for the dollars spent. This entails a knowledge of the going market; on this point, even most experienced boatmen will fail. Paying too much for a good boat is a better situation than buying a bad boat, but it is still not completely satisfactory.

None of the foregoing cautions applies if the purchase is of a new boat from a factory-accredited dealer. Then the sales price is fixed although, admittedly, haggling often can reduce it. There exists a factory warranty and thus some degree of recourse to the dealer. The transaction becomes very similar to the familiar one of buying an automobile; it does not assure the acquisition of a perfect boat but it does eliminate many of the risks.

Nevertheless, the majority of transactions in the pleasure boating world are secondhand, just as they are in cars, and the buyers are in the vulnerable positions already stated. It is thus helpful to evaluate the palliatives.

Selecting a Broker

Yacht brokers are in plentiful supply at almost every marine center, but there still remains the problem of zeroing in on a certain one. Word of mouth, local reputation, convenient location—all play their part in the selection.

The broker/owner or broker/prospective-buyer relationship can become a fairly personal one and thus that evanescent quality, "sympatico," is important. Whether or not this exists is found only by personal contact under the stress of actual negotiations.

Yacht brokers have maintained a high level of ethical conduct, despite the often highly competitive nature of their business. Most are members of their industry trade association.

Brokers

A buying or selling boatman can find a broker's services valuable. First, the broker is in touch with buyers and sellers and thus has a perspective of the market and of current price levels. Second, the broker generally has acted as a preliminary sifter and for his own protection has eliminated listings of unfit merchandise. Third, the broker presumably is a better bargainer and a better salesman than the average individual.

A buyer attempting to act on his own can scan the classified advertising of newspapers and periodicals and haunt a few boatyards or marinas. This will give him leads that he can then run down. He will usually find that, except for the smallest and cheapest items, these boats already are on brokers' lists. As they say in the advertisements for the telephone directories, he could have saved himself a lot of walking. The broker will have minute details of each listed boat catalogued.

The broker acquires his specific boat information by having the prospective lister fill out a form such as the one reproduced in Figure 26-1. Even a quick perusal shows how complete is the data requested; it covers just about everything vital to the mechanical or comfort functioning of the craft. (Remember, however, that it is only human

POWER YACHT

YACHT NAME ....

YACHT TYPE ....

SEDAN .... DBL CABIN ....

COCKPIT .... EXPRESS ....

FLUSH DECK .... FLY BRDG ....

WALK-AROUND DECKS .... TYPE HULL ....

NAVY TOP? .... HARD TOP? ....

LOA .... BEAM .... DRAFT ....

DESIGNER ....

BUILDER ....

YEAR BLT .... RE-BLT ....

DOCUMENTED OR NUMBERED ....

CONSTRUCTION (Material) ....

....

Planking .... Frames ....

Fastenings .... Decks ....

Cockpit Deck ....

SUPERSTRUCTURE: Paint .... Varnish ....

HULL CONDITION AND COMMENTS ....

....

FORMER NAME ....

ENGINE MAKE .... HP .... EA.

Single or Twin .... No. Cyl. ....

Gas or Diesel .... Red Gear ....

Out Drive? .... F/W Cooling? ....

Eng. Year .... Overhauled? ....

Eng. Hours .... Condition ....

Eng. Controls .... Dual? ....

SPEED (Cruis) .... kn/mph @ .... RPM

SPEED (Max) .... kn/mph @ .... RPM

CRUISING RANGE .... Miles

FUEL CONSUMPTION

@ Cruising Speed .... GPH

@ Max Speed .... GPH

FUEL CAPACITY .... Gals

Material of Tanks ....

WATER CAPACITY .... Gals

Material of Tanks ....

VOLTAGE (Lights) .... (Start) ....

AUX. GENERATOR .... MAKE ....

Gas/Dies .... KW .... Vltg ....

BATTERIES .... Voltage ....

CONSTAVOLT .... WIRING 110V .... 220V ....

CHARGICATOR .... POLARITY IND. ....

──────── ACCOMMODATIONS ────────

TOTAL for OWNER and GUESTS .... and CREW ....

STATEROOMS (Double) .... Headroom ....

(Single) .... Headroom ....

Main Salon Berths .... Headroom ....

Other Berths .... Location ....

Toilets .... (Elec) .... (Manual) ....

Chlorinator ....

Showers .... Enclosed ....

Interior Finish ....

Interior Furnishings ....

Deck Furniture ....

CREW QUARTERS

Cabins .... # Berths ....

Toilets .... # Showers ....

GALLEY LOCATION ....

Type Refrigeration ....

Deep Freeze ....

Type Stove .... # Burners ....

Oven .... Broiler ....

Figure 26-1: This typical yacht broker's questionnaire shows the extent of the information he requests.

for an owner to be optimistic.) In addition, many brokers have direct knowledge of their boats by actual visits made aboard during the present or a former ownership.

BROKERS' FEES.

A boat broker is paid for his work in the form of a commission which is figured as a percentage of the selling price. In other words, a certain small, predetermined percentage of the price paid for the boat is retained by the broker and not passed on to the seller.

The commission is fairly uniform throughout the industry and operates on a downward sliding scale that runs from 10 to 5 percent. Most brokers charge 10 percent on the first $10,000 of the sale price, some on the first $20,000; the balance of the selling price is usually charged at 7 percent although some brokers reduce this to 5 percent on very expensive yachts. The terms are fixed at the time of any agreement (not at the time of sale) and it is important that this be done *then*, to avoid subsequent controversy.

It is considered unethical, and it is actually illegal in some states, for a broker to tack his commission on top of the seller's stated selling price. The seller must fix his asking price with the full realization that a commission will be deducted.

BROKERS' FUNCTIONS.

Aside from making a market by bringing buyer and seller together, the broker also acts as a buffer between the two. The broker can serve as an impartial intermediary. When the bid and asked prices are at variance, the broker can cajole one up and the other down. He can be effective in doing this whereas the principals, personally involved, may end in a clash of stubborn determination that can doom the deal.

The transfer of a valuable property like a good boat inevitably involves paperwork; the broker can relieve buyer and seller of this chore. Titles must be cleared, taxes must be paid, various governmental agencies must be satisfied; these services are included in the commission paid to reputable brokers.

Buying Procedures

If the buyer has found the desired boat by direct contact with the owner, for instance through advertisements or word-of-mouth, the deal will be consummated in any manner satisfactory to both parties. If a broker has presented the boat to the buyer, then the procedure will be more ritualistic.

First, the buyer will be asked to back his offer with a deposit or, as the trade calls it, "earnest money." The amount will be between 10 and 20 percent of the bid figure and assures both broker and seller that the buyer is not just fooling around. This deposit will not be passed immediately to the seller; most brokers will hold the check in their possession without even depositing it in a bank account. When the sale is completed, the broker will add this check to the balance paid, deduct his commission, and make the remittance to the seller.

The deposit can be made with certain stipulations. These could be that the boat must pass survey, that certain repairs must be made, that certain equipment must be included, or any other. If these cannot be fulfilled, or if the bid is rejected, the deposit is returned to the buyer. (If the buyer fails to carry through without proper reason for his failure, the deposit could be forfeited.)

Procedures in Selling

Selling a boat, like selling anything else, requires that a buyer first be found. This, in turn, is a matter of communication. Direct advertisements and word-of-mouth can be used to inform prospective buyers, but brokers' listings are usually better. Advertisements often bring idle lookers and the curious who have time on their hands but no serious intentions; a broker can weed out many of these.

Excessive price is the greatest single obstacle to sales. Many owners cannot divorce themselves from their subjective attachment to their boats and confuse this with market value. An experienced broker can often bring such an owner down out of the clouds to a reasonable price level—unfortunately, he can also lose a client by being honest.

More and more brokers are joining in a universal complaint: that owners do not present their boats to best advantage. A boat on display for sale should look like a Navy craft under the command of a spit-and-polish admiral; in actuality, it often looks as though a Russian peasant family had lived on board with its livestock.

Listings

Most brokers list their salable boats without charge to the owner and take their remuneration as commission when and if sold. The listings carry the information requested on the form shown in Figure 26-1 and sometimes also a picture of the boat; these lists are sent to prospects classified on the basis of boat preferences or amount of money they wish to spend. Often the broker also features certain listings in his advertising.

MULTIPLE LISTINGS.

A broker who has been given the exclusive selling right on a boat usually gives it a "multiple listing." This means that he distributes his listing to other brokers and authorizes them to find buyers. He remains in charge and consummates the final deal acceptable to the seller, however. For this service, the listing broker receives a flat 10 percent commission and shares this with the broker who found the buyer.

A multiple listing is preferable to making many individual listings on the same boat with a series of brokers. This can result in brokers competing with each other and losing interest. It can also create some sticky situations.

Surveyors

As stated earlier, a buyer can also acquire experience vicariously by employing a surveyor to inspect the condition of the vessel. Many appraisers for marine insurance companies moonlight as free-lance surveyors. Many retired sea captains and shipwrights also do boat surveying professionally. Surveyors can be found through their advertisements and on recommendation from brokers, marinas, and insurance agents.

A surveyor is engaged on a per-diem basis or on a per-foot basis by the buyer; traveling expenses to the boat in question are also paid. He makes a thorough inspection and submits a report that places greater emphasis on what is wrong than on what is right with the vessel. This report can then become the basis for judgment of the boat's soundness and for estimate of the cost of any needed repairs. Note that surveyors usually disavow legal responsibility for their opinions.

Hull surveys, of course, can have no great meaning unless the vessel is hauled to permit a direct inspection of the bottom. The cost of hauling is also paid by the buyer. Sometimes, if a sale seems imminent, the seller may permit the deduction of the hauling expense from the price.

Trades

Trading the old one in as partial payment for the new one, a common practice with automobiles, is much rarer in the boat business. Brokers are not particularly interested in trade deals because of the difficulty in locating a buyer-seller situation in which both boats are acceptable. When they do consummate a trade deal, they apportion the sales commission between the two parties.

There is more likelihood of making a trade-in transaction with a dealer who carries an inventory of boats. He may be amenable to taking another boat into inventory, plus cash, simultaneously with letting one out.

Chartering

Chartering serves two functions for the charterer and one for the owner. A charterer may wish to try out a boat under actual running conditions for a period of time before buying it; he may also have no desire to own a boat but may wish to use one occasionally. The owner can set his boat to paying its own way during the time he is not using it.

The two kinds of charter and the charter party which seals the bargain are discussed in Chapter 25, together with the legalities attendant to them. Bringing the charterer and the owner together also becomes a matter of communication and, just as in buying and selling, this can be accomplished in many ways. The most common and most effective method is through a broker.

The broker makes arrangements for collecting the payment and acts as intermediary in setting a mutually acceptable type and time of charter. For this service, the broker receives a commission of 15 percent from the owner. An advantage in chartering through a broker is again the fact that he has personal knowledge of the boat and especially the crew and probably has been aboard.

In a demise or bareboat charter (see Chapter 25), the charterer assumes all running expenses including food and wages for his crew. (If he can convince the owner of his experience and ability to handle the craft, the charterer may be permitted to run the boat himself without a professional crew.)

The boat is turned over by the owner completely "found." This means that cooking and eating utensils and even blankets are aboard in addition to the purely navigational gear. Except by special arrangement, linen is not included in the supplies.

The principle of demurrage, well known in railroading, is applied in chartering. If the demurrage is the fault of the owner (late delivery of the boat), the charterer is entitled to a refund or adjustment and, in some cases, even a complete release from his obligation to take the boat. If the craft becomes disabled en route, the charterer also has recourse. The charter party prescribes arbitration as the method for resolving any disputes. When the demurrage is the fault of the charterer (late return of the boat) the owner is entitled to pro-rata extra pay and perhaps also indemnity if it causes him subsequent monetary loss.

The charter party states the area within which the boat must remain and settles the matter of insurance. (All owners are careful about insurance because in admiralty law the *boat* itself, physically, is held liable for infractions and can be seized. See Chapter 25.) The charterer also contracts to use the boat for pleasure purposes only and never in an unlawful manner. Naturally, the charterer is prohibited from incurring any charges or liens against the vessel.

In a demise charter, the charterer furnishes the crew if he himself is not authorized to operate the craft. He does this by signing on a captain with a short form that sets forth the terms of payment or wages, the length of employment, and the captain's qualifications. The captain in turn chooses a mate and any additionally required extra help.

Insurance

Insurance of all kinds has become such an established part of American life that its need for boats hardly requires emphasis. Few people would run an uninsured automobile. Even fewer should operate an uninsured boat with the attendant risks.

Yacht insurance can be placed through most general insurance brokers and many owners simply pass this job on to the agents through whom they insure their homes and cars. However, marine insurance is a highly specialized business; it is more likely, therefore, that a fully comprehensive service can best be had from a broker who devotes his energies mainly to this field. Most yacht brokers also provide boat insurance through their own or affiliated facilities.

Application for insurance is made by filling out a questionnaire which covers even such minute details as whether the fuel fill pipe is tightly connected to the outside deck plate. In addition to the usual identification of the boat by stating its name, year, builder, and overall size, the applicant is asked to state the cost of the craft when new and the price at which he bought it. Inquiry is made about the waters to be navigated, the boat's use for water skiing, and whether any other insurance company ever refused coverage on the boat.

The questions probe the possibility of loss arising from details of the boat's construction. Thus, inquiry is made whether the propeller and rudder project below the keel and whether a protective shoe is provided. Queries concerning the tanks ask about welded, brazed, or soldered seams and the accessibility of the shut-off cocks. The use of liquid petroleum gas on board for cooking brings up questions as to the location of the tanks and the shut-offs and the presence of a pressure gauge.

Reduced rates are offered for powerboats using diesel fuel and having no gasoline on board. Built-in CO_2 fire-extinguishing systems also bring a reduction in insurance cost.

Types of Insurance

The standard yacht policy covers the obvious hazards to a power or sail craft navigating the waters for pleasure. To this basic contract can be added additional protection in the amounts required by any specific owner. The classifications are hull insurance, liability insurance, compensation insurance, and medical payments insurance.

HULL INSURANCE.

The hull, its propulsive and other machinery, all gear necessary for operation, including the dinghy, and the boat's furnishings are covered by hull insurance against all physical loss or damage. Personal possessions carried on board, such as clothing and fishing equipment, are not covered. Some of the boat's gear may be stored on shore and still retain its coverage; policies limit this to between

20 and 50 percent of the amount for which insurance is carried.

Hull insurance does not cover wear-and-tear, deterioration caused by neglect or age or defect, destruction by marine or other vermin, and damage from ice and freezing. "Mysterious disappearance" of equipment is not covered unless conclusive proof of theft can be given. The insurance is in effect during the life of the policy, regardless of whether the hull is afloat or ashore. Lay-up periods are usually specified in climates where year-round use is not likely and during these times the boat must be stored properly.

COLLISION INSURANCE.

An important phase of hull insurance is the provision for collision payment. This is written as a separate coverage; this means that in a collision involving the loss of his boat, the owner will receive full policy payment and in addition an equal amount will be available for payment of resulting claims against him. (The amount available for collision claims is there, of course, even if he does not lose his own boat.)

LIABILITY INSURANCE.

The industry term for liability insurance is P&I, protection and indemnity. This coverage is obtained for an extra premium payment. P&I protects the owner up to the limits of the policy against claims made against him by guests, crew, or outside parties for damages resulting from the boat and its operation for which he may be liable because of his ownership. This is a familiar type of protection for homeowners and automobile owners.

P&I coverage can be extended to include any claims arising when members of the owner's family, his own crew, or his friends operate the boat. The requirement is that the operation be with the owner's knowledge and permission.

A "running down clause" in all-risk policies pays damages to the insured boat plus damages to the other boat involved. Costs of salvage are determined by the LOF (Lloyd's Open Form salvage agreement).

P&I insurance also protects the owner against claims arising from the Federal Longshoreman's and Harbor Worker's Compensation Act. This legislation makes the owner liable for injury or death suffered by any paid employees, other than his own crew, working on his boat. The crew is covered under the original P&I.

MEDICAL PAYMENTS.

An owner often feels that he should pay the medical expenses for a guest or crew member which result from an accident aboard his boat, even though he is not legally liable for the occurrence. The medical payments clause covers such contingencies. Most P&I clauses throw in the medical clause up to $1000 without any extra premium; higher limits are available for additional payment.

An interesting feature of all marine insurance is the concept that the owner must take all necessary and possible steps to limit loss when it occurs. Thus he is empowered to hire towing services if his stranded position involves loss and danger; the insurance company will reimburse him. The criterion is that the owner must act in the best interests of his boat just as though he had no insurance and wanted to protect his investment.

Insurance Costs

Some yacht insurance policies carry a no-loss refund provision. At the expiration of such a policy, the owner is entitled to a refund of up to perhaps 20 percent of the original cost of the insurance if no compensable loss has occurred during its life. This is sometimes refined to an alternative offer of a smaller deduction at the inception of the policy with the same stipulations.

Yacht insurance can be in the form of an "agreed-value contract" or a "cash-value contract." The former is the general form for the average large boat. The latter is written for outboards, houseboats, and small stuff.

A total loss of the boat under the agreed-value contract is paid for by the insurance company with the full agreed sum. No deduction is taken for deterioration. Obviously, therefore, the amount for which such a policy is issued must bear a real relation to the true value of the boat. Understating the value of the boat is of no eventual gain to the owner.

A total loss under the cash-value contract is reimbursed in a different manner. Here the value of the boat at the time of loss is the governing factor and this is determined "by the book." The procedure is a carryover from the standard method of writing automobile insurance.

The familiar deductible clauses also have been borrowed from the auto world and have become a standard fixture of yacht policies. Under these, the owner pays the first certain specified portion of a damage claim (perhaps $100) and in return gets his insurance for a lower premium rate. Generally this deduction is not applied in the event of total loss of the boat.

Loss Recovery

All insurance companies stress the importance of immediate reports of loss to the owner's broker or agent. If at all possible, an estimate of the cost of repair made by a responsible professional source should accompany the report. In most instances the insurance company will send its own surveyor to assess the situation and make his own estimate of the extent of damage and the price of correcting it.

Sometimes the insurance company will make a flat sum reimbursement direct to the owner in return for a quitclaim. It is then up to the owner to stretch this money in whatever way he pleases to accomplish the needed correction. Alternatively, the company may authorize the repairs in a specified boatyard and then pick up the tabs and pay them. This is often the better way, because insurance companies can exert greater leverage than an individual.

Some homeowners' policies with comprehensive-risk clauses include limited coverage for small outboard boats and their motors. It is advisable to have these examined by a person knowledgeable in marine insurance to learn whether they cover the risks inherent in normal boating. An additional yacht-owner's policy may be indicated for full peace of mind.

Wanted and For Sale Ads

For those owners and buyers who like to work without intermediaries, there are always the classified colums of newspapers and boating magazines. Even these often lead to a broker instead of to a principal, however.

Newspapers in such metropolitan boating centers as New York, Chicago, Los Angeles, and Miami maintain special boating departments. Their classified sections offer a great number of sale and purchase possibilities; often these are amplified on one particular day of the week, such as Sunday. Newspaper advertising offers immediacy with a minimum time lag.

Boating magazines, such as *Boating*, *Motorboating*, *Rudder*, and *Yachting*, and tabloids, such as *Soundings*, have the advantage of a restricted, boat-minded readership. However, the time lag between ad placement and ad appearance in periodicals can be a matter of weeks or even months.

One difficulty with many boats advertised for sale is that the owners write the descriptions while still under the spell of total love. It takes a bit of experience on the part of the prospective buyer before he can automatically apply the correct percentage of discount.

27 *Learning the Game*

MANY opportunities exist for the sail- and power-boatman to increase his technical competence. Some of the best of these chances to learn are offered by interested organizations and are free.

The United States Power Squadron and the Coast Guard Auxiliary are the two largest nationwide organizations devoted to furthering the cause of boating safety through education. Both groups schedule many training classes in which beginners are welcome to enroll without cost.

Other means for becoming a competent skipper also are available. Many schools advertise courses in class and in person; some add that rare ingredient—actual instruction on the water. Then, for the few who have access to it, there is the best method of all—tutelage under the eye of an experienced and willing boatman.

United States Power Squadron (USPS)

A small group of dedicated yachtsmen formed this organization in 1914. It weathered two world wars and many accompanying vicissitudes and grew to its present membership of more than 80,000 distributed into 400 squadrons. During this period, more than 2.5 million persons were students in its preliminary courses in seamanship.

The USPS has not deviated from its founding theme of instilling skill in the handling and navigating of yachts—whether they are true marine queens or small outboards. Equally zealous has been the organization's fight against the institution of licensing for pleasure boat operators.

The Power Squadron has successfully maintained that education and not operator licensing is the key to pleasure boating safety. The USPS fiercely believes that licensing would degenerate simply into another form of taxation.

Power Squadron men and their boats went into the service of the nation in World War I. The cycle was repeated in World War II. Presidential citations attest to the help they gave.

The need which every small boat skipper has for thorough knowledge of the rules of the road, of piloting technique, of proper boat handling is emphasized throughout this book and the free USPS classes stress these same subjects. (It follows, quite logically, that a study of the preceding chapters will give you a head start in these classes.)

Safe boat handling has wider implications than the simple moral dictum not to cause injury. It reduces the risk to property and this is of vital interest to insurers and has a bearing on premiums. Very early in the program, insurance companies expressed their appreciation of the USPS education efforts.

The basic classes held each year, one of which is shown in session in the accompanying photograph of Figure 27-1, are the first steps toward membership in the Power Squadron. Successful completion of the examinations given when the lessons end leads to the award of a certificate—and members are chosen from certificate holders. Once membership is achieved, additional more advanced courses restricted to members only may be chosen, on subjects ranging up to celestial navigation. These lead to degrees such as seaman (S), advanced pilot (AP), junior navigator (JN), and finally navigator (N).

The chart designated as 1210TR, which for many years has been a standard training chart, has been supplanted by a new issue. The new training chart covers a section of Long Island Sound and is in the small craft format. (1210TR is a large, full-size chart more unwieldy to handle.) The price of the new chart is 15¢ and it is obtainable from the usual sources.

Members of the United States Power Squadron are privileged to fly the Squadron's flag, illustrated in Figure 27-2. How to do this properly is discussed in the section on Flags on page 597.

Figure 27-2: Members of the United States Power Squadron are privileged to fly this ensign.

Coast Guard Auxiliary

In 1939 Congress authorized the formation of the United States Coast Guard Reserve. This was a quasi-military organization. In 1941 Congress amended this to a civilian

Figure 27-1: Piloting classes like these are held in many locations by the (a) United States Power Squadron and the (b) United States Coast Guard Auxiliary and are free. (Credit—U.S. Power Squadron & U.S. Coast Guard Auxiliary)

system and changed the name to the Coast Guard Auxiliary. The overall plan conceived a reservoir of nautically trained men available in a national emergency plus a continuous force for the advancement of pleasure boating safety.

The Coast Guard Auxiliary distinguished itself during World War II. Its members were on active duty, often serving on their own boats, which were enlisted as temporary government craft. The auxiliarists patrolled harbors, prevented sabotage, and enforced security; by taking over these jobs they released the regular Coast Guard for other duties. Considering the 21,000-mile actual coastal perimeter line of the United States, the CGAux scored a mammoth accomplishment.

The present Coast Guard Auxiliary activity most likely to bring it in contact with the small boat skipper is its system of "courtesy inspections." Under this procedure, the CGAux boards a boat (but only if the owner requests it) and examines the safety equipment carried. All legally required safety gear must be aboard and in good order. Additional equipment not required by law but necessary for safe boat operation also must be present. If everything proves satisfactory, the CGAux inspector will affix an approval decal to windshield or window.

A currently valid Coast Guard Auxiliary decal has real value. It is respected by the Coast Guard to the extent that they usually will not board a vessel carrying it. (See Chapter 25.) This saves the annoyance of heaving to and palavering with a boarding party.

The Coast Guard Auxiliary offers many free courses for introducing neophytes to the arts and pleasures of safe boating. It also runs advanced classes in which the degrees of navigator, senior navigator, and engineer can be won.

The CGAux is based on the concept of a pyramid whose base is the flotilla. A flotilla consists of ten or more boats, radio stations, planes, or combinations of these. Five flotillas form a division, and three divisions constitute a district, the governing HQ. At the very top of the totem pole the CGAux is answerable to the Commandant of the Coast Guard; it is the only civilian group with such official sponsorship.

Members of the Auxiliary are permitted to fly the CGAux ensign. The correct manner of doing this is described in the section on Flags on page 597. The Coast Guard ensign is shown in Figure 27-3.

Many pleasure boatmen, stranded far from home base

Figure 27-3: Members of the United States Coast Guard Auxiliary are privileged to fly this official ensign.

for one reason or another, owe their safe return to the towing service rendered by the CGAux. (See Figure 27-4).

Boat Owners Association of the US (Boat/US)

This is a group of boat owners from all parts of the nation who have banded together for mutual benefit and maintain headquarters in Washington, D.C. Boat/US exerts considerable effort in advising legislators on the needs of pleasure boating. In addition, this organization maintains educational programs for its members and provides insurance for their boats. It is said that financing for the purchase of pleasure craft also can be obtained from BOAT/US by its members.

Schools

Nautical knowledge can also be obtained through commercially established schools, either by classroom attendance, by private tuition, or by mail. The courses offered are at various levels; some aim at qualifying the student to pass the professional Coast Guard examinations while others stress all-around seamanship and still others emphasize sailing techniques. All have value for the serious boatman.

Nautical schooling is even available to the youngster. Several "military academy type" private institutions confine themselves to the naval side of things. The classroom training in marine subjects usually is amplified by actual experience in the school-owned boats.

Sometimes the tuition fee includes the basic instruments a navigator needs. These include dividers, protractors, parallel rules, circular calculators, and even low-cost plastic sextants. (See Chapter 9.)

Nautical Etiquette

Time was when the most mortifying incident in a yacht captain's day proved to be guests coming aboard by the *port* accommodation ladder. Everyone knew that this entry was reserved for the crew; guests properly arrived by the *starboard* accommodation ladder. Think of the snickers by the wielders of binoculars on nearby ships.

In that era nautical etiquette was at a rarefied level. One crewman was occupied in hoisting appropriate flags to the yardarm and then in lowering them: "Owner absent," "owner at meal," "guests aboard." And all activity ceased when the red "crew at meal" pennant flew.

Those were the days when yachts were scaled-down ocean liners, when their tenders exceeded in length most of the boats berthed at today's marinas. Happily those overstressed manners are gone, victims of modern accelerated living and soaring costs. But a more practical etiquette remains and is necessary to smooth an ever-increasing pleasure boat world.

The pleasure-boatman's etiquette is a blend of snatches from naval lore plus the normal behavior of well-bred people ashore. Take, for instance, the ban on rowdy and noisy behavior in a marina or anchorage containing other boats. Surely the same prohibition exists in an apartment house or in any public place.

Suppose you intend to visit a friend on his boat. Do you just climb aboard without a by-your-leave? Do you simply open the door and barge into his house ashore? The mannered yachtsman goes as far as the rail and says: "Request permission to come aboard." Say it with a smile and think of your Navy days, but say it anyway. When a visitor to your own boat says it to you, and your smile broadens as your heart warms, the whole thing will explain itself.

Guests aboard for a cruise often are landlubbers not knowledgeable in the minimal storage space available on a boat or in the vulnerability of decks to hard-soled shoes. A courteous hint about airline plastic bags instead of suitcases and rubber-soled footwear in place of spiked heels avoids embarrassment and saves the pristine surfaces from nicks.

Sometime in the prehistoric life of the teak tree it must have had an insatiable yen for fat. How else explain teak's avid soaking up of every last drop of oil from a dropped potato chip or popcorn? The inevitable solution is to ask guests please not to bring such party snacks aboard because of the unsightly stains they cause.

Even though a skipper, under the law (see Chapter 25), is responsible for his wake, simple good manners should make recourse to legal enforcement unnecessary. Hold down speed in an anchorage and give a thought to the comfort of people on other boats and to the safety of mates working in galleys. Hold down speed in narrow canals and channels so the wake damages neither piers nor the boats tied to them. Pass other craft as neatly as possible and, if you are being passed, slow down and ease the job for both of you.

Heads at best are cantankerous mechanisms and for landlubber guests aboard they are ogres. Explain the mystery with whatever finesse is prescribed by sex and age. Hint that the single head, like a telephone party line, must be used by all in turn with a minimum of friction. (It surely ain't no powder room.)

Many modest craft boastfully are advertised to "sleep six" (or "four" or "eight" or whatever) and this usually is accomplished by converting dinettes, sofas, or other daytime furniture. Of necessity, this makes sleeping time and rising time unanimous—and the well-mannered guest should catch on quickly. Midnight fridge raiding also is frowned upon because the vittles generally are scheduled for the trip.

Etiquette at yacht clubs is a variable thing. There are swanky yacht clubs and clubs not so swanky; in any case it is wisest to follow the local norm and to use good taste. You would not dress in coveralls for a formal club dance. Nor does it make sense to appear in the regalia of an admiral in the Swiss navy when everyone else is attired in casuals.

Flags

In addition to the national ensign and the yacht ensign, "flags" includes the ensigns of the USPS and the CGAux, yacht club burgees, the union jack, owners' private signals, and various flags that indicate conditions on board. The international code flags of letters and numerals could also be included, although they rarely are seen on pleasure boats.

Figure 27-4: The Coast Guard Auxiliary is active in rescue work. Here a CGAux member is towing a disabled pleasure boat.

Standard manuals of flag etiquette all seem to assume that every small boat has two masts complete with yard-arms and trucks as well as jack and stern staffs. The ensuing instructions are equally complex and serve only to confuse the average small boat skipper. By contrast, he can observe the amenities by complying with the few rules that follow.

NATIONAL ENSIGN.

The national ensign is the one universally recognized as our country's flag. It is superior to all others and never is flown below any other. It is hoisted at "sunrise" (about 0800) and lowered at sunset or at the yacht club's sunset gun. The national ensign always is the first to go up; other flags follow.

Powerboats fly the national ensign at the stern staff. The exception is the rare boat with a mast and gaff; this vessel flies the national ensign at the gaff.

Sailboats fly the national ensign at the stern staff while at anchor and three-quarters up the leach of the mainsail while underway. Burgees can be flown at the truck.

YACHT ENSIGN.

Originally, the yacht ensign was reserved for use by documented vessels only, but it may now be flown legally in place of the national ensign by any boat that wishes to do so. It is flown at the stern staff and the rules applicable to its use are the same as those which govern the national ensign.

UNION JACK.

The union jack has very limited use on any vessel smaller than an ocean-going yacht. It could, perhaps, assist in dressing ship during some gala celebration.

USPS ENSIGN.

Members in good standing of the United States Power Squadron may fly the USPS ensign at the stern staff in place of the national ensign or the yacht ensign. If they elect to fly the national ensign or the yacht ensign at the stern staff, then the USPS ensign may additionally be flown at the starboard yardarm.

CGAUX ENSIGN.

The rules governing the flying of the Coast Guard Auxiliary ensign are the same as those given for the USPS ensign.

YACHT CLUB BURGEE.

The burgee of the yacht club to which the owner belongs is flown at the bow staff.

ON-BOARD-CONDITION FLAGS.

These flags (owner absent, etc.) are all flown, although of course only one at a time, from the starboard yardarm. Some are shown in Figure 27-5.

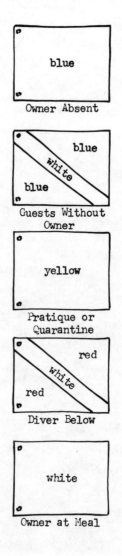

Figure 27-5: These pennants are flown to indicate conditions on board.

FLAG-FLYING TIME.

It can be taken as a general rule that all flags are flown only from sunrise to sunset. Sunrise may be taken arbitrarily as 0800 local time; sunset may be marked by a sunset gun.

Uniforms

Uniforms have lost their importance in pleasure boating. This is a natural result of the metamorphosis from rich man's diversion to everyman's hobby. Nevertheless, there are still some occasions when members of boating organizations can wear uniforms in whole or in part.

The USPS and the CGAux both have regulations governing the dress of their members under various conditions. Many yacht clubs also specify in their constitutions and by-laws guides to member apparel and appearance.

One "uniform" very appropriate for every boatman to have aboard is foul-weather gear. The basic foul-weather gear (but by no means the most comfortable) is the oilskin of the old-time sailboatman. Outfitted in this, a man felt like a knight in armor and had about the same freedom of movement.

Modern foul-weather gear is as supple as civilian rainwear. The materials of which it is made comprise the gamut of synthethics, some inherently waterproof and others chemically treated to resist water.

One difficulty with most foul-weather gear stems from the very fact that it is waterproof: It prevents body moisture from evaporating and traps it so that soon the wearer is in a sea of his own sweat. One attempt at alleviation places ventilating grommets under the armpits and on the back. Much foul-weather gear is made in the bright orange generally considered an emergency color—just in case.

28 *And Now to Graduate*

H AD the preceding pages been a course in an actual school, you would now be on the threshold of graduating into the world as a skipper. True, the degree of "skipper" is not a particularly official title but, as you now know, it is fraught with responsibility. As the skipper you are legally accountable for the safety of your crew, your vessel and for any breach of good seamanship that causes damage to others.

You have learned the rules of the road and realize their importance in enabling marine traffic to proceed in a safe and orderly fashion. You know why a ship floats and what conditions are necessary to make that flotation stable. You understand the internal functioning of engines and can proceed logically in a search for the cause of trouble. Electronics no longer mystifies you, and you can manipulate the knobs and dials which aid navigation.

In short, you are primed to the teeth with theoretical knowledge. Now only practical experience aboard can sharpen your skills and polish you into the true skipper who takes fair weather and foul with equal grace. As all graduates must, you are emerging from the protected cocoon of learning and entering the harsh outside world of doing.

If you are not already a boat owner but contemplate becoming one, then your first question must be: "Sail or power?" Earlier pages have gone into the minutiae of purchase; here we will contemplate only the generalities of the overall choice, really a choice between two different worlds.

The basic fact to remember, aside from all other aspects of your decision, is that sailing requires physical effort. The amount of effort required and whether it is within one man's capabilities or not depend upon the size of the sailboat; but it is physical effort nevertheless. This often causes sailing to be spoken of as a young man's game but the number of grayheads at tillers belies this.

Contrariwise, your greatest effort on a powerboat could be turning the ignition key and moving the engine controls. Powering is closer to the concept of a spectator sport while sailing is a participation sport. Neither of these descriptions is intended to be pejorative; the fun is simply different.

There are other basic dissimilarities between sailboats and powerboats, especially where families are concerned. Foot for foot, the powerboat offers more living space, has room for more of the amenities of creature comfort and allows more of the privacy required where sex and generation differences exist.

Economics should be in your mind when you choose between sail and power. Most boats today are made of fiberglass so maintenance costs are about equal—and minimal. But running costs! The wind is free while the price of fuel is high and keeps zooming. With the large overpowered engines which are today's norm, a trip to the gas dock can take a mean bite out of the weekend fun budget. Here the sailor can keep his money in his pocket and chortle with glee at the stinkpotter's discomfiture.

Speaking of families brings a comparatively new genus of craft into the picture: the houseboat. Manufacturers have brought these vessels to a remarkable degree of compact livability without skyrocketing the price. This could be the best family boat if your boating is to take place on protected waters. Houseboats are the closest things to floating apartments and take the least amount of getting used to by landlubbers.

The boat trailer is another factor that should be considered when you are making your decision. The trailer can make boating waters accessible even though you live far from them. It allows you a wider choice of cruising areas than you ever could achieve by water alone without using the intervening highways. Boat ramps are so common now that it is hard to find a marina or public marine area without a launching place, so your range is almost limitless.

Not the least of the trailer's advantages is the reduction in upkeep cost which it can make possible. By leaving the boat on its trailer in the backyard between voyages, the cost of marina slip rental is avoided. Not only that, but bottom painting becomes almost unnecessary. (The ability to be left out of the water for periods of time is one of the virtues of fiberglass; wood cannot match this because it dries out, shrinks and becomes leaky.)

One thing to bear in mind about prospective trailering: It automatically limits the size of your boat. Overall load width is limited to eight feet by almost all state highway laws and this means that the boat's beam cannot exceed this. Indirectly, this also puts a limit on the overall length.

Surprisingly, the annual upkeep and replacement expenses for sailman and powerman come out close to equal. Sails don't look like much money until you have to pay the bills for tear repairs and new suits. And every automobile owner knows that engines just do not seem to contain any inexpensive parts when failure occurs.

A further choice you must make concerns motive power. This applies to sailboats with auxiliaries as well as to powerboats. Will it be gasoline or diesel? (Small sailboats that hang their horses over the transom are of course restricted to gasoline outboard motors.)

Millions of boats use gasoline with an infinitesimal percentage of reports of trouble, yet there is a well-grounded reason for fear of the stuff; it *is* liquid dynamite. Diesel, on the other hand, is monotonously safe. Even the staid insurance companies admit this in their premium structure. Although diesel fuel springs instantly to life in an engine, it takes a great deal of coaxing to make it burn anywhere else. For family boats with children on board, diesel engines are great mind-pacifiers.

The sad fact is that diesel engines cost more than gasoline power engines of equal rating. Part of this is due to the much small number of diesels produced; part to the heavier and sturdier construction of these oil burners. To

their advantage is the greater longevity of diesels, their simplicity, their reliability and the lower cost of their fuel. All these bits of information must be fed into your mental computer and then you must cogitate—perhaps on a tie line with the mate. No one can give you a pat answer.

Should your boat selection be a planing hull between 14 and 24 feet in length, you can adopt a new wrinkle in propulsion—jet drive. This does away with propellers and rudders and is ideal for water skiing and similar fast runs. The jet drive allows the boat to run in shallower water than would a prop drive and to some extent under weedy conditions that would foul a conventional screw. But a prerequisite to this installation must be that you intend to travel fast all the time; the jet drive loses its efficiency when you throttle down to piddling speeds. A great plus for this scheme of propulsion is its safety. No moving parts are out where swimmers or anyone else can get hurt by them. (See Figure 28-1.)

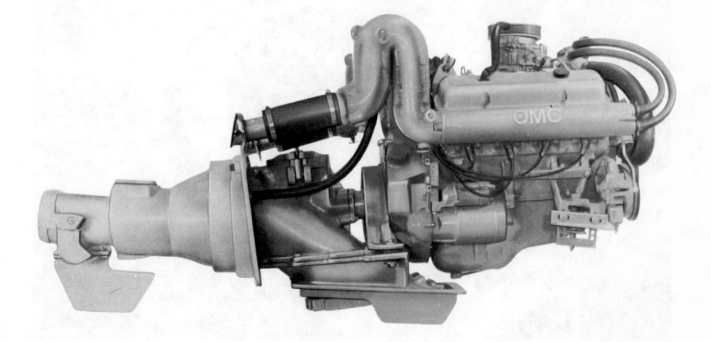

Figure 28-1: This is the complete hookup of engine, pump and nozzle for jet drive. The rudder at the far left increases steering effect at low speeds. The deflector makes reverse possible.

A recent development in the jet drive field is an outboard motor version for dinghies and rowboats. It permits trolling in water just deep enough to float the boat as well as beaching on the shore without worrying about prop damage. (See Figure 28-2.)

Often the total financial answer is a rude shock that can derail the desire to buy a boat. At such times the thought occurs of owning a boat in partnership with friends or relatives. The cure is much worse than the disease. I am certain that many unsolved murders could

be traced to boat-owning partnerships by boat-minded detectives. The scheme just does not work except perhaps among the few saints still left on earth.

Financing is an ingrained facet of American life and it has proved its worth in boating by making new vistas of enjoyment possible for countless economically average people. But this, too, should be considered carefully. Lending institutions have become as competitive as supermarkets and therefore it pays to shop for lowest rates. There is very little fun left in a boat that is breaking your

Figure 28-2: This adaptation of an outboard motor and a pump brings jet drive down into the realm of dinghies and small fishing boats. The rig is excellent for trolling in very shallow water.

The boats are to blame. Their designers have ignored back with its payments.

In addition to the foregoing factors, there are still more forks in the road to a final choice. Is it your intention to race, to cruise, to fish or just to be a marina navigator fast to the pier with a cocktail in your hand and friends aboard? Each activity points to a different kind of boat and no one boat will fill all slots. Perusing catalogs, talking to similarly minded boat owners and haunting salesrooms can provide the answer.

The new boat you buy will be legally equipped—and often no more than that. This may sound good but is just barely minimal. You should have a great deal more equipment on board for safe boating and this means a further drain on the pocketbook. Just as with automobiles, the "extras" and the "options" can deplete the cash reserve and make a totally different picture out of the purchase.

The preceding pages have made you familiar with all available boat equipment and have explained the pluses and the minuses. From a strictly nautical point of view, excluding all economic factors, how much optional equipment you should install is determined by the use you will make of the craft. Obviously, offshore navigation requires more instrumental assistance than river piloting.

A radiotelephone should be a number one "must." With this electronic safeguard aboard you are never out of touch with help when you need it or even with important business matters. The latest law has complicated this situation a bit because it requires that a VHF phone be installed before a permit will be issued for longer-range radio.

When all else has been said and has been done, insurance pops over the horizon as still another need for spending money. Insurance is not cheap; as more and more people take to the water and the exposure risk increases, premiums will go even higher. The cost of insurance seems a waste—until the moment when you need it; then it proves to be the best investment ever. An earlier chapter unravels some of the mysteries of this ancient form of loss protection and urges you to deal with a specialist.

A nearly universal problem among boatmen is that women do not like boats. I do not refer to the languid beauties who adorn top decks with bikinis carefully adjusted to minimum legal limits. I mean wives, mates, the real women in men's lives.

the female nesting instinct, the inborn need for a cozy comfortable home, even afloat. This is something you must bear in mind when shopping for family boating. That oh-so-cute forward vee berth which looks so appealing in the showroom can become a triangular hell underway if its dimensions are skimped. So stretch out in it, move around in it, check it, get the mate's opinion before you put pen to checkbook.

This same idea of simulating future life aboard goes for all other spaces in the boat whether or not it has a cabin. Even the walk forward to the bow from the wheel of a runabout can be a bother if the design is not right.

Check all mooring fittings carefully. Are they there for mere nautical decoration or can they take real service? Are they through-bolted or just fastened with short screws and a prayer?

The final summation of your boat-buying venture gets down to the nitty gritty of whether to purchase new or used. Here the thinking should become familiar to you because it parallels your experience over the years in trading automobiles.

On the plus side of buying used: A dollar buys more used boat than new boat. The previous owner has already taken the heavy depreciation which a new purchase entails. The chances are that a great deal of equipment is on board which would be optional and cost extra on a new boat. Often the seller is in a tight spot and really offers a bargain.

The minus side concerns itself mostly with the fact that, if something goes wrong, your recourse is doubtful unless the seller is an established dealer who wants you for a future customer. Nor is there any way of x-raying a used boat or its engine to learn how much longer it can resist the eventual urge to give up its ghost. (Sadly, this also is true of the skipper.)

Finally, the sweet pain of coming to a decision is ended. You have made your choice. The intricacies of paper work and finance are behind you. You own a boat. You really feel like a skipper and people address you with "Hi, Cap'n!"

What now? Remember the violin virtuoso who was asked how to get to Carnegie Hall? His answer was "Practice, practice, practice!" And that is exactly how you become a virtuoso skipper—by practice, practice and more practice.

Earlier in this book the various skills in which you must

become proficient are outlined carefully. Some are identical for power and sail, others are relevant to only one or the other. Whichever skills suit your new status, keep at them until you are letter-perfect. The sea is a tough mistress who does not forgive and who makes no allowance for your ignorance when she is angry.

Unless you carry horseshoes in your pockets and are an adopted child of the gods, you are bound to make boo-boos. One day, in landing, you will ram a pier as though you intended to move it several feet inland. Old-timers will smile tolerantly as you stammer the same excuse they themselves made way back when: "My reverse gear didn't take hold!"

You will run aground—and incidentally by no means is that a sign of the novice; it happens to the saltiest salts in the business. An old saying claims that a skipper who never has run aground just never has cruised anywhere. Nevertheless, running aground is always embarrassing and sometimes is costly and dangerous in addition.

The first few seconds are what count the most when you do run aground. A quick reverse at the instant of touching could save your pride and a lot of trouble. If

that does not do the trick forget the engines for a bit because power could make things worse. Now is the time to pull your wits together and think. Perhaps a rising tide will help you automatically.

Analyze the situation, check where the hull is touching. Which is the best direction to deeper water? Is the bottom soft enough so that you could do a bit of horsing around without damage or is it hard enough to chew your hull? Can you get out of your scrape without help or is it time to get on the radio?

Don't let the foregoing create a doleful picture in your mind and scare you. Most groundings don't amount to a tinker's damn, especially if you are reasonably near the navigable channel where you should be. A little shiver as she touches, a fast reverse with held breath and crossed fingers and back—she's all clear! Clever skippers do this so fast their landlubber passengers never even notice.

Powerboats, particularly twin screwers, are more vulnerable in groundings than are sailboats. Propellers are the most likely parts to be damaged. This is equally true not only in grounding but simply in striking debris. The single screw prop on both powerboat and auxiliary gets a

Figure 28-3: The repaired propeller has just been scribed with the median pitch line to enable further checking.

certain amount of protection from the keel ahead of it.

The one good thing about propeller damage is that it looks awful but hardly ever is as bad as it looks. It is simply amazing how a skilled mechanic can unroll a torn and curled blade, fill in the missing spots with brazing rod and then grind the whole back to its original shape. He then checks the pitch and restores it if necessary with knowing taps of a heavy leather hammer. Presto! Just as good as new! Figure 28-3 and 28-4 illustrate two steps in repairing a propeller.

As you begin active cruising, you will draw upon much of the information in the previous pages of this book. But actual conditions on the water may not always be as clear-cut as the illustrations and the text would lead you to believe. Buoys do not stand out in full pristine glory; as a matter of fact, even the gulls roosting on them often must don their spectacles to read the numbers.

Many markers on the Intracoastal are in dilapidated condition, some so much so that it becomes difficult to tell red from black. As you have already been warned from your reading, some buoys may be totally absent for one cause or another. Your judgment and your dead reckoning

must come to the rescue.

The rules of the road make certain signals mandatory. You know this because of your studies in an early chapter —but it quickly develops that the other guy does not. How can you expect results by signaling someone who is not familiar with the signals? Again, your judgment, tolerance and good seamanship must see both of you through. And that is not just being a good Samaritan; it is legally required by Article and Rule 27.

A small boatman's greatest concern is weather. A chapter on weather gave you the rudiments but only constant observation of Mother Nature's moods can sharpen your reactions to the point where your forecasts are an asset to safe boating. The secrets are held by the wind and the clouds and can be deciphered mostly by cloud appearance. Soft cloud masses that seem to coagulate into definite outlines are a sign of forthcoming trouble. Some signs are obvious, such as halos around the moon and sun; others are more subtle and will test your skill. The crackles and sizzles on an AM radio are a thunderstorm warning that small craft should heed.

Sooner or later you are going to get caught out in a fog

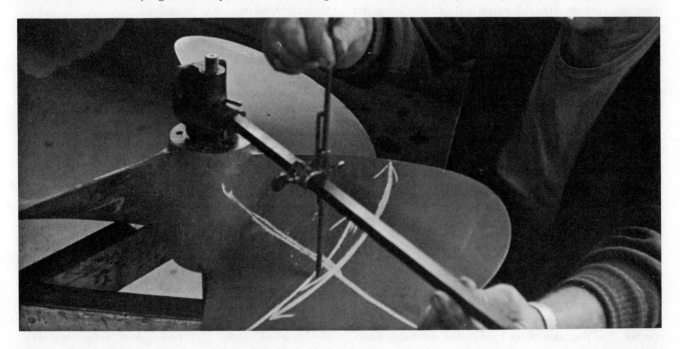

Figure 28-4: The pitch gauge follows the median pitch line and tells whether or not the blade is correctly angled. Corrections are made with heavy leather hammers.

—and it will scare you the first time and still scare you a little the umpteenth time. Fog suspends you in a void and unless you keep yourself under control, you will begin to doubt the compass and eventually will get yourself into a state of panic.

The most prudent course in heavy fog is to get out of the fairway, anchor and religiously continue to give the required fog signals. This may seem like a lack of spinal rigidity but you will be safe—provided that nearby traffic keeps a sharp watch and notes your presence.

Once you gain confidence in your boat and in your guiding equipment, it is not too difficult to run in fog, remembering of course that the rules specify slow speed. The important point is to know where you are when the fog closes in and to use that as a point of departure. It should go without saying that you need a chart.

A buoy which you can identify on the chart is a fine point of departure. From it you can lay a compass course to the next aid to navigation and compute how soon you should arrive there.

If you fail to pick up that next aid within a reasonable (and small) overshoot, stop. Something has gone awry (compass, current, wind, your steering) and now the safest procedure is to drop the hook and wait it out with the required fog signals, of course. It is as important to know when to give up as when to continue.

Continuous weather information is becoming available to the skipper more and more easily. The latest (and perhaps best) sources are the Weather Bureau broadcasts on 162. Mcs. It is worthwhile to have aboard an FM radio receiver that tunes to this frequency.

Once upon a time courtesy ruled on the nation's highways. Passing cars stopped to help a motorist stalled at the side of the road. A driver managed his car so that both he and the other fellow could enjoy driving. Unfortunately, those days are gone and now it is devil take the hindmost.

Happily, some courtesy still remains on the nation's waterways and it would be a fine gesture for every new skipper to add a little more. The pleasant, free and easy way that pleasure boat skippers have with each other makes courtesy a natural byproduct. The combination of courtesy and the rules of the road makes great safe boating insurance.

A new boat in the family often leads to overenthusiastic invitations to neighbors and friends and before you know it you have overloading. This is a serious danger to be avoided at all times. Overloading is the prime cause of boating accidents.

You cannot find a logical excuse for overloading. In the first place, common sense alone should indicate what is a load and what is an overload. Second, all modern small boats are marked by their makers with the exact poundage and the exact number of people which the vessel can carry safely. This information is on a plate in a prominent place in the hull.

Overpowering is another common reason for accidents. This is inexcusable because the manufacturers also inscribe the hull with the maximum recommended horsepower.

If the number of your passengers is within the safely allowed maximum, how they are distributed and how they act is next in importance. The all-too-common practice of riding on the bow with legs dangling is an invitation to tragedy and in some states is even illegal. The bow rider is vulnerable in a crash and he is equally vulnerable in a sudden stop. In the latter case he is pitched overboard and stands an excellent chance of being run over and then chopped up by the propeller.

Early in this book you learned about metacentric height and the center of gravity and the effect these have on stability. People walking about in a small boat affect both strongly and therefore endanger the craft's stability and its safety. Distribute your passengers properly when they come aboard and try to keep them put. (Obviously, the larger the boat the less effect each person will have and the more liberty can be allowed him.)

Most likely you will have a "crew" consisting of mom, or the kids, or a friend, or a neighbor or whoever. They can be a boon or a headache and which they turn out to be is largely dependent upon you. They will be inexperienced and it will be up to you to guide them into the groove. Guide, not bully.

In studying this book you have ingested a great amount of nautical knowledge. Certain portions of this you must now impart to your crew. By knowing why they are doing what they are doing, their enjoyment and their efficiency will both increase—as will their helpfulness to you.

Above all, avoid that commodore-of-the-royal-navy attitude. It defeats its own purpose and creates only resentment.

It is quite possible that you passed over lightly the section in this book explaining knots. Knots do not seem very important until you are faced with a storm and must quickly tie a knot that will hold the boat, come the worst. Consider that you are not really a good knot-tier until you can tie a perfect knot with your eyes closed. (That's to take care of a future dark and stormy night.)

Unless you trailer your boat home after each trip, you will have much to do with marinas and boatyards. Unfortunately, there is not much love involved in this facet of pleasure boating. Boatmen think marina owners are robbers and marina people consider most pleasure-boat owners unrealistic and impossible to please. Of course neither description is true.

Marinas and boatyards are expensive and often their charges seem exorbitant, there is no getting away from that. However, there are economic reasons. Boatmen often do not get the service to which they are entitled and for which they pay and they blame management. But management is at the mercy of a labor force which has lost the pride of accomplishment and does not give a hang about pleasing customers. At present there is no hint of a solution.

The net result of all this will be that if you do not start out as a do-it-yourselfer you will become one. And that is not half as bad or as arduous as it sounds. Much of the fun in pleasure boating lies in husbandry. Afloat and underway you are the skipper; at other times you must be the boat's husband. It behooves you to become handy.

Almost every mechanical and nautical item on board your boat has been dissected and explained in earlier text. A little study should enable you to navigate safely through the innards of all these devices. Remember, however, that the circuits of radio transmitters and radars are off limits to all except those who hold a second-class or better radio operator's license.

Much husbandry is involved in operations with which you doubtless already are familiar: painting and a bit of joiner work here and there for repairs. A good hand with a paintbrush, who also is conscientious about prior sanding and preparation, can do a great deal toward keeping a boat looking spry. Well-kept boats, like well-kept women, show the care lavished upon them.

Aside from pride of ownership, maintaining your boat in top condition is good business. Value is kept high should you ever want to sell. Manufacturers' warranties, too, are affected because most require a certain amount

and grade of service in order to keep the warranty alive.

The amount of work you must do on your craft and when you do it naturally are determined to a large extent by your geographical location. Northern boatmen have long seasons of layup during which maintenance can proceed leisurely on and off the boat. Southern boatmen enjoy year-round sailing—and year-round battles with marine grasses and organisms.

One great advantage of doing your own maintenance work is the familiarity it gives you with every part of your boat. This knowledge can become priceless in an emergency underway. You will know just where the fuse or the valve or any other offending gizmo is located and you will have learned what to do about getting it back in service.

It is wise to develop a regular system for your husbandry because this assures that things will be done. Just what that system will be, however, must be left to your own style of procedure.

There is a good likelihood that you will join some boating organization because pleasure boating is a gregarious, friendly undertaking. It could be the local yacht club or the Squadron or the Auxiliary or even several of these. Some are purely social, others render general boating services. One of the latter is the pleasure-boat inspection offered by the U.S. Coast Guard Auxiliary. You would be wise to make use of this.

The Auxiliary makes its inspections only at the direct request of the boat owner and in his presence. A decal is awarded to boats that pass—and passing requires that a great deal more safety equipment be on board than is legally necessary. Squadron and Auxiliary both offer free seamanship classes which you would do well to attend. (Your study of this book should give you a good leg on these courses.)

One day you may raft up with other boats and it is well to know what to do and what not to do. In rafting, a number of boats tie up together at a mooring or anchorage so that you can walk from deck to deck. The largest boat usually is chosen as the mother ship about which the others tie. Plenty of fendering is in order; this protects both hulls and owners' tempers. Only the mother ship is anchored or moored and her ground tackle must be adequate for the total raft. All boats swing with the mother in response to tides, winds and currents.

The visiting from ship to ship and the merriment go on,

often into the wee hours. By then skippers more than likely have lost the ambition to break up and seek individual anchorage—although generally it is much safer to do so because of the possibility of night storms.

Rafting puts a great strain on the deck fittings of the mother ship and proportionately lesser strains on the satellites around her. Hence the adequacy of chocks and bitts and cleats should be considered before rafting up.

It has always been a tradition of the sea that ships help other ships in distress. The latest laws now make it almost mandatory for you to offer help to a fellow boatman in trouble. But only up to a point.

You are not required nor expected to endanger your crew, your ship or yourself in coming to someone's rescue. Here again, common sense is the best arbiter. It certainly would not help matters if both distressed ship and rescue ship got themselves into an identical mess. The next rescuer would be confronted with twice the problem of the first.

What is even more important, the latest law lets you get at the job of rescue without fear of later recriminations. You cannot now be held liable for any damage caused by your rescue efforts if the actions you took would normally have been taken by any other person of good faith and average knowledge.

Most pleasure skippers are of such goodwill and so anxious to help anyone in trouble on the water that the problem really becomes one of curbing overenthusiasm. For instance, pulling someone off a grounding *seems* simple enough but it has inbuilt dangers. Are the deck fittings strong enough for the severe and sudden loads? Will the towline part and snap back like a huge rubber band? Will current or wind force you into a predicament exactly like that of the boat you are trying to succor?

Often, when you meet a boat in distress that does not involve taking aboard victims immediately, you will serve the best interests of all concerned by standing by and lending moral support while you put in a call for the experts.

Since we now have run the gamut from the purchase of your boat all the way to your role as a rescuer of ships in distress, it is time to stop. Like the oratory at any graduation, it must come to a welcome end. Happy and, above all, *safe* boating as you take the helm.

Glossary

ABAFT toward or at the stern

ABEAM directly off the port or starboard sides of the vessel

ABREAST alongside of the vessel

ADRIFT accidentally broken away from mooring or pier or anchorage

AFORE ahead of

AFT near the stern

AFTER toward the stern or the sternward half of the vessel

AGROUND wholly or partially resting on the bottom

AHEAD to or from the direction in which the vessel is moving

ALOFT overhead, usually in the rigging

AMIDSHIPS the central portion of a ship

ANCHOR LIGHT a white light at the mast top displayed while anchored

ANCHOR RODE the anchor line or rope

APOGEE the point farthest from the earth in the orbit of the moon

APPARENT WIND the wind direction felt from a moving ship

ASPECT RATIO the ratio between width and height of a rectangle

ASTERN aft of the ship

ATHWARTSHIP at a right angle to the ship's length

AZIMUTH the horizontal angle between the reference point and an object

BACK said of a counterclockwise wind shift in the northern hemisphere (clockwise in the southern hemisphere)

BACKING a counterclockwise wind shift; reversing

BACKSTAY part of the standing rigging leading from mast top to a point abaft the mast

BAIL to remove water from the bilge

BALLAST a heavy weight placed low in the hull to lower the center of gravity

BALLOON a large billowing jib

BAR a sand hill projecting up from the bottom of the water

BARNACLE a mollusk which attaches itself to ship bottoms

BATTEN a narrow strip of wood, plastic or metal to stiffen the leach of a sail

BEACON a lighted navigational aid (a *day*beacon is an unlighted marker)

BEAM the maximum width of a ship

BEAM ENDS a description of a vessel on its sides

BEARING the horizontal angle measured clockwise from 0° to 360°

BEATING sailing almost into the wind

BEAUFORT SCALE a system of indicating wind force by number

BELAY a nautical command meaning to cease

BELOW lower than the deck

BEND to tie or attach a line to or to fasten to

BILGE the lowest internal portion of a hull; also the equivalent outside

BILGE KEEL a strake on the outside of a hull to reduce rolling

BINNACLE the housing which contains the compass

BITT a heavy post protruding through the deck to which lines can be secured

BITTER END the end of a line or rope

BLOCK a pulley

BOBBING (A LIGHT) raising and lowering the head when viewing a distant light

BOLLARD a short thick post on a pier for tying up ships

BOOM a horizontal spar at the bottom of a sail attached to the mast

BOW the forward end of a ship

BOW LINE a mooring line coming from the bow

BOWLINE (bo lin) a common and useful rope knot

BOWSPRIT a spar extending forward from the bow

BROACH involuntary swing to parallel with the waves

BROAD ON directly off bow beam or quarter (specify which)

BROAD REACH the points of sailing between a beam reach and a run

BROADSIDE in a direction parallel to the side of the ship

BULKHEAD the "walls" which divide the interior of a hull

BULWARKS the portion of the hull extending above the deck

BUOY a floating marker

BURGEE a triangular flag ending in a point or swallowtail

CABLE LAID the normal method of laying up a rope with three strands

CAMBER the athwartship curvature of a deck

CAPSIZE to turn over

CARDINAL POINTS north, south, east and west

CARLING short support between beams

CARVEL a type of wooden hull construction in which the planks abut smoothly

CATAMARAN a boat with two hulls rigidly connected

CATBOAT a wide-beamed sailboat with one sail

CAULK to fill the gap between planks

CAVITATION propeller slippage due to ingested air

CEILING the inside "wall" covering the frames in a hull

CENTERBOARD a board passed down through a slot in the hull to provide lateral resistance

CENTER OF GRAVITY the imaginary point from which all weight can be considered to act

CHAIN PLATE a fitting at the sides of a hull to which shrouds are attached

CHARLEY NOBLE a protective cap for the smoke pipe from the galley

CHINE the line at which sides and bottom of a hull meet

CHOCK a fitting for guiding rope to a cleat or bitt

CLAMP a longitudinal support member for deck beams

CLEAT a pronged fitting to which ropes are fastened

CLEW the sail corner between leech and foot

CLINKER BUILT overlapping strip (lapstrake) hull construction

CLOSE-HAULED sails trimmed in toward the center line for sailing close to the wind

CLOSE REACH points of sailing between the beam reach and the beat

COAMING a water-stopping strip around a deck opening

COCKPIT an open space in the hull, usually aft, lower than the deck

COMPANIONWAY a passage below decks

COMPENSATE to adjust a compass to minimize deviation

COORDINATE a number referring to east-west or north-south location

CRINGLE a grommet in a sail to prevent chafe by the attached line

CROW'S NEST an observation post high on a mast

CUDDY a small cabin usually on a sailboat

CURSOR a rotatable ring marked in degrees over a compass, pelorus, etc.

DAGGER BOARD a slidable centerboard

DAVIT a crane-like post for hoisting anchors or dinghies

DEADLIGHT a porthole which does not open (fixed glass)

DEADRISE the height from the top of the keel to the chine

DEEP SIX colloquial for the bottom

DEPARTURE the distance made good to the east or to the west by a ship on her course

DEVIATION the disturbing effect on the compass of a ship's own magnetic field

DIAPHONE a sound-producing device used as an aid to navigation

DINGHY a small open boat used as a tender

DISPLACEMENT weight of water equivalent to the weight of the ship

DIURNAL recurring daily (semi-diurnal, twice daily)

DOG WATCH a two-hour watch (instead of four) to break the watch cycle

DOLPHIN a large heavy spar or group of spars for mooring ships

DORY a long, narrow, flat-bottomed open boat

DOUSE to drop sails quickly

DOWNHAUL a line or block and fall used to hold down the foot of a sail

DRAFT the depth of a hull from waterline to keel

DRIFT the velocity, in knots, of a current

DROGUE a sea anchor

DUMB COMPASS a pelorus

EBB TIDE the flow of water back to the sea after high tide

ECHO SOUNDER a depth sounder

ECLIPTIC the apparent path of the sun through the heavens

ELECTROLYSIS the decomposition of a metal by an electric current

ENSIGN a national flag or the flag of an organization

ENTRANCE the portion of the bow which cuts the water

EQUINOX the time when the sun crosses the equator

EYE a fixed closed loop at the end of a rope

FAIRLEAD a guide for a working line

FAKE to lay a line down in a figure eight pattern

FATHOM a unit of depth equivalent to six feet

FEND OFF to push a boat clear of an obstruction

FID a pointed, carrot-shaped tool used for splicing rope

FIX a mark on a chart showing the accurate position of a ship

FLARE a concave bulge spreading outward at the bow of a ship

FLOOR the inside bottom of a hull

FLUKE the point area of an anchor

FLY the horizontal length of a flag

FORE a prefix meaning to or at the forward part of the ship

FORECASTLE (fo'c'sle) the forward part of the hull under the deck

FOREMAST the mast nearest the bow

FOUNDER to sink

FRAMES athwartship structural members that give shape to the hull

FREEBOARD the height to the lowest point above the waterline at which water could come aboard

FURL to lower and secure a sail

GAFF a spar at the head of a four-sided sail

GALLEY the ship's kitchen

GANGWAY the ramp leading up to a ship from pier or float

GARBOARD STRAKE the plank just above the keel

GENOA a very large jib

GHOSTING sailing on a wind of minimum force

GIMBALS connected hinged rings to keep a compass or other instrument level

GOOSENECK the ring at the mast end of a boom

GRANNY an incorrectly tied square knot

GRAPNEL a many-clawed large hook used for retrieving articles from the bottom

GREAT CIRCLE the shortest distance over the earth between two points

GRIBBLE one of a genus of animalcules that can bore into and digest wood

GROMMET a metal (or plastic) insert to strengthen a hole

GROUND TACKLE the anchor with its chains, ropes, etc.

GROUND WAVE radio energy which travels through or along the ground

GUDGEONS fittings on the transom which accept the pintles of a rudder

GUNKHOLING exploring in shallow bywaters

GUNWALE (gun'nel) the strip over the topmost strake of a hull

GUY a wire supporting and steadying an upright object

HAIL to call

HALYARD a line for hoisting sails or flags

HARD ALEE a warning that the helmsman is going to put the ship about

HARD OVER either the port or starboard extreme of the helm

HATCH an opening in a deck giving access to below

HAWSEHOLE a hole in the side of the bow through which the anchor line passes

HAWSER a very heavy line used for mooring

HEAD a sea-going toilet

HEAVE TO to stop dead in the water

HEEL to lean to one side

HOG a hull bottom distorted by being lower at the ends than at the middle, like a hog's back

HORIZON the distant line where sea and sky apparently meet

HULL SPEED the maximum practical speed of a displacement hull of given length

HUNT to oscillate about a midpoint

INBOARD a boat with engines inside the hull (as distinct from outboard)

IN IRONS (or in stays) a point of no headway when coming about from one tack to another

INSHORE landward or toward the shore

IONOSPHERE an ionized gaseous shell enclosing the earth

ISOBAR a line connecting points of equal barometric pressure

ISOGON a line connecting points with the same magnetic variation

ISOTHERM a line connecting points of equal temperature

JACK short for Union Jack

JACK STAFF a short flagstaff at the bow

JACOBS LADDER a rope ladder over the side of a hull

JETTY a pier projecting into the sea to counteract current

JIB a triangular sail set on a stay forward of the mast

JIBE a maneuver with wind astern in which the mainsail swings from one side to the other

JIBSHEET the line which controls the jib

JOLLY BOAT a dinghy hoisted at the stern

JURY RIG seagoing term for a temporary or improvised structure

KEDGE a small anchor generally used for freeing a grounded boat

KEEL a vertical surface at the bottom of a hull to provide lateral resistance

KEELSON a timber placed inside over the keel

KETCH a sailboat with a mainmast and a smaller mizzen-mast stepped forward of the rudder post

KILO a prefix meaning one thousand

KNEE a right-angled timber acting as a bracket between horizontal and vertical members

KNOT a speed of one nautical mile per hour

LANYARD a short piece of rope used as a handle or to secure an object

LAPSTRAKE same as clinker built

LASHING any binding or fastening with light line

LATITUDE the distance measured as an angle north or south of the equator

LAZARETTE the enclosed storage space at the stern in the hull

LEACH the after edge of a sail

LEAD LINE (led) a marked line for determining depth of water

LEE SIDE the side away from the wind

LEE SHORE the shore upon which the wind is blowing

LEEWARD (loo'ard) toward the lee

LEEWAY undesired sideward travel of a ship off her intended course

LIE TO to head into the wind with a sailboat and remain almost motionless

LIMBERHOLE hole through frame in the bilge to facilitate pumping out

LINE OF POSITION (LOP) a line on a chart along any part of which the boat may be

LIST to lean to one side

LOA abbreviation for length overall

LOCKER seagoing name for any chest, closet or box

LOG a record of events occurring aboard; taffrail log—a device used for measuring speed through the water

LONGITUDE the distance measured as an angle east or west of Greenwich, England

LOOM the glow visible in the heavens before a light actually is seen

LUBBER someone unused to being aboard ship

LUBBER'S LINE a line over or parallel to the keel of a vessel

LUFF to head into the wind thereby causing the sails to flap (luff)

LUNAR having to do with the moon

LUNCH HOOK a small anchor used for short stops in good weather

LWL an abbreviation for length at the waterline

MAGNETIC COURSE a course determined with the magnetic pole as a reference

MAKE SAIL to set sail and get way on

MANEUVERING BOARD a plotting sheet laid out in polar coordinates

MANILA a rope fiber from the Philippines

MAST PARTNERS two encircling members to which the mast transmits its push

MARINE BORER a marine organism (teredo) which destroys wood planking

MARINE RAILWAY tracks at a boatyard leading into the water for hauling ships

MAYDAY prefix to a radio call for help by a ship in distress (m'aidez)

MEAN SUN an imaginary sun which "moves" at a uniform rate

MEGA prefix meaning one million

MERIDIAN the great circle formed by a plane passing through both poles and the earth's center

MESSENGER a weight sent down an anchor rode to improve anchor holding power

METACENTER the meeting point of a line through the center of gravity and the center of buoyancy during a slight heel

MAINSHEET the line which controls the mainsail

MILLI prefix meaning one-thousandth

MIZZEN the shorter aftermast of a ketch, yawl, schooner and others

MONKEY LOOP an indeterminate circle of position from three sightings

MONKEY RAIL a low guard rail at the stern deck

MOORING a designated anchoring spot or a buoy floating at the end of an anchor line

MUSHROOM an anchor shaped like a mushroom

NADIR the lowest point in an orbit

NAUTICAL MILE the distance of one degree of latitude (6,080 feet)

NAVIGABLE WATER legally, water which connects with the sea or which permits navigation between two states or to a foreign country

NEAP TIDE the decreased tidal action occurring at first and last quarter moons

NIMBUS a rain cloud

NULL the point of least signal

NUN a buoy with a conical top, usually red

OAKUM a fibrous material used for caulking seams

OCCLUDED FRONT an intermingled cold front and warm front

OCCULTING a system of flashing in which the ons are longer than the offs

OCTANT a sextant with only an eighth instead of a sixth of a circle scale

OMNIDIRECTIONAL effective in all directions

ORDINATE the vertical direction in a system of coordinates

OUTHAUL the line which hauls the sail clew to the end of the boom

PAINTER a short line attached to the bow of a dinghy

PAN (pawn) prefix to a message concerning safety of ship or personnel but not actual distress; a radio emergency call less urgent than mayday

PARALLAX the difference between the true and the apparent direction of sighting

PARCEL to protect a line from wear by covering it with canvas or similar material

PARTNERS short structural members to support the mast where it goes down through the deck

PELORUS an instrument resembling a compass but without magnetic ability

PERIGEE the point in the moon's travel at which it is closest to the earth

PILE (or spile) a vertical post driven into the bottom as a mooring for ships

PINTLE the fitting on a detachable rudder which fits into the gudgeon

PITCH the up and down movement of bow and stern in response to seas; also a measurement of propeller angle

PITCHPOLE to pitch down end over end, as from the top of a wave

PLANE SAILING solving navigational problems by considering the earth to be flat

PLANING SPEED the minimum speed needed by a planing hull to rise on plane

PLUMB vertical

PONTOON a float

POOPED inundated by a wave coming over the transom

PORPOISING moving forward with short leaps from the water (like a porpoise)

PORT the left side of the ship as you face the front

PRAM a small boat with a square bow

PREVAILING WIND the normal wind for a given place at a given time of year

PURCHASE an application of mechanical power

QUADRANT a quarter-circular fitting at the top of a rudder post

QUADRANTAL ERROR a compass error which changes with each quarter turn of a steel ship

QUARTER the side of the hull near the stern

QUARTERDECK the deck at the quarters of a vessel

QUARTERING running at an angle to the sea

RABBET a groove in a structural member into which another fits and is fastened

RADIATION FOG a ground fog caused by condensation

RAKE an inclination forward or aft from the vertical

RANGE a line of position formed by two fixed objects

RATLINE short line which forms the step between shrouds for climbing the mast

REACH a point of sailing with the wind near the beam

READY ABOUT the helmsman's warning that he is putting the ship about on the other tack

REEF to reduce sails, usually because of increasing wind

REFRACTION the change in direction of a light beam passing from air to water

RESOLUTION the ability to separate two close objects observed at a distance

RHUMB LINE a course line on a chart crossing all meridians at the same angle

RIBS more properly called frames, which see

RIGHTING MOMENT the torque by which a ship rights herself from a heel

ROACH a curve in the leach of a sail to improve its aerodynamicity

RODE anchor line and chain

ROLL the side to side swaying of a ship in a sea

ROOSTER TAIL water and spray kicked up at the stern by fast spinning props

RUB RAIL a molding, usually metal, around the hull, which acts as a bumper

RUDDER a swingable flat vertical surface at the stern which steers the boat

RUN a point of sailing with the wind astern

RUNNING FIX a fix established by moving an LOP ahead with time

RUNNING LIGHTS red and green side lights plus stern and bow lights

RUNNING RIGGING the lines which control the sails (the sheets)

SAG distortion in a hull whereby the keel ends are lower than the center

SALOON (or salon) the main cabin of a vessel

SAMSON POST a bitt at the bow used for making fast

SCALE the relation between distance on a chart and the actual distance

SCANTLING a piece of timber used in ship construction

SCARF a joint made between two members by tapering and overlapping them

SCUPPER an opening on the deck through which water drains

SCUTTLE to sink a vessel

SEA ANCHOR an object towed by a ship in order to restrict the ship's movement

SECURE nautical term for making fast

SECURITY (say cur i tay) prefix to a message concerning safety of navigation

SEICHE extreme fluctuations in depth in the Great Lakes

SEMI-DIURNAL occurring in cycles of half a day

SEXTANT an instrument for measuring angles visually

SHACKLE an openable link in a chain

SHAFT LOG the timber or member through which the prop shaft protrudes

SHEAVE (shiv) a grooved pulley wheel

SHEER the curve of a deck as seen from the side

SHEER STRAKE the topmost plank in a hull

SHEET a line used for controlling a sail

SHELF a longitudinal member supporting the deck beams

SHOE a strip fastened to the bottom of a keel

SHROUD a rope which guys the mast from the side

SIDEREAL pertaining to the stars

SISTER FRAME a partial frame fastened to the side of a broken or weak frame

SKEG a member running out from the keel to support the rudder post

SLACK WATER the current at the instant it is not moving in or out

SLEEPERS bracket-like members connecting the transom to structural members

SMALL STUFF line with a small diameter

SOLE seagoing term for a floor of a cabin or cockpit

SOLSTICE the point at which the sun is farthest north or south of the ecliptic

SOUND to measure the depth of water

SPAR an inclusive name for a mast, boom, yard or similar member

SPAR VARNISH a varnish especially formulated to take the weather

SPINNAKER a large, balloon-like sail used at the bow

SPLICE a joint between two ropes made by interleaving the strands

SPRING LINE a docking line running aft from the bow or forward from the quarter

STADIMETER an instrument for measuring the distance to an object of known height

STANCHION a post supporting a rail

STAND the tide at the instant of its lowest or highest point

STATUTE MILE the unit of land distance (5,280 feet)

STAY a fore and aft guy for a mast

STOCK the crossbar in the shank of an anchor

STOPWATER a dowel in the center of a joint to prevent leakage

STOVE smashed in by a collision or accident

STOW nautical term for packing away

STRAKE a length of hull planking

STRINGER a sturdy fore and aft structural member in the bilge

STRUT a fitting for supporting the extended propeller shaft

SWELL an undulating breakerless motion of the sea surface

TABLING the foldover or hem on the edges of sails

TACK the relationship between the direction of the wind and the direction the sailboat is moving

TAFFRAIL a stern rail of a ship

TARPAULIN a large piece of canvas used as a protective cover

TENDER a small boat used as a dinghy

TEREDO one of a genus of animalcules that can bore into and digest wood

THWART the seat in a rowboat

TILLER the long leverage arm attached to the rudder post

TOPPING LIFT a line from boom end to mast head

TOPSIDES the portion of the hull above the waterline

TORQUE a twisting force

TRACK the plotted path of a ship

TRANSOM the outside stern of a hull

TRAVELER an athwartship track from which a line controls the boom

TRIM the attitude of a vessel with reference to the water surface

TRIP LINE a line attached to the crown of an anchor to bring it up backwards

TRUCK the very top of the mast

TRUNK the upper part of a cabin rising through the deck

TUMBLE HOME inward sloping of a portion of the hull

TURNBUCKLE a device with a lefthand and a righthand screw for tightening stays

UNBEND to untie

UNCORRECT to change from true direction to magnetic or compass bearing

UNDERWAY a ship afloat that is not tied or anchored

UNSHIP to take away or remove from a secure position

UNSTABLE AIR warm moist air near the ground

VANG tackle used for controlling a boom

VARIATION changes in the direction of the earth's magnetic field

VECTOR a line which represents the direction and the magnitude of a force

VEER wind changing in a clockwise direction in the northern hemisphere and counterclockwise in the southern hemisphere

VERNIER a device for dividing a scale into finer graduations

VHF very high frequency

WAKE the surface turbulence left by a ship in motion

WARD ROOM on naval vessels, a room reserved for commissioned officers

WARP to inch a ship into a pier with external force, without use of its own power

WATCH a seagoing tour of duty

WEATHER HELM the tendency of a ship to head into the wind

WEDGES tapered pieces under the stern of a powerboat to keep it from squatting

WEIGH nautical term for lifting

WELL FOUND said of a ship that is fully equipped

WHEEL the steering wheel; colloquially, the propeller

WHIP to bind, as the end of a rope, with small twine or small stuff

WHISKERS colloquial term for long grasses that attach themselves to the hull underside

WINDWARD the direction toward the wind

WING AND WING running before the wind with jib on one side and main on the other

WORK said of structural parts that have loosened sufficiently to move against each other

WORM to wind a rope in a spiral with small stuff

X-BAND the radio frequencies lying roughly between 5,000 and 10,000 Mcs.

YARD a spar from which a square sail is hung

YARDARM the crosspiece near the top of a mast

YAW movement to right and left of the desired course

YAWL a sailing ship with a mizzenmast aft of the rudder post in addition to the mainmast

Index

C

HOW TO USE THIS BOOK
TO HELP YOU MASTER THE COURSES
GIVEN BY THE USPS AND CGAUX.

Listed below are the page references which will illuminate the subject matter in each of the lessons of both courses. If you read the indicated pages prior to going to class, your understanding of the classroom work will be greatly facilitated.

USPS
BOATING COURSE

CGAUX
BOATING SAFETY & SEAMANSHIP

ADDITIONAL PHOTO CREDITS

79—Stanley Rosenfeld
101—Stanley Rosenfeld
115—M.E. Warren (Photo Researchers)
117—Stanley Rosenfeld
122—Stanley Rosenfeld
123—Stanley Rosenfeld
138A—Rohn Engh (Photo Researchers)
138B—David Rosenfeld (Photo Researchers)
139—David Rosenfeld (Photo Researchers)
141—Stanley Rosenfeld
161—Morris Rosenfeld
165—Stanley Rosenfeld Also used on page 171B
170–171A—Elliott Erwitt (Magnum)
188—Morris Rosenfeld
191—I.T.T. Decca Marine
221—Kimball Products, Inc.
223—Stanley Rosenfeld
247—Stanley Rosenfeld
265—Morris Rosenfeld
270—Stanley Rosenfeld
271A—Wayne Miller (Magnum)
271B—Wayne Miller (Magnum)
271C—Erich Hartmann (Magnum)
287—Morris Rosenfeld
288A—Stanley Rosenfeld
288B—Morris Rosenfeld
289C—Morris Rosenfeld
290–291—Morris Rosenfeld
293C—Morris Rosenfeld
293D—Morris Rosenfeld
297—National Association of Engine and Boat Manufacturers
302—National Association of Engine and Boat Manufacturers
303—National Association of Engine and Boat Manufacturers
316A—Ed Finley (Photo Researchers)
316B—Stanley Rosenfeld
317C—National Association of Engine and Boat Manufacturers
318—National Association of Engine and Boat Manufacturers
319—National Association of Engine and Boat Manufacturers
320A—Stanley Rosenfeld
320B—Morris Rosenfeld
321C—National Association of Engine and Boat Manufacturers
323—Stanley Rosenfeld
329—National Association of Engine and Boat Manufacturers
333—Morris Rosenfeld
348—Morris Rosenfeld
349B—National Association of Engine and Boat Manufacturers

349C—Stanley Rosenfeld
355—Stanley Rosenfeld
357—Morris Rosenfeld
378—David Rosenfeld (Photo Researchers)
379—Sea Line
381—Stanley Rosenfeld
400—Stanley Rosenfeld
401A—U.S. Coast Guard Photo
401B—U.S. Coast Guard Photo
402A—Martin Ray (Bermuda News Bureau)
402B—Stanley Rosenfeld
402C—Stanley Rosenfeld
403—David Rosenfeld (Photo Researchers)
405—Stanley Rosenfeld
440A—Bettmann Archive
440B—Brown Brothers
441—Bettmann Archive
442A—Brown Brothers
442B—Culver Pictures
443A—Brown Brothers
443B—Brown Brothers
443C—Brown Brothers
444—Brown Brothers
445—Brown Brothers
451—"ESSA" Photo
455—Morris Rosenfeld
461A—U.S. Department of Commerce Weather Bureau
461B—U.S. Department of Commerce Weather Bureau
465—Morris Rosenfeld
467—Stanley Rosenfeld
485—Stanley Rosenfeld
492—Stanley Rosenfeld
493A—Stanley Rosenfeld
493B—H.A. Bruno & Associates, Inc.
495—Stanley Rosenfeld
505—Morris Rosenfeld
515—David Rosenfeld (Photo Researchers)
517—Bertrand De Geofroy (Photo Researchers)
533—Morris Rosenfeld
537—Stanley Rosenfeld
539—Bill Robinson
543—Glastron
567—Morris Rosenfeld
570—Stanley Rosenfeld
581—Bermuda News Bureau
585—Russ Kinne (Photo Researchers)
587—Bermuda News Bureau
591—Stanley Rosenfeld
593—Wayne Miller (Magnum)
598–599—Official Coast Guard Photo
601—Stanley Rosenfeld

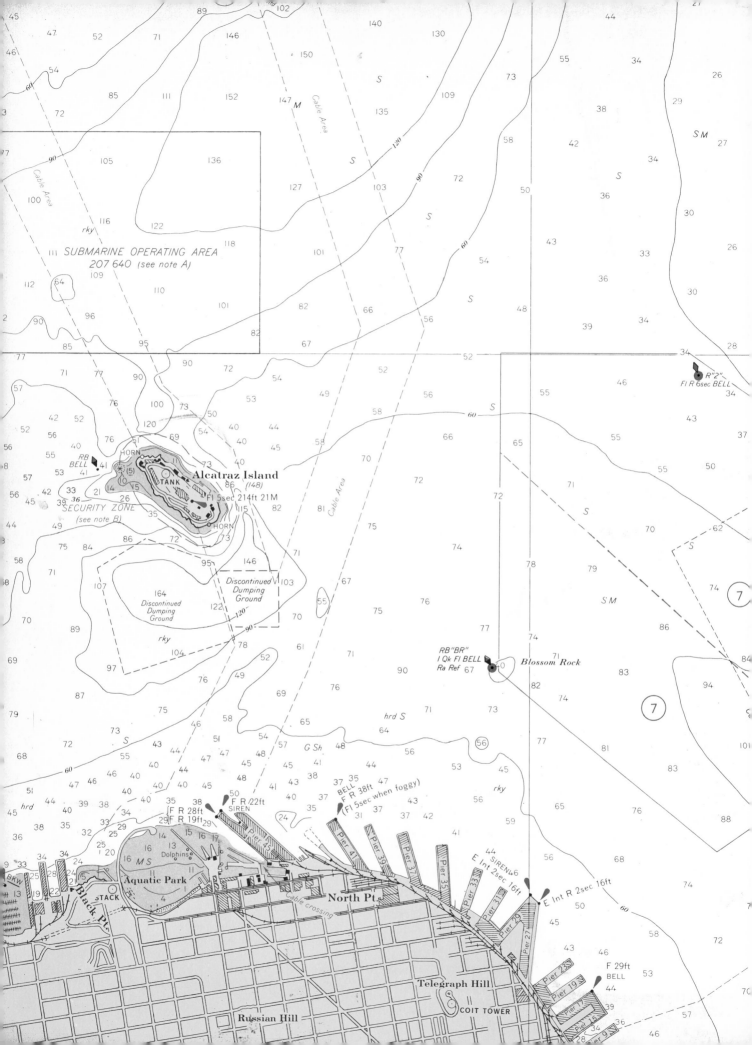